Nepal

Hugh Finlay

LONELY PLANET PUBLICATIONS
Melbourne • Oakland • London • Paris

NEPAL

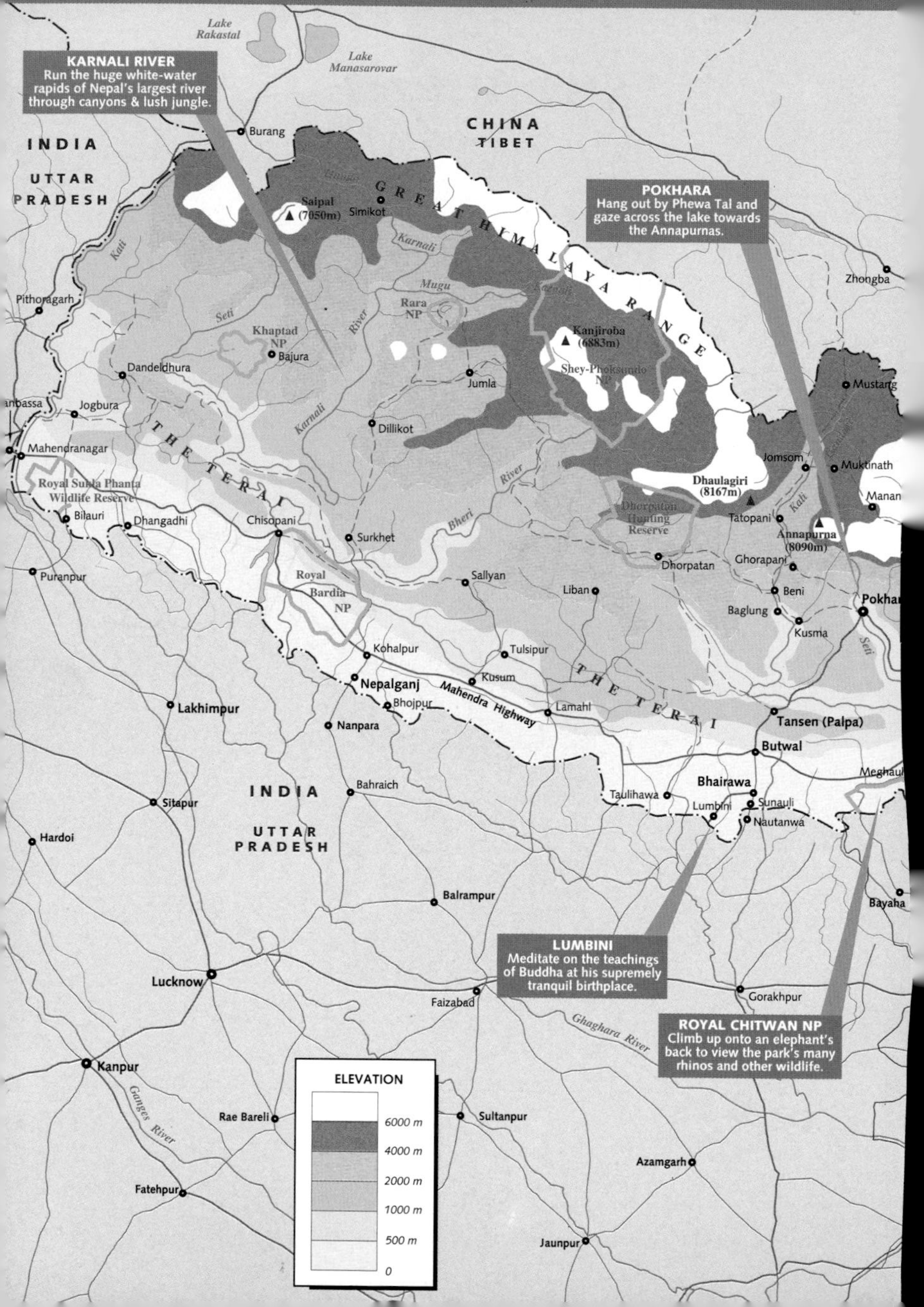

KARNALI RIVER
Run the huge white-water rapids of Nepal's largest river through canyons & lush jungle.

POKHARA
Hang out by Phewa Tal and gaze across the lake towards the Annapurnas.

LUMBINI
Meditate on the teachings of Buddha at his supremely tranquil birthplace.

ROYAL CHITWAN NP
Climb up onto an elephant's back to view the park's many rhinos and other wildlife.

ELEVATION
6000 m
4000 m
2000 m
1000 m
500 m
0

Lake Rakastal
Lake Manasarovar
CHINA
TIBET
INDIA
UTTAR PRADESH
Burang
GREAT HIMALAYA RANGE
Saipal (7050m)
Simikot
Karnali
Kali
Mugu
Rara NP
Seti
Khaptad NP
Bajura
River
Kanjiroba (6883m)
Shey-Phoksundo NP
Jumla
Zhongba
Mustang
Pithoragarh
Dandeldhura
anbassa
Jogbura
Dillikot
THE TERAI
Mahendranagar
Royal Sukla Phanta Wildlife Reserve
Bilauri
Dhangadhi
Chisopani
Surkhet
Bheri
Jomsom
Muktinath
Dhaulagiri (8167m)
Manan
Dhorpatan Hunting Reserve
Tatopani
Annapurna (8090m)
Dhorpatan
Ghorapani
Puranpur
Royal Bardia NP
Sallyan
Liban
Beni
Pokhar
Baglung
Kusma
Kohalpur
Tulsipur
Kusum
Nepalganj
Mahendra Highway
Bhojpur
Lamahi
Lakhimpur
Nanpara
Tansen (Palpa)
Butwal
Bhairawa
Meghaul
Bahraich
Taulihawa
Lumbini
Sunauli
Nautanwa
Sitapur
INDIA
UTTAR PRADESH
Hardoi
Balrampur
Bayaha
Lucknow
Faizabad
Gorakhpur
Ghaghara River
Kanpur
Ganges River
Rae Bareli
Sultanpur
Azamgarh
Fatehpur
Jaunpur

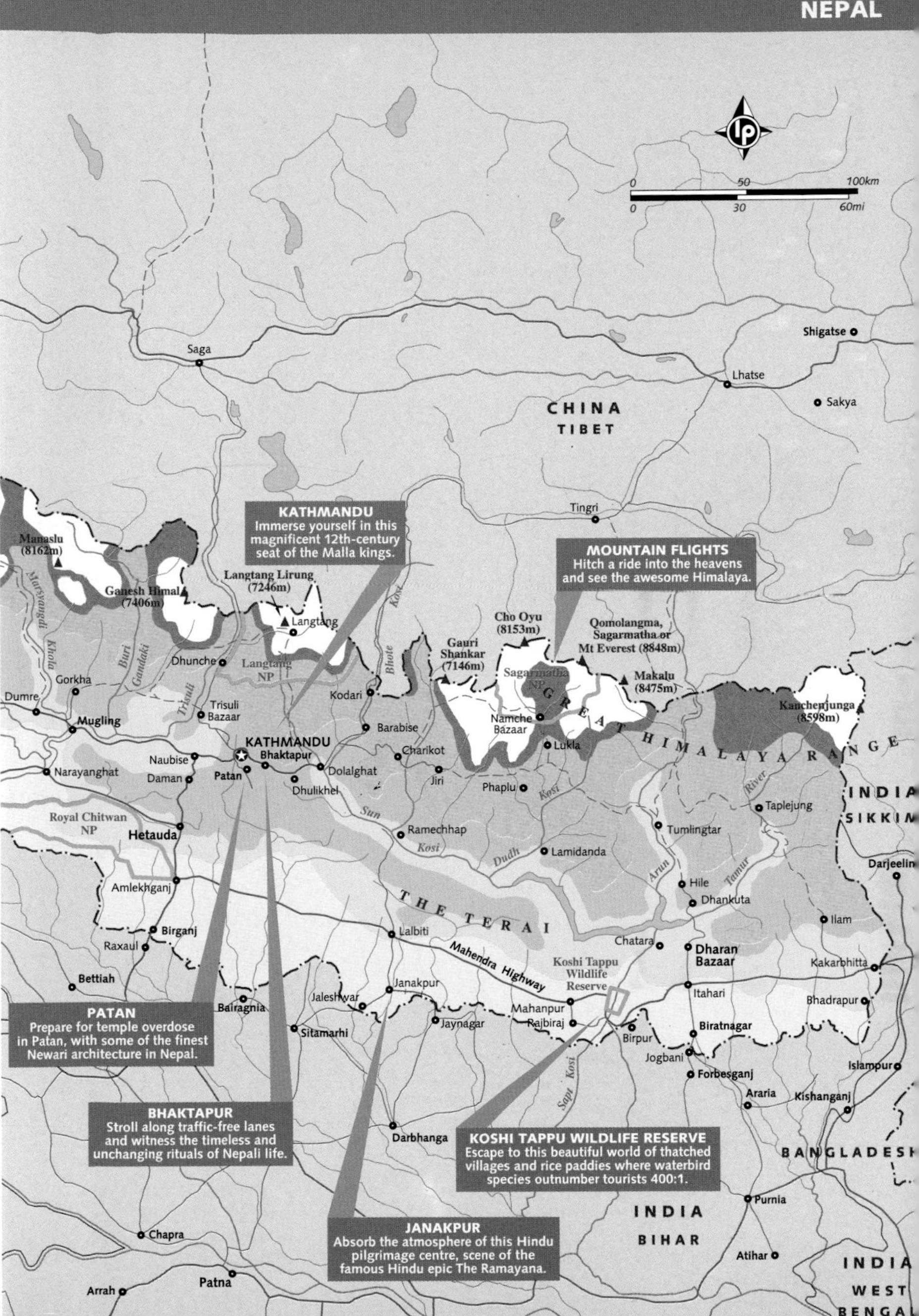

KATHMANDU
Immerse yourself in this magnificent 12th-century seat of the Malla kings.
MOUNTAIN FLIGHTS
Hitch a ride into the heavens and see the awesome Himalaya.
PATAN
Prepare for temple overdose in Patan, with some of the finest Newari architecture in Nepal.
BHAKTAPUR
Stroll along traffic-free lanes and witness the timeless and unchanging rituals of Nepali life.
KOSHI TAPPU WILDLIFE RESERVE
Escape to this beautiful world of thatched villages and rice paddies where waterbird species outnumber tourists 400:1.
JANAKPUR
Absorb the atmosphere of this Hindu pilgrimage centre, scene of the famous Hindu epic The Ramayana.
CHINA
TIBET
INDIA
BIHAR
SIKKIM
BANGLADESH
WEST BENGAL
THE TERAI
GREAT HIMALAYA RANGE
Manaslu (8162m)
Ganesh Himal (7406m)
Langtang Lirung (7246m)
Gauri Shankar (7146m)
Cho Oyu (8153m)
Qomolangma, Sagarmatha or Mt Everest (8848m)
Makalu (8475m)
Kanchenjunga (8598m)
Saga
Lhatse
Shigatse
Sakya
Tingri
Dhunche
Langtang
Langtang NP
Gorkha
Dumre
Mugling
Trisuli Bazaar
Kodari
Barabise
KATHMANDU
Bhaktapur
Patan
Naubise
Daman
Narayanghat
Dolalghat
Dhulikhel
Charikot
Jiri
Namche Bazaar
Lukla
Phaplu
Royal Chitwan NP
Hetauda
Ramechhap
Lamidanda
Tumlingtar
Taplejung
Hile
Dhankuta
Amlekhganj
Birganj
Raxaul
Bettiah
Lalbiti
Mahendra Highway
Koshi Tappu Wildlife Reserve
Chatara
Dharan Bazaar
Ilam
Kakarbhitta
Bhadrapur
Itahari
Biratnagar
Birpur
Jogbani
Forbesganj
Araria
Kishanganj
Islampur
Darjeeling
Janakpur
Jaleshwar
Bairagnia
Sitamarhi
Jaynagar
Mahanpur
Rajbiraj
Darbhanga
Purnia
Atihar
Chapra
Patna
Arrah
0 50 100km
0 30 60mi

Nepal
5th edition – August 2001
6-monthly updates of this title available free on
www.lonelyplanet.com/upgrades
First published – October 1990

Published by
Lonely Planet Publications Pty Ltd ABN 36 005 607 983
90 Maribyrnong St, Footscray, Victoria 3011, Australia

Lonely Planet Offices
Australia Locked Bag 1, Footscray, Victoria 3011
USA 150 Linden St, Oakland, CA 94607
UK 10a Spring Place, London NW5 3BH
France 1 rue du Dahomey, 75011 Paris

Photographs
Many of the images in this guide are available for licensing from Lonely Planet Images.
email: lpi@lonelyplanet.com.au

Front cover photograph
Kathmandu Valley – Swayambhunath (Hannah Levy)

ISBN 1 86450 247 9

Printed by The Bookmaker International Ltd
Printed in China

Contents – Text

Contents – Maps

INTRODUCTION

FACTS ABOUT NEPAL

GETTING AROUND

KATHMANDU

AROUND THE KATHMANDU VALLEY

POKHARA

THE TERAI

TREKKING

RAFTING & KAYAKING

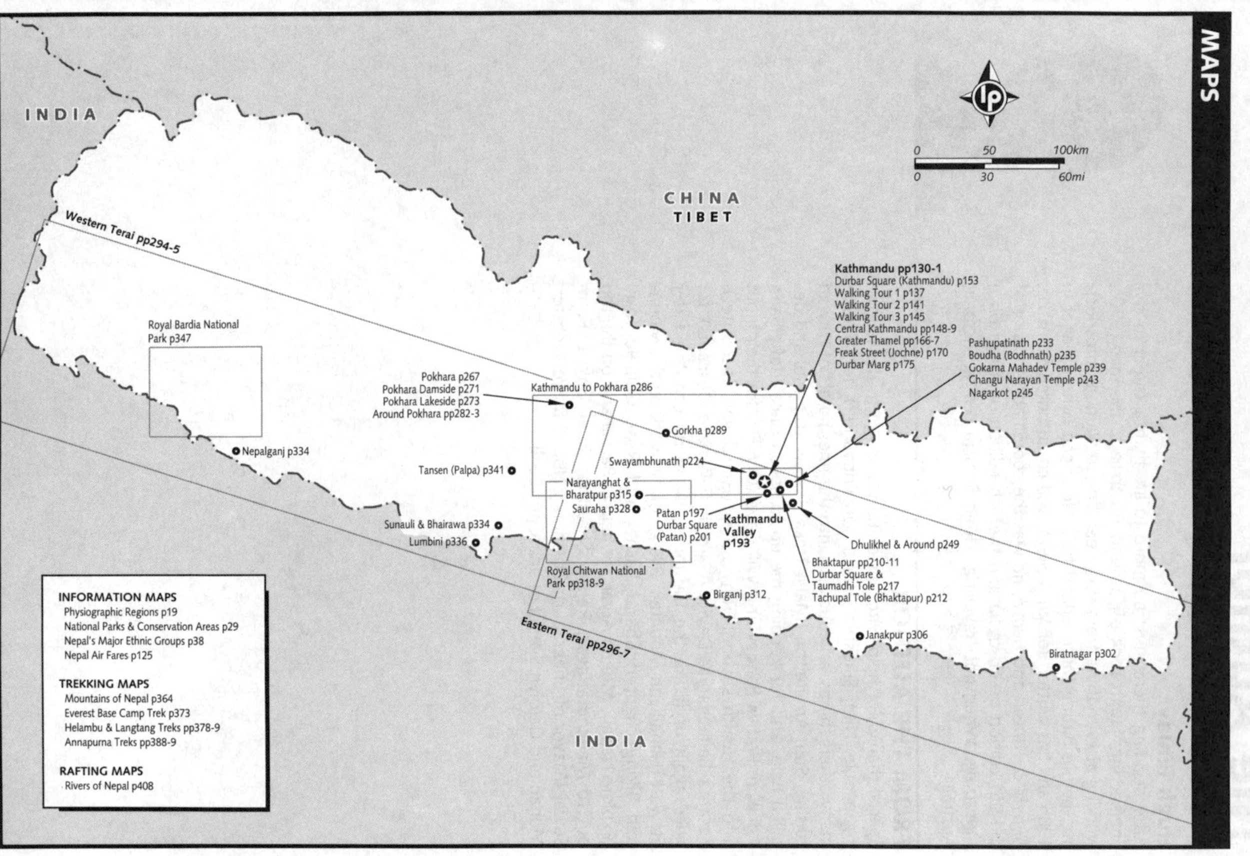
MAPS
INDIA
CHINA
TIBET
0 50 100km
0 30 60mi
Western Terai pp294-5
Royal Bardia National
Park p347
Nepalganj p334
Pokhara p267
Pokhara Damside p271
Pokhara Lakeside p273
Around Pokhara pp282-3
Kathmandu to Pokhara p286
Gorkha p289
Tansen (Palpa) p341
Narayanghat &
Bharatpur p315
Sauraha p328
Sunauli & Bhairawa p334
Lumbini p336
Royal Chitwan National
Park pp318-9
Swayambhunath p224
Patan p197
Durbar Square
(Patan) p201
Kathmandu
Valley
p193
Kathmandu pp130-1
Durbar Square (Kathmandu) p153
Walking Tour 1 p137
Walking Tour 2 p141
Walking Tour 3 p145
Central Kathmandu pp148-9
Greater Thamel pp166-7
Freak Street (Jochne) p170
Durbar Marg p175
Pashupatinath p233
Boudha (Bodhnath) p235
Gokarna Mahadev Temple p239
Changu Narayan Temple p243
Nagarkot p245
Dhulikhel & Around p249
Bhaktapur pp210-11
Durbar Square &
Taumadhi Tole p217
Tachupal Tole (Bhaktapur) p212
Birganj p312
Janakpur p306
Biratnagar p302
Eastern Terai pp296-7
INDIA
INFORMATION MAPS
Physiographic Regions p19
National Parks & Conservation Areas p29
Nepal's Major Ethnic Groups p38
Nepal Air Fares p125
TREKKING MAPS
Mountains of Nepal p364
Everest Base Camp Trek p373
Helambu & Langtang Treks pp378-9
Annapurna Treks pp388-9
RAFTING MAPS
Rivers of Nepal p408

The Author

Hugh Finlay

After deciding there must be more to life than a career in civil engineering, Hugh took off around Australia in the mid-1970s, working at everything from spray painting to diamond prospecting, before hitting the overland trail. He joined Lonely Planet in 1985 and has written *Jordan & Syria*, and co-authored *Morocco, Algeria & Tunisia* and *Kenya*; he was the coordinating author of the 9th edition of *Australia* and the 9th edition of *Africa on a shoestring*. When not travelling, Hugh lives in central Victoria, Australia.

FROM THE AUTHOR

Special thanks for help with this edition must go to the following people: Niraj Shrestha (Himalayan Encounter), for, among many others things, an education into the finer points of Newari cuisine; Stan Armington (Malla Treks) for his insightful and detailed help, and for keeping me up to speed once I left; Badri Adhikari; Prativa Pandey and Will Cave (CIWEC) for their input into the Health section; Tony Jones (Himalayan Encounter); Basanta Bajracharya; David Allardice (Ultimate Descents) for once again updating the Rafting & Kayaking chapter; Peter Stewart (Himalayan Mountain Bikes) for his work on the Mountain Biking chapter; Bharat Basnet and Rose Chipalu Joshi (Explore Nepal); Mohan Aryal, for help in Bardia and on the trip out to Mahendranagar; Rajeev Shrestha; Rajan Sakya; Prem Suwal (Mayor of Bhaktapur); Lt Col Ian Noble; Steve Webster; Mohan and Carolyn Syangbo; and Chris Beall.

This Book

The first five editions of Lonely Planet's *Kathmandu & the Kingdom of Nepal* guide were the work of Nepali writer Prakash A Raj. In 1989 Tony Wheeler and Richard Everist completely rewrote the book (renaming it *Nepal*) to bring it into line with other Lonely Planet guidebooks. In 1992 Richard Everist researched the 2nd edition.

This is the third edition of *Nepal* that Hugh Finlay has researched. The Geography, Flora & Fauna and Ecology sections were originally written by Lewis Underwood. The Mountain Biking chapter was originally written by John Prosser; it was updated for the 4th and current edition by Peter Stewart. David Allardice, operations manager for Ultimate Descents International and co-author of *White Water Nepal*, originally wrote the Rafting & Kayaking chapter for the 2nd edition. He updated the chapter for the 4th and current editions, with the able assistance of Ravi Fry, also of Ultimate Descents. Stan Armington, author of Lonely Planet's *Trekking in the Nepal Himalaya*, helped update the Trekking chapter for this edition.

FROM THE PUBLISHER

The coordinating editor for this fifth edition of Nepal was Susan Holtham. Her editorial team comprised Kerryn Burgess, Hilary Rogers, Evan Jones, Kim Hutchins, Jenny Mullaly, Thalia Kalkipsakis and Shelley Muir.

Rod Zandbergs coordinated the mapping and layout of this edition, with cartographic assistance from Amanda Sierp, Barbara Benson, Hunor Csutoros and new recruit Huw Fowles. Brett Moore assisted with layout, Shahara Ahmed supplied the climate charts, Quentin Frayne updated the language chapter and Jenny Jones designed the cover. From Lonely Planet Images, Matt King liaised with the illustrators, Annie Horner sourced the colour images and the chapter end illustration was drawn by Martin Harris. The colour artwork for the Gods of Nepal special section was drawn by Professor TC Mafapuria.

THANKS
Many thanks to the travellers who used the last edition and wrote to us with helpful hints, advice and interesting anecdotes. Your names appear in the back of this book.

Foreword

ABOUT LONELY PLANET GUIDEBOOKS

The story begins with a classic travel adventure: Tony and Maureen Wheeler's 1972 journey across Europe and Asia to Australia. Useful information about the overland trail did not exist at that time, so Tony and Maureen published the first Lonely Planet guidebook to meet a growing need.

From a kitchen table, then from a tiny office in Melbourne (Australia), Lonely Planet has become the largest independent travel publisher in the world, an international company with offices in Melbourne, Oakland (USA), London (UK) and Paris (France).

Today Lonely Planet guidebooks cover the globe. There is an ever-growing list of books and there's information in a variety of forms and media. Some things haven't changed. The main aim is still to help make it possible for adventurous travellers to get out there – to explore and better understand the world.

At Lonely Planet we believe travellers can make a positive contribution to the countries they visit – if they respect their host communities and spend their money wisely. Since 1986 a percentage of the income from each book has been donated to aid projects and human rights campaigns.

Updates Lonely Planet thoroughly updates each guidebook as often as possible. This usually means there are around two years between editions, although for more unusual or more stable destinations the gap can be longer. Check the imprint page (following the colour map at the beginning of the book) for publication dates.

Between editions up-to-date information is available in two free newsletters – the paper *Planet Talk* and email *Comet* (to subscribe, contact any Lonely Planet office) – and on our Web site at www.lonelyplanet.com. The *Upgrades* section of the Web site covers a number of important and volatile destinations and is regularly updated by Lonely Planet authors. *Scoop* covers news and current affairs relevant to travellers. And, lastly, the *Thorn Tree* bulletin board and *Postcards* section of the site carry unverified, but fascinating, reports from travellers.

Correspondence The process of creating new editions begins with the letters, postcards and emails received from travellers. This correspondence often includes suggestions, criticisms and comments about the current editions. Interesting excerpts are immediately passed on via newsletters and the Web site, and everything goes to our authors to be verified when they're researching on the road. We're keen to get more feedback from organisations or individuals who represent communities visited by travellers.

Lonely Planet gathers information for everyone who's curious about the planet – and especially for those who explore it first-hand. Through guidebooks, phrasebooks, activity guides, maps, literature, newsletters, image library, TV series and Web site we act as an information exchange for a worldwide community of travellers.

Research Authors aim to gather sufficient practical information to enable travellers to make informed choices and to make the mechanics of a journey run smoothly. They also research historical and cultural background to help enrich the travel experience and allow travellers to understand and respond appropriately to cultural and environmental issues.

Authors don't stay in every hotel because that would mean spending a couple of months in each medium-sized city and, no, they don't eat at every restaurant because that would mean stretching belts beyond capacity. They do visit hotels and restaurants to check standards and prices, but feedback based on readers' direct experiences can be very helpful.

Many of our authors work undercover, others aren't so secretive. None of them accept freebies in exchange for positive write-ups. And none of our guidebooks contain any advertising.

Production Authors submit their raw manuscripts and maps to offices in Australia, USA, UK or France. Editors and cartographers – all experienced travellers themselves – then begin the process of assembling the pieces. When the book finally hits the shops, some things are already out of date, we start getting feedback from readers and the process begins again…

WARNING & REQUEST

Things change – prices go up, schedules change, good places go bad and bad places go bankrupt – nothing stays the same. So, if you find things better or worse, recently opened or long since closed, please tell us and help make the next edition even more accurate and useful. We genuinely value all the feedback we receive. A well-travelled team reads and acknowledges every letter, postcard and email and ensures that every morsel of information finds its way to the appropriate authors, editors and cartographers for verification.

Everyone who writes to us will find their name in the next edition of the appropriate guidebook. They will also receive the latest issue of *Planet Talk*, our quarterly printed newsletter, or *Comet*, our monthly email newsletter. Subscriptions to both newsletters are free. The very best contributions will be rewarded with a free guidebook.

Excerpts from your correspondence may appear in new editions of Lonely Planet guidebooks, the Lonely Planet Web site, *Planet Talk* or *Comet*, so please let us know if you *don't* want your letter published or your name acknowledged.

Send all correspondence to the Lonely Planet office closest to you:

Australia: Locked Bag 1, Footscray, Victoria 3011
USA: 150 Linden St, Oakland, CA 94607
UK: 10A Spring Place, London NW5 3BH
France: 1 rue du Dahomey, 75011 Paris

Or email us at: talk2us@lonelyplanet.com.au

For news, views and updates see our Web site: www.lonelyplanet.com

HOW TO USE A LONELY PLANET GUIDEBOOK

The best way to use a Lonely Planet guidebook is any way you choose. At Lonely Planet we believe the most memorable travel experiences are often those that are unexpected, and the finest discoveries are those you make yourself. Guidebooks are not intended to be used as if they provide a detailed set of infallible instructions!

Contents All Lonely Planet guidebooks follow roughly the same format. The Facts about the Destination chapters or sections give background information ranging from history to weather. Facts for the Visitor gives practical information on issues like visas and health. Getting There & Away gives a brief starting point for researching travel to and from the destination. Getting Around gives an overview of the transport options when you arrive.

The peculiar demands of each destination determine how subsequent chapters are broken up, but some things remain constant. We always start with background, then proceed to sights, places to stay, places to eat, entertainment, getting there and away, and getting around information – in that order.

Heading Hierarchy Lonely Planet headings are used in a strict hierarchical structure that can be visualised as a set of Russian dolls. Each heading (and its following text) is encompassed by any preceding heading that is higher on the hierarchical ladder.

Entry Points We do not assume guidebooks will be read from beginning to end, but that people will dip into them. The traditional entry points are the list of contents and the index. In addition, however, some books have a complete list of maps and an index map illustrating map coverage.

There may also be a colour map that shows highlights. These highlights are dealt with in greater detail in the Facts for the Visitor chapter, along with planning questions and suggested itineraries. Each chapter covering a geographical region usually begins with a locator map and another list of highlights. Once you find something of interest in a list of highlights, turn to the index.

Maps Maps play a crucial role in Lonely Planet guidebooks and include a huge amount of information. A legend is printed on the back page. We seek to have complete consistency between maps and text, and to have every important place in the text captured on a map. Map key numbers usually start in the top left corner.

Although inclusion in a guidebook usually implies a recommendation we cannot list every good place. Exclusion does not necessarily imply criticism. In fact there are a number of reasons why we might exclude a place – sometimes it is simply inappropriate to encourage an influx of travellers.

Introduction

Draped along the greatest heights of the Himalaya, the kingdom of Nepal is a land of eternal fascination, a place where the ice-cold of the high Himalaya meets the heat of the steamy Indian plains. It's a land of ancient history, colourful cultures and people, superb scenery and some of the best trekking on earth.

Nepal's history is shaped by its geographical location, between the fertile plains of India and the desert-like plateau of Tibet. Its position between India and China has meant that Nepal has at times played the role of intermediary – a canny trader between two great powers – while at other times it has faced the threat of invasion. Internally its history is just as dynamic, with city-states in the hills vying with each other for power until one powerful king, Prithvi Narayan Shah, overran them all. The three great towns of the Kathmandu Valley – Kathmandu, Patan and Bhaktapur – still bear witness to their days as fiercely competitive medieval minikingdoms. Indeed, in Nepal it's possible to mentally turn back the clock to the medieval era, such is the evocative power of the country.

Behind the time-worn temples and palaces of the Kathmandu Valley, above and beyond the hills that ring the valley, another 'kingdom' rises skyward. The 'abode of snows' (Sanskrit for 'Himalaya') is a natural kingdom and a magnet for trekkers, mountaineers and adventurers from around the world. Fortunately you don't have to be a Sherpa and your surname doesn't have to be Hillary, Messner or Bonington for you to get in among these great mountains. With a

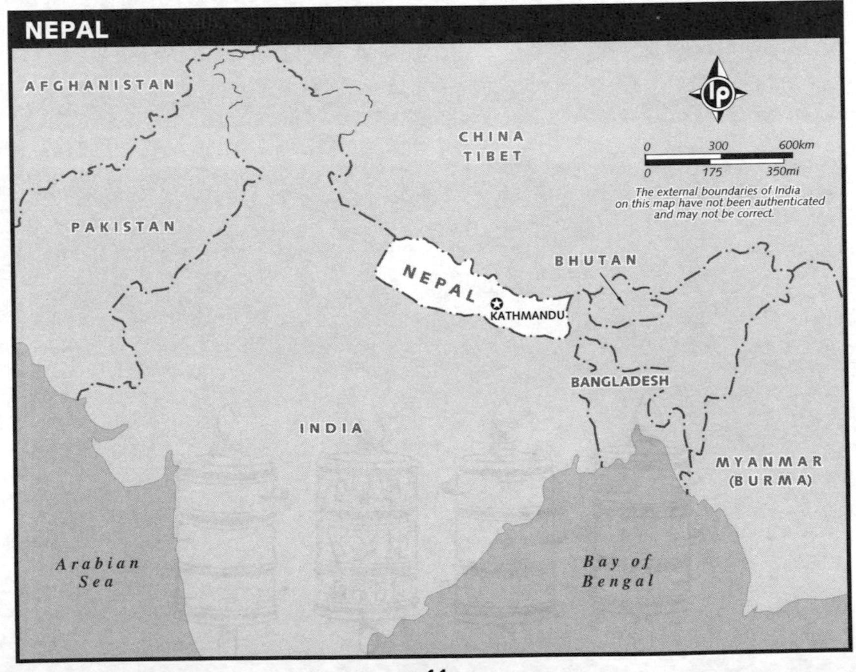

dash of enterprise and a modicum of fitness most travellers can walk the trails that lead into the roadless heights of the Himalaya. One trek is rarely enough and many visitors soon find themselves planning to return.

Fascinating old towns, magnificent temples and great trekking are not all Nepal has to offer. Many visitors come to Nepal expecting to find these things, but also discover how amazingly rich and diverse the local culture is, and how friendly Nepalis can be.

Nepal has some of the world's premier white-water rafting and kayaking opportunities, as well as offering mountain biking and other adventure sports such as canyoning and paragliding. And for those that get their thrills at less than adrenaline-rush speed, the national parks of the lowland Terai region offer wildlife-spotting safaris by elephant.

It's an amazingly diverse country that offers something for everyone – and it usually ends up doing so more than once!

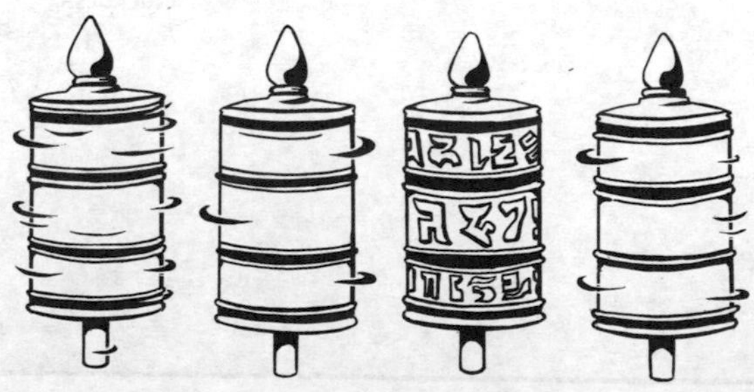

Facts about Nepal

HISTORY

In many ways – historically, culturally and linguistically – Nepal has been the meeting point between the Mongoloid peoples of Asia (who speak Tibeto-Burmese languages) and the Caucasoid peoples of the Indian plains (who speak Indo-European languages). In earlier times, Nepal was able to exploit its position as an intermediary in the trade between India and China. Today, the country continues to take advantage of its strategic position between these two uneasy giants.

Over the centuries, the boundaries of Nepal have extended to include huge tracts of neighbouring India, or contracted to little more than the Kathmandu Valley and a handful of surrounding city-states.

Legends recount that the Kathmandu Valley was once a great lake and that Manjushri broached the valley wall with a magical sword, draining the water and creating the Kathmandu Valley we know. Or perhaps it wasn't Manjushri; he was, after all, a Buddhist from China. Hindus claim it was Krishna who performed the mighty deed, hurling a thunderbolt to create the Chobar Gorge. Choose whichever legend you prefer, but scientists agree that the valley was submerged at one time and the rivers of the valley do indeed flow southward through the narrow Chobar Gorge.

The Kiratis

Recorded history begins with the Kiratis, Mongoloid people who arrived in Nepal from the east around the 7th or 8th century BC. Although they are the first known rulers of the Kathmandu Valley, and Yalambar (the first of their kings) is mentioned in the Hindu epic the *Mahabharata*, little more is known about them.

It was during the Kirati period that Buddhism first arrived in the country; indeed it is claimed that during the reign of the seventh of the 28 Kirati kings, Buddha, together with his disciple Ananda, visited the valley and stayed for a time in Patan.

Other accounts of the Kirati period include a 4th century BC description of the Kiratis' sheep-breeding and agricultural activities. Around the 2nd century BC, the great Indian Buddhist emperor Ashoka visited Nepal and erected a pillar at the Buddha's birthplace at Lumbini, south of Pokhara near the present-day Indian border. Ashoka also visited the Kathmandu Valley, and evidence of four stupas he erected around Patan can still be clearly seen. Ashoka may have also enlarged the stupas at Bodhnath and Swayambhunath. His daughter Charumati was said to have founded Chabahil, a village on the road between Kathmandu and Bodhnath, which has now been swallowed up by the capital. There is a stupa, which is a smaller version of the one at Bodhnath, and a monastery here that are claimed to date back to Charumati's time in Nepal.

Kirati domination ended around 300 AD but the Rai and Limbu people of eastern Nepal are said to be modern descendants.

The Licchavis

Buddhism faded and Hinduism reasserted itself with the Licchavis, Indo-Aryan people who invaded from northern India about 300 AD and overthrew the last Kirati king. They brought with them the caste divisions that continue in Nepal to this day, but they also ushered in a golden age of Nepali art and architecture.

Manadeva I established the Licchavis' political and military might; an inscription dated to 476 AD telling of his prowess can be seen at the beautiful Changu Narayan Temple in the eastern part of the Kathmandu Valley. His successor, Manadeva II, left numerous stone inscriptions around his kingdom, most of them commenting on what a wonderful mother he had and how he wouldn't have got anywhere without her.

The Thakuris

Amsuvarman, the first Thakuri king, came to power in 602 AD, succeeding his Licchavi father-in-law. Amsuvarman consolidated his power with strategic family connections to the north and south. His daughter Bhrikuti married a Tibetan prince and collected the Buddha's begging bowl in her wedding dowry. She was said to be a reincarnation of Tibetan Buddhism's Green Tara, seen on many *thangkas* (Tibetan paintings on cotton). Meanwhile in Nepal, Amsuvarman constructed a marvellous seven-storey palace at Deopatan near Pashupatinath, and contemporary accounts speak with wonder of his luxurious life.

Amsuvarman's was the first of three Thakuri dynasties and although the centuries that followed were a time of invasion and turmoil, the Kathmandu Valley's strategic location ensured the kingdom's survival and growth. It is believed that the city of Kantipur, today's Kathmandu, was founded around the 10th century by Gunakamadeva. His Kasthamandap (House of Wood) gave the city its name and can be seen in Kathmandu's Durbar Square.

The Golden Age of the Mallas

In 1200, so another legend goes, King Arideva was wrestling when news came of the birth of his son. He instantly awarded his son the title *malla* (wrestler) and thus founded the illustrious Malla dynasty. This golden age saw great wealth flow to the valley and the kingdom's architects constructed many of the wonderful buildings still seen in Nepal today, but the early Malla years saw a series of terrible disasters. A huge earthquake shook the valley and killed thousands, an invasion from the north-west followed, and the town of Patan was destroyed in 1311.

The Hindu Mallas were followers of Shiva but were considered to be incarnations of the god Vishnu, and their tolerance of Buddhism allowed the Himalayan Tantric form of the religion to continue to flourish. An aristocracy grew up under the Malla rulers and the Hindu caste rules were strengthened and became more rigid. Hari Singh, who arrived in

Warning about Figures, Dates & Names

There doesn't seem to be an entirely correct reference for anything in Nepal. For example, we've seen half a dozen different figures for the number of square kilometres that Nepal occupies. And we lost track of how many times sources A, B and C said Temple 1 is to the right, Temple 2 is to the left while sources X, Y and Z said the opposite. It's open to contention which of the three Taleju temples in Patan's Durbar Square is which. When temples were built is also a matter of speculation: Some sources give a date of construction for a certain temple and the period of reign for the king who built it, and yet the two do not coincide.

Many temples in Nepal have alternative names. For example, Vishnu Temple in Patan's Durbar Square is referred to as Jagannarayan or Charnarayan Temple; the great Shiva Temple in Kathmandu's Durbar Square is sometimes called Maju Deval, at other times simply Shiva Temple. Where possible, alternative names that are commonly used have been provided in this book.

Mandir simply means 'temple' – generally we have used the English word except in cases where mandir is always used, as with the Krishna Mandir in Patan.

Further confusion can be caused by different systems of transliteration from Sanskrit – the letter 'h' appears in some systems, but doesn't appear in others, so you may see Manjushri and Manjusri, Machhendranath and Machendranath. The letters 'b' and 'v' are also used interchangeably in different systems – Shiva's fearsome manifestation can be Bhairab or Bhairav; Vishnu is often written as Bishnu; and the Nepali word for the Tibetan thunderbolt symbol can be a *bajra* or a *vajra*.

Confusion may also be caused by different places having the same name; in the Annapurna region there are two villages called Phedi, and there are at least three places called Chisopani.

Finally, texts differ in their use of the words Nepali and Nepalese. In this book we have used Nepali both for the language and for other terms relating to the country and its people.

the valley some time between 1325 and 1330, was one of the best-known early Malla rulers and through him Taleju Bhawani became the royal goddess of Nepal. Hari Singh's southern Indian followers may have been the Newars whose name the people of the Kathmandu Valley take to this day.

During this period Nepal began to divide into numerous frequently feuding city-states. The hill country became more densely settled as agricultural techniques improved, but a Muslim invasion from Bengal swept through the valley, leaving in its wake damaged Hindu and Buddhist shrines. The wave of Muslim destruction soon passed Nepal, but in India the damage was more widespread and many Hindus were driven from the plains, establishing more small Rajput principalities in the hills and mountains of Nepal. The country we know today was divided at that time into 46 separate small states. These kingdoms minted their own coins and maintained standing armies.

In Kathmandu, Patan and Bhaktapur – the three greatest towns of the Kathmandu Valley, which remain to this day – were independent kingdoms with powerful kings who encouraged the construction of many temples and the creation of many enduring works of art. Each city centred on the king's palace, with the nobility and high castes concentrated close to the centre. High walls were built to fend off the city's neighbours.

In 1372, however, Jayasthiti Malla founded the third Malla dynasty and took first Patan, then, 10 years later, Bhaktapur, to unify the whole valley. In the 15th century, Malla art and culture reached their peak and during the reign of Yaksha Malla (1428–82) the kingdom extended south to the Ganges River, north to the edge of Tibet, west to the Kali Gandaki River and east to Sikkim. With Yaksha Malla's death, the kingdom again split into small warring states and another two centuries of conflict followed. Trade was booming, agriculture continued to improve and the valley towns enjoyed an orgy of temple and palace construction, but the constant squabbling of the Malla kingdoms opened the door to a new dynasty.

The Shah Dynasty Unifies Nepal

From the tiny kingdom of Gorkha, halfway between Kathmandu and Pokhara, the Shah kings gradually strengthened and extended their power while dreaming of conquering the rich Kathmandu Valley. In 1768, Prithvi Narayan Shah, ninth of the Shah kings, conquered the valley and moved his capital to Kathmandu. The Shah dynasty, which continues to this day, was established.

From this new base the kingdom's power continued to expand, until a clash with the Chinese in Tibet led to an ignominious defeat. The Nepalis had first fought the Chinese in 1790, but by 1792 the Chinese army had struck back and in the ensuing treaty the Nepalis had to stop their attacks on Tibet and pay tribute to the Chinese emperor in Beijing; the payments continued until 1912.

British power on the subcontinent was growing at this time and a British envoy arrived in Kathmandu in 1792, too late to aid the Nepalis against the Chinese invasion. Despite treaties with the British, the expanding Nepali boundaries, stretching all the way from Kashmir to Sikkim by the early 19th century, were bound to cause problems with the Raj, and disputes over the Terai (the lowlands south of the Himalayan foothills) led to war with the British.

In 1810 Nepal was approximately twice its current size, but the 1816 Sugauli treaty with the British ended its growth. Britain took Sikkim and most of the Terai, and Nepal's present-day eastern and western borders were established. Some of the land was restored to Nepal in 1858 as a reward for Nepali support for the British during the Indian Mutiny (or Indian Uprising or War of Independence as it is referred to in modern India).

The Sugauli treaty opened the door for Indian business influence in Nepal. A century later, when new direct trade routes were established between India and Tibet, the Nepalis began to lose their influence as an intermediary in trade between the two countries. A British resident was sent to Kathmandu to keep an eye on things. The Nepalis, less than entranced with the British, allotted him a piece of land which they considered to be disease-prone and a haven for evil spirits, but the British stiff upper lip prevailed. In fact the defeat by the British had so rankled the Nepalis that they shut off all foreign contact and from 1816 right through to 1951 the country's borders were firmly closed to outsiders. The British residents in Kathmandu were the only Westerners to set eyes on Nepal for more than 100 years.

Many Nepali eyes were, however, viewing the outside world. The British were so impressed by the fighting qualities of the Nepalis that they brought mercenaries, known as Gurkhas, into the British army. Gurkha mercenaries have fought in the British army ever since, even spreading fear among the Argentineans during the Falklands War in 1982. Gurkha earnings are an important element of Nepal's income today and although the importance of Gurkha troops to Britain is diminishing, various other nations are only too happy to pay for their soldiering abilities. The Sultan of Brunei, for example, has a contingent of Gurkha troops.

The Ranas

Although the Shah dynasty continued in power, a curious palace revolt occurred in 1846 when Jung Bahadur Rana engineered the Kot Massacre.

Jung Bahadur was an ambitious and ruthless young Chhetri noble from western Nepal. Taking advantage of the complex, often bloody, power struggles within the ruling family, he developed his own power base. On 15 September 1846, he initiated a decisive coup. His soldiers massacred several hundred of the most important men in the kingdom – noblemen, soldiers and courtiers – while they were assembled in the Kot courtyard adjoining Kathmandu's Durbar Square. Jung Bahadur took the title of prime minister and changed his family name to the more prestigious Rana. Later, he extended his title to maharaja and then made the title hereditary. The Ranas became a second 'royal family' within the kingdom and held the real power, keeping the Shah kings as pampered figureheads.

For more than a century the hereditary family of Rana prime ministers held power and although development in Nepal stagnated, the country did manage to preserve its independence during the period when European colonial powers were snatching up virtually every country unable to defend itself. Nepal was never ruled by a colonial power, but it was almost completely isolated from the outside world right through the Rana period. Only on rare occasions were visitors allowed into Nepal and even then they were only allowed to visit a very limited part of the country.

Jung Bahadur Rana travelled to Europe in 1850 and brought back a taste for neoclassical architecture (examples of it can be seen in Kathmandu today). To the Ranas' credit, *suttee* (the Hindu practice of casting widows on their husband's funeral pyre) was abolished, forced labour was ended, and a school and a college were established in Kathmandu. But while the Ranas and their relations lived luxurious lives in huge Kathmandu palaces, the peasants in the hills were locked in a medieval existence.

Elsewhere in the region dramatic changes were taking place. After WWII, India gained its independence and a revolution took place in China. Tibetan refugees fled into Nepal when the new People's Republic of China annexed Tibet, and Nepal became a buffer zone between the two Asian giants. The turmoil naturally spread over Nepal's closed borders, and while one Rana made moves towards liberalising the country's moribund political system, another attempted to move towards stronger central control. Under the charismatic BP Koirala, the Nepali Congress party, supported by the ruling Indian Congress party, was established by many Nepalis and even by some Rana family members.

At the same time King Tribhuvan, forgotten in his palace, was being primed to overthrow the Ranas.

The Shahs' Restoration

In late 1950 King Tribhuvan escaped from his palace to the Indian embassy and from there to India. Meanwhile, BP Koirala's forces managed to take most of the Terai from the Ranas and established a provisional government which ruled from the border town of Birganj. Nepal was in turmoil, but there was no clear victor. Finally, India exerted its influence and negotiated a solution. King Tribhuvan returned to Nepal in 1951 and set up a new government composed of Ranas and commoners from BP Koirala's Nepali Congress.

Although Nepal gradually reopened its long-closed doors and established relations with many other nations, dreams of a new democratic system were not permanently realised. King Tribhuvan died in 1955 and was followed by his son Mahendra. A new constitution provided for a parliamentary system of government and in 1959 Nepal held its first general election. The Nepali Congress won a clear victory, somewhat to the king's surprise, and BP Koirala became the new prime minister. In late 1960, however, the king decided the government wasn't working to his taste and had the cabinet arrested. Political parties were banned and the king swapped his ceremonial role for real control.

In 1962 King Mahendra decided that a partyless, indirect *panchayat* (council) system of government was more appropriate to Nepal. Local panchayats chose representatives for district panchayats, which in turn were represented in the National Panchayat. The real power, however, remained with the king. He retained executive power, directly chose 16 members of the 35-member National Panchayat, and appointed the prime minister and his cabinet. Political parties continued to be banned.

In 1972 Mahendra died and was succeeded by his son Birendra, who had been educated at Eton and Harvard. Birendra's view that Nepal now had the correct political system was not supported by everybody, however. Popular discontent with slow development, corrupt officials and rising costs simmered in the 1970s. In 1979 the smouldering anger finally exploded into violent riots in Kathmandu, and King Birendra announced that a referendum would be held to choose between the panchayat system and one that would permit political parties to operate.

BP Koirala, who had been in jail or in self-imposed exile since 1960, was allowed to campaign but the 1980 referendum result was 55% to 45% in favour of the panchayat system.

Nevertheless, the king had already declared that whichever way the vote went, the people would elect the country's legislature for a five-year term and it, in turn, would elect the prime minister. The king, however, would continue to directly appoint 20% of the legislature, and all candidates would have to be members of one of six government-approved organisations and stand under their own name, not as a representative of any party. The first elections under this system were held in 1981.

On the surface, the panchayat system, which allowed a secret vote and universal suffrage, did not appear to be dictatorial: The constitution theoretically guaranteed freedom of speech and peaceful assembly, as well as the right to form unions and associations (so long as they were not motivated by party politics).

The reality was somewhat different. Nepal's military and police apparatus were among the least publicly accountable in the world and there was strict censorship. Mass arrests, torture and beatings of suspected activists are well documented, and the leaders of the main opposition, the Nepali Congress, spent the years between 1960 and 1990 in and out of prison. (BP Koirala died in 1983.)

Until early 1990, the king wielded considerable power. It is difficult to know quite how much – the inner workings of the palace and the king's relationships with members of the cabinet were not made public – but the constitution guaranteed his supremacy and the National Panchayat basically acted as a rubber stamp.

The aristocracy, in general, managed to retain its influence and wealth (the king and his brothers are all married to Ranas) and the panchayat system did not seem to cramp its style. Firm figures are impossible to find, but it is generally accepted that a huge portion of foreign aid (perhaps up to 50%) was routinely creamed off into royal and ministerial accounts.

People Power

In 1989 the opposition parties formed a coalition to fight for a multiparty democracy with the king as constitutional head; the upsurge of protest was called the Jana Andolan, or People's Movement. Popular support was motivated in part by economic problems caused by an Indian government blockade, and in part by widespread discontent with blatant corruption.

In February 1990 the government responded to nonviolent protest meetings with bullets, tear gas, thousands of arrests and torture. However, after several months of intermittent rioting, curfews, a successful strike, and pressure from various foreign aid donors, the government was forced to back down. The people's victory did not come cheaply. Estimates of the number who died reach to more than 300.

On 9 April, the king announced on national radio that he was lifting the ban on political parties and on 16 April he asked the opposition to lead an interim government. He also announced his readiness to accept a role as a constitutional monarch.

Democracy

In May 1991, 20 parties contested a general election for a 205-seat parliament. The Nepali Congress and a communist party were the two major players. The Nepali Congress won power with around 38% of the vote. The Communist Party of Nepal-Unified Marxist-Leninist (CPN-UML) won 28%. The next largest party, the United People's Front, received only 5% of the vote.

In the years immediately following the 1991 election, the political atmosphere in the country was uneasy. For those on the right of the political spectrum, the king's popularity never waned. Many ordinary people, however, had unrealistically high expectations and they were unsettled by political infighting and hurt by price rises. Economic pressures were intense and in April 1992 a general strike degenerated into street violence between protesters and police, and resulted in a number of deaths.

In late 1994 the Nepali Congress government, led by GP Koirala, (the youngest brother of BP Koirala) called a midterm election. The outcome failed to give any party a clear mandate, and in the end the communist CPN-UML won out, in coalition with the third major party, the Rastriya Prajatantra Party (RPP), the old panchayats, and with the support of the Nepali Congress. It's one of the very few times in the world that a communist government has come to power by popular vote.

Political stability remained elusive, infighting and factionalism were rife, and within nine months the Congress had withdrawn its support for the CPN, fearing the communists were becoming too well entrenched. A new Congress government was formed, with the support of the opportunistic RPP.

The main feature of Nepali democracy in the late 1990s was its changeability: Coalitions (often seemingly idealistically contradictory) were formed and broken with alarming frequency, opportunism and corruption were everywhere, and governments came and went with startling regularity.

The most recent elections were held in May 1999. These saw the Nepali Congress win power with a healthy majority and KP Bhattarai installed as prime minister. Bhattarai was toppled by former Congress leader GP Koirala in March 2000.

Factionalism still plagues Nepal's political parties, particularly the ruling Nepali Congress. At the time of research, the leader and prime minister, GP Koirala, was engaged in a bitter struggle for ascendancy with former Congress leader and prime minister Sher Bahadur Deuba. While these two old men squabble for supremacy it seems they are quite prepared to see the country fall apart around them – major issues facing the government at the time of research included the Maoist insurgency (see the boxed text 'People's War' under Government & Politics later in this chapter) and civil unrest in the Kathmandu Valley and elsewhere. After a decade of democracy it seems increasing numbers of Nepalis, particularly young Nepalis, are utterly disillusioned with the whole system, and are increasingly prepared to take to the streets to protest against it – riots in late 2000 left a number of people dead in the Kathmandu Valley. The riots were ostensibly a protest against an anti-Nepal slur allegedly made by a well-known Indian actor, but this was just a catalyst for the venting of much wider frustrations which have been simmering for some time. The government seems unwilling to take the lead in resolving these issues and the country looks set for a period of major political instability.

This instability is further complicated by a fragile economy, extreme poverty, illiteracy, and an ethnically and religiously fragmented population that is continuing to grow at a high rate.

There is no doubt that there exists within the nation's political parties a will to change, but as long as those in power are in such a position of insecurity, little real change is likely.

GEOGRAPHY

In length and breadth, Nepal is just another small country. In height, it's number one in the world. Nepal stretches from north-west to south-east about 800km and varies in width from around 90km to 230km. This gives it a total area of just 147,181 sq km according to the official figures.

Within that small area, however, is the greatest range of altitude to be seen on Earth – starting with the Terai, only 100m or so above sea level, and finishing at the top of Mt Everest (8848m), the world's highest point.

Often a visitor's overriding goal is to see the mountains, especially Everest and Annapurna. However, to exclude the people, flowers, birds and wildlife from the experience is to miss the essence of the country.

Physiographic Regions

Nepal consists of several physiographic regions, or natural zones: the plains in the south, four mountain ranges, and the valleys lying between them. The lowlands with their fertile soils, and the southern slopes of the mountains with sunny exposures, allow for cultivation and are the main inhabited regions.

The Terai Seen from the air, the Gangetic plain is a flat monotonous expanse that comes to a sudden halt as it turns into

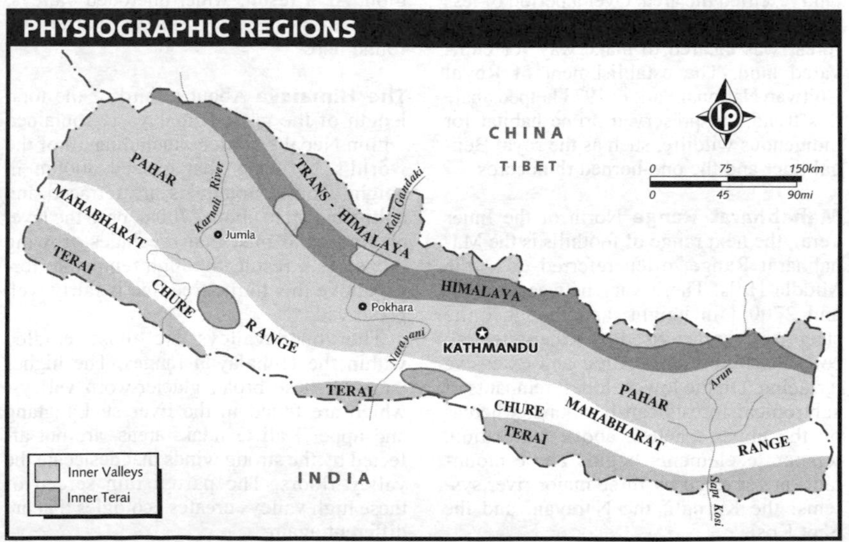

mountainous relief. The last of this landscape, about 100m above sea level, encroaches up to 40km into Nepal and is known as the Terai (sometimes written Tarai). This region is a montage of paddy fields, interspersed with oases of mango groves, bamboo stands and villages beneath scattered palms.

Chure Hills Known as the Siwalik Hills in India, these are the first of the four mountain ranges and run the length of the country. They have an average height of 900m, but are as high as 1350m in places. This range separates the Terai from the Inner Terai and harbours the fossilised remains of many mammals no longer typical of Eurasia.

Inner Terai Between the Chure Hills and the next range of foothills are longitudinal basins about 150m above sea level, formed by east–west flowing rivers and called the Inner Terai. Before the introduction of the insecticide DDT in the 1950s, the Terai was inhabited only by the Tharus, who demonstrated a partial resistance to malaria.

After the eradication of malaria, a large number of hill people looking for fertile land resettled the area. Over a period of less than a decade, more than 50% of the natural forest was cleared to make way for cultivated land. The establishment of Royal Chitwan National Park in 1973 helped abate this trend and preserved prime habitat for indigenous wildlife, such as the royal Bengal tiger and the one-horned rhinoceros.

Mahabharat Range North of the Inner Terai, the next range of foothills is the Mahabharat Range, often referred to as the Middle Hills. These vary between 1500m and 2700m in height, and though quite steep, are characterised by water-retentive soils that allow cultivation and extensive terracing. On the lower slopes, remnants of subtropical forests can be found, whereas on the upper reaches, above cultivation, temperate elements begin. These mountains are severed by three major river systems: the Karnali, the Narayani and the Sapt Kosi.

Pahar Zone Between the Mahabharat Range and the Himalaya lies a broad belt referred to as the midlands, or the Pahar zone. This includes fertile valleys (previously large lakes) such as Kathmandu, Banepa and Pokhara. This area, which has been inhabited for centuries, supports nearly half of Nepal's population. As a result, the central and eastern parts of this zone have been extensively cultivated. Ranging mostly between 1000m and 2000m, subtropical and lower temperate forests are found here, but have been disrupted by fuel and fodder gathering.

The Pokhara area is unique, not only because of its magnificent setting at the foot of the Annapurna massif, but also because there is no formidable barrier directly to the south to obstruct the spring and monsoon rain clouds. Consequently, it is subjected to abnormally high rainfall, which limits cultivation to under 2000m. Red laterite soils are typical of such areas, where most minerals except for iron and aluminium oxide are leached out of the soil.

Conversely, the Humla-Jumla area in the west is protected to the south by ranges over 4000m in height that prevent much of the monsoon moisture from reaching this region. As a result, wide, uneroded valleys, snowless peaks and drier vegetation are found here.

The Himalaya About a third of the total length of the great Himalaya is contained within Nepal's borders, including 10 of the world's 14 peaks that exceed 8000m in height. These mountains are terraced and cultivated up to about 2700m, or to the level of cloud and mist that precludes growing crops. As a result, the high temperate forest above this to the tree line is fairly well preserved.

The inner valleys are those cradled within the Himalayan ranges. The higher parts of these broad glacier-worn valleys, which are found in the Everest, Langtang and upper Kali Gandaki areas, are not affected by the strong winds that desiccate the valley floors. The partial rain screen of these high valleys creates ecologies that are different again.

The Trans-Himalaya North of the Himalaya is the high desert region, similar to the Tibetan plateau. This area encompasses the arid valleys of Mustang, Manang and Dolpo, as well as the Tibetan marginals (the fourth range of mountains, which sweeps from central to north-western Nepal, averaging below 6000m in height). The trans-Himalaya is in the rain-shadow area and receives significantly less precipitation than the southern slopes. Uneroded crags, spires and formations like crumbling fortresses are typical of this stark landscape.

GEOLOGY

Imagine the space Nepal occupies as an open expanse of water, once part of the Mediterranean Sea, and the Tibetan plateau, or 'roof of the world', as a beachfront property. This was the setting until about 60 million years ago, before the Indo-Australian plate's collision with the Eurasian continent. As the former was pushed under Eurasia, Earth's crust buckled and folded and mountain building began.

The upheaval of mountains caused the temporary obstruction of rivers that once flowed unimpeded from Eurasia to the sea. However, on the southern slopes of the young mountains, new rivers formed as trapped moist winds off the tropical sea rose and precipitated. As the mountains continued to rise and the gradient became steeper, these rivers cut deeper and deeper into the terrain.

The continual crunching of the two plates, augmented by phases of crustal uplifting, created yet new mountain ranges, and once again the rivers' courses were interrupted. If the forces of erosion eventually prevailed, long east-west valleys were formed. If not, lakes resulted.

The colossal outcome was the formation of four major mountain systems running north-west by south-east, incised by the north–south gorges of not only new rivers, but also the original ones whose watersheds in Tibet are older than the mountains themselves. In conjunction with the innumerable rogue ridges that jut out from the main ranges, the terrain can be likened to a complex maze of ceilingless rooms.

The mountain-building process continues today, not only displacing material laterally, but also sending the ranges even higher and resulting in natural erosion, landslides, silt-laden rivers, rock faults and earthquakes.

CLIMATE

Nepal has a typical monsoonal, two-season year. There's the dry season from October to May and there's the wet season (the monsoon) from June to September.

In summer (May to September) Kathmandu can get very hot, with temperatures often above 30°C (May and the early part of June, before the monsoon, are the hottest). Even in winter (October to April) the bright sunny days often reach 20°C, although with nightfall the mercury may plummet to near freezing. It never snows in the Kathmandu Valley, and higher up the

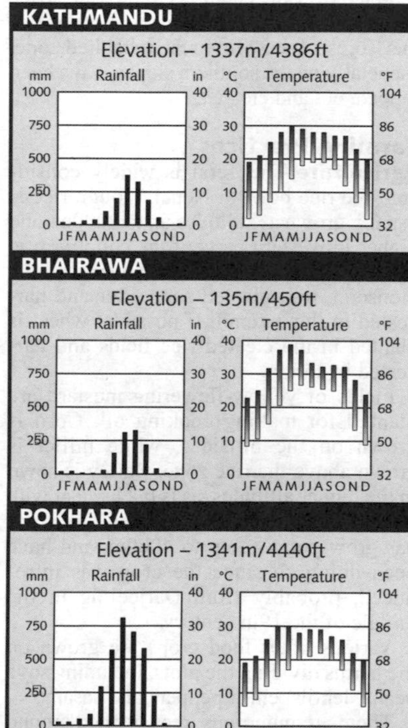

coldest weather is also the driest weather, so snow is unusual. Because of its lower altitude Pokhara is warmer and more pleasant than Kathmandu during winter, but hotter when the temperature builds up and wetter during the monsoon.

Surprisingly, Kathmandu is farther south than New Delhi. Nepal is about 1500km closer to the equator than the Alps in Europe, so the snow line is much higher.

For information about the importance of climatic factors in planning a visit to Nepal, see When to Go under Planning in the Facts for the Visitor chapter.

ECOLOGY & ENVIRONMENT

Much of the land between the Himalaya and the Terai has been vigorously modified by human activities and represents the lifeblood of Nepal. This land has been worked and sculpted over the centuries to provide space for crops, animals and houses. Because of this, forests lying within the inhabited zone, especially on the southern slopes, have been lopped, cut and cleared.

Farming Practices

Agriculture The Terai is widely considered the rice bowl of Nepal, though rice is usually grown at altitudes up to 2000m, and higher in western parts of the country. It is usually planted before the advent of the monsoon, transplanted soon after and harvested in the autumn. If possible, wheat is planted in the cleared rice fields and harvested in spring.

Fields of yellow-flowering mustard are planted for making cooking oil. Corn is grown on the hillsides, while millet is grown above the rice zone. Barley is sown in the higher altitudes, as is buckwheat with its pink and white flower cluster. The Sherpas grow potatoes up to 4000m, and have been doing so since the crop was introduced, probably from Darjeeling in the middle of the 19th century.

Various other food crops are grown on the berms dividing the plots, including soya beans, lentils, chilli peppers and sesame.

There are numerous trees planted around villages and fields, all for some kind of purpose, whether for shade, fruit, fodder or medicine. Bananas, mangoes, papaya, citrus fruits, peaches and apples have all brought new income to the remote hill areas.

Fodder such as rice stalks and corn sheaves is often dried and stored in trees, while seed corn is stored under the eaves of houses.

A variety of fig trees provide shade for pilgrims and travellers. The magnificent mushrooming canopies of banyan and pipal trees are unmistakable, usually found together atop a stone dais designed for accommodating porters' loads. The Buddha is believed to have attained enlightenment under a pipal tree, and Hindus see the pipal as an embodiment of Narayan (Vishnu). Hindus also revere the banyan as an embodiment of Lakshmi, the goddess of wealth.

Bamboo grows under a variety of conditions and is found throughout Nepal. Another common feature in villages are kitchen gardens comprising greens, beans, turnips, radishes, pumpkins, cucumbers, taro and squash. Bauhinia, with its distinctive camel-hoof leaves and orchid-like flowers, is grown near houses, the leaves for fodder and the flowers cooked or pickled. In the west, plots of tobacco are commonly seen in villages, as are fields of cannabis, grown for hemp. In addition, stinging nettles are picked with tongs, rendered harmless by boiling and eaten as greens.

Eupatorium is a red-stemmed daisy with heart-shaped leaves; it's called *ban mara* (death of forest) by Nepalis. A native of Latin America introduced into the Himalaya during the 19th century, it invades subtropical and temperate zones, and is widespread. Covering deforested hillsides, it is unpalatable, even for sheep and goats, and is a prime indicator of environmental degradation.

Animal Husbandry Bovines play an important role in rural and urban Nepal. Cows are sacred, and are not slaughtered or used as beasts of burden – they bear calves, and provide milk and multipurpose dung. In the Kathmandu Valley, the cows wandering and sleeping in the streets have been let loose by pious Hindus. Because the bull is Shiva's steed, bulls are also considered holy and generally are not used to pull ploughs in the valley. The beasts of burden on the lowlands are usually castrated bulls, or oxen.

Water buffaloes belong to a different genus, but are still lumped with the bovines. These animals lose their body hair as they mature, and must wallow to dissipate heat and protect themselves from the sun. The males are used as beasts of burden and are butchered. The females produce a creamy milk, which is also converted into yogurt.

Long-haired yaks, no longer found in the wilds of Nepal, are very temperamental and are used mostly for stud service. The yaks generally seen are hybrids, which have confusing names. The female yak is called a *nak*. The nak and the male yak can be crossbred with cattle, which produces a more docile creature suitable for carrying loads. In the Everest region the male is called a *dzopkyo* or *zopkiok* and the female a *dzum* or *zhum*. The dzum lactates well and produces a better-quality milk than the nak. The second generation of these hybrids is sterile.

In the Kali Gandaki and on the southern approaches to the Everest region, donkeys and mules are used as pack animals. These beasts are often adorned with headgear of dyed plumes and mirrors, and collars of bells.

Conservation

As long as Nepalis marry early, feel uncertain about infant survival, and desire sons to look after them in their old age and to perform funeral rites, the population of Nepal will continue to burgeon. With population demands, the forests will continue to be depleted, erosion caused by humans will compound that which is natural, water supplies will dry up and floods will inundate the lowlands.

The visitor should not, however, adopt the role of the vociferous critic. Nepal is making positive changes, but traditional societies require long lead times for change. There are various alternative energy schemes under way. The Annapurna

KEEP Nepal Green

If you want to find out about environmental conservation, or just talk to someone about where and how to trek, visit the Kathmandu Environmental Education Project (KEEP), which operates the Travellers' Information Centre in Kathmandu (see Information in the Kathmandu chapter for details).

Visitors can get information on how to minimise their negative impact and maximise their positive impact. Displays and hand-outs illustrate practical dos and don'ts, and there are also professional Nepali staff and Western volunteers to deal with specific questions. During trekking seasons a slide show on conservation practices and a talk on prevention of acute mountain sickness (AMS) is given every afternoon.

Green-Keeper's coffee shop sells freshly brewed coffee, home-made cakes and cookies, KEEP T-shirts, biodegradable soaps, sun screen, lip balm, and other items useful for ecologically sound trekking. Guidebooks, periodicals and maps are available in the library. A journal records trekkers' comments on treks, and an outside notice board carries notices from people selling gear, looking for trekking partners, looking for friends... Although KEEP information is particularly useful for individual trekkers, it is also helpful for group trekkers, mountaineers and city sightseers – everyone is welcome. Eventually, KEEP hopes to become a clearing house for information on the environment and conservation for the entire Himalaya region.

Visitor contributions are much appreciated. An annual fee of US$20 for individuals, US$50 for businesses and institutions, US$160 for life, and US$200 to US$500 for 'Friends of KEEP' entitles members to the biannual newsletter and a KEEP T-shirt. KEEP has nonprofit, charitable status.

For more information, contact KEEP (☎ 259275, ⓔ tours@keep.wlink.com.np), PO Box 9178, Thamel, Kathmandu.

Conservation Area Project (ACAP) takes an innovative approach, not only incorporating alternative energy developments, forest conservation and environmental education, but also being an effective strategy for getting the Nepali people directly involved in determining their own destiny.

Conservation is typically a concept of affluent countries with land and resources to spare, a luxury unknown in the Third World. With dwindling space and forests, it is difficult for a farmer to grasp why land should be set aside for tigers and rhinos, especially when they ravage crops, take domestic animals and generally make a hard life even harder.

Visitors should ensure that they minimise their impact on the environment. Trekking groups and individuals staying in lodges should insist that kerosene, as opposed to firewood, is used for cooking meals and heating water. You should also minimise the use of nonbiodegradable products (especially plastic and batteries), as there are no facilities for their disposal. One potential nightmare is the trend to the sale of water in plastic bottles, which are expensive and completely unnecessary if you carry your own water bottle and iodine.

See the Trekking chapter for more information on minimising your impact on the environment.

FLORA

There are 6500 known species of trees, shrubs and wildflowers in Nepal. In the temperate areas the flowers emerge as winter recedes and the rivers swell with snow melt, while in the subtropics, the bloom is triggered by warmer temperatures and spring showers.

The height of floral glory can be witnessed in March and April when rhododendrons burst into colour. The huge magnolias of the east with their showy white flowers borne on bare branches are also spectacular, as are the orchids (there are more than 300 species in Nepal).

In the post-monsoon season, when most people choose to visit, the flowers of summer are all but gone, save for some straggler blooms and those not palatable to grazing animals. However, in the subtropical and lower temperate areas, some wildflowers that have survived environmental degradation include pink luculia, mauve osbeckia and yellow St John's wort. Flowering cherry trees also add colour to the autumn village scenes, as do, in the temperate areas, blue gentians. Otherwise, one can enjoy the autumn yellows of withering maples and ginger, and the reds of barberry shrubs. When the dark temperate forests are back lit, the moss appears luminescent, and the epiphytic ferns and orchids shine like tiny paper lanterns.

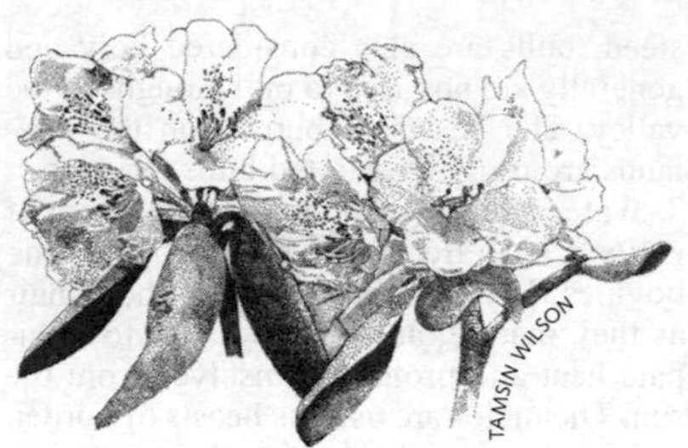

The rhododendron is Nepal's national flower – look for them in March and April.

In the Kathmandu Valley, Australians will find familiar silky oak with its spring golden inflorescence, and bottlebrush and eucalyptus. Though these trees are fast-growing timber species in their native country, in the valley they are planted as ornamentals, along with cherry, poplar and jacaranda. Historically, the Nepalis have been avid gardeners of such exotics as hibiscus, camellia, cosmos, salvia and marigold.

Tropical Zone

Up to 300m

Sal *(Shorea robusta)*, a broad-leaved, semi-deciduous hardwood, dominates here. The leaves are used for 'disposable' plates, and the wood is used for construction. There is also a deciduous moist forest in this zone, of acacia and rosewood, as well as open areas of tall elephant grass. The grass areas are burned off in winter, which helps preserve them. These forest types are typical of the Chure and the Inner Terai.

Subtropical Zone

1000m to 2000m

The dominant species east of the Kali Gandaki are the true chestnuts and a member of the tea family, schima. Because of the popularity of chestnut wood as a source of fuel, it is often depleted. In the west, the chir pine is found on all aspects.

Lower Temperate Zone

1700m to 2700m

Evergreen oaks are indigenous to this zone. In the east, the oaks of the wet forests are festooned with moss and epiphytes and have dense understoreys.

A common wet forest that occurs mostly on north and west faces in western Nepal comprises horse chestnut, maple and walnut. Alder and birch are prevalent along watercourses.

Homogeneous blue-pine forests occur extensively in the west, mostly on south faces, and range to the tree line. This species is hardy and fire resistant, thriving in habitats modified by humans.

Upper Temperate Zone

2400m to 4000m

Another evergreen oak that is widespread throughout the dry forests of the west exhibits two types of leaves: The young ones are spiny, while the older ones have leaf margins. In the east, this species is confined to southern slopes, but is heavily cut for fodder and fuel.

The spectacular wet rhododendron forests are interspersed with hemlock and fir. *Rhododendron arboreum*, the national flower, reaches heights of 18m and ranges in colour from red to white. There are more than 30 species of rhododendron in Nepal, but these are found more extensively in the east than the west. Unfortunately, this tree is felled for fuel or turned into charcoal.

Subalpine Zone

3000m to 4000m

Silver fir mixed with oak and birch extends to the tree line in the west. East of the Kali Gandaki, only birch is found to the tree line.

Alpine Zone

4000m to Snow Line

In this realm above the tree line, vegetation must cope with extremes in ground temperatures, and moisture levels that range from nothing in winter to profuse in summer. Only the most tenacious of wildflowers thrive here. In the trans-Himalaya, the vegetation is restricted to the arid-adapted species of the Tibetan plateau.

FAUNA

Birds

More than 800 bird species are known in Nepal, more than in Canada and the USA combined, or nearly 10% of the world's species! Resident bird numbers are augmented by migratory species, as well as winter and summer visitors.

Eight species of stork have been identified along the watercourses of the Terai. Similar in appearance are the cranes, though these are not as well represented, save for the demoiselle cranes that fly down the Kali Gandaki and Dudh Kosi for the winter, before returning in spring to their Tibetan nesting grounds. Herons and egrets are quite common in the tropics and subtropics.

Most of the waterfowl are migratory. Many can be seen at the Kosi Barrage in the eastern Terai and in the Chitwan and Bardia areas. The bar-headed goose has been observed flying at altitudes near 8000m.

Raptors or birds of prey are especially prevalent with the onset of winter. One of the first raptors to leave is the small Eurasian kestrel that must flap its wings at regular intervals, or rapidly when hovering, as distinct from the Himalayan griffon, a heavy bird that must wait for thermal updraughts to allow its soaring, gliding flight. The griffon, along with the lammergeier, with a wingspan of nearly 3m, are carrion eaters, though often mistaken for eagles. There are, however, true eagles present, including the resident golden eagle common in the Khumbu, as well as other species that are known to migrate in large numbers in the Kali Gandaki region. Many medium-sized raptors have highly variable plumages and are difficult to identify in the sky.

There are six species of pheasant in Nepal, including the national bird, the impeyan pheasant, the male of which has a plumage of iridescent colours. These birds are known as downhill fliers, as they do not fly, per se, and must walk uphill! The cheer and koklas pheasants are only found west of the Kali Gandaki, while the kalij pheasant is common throughout Nepal.

Nepal hosts 17 species of cuckoo, which are characterised by their distinctive calls. Arriving in March, they herald the coming of spring. The Indian cuckoo is recognised by its *'kaphal pakyo'* call, which announces in Nepali that the fruit of the box myrtle is ripe. The common hawk cuckoo has a repetitious call that rises in a crescendo and sounds like 'brain fever' – or so it was described by British sahibs as they lay sweating with malarial fevers. Most cuckoos are social parasites, meaning they lay their eggs in the nests of other species.

One of the most colourful, varied and vocal families is the timalids, or babblers and laughing thrushes, common from the tropical Terai to the upper temperate forest. They range in length from 8cm to 33cm, and live in both terrestrial and arboreal habitats. They are found individually or in large, foraging parties, and can often be identified by their raucous calls. The black-capped sibia with its constant prattle and ringing song is an integral part of the wet temperate forests. The spiny babbler is Nepal's only endemic species.

Nepal is home to 15 members of the crow family. The two species of blue magpies are similar in appearance, but each species occupies a different altitudinal range: The red-billed blue magpie is a resident of the subtropical zone, while the yellow-billed blue magpie is found in the temperates. Both species are spectacular. Likewise, two species of treepies are very similar in appearance, but the Indian treepie prefers the tropics, while the Himalayan species lives in the subtropics and temperates. Above the tree line, two species of chough, congregating in large flocks in winter, are prevalent. Though the two species often overlap in range, the yellow-billed chough is found higher and is known to enter mountaineers' tents high on Everest. Another member of the crow family, also bold and conspicuous in the trans-Himalayan region, is the large raven.

Besides such families as kingfishers, bee-eaters, drongos, minivets, parakeets and sunbirds, there are a host of others, including 30 species of flycatchers and nearly 60 species of thrushes and warblers.

In the Kathmandu Valley, sparrows and pigeons demonstrate adaptability to urban centres by their sheer numbers. Dark kites, hawk-like birds with forked tails, are common over the city. At sunset, loose groups of crows, mynahs, egrets and kites fly to their respective roosts. Pulchowki, Nagarjun and Shivapuri are excellent areas for finding birds of subtropical and temperate habitats.

In the Pokhara region, the Indian roller is conspicuous when it takes flight and flashes the iridescent turquoise on its wings. Otherwise, while perched, it appears as a plain brown bird. Local superstition has it that if someone about to embark on a journey sees a roller going their way it is a good omen. If they see a crow, however, it is a bad omen and the trip is aborted. Many trips must be destined for delay thanks to the presence of the common crow!

Mammals

As one might expect, because of habitat degeneration from both natural and human causes, opportunities for seeing wildlife are usually restricted to national parks, reserves and western Nepal, where the population is sparse. Wildlife numbers have also been thinned by poaching for pelts and for other animal parts that are considered to be delicacies or medicinally valuable. Animals are also hunted because of the damage they inflict on crops and domestic animals.

At the top of the food chain is the royal Bengal tiger, the most magnificent cat, which is solitary and territorial. Males have territorial ranges that encompass those of two or three females and may span as much as 100 sq km. Royal Chitwan National Park in the Inner Terai and Royal Bardia National Park in the western Terai protect sufficient habitat to sustain viable breeding populations.

The spotted leopard is an avid tree climber and is more elusive than the tiger. Like the tiger, this nocturnal creature has been known to prefer human flesh when it has grown old or been maimed. Humans are easy prey, and once the taste is acquired, eaters of human flesh lose interest in their natural prey. Local people liken the spotted leopard to an evil spirit because its success at evading hunters suggests it can read minds.

The snow leopard is often protected from hunters, not only by national parks, but also because it inhabits inhospitable domains above the tree line and sensitive border regions. Its territory depends upon the ranges of ungulate (hoofed) herds, its prey species. Packs of wolves compete directly and when territories overlap, the solitary snow leopard will be displaced.

The one-horned rhinoceros is the largest of three Asian species and is a distinct genus from the two-horned African rhinos. It has poor eyesight, and though it weighs up to two tonnes, it is amazingly quick. Anyone who encounters a mother with its calf is likely to witness a charge, which is disconcertingly swift, even if you are on an elephant. The rhino is a denizen of the grasslands of the Inner Terai, specifically the Chitwan Valley, although it has also been reintroduced to Royal Bardia National Park and Royal Sukla Phanta Wildlife Reserve.

The Asian (Indian) elephant, like the one-horned rhino, is different from its African relative, belonging to a separate genus. The only wild elephants known to exist in Nepal are in the western part of the Terai and Chure Hills, though individuals often range across the border from India. Elephants are known to maintain matriarchal societies, and females up to 60 years of age bear calves. Though elephants may reach 80 years of age, their life spans are determined by dentition. Molars are replaced as they wear down, but only up to six times. When the final set is worn, the animal dies of starvation.

Periodically, male and occasionally female elephants enter a 'musth' condition that makes them excitable and highly aggressive. While in this agitated state they have been known to trample villages. When a herd goes on the rampage, outsiders or

Tea with the Mayor

I spent a month in a small town called Gularia in the far west of Nepal as part of an Australian conservation expedition in early 2001. Tourists don't really go there, so we received a lot of curious and friendly attention. We would walk the six dusty kilometres to our research site with little children running along beside us shouting 'Namaste!'. Often a university student or two would cycle alongside and converse animatedly with us in English. Even the local mayor and his councillors welcomed us with a rooftop tea party!

The conservation work involved collecting information on a rare antelope called the black buck. There are only 45 left in Nepal; they live in a small reserve about 6km from Gularia (a day trip from Royal Bardia National Park). I had contacted a Nepalese NGO (which I found on the Internet), which suggested the project and oversaw our work. This aspect was really important to us: We wanted our work to directly help the Nepalese and the environment. Each day we observed the animals, collected information, pulled out noxious weeds and dug waterholes. With the help of an interpreter we also interviewed local villagers in their homes about the situation.

The effort and hope of the Nepalese people to conserve this endangered animal despite enormous odds was impressive. We made many friends and had the unique privilege of becoming part of the daily routine of the town, joining in on everything from local weddings to Muslim festivals. I would recommend conservation work to any traveller who wants to really understand the places they visit and to give something back.

See the boxed text 'KEEP Nepal Green' earlier in this chapter for more information on conservation in Nepal.

Miranda Wills

non-Hindus are often summoned to deal with the problem, as the elephant is considered a holy animal by Hindus (because of the much-loved Ganesh, the elephant-headed god of the Hindu pantheon).

There are several species of deer, but most are confined to the lowlands. The spotted deer is probably the most beautiful, while the sambar is the largest. The muntjac, or barking deer, which usually makes its presence known by its sharp, one-note alarm call, is found at altitudes up to 2400m, while the unusual musk deer, which has antelope-like features and is only 50cm high at the shoulder, ranges even higher.

There are two primates: the rhesus macaque and the common langur. The rhesus is earth-coloured, with a short tail and travels on the ground in a large, structured troop, unafraid of humans. The langur is arboreal, with a black face, grey fur, and long limbs and tail. Because of Hanuman, the monkey god in the Hindu epic the *Ramayana*, both species are considered holy and are well protected. The rhesus ranges from the Terai up to 2400m, while the langur goes up to 3600m.

In the Kathmandu Valley, rhesus macaques at the Swayambhunath and Pashupatinath temples take advantage of their holy status and relieve worshippers of their picnic lunches and consecrated food.

Two even-toed ungulate mammals are found in the alpine regions. They are the Himalayan tahr, a near-true goat, and the blue sheep, which is genetically stranded somewhere between the goat and the sheep. The male tahr poses majestically in its flowing mane on the grassy slopes of inner valleys, while the blue sheep turns a bluish-grey in winter and is found in the trans-Himalayan region.

The Himalayan black bear is omnivorous and a bane to corn crops in the temperate forests. Though it rarely attacks humans, its poor eyesight may lead it to interpret a standing person as making a threatening gesture and to attack. If so, the best defence is not to run, but to lie face down on the ground, this is particularly effective when one is wearing a backpack. Nepal's bears are known to roam in winter instead of hibernating.

There are some prominent canines, though behaviourally they are fairly shy. The jackal, with its eerie howling that sets village dogs barking at night, ranges from the Terai to alpine regions. It is both a hunter and a scavenger, and will take chickens and raid crops.

The pika, or mouse hare, is the common guinea-pig-like mammal of the inner valleys, often seen scurrying nervously between rocks. The marmot of western Nepal is a large rodent; it commonly dwells in the trans-Himalaya. The marmot is also found in Sikkim and Bhutan, but not eastern Nepal – such gaps in speciation are not uncommon across the Himalaya.

Noisy colonies of flying foxes or fruit bats have chosen the trees near the Royal Palace in Kathmandu and the chir pines at the entrance to Bhaktapur as their haunts. They are known to fly great distances at night to raid orchards, before returning at dawn. They have adequate eyesight for their feeding habits and do not require the sonar system of insectivorous bats.

Pulchowki, Nagarjun and Shivapuri are good areas for possible sightings of small mammals.

Reptiles

There are two indigenous species of crocodile: the gharial and the marsh mugger. The gharial inhabits rivers and is a prehistoric-looking fish-eating creature with bulging eyes and a long, narrow snout. The marsh mugger prefers stagnant water and is omnivorous, feeding on anything within reach. Because of the value of its hide and eggs, the gharial was hunted to the brink of extinction, but has increased in numbers since the establishment of a hatchery and rearing centre in Chitwan. Both crocodiles inhabit the Terai.

Though venomous snakes such as cobras, vipers and kraits are present, the chance of encountering one is small, not only because of their usual evasive tactics, but also because they are indiscriminately slaughtered. The majority of species are found in the Terai, though the mountain pit viper is known higher up, along with a few other nonvenomous species.

NATIONAL PARKS & CONSERVATION AREAS

Nepal has national parks and wildlife reserves that protect every significant ecological system in the country – from the tropical plains of the Terai and the fertile midland valleys, to the highest mountains in the world.

Around 16,650 sq km are protected, or 11.3% of the country's area, and you can add another 2600 sq km if you include the Annapurna Conservation Area. Considering the strength of the demand for land, there has been a particularly impressive commitment to conservation.

Travellers are almost certain to visit a protected area: the Sagarmatha National Park includes Mt Everest; the Annapurna Conservation Area includes many of the most popular treks around the Annapurna *himal* (range or massif with permanent snow); and Royal Chitwan National Park is famous for its elephant-back safaris in search of royal Bengal tigers and one-horned rhinoceroses.

All visitors are charged Rs 500 per day to enter a park or reserve, and Rs 2000 to enter the Annapurna Conservation Area. There is no fee for using a camera or video camera within the parks. The Department of National Parks & Wildlife Conservation (☎ 01-220912) can be contacted through PO Box 860, Babar Mahal, Kathmandu.

The problems Nepal has faced in setting aside areas for conservation are more acute than those faced in most industrially developed countries, but the Nepalis are responding by developing new management concepts – it is not possible or desirable to set aside areas of land that are totally untouched by humans.

Firstly, very little of Nepal can be accurately described as wilderness. Most of the country is, in some way, used by humans. Virtually every possible square metre of arable land is used for farming; the remaining forests are utilised for firewood and hunting; the high country is used for hunting and grazing; and the whole country is crisscrossed with trade routes. The only exceptions are several royal hunting reserves, some of the Terai (large parts of which were virtually untouched until the 1950s) and mountain peaks at high altitude.

Secondly, developing national parks and conservation areas by following the Western

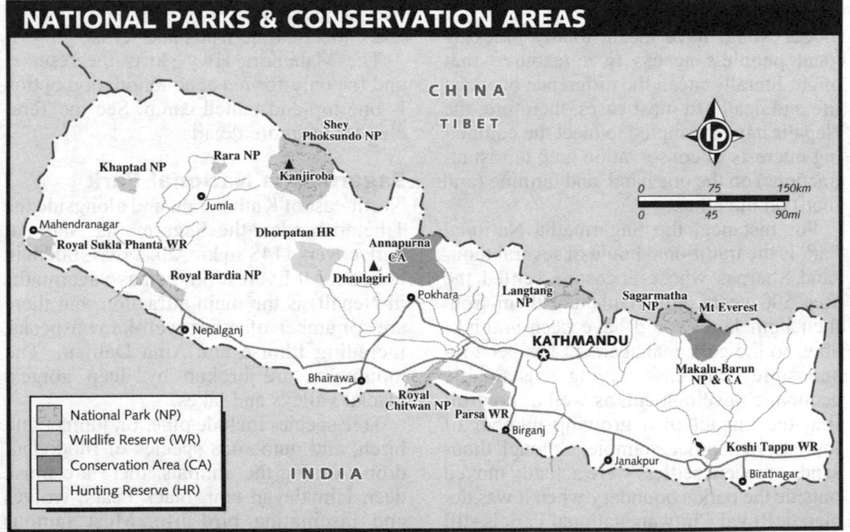

SIMON BORG

The magnificent royal Bengal tiger is a focus of conservation efforts in Nepal.

model would have meant totally blocking local people's access to a resource that might literally mean the difference between life and death. In most cases, therefore, the Nepalis have attempted to meet the competing interests of conservation (and tourist attractions) on the one hand, and farming (and food) on the other.

For instance, the Sagarmatha National Park is the traditional home of several thousand Sherpas whose ancestors settled the area 500 years ago. Banishing them from their homeland would have been unthinkable, so the park management has been responsible for encouraging sustainable economic development, as well as controlling the impact of a growing number of tourists. In another example, although thousands of recent settlers were actually moved outside the park's boundary when it was declared, Royal Chitwan National Park is still used by the settlers as an important source of thatching grass, which is harvested every year.

Despite these essential compromises, there have been some notable successes. The magnificent royal Bengal tiger has been saved in Chitwan and there have been impressive achievements in the Sagarmatha National Park and the Annapurna Conservation Area near Pokhara – in forestry, agriculture, health and education, as well as in protecting the most spectacular scenery in the world.

Koshi Tappu Wildlife Reserve

The Koshi Tappu Wildlife Reserve is a small reserve (175 sq km) that lies on the beautiful flood plain of the Sapt Kosi in eastern Nepal. It runs north from the massive Kosi Barrage and the Indian border.

The reserve is often flooded during the monsoon, although mostly to shallow depths only. It is, nonetheless, home to the last surviving group of wild buffalo (around 200) and several species of deer. The vegetation is mainly grassland, with some mixed riverine forest. A total of 280 different species of birds – including many migratory birds – have been recorded. Local villagers harvest grasses for thatching, and also fish and collect edible fruits and ferns.

The Mahendra Hwy skirts the reserve, and the only formal accommodation option is one top-end tented camp. See the Terai chapter for more details.

Sagarmatha National Park

North-east of Kathmandu and alongside the Tibetan border, the Sagarmatha National Park covers 1148 sq km, all above 3000m in altitude. Mt Everest (known as Sagarmatha in Nepali) is the main attraction, but there are a number of other well-known peaks, including Lhotse and Ama Dablam. The mountains are broken by deep gorges, glacial valleys and lakes.

Tree species include pine, fir, juniper and birch, and numerous species of rhododendron. Among the animals, there are musk deer, Himalayan tahr, black bears, wolves and fascinating bird life. Most famous would be the beautiful impeyan pheasant, Nepal's national bird, but there are choughs, snow pigeons and Himalayan griffons, among 130 bird species.

More than 3500 Sherpas use the park for cropping and grazing (their villages are not included in the park proper) and their unique culture provides yet another reason to visit. There are several important monasteries. For detailed information on this park try to find a copy of *Mt Everest National Park: Sagarmatha, Mother of the Universe* by Margaret Jefferies, an excellent book that gives fascinating background information and has some magnificent photos.

This seems to be one of the most popular trekking regions in the country, but it's only accessible on foot, with the nearest airstrip at Lukla and the road head at Jiri. Many trekkers visit, lured by the highest and most spectacular mountain scenery in the world and by Sherpa culture. See the Trekking chapter for information on trekking in the park.

Makalu-Barun National Park & Conservation Area

The Makalu-Barun National Park and Conservation Area, just to the east of Mt Everest, was proclaimed in November 1992. It covers 2330 sq km. Its boundaries are marked by the Arun River to the east and the Sagarmatha National Park to the north-west. Its northern boundary is the Qomolangma (Mt Everest) Nature Preserve (35,000 sq km) in Tibet. Together these three parks protect a vast area around the Everest massif.

The park includes Makalu, at 8463m the fifth-highest mountain in the world, and each year a small number of trekkers walk in to the base camp. Elevations range from 435m on the Arun River to the 8000m summits of the *himal* (a himal is a range or massif with permanent snow). Nearly all ecological zones, from subtropical forest to the alpine snows of the Himalaya, are found in the area. In the valleys you can find some of the last remaining tracts of pristine mountain landscape in Nepal. The area is rich in plant and animal diversity.

The wilderness area has the status of a national park, but the surrounding regions, which are home to more than 32,000 people, are being managed according to the model pioneered by the ACAP. The majority of people are Rai, followed by Sherpa and Tibetan-speaking groups.

There is an airstrip at Tumlingtar about 10km south of Khandbari.

Royal Chitwan National Park

South-west of Kathmandu, near the Indian border on the tropical Terai, Royal Chitwan National Park and the contiguous Parsa Wildlife Reserve cover just over 1431 sq km. The park includes a section of the Chure Hills and the Rapti, Narayani and Reu Valleys.

Sal forest covers 70% of the park, with the remainder consisting of grasslands and riverine forests. The park is home to the only significant number of one-horned rhinoceroses surviving in Nepal, and to other endangered species such as the royal Bengal tiger, the Gangetic dolphin and the gharial crocodile. Altogether, there are more than 43 species of large mammals and over 450 species of birds. There are no human communities living in the park, but the surrounding countryside is intensively cultivated.

For detailed information on this park, try to find a copy of *Royal Chitwan National Park: Wildlife Heritage of Nepal* by Hemanta R Mishra and Margaret Jefferies; some of the photos are magnificent.

The park is easily accessible by road, and accommodation ranges from five-star and expensive, to zero-star and cheap. Many people visit for two or three days (especially if they are going to or from India) and take an elephant safari through the forest. See the Royal Chitwan National Park section in the Terai chapter for more details.

Annapurna Conservation Area

North of Pokhara and extending to the Tibetan border, the Annapurna Conservation Area covers 2600 sq km. It includes the Annapurna peaks, the famous Annapurna Sanctuary and a significant section of the Kali Gandaki Valley.

The conservation area is run by the Annapurna Conservation Area Project (ACAP), a nongovernmental, nonprofit organisation funded by various trusts. The project's primary objectives are to improve local standards of living, to protect the environment and to develop more sensitive forms of tourism.

This is the most popular trekking region in Nepal, especially for individual trekkers, and this influx of visitors has added to the pre-existing problems in the mountains. The trekkers' demands for heating and hot water have led to increased deforestation, there are litter and sanitation problems, and wildlife has been driven away from many parts.

In response, ACAP has started work on a number of projects, such as forestry nurseries, introducing wood-saving technologies (eg, efficient stoves), banning fires altogether in certain areas, and building rubbish tips, latrines and water treatment stations for drinking water. Many problems still remain, and it is vital that trekkers cooperate with these and other initiatives. If you would like more information on ACAP activities, visit the ACAP offices in Kathmandu or Pokhara (see those chapters for details).

The treks around the Annapurna himal are undoubtedly some of the best in the world – not only for the grandeur of the mountains, but for the variety of fascinating cultures you can visit (Bhotiya, Tibetan, Tamang, Magar, Gurung, Thakali and others). The area is easily accessible from Pokhara and there is an airstrip at Jomsom. See the Trekking chapter for more information.

Langtang National Park

This is the nearest national park to Kathmandu, extending from 32km north of Kathmandu to the Tibetan border, and covering 1710 sq km. The park encloses the catchments for two major rivers – the Trisuli and the Sun Kosi – and several 7000m mountains.

The complex topography and geology of the area together with the varied climatic patterns means there is a wide variety of vegetation types and animals. There are small areas of subtropical forest below 1000m, then temperate oak and pine forests, subalpine juniper, larch and birch, and finally alpine scrub, rocks and snow. The fauna includes lesser or red pandas, muntjac, musk deer, black bears, monkeys, ghorals and serows (so-called goat-antelopes).

About 45 villages lie within the park boundaries (although they do not come under park jurisdiction). In total, around 18,000 people depend on the park's resources, mainly for wood and pasture land. There are several ethnic groups, but the majority of the people are Tamangs (settlers originally from Tibet and followers of the pre-Buddhist Bön religion).

There are a number of popular treks in the park, varying in length and difficulty. There is road access to Dhunche (near the park headquarters) from Kathmandu, or you can walk in from Sundarijal or Panchkhal, or from Chatara or Tatopani on the Kodari road. See the Trekking chapter for more details.

Dhorpatan Hunting Reserve

The Dhorpatan Hunting Reserve lies in the Dhaulagiri himal in western Nepal. It is characterised by a dry climate in the north and well-developed, mixed hardwood forests at lower elevations.

The 1325 sq km reserve is one of the prime habitats of the blue sheep, a highly prized trophy animal. Other 'game' animals include the ghoral, serow, Himalayan tahr, black bear, deer, pheasant and partridge.

The only access, unless you have a helicopter, is by foot from Jelbang.

Shey Phoksundo National Park

At 3555 sq km, the Shey Phoksundo National Park is the largest park in Nepal. It encompasses the Kanjiroba himal in western Nepal and runs north to the Tibetan border.

The park stretches across all possible vegetation zones – from the luxuriant forests of the lower Himalaya to the near desert of the Tibetan plateau. Typical animals include the Tibetan hare, the Himalayan weasel and the beautiful snow leopard. Lake Phoksundo and the Shey Monastery are the two main attractions in the park, but the entire region has been little touched by the modern era.

Very few people visit this region, partly because access has, in the past, been officially restricted, and because it entails a dangerous 14-day trek from Pokhara. Permits can be arranged through trekking companies. See *Trekking in the Hidden Land of Dolpa-Tarap & Shey Poksumdo* by Paolo Gondoni (available at Pilgrims Book House, Kathmandu) for more detailed information. According to information from the national parks department, it takes two days to walk to the entrance gate at Sumduwa from Dunai, the district headquarters for Dolpo.

Rara National Park

In little-visited western Nepal, the 106 sq km Rara National Park was established to preserve the catchment and surrounds of the beautiful Rara Lake – a clear high-altitude lake ringed with pine, spruce and juniper forests and snow-capped peaks. The lake is the largest in Nepal (10.8 sq km) and is an important water-bird habitat.

The only way to get to Rara Lake is a strenuous three-day trek from the airstrip at Jumla, or a 10-day trek from the road head at Surkhat. Trekking in this area is much more difficult than in eastern or central Nepal. See Lonely Planet's *Trekking in the Nepal Himalaya* for more details.

Royal Bardia National Park

In the western Terai, bordering the Geruwa (a branch of the Karnali River), this 968 sq km reserve is reminiscent in many ways of Royal Chitwan National Park. The relative difficulty of access, however, means it is much less popular. But there is a higher likelihood of seeing a royal Bengal tiger.

The reserve is bordered to the north by the Chure Hills, but is predominantly flat and dominated by sal forests and grasslands. As well as tigers, there are blue bulls, a variety of deer, a few wild elephants and

Watch out for the introduced one-horned rhinoceros at Royal Bardia National Park.

a small herd of introduced rhinoceros. If you're lucky you might also see Gangetic dolphins in the river.

The park is 2½ hours by road from Nepalganj and there is accommodation available, ranging from budget to top of the range. See Royal Bardia National Park in the Western Terai section of the Terai chapter for more details.

Khaptad National Park

Another rarely visited park, Khaptad covers 225 sq km in far western Nepal. Lying at around 3000m, it is largely a rolling plateau with grasslands and oak and coniferous forests.

Royal Sukla Phanta Wildlife Reserve

This 305 sq km reserve lies in the far southwestern corner of Nepal on the Indian border. It covers a riverine flood plain, dominated by sal forest, but like both Royal Chitwan and Royal Bardia National Parks, there are also grasslands, which make it ideal for wildlife observation.

Sukla Phanta is one of the last strongholds of the endangered swamp deer (now thought to number about 2000 here), but there are also around 35 tigers and an estimated 45 wild elephants, as well as leopards and a variety of birds.

Access to the park is by road from Mahendranagar and it is possible to stay in a tented camp. See the Terai chapter for more details.

GOVERNMENT & POLITICS

In April 1990, the Jana Andolan, or People's Movement, forced King Birendra to abandon the panchayat system that had been established by his father and under which the king enjoyed virtually sole power. (See under The Shahs' Restoration in the History section earlier in this chapter for more information.)

A new constitution was adopted in November 1990. It provided for a constitutional monarchy, universal adult franchise and a multiparty parliamentary system. Members of the 205-seat Pratinidhi Sabha (House of Representatives) are elected every five years according to the first-past-the-post system.

In the May 1991 elections, the Nepali Congress party won 110 seats, giving it a simple majority, and formed the government with GP Koirala as prime minister. In the decade since then, Nepal has had more than a dozen governments, many of them frail coalitions that lasted less than a year. At the time of writing, the prime minister was GP Koirala (again), who toppled fellow Nepali Congress leader KP Bhattarai in March 2000.

Members of the 60-seat Rastriya Sabha (National Assembly) have a six-year tenure; a third retire every two years. Thirty-five members are elected by proportional representation, 15 members are elected by local government representatives, and 10 members are nominated by the king.

People's War

Since 13 February 1996, the Communist Party of Nepal (Maoist) has been waging a People's War in the hills of Nepal against the Nepali state. Formed in 1995 after innumerable splits in the country's communist movement, the extremist party advocates the establishment of a communist republic in place of the existing constitutional Hindu monarchy.

The 'War' itself started after the Maoists presented the then prime minister with a 40-point charter of demands that ranged from favourable state policies towards backward communities to an assertive Nepali identity, from better governance to an aggressive posture against India. The government chose to keep mum on the Maoist demands and within 10 days the Maoists attacked police stations in two western Nepal districts and began the insurgency that as of the end of 2000 had killed 1513 people, with a further 256 injured and 380 kidnapped (government figures).

The initial government reaction to a force armed with ancient muskets and *khukuris* (traditional knives) took the form of reprisals in areas considered Maoist strongholds. It backfired badly since it only succeeded in alienating the local people. As the fighting continued, the Maoist arsenal got more and more sophisticated with the addition of guns looted from the police, home-made explosives, and, it is believed, automatic weapons (although the last have not been used so far). Recent events have shown that the civilian police is incapable in dealing with the rebels and in early 2001 preparations were underway to set up a paramilitary force after which the violence is likely to escalate.

Although officially 46 of Nepal's 75 districts have been classified as 'highly affected', and another 20 (including Kathmandu) as 'affected' by the Maoist insurgency, the real fighting has so far been confined to the remote districts far away from the power centre in the capital. Analysts believe that this is one reason why the State has not actively responded to what is shaping up as a real national crisis.

So far there is no record of foreigners being attacked although practically all the popular trekking routes pass through 'Maoist affected' areas. One reason could be that trekking provides direct employment to the working class and hence is ideologically palatable to the Maoists. Another could be that trekking companies are known to be paying 'safe-passage' money to the Maoists, although none would admit it publicly. There have been stray reports of tourist groups robbed but there is enough reason to believe that at least some of these were perpetrated by small-time thugs using the Maoists as a cover.

Deepak Thapa, journalist for the *Nepali Times*

ECONOMY

Judged by Western standards, Nepal is one of the poorest countries in the world, with an estimated gross domestic product (GDP) of only US$240 per person in 2000. To a certain extent, this suggests an overly bleak picture because more than 90% of the population consists of subsistence farmers operating outside the cash economy, and things are likely to remain this way.

Agriculture

Around 40% of GDP is accounted for by agriculture (including fisheries and forestry). At present, most farmers succeed in meeting their basic needs and producing a small surplus for cash sales. Indeed aid workers have been known to bemoan the fact that they can't convince peasant farmers to work harder and produce additional cash crops.

The problem is that the rewards are not believed to be worth the effort. After all, if a family has food, a house, and perhaps access to a TV and bicycle, what more could they want – or realistically aspire to?

In the late 1970s Nepal actually exported large quantities of rice. The development of the Terai opened up new land, temporarily relieving some of the population pressure in the hills, and the so-called green revolution (utilising improved seeds, artificial fertilisers and pesticides) led to increased productivity. The population, however, has again begun to grow more rapidly than production, and Nepal has to import rice to meet its needs. It is a net importer of food, and food imports rose to US$105 million in 2000.

The average size of land-holdings has continued to drop; it now stands at around 0.7 hectares in the hills and a little over 1 hectare in the Terai. In a good year, half a hectare in the hills around Kathmandu might produce around 1000kg of rice and 500kg of mixed vegetables, but if the farmer does not own the land up to 50% of this production will go to the owner as rent. Although there are theoretical limits on the amount of land an individual may own, tenant farmers are still common and many are in debt to moneylenders.

Where possible, crops are supplemented with livestock (especially in the mountain areas), but the animals are often of poor quality, partly because there is a serious shortage of fodder, especially in winter. One of the important uses of Nepal's remaining forests is as a source of animal fodder; unfortunately this can also lead to unsustainable damage. For more information on agriculture and animal husbandry in Nepal, see Ecology earlier in this chapter.

Manufacturing & Services

For many Nepalis there's not much food to spare, especially if the rains fail. Although outright starvation is rare, undernourishment is very common, particularly in the undeveloped west of the country. A growing number of people are forced to seek seasonal work, or rely on money that is repatriated by other family members, to supplement what they can produce from their land.

Unfortunately, Nepal's embryonic manufacturing industries (mainly on the Terai) and service sector are unable to meet the demand for work, so there is significant underemployment. Manufacturing and industry account for around 30% of GDP, up from around 20% just a decade ago.

Perhaps the most amazing success story of the last few decades, has been that of Tibetan carpets. Although weaving is an indigenous craft, in 1960 the Nepal International Tibetan Refugee Relief Committee, with the support of the Swiss government, began encouraging Tibetan refugees in Patan, to make and sell carpets. Today, Nepal exports more than 244,000 sq metres of rugs (down from a peak of 300,000 sq metres in the 1990s), valued at around US$135 million. This industry accounts for around 50% of the country's exports of manufactured goods (to countries other than India), and employs more than 250,000 workers.

The carpet industry has declined somewhat over recent years, largely because of negative publicity about exploitative work practices (namely child labour) and the use of carcinogenic dyes. While both of these practices are supposedly illegal, they still continue.

For many people, however, the only accessible source of income is the tourist trade either as a market for handicrafts and other small-scale businesses (lodges, shops, travel agencies etc) or as an employee (hotel staff, porters etc). Others work as day labourers for wealthy farmers, or try to pick up menial work in Kathmandu.

Foreign Exchange & Trade

Tourism accounts for 22% of foreign exchange earnings, although there is some debate over how much of this leaks out of the country again in paying for the goods and services that Westerners require. This makes the country particularly vulnerable to fluctuations in the number of tourist arrivals. With around 25% of all arrivals by air being Indians, any negative impact, such as the hijacking of the Indian Airlines jet from Kathmandu Airport on 24 December 1999, can have disastrous effects on the economy – arrivals of Indian tourists were down by a massive 32% in 2000 compared with 1999.

Some cynics claim that the two mainstays of the Nepali economy are really smuggling and foreign aid: There are no official figures for the smuggling, but foreign aid accounts for 14% of hard-currency receipts.

Nepal has always been an intermediary between India and China. More recently, it has become a transit point for goods from Japan, Singapore and Hong Kong. It is claimed that many goods travel in a circuit from India to Nepal and back to India.

Nepal's trade is dominated by India and many activities within the country are Indian-owned or controlled. In the 1998–99 financial year Nepal had a trade deficit with India of an estimated Rs 20,000 million.

Development

It is hard to be optimistic when looking at the prospects for Nepal, despite the ingenuity of the Nepali people. The growing population threatens to overwhelm the developments that have already taken place, and future developments will always be hampered by the impossible terrain.

Whether the country can continue to carry the population it already has – given that soils and forests are already being exploited at unsustainable levels – might even be questioned. For a very large number of peasant families, existence appears set to become increasingly perilous. This is likely to lead to increased migration to the Kathmandu Valley (where resources are already strained), to the Terai and to India.

In Kathmandu, the gulf between rich and poor is extreme. The aristocracy wields considerable power and influence, and many of its members lead lives that are extraordinarily privileged. These feudal survivors have been joined by a new business elite, whose strikingly ugly houses now dot the outskirts of Kathmandu. Corruption is endemic at every level of government.

The challenges facing Nepal are clearly immense. A large proportion of the population (42%) lives in poverty and nearly 60% is illiterate. Health services, especially outside the Kathmandu Valley, are limited – the ratio of doctors to people was one to 15,000 in 1991, and there were only 4700 hospital beds. The average life expectancy is 57 years.

Since most people are dependent on agriculture, this is the most important area for development. Much can be done to increase and sustain productivity, but here as elsewhere, the topography means there is an amazing diversity of problems, not least of which is reaching the isolated valleys and ridges where so many of the people live.

On the positive side, education is spreading into distant valleys, and trekkers are likely to come across thriving primary schools in the most remote areas. Also highly visible are the improvements in Nepal's communications network. The telephone system links all major towns, and roads continue to extend farther and farther into distant parts of the country. Often, however, new roads bring undesirable social changes (thanks to an influx of outsiders and trade goods, and the facilitation of migration to the cities), and some question whether the huge sums of money involved in road construction and maintenance might not be better allocated to expanding and improving the existing network of walking tracks and bridges.

Nepal's physical resources are extremely limited. There are few accessible minerals, and there is little unexploited arable land. There are, however, great hydroelectric power resources, although the market for them is likely to be found in India, and the capital and ecological costs involved in construction are huge.

Foreign Aid

Foreign aid sounds as if it should be a wonderful industry – on the surface, totally non-polluting and ecologically sound. Nepal has lots of it and the end result is highly questionable. If you're interested in the impact of foreign aid on a country like Nepal, the magazine *Himal* regularly has articles that will provide food for thought.

Two other books, accounts of travels in Nepal, are enlightening. Peter Somerville-Large's *To the Navel of the World* contrasts the successful, heavily touristed and aided Solu Khumbu region of the Sherpas in eastern Nepal with the neglected areas of the far north-west. While critics debate the damage caused by tourism it seems hardly likely that the people living in the areas where trekkers and aid projects are plentiful would willingly switch to the areas of Nepal that are still 'off limits'.

Charlie Pye-Smith's *Travels in Nepal* was essentially a trek from one aid project to another and what he saw was not always a pretty sight. Too often the projects were pointless, or imposed without consultation with the locals, or without adequate understanding of the local physical and cultural environment. Often the only people who benefited were the foreign companies that supplied the equipment and expertise and the affluent Nepalis who skimmed off a profit as the project passed by them.

Pye-Smith contends that most aid donors look for big projects (they like to have something visible to show off) and that government officials like the big ones too (there's more likely to be something in it for them). The projects that actually work, however, are much closer to ground level. Pye-Smith describes disastrous Japanese irrigation projects, ill-planned Austrian hydroelectric power projects and well-meaning but inept US ecological projects, but also tells of a British agricultural project near Dhankuta in the east which really seemed to work, and an Australian forestry project which operated on a shoestring and seemed to work much better because of that.

He concludes, however, by questioning the whole basis of foreign aid in Nepal. Along the way he turns up many interesting thoughts. Hydroelectric power, for example, is touted as an enormous energy saver but its main use is for electric lighting. Lighting powered by hydroelectricity is much cheaper than that powered by kerosene, and a great deal of expensive kerosene can be saved. But Pye-Smith argues that with cheap lighting people stay up later and when they stay up they burn firewood. The end result of providing hydroelectric power can actually be an increase in the consumption of scarce timber.

One aid project disaster he observed was a tree-planting exercise where the trees were not only badly planted but planted in an area where the first monsoon deluge washed them away. This totally wasted plantation was fenced in by cutting down healthy trees! Even the horror story of Himalayan deforestation is brought into question. 'The only number which has any scientific validity at all in the Himalaya is sixty-seven', he writes. This is the factor by which estimates of per-capita firewood consumption vary.

In the nearly 15 years that have passed since the publication of Pye-Smith's work, much has changed and yet much has remained the same when it comes to foreign aid. Nepal is still not short of donors willing to pour money into the country – what has changed is that there has been a shift away from direct involvement to management of aid money and projects by local NGOs. The result has been a proliferation of NGOs and not necessarily any more effective spending of aid funds. Corruption and inefficiency are as rife here as anywhere in government, and cynics will happily tell you that for every aid dollar which gets spent on a project, a further two dollars or more gets siphoned off before it ever has a chance to reach the intended beneficiaries.

POPULATION

Nepal's population stands at around 23.4 million (2001 estimate). The population growth rate is a high 2.43%. The largest city is Kathmandu, the capital, with 500,000 people, although the population of the Kathmandu Valley is around one million.

In the mountains the rate of population increase is lower than in the Terai, but this is because many people are migrating in search of land and work. Despite (or because of) extremely high rates of infant mortality and the life expectancy of only 57 years, the overall annual rate of population increase is high, putting enormous pressures on Nepal's fragile ecology.

PEOPLE

Like the geography, the population of Nepal is extremely diverse and highly complex. Simplistically, Nepal is the meeting point of the Indo-Aryan people of India and the Tibeto-Burmese of the Himalaya, but this gives little hint of the dynamic ethnic mosaic that has developed and continues to change to this day.

In a south–north direction, as you move from the plains to the mountains, the ethnic map can be roughly divided into layers: the Himalaya, the midlands or Pahar zone, and the Terai. Each zone is dominated by characteristic ethnic groups whose agriculture and lifestyles are adapted to suit the physical constraints of their environment. (See Geography earlier in this chapter for more detail on the physiographic features of each area.) These zones can be further subdivided from east to west, with different groups in the east, central and western regions of each zone.

Himalayan Zone

In the Himalayan zone, the people are Mongoloids of Tibetan descent. They are known in Nepali as Bhotiya or Bhote, terms that are now often considered derogatory because the Shah and Rana regimes categorised Bhotiya as untouchables who could legally be enslaved.

Most Bhotiya identify with a particular region, and attach the suffix *pa* (people) to their name. These include the Sherpas of the Everest region, the Manangpa of the Manang region north of the Annapurna himal, and the Lopa of the Mustang region. This group also includes Thakalis, who are the

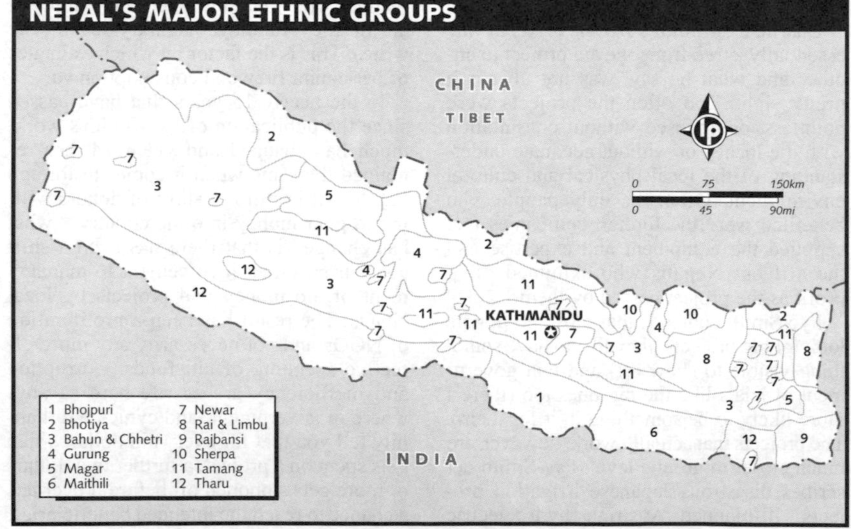

well-known innkeepers from the Thak Khola (Kali Gandaki) on the Jomsom Trek, and Tamangs, around the Kathmandu Valley and the Langtang region.

With a few exceptions in the far west, all these people are Buddhist and have a culture similar to that of Tibetans.

Thakalis Originating along the Kali Gandaki Valley in central Nepal, the Thakalis are a Tibeto-Burmese people who have become the entrepreneurs of Nepal. They honed these skills from the days when they played an important part in the salt trade between the subcontinent and Tibet but now they are found in many areas of modern commercial life. Originally Buddhist, many pragmatic Thakalis have now adopted Hinduism.

Most Thakalis have small farms, but travellers will regularly meet them in their adopted roles as hoteliers. Many small hotels in Nepal are run by Thakalis; the Pokhara to Jomsom trek along the Kali Gandaki Valley is the best 'village inn' trek in Nepal, because of the numerous Thakali lodges along this route through their homeland. The actual number of Thakalis is very small.

Tamangs Tamangs are the largest Tibeto-Burmese ethnic group in Nepal, but little is known of their history. Tamangs are now sedentary farmers and labourers. Their appearance, language and Buddhist beliefs all bear testimony to their origins. Indeed, many of the 'Tibetan' souvenirs for sale in Kathmandu are actually made by Tamangs.

Around half the Himalayan zone of Nepal is inhabited by Tamangs, and it is likely they have been there longer than any other group. Tamangs dominate the high hills surrounding the Kathmandu Valley and the central Himalayan zone, especially in the Langtang region. Their homesteads, unlike the Newars', are often solitary. Houses may be constructed out of brick or stone, but they are often modest in size, with a porch, a courtyard, a mud finish and a thatched roof.

Many Tamangs have been influenced in their dress by both Western and Newari styles. Traditionally, women wear a colourful wraparound skirt, a blouse, jacket and scarf. On important occasions they wear chunky gold or brass earrings and nose rings set with semiprecious stones. Men wear loincloths or the traditional Newari pants, short-sleeved jackets and *topis* (caps). Both men and women wear several metres of cloth wrapped around the waist.

Tamangs' religion is closely associated with Tibetan Buddhism (see Religion later in this chapter). Some Tamangs follow Bön, the pre-Buddhist religion of Tibet. In Tamang areas you are certain to come across *chortens* (Tibetan Buddhist stupas with a square base, topped with a dome), and *mani* walls. Manis are prayer stones engraved with mantras.

Tamangs are one of the largest groups in Nepal, but they have been seriously exploited, especially since the unification of Nepal under the Shahs. In the 19th century their legally defined status was the lowest of any hill people, and much of their land was distributed to Bahuns and Chhetris.

Tamangs were relegated to bonded labour, and were dependent on menial work, particularly as porters. They were prevented from joining the government or the military (unlike many other hill groups). Tamangs remain, in general, extremely poor, and continue to work as *thela gada* (cart pushers), rickshaw pullers, autorickshaw drivers and porters. They produce the bulk of the thangka paintings sold in Kathmandu, and many of the Tibetan carpets. Many Tamang women have been forced into prostitution, in both Nepal and India.

Tibetans Mongoloid people from Tibet have settled in Nepal for thousands of years, but the most recent arrivals have been refugees. In 1950 the communist People's Republic of China overpowered the Tibetan army. For the next eight years the Chinese made a heavy-handed attempt to bring the Tibetans into the communist fold, including the imposition of inappropriate agricultural policies that led to mass famine. In March of 1959 a Tibetan uprising was brutally crushed, and the Dalai Lama, Tibet's spiritual and political leader, fled to India. Thousands of Tibetans followed him across the Himalaya.

There are currently around 120,000 Tibetans in exile, and about 12,000 of them are in Nepal, mostly in Kathmandu and Pokhara. Although their numbers are only small, they have a high profile, partly because of the important role they play in tourism. Many hotels and restaurants in Kathmandu are owned or operated by Tibetans. They have also been responsible for the extraordinary success story of the Tibetan carpet industry, which in 30 years has grown from nothing to being the largest single employer in the country. (See the Economy section earlier in this chapter.)

Tibetans are devout Buddhists and their arrival in the valley has rejuvenated a number of important religious sites, most notably the stupas at Swayambhunath and Boudha. A number of large new monasteries have been established.

Sherpas Living high in the mountains of eastern and central Nepal, in particular in the Solu Khumbu region at the foot of Mt Everest, the Sherpas are probably the best known Nepali ethnic group. Originally from Tibet, they settled in the area about 500 years ago, and were probably nomadic herders until the introduction of the potato in the middle of the 19th century. The relative increase in wealth that this new crop created allowed them to settle in permanent villages and to create a number of monasteries known as *gompas*.

The Sherpas are Buddhists, and in the 20th century their name has become synonymous with mountaineering and trekking. Not all *sherpas* – the small-'s' word describes a trek guide or mountaineer – are Sherpas, but many of them are, and they've won worldwide fame for their skill, hardiness and loyalty.

Midlands Zone

In the east of the midlands zone, one finds the Kirati (also known as Kiranti) people, who are divided into the Rai and Limbu groups. These groups are also Mongoloid peoples who speak various Tibeto-Burmese languages. Their religion is shamanistic – neither Buddhist nor Hindu – but Hinduism

MICK WELDON

Sherpas (and Sherpanis) are known worldwide for their hardiness

is becoming increasingly influential. The Kirati entered Nepal from the north and east and founded a kingdom in the Kathmandu Valley around the 7th century BC that continued for 1000 years. Independent Kirati kingdoms survived in the east until the end of the 18th century.

In the central midlands around the Kathmandu Valley live the Newars. Some believe the Newars are Kirati; others believe they are survivors from a still older group. They have absorbed successive waves of immigrants and created a religious environment that is in many ways a synthesis of Hinduism and Buddhism.

In the central midlands around the Kali Gandaki, the two main groups are the Magar and the Gurung. Both groups are Mongoloid and speak Tibeto-Burmese languages, which indicates they came from Tibet, although no-one knows when. The Gurungs tend to occupy middle elevations to the southern flanks of the Annapurna massif, while the Magars tend to occupy the lower elevations.

The Gurungs' shamanistic religion is under pressure from Hinduism in the south and Buddhism in the north. The Magars have long been Hindu, and have developed close ties with the Indo-Aryan Khas, farther to the west. In many cases they have taken the high-status Chhetri (Kshatriya) caste. Until the 18th century, Magar kingdoms dominated the region. The most famous was Palpa, with its capital at Tansen, which fought alongside Gorkha at the beginning of Prithvi Narayan Shah's expansionist wars.

In the western midlands, the situation becomes confusing, partly because there are few written historical records and ethnicity becomes confused with caste. The area is dominated by Khas, an Indo-Aryan people whose language has evolved into present-day Nepali. The numbers of Khas have been continually supplemented by the arrival of Parbatiyas (Hindus of varying caste and ethnicity) from the Indian plains. In the 12th century the Khas, who controlled a large empire, were joined by Bahun (Brahmin) and Chhetri refugees from the Muslim invasion of India. Although the Khas were technically low caste, many were given the high Chhetri caste by the Bahun, and the children of Bahun men and Khas women were also made Chhetris.

The unusual fluidity of caste allowed ambitious families to adopt higher castes – the most powerful Chhetris from among the Khas and Magar became Thakuris. The Khas empire fragmented into many small kingdoms ruled by powerful families who further embellished their pedigrees by claiming royal antecedents in India. After Prithvi Narayan Shah's triumph, many Bahuns and Chhetris were rewarded with grants of land in central and eastern Nepal, and since then they have spread throughout the country. In the west, however, they are numerically dominant.

Rais & Limbus These two large groups are known as Kirati people, the descendants of the Kiratis who formed the first recorded kingdom in the Kathmandu Valley. They now live in the eastern midlands, and many have migrated to the eastern Terai. Large numbers find employment with Gurkha regiments.

They are Tibeto-Burmese people, but their traditional religion is distinct from both Buddhism and Hinduism, although Hinduism is exerting a growing influence. The traditional religion is entirely oral and is based on the periodic appeasement of ancestor divinities and nature spirits; there are priests, elders and shamans. Rais and Limbus both bury their dead. The Limbus use a common burial site and erect a whitewashed rectangular grave marker with three levels for women, four for men.

The Rais and Limbus cultivate wet and dry fields, and slash-and-burn shifting agriculture is still important in places. In the hills, most villages are scattered and the houses are small one-storey edifices built of stone. Along the Arun River and in the Terai, the houses are often timber and bamboo, built on high wooden piles. In the Terai, these houses can be large, and are often surrounded by a verandah.

Newars The Newars of the Kathmandu Valley, who make up around 6% of the total population, are a good example of the result of this Himalayan melting pot. They number about 1.1 million and speak Newari, a language distinct from Tibetan, Nepali or Hindi, and they follow a version of Hinduism with many Buddhist overtones.

It is not surprising that the Newar people were influenced by Tibet and India. What is surprising is their creative response to this stimulus, which actually led to a genuine exchange with their giant neighbours. Medieval Newari society has left a religious, architectural and artistic legacy that is unique, and spectacular by any standard.

Although most Newars have Mongoloid physical characteristics, some don't, so their origins are shrouded in mystery. It is generally accepted that they are a mixture of many different peoples who were attracted to the valley, possibly originating with the Kiratis, or an even earlier group.

Perhaps the Newars' most striking characteristic is their love of communal life; Newari houses are invariably clustered together, usually around sites of religious significance. Although their economy was centred on agriculture and trade, they created sophisticated urban communities which catered to a breadth of human needs in an integrated way that has rarely been matched.

Always traders and merchants, the Newars continue to fill this role throughout the kingdom. Their proximity to the centre of power has also led to them having a disproportionate influence in the bureaucracies of Kathmandu. Many now live in depressingly ugly bungalows on the outskirts of the city proper, and many of their traditions are on the wane.

Newari Architecture The most important social unit was the family and the family house was the starting point for urban planning. Rich Newars built handsomely proportioned brick houses that were up to five storeys high, but more usually three or four with tiled roofs. Symbolically a Newari house becomes ritually purer as you ascend floors. The *chhyali* (ground floor) is not considered suitable for living in, and is used for commerce or the stabling of animals, or both. The *mattan* (first floor) consists of a bedroom and a room for visitors. Windows are small and latticed for both privacy and security. The *chota* (second floor) is the most active floor in the house and holds the living room, bedrooms and workroom for weaving and the like. It also houses a *dhukuti* (storeroom). Windows on this floor are larger and have outward-opening shutters. The *baiga* (attic floor) has the kitchen and dining room, a *pujakuthi* (shrine room) and a roof terrace.

A community developed when a series of houses was built in a rectangle around a *chowk* (courtyard or square). The chowk, often with running water and a temple or shrine, was the centre of day-to-day life, and still is today to a large extent. Here, the markets buzz, children play, women chat and work (weaving, washing, drying grain), old people doze in the sun, men talk over the community's business and religious ceremonies take place.

The cities and towns of the Kathmandu Valley were made up of a compact network of these interlocking squares, courtyards, twisting alleyways, ponds and temples, often centred on a main square. Fortunately, much of this tradition remains. Decorated with carved windows and doorways, statues and shrines, and humming with gregarious people, a Newari town is a remarkable synthesis of art and everyday life.

Newari Religion The vast majority of Newars are Hindu and fall under a caste system, although there is still a significant minority of Buddhists. This simplistic description, however, masks an incredibly diverse and complex system of beliefs.

Since the 5th century, kings and aristocrats have been Hindu and their influence gradually led to Buddhists adopting castes and a hereditary priesthood (the Banrhas). The many collapsing *bahals* (monasteries) testify to a long-gone Buddhist golden age.

The result is that a purist from either religion would not recognise many of the Newari gods or the practices that go into their worship. For not only have aspects of both religions combined, they have been added to by a Tantric tradition, Tibetan Buddhism and even older local deities and beliefs.

This has led to a confusing proliferation of gods who are often hybrids unashamedly shuffled from one pantheon to another. There are literally hundreds of these divinities, and more than 150 days of festivals a year to celebrate them. From a functional point of view, most people are free to follow whatever gods and goddesses particularly appeal to them, so theological consistency (including the distinction between Hinduism and Buddhism) is irrelevant, certainly to the people themselves. (See Religion later in this chapter for more details.)

Gurungs The Gurungs tend to live in higher country and generally farther to the east than the Magars, but otherwise are similar to them in many respects. Their homeland is the central midlands, ranging from Gorkha and Baglung to quite high on the southern slopes of the Annapurnas. They are a Tibeto-Burmese people with a unique shamanistic religion that is gradually giving way to Hinduism and Buddhism.

Gurungs are farmers, raising rice, wheat, maize and millet. Sheep husbandry is also important, with village families contributing a handful of sheep to a larger village flock. During the summer months they move their sheep to higher pastures, then with the end of the monsoon they bring them down to the villages. Like the Magars, the Gurungs often work as Gurkha soldiers.

Magars A numerically large group (around 8% of the total population), the Magars are a Tibeto-Burmese people who live in many parts of the midlands zone of western and central Nepal. Until the 18th century they had their own kingdoms, but they also had close contact with the Hindu Indo-Aryans in the west. This led to a gradual increase in Hindu influence and cultural assimilation. Nowadays in terms of religion, farming practices, housing and dress, they are hard to distinguish from Chhetris.

The Magars are farmers, and renowned soldiers; they fought with Prithvi Narayan Shah, and their kingdom of Palpa (based at Tansen) was one of the last to be incorporated into the new unified Nepal. Their martial qualities have been recognised by the British and Indian armies; Magars are the single largest group in the Gurkha regiments. Gurkha earnings play an enormously important role, both in improving living standards in the villages, and in the Nepali economy as a whole.

The Magars generally live in two-storey rectangular or square thatched houses washed in red clay. Historically, these houses were often round or oval in shape.

Bahuns & Chhetris In Hindu theory there is no relationship between caste and ethnicity, so Bahuns and Chhetris are simply the two highest castes (Brahmin priests and Kshatriya warriors respectively). In Nepal, however, most Bahuns and Chhetris are from the Khas kingdoms that flourished in western Nepal for at least a millennium before the unification of Nepal. Today they account for around 30% of the total population.

The Khas are Indo-Aryans who migrated to Nepal over the centuries; in the Middle Ages their numbers, and their consciousness of caste, were supplemented by refugees from the Muslim invasions of India. The progeny of Bahun men and hill women were considered Chhetri, and a number of high-status families from other hill groups have also adopted Chhetri status, so some do have Mongoloid tribal ancestry.

Bahuns and Chhetris played an important role in the court and armies of Prithvi Narayan Shah, and after unification they were rewarded with lands throughout the country. The Khas' language, Khas Kura, became the national language of Nepal, and the position of Bahuns and Chhetris at the top of the heap was religiously, culturally and legally enforced. Ever since, they have dominated the processes of government in Kathmandu.

Outside of the valley, the majority of Bahuns and Chhetris, however, are simple peasant farmers, indistinguishable in most respects from their neighbours. Sometimes their wealth is reflected by relatively large houses (compared with those of neighbouring tribal groups). Most of these people live in two-storey stone or mud-brick thatched houses that are washed with lime or red ochre. Many had roles as tax collectors under the Shah and Rana regimes, and to this day many are moneylenders with a great deal of power.

All Bahuns and Chhetris are Hindu, but the Bahuns tend to be more caste-conscious and orthodox than other Nepali Hindus and this sometimes creates difficulties in their relationship with 'untouchable' Westerners. Many are vegetarians and do not drink alcohol; marriages are arranged within the caste.

There is no particular cultural dress by which they can be recognised but men in both castes wear a sacred thread – the *janai* (see Janai Purnima in the 'Festivals of Nepal' Special Section).

Terai Zone

Until the eradication of malaria in the 1950s, the only people to live in the valleys of the Inner Terai, and along much of the length of the Terai proper, were Tharus and a few small associated groups. Most Tharus, though not all, have a Mongoloid appearance. There is considerable speculation, but there are no hard facts, about where they originated. Their religion is animist, with increasingly important Hindu overtones.

Along the Terai proper, a number of numerically significant groups straddle the border between India and Nepal. In the eastern Terai, Mithila people dominate; in the central Terai, Bhojpuri-speaking people dominate, and in the western Terai, Abadhi-speaking people are significant. All these are essentially cultures of the Gangetic plain, and Hindu caste structure is strictly upheld. In various parts, notably around Nepalganj and Lumbini, there are also large numbers of Muslims.

Since the Terai has been opened for development, it has also been settled by large numbers of people from the midlands – every group is represented.

Tharus One of the most visible groups in the Terai is the Tharus, a race who are believed to be the earliest inhabitants of the Terai (and they're even thought to be immune to malaria). About one million Tharu speakers inhabit the length of the Terai, including the Inner Terai around Chitwan, although they primarily live in the west. There are caste-like distinctions between different Tharu groups or tribes. Most have Mongoloid physical features.

Nobody is sure where they came from, although some believe they are the descendants of the Rajputs (from Rajasthan), who sent their women and children away to escape Mughal invaders in the 16th century. The women later married into local tribes. Another belief is that they are descended from the royal Sakya clan, Buddha's family, although they cannot be described as Buddhist.

Customarily the women were heavily tattooed, although these days this is unusual and tattoos are rarely seen on young women. Some groups wear simple white saris, others colourful calf-length dresses and a short blouse or bodice that exposes their belly. Tharu houses have mud-rendered walls and thatched roofs; they are high, dark and cool, with few if any windows. Reliefs of domestic animals are often moulded on the mud walls.

Apart from farming, Tharus also hunt and fish. In particular, groups of young women and children will often be seen heading off on fishing expeditions. Their beliefs are largely animistic, although increasingly influenced by Hinduism, and they live a life that is cleverly adapted to their environment.

Many Tharus are heavily exploited by newly arrived hill people or *zamindars* (landlords). Large numbers fell into debt and entered into a form of bonded labour (known as the *kamaiya* system) little different from slavery. In 2000 the *kamaiyas* (bonded labourers) were granted freedom from this system by government legislation. While the legislation is laudable, there was little follow-up resourcing of these landless people who suddenly found themselves with no work and nowhere to live. Consequently, in most Terai towns in western Nepal you'll see squatter settlements, and most of these squatters are former kamaiyas. After much outcry the government provided some relief for these people, with provision of limited money and the promise of land, and at least one foreign aid organisation has taken up the cause.

EDUCATION

While education is gradually spreading to the small villages, it has been a slow process, especially in the mountains. At 60%, the illiteracy rate in the country is uncomfortably high.

A complicating factor is that the country faces an acute shortage of qualified teachers. There are currently around 92,000 primary-school teachers in Nepal, and more than half of these have no formal teacher training. Official primary enrolments stand at around 3.6 million, which translates to one qualified teacher for every 88 enrolled children. On top of this are all the children who are not even enrolled because their families can't afford to lose an able-bodied worker from their land-holding.

The public education sector is augmented by private schools, which have proliferated in the past decade – seemingly every town you pass through has a high number of 'English Medium Boarding Schools'. On the surface this is a good thing, but unfortunately the reality is somewhat less encouraging. With profit being the bottom line of any business, it seems many of these schools are business ventures first and foremost; the education side of things comes a poor second. Parents have to pay anything from Rs 90 to Rs 200 a month for their children to attend such schools.

It is a sad fact that the standard of education offered by the free government schools is also lacking.

ARTS

The whole Kathmandu Valley could be seen by a traveller as one enormous art gallery and museum; the arts and architecture in Nepal are inextricably intermingled. The finest woodcarving and the best sculpture are often part of a building – a temple is simply not a temple without its finely carved roof struts. The crafts also reflect the uniquely Nepali melting pot where religious art has Tantric Hindu and Buddhist overtones and the dividing line between one religion and another is hard to discern.

Lydia Aran's *The Art of Nepal* is a handy and interesting introduction to Nepali art and its religious background. There are detailed descriptions of the many Hindu, Buddhist and Hindu-Buddhist deities and their associated religious terminology. This book is particularly interesting because it concentrates on the art still in Nepal, as opposed to objects in overseas museums and private collections.

Architecture & Sculpture

The earliest architecture in the Kathmandu Valley has faded with history. The four Ashoka stupas of Patan are simply grassy mounds today, and the great stupas of Swayambhunath and Boudha have undoubtedly changed many times over the centuries. Nevertheless, these simple hemispherical Buddhist structures are essentially unchanged from their earliest appearance – they're simply a solid mound rising from the ground and topped with a spire. You can find similar Buddhist stupas in Sri Lanka, Myanmar (Burma) and Thailand.

The Licchavi period from the 4th to 9th centuries AD was a golden age for Nepal, and while the temples may have disappeared the superb stone sculptures can still be found. Many temples around the valley have beautiful pieces of Licchavi craftwork in their courtyards; the temple of Changu Narayan at the eastern end of the valley is a particularly good example. The great reclining Vishnu image at Budhanilkantha is another wonderful example of Licchavi stonework. The Licchavis undoubtedly worked in wood as well, but no wooden buildings or carvings survive from that era.

It was in the Malla period that Nepali artistry with wood really came into its own. The earliest woodcarving in the valley dates from the 12th and 13th centuries and includes the roof struts of the great Basantapur Tower in Hanuman Dhoka (the old Royal Palace) in Kathmandu's Durbar Square, and the Kasthamandap building, also in the square. The Uku Bahal in Patan also dates from this period, but you have to go out of the valley to Panauti, near Banepa, to find one of the oldest and finest survivors in the shape of the Indreshwar Mahadev Temple.

The artistic skills of the Newar people of the valley flourished under the Mallas, and not only woodcarving but metalwork, terracotta, brickwork, stone sculptures and other crafts all enjoyed a long golden age. The finest metalwork includes the images of the two Tara goddesses at Swayambhunath, and the river goddesses Ganga and Jamuna, standing guard in the palace of Patan.

The popularity of the multiroofed Nepali pagoda design in China and eastern Asia is credited to the architect Arniko, who with 24 assistants visited Tibet in the late 13th century and later worked for the Ming emperor. The road to the Tibetan border is named the Arniko Hwy in his honour. The contact with Tibet also began to influence Nepali artists, and vivid Tibetan colours and fantastic Tibetan creatures started to appear in Nepali art and architecture.

Temple Architecture

Newar Pagoda Temples

The distinctive Newar pagoda temples are a major feature of the Kathmandu Valley skyline. While strictly speaking they are neither wholly Newari nor pagodas, the term has been widely adopted to describe the temples of the Kathmandu Valley.

The temples are generally square in design, and may be either Hindu or Buddhist (or both in the case of mother goddesses). On rare occasions temples are rectangular or octagonal, but this depends on the god being worshipped; Krishna, for example, can occupy octagonal temples, whereas Ganesh, Shiva and Vishnu can only inhabit square temples.

The major feature of the temples is the tiered roof, which may have one to five tiers, with two or three being the most common. In the valley there are two temples with four roofs and another two with five (Kumbeshwar at Patan and Nyatapola at Bhaktapur). The sloping roofs are usually covered with distinctive *jhingati* (baked clay tiles), although richer temples will often have one roof of gilded copper. The *gajur* (pinnacle of the temple) is usually bell-shaped and made of baked clay or gilded copper.

The temples are usually built on a stepped plinth, which may be as high as or even higher than the temple itself. In some cases the number of steps on the plinth corresponds with the number of roofs on the temple.

The temple building itself has just a small sanctum, known as a *garbha-griha* (literally 'womb room') housing the deity. Worshippers practise individually, with devotees standing outside the door to make their supplications. The only people permitted to actually enter the sanctum are *pujari* (temple priests).

Perhaps the most interesting feature of the temples is the detailed decoration, which is only evident close up. Under each roof there are often brass or other metal decorations, such as *kinkinimala* (rows of small bells) or embossed metal banners. The metal streamer that often hangs from above the uppermost roof to below the level of the lowest roof (such as on the Golden Temple in Patan) is called a *pataka*. Its function is to give the deity a means of descending to earth.

The other major decorative elements are the wooden struts that support the roofs. The intricate carvings are usually of deities associated with the temple deity or of the *vahana* (deity's vehicle). Occasionally the designs are merely floral, and there are a number of temples where the carvings depict explicit sexual acts, often involving animals. One theory is that these have been put on temples to deter the goddess of lightning, who is a virgin.

ALL ILLUSTRATIONS BY KELLI HAMBLET

The staggered roof of the Nyatapola Temple at Taumadhi Tole dominates the Bhaktapur skyline.

Temple Architecture

Stupas

The Buddhist stupas of the Kathmandu Valley – particularly the stupas of Swayambhunath and Boudha (also known as Bodhnath) – are among the most impressive and most visited monuments in Nepal.

The earliest stupas in India were merely domed burial mounds, but they have evolved over the centuries to become complex structures which represent the Buddha and Buddhist philosophy.

The lowest level of the stupa is the plinth, which may be simply a square platform, but may also be terraced, as at Boudha. On top of the plinth is the hemispherical *kumbha* (dome; kumbha literally means 'pot'), which is usually whitewashed each year.

Atop the dome is a spire, which always consists of a number of elements. Immediately on top of the dome is a *harmika*, a square base usually painted on each side with a pair of eyes, which most people believe represent the all-seeing nature of the Buddha.

Topping the harmika is a tapering section of 13 stages, which are said to represent the 13 stages of perfection. At the very peak is a gilt parasol, which symbolises royalty.

The all-seeing Swayambhunath Buddhist stupa, one of the most recognised and popular temples in Nepal.

Shikhara Temples

The second most common temples are the shikhara temples, which have a heavy Indian influence. The temples are so named because their tapering tower resembles a *shikhara* (in Sanskrit, a mountain peak). Although the shikhara style developed in India in the 6th century, it first appeared in Nepal in the late Licchavi period in the 9th century.

The main feature is the tapering, pyramidal tower, which is often surrounded by four similar but smaller towers, and these may be located on porches over the shrine's entrances. The tower is usually built on a square stepped plinth. A quite good example of a shikhara temple is the Shiva Temple in Bhaktapur's Durbar Square.

Occasionally the shikhara temple follows the same basic design but is much more elaborate, with porches and small turrets seemingly all over the place. The Krishna Mandir and the octagonal Krishna Temple, both in Patan's Durbar Square, are excellent examples.

Krishna Mandir, Patan Durbar Square

The last centuries of the Malla period saw temple after temple rise over the Kathmandu Valley skyline. The squabbling city-states of Kathmandu, Patan and Bhaktapur vied with each other to raise yet more glorious temples and palaces. Much of the construction was still in the traditional multiroofed Nepali pagoda style but there was also a great deal of Indian influence, as seen in the stone Krishna Mandir of Patan's Durbar Square, the spires of the Mahabouddha Temple in Patan, and the two temples at the top of the stairway to Swayambhunath.

With the invasion of the valley by Prithvi Narayan Shah from Gorkha, the great age of Nepali architecture came to a dramatic end. The great woodcarved temples and palaces in the valley today mainly date from that brilliant period prior to 1767. Although the skills used to build them have lain dormant in the centuries since then, these skills are still alive and well. When the Hanuman Dhoka palace in Kathmandu and the Tachupal Tole buildings in Bhaktapur were restored in the 1970s, the work was done by purely traditional means and with craftwork every bit as good as in the past. More recently the Chyasilin Mandapa in Bhaktapur, completely destroyed in the great earthquake of 1934, was totally rebuilt in 1989–90, again using traditional skills.

Painting

Nepal has a long history of painting, and some high-quality traditional work is still being done today. The earliest Newari paintings were illuminated manuscripts dating from the 11th century. These were followed by miniature paintings influenced by the miniature styles of northern India, and then by scrolls and murals. By this time the Tibetan influence was starting to make itself felt on Newari painting, although from the 14th to 16th centuries the Newars also had a great influence on Tibetan art.

Today some of the best examples of old Newari painting are hung in temples where they are rarely seen, but the art gallery in Bhaktapur has a fine collection and is an excellent introduction to the development of art in Nepal. Newari artists have their own special caste of Chitrakar. For more information on painting in Nepal today, see Thangkas under Shopping in the Facts for the Visitor chapter.

Music & Dance

Despite the pervasiveness of Western music, Nepali music hangs in the air, whether it is the plaintive notes of a flute or the gentle twang of the four-stringed *saringhi*. Although the *gaines*, traditional professional musicians, are a dying breed, they can still be heard. The folk music of rural Nepal still has a strong following and the gaines are often storytellers as well.

The *damais* are modern professional musicians, all drawn from the tailor caste, who form the backbone of wedding bands. This music can definitely be hard on Western ears, falling uncomfortably close to the painful standards of Indian bus music. The blaring wail of long Tibetan horns at Buddhist religious sites probably also qualifies for the unlistenable category.

Dance has a long and strong history in Nepal, both in cheerfully performed folk dances and in the more formal classical dances. The Newars of the Kathmandu Valley are the chief exponents of classical dancing, but there are also masked dances with a Tantric background, and the colourful masked dances of Bhaktapur (performed during the Indra Jatra festival each year).

Some of the more important traditional dances include Bajrayogini, based on Tantric Buddhism; Bhairavkali, a classical dance of Shiva and Kali; Bhojpuri, a popular dance from the Terai; Jhagad, from the eastern Terai; Lakhe, a mask dance of the Newars; and Sangini, which is a prayer dance from the women of the Bahun-Chhetri.

Literature

Nepal does not have a long literary tradition; it dates back only to the 19th century to the works of Bhanubhakta Acharya (1814–68). Bhanubhakta was the first person to really break away from the strong influence of Indian literature and compose truly Nepali verse. He is most famous for his rendering of the *Ramayana* into Nepali.

This was far more than just a straightforward translation; it was instead a 'Nepalised' version of the Hindu epic.

Further development of Nepali literature was hindered by the fact that until the 20th century, very little written Nepali was published. The Rana regime sought to promote Nepali literature early in the 20th century with the establishment of the Gorkha Language Publication Committee in 1913. This body virtually had a monopoly over Nepali publishing, and because of its heavy censorship role came to be regarded with suspicion by writers and poets, who chose to have their work published in India. Indeed, a number of Nepali periodicals appeared in India for this very reason.

It was only in the 1930s that Nepal's first literary journal, *Sharada*, appeared. It was published monthly right up until 1963 and gave many aspiring writers the chance to have their work published.

Important writers and poets include Lekhnath Paudyal, Balkrishna Sama, Lakshmiprasad Devkota, Daulat Bikram Bishtha and Guruprasad Mainali.

SOCIETY & CONDUCT

Nepal has always been a dividing line between civilisations and cultures, and a crossroads for the flow of commerce and culture. Here the plains of the subcontinent climb up to the high plateau of Tibet, the languages and people of India give way to those of China, and the Hindu religion blends into Buddhism. Nepal, the land in the middle, is often a complex blend of the two influences and this variation is further complicated by the diversity of ethnic groups within the country.

Newari Traditional Culture

Customs The Newars are divided into castes, whether they nominally consider themselves Hindu or Buddhist, and these include untouchables (tinkers, butchers and some others). Caste rules are not quite as rigid as in some parts of India, but intermarriage is still rare and untouchables are still grossly disadvantaged.

The usual dress for a Newari woman is a sari and blouse, often with a shawl. The men wear *surwal* (trousers with a baggy seat that are tighter around the calves, like jodhpurs), a *daura* (thigh-length double-breasted shirt), a vest (waistcoat) or coat and the traditional *topi* (Nepali cap). The most distinctive caste is the Jyapu, who are farmers, and many of them still lead highly traditional lives. Jyapu women wear a black sari with a red border, while the men often wear the traditional trousers and shirt with a long piece of cotton wrapped around the waist. They prefer to carry goods on a shoulder pole.

Newari children undergo a number of *samskara* (rites of passage) as they grow up. The *namakarana* (naming rite) is performed by the priests and chief of the clan, and the family astrologer gives the child its public and secret name. The next rite is the *machajanko* (rice feeding), which celebrates the child's presence on earth and wishes them a smooth life. Next for boys comes the *busakha*, performed between the ages of three and seven, when the head is shaved, leaving just a small tuft. This is an occasion of great feasting and animals are sacrificed. This is followed by the fixing of a kaitapuja (loincloth), which marks a commitment by the boy to bachelorhood and self-control. Girls undergo *Ihi* (a symbolic marriage to Vishnu) between the ages of five and 11, and at this time the girl begins to wear a thick cotton thread. The Ihi samskara venerates chastity and guarantees the girl a choice of husband. This is followed by a *barha* (menarche rite), which protects the girl's virginity and safeguards against passion.

Weddings are usually negotiated through a *lami* (mediator), and take place at times deemed auspicious by the family astrologer. The bride is taken in a noisy procession to the groom's house where she is received with an oil lamp and the key to the house. The *chipka thiyeke* samskara involves the serving of 84 (!) traditional dishes and is a symbol of the couple's union.

The first *janko* (old-age samskara) takes place at 77 years, seven months and seven days, the second at 83 years, four months and four days and the third – if you make it that far! – at 99 years, nine months and nine days.

The final samskara is *sithan* (cremation), which marks the body's move to its final destination.

Traditionally, men were members of a unique cooperative institution known as a *guthi*. This is a religious and social group based on family and other local links. Guthis may own land and are often responsible for the upkeep of particular temples and financing particular rites, as well as the welfare of their members.

Dos & Don'ts

The challenge for you as a visitor to Nepal is to respect the rights and beliefs of the local people, and to minimise your impact – culturally and environmentally. Remember Nepal is not an adventure park or museum established for your convenience, but home to a vital, changing culture. Life for many is extremely hard, but despite the scarcity of material possessions, Nepal has many qualities that shame the so-called 'developed' world.

Your very presence in Nepal will have an effect – an increasing number of people say a negative one. In a totally different culture it is also inevitable that the visitor will make some gaffe at some point. Most Nepalis make allowances, but they do appreciate it when a genuine effort is made to observe local customs. Following is a collection of simple suggestions that will help you to avoid offence.

Dress Dress appropriately – shorts and revealing clothes are unsuitable for women. Shorts are acceptable for men only when trekking; going without a shirt anywhere is not. Nudity is unacceptable anywhere.

Behaviour Public displays of affection are frowned upon. Nepali men often walk around hand in hand, but this does not have the same implications as it does in San Francisco!

Raising your voice or shouting shows extreme bad manners and will not solve your problem, whatever it might be. Always try to remain cool, calm and collected.

Bodily contact is rarely made, even for shaking hands, although among Nepali men with frequent Western connections it is becoming more accepted. Never touch anything or point at anything with your feet, the 'lowest' part of the body. In contrast, the head is spiritually the 'highest' part of the body, so don't pat children on the head.

Don't inquire about a person's caste.

Nepalis do not like to give negative answers or no answer at all: If you are given a wrong direction or told a place is much nearer than it turns out to be, it may be through fear of disappointing you!

Don't encourage begging children. If you want to help, there are lots of excellent aid organisations which will make good use of your contribution, and local schools will be only too happy with a gift of ballpoint pens.

For more information, see Begging later in this chapter.

Visiting a Temple Always walk clockwise around Buddhist stupas, chortens and mani walls. Always remove your shoes before entering a Buddhist or Hindu temple or sanctuary. You may also have to remove any items made from leather, such as belts and bags. Many Hindu temples do not permit Westerners to enter.

It's the custom to give a *khata* (white scarf) to a Buddhist priest when you are introduced. The honorific title Rimpoche (Precious One) is usually bestowed on priests. The scarves can easily be found in Tibetan shops.

Visiting a Nepali Home Fire is sacred, so do not throw rubbish into it. This applies particularly to a kitchen fire in a Nepali home, and in theory applies to trekkers' campfires. In practice, burning the garbage before leaving camp is accepted, but it's probably best to wait until just before you leave camp to do it; certainly don't do it before cooking. In a Nepali home the kitchen is off limits to strangers.

Avoid 'polluting' food by inadvertently touching it or bringing it into contact with a used plate or utensil. Using your own fork or spoon to serve more food is not acceptable. Putting your used plate on a buffet table risks making the food still on the table *jutho* (polluted). Notice how Nepalis drink from a cup or water vessel without letting it touch their lips.

Always remove your shoes before entering a Nepali home.

Photography Do not intrude with a camera, unless it is clearly OK with the people you are photographing. Ask before entering a temple compound whether it is permissible to enter and take photographs. Do not exchange addresses or offer copies of photos unless you definitely intend to follow it up later. For more information, see Photography & Video in the Facts for the Visitor chapter.

Begging Various kinds of begging is relatively common in Nepal, partly because both Hinduism and Buddhism encourage the giving of alms. This presents many visitors with a heart-rending moral dilemma. Should you give? Sometimes, especially if you've just spent Rs 500 on drinks, it seems grotesque to ignore someone who is genuinely in need. It is often worth checking to see how the local Nepalis react; if they give, it's a reasonably safe assumption that the beneficiary is genuine.

Around the main religious shrines, especially Pashupatinath, there are long lines of beggars. Pilgrims customarily give a coin to everyone in the line (there are special money-changers nearby who will change notes for small-denomination coins). This is a culturally sanctioned and traditional form, but most Westerners find it difficult to deal with, and are not really expected to give. *Sadhus* (holy men) are another special case, and are usually completely dependent on alms. There are plenty of con artists among their ranks, but equally, plenty of genuine holy men.

The main tourist centres, especially Thamel and Durbar Marg, have also attracted numbers of beggars. Here, Westerners are expected to give, although whether they should is another matter – there are even signs up around Thamel asking visitors not to give to beggars.

Thamel attracts many of Kathmandu's estimated 1000-plus street kids. Giving to them, however, is at best a double-edged sword. Firstly, the lure of easy money attracts kids onto the streets in the first place, and then gives them a powerful incentive to remain. Secondly, it's a dog-eat-dog world: Children who are seen receiving money may well be beaten up and have it stolen.

Also highly visible are women (often from India), usually clutching one or two children. Rumours suggest these women are often part of organised begging rings, and that the money they receive is passed on to a Fagan-like figure. By giving to them, you are encouraging a further influx of people into Kathmandu where very few facilities exist for them.

Although the blind and lepers are probably genuinely dependent on begging for their survival, long-term solutions are offered by See Nepal (☎ 475927), PO Box 501, Kathmandu; and the Leprosy Hospital (☎ 290545), PO Box 151, Anandban, Kathmandu.

See Nepal is an innovative and effective program well known to most Australians because of the involvement of the late Professor Fred Hollows. Many forms of blindness are dealt with in rural clinics; often, relatively simple treatments and surgical techniques can restore people's sight. See Nepal has opened a factory in Nepal which manufactures the plastic lenses used in cataract operations. Excess production will be exported to India and China and any profits will be ploughed back into the program, hopefully making it self-sustaining. In the meantime, See Nepal can do with donations.

In the countryside, visitors will quickly be discovered by small children who chant a mantra that sounds something like: 'bonbonpenonerupeeee?'. Someone, somewhere, started giving children sweets (bonbons), pens and money, and it sometimes seems that every child in Nepal now tries their luck. Do not encourage this behaviour. Most Nepalis find it offensive and demeaning (as do most visitors), and it encourages a whole range of unhealthy attitudes.

For some suggestions on how you can support alternatives to begging, by shopping at community-based craft organisations, for example, see Shopping in the Facts for the Visitor chapter.

RELIGION

In Nepal, Hinduism and Buddhism are mingled into a complex blend which is often impossible to separate. The Buddha was actually born in Nepal but the Buddhist religion first arrived in the country around 250 BC, introduced, so it is said, by the great Indian Buddhist emperor Ashoka himself. Later, Buddhism gave way to Hinduism but from around the 8th century AD the Tantric form of Buddhism practised in Tibet began to make its way across the Himalaya into Nepal. Today Buddhism is practised mainly by the people of the high Himalaya, such as the Sherpas and Tamangs, and by the Tibetan refugees who have settled in Nepal.

Officially Nepal is a Hindu country but in practice the religion is a strange blend of Hindu and Buddhist beliefs with a pantheon of Tantric deities tagged on to the list of Hindu gods or, in many cases, inextricably blended with them. Thus Avalokiteshvara, the prime Bodhisattva of this Buddhist era, becomes Lokeshvara, a manifestation of the Hindu god Shiva, and then appears as Machhendranath, one of the most popular gods of the Kathmandu Valley. Is he Hindu or Buddhist? Nobody can tell. Hindu temples have been marked differently on maps, but the distinction is somewhat arbitrary.

Although the vast majority of the population is Hindu (86.5%) or Buddhist (7.8%), there are also small groups of Muslims (3.5%) and Christians (0.2%).

Hinduism

India, Bali, Mauritius and possibly Fiji are the only places apart from Nepal where Hinduism predominates, but it is the largest religion in Asia in terms of the number of adherents. Hinduism is one of the oldest extant religions, with firm roots extending back to beyond 1000 BC.

The Indus Valley civilisation developed a religion that showed a close relationship to Hinduism in many ways. Later, it further developed on the subcontinent through the combined religious practices of the Dravidians and the Aryan invaders who arrived in northern India around 1500 BC. Around 1000 BC, the Vedic scriptures were introduced and gave the first loose framework to the religion.

Hinduism today has a number of holy books, the most important being the four *Vedas*, the 'divine knowledge' that is the foundation of Hindu philosophy. The *Upanishads* are contained within the *Vedas* and delve into the metaphysical nature of the universe and soul. The *Mahabharata* is an epic poem describing in over 220,000 lines the battles between the Kauravas and the Pandavas. It contains the story of Rama, and it is probable that the most famous Hindu epic, the *Ramayana*, was based on this. The *Bhagavad Gita* is a famous episode of the *Mahabharata* where Krishna relates his philosophies to Arjuna.

Hinduism postulates that we will all go through a series of rebirths or reincarnations that eventually lead to *moksha*, the spiritual salvation that frees one from the cycle of rebirths. With each rebirth you can move closer to or further from eventual moksha; the deciding factor is your karma, which is literally a law of cause and effect. Bad actions during your life result in bad karma, which ends in a lower reincarnation. Conversely, if your deeds and actions have been good you will

The Ages of Brahma

Each universe has a Brahma who lives for 100 years, Brahma years, that is, which are much longer than our Earth years. Each day in a Brahma year is a Kalpa, and each Kalpa or Brahma day is in turn divided into 1000 Mahayugas or Great Ages.

In a single Great Age there are four Yugas, which follow a prescribed pattern. In the first Yuga everything is fine, but in the second Yuga evil makes its appearance and the eternal struggle between good and evil commences. In the third Yuga, good is in serious trouble and in the fourth Yuga, the Kaliyuga, evil comes out on top and it's time for Vishnu to take on his 10th incarnation as Kalki the destroyer and bring the whole mess to a quick end.

And where are we currently in this cycle of existence? About halfway through the fourth Yuga.

reincarnate on a higher level and be a step closer to eventual freedom from rebirth.

Dharma is the natural law that defines the total social, ethical and spiritual harmony of your life. There are three categories of dharma, the first being the eternal harmony that involves the whole universe. The second category is the dharma that controls castes and the relations between castes. The third dharma is the moral code that an individual should follow.

The Hindu religion has three basic practices. These are puja or worship, the cremation of the dead, and the rules and regulations of the caste system. There are four main castes: the Brahmin, or priest caste; the Kshatriya, or soldiers and governors; the Vaisyas, or tradespeople and farmers; and the Sudras, or menial workers and craftspeople. These castes are then subdivided, although this is not taken to the same extreme in Nepal as in India. Beneath all the castes are the Harijans, or untouchables, the lowest, casteless class for whom all the most menial and degrading tasks are reserved.

Despite common misconceptions, it is possible to become a Hindu, although Hinduism itself is not a proselytising religion. Once you are a Hindu you cannot change your caste – you're born into it and are stuck with your lot in life for the rest of that lifetime. Nevertheless the concepts of Hinduism have a great attraction for many Westerners and India's 'export gurus' are numerous and successful.

A guru is not so much a teacher as a spiritual guide, somebody who by example or simply by their presence indicates what path you should follow. In a spiritual search one always needs a guru. A sadhu is an individual male on a spiritual search. Sadhus are an easily recognised group, usually wandering around half-naked, smeared in dust, with their hair and beard matted.

See the special section 'The Gods of Nepal' for an illustrated guide to some of the more popular of Nepal's Hindu pantheon.

Buddhism

Strictly speaking, Buddhism is not a religion, since it is centred not on a god, but on a system of philosophy and a code of morality. Buddhism was founded in northern India in about 500 BC when Siddhartha Gautama, born a prince, achieved enlightenment. According to some, Gautama Buddha was not the first Buddha but the fourth, and he is not expected to be the last 'enlightened one'. Buddhists believe that the achievement of enlightenment is the goal of every being, so eventually we will all reach buddhahood.

The Buddha never wrote down his dharma (teachings), and a schism that developed later means today there are two major Buddhist schools. The Theravada (Doctrine of the Elders), or Hinayana, holds that the path to nirvana, the eventual aim of all Buddhists, is an individual pursuit. In contrast, the Mahayana school holds that the combined belief of its followers will eventually be great enough to encompass all of humanity and bear it to salvation. To some, the less austere and ascetic Mahayana school is considered a 'soft option'. Today it is practised mainly in Vietnam, Japan and China, while the Hinayana school is followed in Sri Lanka, Myanmar (Burma) and Thailand. There are still other, sometimes more esoteric, divisions of Buddhism, including the Tantric Buddhism of Tibet, which is the version found in Nepal.

Buddha renounced material life to search for enlightenment but, unlike other prophets, found that starvation did not lead to discovery. He developed his rule of the 'middle way' (moderation in all things). Buddha taught that all life is suffering – suffering comes from our sensual desires and their illusion of importance. By following the 'eightfold path' these desires will be extinguished and a state of nirvana, where our desires are extinct and we are free from their delusions, will be reached. Following this process requires going through a series of rebirths until the goal is reached and no more rebirths into the world of suffering are necessary. The path that takes you through this cycle of births is karma, but this is not simply fate. Karma is a law of cause and effect; your actions in one life determine the role you will play and what you will have to go through in your next life.

In India, Buddhism developed rapidly when it was embraced by the great emperor

Ashoka. As his empire extended over much of the subcontinent, so Buddhism was carried forth. Later, however, Buddhism began to contract in India because it had never really taken a hold on the great mass of people. As Hinduism revived, Buddhism in India was gradually reabsorbed into the older religion.

Tibetan Buddhism There are four major schools of Tibetan Buddhism and all of them are represented in the Kathmandu Valley: Nyingmapa, Kargyupa, Sakyapa and Gelugpa. The differences are quite esoteric, with their roots often in political as well as major theological disputes.

The Indian sage Padmasambhava (also known as Guru Rimpoche) is credited with establishing Buddhism in Tibet in the 8th century, when he helped build a gompa at Samye. The Nyingmapa order, sometimes referred to as the Old One, traces its origins back to Padmasambhava. The Kargyupa (Whispered Transmission) order was established by Marpa in the 11th century and has a strong Tantric influence. Marpa's most famous disciple was Milarepa, Tibet's most revered poet.

The Sakyapa was also founded in the 11th century and rose to a position where it ruled Tibet (with the support of the Mongols) until it came into conflict with the Gelugpa (Virtuous) order, which had been founded in the 14th century by Tsongkhapa.

The Gelugpa were celibate and advocated monastic discipline. The school introduced the system of reincarnated spiritual leaders and ultimately came to power – again with the support of the Mongols – in the late 17th century. It was a Mongol ruler who conferred the title Dalai Lama (Ocean of Wisdom) on its leader. The Gelugpa completely isolated Tibet and maintained a strict theocratic state.

In some texts, Tibetan Buddhism may be referred to as Lamaism, and the Gelugpa are known as the Yellow Hats, while the other schools are sometimes collectively identified as the Red Hats.

Islam

Nepal's small population of Muslims (around 750,000 people, or 3.5% of the total population) originated in different parts of Asia, and today are mainly found close to the border with India and in a handful of isolated villages.

The first Muslims, who were mostly Kashmiri traders, arrived in the Kathmandu Valley in the 15th century. A second group arrived in the 17th century from northern India, and they primarily manufactured armaments for the small hill states. The descendants of these early immigrants today speak Nepali and are indistinguishable from upper-caste Hindus.

The largest Muslim group are the Terai Muslims, many of whom arrived before unification. Others gradually drifted north from India, especially following the War of Independence in 1857. Many of them still have strong ties with the Muslim communities in the Indian states of Bihar and Uttar Pradesh.

A number of Tibetan Muslims arrived in the country along with their Buddhist counterparts following the 1959 Chinese overthrow of Tibet.

Unlike in India, where communal tension is a major problem, Nepal's Hindu and Muslim communities seem able to coexist peacefully.

LANGUAGE

Nepal's diverse ethnic groups speak many languages; Nepali functions as the national language and it allows all of these groups to communicate with each other.

As is usually the case, English is the language of tourism; visitors will find that most of the people they deal with in both the Kathmandu Valley and in Pokhara will speak at least some English. English is widely understood along the main trekking trails.

Once away from the main tourist areas of the Kathmandu Valley, Pokhara and Royal Chitwan National Park, the amount of signage in English decreases markedly. While this is an inconvenience if you can't read Nepali, travelling is still easy and there is usually someone around who speaks at least some English.

For a basic guide to Nepali, see the Language chapter at the end of this book; for much more detailed information see Lonely Planet's *Nepali phrasebook*.

THE GODS OF NEPAL

Westerners may have trouble understanding Hinduism principally because of its vast pantheon of gods. In fact you can look upon all these different gods simply as pictorial representations of the many attributes of a god. The one omnipresent god usually has three physical representations: Brahma is the creator, Vishnu is the preserver and Shiva is the destroyer and reproducer. All three gods are usually shown with four arms.

Each god has an associated animal known as the 'vehicle' on which they ride, as well as a consort with certain attributes and abilities. Generally each god also holds symbols. You can often pick out which god is represented by identifying either the vehicle or the symbols.

Most temples are dedicated to one or another of the gods, but most Hindus profess to be either Vaishnavites (followers of Vishnu) or Shaivites (followers of Shiva). A variety of lesser gods and goddesses also crowd the scene. The cow is, of course, the holy animal of Hinduism.

The definitions that follow include the most interesting and most frequently encountered 'big names', plus associated consorts, vehicles and religious terminology.

Incarnations, Manifestations & Aspects

There's a subtle difference between these three possibilities. Vishnu has incarnations – 10 of them in all. They include Narsingha the man-lion, Krishna the cowherd and Buddha the teacher. Shiva, on the other hand, may be the god of 1000 names but these are manifestations – what he shows himself as – not incarnations. When you start to look at the Buddhist 'gods' their various appearances are aspects rather than incarnations or manifestations.

Brahma Despite his supreme position, Brahma appears much less often than Shiva or Vishnu. Like those gods, Brahma has four arms, but he also has four heads, to represent his all-seeing presence. The four *Vedas* are supposed to have emanated from his mouths.

Saraswati The goddess of learning and consort of Brahma, Saraswati rides upon a white swan and holds the stringed musical instrument known as a *veena*.

Shiva As creator and destroyer, Shiva is probably the most important god in Nepal – so it's important to keep on his good side! Shiva is often represented by the phallic lingam, symbolic of his creative role. His vehicle is the bull Nandi and you'll often see this figure outside Shiva temples. The symbol most often seen in Shiva's hand is the trident.

Shiva is also known as Nataraja, the cosmic dancer whose dance shook the cosmos and created the world. Shiva's home is Mt Kailash in the Himalaya and he's also supposed to be keen on smoking hashish. He takes various forms including peaceful Pashupati and destructive Bhairab.

Inset: The meditative faces of Brahma

Pashupati In the Kathmandu Valley Shiva is most popularly worshipped as Pashupati, the lord of the beasts. As the keeper of all living things, Pashupati is Shiva in a good mood, and the temple of Pashupatinath is the most important Hindu temple in the country.

Bhairab In Nepal, Shiva appears as Bhairab when he is in his fearful or 'terrific' form. Bhairab can appear in 64 different ways, but none of them is pretty. Typically he has multiple arms, each clutching a weapon; he dances on a body and wears a headdress of skulls. More skulls dangle from his belt, and his staring eyes and bared fangs complete the picture. Usually Bhairab is black, carries a cup made from a human skull and is attended by a dog. The gruesome figure of Bhairab near the Hanuman Dhoka palace entrance in Kathmandu is a good example of this fearsome god at his worst.

Tara Another deity who appears in both the Hindu and Buddhist pantheons is the Tara goddess. There are actually 108 different Taras, but the best known are Green Tara and White Tara. The Taras are two of the *shaktis* (female consorts) to the Dhyani Buddhas. (For more information on the Dhyani Buddhas, see the boxed text 'The Dhyani Buddhas' in the Around the Kathmandu Valley chapter.)

Shakti While Shakti the goddess is Shiva's consort, shakti is the creative or reproductive energy of the gods, which often manifests in their consorts. A Hindu god's shakti is far more than just a companion. A shakti often symbolises certain parts of a god's personality, so while Shiva is the god of both creation and destruction, it is often his shakti, Parvati, manifesting as Kali or Durga, who handles the destructive business and demands the blood sacrifices.

The Kathmandu Valley has numerous shrines and temples dedicated to the great goddesses, including four shrines dedicated to the Joginis, the mystical goddesses who are the female counterpart to the Bhairabs. These shrines are found near Sankhu at the eastern end of the valley, at Guhyeshwari near Pashupatinath, at Pharping and at Vijeshwari.

Parvati Shiva's shakti is Parvati the beautiful, and she is the dynamic element in their relationship. Just as Shiva is also known as Mahadev, the Great God, so she is Mahadevi, the Great Goddess. Just as Shiva is often symbolised by the phallic lingam, so his shakti's symbol is the yoni, representing the female sex organ. Their relationship is a sexual one and it is often Parvati who is the energetic and dominant partner.

Shiva's shakti has as many forms as Shiva himself. She may be peaceful Parvati but she may also be fearsome Kali, the black goddess, or Durga, the terrible. In these terrific forms she holds a variety of weapons in her hands, struggles with demons and rides a lion. As Kali, the fiercest of the gods and goddesses, she demands sacrifices and wears a garland of skulls.

Brahma
Four heads represent an all-seeing presence

Saraswati
The goddess of learning and consort of Brahma

Shiva
The creator and destroyer, with his vehicle Nandi the bull

Bhairab
The fearful manifestation of Shiva

Kali
The black goddess, Parvati's fiercest manifestation

Parvati
The peaceful shakti of Shiva

Durga
Durga the terrible, another Parvati form

Seto (white) Machhendranath
In both his white (above) and red (below) forms, Machhendranath is protector of the Kathmandu Valley

Ganesh
God of prosperity and wisdom

Rato (red) Machhendranath

Hanuman
The helpful monkey god

Krishna
The gentle and much-loved incarnation of Vishnu

Garuda
The man-bird vehicle of Vishnu

Vishnu
The creator and preserver

Machhendranath A strictly Nepali Hindu god, Machhendranath has power over the rains and the monsoon and is regarded as protector of the Kathmandu Valley. It's typical of the intermingling of Hindu and Buddhist beliefs in Nepal that, in the Kathmandu Valley at least, Machhendranath has come to be thought of as an incarnation of Avalokiteshvara, the Bodhisattva of our era. In actual fact the connection from Avalokiteshvara to Machhendranath is not quite so direct. Purely Buddhist Avalokiteshvara is linked with Shiva through Lokeshvara, the lord of the world. Machhendranath is then a manifestation of Lokeshvara.

There are two forms of Machhendranath based on colour and features: Seto (White) Machhendranath of Kathmandu and Rato (Red) Machhendranath of Patan. Some scholars say that they are the same god, but for others they are different.

Ganesh With his elephant head, Ganesh is probably the most easily recognised of the gods and also the most popular. Ganesh is the god of prosperity and wisdom and there are many Ganesh shrines and temples in Nepal. Ganesh's parents are Shiva and Parvati and he obtained his elephant head thanks to his father's notorious temper. Coming back from a long trip, Shiva discovered Parvati in bed with a young man. Not pausing to think that their son might have grown up a little during his absence, Shiva lopped his head off! Parvati then forced him to bring his son back to life, but he could only do so by giving him the head of the first living thing he saw – which happened to be an elephant.

Hanuman The monkey god Hanuman is the important character from the *Ramayana* who came to the aid of Rama – he helped to defeat the evil Rawana and release Sita from his grasp. Hanuman's trustworthy and alert nature is commemorated by the many statues of Hanuman seen guarding palace entrances. The best known in Nepal is the image of Hanuman that stands beside the old Royal Palace entrance in Kathmandu, and indeed gives the old palace its name of Hanuman Dhoka.

Hanuman also has an important medicinal connection in Nepal and other Hindu countries. The *Ramayana* recounts a legend of how Rama, desperately needed a rare herb grown only in the Himalaya region, and sent Hanuman to procure it for him. Unfortunately, by the time he finally arrived in the mountains Hanuman had forgotten which particular herb he had been asked to bring back to Rama, but he got around the problem by simply grabbing a whole mountain, confident that at least somewhere on the mountain would be the required plant.

On the walls of the Bir Hospital in Kathmandu you can see a large illustration of Hanuman flying through the air, tightly clasping a whole mountain.

Vishnu Although in Nepal, where he often appears as Narayan, he also plays a role in the creation of the universe, Vishnu is the preserver. Narayan is the reclining Vishnu, sleeping on the cosmic ocean, and from his navel appears Brahma, who creates the universe.

Vishnu has four arms and can often be identified by the symbols he holds: the conch shell or *sankha*, the disc-like weapon known as a *chakra*, the stick-like weapon known as a *gada*, and a lotus flower or *padma*. Vishnu's vehicle is the faithful man-bird Garuda, and a winged Garuda will often be seen kneeling reverently in front of a Vishnu temple. Garuda has an intense hatred of snakes and is often seen destroying them. Vishnu's shakti is Lakshmi, the goddess of wealth and prosperity.

Vishnu has 10 incarnations, starting with Matsya, the fish. Then he appeared as Kurma, the tortoise on which the universe is built. Number three was his boar incarnation as Varaha, who bravely destroyed a demon who would have drowned the world. Vishnu was again in a demon destroying mood in incarnation four as Narsingha (or Narsimha), half man and half lion. (See the boxed text 'Narsingha' in the Around the Kathmandu Valley chapter for an explanation of the legend behind this incarnation.)

Still facing difficulties from demons, Vishnu's next incarnation was Vamana, the dwarf who reclaimed the world from the demon-king Bali. The dwarf politely asked the demon for a patch of ground upon which to meditate, saying that the patch need only be big enough that he, the dwarf, could walk across it in three paces. The demon agreed, only to see the dwarf swell into a giant who strode across the universe in three gigantic steps.

In his sixth incarnation Vishnu appeared as Parasurama, a war-like Brahman who proceeded to put the warrior-caste Chhetris in their place.

Incarnation seven was as Rama, the hero of the *Ramayana* who, with help from Hanuman the monkey god, rescued his beautiful wife Sita from the clutches of Rawana, evil king of Lanka. Sita is believed to have been born in Janakpur, and this is also where she and Rama married.

Incarnation eight was the gentle and much-loved Krishna, the fun-loving cowherd, who dallied with the *gopis* (milkmaids), danced, played his flute and still managed to remain devoted to his wife Radha.

For number nine Vishnu appeared as the teacher, the Buddha. Of course, Buddhists don't accept that Buddha was just an incarnation of some other religion's god, but perhaps it was just a ploy to bring Hindu converts back into the fold.

Incarnation 10? Well, we haven't seen that one yet, but it will be as Kalki the destroyer, when Vishnu wields the sword that will destroy the world at the end of the Kaliyuga, the age we are currently in.

Facts for the Visitor

SUGGESTED ITINERARIES

While many people come to Nepal just to trek in the Himalaya, there is indeed a great deal more to the country. The Kathmandu Valley is worth devoting at least a week to in itself, although most people seem to fly in and get out as quickly as possible. The temples at Patan, Bhaktapur, Swayambhunath, Pashupatinath and Boudha should not be missed.

The Terai, the lowland strip that runs the width of the country, is a fascinating area that is often completely overlooked by foreign visitors but which has a great deal to offer. Visiting the Royal Chitwan and Royal Bardia National Parks in the Terai offers visitors a chance to see an incredible variety of bird and animal life, including the royal Bengal tiger and the rhinoceros. Other Terai towns, such as Janakpur and Lumbini, are significant religious sites and are also worth a visit.

One Week

With so much to see and do in Nepal, there's not much point coming just for a week, but if that's all the time you have you could have a good look around the highlights of the Kathmandu Valley in a week. The cities of Kathmandu, Bhaktapur and Patan are the major attractions, with their evocative city squares and magnificent ancient architecture.

Two Weeks

With two weeks up your sleeve, there's more scope to look around a bit, but this is still not enough time to do any serious exploration. In addition to the Kathmandu Valley, you could take up one of a number of other options: a short trek into the Himalayan foothills; a visit to the beautiful and relaxing lakeside city of Pokhara; or a trip to Royal Chitwan National Park in the Terai, where you will hopefully catch sight of (among other wildlife) a rhinoceros and a royal Bengal tiger.

One Month

One month is really the minimum time needed to get a good feel for Nepal. The Kathmandu Valley is worth a week (although many people give it just a day or two at either end of their trip). You could then do an extended trek (such as the Everest Base Camp) or a shorter trek (say, two weeks) and slot in a visit to Pokhara and Royal Chitwan National Park.

Two Months

Those lucky souls with two months at their disposal should have no difficulty in spending that time in Nepal, particularly if trekking is on the agenda. The longer treks, such as the Annapurna Circuit and the Everest Base Camp trek, take at least a good three weeks, and with the juggling around to and from the trail head, it's best to put aside four weeks. This still leaves another four weeks for Kathmandu and Pokhara, and also gives you the chance to explore the Terai, a fascinating area that is overlooked by most visitors. The main attractions of the Terai are the national parks, conservation areas and wildlife reserves: Royal Chitwan and Royal Bardia national parks and Koshi Tappu Wildlife Reserve are all well worth visiting.

Highlights of Nepal

Himalayan Views

- **Nagarkot** On the rim of the Kathmandu Valley, Nagarkot is one of the best and most popular places for sweeping views. Many people stay overnight at one of the many lodges to catch the sunrise.
- **Dhulikhel & Kakani** On opposite edges of the Kathmandu Valley rim, both places offer great views and are far less touristy than Nagarkot.
- **Daman** About 70km south of Kathmandu on the old highway, Daman has simply stunning mountain views of Dhaulagiri in the west across to Everest in the east.
- **Mountain Flights** Early morning mountain flights out of Kathmandu take you on a loop around the world's major peaks and offer unsurpassed views.

Pilgrimage Sites

- **Pashupatinath Temple** This temple in Kathmandu is one of the major Hindu temples of the subcontinent, and during the festival of Maha Shivaratri in February–March the whole place throngs with thousands of pilgrims.
- **Lumbini** On the Terai close to the Indian border, Lumbini is the birthplace of the Buddha and is a special place for Buddhist pilgrims. A number of countries have already built monasteries here and there are plans for more. It is a peaceful place best visited in the cooler months.
- **Janakpur** In the eastern Terai, this is one of the best places to absorb the atmosphere of a Hindu pilgrimage centre. The temple to Sita attracts huge numbers of pilgrims, especially during the festival of Sita Bibaha Panchami in November–December.

Architectural Marvels

- **Kathmandu, Patan & Bhaktapur** These three royal cities of the Kathmandu Valley each have superb World Heritage–Listed Durbar Squares, where centuries-old palaces bear testimony to the strength of Newari culture.

PLANNING

Lonely Planet's *Read This First: Asia* gives handy hints for the first-time visitor to the region.

When to Go

Climatic factors are very important in planning when to visit Nepal. October to November, the start of the dry season, is in many ways the best time. With the monsoon only recently finished, the countryside is green and lush and Nepal is at its most beautiful. Rice is harvested and there are some important and colourful festivals to enjoy. However, bear in mind that these festivals can be disruptive (see Public Holidays later in this chapter). At this time of year the air is sparkling clean, visibility is excellent and the Himalayan views are as near perfect as you could ever hope for. Furthermore, the weather is still balmy, neither too hot (as it can be towards the end of the dry season or during the monsoon) nor too cold (as it can be at the height of winter). For obvious reasons, this is also the high tourist season.

In December and January the climate and visibility are still good, though it can get very cold. Trekkers need to be well prepared, as snow can be encountered on high-altitude treks. Heading for the Everest Base Camp at this time of year can be a real feat of endurance and the Annapurna Circuit trek is often closed by snow on the Thorung La. Down in Kathmandu, the cheaper hotels – where there is no heating – are often chilly and gloomy in the evenings.

From February to April, the tail end of the dry season, is a good second-best time to visit. The weather gets warmer so high altitude treks are no longer as arduous, although

Highlights of Nepal

- **Buddhist Stupas** The stupas of Swayambhunath and Boudha (also known as Bodhnath), close to Kathmandu, are fine examples of Buddhist temple architecture and are a great place to observe Buddhist religion.

Traveller Hang-Outs

- **Pokhara** It's hard to go past Pokhara, with its lakeside location, relaxed atmosphere and potential for exploration on foot or by boat.
- **Freak Street** In Kathmandu, Freak St has been on the overland trail for the best part of 30 years. Although now a shadow of its former self, it still conjures up images of hippies and hashish.

Adrenaline Fixes

- **Bungy Jumping** Try the highest commercial bungy jump on earth at the Last Resort, close to the Tibetan border north-east of Kathmandu.
- **White-Water Rafting** A highlight of travel to Nepal, is white-water rafting on some of the world's wildest rivers. Kayaking is rapidly gaining in popularity too.
- **Parasailing** Near the lake in Pokhara, parasailing is one of the latest ways to get high in Nepal.
- **Hot-Air Ballooning** A dawn ride above the Kathmandu Valley is a little more sedate than parasailing, but is nevertheless a superb experience – there's the added bonus of excellent views of the Himalaya.

Wildlife Adventures

- **Elephant Safaris** In the Royal Bardia and Royal Chitwan National Parks, an elephant safari is a superb way to track the elusive royal Bengal tiger or the sometimes aggressive Indian one-horned rhinoceros.
- **Koshi Tappu Wildlife Reserve** In the eastern Terai, this reserve has a high concentration of migratory birds and is well off the tourist circuit, making it an ideal escape from the crowds.

by the end of the dry season, before the monsoon breaks, it starts to get too hot for comfort. Visibility is not as good as earlier in the dry season because the country is very dry at this time, and dust in the air reduces that crystal Himalayan clarity. As compensation, Nepal's wonderful rhododendrons and many other flowers are in bloom, so there's plenty of colour to be seen along the trekking trails.

May and the early part of June are not the best months to visit as it is extremely hot and dusty and the coming monsoon seems to hang over you like a threat.

Mid-June to September, when the monsoon finally arrives, is the least popular time to visit Nepal. The rains wash the dust out of the air, but the clouds obscure the mountains so you're unlikely to enjoy more than a rare glimpse of the Himalaya. Although it doesn't rain all day it usually rains every day and the trails and roads will be muddy and plagued by leeches. Despite this, it is possible to trek during the monsoon, although high rivers may further complicate matters, and it's not as pleasant as at other times of year. Landslides sometimes block roads during the monsoon but many visitors still come to Nepal from India – the weather is even less pleasant down on the plains. The latter part of the monsoon, the months of August and September, is a time of festivals, which will certainly enliven a visit to Kathmandu.

Maps

An interesting account of the history of mapping in Nepal is found in Harka Gurung's *Maps of Nepal,* which covers historic maps right up to the trekking maps of the early 1980s.

The Research Scheme *Nepal Himalaya* maps are better known as Schneider maps, after their cartographer. These are the best trekking maps available, although their price is as high as their quality. The series covers the routes into the Everest region in six separate maps, as well as the Langtang and Annapurna areas.

There are many locally produced maps available in Nepal that are much cheaper and for most trekkers prove quite adequate. The main series are produced by Himalayan Maphouse, and these include Nepa Maps and Himalaya Kartographisches Institut brand names. They are all good quality colour maps and cost Rs 150 each. Nepa Maps also has reasonable pocket maps to Kathmandu and Pokhara for a bargain Rs 50 each.

Topographic map sheets at 1:25,000 scale are available for large areas of the country, mainly the east. This is an ongoing Finnish-Nepali joint program and is the result of aerial photographs taken in the past few years. As a result, the maps are very accurate but are unsuitable for trekking as the trails aren't always marked. The maps are available in Kathmandu from the Topography Department of the Survey Ministry, at New Baneshwar on the Bhaktapur road, for Rs 80 per sheet.

Setting the standard for maps in Nepal is Karto-Atelier. These locally made maps are a result of German-Nepali collaboration and are simply outstanding. Currently there are maps to Kathmandu, Pokhara and a route map for Kathmandu to Everest. The catch is that they cost Rs 800 each!

The Kathmandu City Map is a new addition to the Lonely Planet. As well as detailed maps of Kathmandu, this handy fold-out map also features maps of Patan and Bhaktapur, a walking tour, glossary and comprehensive index.

The problem with most of the detailed maps of Nepal is that villages often have widely diverse names and their actual position is often equally open to interpretation. Reality, when you're there on foot, is often very different from what the map says. Even the Schneider maps often have highly original versions of common place names.

What to Bring

Nepal's climatic variations due to altitude mean that at certain times of year you'll have to come prepared for almost any weather. If you're in Nepal during the winter you'll find it's T-shirt weather in the Terai, but up at the Everest Base Camp you'll want the best thermal or duck-down gear money can buy!

In the Kathmandu Valley the daytime weather is pleasant year-round, but in winter the temperature drops as soon as the sun sets, or even goes behind a cloud. It never reaches freezing in the valley, however, so it's sweater or warm-jacket weather, nothing worse. Climb higher to the valley edge at Nagarkot and you will find it gets much colder. If you plan to ride a bicycle, or have a respiratory problem, Kathmandu's air pollution is sufficiently bad to justify a mask.

During the monsoon you'll need an umbrella or a raincoat, particularly in Pokhara where the rainfall is much heavier than in Kathmandu. In the first month after the monsoon it can be pleasantly warm, even on treks, as long as you're sticking to lower altitudes.

Sunglasses, a hat and covering for unprotected skin are all necessary on high altitude treks or for prolonged exposure in the Terai (see the Trekking chapter for more information on trekking necessities).

Most clothing is easily and cheaply available in Nepal so if there's any question about bringing a particular item, leave it behind – you can always buy one if you need it.

Most toiletries are readily available, including toilet paper. Women should, however, bring tampons if needed. Ear plugs can be more than a luxury if you sleep lightly – cheap hotels and lodges are often very noisy. If you plan on staying in cheap hotels a padlock can be useful to prevent theft from your room (hotels in this category often lock the doors with a latch and padlock).

If you're visiting Royal Chitwan National Park or other places in the Terai a good insect repellent is a near necessity. Bring a torch (flashlight) for trekking and for power cuts.

RESPONSIBLE TOURISM

Tourism is generally having a big environmental and social impact in Nepal, and a large part of this comes through the trekking industry. Trekking areas have suffered seriously from the sheer weight of visitor numbers, and in many cases there hasn't been the necessary will or resources (or both) to enforce regulations. The local communities that live in or around trekking routes have also been hugely affected. See also the Trekking chapter for responsible trekking advice.

A few tour operators are making conscious efforts to diversify in an effort to address these problems, but it's slow going. The best companies are those that have a serious commitment to protecting the fragile ecosystems in these and other areas, and which direct at least some portion of profits back into local communities. Although these won't always be the cheapest ones, the extra money you spend is an important way that you can contribute to the future of the areas that you visit.

Explore Nepal (☎ 01-248942, ⓔ explore.mos.com.np), PO Box 536, Kamaladi, Kathmandu, is a very environmentally conscious trekking company. The director, Bharat Basnet, was at the forefront of the successful campaign to have Vikram tempos banned from the Kathmandu Valley. The company operates a number of 'clean-up treks', where participants are involved in helping clean up villages along the trekking routes. For more information see the Web site www.explore-nepal-group.com.np/environment/cleanup.htm (sometimes a little out of date).

When evaluating a company based on environmental criteria, try to distinguish between mere lip service and real action; contact the various bodies such as Kathmandu Environmental Education Program (KEEP; ☎ 259275, ⓔ tours@keep.wlink.com.np) to learn about environmental and tourism-related issues in the areas you wish to visit.

Another dimension of responsible tourism is the manner and attitude that visitors assume towards local people. Respect is of the utmost importance, both in personal dealings as well as in your overall behaviour and your style of dress (see Society & Conduct in the Facts about Nepal chapter for more details on how not to cause offence).

TOURIST OFFICES

The Ministry of Tourism does not overdo things; there is very little printed information available and the handful of tourist offices around the country are of extremely limited use.

The Nepal Tourism Board (☎ 01-256909, ⓔ info@ntb.wlink.com.np) operates an office in Kathmandu's Tribhuvan airport, and has leaflets and maps. The tourist office in the Tourist Service Centre, east of Tundikhel in central Kathmandu, has government publications and an information counter. You can surf its Web site at www.welcomenepal.com.

There are also tourist offices in Pokhara, Bhairawa, Birganj, Janakpur and Kakarbhitta. Again, these are virtually useless unless you have a specific inquiry. See the Terai and Pokhara chapters for contact details.

VISAS & DOCUMENTS

Visas

All foreigners, except Indians, must have a visa. Nepali embassies and consulates overseas issue visas, or they can be issued on the spot when you arrive in Nepal, either at Kathmandu's Tribhuvan airport or at any road border. If you stay in Nepal for longer than the duration of your initial 60-day visa, you will require a visa extension. Children under 10 do not need a visa. A Nepali visa is valid for entry for three months from the date of issue. Do not apply too soon or it will not be valid when you arrive in Kathmandu.

You can download a visa form from the Nepali Embassy in Washington DC at www.newweb.net/nepal_embassy/visaform.htm.

To obtain a visa on arrival by air in Nepal you must fill in an application form. In theory you should have a photograph, though this requirement is overlooked if you don't have one. Visa application forms are available on a table in the arrival hall; most airlines do not provide this form on the flight. To get a jump on the immigration queue, you can download the visa-on-arrival form from www.treks.com.np/visa. The following visas are available:

duration	type	cost (US$)
60 days	single entry	$30
60 days	double entry	$55
60 days	multiple entry	$70–90

The double- and multiple-entry visas are useful if you are planning a side trip to Tibet, Bhutan or India. At Kathmandu's Tribhuvan airport the fee is payable only in US dollars cash, and it's a good idea to have the exact amount on hand as change may be scarce. At land borders, officials may also demand payment in dollars cash, so be prepared for this.

If you have already visited Nepal during the same calendar year the visa fee is US$50 for a 30-day visa. Much of the time you spend in the visa-on-arrival queue is waiting while officers scour your passport for previous entry stamps.

Don't overstay a visa. You can pay a fine of US$2 per day at the airport if you have overstayed less than seven days. If you overstay longer, you might not be allowed to board your departing flight. In such cases, you will be sent back to the immigration office to settle the situation there.

There is no advantage organising a visa in advance except for the time you may save at the airport when you arrive – though sometimes the visa-on-arrival queue moves faster than the queue for those who have a visa. If you are arriving by road, it might save some hassle and delay if you already have a visa, but you can get one at any road border post, even the funky Kodari checkpoint on the road to Tibet.

Visa Extensions Visa extensions cost US$50 (payable in rupees) for a 30-day extension. You get a 30-day extension whether you are staying for an extra one day or 30 days. To get a visa extension in Kathmandu, go to the Immigration Office (☎ 01-494273). For more details see Information in the Kathmandu chapter.

Visa extensions are normally available the following day, but during the busy season you should allow up to three working days for an extension to be processed. At peak times the queues are long and the formalities are tedious.

For a fee, trekking and travel agencies can assist with the visa extension process and can usually save you the time and tedium of queuing.

Every visa extension requires your passport, money, photos and an application form. Collect all these before you join the queue. There are several instant photo shops near the immigration office, but Polaroid photos are expensive. If you plan ahead, there are many photographers in Kathmandu and Pokhara who will provide passport photos within a day.

You can extend your visa up to a total stay of 150 days without undue formality. However, you are only allowed to stay in Nepal for a total of 150 days in a calendar year (which is counted as January to December) on a tourist visa.

Re-entry Permits

If you are travelling from Nepal to India or Tibet and returning to Kathmandu within 30 days you should either buy a double-entry visa or get a re-entry permit before you leave Nepal. This is an easy process at the immigration office and costs US$25. Don't overlook it or you may be obliged to pay excessive visa fees on your return.

Trekking Permits

Trekking permits are not required for the main trekking areas of Everest, Annapurna and Langtang. The national park and conservation area fees have not been abolished, and in fact have recently risen substantially: It now costs Rs 2000 to enter the Annapurna Conservation Area. Permit requirements for all remote regions are still in effect.

Trekking permits are only issued (and extended) at the immigration offices in Kathmandu and Pokhara. See Permits in the Trekking chapter for more details.

Travel Insurance

A travel insurance policy to cover theft, loss and medical problems is a good idea. There is a wide variety of policies available, so check the small print. Some policies specifically exclude 'dangerous activities', which can include trekking.

You may prefer a policy that pays doctors or hospitals directly rather than you having to pay on the spot and claim later. If you have to claim later make sure you keep all documentation. Some policies ask you to call back (reverse charges) to a centre in your home country where an immediate assessment of your problem is made.

Check that the policy covers an emergency flight home.

Other Documents

If you think you might drive a car or ride a motorcycle while in Nepal then it is worth having an international driving permit.

When travelling in Asia it's a good idea to keep a number of passport photos with your passport so they are immediately handy for trekking permits, visa applications and other official documents. Passport photos are easily and cheaply obtained in Kathmandu – these cost around Rs 100 for four in black and white or Rs 150 for four in colour.

EMBASSIES & CONSULATES

Nepali Embassies & Consulates

Australia
Sydney: (☎ 9328 7062, fax 9340 1084) PO Box 474, Edgecliff, NSW 2027
Perth: (☎ 9386 2102, ⓔ gregcam@iinet.net.au) Suite 2, 16 Robinson St, Nedlands, WA 6009
Brisbane: (☎ 3220 2007, ⓔ konbridge@selcom.com.au) Level 7, 344 Queen St, Brisbane, Qld 4000

Bangladesh
(☎ 601890, fax 882 6401, ⓔ rnedhaka@bdmail.net) United Nations Rd, Road 2, Baridhara, Dhaka

Belgium
(☎ 346 2658, fax 344 1361, ⓔ rne.bru@skynet.be) Ave Winston Churchill 68, 1180 Brussels

Canada
(☎ 865 0200, fax 865 0904) Royal Bank Plaza, PO Box 33, Toronto, Ontario M5J 2J9

China
(☎ 6532 1795, fax 6532 3251, ⓔ rnebc@public.netchina.com.cn) No 1, Xi Liu Jie, Sanlitun Lu, Beijing 100600 (see also Tibet)

Denmark
(☎ 3927 3175, fax 3920 1245, ⓔ janus@janus-as.dk) Aldersrogarde 3A, 2100 Kobenhavn

France
(☎ 01 46 22 48 67, fax 01 42 27 08 65, ⓔ nepal@worldnet.fr) 45 bis Rue des Acacias, 75017 Paris

Germany
(☎ 3435 9920, fax 3435 9906) Guerickestrasse 27, 10587 Berlin-Charlottenburg

India
New Delhi: (☎ 332 7361, fax 332 6857, ⓔ ramjanki@vsnl.net.in) 1 Barakhamba Rd, New Delhi 110001
Kolkata (Calcutta): (☎ 479 1117, fax 479 1410, ⓔ rncg@cal.vsnl.net) 1 National Library Ave, Alipore, Kolkata 700027

Italy
(☎ 3545 0656, fax 3542 0720, ⓔ info@mappatour.it) Piazzale Medaglie d'Oro 20, Rome 00136

Japan
(☎ 3705 5558, fax 3705 8264, ⓔ nepembjp@big.or.jp) 14–19 Tokoroki 7-chome, Setagaya-ku, Tokyo 158-0082

Myanmar (Burma)
(☎ 545 880, fax 549 803) 16 Natmauk Yeiktha (Park Ave), PO Box 84, Yangon (Rangoon)

Pakistan
(☎ 828 838, fax 828 839, ⓔ nepem@isb.comsats.net.pak) House 11, Street 84, G-6/4, Islamabad

Russia
(☎ 244 0215, fax 244 0000, ⓔ nepal@orc.russia) 2nd Neopalimovsky Pereulok 14/7, Moscow

Singapore
(☎ 336 1677, fax 337 1737) 1 North Bridge Rd, 18-05 High St Centre, Singapore 0617

Spain
(☎ 447 0987, fax 447 1023) Viriato 41b, Dacha, 28010 Madrid

Switzerland
(☎ 201 4515, fax 201 4435) Bleicherweg 33, CH-8027 Zurich

Thailand
(☎ 391 7240, fax 381 2406, ⓔ nepembkk@asiaaccess.net.th) 189 Soi 71, Sukhumvit Rd, Prakanong, Bangkok 10110

Tibet
(☎ 682 2881, fax 683 6890 ⓔ rncglx@public.ls.xz.cn) Norbulingka Rd 13, Lhasa, Tibet Autonomous Region

UK
(☎ 020-7229 1594, fax 7792 9861, ⓔ rnelondon@compuserve.com) 12A Kensington Palace Gardens, London W8 4QU

USA
San Francisco: (☎ 434 1111, fax 434 3130, ⓔ skelly@blumcapital.com) Suite 400, 909 Montgomery St, San Francisco, California 94133
Washington: (☎ 667 4550, fax 667 5534, ⓔ nepali@erols.com) 2131 Leroy Place NW, Washington DC 20008

Embassies & Consulates in Nepal

Travellers continuing beyond Nepal may need visas for Bangladesh, China, India, Myanmar (Burma) or Thailand. The only visas for Tibet (actually visas for China) dished out in Kathmandu are for organised groups; individuals wishing to travel to Tibet should get a visa before arriving in Nepal (Delhi is a good place to get them). See Tibet under Land in the Getting There & Away chapter for advice about travelling independently in Tibet.

Many foreign embassies in Kathmandu are clustered around the north-east of the centre and include the following:

Australia (☎ 371678, fax 371533) Bansbari. Just beyond the Ring Rd in Maharajganj.
Bangladesh (☎ 372843, fax 373265) Maharajganj. Open from 9 am to 1.15 pm and 2 to 5 pm Monday to Friday; tourist visas are not issued here, but are available on arrival in Dhaka.
China (☎ 411740, fax 414045) Baluwatar. Open from 9 am to noon and 3 to 5 pm Monday to Friday; visa applications are accepted Monday, Wednesday and Friday from 9.30 to 11.30 am; passports will be returned the next working day.
France (☎ 413332, fax 419968, ⓔ ambafr@mos.com.np) Lazimpat
Germany (☎ 412786, fax 416899) Gyaneshwar
India (☎ 410900, fax 413132, ⓔ indemb@mos.com.np) Lainchhaur. Open from 9 am to 1 pm and 1.30 to 5 pm Monday to Friday; accepts visa applications from 9.30 am to 12.30 pm (collect visas from 4 to 5 pm). Allow seven to 10 days for processing of tourist visas; transit visas (valid for 15 days from date of issue) are issued the same day. One photo is required. The cost varies according to nationality, but is around Rs 2800!
Israel (☎ 411811, fax 413920, ⓔ israelm@mos.com.np) Bishramalaya House, Lazimpat.
Italy (☎ 252801, fax 255218, ⓔ negroup@mos.com.np) IJ Plaza, Maharajganj.
Japan (☎ 426680, fax 414101) Pani Pokhari.
Myanmar (Burma) (☎ 521788, fax 523402) Chakupat, near Patan Dhoka (City Gate), Patan. Open from 9.30 am to 1 pm and 2 to 4.30 pm Monday to Friday; visa applications accepted mornings only. Fourteen-day visas are available, four photos are required, 24-hour turnaround; the cost is US$20.
Pakistan (☎ 374024, fax 374012) Narayan Gopal Chowk, Ring Rd, Maharajganj. Open from 9 am to 5 pm Monday to Friday.
Russia (☎ 412155, fax 416571) Baluwatar.
Thailand (☎ 371410, fax 371408) Bansbari. Open from 8.30 am to 12.30 pm and 1.30 to 4.30 pm Monday to Friday; visa applications accepted from 9.30 am to 12.30 pm, two photos required, 24-hour turnaround; the cost is about US$10.
UK (☎ 410583, fax 411789) Lainchhaur.
USA (☎ 411179, fax 419963) Pani Pokhari.

It's important to realise what your own embassy – the embassy of the country of which you are a citizen – can and can't do to help you if you get into trouble.

Generally speaking, it won't be much help in emergencies if the trouble you're in is remotely your own fault. Remember that you are bound by the laws of the country you are in. Your embassy will not be sympathetic if you end up in jail after committing a crime locally, even if such actions are legal in your own country.

Officials of all embassies in Nepal stress the benefits of registering with them, telling them where you are trekking, and reporting in again when you return. The offices of KEEP and the Himalayan Rescue Association (HRA, see Information in the Kathmandu chapter for details) have forms from most embassies, so it's simple to provide the information.

In genuine emergencies you might get some assistance, but only if other channels have been exhausted. For example, if you need to get home urgently, a free ticket home is exceedingly unlikely – the embassy would expect you to have insurance. If you have all your money and documents stolen, it might assist with getting a new passport, but a loan for onward travel is out of the question.

CUSTOMS

All baggage is X-rayed on arrival and departure. In addition to the import and export of drugs, customs is concerned with the illegal export of antiques. You may not import Nepali rupees, and only nationals of Nepal and India may import Indian currency. There is no restriction on bringing in either cash or travellers cheques, but the amount taken out at departure should not exceed the amount brought in. Officially you should declare cash or travellers cheques in excess of US$2000, or the equivalent, but no-one seems to bother with this.

Visitors are permitted to import the following articles for their personal use (and we quote):

Cigarettes, 200 sticks; cigars, 50 sticks; alcoholic liquor, one bottle not exceeding 1.15 litre; one binocular; one movie camera with 12 rolls of film; one video camera; one ordinary camera with 15 rolls of film; one tape recorder with 15 tape reels or cassettes; one perambulator; one bicycle; and one stick.

Antiques

Customs' main concern is preventing the export of antique works of art – with good reason as Nepal has a great many treasures, many kept under conditions of very light security. It would be a great shame if international art thieves and 'collectors' forced more of it to be kept under lock and key. Unfortunately a lucrative international market has led to the theft of a staggering amount of irreplaceable art.

It is very unlikely that souvenirs sold to travellers will be antique (despite the claims of the vendors), but if there is any doubt, they should be cleared and a certificate obtained from the Department of Archaeology (☎ 01-250683) in the National Archives building on Ramshah Path, Kathmandu. If you visit between 10 am and 1 pm you should be able to pick up a certificate by 5 pm the same day. These controls also apply to the export of precious and semiprecious stones.

Animal Furs & Trophies

Unfortunately, there is still a thriving trade in animal furs and trophies, despite the fact that this is also officially prohibited. Many seriously endangered species, including the beautiful snow leopard, are still being hunted for valuable parts of their corpses.

As long as there's a market, this will continue. The argument that because the animal is already dead there is no further harm caused by having its skin made into a coat is entirely spurious. If there is any cosmic justice, those that encourage the trade will be reincarnated as rabbits on fur farms in Siberia!

MONEY

Currency

The Nepali rupee (Rs) is divided into 100 paisa (p). There are coins for denominations of five, 10, 25 and 50 paisa, and for one, two, five and 10 rupees, although as the rupee coins are not in wide circulation and prices are generally rounded to the nearest rupee, you often don't come across any coins at all. This is a great contrast to a time not long ago, when once outside the Kathmandu Valley, it was rare to see any paper money. Mountaineering books from the 1950s often comment on the porters whose sole duty was to carry the expedition's money – in cold, hard cash.

Bank notes come in denominations of one, two, five, 10, 20, 50, 100, 500 and 1000 rupees. There are also a few Rs 250 notes, which were issued recently to commemorate the king's golden jubilee. Away from major centres, changing a Rs 1000 note can be very difficult, so it is always wise to have at least some of your money in small denomination notes. Even in Kathmandu, many small businesses – especially rickshaw and taxi drivers – simply don't have sufficient spare money to allow them the luxury of carrying a wad of change.

Note that dollar prices quoted in this book are US dollars.

Exchange Rates

country	unit		rupee
Australia	A$1	=	Rs 37
European Union	€1	=	Rs 67
France	1FF	=	Rs 10
Germany	DM1	=	Rs 34
India	INRs 100	=	Rs 160
Japan	¥100	=	Rs 60
UK	UK£1	=	Rs 106
USA	US$1	=	Rs 74

Exchanging Money

Major international currencies, including the US dollar and pounds sterling, are readily accepted. In Nepal the Indian rupee is also like a hard currency – the Nepali rupee is pegged to the Indian rupee at the rate of INRs 100 = NRs 160. Be aware that Indian Rs 500 notes are not accepted anywhere in Nepal, apparently due to forgeries.

Hard Currency When you change money officially, you are required to show your passport, and you are issued with a foreign exchange encashment receipt showing your identity and the amount of hard currency you have changed. Hang onto the receipts as they have a number of potential uses.

Many upmarket hotels and businesses are obliged by the government to demand payment in hard currency; they will also accept rupees, but only if you can show a foreign exchange encashment receipt that covers the amount you owe them. In practice this regulation seems to be widely disregarded and you are rarely asked to prove the source of your rupees.

Airlines are also required to charge tourists in hard currency, but most seem unwilling to accept anything other than cash, travellers cheques or credit cards. Budget hotels, bus companies and most small businesses are usually only too happy to get rupees and do not muck around with encashment receipts.

If you leave Nepal via Kathmandu's Tribhuvan airport, the downstairs exchange counter will re-exchange up to 15% of the amount shown on 'unused' exchange certificates. The receipts used for re-exchange are kept by the bank, so make sure you have photocopies if you need them for other purposes. Be warned that official re-exchange is not possible at any bank branches at the border crossings.

ATMs Nepal Grindlays Bank has ATMs in Kathmandu and Pokhara; you can get cash advances on both Visa and MasterCard. These ATMs are accessible 24 hours a day. See the Kathmandu and Pokhara maps in their respective chapters for locations.

Some other banks, such as the Himalayan Bank, also have ATMs but these only accept local cards.

Credit Cards Major credit cards are widely accepted at mid-range and better hotels, restaurants and fancy shops in the Kathmandu Valley and at Pokhara. Elsewhere it's safer to assume that credit cards won't be accepted, and so you will need to carry enough cash or travellers cheques to cover your costs.

Branches of Nepal Grindlays bank are able to make cash advances against Visa and MasterCard in Nepali rupees (no charge), and will also sell you foreign currency travellers cheques against the cards with a 2% commission.

The American Express (AmEx) agent is Yeti Travels in Kathmandu (see Money under Information in the Kathmandu chapter). They advance travellers cheques to card holders for a standard 1% commission.

International Transfers If you do not follow the right steps, money transfers from overseas can be very time-consuming. Pin down every possible detail, ensure that you know which bank the money is going to, make sure they have your name exactly right and if possible ensure that you are notified of the transfer at the same time as the bank. It's important to choose the right bank as well – check that your bank has links with a bank in Nepal and does not have to operate through an intermediary.

Western Union claims it can transfer money from many countries to Nepal in 24 hours. The agent is in Kathmandu (see Money under Information in the Kathmandu chapter).

Black Market The once-thriving black market is pretty subdued these days. Touts around Thamel in Kathmandu and Lakeside in Pokhara still offer to change money, but the premium over the bank rate is usually less than 5%, so it's hardly worth the (small) risk. It is, of course, illegal.

Banks & Moneychangers Official exchange rates are set by the government's

Nepal Rastra Bank. Rates at the private banks vary, but are generally not far from the official rate. The daily *Rising Nepal* and *Kathmandu Post* newspapers list the Nepal Rastra Bank's rate, providing a useful reference point.

There are exchange counters at the international terminal at Kathmandu's Tribhuvan airport and banks and/or moneychangers at the various border crossings. Pokhara and the major border towns also have official moneychanging facilities, but changing travellers cheques can be difficult elsewhere in the country, even in some quite large towns. If you are going trekking try and take enough small denomination cash with you to last the whole trek.

The usual banking hours are 10 am to 2 pm Sunday to Thursday, and until noon on Friday.

The best private banks are the Nepal Bank Ltd, Nepal Grindlays Bank, Himalayan Bank and the Bank of Kathmandu. Some hotels and resorts are also licensed to change money, and while their rates are usually OK it's best to check first. Rates and commissions vary from bank to bank, so it pays to shop around.

In addition to the banks there are licensed moneychangers in Kathmandu, Pokhara, Birganj, Kakarbhitta and Sunauli/Bhairawa. The rates are often marginally better than the banks, but the commissions are higher, so check before changing. The big advantages of the moneychangers over the banks is that they have much longer opening hours (typically from 9 am to 7 pm often seven days a week) and that they are also much quicker, the whole process often taking no more than a few minutes.

Many of the licensed moneychangers do not offer exchange receipts, which makes any transactions with them basically legal blackmarket transactions. Because they don't offer receipts, you should in many cases be able to negotiate better rates then those posted on their boards.

Security

While it is still uncommon, petty theft is on the rise in Nepal so it pays to be cautious. Money is best carried in a money belt or pouch worn under your clothes. Keep enough cash at the ready to deal with everyday transactions, and keep the rest stashed so you don't need to bring out large wads of cash in public.

When changing money or getting cash from an ATM, always put your cash away safely before moving off.

Costs

If you stay in rock-bottom accommodation and survive on a predominantly Nepali diet you could live in Nepal for less than US$5 a day. On an independent 'village inn' or 'teahouse' trek your living costs are likely to be around that level.

On the other hand if you stay in comfortable hotels (say US$10 to US$20 for a double room), sit down to eat in popular tourist oriented restaurants, rent bicycles and take taxis from time to time your living costs could be around US$20 to US$30 a day.

At the top end it is possible to spend US$200 a night for a five-star double room in Kathmandu; a meal for two in one of Nepal's very best restaurants can cost US$40 to US$60; and a deluxe trek booked from overseas can cost US$100 a day.

Residents should bear in mind that most of the major upmarket tour and trekking operators offer significant discounts, so make your resident status clear when you ask for prices and make bookings.

Tipping & Bargaining

Tipping is prevalent in Kathmandu. In expensive establishments you should tip up to 10%, while in smaller places some loose change or Rs 25 will be most appreciated (do not worry about it in the really cheap restaurants). Taxi drivers don't expect to be tipped.

Before bargaining, try to establish a fair price by talking to local people and other travellers. Paying too much feeds inflation, while paying too little denies the locals a reasonable return for their efforts and investments. Not everything is subject to bargaining: You should respect standard food, accommodation and entry charges, and follow the going rate for services.

Bargaining should never be treated as a matter of life and death importance – it's usually regarded as an integral part of a transaction and is, ideally, an enjoyable social exchange. Nepalis do not ever appreciate aggressive behaviour. A good deal is when both parties are happy. Try to remember that Rs 10 might make quite a difference to the seller, but in hard currency it amounts to very little (less than US$0.15).

Taxes

Most hotels and restaurants in the mid to upper range charge 10% VAT tax, on top of which is slapped a 2% Tourism Service Charge. Hotel employees have recently been campaigning for an additional 10% service charge to be added to hotel bills, which would bring the total tax take to 22%. The move is opposed by the Hotel Association of Nepal (HAN) and has thus far been resisted by the government.

POST & COMMUNICATIONS

Post

The postal service to and from Nepal is, at best, erratic and can be extremely slow. But just to surprise you, things can also be amazingly efficient. Most articles do finally arrive at their destination, but they can take weeks.

Poste restante services are quite well organised, but as with other Asian countries ask people writing to you to print your family name clearly and underline it. Misfiled mail often results from confusion between family names and given names.

Most bookshops in Thamel, including Pilgrims Book House, also sell stamps and deliver postcards to the post office, which is much easier than making a special trip to the post office yourself.

Airmail rates for a letter/postcard are Rs 1 within Nepal and to India, Rs 30/18 to the USA and Australia and Rs 25/15 to Europe and the UK.

Parcel Post Having stocked up on souvenirs and gifts in Nepal, many people take the opportunity of sending them home from Kathmandu. Parcel post is not cheap or quick, but the service is reliable.

The contents of a parcel must be inspected by officials before it is wrapped so do not take it to the post office already wrapped. There are packers at the Kathmandu foreign post office who will package it for a small fee. The maximum weight for seamail is 20kg; for airmail it's 10kg.

See also Shopping at the end of this chapter for details on sending things home by courier, which is even more expensive.

Telephone

Thankfully the telephone system works pretty well, and it's easy to make local, STD and international calls. Reverse-charge (collect) calls can only be made to Canada, Japan, the USA and the UK.

The cheapest and most convenient way to make calls is through one of the hundreds of private call centres that have sprung up across the country. Look for signs advertising STD/ISD services (STD is an abbreviation for subscriber trunk dialling). It's really only worth using the government telegraph offices if you need to make a call in the middle of the night when other places are closed.

With the private operators, expect to pay around Rs 170 per minute to Australia, France, the UK and the USA, around Rs 185 to New Zealand and Germany and around Rs 215 to Israel. Many of the hotels also have direct-dial facilities, but always check their charges before you make a call.

Internet phone calls are cheapest of all. These are only available in Kathmandu, and are technically illegal. Nevertheless, they are the preferred option these days as it means calls to just about anywhere cost less than Rs 30 per minute (Rs 10 to the USA). There is some delay in the line when making Internet calls, but it is fine for most purposes.

The international country code for Nepal is ☎ 977. For outgoing international calls the international access number is ☎ 00, which is followed by the country code.

Email & Internet Access

Consider opening a free email account such as eKno (www.ekno.lonelyplanet.com), Hotmail (www.hotmail.com) or Yahoo! Mail (mail.yahoo.com). You can then access your mail from any Web-connected computer worldwide. Email and Internet services are offered by dozens of places in Kathmandu (Rs 1 per minute) and Pokhara (Rs 7 per minute). Internet access is also available in most other towns, but connections are usually slow and relatively expensive, as connection may involve an STD call to Kathmandu. See the city maps in the Kathmandu and Pokhara chapters for locations.

For those looking for their own Internet account there are numerous Internet service providers in Nepal including:

Computerland Communication System
www.ccsl.com.np
Mercantile Communications
www.mos.com.np
Nepal Telecommunication Corporation
www.ntc.com.np
Worldlink
www.wlink.com.np

INTERNET RESOURCES

The World Wide Web is a rich resource for travellers. You can research your trip, hunt down bargain airfares, book hotels, check on weather conditions or chat with locals and other travellers about the best places to visit (or avoid).

A good place to start your Web explorations is the Lonely Planet Web site (www.lonelyplanet.com). Here you'll find succinct summaries on travelling to most places on earth, postcards from other travellers and the Thorn Tree bulletin board, where you can ask questions before you go or dispense advice when you get back. You can also find travel news and updates to many of our most popular guidebooks, and the subWWWay section links you to the most useful travel resources elsewhere on the Web.

There are a number of interesting sites that carry a great deal of information about Nepal. The following sites also have excellent links:

Above the Clouds Featuring lots of mouth watering photographs of treks in Nepal and Tibet.
www2.gorp.com/abvclds/

Catmando.com A hip version of the following gateway sites with lots of ads as well as a link to Radio Nepal.
www.catmando.com

Explore Nepal A good gateway information site with many links set up by category.
www.explorenepal.com

Himalayan Explorers Club (HEC) This non-profit Western and Nepali organisation exists to facilitate good environmentally sound experiences for travellers. Whether it's volunteer teaching you're after or if you just want to hang in the clubhouse, check out this site.
www.hec.org

Nepal Home Page A site with good information, pictures and a FAQ page.
www.info-nepal.com

Nepal.Com Another gateway site notable for its pretty pictures.
www.nepal.com

Nepalnews.Com This is an excellent site with daily news items which also carries links to all major online news media in Nepal.
www.nepalnews.com

NepalSearch.Com Another gateway site, which offers free email 'postal service' to anywhere within the country.
www.nepalsearch.com

Trekinfo.Com You guessed it – all the trekking information about the region that you'll need to get started.
www.trekinfo.com

VisitNepal.Com A comprehensive site with detailed information for travellers and many links to companies and organisations within the country.
www.visitnepal.com

BOOKS

There is no shortage of books about Nepal – the Himalaya and heroic mountaineers, colourful religions and exotic temples, the history and brave Gurkhas have all inspired writers and photographers; the results are piled high in numerous bookshops in Nepal, of which there is a surprisingly good selection. Most are in Kathmandu and Pokhara.

Most books are published in different editions by different publishers in different countries. As a result, a book might be a hardcover rarity in one country, yet readily available in paperback in another. Fortunately, bookshops and libraries search by title or author, so your local bookshop or library is able to advise you on the availability of the following recommendations. These are only some of the more interesting titles and include books that are long out of print and others that may only be available in Nepal.

Lonely Planet

There are a number of Lonely Planet books that are of interest to visitors to Nepal.

Read This First: Asia & India Invaluable for first-time travellers to the region.

Shopping for Buddhas by Jeff Greenwald. Part of the Journeys travel literature series, this is an astute and funny book about the author's travels in Nepal, motivated by the obsessive pursuit of a perfect Buddha statue.

Nepali phrasebook A valuable introduction to the language.

Travel with Children by Maureen Wheeler. A handy reference for travellers who want to take the kids.

Trekking in the Nepal Himalaya by Stan Armington. This covers everything you need to know before setting out on a trek in Nepal. The book includes day-by-day coverage of all the main trekking routes, with an excellent medical section covering the problems likely to be encountered in the mountains.

Buddhist Stupas in Asia: The Shape of Perfection This is a full colour hardback pictorial that explores the spread of Buddhism and stupa building across India and Asia.

Guidebooks

Nepal by Tom Le Bas. One of the Insight series of photographic coffee–table type guides.

Nepal Namaste by Robert Rieffel. An excellent locally produced English-language book with all sorts of odd titbits of information.

The Himalaya Experience by Jonathan Chester. An interesting, colourful appetite-whetter for the entire Himalayan region. It has a great deal of information about trekking and climbing as well as some wonderful photographs.

An Introduction to the Hanuman Dhoka is no longer readily available, but it gives a good short description of the buildings around the Durbar Square area of Kathmandu.

Kathmandu – The Hidden City by Annick Holle. A small, locally produced English-language book, which takes you on a number of walks around Kathmandu, revealing some of the lesser-known backstreets where tourists rarely get to. It is definitely for the dedicated sightseer.

Mountaineering

There can be few activities that seem to so inspire people to write about them as that of mountaineering. Every first ascent of a Himalayan peak seems to have resulted in a book about it, together with the numerous other books about the mountains written simply because it seemed a good idea.

The Ascent of Rum Doodle by WE Bowman. A classic spoof of these often all-too-serious tomes.

Nepal Himalaya by HW Tilman. A rarity among mountaineering books in that it gives an often-amusing account of some early trekking expeditions together with the odd mountain assault which had, by today's standards, an amazing lack of advance planning. Although Tilman was a Himalayan mountaineering pioneer he has probably contributed even more to the current popularity of trekking. His book has been republished together with other Tilman classics in ***The Seven Mountain-Travel Books***. Tilman's dry wit is quite delightful.

Annapurna by Maurice Herzog. A mountaineering classic. Herzog led the first group to reach the top of an 8000m peak, but the descent turned into a frostbitten nightmare taking them to the very outer edges of human endurance.

Naturally, there are numerous books about climbing Everest.

Forerunners to Everest by Rene Dittert, Gabriel Chevalley & Raymond Lambert. Describes the two Swiss expeditions to Everest in 1952 and includes a good description of the old expedition route march.

The Conquest of Everest by Sir John Hunt. The official account of the first successful climb of the world's highest mountain.

Everest by Walt Unsworth. Probably the best history of Everest mountaineering.

Annapurna South Face by Chris Bonington. Describes in detail the planning that goes into making a major expedition, the complicated logistics of the actual climb, and makes an authoritative account of a highly technical assault on a difficult face. In the 1970s unconquered peaks were few and far between so attention turned to climbing by more difficult or spectacular routes. This was technical climbing of a high order and Englishman Chris Bonington's various expeditions were the best-known examples of the craft.

Everest the Hard Way, also by Chris Bonington. Describes his expedition's first ascent of the south-western face in 1975. This climb was a perfectly planned and executed race to the top, and the book is illustrated with superb mountain photography. Despite his record of leading some of the most acclaimed mountaineering expeditions of the time, Bonington did not reach the top of Everest until 1985, when he set a record as the oldest Everest summiteer. He was 50-years-old at the time but just nine days later his record fell to 55-year-old American climber Dick Bass.

Many people come, looking, looking by Galen Rowell. By the renowned mountain photographer, this is a thought-provoking study of the impact of trekking and mountaineering on the Himalayan region. There's a good description of the Annapurna Circuit trek and a quick side-trip to knock off a little 6000m peak.

Annapurna to Dhaulagiri by Harka Gurung. Covers the ten-year period between 1950 and 1960, when most of Nepal's major peaks 'fell' to mountaineering expeditions.

Himalaya by Herbert Tichy. Describes the author's journeys in the region from the 1930s, including his ascent of Cho Oyu, the third-highest peak climbed at that time.

Into Thin Air by Jon Krakauer. Recounts the disastrous Everest expedition of 1996 in which eight climbers died. This was a controversial expedition as there were a number of inexperienced, paying climbers.

The Trekking Peaks of Nepal by Bill O'Connor. A complete description of the climbing routes up Nepal's 18 'trekking peaks'.

Trekking, Biking & Rafting

Trekking in Nepal: A Traveler's Guide by Stephen Bezruchka. Covers all the main trekking routes with detailed descriptions, and is probably the best all-round reference for the individual trekker.

Trekking in the Everest Region by Jamie McGuiness. One of the excellent Trailblazer series, with separate guides to Langtang and the Annapurna regions.

Treks on the Kathmandu Valley Rim by Alton C Byers III. Details a number of one-day and overnight treks near Kathmandu.

Kathmandu: Bikes & Hikes by resident James Giambrone. Gives details on 10 hikes and 11 mountain-bike rides around the valley; it also has a decent fold-out map, although it's now somewhat dated.

White Water Nepal by Peter Knowles. Anyone who is seriously interested in rafting and kayaking, and especially anyone contemplating a private expedition, should get hold of this book, which is widely available in Kathmandu. It has detailed information on river trips, 60 maps, river profiles and hydrographs, plus advice on equipment and health – in short all the information a prospective 'river runner' could want.

A Winter in Nepal by John Morris. Recounts in a very readable fashion a trek from Kathmandu to Pokhara. Like other accounts of the time it's interesting to compare it with the situation today – there was no Kathmandu to Pokhara road in those days. Morris was a retired British army Gurkha officer and his ability to speak Nepali gives him an excellent insight into Nepali life.

The Snow Leopard by Peter Matthiessen. This is, on one level, an account of a trek from Pokhara up to Dolpo in the west of Nepal, keeping an eye open for snow leopards on the way. On other levels, however, it's clear the author is searching for much more than rare wildlife and this widely acclaimed book doggedly pursues 'the big questions' with the Himalaya as a background.

Stones of Silence by George Schaller. Matthiessen's companion on the above trek, this work includes the same journey, and an account of various journeys in the Himalaya.

History & Politics

Although browsing through a good Kathmandu bookshop will reveal plenty of histories of Nepal, there is no definitive book that tells it all in a readable fashion. In particular there has been little documentation of recent events in Nepal, especially the push for greater democracy and the underlying political unrest.

Fatalism & Development – Nepal's Struggle for Modernization by Dor Bahadur Bista. An often controversial analysis of Nepali society and its dynamics. It has a very good historical introduction, and the author looks especially critically at the role of the caste system.

Travels in Nepal by Charlie Pye-Smith. A travel account on one level, but the author's travels around the country are highly directed – he was there to study the impacts and benefits of foreign aid to Nepal, and his conclusions are incisive and interesting. In between the aid projects he chain-smokes his way around quite a few interesting places and then appears to finish up as much in love with the country as many other less single-minded visitors! See Foreign Aid under Economy in the Facts about Nepal chapter for more about this book.

The Wildest Dreams of Kew by Jeremy Bernstein. A rather dated account of Nepal, which covers the country's history in a very readable style and includes an interesting trek to the Everest Base Camp.

Heroes & Builders of Nepal by Rishikesh Shaha. A brief volume detailing the lives of some of Nepal's early historical figures.

The Challenge to Democracy by T Louise Brown. An excellent reference on Nepal's political history up until around 1996, but with a price tag of US$85, it's for the dedicated.

Democracy without Roots by Jan Sharma. A lucid account of Nepali politics post-1990.

Culture, People & Festivals

Festivals of Nepal by Mary Anderson is an excellent (but getting a bit old) rundown on Nepal's many festivals and includes interesting accounts of many of the legends and tales behind them. There is also a great deal of background information about the Hindu religion.

Nepalese Festivals by Jim Goodman. Another worthwhile festivals reference.

The Gods of Nepal by Mary Rubel. A detailed description of Hindu and Buddhist deities.

People of Nepal by the Nepali anthropologist Dor Bahadur Bista. Describes the many and diverse ethnic groupings found in the country.

Ethnic Groups of Nepal by DB Shrestha & CB Singh. A similar work to ***People of Nepal***.

Sherpas of Nepal by C Von Furer Haimendorf. Focuses on the Sherpas of the Everest region in a rather dry and academic manner.

Himalayan Traders also by C Von Furer Haimendorf. A rather more readable follow-up, concentrating on the changes in trading patterns and cultures among Nepal's Himalayan people.

Tiger for Breakfast by Michel Peissel. A biography of the colourful gentleman who was probably the best-known resident expatriate in the kingdom: Boris Lissanevitch of the Royal Hotel and Yak & Yeti Restaurant in Kathmandu.

Bending Bamboo, Changing Winds by Eva Kipps. Depicts the lives of a number of Nepali village women.

Nepali Aama by Broughton Coburn. Details the life of a remarkable Gurung woman and gives an interesting insight into the life of Nepali women.

The Violet Shyness of Their Eyes: Notes from Nepal by Barbara J Scot. Gives a fascinating insight into the lives and roles of women in Nepal.

Natural History

The Heart of the Jungle by KK Gurung. Details the wildlife of Royal Chitwan National Park.

Indian Wildlife covers all the national parks on the subcontinent, including Royal Chitwan and Royal Bardia in Nepal with APA's usual high standards of photography.

Birds of Nepal by Robert Fleming Sr, Robert Fleming Jr & Lain Singh Bangdel. A field guide to Nepal's many hundreds of birds.

Himalayan Flowers & Trees by Dorothy Mierow & Tirtha Bahadur Shrestha. This is the best available field guide to the plants of Nepal.

A Popular Guide to the Birds & Mammals of the Annapurna Conservation Area by Carol Inskipp.

Birdwatchers' Guide to Nepal by Carol Inskipp.

Flowers of the Himalaya by Oleg Polunin & Adam Stainton.

Forests of Nepal by Adam Stainton.

Mount Everest National Park: Sagarmatha, Mother of the Universe by Margaret Jefferies.

Nepal's Forest Birds: Their Status and Conservation by Carol Inskipp.

Royal Chitwan National Park: Wildlife Heritage of Nepal by Hemanta R Mishra & Margaret Jefferies.

Trees & Shrubs of Nepal & the Himalaya by Adrian & Jimmie Storrs.

Architecture & the Arts

The Art of Nepal by Lydia Aran. This book is readily available in Nepal and concentrates on the art that can actually be seen in the country. See Arts in the Facts about Nepal chapter for more on this book.

Kathmandu Valley, Vols I & II by Austrian publisher Anton Schroll. These are two exhaustive studies of the architecture of the Kathmandu Valley. Volume I covers the most important temples and buildings in great detail while Volume II has individual plans of a great many temples and buildings. This is strictly for academics, but it's amusing to see how many other guidebooks have used these titles in their research. Often they've even copied the mistakes!

The Traditional Architecture of Kathmandu Valley by Wolfgang Korn. This book has some superb line drawings showing the most important architectural forms, along with interesting text describing their historical development.

Nepal by Michael Hutt. An excellent guide to the art and architecture of the Kathmandu Valley. The book outlines in some depth the main forms of art and architecture, and then goes on to describe specific sites within the valley, often with layout plans. It also features excellent colour plates, as well as black-and-white photos.

Nepal Mandala – A Cultural Study of the Kathmandu Valley by Mary Shepherd Sluiser. Another two-volume academic study of the valley. Volume II is full of excellent photographs.

Nepal – Art Treasures from the Himalaya by Waldschmidt. Describes and illustrates many Nepali works of art.

Himalayan Art by Madanjeet Singh. Covers the art of the whole Himalayan region, again with excellent photographs.

Kathmandu Valley Towns by Fran Hosken. About the temples, people, history and festivals of the towns of the Kathmandu Valley. The book is illustrated with a great many black-and-white and colour photographs.

Erotic Themes of Nepal by Trilok Chandra Majupuria & Indra Majupuria. An interesting locally produced book on the erotic art seen on some temples, although it has to work hard to make a book-length study of the subject!

Tibetan Rugs by Hallvard Kåre Kuloøy. A fascinating and well-illustrated introduction to the subject. If you enjoy the Tibetan rugs made in Nepal you may be a litte disappointed to find that the author summarily dismisses modern rugs as doing 'very little justice to a very splendid tradition'.

Himalayan Voices by Michael Hutt. Subtitled ***An Introduction to Modern Nepali Literature***, this book includes work by contemporary poets and short-story writers.

General

Nepal – the Kingdom in the Himalaya by Toni Hagen. One of the most complete studies of Nepal's people, geography and geology. Hagen has travelled extensively through Nepal since the 1950s, and the book reflects his intimate knowledge of the country and also has fine colour plates. This book is now in its fourth edition, and is one of the best and most up-to-date references available.

To the Navel of the World by Peter Somerville-Large. An amusingly written account of a saunter around Nepal and Tibet. The author does some deep-winter trekking, using yaks, in the Solu Khumbu and up to the Everest Base Camp. His encounters with tourism in remote locations are very funny.

Video Night in Kathmandu by Pico Iyer. This book gallivants all around Asia, but the chapter on Nepal has some astute and amusing observations on the collision between Nepali tradition and Western culture, particularly video culture.

The Waiting Land: A Spell in Nepal by Dervla Murphy. An interesting account of a visit to Nepal at a time when great changes were at hand. She tells of her time spent in a Tibetan refugee camp near Pokhara, and of her travels in the Langtang region.

Mister Raja's Neighbourhood by Jeff Greenwald. This book gives an amusing account of the author's travels in Nepal.

Escape from Kathmandu by Kim Stanley Robinson. This is an off-the-wall romp around Nepal. Adventures include helping a captured yeti, an illegal ascent of Everest with a reincarnated lama (Tibetan Bhuddist monk), an attempt to kidnap King Birendra, a visit to the imaginary place of Shambhala, a very logical explanation for why Prince Charles is the way he is, and the best ever description of what they do to Kathmandu while you're away trekking.

Misery Behind the Looms A sobering account of the plight of the young children who are forced to work in abhorrent conditions in the carpet factories of the Kathmandu Valley.

Travelers' Tales Nepal One in a series published by Travelers' Tales Inc, this book is a collection of 37 interesting and wide-ranging stories from a variety of writers, including Peter Matthiessen and Jimmy Carter.

FILMS

Despite its stunning scenery, Nepal is used as a film location surprisingly rarely. Recently the film *Everest*, shot in the impressive Imax format, has proved very popular and is credited by some as having significantly boosted the number of people wanting to trek in the Everest region in recent years.

Bhaktapur's Durbar Square was made over and used for the set of Bertolucci's *Little Buddha*.

More recently, Oscar-nominated, Nepali-French co-production *Caravan*, directed by Eric Valli, has been a huge success. It was renamed for sales abroad as *Himalaya*. While the story only just manages to hold together, the film has some of the most stunning photography of Nepal that you're ever likely to see. It was shot mostly in the Upper Dolpo district of western Nepal.

Basantpur by Neer Shah, the co-producer of *Caravan*, is a recent Nepali film depicting the intrigues and conspiracies of life at the Rana court. While it owes something to Bollywood 'masala movies' (a little bit of everything), it is based on a historical novel written nearly 60 years ago.

CD-ROMS

The Nepal Tourism Board (NTB) has produced a surprisingly slick, interactive CD-ROM on Nepal. Called *Experience it in Nepal*, it has video clips, directories of various government, tourism and private sector bodies such as airlines, trekking companies and hotels. The test will be whether (and how) often it is updated. It is available from the Tourist Service Center at Bhrikuti Mandap in central Kathmandu for Rs 100.

NEWSPAPERS & MAGAZINES

Nepal's main English-language daily paper, *Rising Nepal*, is basically a government mouthpiece. It covers most important international news while events in Nepal are reported in a very individual style.

For a more balanced view of local issues there's the daily *Kathmandu Post*, which is not too bad. The international news is patchy and it mostly reports on regional issues.

The paper that really tackles the main issues in depth is the weekly *Nepali Times*, which gives some interesting insights into the local political scene. *Spotlight* is a local weekly current affairs magazine that is also worth a look.

For international news you'll have to look farther afield. The *International Herald Tribune* is widely available in Kathmandu – at a price. *Time* and *Newsweek* are readily available and Indian dailies such as the *Statesman* or the *Times of India* can also be found.

The glossy *Travellers Nepal* and *Nepal Traveller* are competing free monthly tourist magazines distributed at many hotels. They often have interesting articles about sightseeing, festivals, trekking and other activities in Nepal, in addition to directories of airlines, embassies, etc. Another information periodical with useful listings is *Kathmandu Flea Market*. It is distributed free around Thamel.

Himal South Asia is a bimonthly magazine mainly devoted to development and environment issues. It's an excellent publication with top-class contributors.

There are also a number of Nepali newspapers and magazines online. The best place to access them is from the Nepal news.com Web site (see Internet Resources earlier in this chapter).

RADIO & TV

Radio Nepal has news bulletins in English at 8 am, 1.05 and 8 pm daily (for a text version 'tune in' online at www.catmando.com).

Nepal Television is the local station, which has an English news bulletin at 10 pm.

Satellite TV is widespread. Most upmarket hotels have dishes, and you can watch everything from the BBC World Service to MTV and American wrestling.

In the Kathmandu Valley, two popular commercial FM radio stations playing contemporary Western and local music are Kantipur FM (96.1 MHz) and Hits FM (92.1 MHz). A station that plays a bit of everything, from John Lennon to Ravi Shankar, is HBC FM (104 MHz).

PHOTOGRAPHY & VIDEO

Bringing a video camera to Nepal poses no real problem, and there are no video fees to worry about. The exception to this is in Upper Mustang where an outrageous fee is levied.

Film & Equipment

In Kathmandu and Pokhara there are numerous camera and film shops, and good-quality film is readily available. Do check, however, that the packaging has not been tampered with, and that the expiry date has not been exceeded. If in doubt, open the cardboard packaging and check, but you are extremely unlikely to be ripped off in the larger shops. Out in the smaller cities and towns, film is also available, but there is little choice and even greater chance of coming across expired film.

Colour-print film can be processed rapidly, competently and economically in Kathmandu and Pokhara, and there are numerous places offering a same-day service for print film (see Photo Shops under Information in the Kathmandu chapter).

The developing charge is typically Rs 40 plus around Rs 5 for each print.

Typically, Fujicolor 100 36-exposure colour film costs about Rs 150, Fujichrome 36-exposure slide film about Rs 345, and Ektachrome 200 36-exposure slide film about Rs 500.

New camera equipment is surprisingly cheap in Nepal. The range of cameras and lenses is also good, although digital cameras have yet to come on the scene. New Rd in central kathmandu is the best place to look. Just be sure to ascertain whether what you are buying has an international warranty.

Technical Tips

Nepal is an exceptionally scenic country so bring plenty of film. It can also provide you with some challenging photo opportunities. For great shots you need a variety of lenses, from a wide-angle lens if you're shooting inside compact temple compounds to a long telephoto lens if you're after perfect mountain shots or close-ups of wildlife. A polarising filter is useful to increase contrast and bring out the blue of the sky.

Remember to allow for the exceptional intensity of mountain light when setting exposures at high altitude. At the other extreme it's surprising how often you find the light in Nepal is insufficient. Early in the morning, in dense jungle in Royal Chitwan National Park, or in gloomy temples and narrow streets, you may often find yourself wishing you had high-speed film. A flash is often necessary for shots inside temples or to 'fill in' shots of sculptures and reliefs.

Restrictions

It is not uncommon for temple guardians to disallow photos of their temple, and these wishes should be respected. It's probably wise not to take photos of army camps.

Photographing People

Most Nepalis are content to have their photograph taken, but always get permission first. Sherpa people are an exception and can be very camera shy. Bear in mind that if someone poses for you (especially those saintly sadhus or holy men), they may insist on being given *baksheesh* (donations).

Respect people's privacy and bear in mind that most Nepalis are extremely modest. Although people carry out many activities in public (they have no choice), it does not follow that passers-by have the right to watch or take photographs. Riverbanks and village wells, for example, are often used as bathrooms, but the users expect as much consideration and privacy as you would in your own house.

Religious ceremonies are also often private affairs, so first ask yourself whether it would be acceptable for a tourist to intrude and to take photographs at a corresponding ceremony in your home country – then get explicit permission from the senior participants. The behaviour of many would-be National Geographic photographers at places such as Pashupatinath in the Kathmandu Valley (the most holy cremation site in Nepal) is horrendous. Imagine the outrage a busload of scantily clad, camera-toting tourists would create if they invaded a family funeral in the West.

Airport Security

All luggage (including carry-on cabin baggage) is X-rayed at Kathmandu's Tribhuvan airport on the way in and the way out of the country; signs on the X-ray equipment specifically state that the machines are not film-safe for undeveloped film. Be warned – have exposed film inspected manually when leaving the country.

TIME

Nepal is five hours and 45 minutes ahead of GMT; this curious time differential is intended to make it very clear that Nepal is a separate place to India, where the time is five hours and 30 minutes ahead of GMT!

When it's noon in Nepal it's 1.15 am in New York, 6.15 am in London, 1.15 pm in Bangkok, 2.15 pm in Tibet, 4.15pm in Sydney and 10.15 pm the previous day in Los Angeles, not allowing for daylight saving or other local variations.

ELECTRICITY

Electricity is only found in major towns and some odd outposts such as Namche Bazaar in the Solu Khumbu. When available it is 220V/50 cycles – 120V appliances from the USA will need a transformer.

Sockets usually take the three-round-pin plugs, sometimes the small variety, sometimes the large. Some sockets take plugs with two round pins.

Outside Kathmandu blackouts are a fact of life and can be random or regular. In winter, power shortages are endemic, especially if there has been low rainfall in the previous monsoon (which means water flow is reduced and the hydroelectric resources have to be rationed).

Power surges are also likely. If you are using expensive equipment (computers, TVs, fridges etc) it is worth buying a volt guard with spike suppressor (meaning an automatic cut-off switch). These are widely available from most electronic shops for around Rs 1000.

LAUNDRY

There are no public laundrettes in Nepal. Hotels generally discourage guests from doing their own laundry, especially in Kathmandu where water shortages are common. Most hotels have a laundry service, and this is generally very reasonably priced.

TOILETS

Throughout the country, the 'squat toilet' is the norm except in hotels and guesthouses geared toward tourists and international business travellers.

Next to the typical squat toilet is a bucket and/or tap. This water supply has a twofold function: flushing the toilet and cleaning the nether regions (with the left hand only) while still squatting over the toilet. More rustic toilets in rural areas may simply consist of a few planks over a hole in the ground.

Public toilets are rare, but can usually be found in bus stations, larger hotel lobbies and airports, although the cleanliness may leave a bit to be desired. While on the road between towns and villages, it is acceptable to go discreetly behind a tree or bush.

HEALTH

Travel health depends on your predeparture preparations, your daily health care while travelling and how you handle any medical problem that may develop. While the potential dangers can seem quite frightening, in reality few travellers experience anything more than an upset stomach.

Predeparture Planning

Make sure you're healthy before you start travelling. If you are going on a long trip make sure your teeth are OK. If you wear glasses always take a spare pair and your prescription.

If you require a particular medication take an adequate supply, as it may not be available locally. Take part of the packaging showing the generic name rather than the brand, which will make getting replacements easier. Have a legible prescription or letter from your doctor to show that you legally use the medication to avoid any problems.

Anyone with known heart disease should carry a recent copy of their ECG. This is useful in aiding quick diagnosis of problems that may arise.

Immunisations Plan ahead for getting your vaccinations; some of them require more than one injection, while some vaccinations should not be given together. Note that some vaccinations should not be given during pregnancy or to people with allergies – discuss this with your doctor.

It is recommended you seek medical advice at least six weeks before travel. Be aware that there is often a greater risk of disease with children and during pregnancy.

Discuss your requirements with your doctor, but vaccinations you should consider for this trip include the following (for more details about the diseases themselves, see the individual disease entries later in this section).

Diphtheria & Tetanus Vaccinations for these two diseases are usually combined and are recommended for everyone. After an initial course of three injections (usually given in childhood), boosters are necessary every 10 years.

Polio Although virtually nonexistent in the West these days, polio is still prevalent in Nepal. Keep up to date with this vaccination, normally given in childhood, with a booster (drops of vaccine on a sugar cube) once as an adult.

Hepatitis A The hepatitis A vaccine (eg Avaxim, Havrix 1440 or VAQTA) provides long-term immunity (possibly for more than 10 years) after an initial injection and a booster at six to 12 months. Alternatively, an injection of gamma globulin can provide short-term protection against hepatitis A for two to four months, depending on the dose given. It is not a vaccine, but is a ready-made antibody collected from blood donations. It is reasonably effective and, unlike the vaccine, it is protective immediately. Hepatitis A vaccine is also available in a combined form (Twinrix) with hepatitis B vaccine. Three injections over a six-month period are required, the first two providing substantial protection against hepatitis A.

Typhoid Vaccination against typhoid is never 100% effective but it does offer good protection. It is advisable for travel to Nepal, and is available either as an injection or as capsules to be taken orally.

Cholera Despite the existence of cholera in Asia, cholera vaccination is not required and the chance of actually catching the disease as a traveller is virtually nil. The vaccine is poorly protective and is not recommended.

Hepatitis B Travellers who should consider vaccination against hepatitis B include those on a long trip, as well as those visiting countries where there are high levels of hepatitis B infection, where blood transfusions may not be adequately screened or where sexual contact or needle sharing is a possibility. Vaccination involves three injections over six months.

Yellow Fever A yellow fever vaccine is the only vaccine that is a legal requirement for entry into many countries, including Nepal, but this only applies when coming from an infected area (parts of Africa and South America).

Rabies This is a viral brain infection transmitted to humans from animals, usually dogs. Vaccination should be considered by those who will spend a month or longer in a country where rabies is common, especially if they are cycling, handling animals, caving or travelling to remote areas, and particularly for children (who may not report a bite). Pre-travel rabies vaccination involves having three injections over 21 to 28 days. If someone who has been vaccinated is bitten or scratched by an animal, they will require two booster injections of vaccine; those not vaccinated require more. The human rabies immune globulin (HRIG) is available in Kathmandu.

Japanese B Encephalitis Consider vaccination against this mosquito-borne disease if spending a month or longer in the Terai during the monsoon. Vaccination involves three injections over 30 days.

Meningococcal Meningitis Centers for Disease Control (CDC) in the USA has taken off its recommendation for this vaccine for travel to Nepal, but it is a very safe, cheap and highly effective vaccine that should be considered by long term travellers and expats.

Tuberculosis (TB) Although TB is endemic in Nepal, the risk to travellers is very low, unless you will be living with or closely associated with local people. Vaccination against TB is not recommended for casual visitors to Nepal.

Medical Kit Check List

Following is a list of items you should consider including in your medical kit. Bear in mind that prescription drugs are available over the counter in Nepal, usually at very low prices.

- ☐ **Antibiotics** – consider including these if you're travelling well off the beaten track; see your doctor, as they must be prescribed, and carry the prescription with you
- ☐ **Antifungal cream or powder** – for fungal skin infections and thrush
- ☐ **Antihistamine** – for allergies, eg, hay fever; to ease the itch from insect bites or stings; and to prevent motion sickness
- ☐ **Antiseptic** (such as povidone-iodine) – for cuts and grazes
- ☐ **Aspirin or paracetamol** – for pain or fever
- ☐ **Bandages, Band-Aids** (plasters) and other wound dressings
- ☐ **Calamine lotion, sting relief spray or aloe vera** – to ease irritation from sunburn and insect bites or stings
- ☐ **Cold & flu tablets, throat lozenges** and **nasal decongestant**
- ☐ **Insect repellent, sunscreen, lip balm** and **eye drops**
- ☐ **Loperamide or diphenoxylate** – 'blockers' for diarrhoea (for use in emergency only)
- ☐ **Multivitamins** – consider for long trips, when dietary vitamin intake may be inadequate
- ☐ **Prochlorperazine or metaclopramide** – for nausea and vomiting
- ☐ **Rehydration mixture** – to prevent dehydration, eg, due to severe diarrhoea; particularly important when travelling with children
- ☐ **Scissors, tweezers and thermometer** (note that mercury thermometers are prohibited by airlines)
- ☐ **Syringes and needles** – in case you need injections in a country with medical hygiene problems. Ask your doctor for a note explaining why you have them.
- ☐ **Water purification tablets or iodine**

Malaria Medication Antimalarial drugs do not prevent you from being infected, but do kill the malaria parasites during a stage in their development and significantly reduce the risk of becoming very ill or dying. Expert advice on medication should be sought, as there are many factors to consider, including the area to be visited (there is virtually no risk of contracting malaria in Nepal outside of the Terai region), the risk of exposure to malaria-carrying mosquitoes, the side effects of medication, your medical history and whether you are a child or an adult or pregnant.

Health Insurance Make sure that you have adequate health insurance. See Travel Insurance under Visas & Documents earlier in this chapter for details.

Travel Health Guides If you are planning to be away or travelling in remote areas for a long period of time, you may like to consider buying and carrying a more detailed health guide.

CDC's Complete Guide to Healthy Travel, Open Road Publishing, 1997. The US Centers for Disease Control and Prevention recommendations for international travel.

Healthy Travel Asia & India, Dr Isabelle Young, Lonely Planet Publications, 2000. Packed with answers to all the common health questions.

Travel with Children, Maureen Wheeler, Lonely Planet Publications, 1995. Includes advice on travel health for younger children.

Travellers' Health, Dr Richard Dawood, Oxford University Press, 1995. Comprehensive, easy to read, authoritative and highly recommended, although it's rather large to lug around.

Where There Is No Doctor, David Werner, Macmillan, 1994. This is a very detailed guide, which is intended for a person such as a Peace Corps worker, going to work in an underdeveloped country.

Online Health Guides There are also a number of excellent travel health sites on the Internet.

CIWEC Clinic Travel Medicine Center This interactive Web site is excellent for medical advice on travel in Nepal. Email advice is possible. www.ciwec-clinic.com

Lonely Planet Follow the Health link for plenty of information including links to the World Health Organization (WHO) and the US Centers for Disease Control and Prevention (CDC). www.lonelyplanet.com

Nutrition

If your diet is poor or limited in variety, if you're travelling hard and fast and therefore missing meals or if you simply lose your appetite, you can soon start to lose weight and place your health at risk.

Make sure your diet is well balanced. Cooked eggs, tofu, beans, lentils (*dal* in Nepali) and nuts are all safe ways to get protein. Fruit you can peel (bananas, oranges or mandarins for example) is usually safe (melons can harbour bacteria in their flesh and are best avoided) and a good source of vitamins. Try to eat plenty of grains (including rice) and bread. Remember that although food is generally safer if it is cooked well, overcooked food loses much of its nutritional value. If your diet isn't well balanced or if your food intake is insufficient, it's a good idea to take vitamin and iron pills.

In hot climates make sure you drink enough – don't rely on feeling thirsty to indicate when you should drink. Not needing to urinate or small amounts of very dark yellow urine is a danger sign. Always carry a water bottle with you on long trips. Excessive sweating can lead to loss of salt and therefore muscle cramping. Salt tablets are not a good idea as a preventative, but in places where salt is not used much, adding salt to food can help.

Basic Rules

Food This is generally safe in Nepal and what you eat is probably more significant than where you eat it – the salads in good Thamel restaurants are as clean as anywhere in the world, and the kitchens of five-star hotels are not immune to wandering flies and other sources of contamination.

Meat in Nepal, including the beef imported from India, is generally of a high standard. There is little evidence that meat is a cause of illness *per se*, although in very rare cases it can cause tapeworms and trichinosis.

Meat storage is the important factor, and any meat – but especially chicken – can contaminate other food stored close by.

Vegetables and fruit should be washed with purified water or peeled where possible. Beware of ice cream that is sold in the street or anywhere it might have been melted and refrozen; if there's any doubt (eg, a power cut in the last day or two), steer well clear.

See also the Food & Drinks section later in this chapter.

Water The number one rule is *be careful of the water* and especially ice. It is not safe to drink tap water in Nepal.

If you don't know for certain that the water is safe, assume the worst. Bottled water is available everywhere and is safe to drink, but the unrecyclable plastic bottles are creating a huge litter problem. The best way not to contribute to this is to purify the tap water yourself using iodine. However there are some people for whom iodine is unsuitable, notably pregnant women and those with iodine allergies and thyroid problems.

Take care with fruit juice, particularly if water may have been added. Milk should be treated with suspicion as it is often unpasteurised, though boiled milk is fine if it is kept hygienically. Tea or coffee should be OK, since the water should have been boiled.

Water Purification The simplest way of purifying water is to boil it thoroughly. Vigorous boiling is enough to kill most pathogens, even at an altitude where the boiling point is lower (at Everest Base Camp water boils at 83°C).

Consider purchasing a water filter for a long trip. There are two main kinds of filter. Total filters take out all parasites, bacteria and viruses and make water safe to drink. They are often expensive, but can be more cost effective than buying bottled water. Simple filters (which could even be a nylon mesh bag) take out dirt and larger foreign bodies from the water so that chemical solutions work much more effectively; if water is dirty, chemical solutions may not work at all. It's very important when buying a filter to read the specifications, so that you know exactly what it removes from the water and what it doesn't. Simple filtering will not remove all dangerous organisms, so if you cannot boil water it should be treated chemically. Chlorine and iodine will kill many pathogens, including parasites such as giardia and amoebic cysts, but cyclospora and cryptosporidium cysts are both highly resistant to chemical treatment.

Environmental Hazards

Acute Mountain Sickness Lack of oxygen at high altitudes (over 2500m) affects most people to some extent. The effect, which may be mild or severe, occurs because less oxygen reaches the muscles and the brain at high altitude, requiring the heart and lungs to compensate by working harder. Symptoms of acute mountain sickness (AMS) or altitude sickness usually develop during the first 24 to 48 hours at altitude. Mild symptoms include headache, lethargy, dizziness, difficulty sleeping and loss of appetite. AMS may become more severe without warning and can be fatal. Severe symptoms include breathlessness, a dry, irritable cough (which may progress to the production of pink, frothy sputum), severe headache, lack of coordination and balance, confusion, irrational behaviour, vomiting, drowsiness and eventually unconsciousness. There is no hard-and-fast rule as to what is too high: AMS has been fatal at 3000m, although from 3500 to 4500m is the usual range. More important than absolute altitude is the rate of ascent – problems are more likely to occur as a result of ascending too fast and a lack of acclimatisation.

Treat mild symptoms by resting at the same altitude until recovery, usually a day or two. Paracetamol or aspirin can be taken for headaches. If symptoms persist or become worse, however, *immediate descent is necessary*; even 500m can help. Drug treatments should never be used to avoid descent or to enable further ascent.

The drugs acetazolamide and dexamethasone are recommended by some doctors for the prevention of AMS; however, their use is controversial. They can reduce the symptoms, but they may also mask warning signs – severe and fatal AMS has occurred in people taking these drugs. In general we do not recommend them for travellers.

To help prevent AMS:

- Ascend slowly – have frequent rest days, spending two to three nights at each rise of 1000m. If you reach a high altitude by trekking, acclimatisation takes place gradually and you are less likely to be affected than if you fly directly to high altitude.
- It is always wise to sleep at a lower altitude than the greatest height reached during the day if possible. Also, once above 3000m, care should be taken not to increase the sleeping altitude by more than 300m per day.
- Drink extra fluids. The mountain air is dry and cold, and moisture is lost as you breathe.
- Evaporation of sweat may occur unnoticed and result in dehydration.
- Eat light, high-carbohydrate meals for more energy.
- Avoid alcohol as it may increase the risk of dehydration.
- Avoid sedatives.

Heat Exhaustion Dehydration and salt deficiency can cause heat exhaustion. Take time to acclimatise to high temperatures, drink sufficient liquids and do not do anything too physically demanding.

Salt deficiency is characterised by fatigue, lethargy, headaches, giddiness and muscle cramps; salt tablets won't help – adding extra salt to your food is better.

Everyday Health

Normal body temperature is up to 37°C (98.6°F); more than 2°C (4°F) higher indicates a high fever. The normal adult pulse rate is 60 to 100 per minute (children 80 to 100, babies 100 to 140). As a general rule the pulse increases about 20 beats per minute for each 1°C (2°F) rise in fever.

Respiration (breathing) rate is also an indicator of illness. Count the number of breaths per minute: Between 12 and 20 is normal for adults and older children (up to 30 for younger children, 40 for babies). People with a high fever or serious respiratory illness breathe more quickly than normal. More than 40 shallow breaths a minute may indicate pneumonia.

Anhidrotic heat exhaustion is a rare form of heat exhaustion that is caused by an inability to sweat. It tends to affect people who have been in a hot climate for some time, rather than newcomers. It can progress to heatstroke. Treatment involves removal to a cooler climate.

Heatstroke This serious, occasionally fatal, condition can occur if the body's heat-regulating mechanism breaks down and the body temperature rises to dangerous levels. Long, continuous periods of exposure to high temperatures and insufficient fluids can leave you vulnerable to heatstroke.

The symptoms include a sense of feeling unwell, not sweating very much (or at all) and a high body temperature (39° to 41°C or 102° to 106°F). Where sweating has ceased, the skin becomes flushed and red. Severe, throbbing headaches and lack of coordination will also occur, and the sufferer may be confused or aggressive. Eventually the victim will become delirious or convulse. Hospitalisation is essential, but in the interim get victims out of the sun, remove their clothing, cover them with a wet sheet or towel and then fan continually. Give fluids if they are conscious.

Hypothermia Too much cold can be just as dangerous as too much heat. If you are trekking at high altitudes or simply taking a long bus trip over mountains, particularly at night, be prepared. In Nepal's mountain regions you should always be prepared for cold, wet or windy conditions even if you're just out walking or hitching.

Hypothermia occurs when the body loses heat faster than it can produce it and the core temperature of the body falls. It is surprisingly easy to progress from very cold to dangerously cold due to a combination of wind, wet clothing, fatigue and hunger, even if the air temperature is above freezing. It is best to dress in layers; silk, wool and some of the new artificial fibres are all good insulating materials. A hat is important, as a lot of heat is lost through the head. A strong, waterproof outer layer (and a 'space' blanket for emergencies) is essential. Carry basic supplies, including fluid and food containing simple sugars, to generate heat quickly.

Symptoms of hypothermia are exhaustion, numb skin (particularly toes and fingers), shivering, slurred speech, irrational or violent behaviour, lethargy, stumbling, dizzy spells, muscle cramps and violent bursts of energy. Irrationality may take the form of sufferers claiming they are warm and trying to take off their clothes.

To treat mild hypothermia, first get the person out of the wind and/or rain, remove their clothing if it's wet and replace it with dry, warm clothing. Give them hot liquids (not alcohol) and some high-kilojoule, easily digestible food. Do not rub victims; instead, allow them to slowly warm themselves. This should be enough to treat the early stages of hypothermia. The early recognition and treatment of mild hypothermia is the only way to prevent severe hypothermia, which is a critical condition.

Motion Sickness Eating lightly before and during a trip will reduce the chances of motion sickness. If you are prone to motion sickness try to find a place that minimises movement – near the wing on aircraft, near the centre on buses. Fresh air usually helps; reading and cigarette smoke don't. Commercial motion-sickness preparations, which can cause drowsiness, have to be taken before the trip commences. Ginger (available in capsule form) and peppermint (including mint-flavoured sweets) are natural preventatives.

Prickly Heat Prickly heat is an itchy rash caused by excessive perspiration trapped under the skin. It usually strikes people who have just arrived in a hot climate. Keeping cool, bathing often, drying the skin and using a mild talcum or prickly heat powder or resorting to air-conditioning may help.

Sunburn In the tropics, the desert or at high altitude you can get sunburnt surprisingly quickly, even through cloud. Use a sunscreen, a hat, and a barrier cream for your nose and lips. Calamine lotion or a commercial after-sun preparation are good for mild sunburn. Protect your eyes with good quality sunglasses, particularly if you will be near water, sand or snow.

Infectious Diseases

Diarrhoea Simple things such as a change of water, food or climate can all cause a mild bout of diarrhoea, but a few rushed toilet trips with no other symptoms is not indicative of a major problem.

Dehydration is the main danger with any diarrhoea, particularly in children or the elderly, as dehydration can occur quite quickly. Under all circumstances *fluid replacement* (at least equal to the volume being lost) is the most important thing to remember. Weak black tea with a little sugar, soda water, or soft drinks allowed to go flat and diluted 50% with clean water are all good. With severe diarrhoea a rehydrating solution is preferable to replace lost minerals and salts. Commercially available oral rehydration salts (ORS) are very useful; add them to boiled or bottled water. In an emergency you can make up a solution of six teaspoons of sugar and a half teaspoon of salt to a litre of boiled or bottled water. Urine output is the best guide to the adequacy of replacement – if you have small amounts of concentrated urine, you need to drink more. Keep drinking small amounts often. Stick to a bland diet as you recover.

Gut-paralysing drugs such as loperamide or diphenoxylate can be used to bring relief from the symptoms, although they do not actually cure the problem. Only use these drugs if you do not have access to toilets, eg, if you *must* travel. Note that these drugs are not recommended for children under 12 years.

In certain situations antibiotics may be required: diarrhoea with blood or mucus (dysentery), any diarrhoea with fever, profuse watery diarrhoea, persistent diarrhoea not improving after 48 hours and severe diarrhoea. In these situations, having paid attention to maintaining your hydration, it would be wise to be assessed by a doctor. Severe diarrhoea is usually bacterial in origin and this should be confirmed by a stool test.

Where this is not possible the recommended drugs for the treatment of bacterial diarrhoea are norfloxacin 400mg twice daily or ciprofloxacin 500mg twice daily for three days. However, these are not recommended for children or pregnant women, and should be avoided by those with diarrhoea and fever or bloody diarrhoea. The drug of choice for children would be naladixic acid, with the dosage dependent on weight. A five-day course is given.

Giardiasis & Amoebic Dysentery Two other causes of persistent diarrhoea in travellers are giardiasis and amoebic dysentery.

Giardiasis is caused by a common parasite, *Giardia lamblia*. Symptoms include stomach cramps, nausea, a bloated stomach, watery, foul-smelling diarrhoea and frequent gas. Giardiasis can appear several weeks after you have been exposed to the parasite. The symptoms may disappear for a few days and then return; this can go on for several weeks.

Amoebic dysentery, caused by the protozoan *Entamoeba histolytica*, is characterised by a gradual onset of low-grade diarrhoea, often with blood and mucus. Cramping abdominal pain and vomiting are less likely than in other types of diarrhoea, and fever may not be present. It will persist until treated and can recur and cause other health problems.

You should seek medical advice if you think you have giardiasis or amoebic dysentery, but where this is not possible, tinidazole or metronidazole are the recommended drugs. Treatment is a 2g single dose of tinidazole or 400mg of metronidazole three times daily for five to 10 days.

Fungal Infections Fungal infections occur more commonly in hot weather and are usually found on the scalp, between the toes (athlete's foot) or fingers, in the groin and on the body (ringworm). You get ringworm (which is a fungal infection, not a worm) from infected animals or other people. Moisture encourages these infections.

To prevent fungal infections wear loose, comfortable clothes, avoid artificial fibres, wash frequently and dry yourself carefully. If you do get an infection, wash the infected area daily with a disinfectant or medicated soap and water, and rinse and dry well. Apply an antifungal cream or powder such as tolnaftate. Try to expose the infected area to air or sunlight as much as possible and wash all towels and underwear in hot water, change them often and let them dry in the sun.

Hepatitis This is a general term for inflammation of the liver, the most common cause of which is an infection with one of the hepatitis viruses. Viral hepatitis is a worldwide problem and is particularly prevalent in Asia. There are several different viruses that cause hepatitis, and they differ in the way that they are transmitted. The symptoms are similar in all forms of the illness, and include fever, chills, headache, fatigue, feelings of weakness and aches and pains, followed by loss of appetite, nausea, vomiting, abdominal pain, dark urine, light-coloured faeces, jaundiced (yellow) skin and yellowing of the whites of the eyes. People who have had hepatitis should avoid alcohol for some time after the illness, as the liver needs time to recover.

Hepatitis A is transmitted by contaminated food and drinking water. You should seek medical advice, but there is not much you can do apart from resting, drinking lots of fluids, eating lightly and avoiding fatty foods.

Hepatitis E is transmitted in the same way as hepatitis A; it can be particularly serious in pregnant women, and is a common cause of hepatitis in Nepal.

There are almost 300 million chronic carriers of **hepatitis B** in the world. It is spread through contact with infected blood, blood products or body fluids, eg, through sexual contact, unsterilised needles and blood transfusions, or contact with blood via small breaks in the skin. Other risk situations include having a shave and tattooing or body piercing with contaminated equipment. The symptoms of hepatitis B may be more severe than type A and the disease can lead to long term problems such as chronic liver damage, liver cancer or a long term carrier state. Hepatitis C and D are spread in the same way as hepatitis B and can also lead to long term complications.

There are vaccines against hepatitis A and B, but there are currently no vaccines against the other types of hepatitis. Following the basic rules about food and water (hepatitis A and E) and avoiding risk situations (hepatitis B, C and D) are important preventative measures.

HIV/AIDS Infection with the human immunodeficiency virus (HIV) may lead to acquired immune deficiency syndrome (AIDS), which is a fatal disease. Any exposure to contaminated blood, blood products or body fluids may put the individual at risk. The disease is often transmitted through sexual contact or dirty needles – thus vaccinations, acupuncture, tattooing and body piercing can potentially be as dangerous as intravenous drug use. HIV/ AIDS can also be spread through infected blood transfusions; in Nepal, blood is screened for HIV but the test may miss the disease in the 'window period' when it is not easily detected.

If you do need an injection, ask to see the syringe unwrapped in front of you, or take a needle and syringe pack with you (available from pharmacies in Nepal).

Fear of HIV infection should never preclude treatment for suspected serious medical conditions.

Intestinal Worms These parasites are most common in rural, tropical areas. The different worms have different ways of infecting people. Some may be ingested on food such as undercooked meat (eg, tapeworms) and some enter through your skin (eg, hookworms). Infestations may not show up for some time and hardly ever cause symptoms. Although they are generally not serious, if left untreated some can cause severe health problems later. After an extended visit consider having a stool test when you return home to check for these and determine the appropriate treatment.

Meningococcal Meningitis This serious disease can be fatal. Epidemics occurred in Nepal in the 1980s but none have occurred since.

A fever, severe headache, sensitivity to light and neck stiffness, which prevents forward bending of the head, are the first symptoms of this strain of meningitis. There may also be purple patches on the skin. Death can occur within a few hours, so urgent medical treatment is required.

Trekkers to rural areas of Nepal should be particularly careful, as the disease is spread by close contact with people who carry it in their throats and noses and spread it through coughs and sneezes; they may not be aware that they are carriers. Lodges in the hills where travellers spend the night are prime spots for the spread of infection.

Treatment for meningitis is large doses of penicillin given intravenously, or chloramphenicol injections.

AIDS & Prostitution in Nepal

HIV/AIDS has become a major problem in Nepal. Official figures reveal that over 2500 people in Nepal died from AIDS-related illnesses in 1999. There are an estimated 35,000 Nepalis infected with the virus, and more than 10,000 intravenous drug users in Nepal who are at risk of contracting the virus. A public education program has been implemented, and along roadsides throughout the country you'll see billboards with cartoon pictures of condoms.

Although prostitution exists in Nepal, particularly in the border towns and along the main truck routes, it is virtually invisible to Western visitors. It is believed that over 100,000 Nepali women work in Indian brothels, often in conditions resembling slavery, and over 30,000 of these women are estimated to be HIV positive. When obvious AIDS symptoms force these women out of work, some manage to return to Nepal. However, they are shunned by their families and there is virtually no assistance available to them or their children.

Up to half a million Nepali men seek seasonal work in Indian cities, and as with migrant workers elsewhere, it is likely that many patronise brothels while they are away.

Sexually Transmitted Diseases (STDs) HIV/AIDS and hepatitis B, C and D can be transmitted through sexual contact (see the Hepatitis and HIV/AIDS sections earlier in this chapter). Some other sexually transmitted diseases include gonorrhoea, herpes and syphilis; sores, blisters or rashes around the genitals and discharges or pain when urinating are common symptoms. In some STDs, such as wart virus or chlamydia, symptoms may be less marked or not observed at all, especially in women. Chlamydia infection can cause infertility in both men and women before any symptoms have been noticed. Syphilis symptoms eventually disappear completely but the disease continues and can cause severe problems in later years.

While abstinence from sexual contact is the only 100% effective prevention, using condoms is also effective. The treatment of gonorrhoea and syphilis is with antibiotics. The different STDs each require specific antibiotics.

Typhoid Contaminated water and food causes this dangerous gut infection, and medical help must be sought.

In its early stages sufferers may feel they have a bad cold or flu on the way, as early symptoms are a headache, body aches and a fever which rises a little each day until it is around 40°C (104°F) or more. The victim's pulse is often slow relative to the degree of fever present – unlike a normal fever where the pulse increases. There may also be vomiting, abdominal pain, diarrhoea or constipation.

In the second week the high fever and slow pulse continue and a few pink spots may appear on the body; trembling, delirium, weakness, weight loss and dehydration may occur. Complications such as pneumonia, perforated bowel or meningitis may occur.

Insect-Borne Diseases

Malaria This serious and potentially fatal disease is spread by mosquito bites. It is not found in the tourist areas of Nepal – the Kathmandu Valley, Pokhara, and the Himalaya – but is known to exist in the lowland Terai region throughout the year. The risk in Royal Chitwan National Park is extremely low except in the hot months of June, July and August, when the risk is simply low.

If you are travelling in endemic areas it is extremely important to avoid mosquito bites and to take tablets to prevent this disease. Symptoms range from fever, chills and sweating, headache, diarrhoea and abdominal pains to a vague feeling of ill-health. Return to Kathmandu and seek medical help immediately if malaria is suspected. Most health facilities in Nepal are not able to diagnose malaria adequately. Without treatment malaria can rapidly become more serious and can be fatal.

If medical care is not available, malaria tablets can be used for treatment. You need to use a malaria tablet that is different from the one you were taking when you contracted malaria. The standard treatment dose of mefloquine is two 250mg tablets and a further two tablets six hours later. For Fansidar, it's a single dose of three tablets. If you were previously taking mefloquine and cannot obtain Fansidar, then the other alternative is Malarone (atovaquone-proguanil; four tablets once daily for three days). There is a greater risk of side effects with these dosages than in normal use if used with mefloquine, so medical advice must be obtained even if self treatment is undertaken. See also Malaria Medication earlier in the Health section.

Travellers are advised to avoid mosquito bites at all times by observing the following advice:

- wear light-coloured clothing
- wear long trousers and long-sleeved shirts
- use mosquito repellents containing the compound DEET on exposed areas (prolonged overuse of DEET may be harmful, especially to children, but its use is considered preferable to being bitten by disease-transmitting mosquitoes)
- avoid perfumes or aftershave
- use a mosquito net impregnated with mosquito repellent (permethrin) – it may be worth taking your own

Dengue Fever This viral disease is transmitted by mosquitoes and is fast becoming one of the top public health problems in the tropical world. It has not been detected in Nepal so far, although it certainly does exist in northern India. Unlike the malaria mosquito, the *Aedes aegypti* mosquito, which transmits the dengue virus, is most active during the day, and is found mainly in urban areas in and around human dwellings.

Signs and symptoms of dengue fever include a sudden onset of high fever, headache, joint and muscle pains (hence its old name, 'breakbone fever') and nausea and vomiting. A rash of small red spots sometimes appears three to four days after the onset of fever. In the early phase of illness, dengue may be mistaken for other infectious diseases, including malaria and influenza. Minor bleeding such as nose bleeds may occur in the course of the illness, but this does not necessarily mean that you have progressed to the potentially fatal dengue haemorrhagic fever (DHF). This is a severe illness, characterised by heavy bleeding, which is thought to be a result of a second infection due to a different strain (there are four major strains) and usually affects residents of the country rather than travellers. Recovery even from simple dengue fever may be prolonged, with tiredness lasting for several weeks.

You should seek medical attention as soon as possible if you think you may be infected. A blood test can exclude malaria and indicate the possibility of dengue fever. There is no specific treatment for dengue. Aspirin should be avoided, as it increases the risk of haemorrhaging. There is no vaccine against dengue fever. The best prevention is to avoid mosquito bites at all times (see the previous section on Malaria for advice on avoiding mosquito bites).

Japanese B Encephalitis This viral infection of the brain is transmitted by mosquitoes. Most cases occur in rural areas as the virus exists in pigs and wading birds. Symptoms include fever, headache and alteration in consciousness. Hospitalisation is needed for correct diagnosis and treatment. There is a high mortality rate among those who have symptoms; of those who survive, many are intellectually disabled.

Cuts, Bites & Stings

See Immunisations earlier and Less Common Diseases later for information about rabies, which is passed through animal bites.

Cuts & Scratches Wash well and treat any cut with an antiseptic such as povidone iodine. Where possible avoid bandages and Band-Aids, which can keep wounds wet.

Bedbugs & Lice Bedbugs live in various places, but particularly in dirty mattresses and bedding, evidenced by spots of blood on bedclothes or on the wall. Bedbugs leave itchy bites in neat rows. Calamine lotion or a sting relief spray may help.

All lice cause itching and discomfort. They make themselves at home in your hair (head lice), your clothing (body lice) or in your pubic hair (crabs). You catch lice through direct contact with infected people or by sharing combs, clothing and the like. Powder or shampoo treatment will kill the lice and infected clothing should then be washed in very hot, soapy water and left in the sun to dry.

Bites & Stings Bee and wasp stings are usually painful rather than dangerous. However, in people who are allergic to them severe breathing difficulties may occur and can require urgent medical care. Calamine lotion or a sting relief spray will give relief and ice packs will reduce the pain and swelling.

Leeches These may be present in damp conditions; they attach themselves to your skin to suck your blood. During the monsoon, trekkers often get them on their legs or in their boots. Salt or a lighted cigarette end will make them fall off. Do not pull them off, as the bite is then more likely to become infected. Clean and apply pressure if the point of attachment is bleeding. An insect repellent may keep them away.

Snakes To minimise your chances of being bitten always wear boots, socks and long trousers when walking through undergrowth where snakes may be present. Don't put your hands into holes and crevices.

Snake bites do not cause instantaneous death. Immediately wrap the bitten limb tightly, as you would for a sprained ankle, and then attach a splint to immobilise it. Keep the victim still and seek medical help, if possible with the dead snake for identification. Don't attempt to catch the snake if there is a possibility of being bitten again. Tourniquets and sucking out the poison are now comprehensively discredited.

Women's Health

Gynaecological Problems Antibiotic use, synthetic underwear, sweating and contraceptive pills can lead to fungal vaginal infections, especially when travelling in hot climates. Fungal infections are characterised by a rash, itch and discharge, and can be treated with a vinegar or lemon-juice douche, or with yogurt. Nystatin, miconazole or clotrimazole pessaries or vaginal cream are the usual treatment. Maintaining good personal hygiene and wearing loose-fitting clothes and cotton underwear may help prevent these infections.

STDs are a major cause of vaginal problems. Symptoms of STDs include a smelly discharge, painful intercourse and sometimes a burning sensation when urinating. Medical attention should be sought and sexual partners must also be treated. For more details see Sexually Transmitted Diseases earlier in this section. After complete abstinence, the next best method to avoid problems is to practise safer sex using condoms.

Pregnancy It is not advisable to travel to some places while pregnant because some vaccinations normally used to prevent serious diseases are not advisable during pregnancy. In addition, some diseases are much more serious for the mother (and may increase the risk of a stillborn child) in pregnancy, eg, malaria.

It is generally considered inadvisable to travel to altitudes above around 3650m when pregnant, so any treks going over this height should be avoided.

Most miscarriages occur during the first three months of pregnancy. Miscarriage is not uncommon and can occasionally lead to severe bleeding. The last three months should also be spent within reasonable distance of good medical care. A baby born as early as 24 weeks stands a chance of survival, but only in a good modern hospital.

Pregnant women should avoid all unnecessary medication, although vaccinations and malarial prophylactics should still be taken where needed. Additional care should be taken to prevent illness and particular attention should be paid to diet and nutrition. Alcohol and nicotine, for example, should be avoided.

Less Common Diseases

The following diseases pose a small risk to travellers, and so are only mentioned in passing. Seek medical advice if you think you may have any of these diseases.

Cholera This is the worst of the watery diarrhoeas and medical help should be sought. Outbreaks of cholera are generally widely reported, so you can avoid such problem areas. *Fluid replacement* is the most vital treatment – the risk of dehydration is severe as you may lose up to 20L a day. If there is a delay in getting to hospital, then begin taking the antibiotic tetracycline. The adult dose is 250mg four times daily. It is not recommended for children under nine years or for pregnant women. Tetracycline may help shorten the illness, but adequate fluids are required to save lives.

Rabies This fatal viral infection is found in many countries, including Nepal. Many animals can be infected (such as dogs, cats, bats and monkeys) and it is their saliva that is infectious. Any bite, scratch or even lick (on broken skin) from an animal should be cleaned immediately and thoroughly. Scrub with soap and running water, and then apply alcohol or iodine solution. Medical help should be sought promptly to receive a course of injections to prevent the onset of symptoms and death.

Tetanus This disease is caused by a germ that lives in soil and in the faeces of horses and other animals. It enters the body via breaks in the skin. The first symptom may be discomfort in swallowing, or stiffening of the jaw and neck; this is followed by painful convulsions of the jaw and whole body. The disease can be fatal, but it can be prevented by vaccination.

Tuberculosis This a bacterial infection is usually transmitted from person to person by coughing but which may be transmitted through the consumption of unpasteurised milk. Milk that has been boiled is safe to drink, and the souring of milk to make yogurt or cheese also kills the bacteria. Travellers are at extremely low risk as close household contact with the infected person is usually required before the disease is passed on.

WOMEN TRAVELLERS

Generally speaking, Nepal is a safe country for women travellers. However, as is the case in most countries, women should still be cautious, especially when trekking. Never trek alone, and only trek with companies that have been recommended by trustworthy friends.

It's a good idea to bear in mind that many Nepali men have peculiar ideas about the morality of Western women, given Nepali men's exposure to Western films portraying 'immodest' clothing and inter-racial holiday flings. Dress modestly, which means wearing clothes that cover the shoulders and thighs – take your cue from the local people if you need to gauge what's acceptable. It's amazing to see how many travellers (male as well as female) get around in totally inappropriate clothing.

Sexual harassment is low-key but does exist. One of the most common sources are trekking guides who take advantage of their position of trust and responsibility. It's very difficult to ensure against this, but the best advice is to not trek alone. There's one agency in Pokhara called Chhetri Sisters. It is run by women and specialises in providing women staff for treks (see Organised Tours in the Trekking chapter for contact details).

For women visitors to Nepal the best chance of making contact with local women is to go trekking, as it is really only here that Nepali women have a role that brings them into contact with foreign tourists – running the many teahouses and lodges along the trekking routes. As often as not, the man of the house is a trekking guide or porter, or is away working elsewhere, which leaves women running the lodge.

GAY & LESBIAN TRAVELLERS

There's no gay scene to speak of in Nepal (homosexuality is officially illegal). Gay couples holding hands in public will experience no difficulties, as this is socially acceptable, but public displays of intimacy *by anyone* are frowned upon. See the Web site www.kushnet.com for some information on Nepal's fledgling queer communities, and www.lavenderlinks.com for many links to sites serving the region.

DISABLED TRAVELLERS

Travellers with a physical disability may find it tough going in Nepal. Throughout the country wheelchair facilities, ramps and lifts are virtually nonexistent. It is common for hotels to be multilevel, with most guest rooms on the upper floors, and many places – even mid-range establishments – do not have lifts. This being said, many lodges are built on ground level. Bathrooms equipped with grips and railings are not found anywhere, except perhaps in some of the top-end hotels.

There is no reason why a visit and even a trek could not be custom tailored through a reliable agent for those with reasonable mobility. However, the generally poor state of roads and pavements would make getting around in a wheelchair well-nigh impossible.

SENIOR TRAVELLERS

Older travellers will find that their age will probably command them a certain amount of respect, but on a practical level there are no discounts or other concessions available.

TRAVEL WITH CHILDREN

Surprisingly few people travel with children in Nepal, yet with a bit of planning it is remarkably hassle free. Certainly it's hard work, but then staying home with kids is hard work too, so why not get out and enjoy it? As always, children are great ice breakers, and the local hospitality and friendliness shines through even more.

In the main tourist centres (Kathmandu and Pokhara), most hotels will have triple rooms, and quite often rooms with four beds, which are ideal for families with young children. Finding a room with a bathtub can be a problem, however, especially at the bottom end of the market. Garden space is at a premium in Kathmandu hotels, but many places have a roof garden, and some of these can be good play areas for kids. Check thoroughly, however, as some are definitely not safe for young children.

One of the hardest parts about life on the road with kids in Nepal is eating out at restaurants. While the food is excellent and there's always something on the menu which will appeal to kids – even if it's only chips or banana porridge – service is usually quite slow. By the time the food arrives your kids will be bored stiff and ready to leave (especially if they are really young). You can minimise the hassles by eating breakfast at your hotel, having lunch at a place with a garden (there's plenty of these) where the children can let off steam, and in the evening going to the restaurant armed with pencils, colouring books, stories and other distractions to keep them busy for half an hour. Away from the tourist areas finding food children will eat may be more of a problem. Plain rice is always available, and mixing in some yoghurt livens it up. Children (young ones in particular) usually find the spicy food a bit hard to take. High chairs are virtually nonexistent.

Walking the crowded and narrow streets of Kathmandu can be a hassle with young kids unless you can get them up off the ground – a backpack is ideal, but a pusher or stroller would be more trouble than it's worth unless you bring one of the modern ones with oversize wheels.

One of the most rewarding things to do with kids is to take them trekking in the mountains. Once again, very few people seem to do this yet the experience for everyone is well worth the effort. The main consideration is that to have an easy trip you need to hire enough porters to carry not only your gear but also any young children. This is not as expensive as it sounds, with porters costing around US$4 to US$10 per day. See under Independent Trekking in the Trekking chapter for more details.

If your child needs disposable nappies, these are available in Kathmandu and Pokhara, but for a price – better to bring them with you if possible. Even better would be to use cloth ones, but this can be a headache and you may well decide the convenience of disposable ones is worth it. Bear in mind, however, that disposable nappies are far from disposable – they are in fact almost indestructible – and waste disposal in Nepal is already a major problem.

Check out Lonely Planet's *Travel With Children* for handy hints and advice about the pros and cons of travelling with children.

DANGERS & ANNOYANCES

Personal Safety & Theft

There was a time only five or 10 years ago when personal safety in Nepal was not something you really needed to give much thought to. Sadly these days are gone and while petty theft is not on the scale that exists in many countries, it does exist in Nepal and you need to be aware of this. Reports of theft from hotel rooms in tourist areas (including along trekking routes) is fairly commonplace, and theft with violence is not unheard of.

All the usual common-sense rules apply:

- keep your hotel room locked and don't store valuables there
- don't wear expensive jewellery
- don't make ostentatious displays of money or possessions

One of the most common forms of theft is the rifling of backpacks on the roofs of buses. This is a problem as there are often people riding on the roof, and unless you are there as well (which is only possible some of the time) it is impossible to keep an eye on your bags. Try to make your pack as theft-proof as possible – small padlocks and cover bags are a good deterrent. It is also not unheard of for things to go missing out of backpacks at Kathmandu's Tribhuvan airport – at both international and domestic terminals.

There's little chance of ever retrieving your gear if it is stolen, and even getting a police report for an insurance claim can be difficult. Try the local police station, but if you aren't getting anywhere, go straight to Interpol (☎ 01-412602) at the Police Headquarters in Naxal, Kathmandu; the postal address is PO Box 407. The documentation requires a passport photo and photocopies of your passport and visa; the process takes two days.

Safety while Trekking

Surrounded by Western comforts in Kathmandu, it is easy to forget that Nepal is, in terms of many physical resources, an undeveloped country. This means that people are extremely poor, hygiene is often bad, transport (particularly of the road variety) is dangerous, rescue facilities are limited, and medical facilities are often primitive or nonexistent.

Fired up by the gung ho stories of adventurous travellers, it is also easy to forget that mountainous terrain is always potentially dangerous. Nepal is, of course, a continuous series of the most spectacular mountains in the world, and the risks are correspondingly real.

Only a tiny minority of people do actually end up in trouble, but the tragedy is that accidents can often be avoided or the risks minimised if people have a realistic and common-sensical understanding of where they are and what they are doing, and take a few basic precautions. See the Trekking chapter for more details.

The KEEP and HRA centres, both in Thamel, can give up-to-date information on trekking conditions and health risks. A visit to either or both is strongly recommended (see Information in the Kathmandu chapter). Several embassies and consulates have registration forms at the centres; if they don't, you can register at the actual embassy or consulate. The forms record your name, rough itinerary, insurance details and next of kin, and can obviously speed up a search or medical evacuation.

Strikes & Demonstrations

Nepal's political process involves frequent demonstrations and strikes, and these became even more prevalent in 2000. They are generally peaceful, but any large gathering of people can cause problems. Often there are processions in the street and meetings in Tundikhel, the parade ground in the centre of Kathmandu. If you come across a large group of slogan-chanting youths, it's best to avoid them in case you end up on the downstream side of a police *lathi* charge (a team of police wielding bamboo staves) or worse.

A normal procession or demonstration is a *julus*. If things escalate there may be a *chakka jam* (jam the wheels), when all vehicles stay off the street, or a *bandh*, when not only do vehicles not ply the roads, but all shops, schools and offices are closed. If you're unlucky enough to have booked a flight during one of these events, you may end up walking to the airport or travelling in a bicycle rickshaw at an outrageous price. When roads are closed the government runs blue public buses with armed policemen from the airport to major hotels. Call the Tourist Service Centre (☎ 01-247041) in Kathmandu for details.

Traffic & Pollution

Traffic on the streets of Kathmandu is a rumpus of pollution-belching vehicles with two, three and four wheels wending their way around a mass of people and a variety of animals. The combination of ancient vehicles, low-quality fuel and lack of emission controls makes the streets of Kathmandu particularly dirty, noisy and unpleasant. Traffic rules do exist, but are rarely enforced; be especially careful when crossing streets and riding a bicycle. Traffic is supposed to travel on the left side of the road, but many drivers simply choose the most convenient side. Left turns are allowed without stopping, even at controlled intersections with red lights.

Consider bringing a face mask to filter out dust and emission particles if you plan to ride a bicycle or motorcycle in Kathmandu.

Scams

Be aware if offered deals by gem dealers (especially in Thamel, Kathmandu) that involve you buying stones to sell for a 'vast profit' at home. The dealers' stories vary, but are usually along the lines of the dealer not being able to export the stones without paying heavy taxes, so the idea is you take them and meet the dealer when you get home, he will sell them to his local contact and you both share the profit. Falling for this ruse is not as unusual among travellers as you might expect.

LEGAL MATTERS

Drugs & Jail

Hashish is banned, but illegal or not, it's readily available in Nepal. Possession of a small amount involves little risk, although potential smokers should keep the less-than-salubrious condition of Nepali jails firmly in mind. Don't try taking any out of the country either – travellers have been arrested at the airport on departure.

If you get caught smuggling something serious – drugs or gold – chances are you'll end up in jail, without trial, and will remain there until someone pays for you to get out. Bribery may be an option to avoid jail in the first place, but this is an extremely sensitive area in which to dabble and unless you can do it in a way which is deniable, you may just end up in deeper strife.

And just in case anyone is under any misconceptions about conditions in Nepali jails, then it is sobering to note that a recent report into jail conditions found that there was serious need for reform – malnutrition, physical torture, sexual abuse, inadequate space, poor sanitation and deaths in prisons were all found to be an issue, and the daily entitlement of Rs 15 and 700g of rice does not go far. The fact that the jail buildings are a century old doesn't help either.

Higher than the Himalaya

In Kathmandu's flower-power era in the 1960s and early 1970s, the easy availability of marijuana and hashish was undoubtedly a major attraction for many visitors. In its hippie heyday Kathmandu had hash shops and hash calendars – and hash cookies appeared on every hip restaurant menu. Many of the 'freaks' who congregated in Nepal in those days were high in places other than the Himalaya.

The drug had always been easily available, but its users were mainly sadhus, for whom it has religious importance. Then, in the run-up to King Birendra's coronation, hashish was banned. The next night, possibly in protest, the huge Singh Durbar building – a palace from the Rana period – burnt down.

BUSINESS HOURS

Most government offices in Kathmandu are open from 10 am to 5 pm Sunday to Thursday during summer and 9 am to 4 pm during the winter months (roughly mid-November to mid-February – the winter starting date for the change of hours varies with the Nepali calendar). Offices close at 3 pm on Friday. Saturday is the weekly holiday and most shops and all offices and banks will be closed; note that Sunday is a regular working day. See also Public Holidays following.

PUBLIC HOLIDAYS

Many holidays and festivals affect the working hours of government offices and banks, which close for the following public holidays and some or all of the days of the following festivals (note this list is not exhaustive). See the Major Festivals Calendar in the special section 'Festivals of Nepal' for the exact dates of the festivals as the dates vary annually.

Prithvi Narayan Shah's Birthday 10 January
Basant Panchami January/February
Maha Shivaratri February/March
Democracy Day 18 February
Bisket Jatra (Nepali New Year) 13/14 April
Janai Purnima July/August
Teej August/September
Indra Jatra September
Dasain September/October
Tihar October/November
Queen's Birthday 7 November
Constitution Day 15 December
King's Birthday 28 December

Dasain Stoppages

Dasain (15 days in September or October) is the most important of all Nepali celebrations, perhaps most closely approximated by Christmas and New Year in the West. Tens of thousands of Nepalis hit the road to return home to celebrate with their families. This means the villages are full of life if you are trekking, but it also means that all the buses and planes are fully booked and overflowing, that porters may be hard to find (or more expensive than usual) and that cars are hard to hire. Many hotels and restaurants in regional towns close down completely, and doing business in Kathmandu, outside Thamel, becomes almost impossible.

The most important days, when everything comes to a total halt, are the ninth day (when thousands of animals are sacrificed), and the 10th day (when blessings are received from elder relatives and superiors). Banks and government offices are generally closed from the eighth day of the festival to the 12th day. The final day of Dasain is on the full moon in September or October.

ACTIVITIES

Trekking

Nepal is one of the world's top destinations for trekkers. Trekking gives you a chance to get out into the countryside to places accessible only on foot, meet some of the people from the many diverse ethnic groups and view some of the most spectacular scenery on earth.

There are many destinations, and almost as many ways of getting to them, so some planning is required. However, much of this can easily be done once you arrive in Nepal. See the Trekking chapter for more details.

Mountain Biking

Mountain biking is becoming an increasingly popular recreational pursuit in Nepal. The Kathmandu Valley offers some superb routes, and on most of these you are rewarded with breathtaking Himalayan views. See the Mountain Biking chapter for more details.

Rafting & Kayaking

With the Himalaya in the backyard, it should come as no surprise that Nepal has some of the world's best white-water rafting.

There are literally dozens of companies, most based in Kathmandu, that run white-water trips of all standards that cater to all budgets, to the many rivers of Nepal. See Organised Tours in the Rafting & Kayaking chapter for more details.

Hot-Air Ballooning

For a different view of the Himalaya and the Kathmandu Valley, try viewing it from a basket suspended 1000m above the floor of the valley! One company in Kathmandu operates balloon flights every morning during the high season, and while not cheap, they are undeniably spectacular. See Activities in the Kathmandu chapter for details.

COURSES

Yoga, Buddhist Meditation & Massage

Nepal is a popular place for people to take up spiritual pursuits. Activity is centred around the Kathmandu Valley, although Pokhara is becoming increasingly popular, and there are a number of places and options.

Check the notice boards in Thamel for up-to-date information about yoga and Buddhism courses, and shop around before you commit yourself. A number of courses are regularly advertised.

Ananda Yoga Center (☎ 01-353477, ⓔ ananda@yoga.wlink.com.np), PO Box 1774, Kathmandu Valley. On the edge of the valley overlooking Matatirtha Village this is a nonprofit yoga retreat offering courses in Reiki, yoga and teacher training. Five-day live-in courses cost US$60. Check out their Web site at www.nepalonline.net/yoga.

Himalayan Buddhist Meditation Centre (☎ 01-221875, ⓔ hbmc@mos.com.np) PO Box 817, Kathmandu or visit their office in Kamaladi (see the Cental Kathmandu map). This place has talks, meditation courses (three to five days, Rs 1000 per day), twice-weekly guided meditations,

Yoga is among one of many spiritual and physical pursuits on offer in Nepal.

Reiki treatments (Rs 1500 for 1½ hours) and video showings. This centre is affiliated with the Kopan Monastery. See their Web site at www.dharmatours.com/hbmc.

Kathmandu Center of Healing (☎ 01-413094, ⓔ kch@ancientmassage.com) PO Box 8975, Maharajganj, Kathmandu. This place offers one-month professional courses in Thai massage. These cost around US$500 and include lunch and dormitory accommodation. Five- and 10-day courses are also held from time to time. Other activities, such as yoga, Reiki and belly dancing (!) are available depending on who is at the centre at the time. Their Web site is at www.ancientmassage.com.

Kopan Monastery (☎ 01-481268, ⓔ kopan@ecomail.com.np) PO Box 817, Kathmandu. This monastery, at Kopan north of Boudha, is affiliated with the Himalayan Buddhist Meditation Centre (see earlier in this list). It offers very reasonably priced courses for seven days (US$54) or 10 days (US$80). There's also an annual one-month course (US$300) held in November (see Kopan in the Around the Kathmandu Valley chapter for details). See the Web site at www.kopan-monastery.com.

Nepal Vipassana Center (☎ 01-250581, Kathmandu office) PO Box 12896, Kathmandu. Holds 10-day retreats twice a month at its centre north-east of Kathmandu, near Budhanilkantha. These are serious meditation courses that involve rising at 4.30 am every morning, not talking or making eye contact with anyone over the entire 10 days, and not eating after midday. For students who have already completed at least one 10-day course, hour-long meditation sessions are held twice a week in the city meditation centre in the Jyoti Bhawan building on Kantipath.

Patanjali Yoga Center (☎ 01-278437) A recommended place for yoga west of the city centre in Teku. Five-day courses start every Monday, and these involve attending the centre for three hours per day, and include lunch.

Language

Nepali is not a difficult language to learn, and there are a number of courses available. You will often see signs and notices around Kathmandu advertising language courses, some of them conducted by former Peace Corps workers. Embassies should be able to recommend somewhere that they themselves use.

Most schools offer courses (often around two weeks long) or individual tuition. Expect to pay about US$50 for a two-week course and around US$3 for private hourly tuition.

Places to try in Kathmandu include:

Bud Language Institute (☎ 01-249576)
Insight Nepal (☎ 01-418963)
School of International Languages (☎ 01-211713) at Tribhuvan University
Speed Language Institute (☎ 01-220999), Bagh Bazaar

WORK

For a Western visitor, working in Nepal is very difficult, although it is not impossible. The easiest work to find is teaching English, as there are many private schools and a great demand for English-language lessons. However, at less than US$100 a month the pay is very low. Other possibilities include work with airline offices, travel and trekking agencies, consultants or aid groups but, the prospects are remote.

Officially you need a work permit if you intend to find employment in Nepal and you are supposed to have this before you arrive in the country. Changing from a tourist visa once you are in the country is rarely permissible. The work permit has to be applied for by your employer and you are supposed to leave the country while the paperwork is negotiated. The process can take months.

Volunteer Work

It's possible to get work as a volunteer, and this can be a rewarding experience and one which gives you the opportunity to put something back into the community. Volunteer Work Opportunity Programs (VWOP; ☎ 01-488773, ⓔ bdumre@usa.net) coordinates volunteers to work on projects in various parts of the country. Activities include teaching, agriculture and environment.

Another good source of information is the Himalayan Explorers Club (HEC) in Thamel. They publish the *Nepal Volunteer Handbook*, which outlines the opportunities for volunteering in Nepal, and is updated annually. It is available for US$10 from the HEC office in Thamel (where you can also flick through a copy – see Information in the Kathmandu chapter) or online at the HEC Web site at www.hec.org.

ACCOMMODATION

In Kathmandu and Pokhara there is a very wide variety of accommodation from rock-bottom flea pits to five-star international hotels. The intense competition between the many cheaper places keeps prices down and standards up – Kathmandu has many fine places with pleasant gardens and rooms for less than US$10 a night including private bathroom and hot water. However at peak times, rooms in the four- and five-star places can be in short supply.

The main towns of the Terai all have accommodation ranging from hotels of reasonable standard, where rooms with fans and mosquito nets are around Rs 400, to grimy, basic places catering to local demand from around Rs 50. Some of the cheap places will only have tattered mosquito nets, if any at all.

Elsewhere in the country the choice of hotels can be very limited but there are places to stay along most of the major trekking trails. It's quite possible to trek from lodge to lodge rather than camp site to camp site. On some trails places may be Spartan – the accommodation may be dorm-style or simply an open room to unroll your sleeping bag. Smoke can be a real problem in places where the chimney has yet to make an appearance. At the other extreme, some trails such as the popular Pokhara to Jomsom route have excellent lodges and guesthouses at every stopping place.

FOOD & DRINKS

Nepali Food

Generic Nepali food is distinctly dull. Hindu Nepalis are vegetarian and so meat doesn't feature in local cuisine. Most of the time meals consist of a dish called *dal bhaat tarakari* which is made up of lentil soup, rice and curried vegetables. The occasional dal bhaat tarakari, prepared to tourist tastes in Kathmandu restaurants, can be just fine. Strictly local versions, eaten day in and day out while trekking, can get very boring indeed. See Food & Drink in the Glossary at the end of this book for definitions.

Newari Food In contrast to the generally bland Nepali food, Newari food is varied, spicy and interesting. There is a wide range of interesting dishes available in the increasing number of Kathmandu restaurants serving Nepali food, although these usually serve a somewhat modified version suitable to tourists' tastes. There are a few local Newari restaurants hidden away in the narrow streets of Kathmandu between Durbar Square and Thahiti Tole but you'll need to find a local Newari to track these down and accompany you.

Newaris are great meat eaters. Buff is the meat of choice but pork (called 'wild boar') is also popular. Very little is wasted when a beast is slaughtered, and in true Newari eateries you can find dishes made from just about every imaginable body part or fluid – from fried brains to braised tongue and steamed blood! Spices are heavily used with chilli being at the forefront.

Many Newari dishes are only eaten at particular celebrations or family events. If you are invited to a Newari home you may get a chance to sample some. See Food & Drink in the Glossary at the end of this book.

Eating & Drinking Customs

There are a number of 'rules' and customs relating to eating and drinking in Nepal and a number of ways you can make life much easier for yourself. For a start, the Nepali eating schedule is quite different from that in the West. The morning usually begins with little more than a cup of tea. The main meal is not taken until late morning. In areas where Western visitors are not often seen and even more rarely catered for, finding food will be much simpler if you go along with this schedule.

You can also save yourself a lot of time and frustration if you pay attention to what you order as well as when you order it. In small local restaurants the cooking equipment and facilities are often very primitive.

Places with some experience of catering to Western tastes will often offer amazingly varied menus, but just because they offer 20 different dishes doesn't mean they can fix two of them at the same time. If you and your five friends turn up at some small and remote cafe and order six different dishes you can expect to be waiting for dinner when breakfast time rolls around the next day. In that situation it makes a lot of sense to order the same dish six times! Not only will you save time, but you will also save cooking fuel, which is often firewood.

If you eat dal bhaat tarakari, most local restaurants and roadside stalls will be able to find a spoon (with a dubious past) if you insist, but the custom is to eat with your right hand. The number one eating rule in Nepal, as in much of Asia, is always use your right hand. The left hand, used for washing yourself after defecating, is never used to eat food and certainly should not be used to pass food (or anything at all) to someone else.

Caste rules also play a part in Nepali eating habits. A high-caste Brahmin simply cannot eat food prepared by a lower-caste individual, which effectively bans practising Brahmins from restaurants since they cannot know what is going on behind the kitchen door. And of course some foods are strictly taboo in Nepal. High-caste Hindus and all Brahmins are, ostensibly at least, vegetarian, but carnivorious or not, beef is strictly banned from the menu because the cow is a holy animal.

If you are invited to a meal at a Nepali home you may find that the women of the household remain totally in the background and do not eat with the men or with guests. As in India, even at quite Westernised homes, socialising goes on before the meal rather than afterwards. After the last mouthful is consumed the guests head out the door – nobody hangs around for conversation over the coffee!

Foreign Cuisines

Although the real local food is often limited in its scope, Kathmandu's restaurants offer an amazing variety of dishes. In the days of 'Asia overlanding', when many travellers arrived in Kathmandu having made a long and often wearisome trip through Asia from Europe, Kathmandu's restaurants had a near mythical appeal. Ecstatic reports filtered back along the trail of superb restaurants and fine cuisine.

These days, as most travellers jet straight in from abroad, the food doesn't seem quite so amazing, but Kathmandu's many restaurants still do give international cuisine a damn good try and they will attempt almost anything. There's a special appeal to being high in the Himalaya and being able to choose between not just European and Asian dishes but also almost anything else from Mexican tacos to Japanese sukiyaki. Of course Nepali interpretations of foreign dishes often arrive a little off target but Nepal is a great place to try Tibetan dishes and the Indian food can also be very good.

Such a variety of restaurants is particularly amazing when you consider that in 1955 Kathmandu had just one restaurant. Leave Kathmandu (and Pokhara) behind, however, and you're soon back to dal bhaat tarakari.

Many of the 'international' restaurants use large quantities of imported food. Cows, for instance, are theoretically not killed in Hindu Nepal, so beef is imported frozen from Kolkata (Calcutta) or Delhi. By ordering with a little care, and especially avoiding beef steaks, it is possible to eat local ingredients and prevent the vital foreign currency you are contributing to the economy heading straight out of the country to pay for your luxuries.

Amber Nectar

The locally produced beer is quite good, especially after a hard day's walking or bicycling around the valley. Beer can usually be found in the hills as well, carried there by porters especially for thirsty trekkers, but it is unlikely to be cold. There are a number of locally produced brands that theoretically replicate the original recipes: Tuborg (Danish), Star (German), Iceberg (Indian), San Miguel (Filipino). Star and Iceberg are generally the cheapest, and cost around Rs 90 to Rs 130 in Kathmandu restaurants.

Care in Eating & Drinking

Don't drink the water. This is the prime health rule on the subcontinent and it certainly applies to Nepal. Diarrhoea, dysentery or even hepatitis can all result from indulging in contaminated drinking water.

In actual fact the relative safety of the water varies with the season. Drinking tap water is never a good idea, but during the dry season from around November to April you would probably get away with it, in Kathmandu at least. During the monsoon, however, when the heavy rains wash all sorts of stuff into the water supply, don't even consider it. Drinking boiled and filtered water is a better idea at any time of year and absolutely imperative in the wet season.

Most good restaurants do boil and filter their water, and although there's no way of telling if it has been boiled or not, tea will be safe, because boiling water is essential for its preparation.

Plastic bottles of mineral water are ubiquitous. Although these seem to be safe (mostly anyway), the empty bottles are creating a major litter problem. The best alternative is to have your own water bottle and to treat the water with iodine. This is 100% safe and has the added benefit of not requiring a fire.

At higher altitudes the water is generally safer than it is lower down and in more densely populated areas. Nevertheless, trekkers should never drink water from springs or streams unless they are absolutely positive they are at a higher level than any villages or cattle. In Nepal that is a very hard thing to guarantee and it is always wiser to prepare your drinking water carefully. Chang, the popular Tibetan beer, is generally safe (but may be made with untreated water) and is found along many trekking routes.

Many travellers do develop some sort of stomach upset while in Nepal although fortunately it's usually just travellers diarrhoea. See Health earlier in this chapter for information on diarrhoea and on treating water with iodine.

ENTERTAINMENT

Nepal is not the place to come if you're after the highlife. Nightlife is pretty much restricted to Kathmandu and to a lesser extent Pokhara; in other regional towns and cities it's very much early-to-bed territory.

Kathmandu has an increasing number of bars, mainly in the Thamel area, which stay open late, and there's a couple of low-key nightclubs. There's only one cinema showing Western films, and there are four casinos, all of them attached to five-star hotels.

Cultural dance performances are also held in Kathmandu, and as tourist entertainment at some of the resorts in Chitwan.

SHOPPING

Nepal is a shopper's paradise whether you are looking for a cheap souvenir or a real work of art. Although you can find almost anything in the tourist areas of Kathmandu, there are specialities in different parts of the valley. Wherever you shop remember to bargain, although in shops that are completely tourist-oriented prices tend to be fixed.

One place you could start is the Amrita Craft Collection, south of the Kathmandu Guest House in Chhetrapati, greater Thamel. They have quite a broad collection of crafts and clothing. Subtract 20% from their prices and you get a good benchmark for what you should pay on the street if you are an excellent bargainer.

Remember that antiquities cannot be taken out of the country, and baggage is inspected by Nepali customs with greater thoroughness on departure than on arrival. If you've bought something that could possibly be antique, you should get a receipt and a description of the object from the shop where you bought it.

A permit is required from the Department of Archaeology in order to take any object that looks as if it could be more than 100 years old out of the country. See Customs earlier in this chapter for details.

Ethical Shopping

A number of shops specialise in handicrafts produced by low-income women. These are nonprofit development organisations, so the money actually goes to the craftspeople in the form of fair wages (as opposed to charity), and also in training, product development, and rehabilitation programs.

One of the best of these organisations is Mahaguthi (☎ 521493), PO Box 396, Kathmandu, which was established with the help of Oxfam. It has two shops and sells a wide range of crafts produced by thousands of people. Among other things it runs a program to rehabilitate destitute women and children.

Dhankuta Sisters is an outlet for women from the eastern hills, and Dhukuti also works with low-income women. Dhukuti has a shop on the way to Patan, in Kopundol, just beyond the bridge over the Bagmati River, and another outlet at Lakeside in Pokhara.

In Patan, near the well-known Kumbeshwar Temple, the Kumbeshwar Technical School (☎ 522271), PO Box 2181, Kathmandu, was established to help provide the untouchable community of Patan with skills. They now produce excellent carpets, jumpers and woodwork. See Shopping in the Kathmandu chapter, and under Patan in the Around the Kathmandu Valley chapter.

Thangkas

Thangkas are the traditional Tibetan Buddhist paintings of religious and ceremonial subjects. The subject may be a mandala, the wheel of life, aspects of Buddha or the various Bodhisattvas, fierce protector deities or historical figures. Thangkas are usually colourful and packed with detail in every corner of the painting.

Although there are genuine antique thangkas to be found, it's highly unlikely that anything offered to the average visitor will date from much beyond last week. Judicious use of a smoky fire can add the odd century in no time at all. Thangkas do vary considerably in quality but buy one because you like it, not as a valuable investment.

Thangkas are available in many locations including the Tibetan shops around Boudha. There are good thangka shops in Thamel in Kathmandu and in the Durbar Square shops in Bhaktapur. There's also an outlet near the Pujari Math in Bhaktapur. Thangkas cost anything from Rs 200 to Rs 80,000 and beyond, and like many other crafts the more you see the more you will appreciate the difference between those of average and those of superior quality. Of course size also plays a part in the final price. Traditionally thangkas are framed in silk brocade.

Block Prints

Locally produced rice paper is used for the block prints of Nepali, Tibetan and Chinese deities. They are sold as pictures or are used for calendars, cards and lanterns. A print typically costs from Rs 50 to Rs 300. There's a good selection in the shops of Thamel.

Tibetan Carpets

Carpet-weaving is a major trade in Nepal, brought from Tibet by the refugees who now carry on the craft with great success in their new homes. There are carpet-weavers around the Kathmandu Valley and also in Pokhara. Some of their output is now exported to Tibet, where the Chinese have unfortunately managed to totally stamp out this archaic craft. A genuine Tibetan carpet purchased in Tibet is probably indeed made by Tibetans, but in Nepal. The Tamang people also make carpets.

Jawlakhel, on the southern outskirts of Patan, is the carpet-weaving centre in the valley, there are numerous carpet shops as you enter the area. You can see carpets being woven here and also in other places around the valley, including the Boudha Stupa. There are larger and smaller sizes available, but the traditional size for a Tibetan carpet is 1.8m by 90cm. They're sturdily woven with colourful designs featuring Tibetan Buddhist symbols and dragons. It is more difficult to find the brilliant reds and blues produced by chemical dyes; more often carpets will be in the pale pastel shades of vegetable dyes. Small square carpets are often used to make seat cushions.

Carpet quality depends on knots per inch, and the price is worked out per square metre. A 60-knot carpet costs around Rs 1700 per sq metre, while a 100-knot carpet is Rs 4800 per sq metre.

Clothing & Embroidery

Tibetan and Nepali clothes have always been a popular buy but recently Western fashions made strictly for the tourist market have also become an important industry. You can buy handmade shirts at outlets in Thamel.

There is still a demand for traditional styles such as the Tibetan wool jackets that are popularly known as *yakets*. Nepali coats, crossing over at the front, closed with four ties and traditionally made in purple velvet material, are a popular buy.

Embroidery has always been popular in Nepal and there are lots of little tailor shops around Kathmandu where the sewing machines rattle on until late at night adding colourful dragons and Tibetan symbols to customers' jackets and jeans. Mountaineers like to return from Nepal with jackets carrying the message that this was the Country X, Year Y expedition to Peak Z. You can take your own clothes to be embroidered or buy items already embroidered. Badges are another good buy – you can add a badge to your backpack saying that you walked to the Everest Base Camp or completed the Annapurna Circuit.

A Nepali *topi* or cap is part of Nepali formal wear for a man and they are traditionally made in Bhaktapur. There's a cap shop right beside the Bhairabnath Temple in Bhaktapur, as well as a group of cap specialists between Indra Chowk and Asan Tole in the old part of Kathmandu. Caps typically cost from Rs 50 to Rs 300.

Pashmina

One of the latest hot souvenir items is shawls and scarves made from fine *pashmina* (goats wool). There are literally dozens of shops in Thamel selling pashmina items. The cheapest shawls are a cotton-pashmina blend, and these cost around Rs 1500 for a 1m by 2m shawl. Silk-pashmina blends cost around Rs 2500, while a pure pashmina shawl is around Rs 3500.

Pottery

Terracotta pottery is made in a number of sites but particularly in Thimi and Bhaktapur in the Kathmandu Valley. The Potters' Square, just south of Durbar Square in Bhaktapur, is a wonderful sight. Thousands of pots are neatly lined up across the square while in the shelters around the sides of the square, potters busily turn out more and more.

In Thimi they specialise in making attractive little flowerpots, often in the shape of dragons, elephants or mythical beasts. You can buy them in Thimi or from stalls near Indra Chowk in Kathmandu or Taumadhi Tole in Bhaktapur.

Jewellery

Kathmandu's many small jewellery manufacturers turn out a wide variety of designs with an equally wide range of standards. You can buy jewellery ready-made, ask them to create a design for you or bring in something you would like copied. There are several good shops around greater Thamel, particularly down towards Chhetrapati.

These outlets mainly cater to Western tastes but there are also many shops for the local market as Nepali women, like Indian women, traditionally wear their wealth in jewellery. Cheap ornaments can also be fun; you can buy an armful of glass bangles for a few rupees or colourful beads by the handful.

Masks & Puppets

Papier-mâché masks and colourful puppets are sold at shops in Kathmandu, Patan and Bhaktapur. Thimi is the centre for manufacturing masks, which are used in the traditional masked dances in September – it's interesting to see masks being made there. Ganesh, Bhairab and the Kumari are the most popular subjects for the mask and they make good wall decorations. Prices typically range from around Rs 10 to Rs 500.

Puppets make good buys as gifts for children and are made in Bhaktapur as well as other centres. They're often of multi-armed deities clutching little wooden weapons in each hand. The puppet heads may be made of easily broken clay or more durable papier mâché. Smaller puppets cost from around Rs 100 to Rs 400 but you can also pay from Rs 500 to Rs 1000 for a larger figure. As usual, quality does vary and the more puppets you inspect the more you will begin to appreciate the differences.

Metalwork

Patan is the valley centre for bronze casting and the best variety of metalwork is found in the shops around Patan's Durbar Square. (See Shopping in the Patan section in the Around the Kathmandu Valley chapter for more details.) Often, beautifully made figures featuring the full range of Tantric Buddhist deities can be bought from Rs 2000 to Rs 5000 for good-quality smaller figures. Of course simpler work can be found much more cheaply. The metal game boards and pieces for *bagh chal*, the traditional Nepali game, make a good buy.

Other Crafts

A *khukuri*, the traditional knife of the Gurkhas, can cost from Rs 300 to Rs 2000. Khukuri House, near the Rum Doodle Bar & Restaurant in Paknajol, greater Thamel, is a good place to start looking.

Bhaktapur is the centre for woodcarving, and you can find good objects in and around Tachupal Tole.

Cassettes and CDs of Nepali, Indian and general Himalayan music are a fine souvenir of a visit to Nepal. There are lots of music shops in Kathmandu selling local music as well as pirated Western tapes and CDs.

For all sorts of small souvenirs the huge market area in Basantapur Square in Kathmandu is a good place to browse. Wandering the crowded and bustling market street from Indra Chowk to Asan Tole is always likely to turn up some interesting bargain.

Tibetan crafts include a variety of religious items such as the *dorje* (thunderbolt symbol) and the popular prayer wheels. Tibetans are keen traders, and prices at Boudha and Swayambhunath are often very high.

Tea

Tea is grown in the east of Nepal, close to the border with India near Darjeeling where the finest Indian tea is grown. Ilam and Mai Valley are the best Nepali brands, but they are not cheap. Expect to pay around Rs 600 per kilogram for good Ilam tea, which is not much cheaper than Darjeeling tea.

Sending Purchases Home

By far the best way of getting something back home is to take it with you. Shipping or mailing objects can be fraught with dangers and hidden expenses. For a start, there's no guarantee that it will be sent at all. If you leave your purchase for a shop to mail to you and it never turns up, what can you do? They will say they mailed it and the post office has lost it somewhere along the line, and you will have no idea whether they have or not (nor any way of proving your suspicions).

If an object is shipped to you, you may find that customs charges for clearance and collection at your end add up to more than the initial cost of sending it. Often it would have been worth paying extra to bring it with you in the first place.

Unless you are very sure about the reliability of the shop, do not ask the shop where you made the purchase to send it for you. There are a number of packing companies in Kathmandu, but some of them are no more reliable than a shop might be. Diki Continental Exports (☎ 417681, ⓔ dikicont@mos.com.np), opposite the Hotel Mandap in Thamel, and Sharmasons Movers (☎ 249565, ⓔ pacmov@mos.com.np) are two that have been recommended. The international courier company DHL (☎ 222358) has offices in Kamaladi and in Thamel.

Air freight costs are punitive – around US$40 per kilogram to Europe or Australia, US$50 to the USA. Sea freight is much cheaper than air, but it is also much slower and less reliable – packages are sent overland to Kolkata or Mumbai, and then wait until a full container has been consolidated.

FESTIVALS OF NEPAL

Nepal's colourful holidays and festivals occur virtually year-round and a visit to Nepal is almost certain to coincide with at least one, particularly in the Kathmandu Valley. Certain times of year, particularly August and September towards the end of the monsoon, are packed with festivals. They go a long way towards compensating for the less-than-ideal weather at this time of year.

For interesting accounts of many of the festivals and the legends behind them, see Books earlier in this chapter. See also Public Holidays for more information on business closures and interruptions during these times.

Major Festivals Calendar

As the actual holidays aren't declared more than a year in advance, many of the following dates are estimates only, but should be correct to within a day or so. Check in Nepal for exact dates.

festival	place	2002	2003	2004
Magh Sankranti	Narayanghat, the Terai	mid-Jan	mid-Jan	mid-Jan
Basant Panchami	Swayambhunath, Kathmandu	18 Jan	6 Feb	26 Jan
Losar	Boudha	12 Feb	1 Feb	20 Feb
Maha Shivaratri	Pashupatinath Temple	14 Mar	1 Mar	18 Feb
Holi	countrywide	27 Feb	18 Mar	6 Mar
Chaitra Dasain	countrywide	20 Apr	10 Apr	29 Mar
Bisket Jatra	Bhaktapur	14 Apr	14 Apr	14 Apr
Buddha Jayanti	Swayambhunath, Kathmandu	26 May	16 May	4 May
Naga Panchami	countrywide	13 Aug	3 Aug	22 Jul
Janai Purnima	countrywide	22 Aug	12 Aug	31 July
Gai Jatra	Kathmandu, Bhaktapur	23 Aug	13 Aug	1 Aug
Krishna Jayanti	Patan	30 Aug	19 Aug	6 Sep
Teej	Pashupatinath	9 Sep	29 Aug	16 Sep
Indra Jatra	Kathmandu	20 Sep	9 Sep	27 Sep
Dasain				
Fulpati	countrywide	12 Oct	2 Oct	20 Sep
Vijaya Dashami	countrywide	15 Oct	5 Oct	23 Sep
Kartika Purnima	countrywide	21 Oct	10 Oct	28 Sep
Tihar				
Deepawali	countrywide	4 Nov	25 Oct	12 Nov
Bhai Tika	countrywide	6 Nov	27 Oct	14 Nov
Haribodhini Ekadashi	Budhanilkantha Temple, Kathmandu	15 Nov	5 Nov	25 Oct
Bala Chaturdashi	Pashupatinath	4 Dec	23 Nov	12 Dec
Sita Bibaha Panchami	Janakpur	9 Dec	28 Nov	17 Nov

Inset: The three-day festival of Mani Rimdu features masked dancers. (Photo: Stan Armington)

Lunar Calendar

Nepali holidays and festivals are principally dated by the lunar calendar, falling on days relating to new or full moons. The lunar calendar is divided into bright and dark fortnights. The bright fortnight is the two weeks of the waxing moon, as it grows to become *purnima* (the full moon). The dark fortnight is the two weeks of the waning moon, as the full moon shrinks to become *aunsi* (the new moon).

The Nepali New Year starts on 13 or 14 April with the month of Baisakh, and is 57 years ahead of the Gregorian calendar used in the West. Thus the year 2002 in the West is 2059 in Nepal. The Newars, on the other hand, start their New Year from the day after Deepawali (the third day of Tihar), which falls on the night of the new moon in late October or early November. Their calendar is 880 years behind the Gregorian calendar, so 2002 in the West is 1122 to the Newars of the Kathmandu Valley.

What sometimes seems like a cavalier attitude towards numbering days actually has a logical explanation. The sun rises every 24 hours, but the period between successive moonrises can vary from 22 to 27 hours. Thus several times each year there can be a 'moon day' (the period from one moonrise to the next) which has no sunrise within it, and several others that have two sunrises. Thus the lunar calendar will sometimes jump a day, and on other occasions it will hiccup and repeat a day. Predicting a date far in advance is additionally complicated by the periodic adjustments that have to be made to bring the shorter lunar year back into line with the solar year, which the Gregorian calendar follows. See the Months Conversion Chart following for the corresponding Gregorian months in the Nepali year.

The Major Festivals Calendar covers festival dates through to the end of 2004, hopefully with reasonable accuracy. Check the dates when you're in Kathmandu.

Months Conversion Table

Nepali lunar months	Gregorian months
Magh	January–February
Falgun	February–March
Chaitra	March–April
Baisakh	April–May
Jeth	May–June
Asaar	June–July
Saaun	July–August
Bhadra	August–September
Ashwin	September–October
Kartik	October–November
Mangsir	November–December
Pus	December–January

Left: A full moon rises over the Royal Chitwan National Park, Terai region.
(Photo: Paul Dymond)

January–February

Magh Sankranti The end of the coldest winter months is marked by this festival and ritual bathing, despite the cold, during the Nepali month of Magh. The festival is dated by the movement north of the winter sun and is one of the few festivals not timed by the lunar calendar. Soon after, on the new-moon day, the Tribeni Mela (a *mela* is a fair) is held at various places including Devghat, on the banks of the Narayani River near the town of Narayanghat in the Terai.

Basant Panchami The start of spring is celebrated by honouring Saraswati; since she is the goddess of learning this festival has special importance for students. The shrine to Saraswati just below the platform at the top of Swayambhunath is the most popular locale for the festivities. This is also a particularly auspicious time for weddings.

Losar The New Year for the Tibetan and Bhotiya people commences with the new moon in February and is welcomed with particular fervour at the great Boudha (Bodhnath) stupa. Colourfully dressed lamas parade around the stupa carrying banners and portraits of the Dalai Lama. Ceremonies are also performed at Swayambhunath and in the Tibetan community at Jawlakhel, which is near Patan. Crowds of Tibetans dressed, in their most traditional costumes and furiously twirling their prayer wheels, watch the proceedings. The Sherpa people of the Solu Khumbu region also celebrate at this time.

February–March

Maha Shivaratri Shiva's birthday falls on the new-moon day of the month of Falgun. Festivities take place at all Shiva temples but most particularly at the great Pashupatinath Temple, and devotees flock there not only from all over Nepal but also from all over India.

Many sadhus make the long trek to Nepal for this festival and the king of Nepal will also appear late in the day because Shiva, as Lord Pashupati, is asked to protect Nepal at the conclusion of any official message. The crowds bathing in the Bagmati's holy waters at this time are a colourful and wonderful sight. The sadhus, meanwhile, will be up to all their usual fun and games, whether this is rolling in the ashes, performing impossible feats of yoga or even sticking thorns through their tongues.

Overall, however, Maha Shivaratri is a serene and peaceful festival, which reflects the deep devotion that Hindus hold for their religion.

Right: Sadhu or wandering holy man. (Photo: Greg Elms)

Holi This exciting festival (also known as Fagu) is closely related to the water festivals of Thailand and Myanmar and takes place on the full-moon day in the month of Falgun. By this time, late in the dry season, it is beginning to get rather hot and the water, which is sprayed around so liberally during the festival, is a reminder of the cooling monsoon days to come. Holi is also known as the Festival of Colours and as well as spraying water on everything and everyone, coloured powder (particularly red) and coloured water are also dispensed. Foreigners get special attention, so if you venture out on Holi leave your camera behind (or keep it well protected) and wear old clothes that can get colour-stained.

At one time Holi used to take place on the eight days leading up to the full moon; these days activities are usually restricted to one day.

The festival is said to be inspired by the exploits of Krishna, particularly an incident when he caught his favourite milkmaids sporting in the Jamuna River. A pole supporting a three-tiered umbrella is set up in front of the Basantapur Tower in Durbar Square in the centre of Kathmandu and on the final day the umbrella is taken down and burnt.

Other activities also take place during Holi. Guru Mapa, the demon of the Yitum Bahal in Kathmandu (see Kigal Tole to Yitum Bahal under Walking Tour 1 in the Kathmandu chapter), has his annual feed on Holi night. The inhabitants of Yitum Bahal sacrifice a buffalo on the banks of the Vishnumati River, cook it in the afternoon in their great courtyard and in the middle of the night carry it in huge cauldrons to the Tundikhel where the demon is said to live to this day.

More peacefully, singing and dancing continues until late at night during another cheerful festival in Tarke Gyang on the Helambu Trek.

March–April

Chaitra Dasain Also known as Small Dasain (in contrast with the Big Dasain in September or October) this festival takes place exactly six months prior to the more important one. Like the other Dasain, it's dedicated to Durga and once again it's a bad day for goats and buffaloes who do their unwilling bit for the goddess early in the morning in Kot Square (north of Durbar Square in central Kathmandu).

Seto Machhendranath The Chaitra Dasain sacrifices also signal the start of the Seto (White) Machhendranath festival, a month prior to the much larger and more important Rato (Red) Machhendranath festival in Patan (see April–May section later). The festival starts with removing the image of Seto Machhendranath from the temple at Kel Tole (see the Walking Tour 1 map in the Kathmandu chapter) and placing it on a *rath* or towering and creaky wooden temple chariot. For the next four evenings, the chariot proceeds from one historic location to another eventually arriving at Lagankhel in the south of Kathmandu. There the image is taken down from the chariot and carried back to its starting point in a palanquin while the chariot is disassembled and put away until next year.

Bisket Jatra Nepali New Year starts in mid-April, at the beginning of the month of Baisakh; the Bisket festival in Bhaktapur is the most spectacular welcome for the New Year, and one of the most exciting annual events in the valley. Magh Sankranti is the only other important religious festival set by the solar rather than the lunar calendar.

Bisket is Bhaktapur's great chariot festival, but while in Kathmandu and Patan it is Machhendranath who gets taken for a ride, here it is Bhairab, accompanied by Betal and, in a second chariot, the goddess Bhadrakali. The ponderous chariots of the gods always appear shaky and unsafe, and moving them requires an enormous amount of energy.

From Taumadhi Tole, outside Bhairab's temple in Bhaktapur, the huge temple chariot proceeds around the town, pausing for a huge tug of war between the eastern and western sides of town. The winning side is charged with looking after the images of the gods during their week-long riverside sojourn. After the battle the chariots slither down the steep road leading to the river, where a huge 25m-high *lingam* (phallic symbol) is erected. In the evening of the following day (New Year's day), the pole is pulled down, again in an often violent tug of war. As the pole crashes to the ground, the New Year officially commences.

As is usual in Nepal, legend is piled upon legend. The following tale of a beautiful princess and a valiant prince lies behind the Bisket festival.

The king of Bhaktapur had an insatiable daughter who not only required a new lover each night but left him dead each morning! Finally a brave prince showed up and despite an exhausting session with the princess forced himself to stay awake afterwards. Late that night two thread-like wisps emerged from the beautiful princess' nostrils, and grew into venomous snakes in the night air. Before they could strike and consign the prince to the scrap heap of discarded lovers he drew his sword and killed them both. Of course, as you would hope, the prince and princess married and lived happily ever after and from the top of the towering Bisket lingam stream two banners, symbolic of those two deadly snakes.

Other events take place around Bhaktapur for a week preceding New Year and then for days after. Members of the potters' caste will put up and haul down their own lingam, and processions also carry images of Ganesh, Lakshmi and Mahakali around town. The New Year is also an important time in the valley for ritual bathing, and crowds of hill people visit the Buddhist stupas of Swayambhunath and Boudha.

It takes a lot of push and shove to move the gods around!

Balkumari Jatra Thimi, the smaller town near Bhaktapur, also welcomes the new year with an exciting festival. This event was instituted by King Jagat Jyoti Malla in the early 1600s. It is Balkumari, another of Bhairab's consorts, who is honoured in this festival. All through the first day of the new year devotees crowd around her temple in Thimi and as dusk falls hundreds of *chirags* (ceremonial oil lamps) are lit. Some devotees lie motionless around the temple all night with burning oil lamps balanced on their legs, arms, chests and foreheads.

The next morning men come from the various *toles* or quarters of Thimi and from surrounding villages, each team carrying a *khat* (palanquin) with images of different gods. As the 32 khats whirl around the temple red powder is hurled at them and the ceremony reaches fever pitch as the khat bearing Ganesh arrives from the village of Nagadish. The crowds parade up and down the main street until late in the morning when Ganesh, borne by hundreds of men, makes a break for home, pursued by the other khats. If they can catch Ganesh the activities are prolonged but eventually Ganesh departs and the festival moves on to the Taleju Temple.

Sacrifices are now made to Balkumari and in the small village of Bode another khat festival, with just seven khats rather than 32, takes place. Here a volunteer spends the whole day with an iron spike piercing his tongue. Successful completion of this painful rite brings merit to the whole village as well as the devotee.

April–May

Rato Machhendranath Although Seto and Rato Machhendranath may be the same deity, the Rato or Red Machhendranath festival of Patan is a much more important occasion than the Kathmandu event. Machhendranath is considered to have great powers over rain and, since the monsoon is approaching at this time, this festival is a plea for good rain.

As in Kathmandu, the Rato Machhendranath festival consists of a day-by-day temple chariot procession through the streets of the town, but here it takes a full month to move the chariot from the Pulchowki area – where the image is installed in the chariot – to Jawlakhel, where the chariot is dismantled.

Along the way, the main chariot is accompanied for most of its journey by a second smaller chariot, which contans the image of Rato (Red) Machhendranath's Bodhisattva companion from the Minanath Temple, near the Rato Machhendranath Temple (which is south of Patan's Durbar Square).

The highlight of the festival is the Bhoto Jatra, or showing of the sacred vest. Machhendranath was entrusted with the jewelled vest as there was some dispute as to who owned it. The vest is displayed three times in order to give the owner the chance to claim it – although this does not actually happen. The king of Nepal attends this ceremony, which is also a national holiday.

From Jawlakhel, Rato Machhendranath does not return to his Patan temple, however. He has a second home in the village of Bungamati and he spends six months of each year at this temple, to where he is now conveyed on a khat. Every 12 years, however, the Rato Machhendranath festival becomes an even more important and time-consuming event when the chariot continues all the way out to Bungamati. The next enactment of the complete Patan to Bungamati procession will be in 2003.

The temple chariots used in these processions are immense wooden affairs that have wheels that are metres in diameter and a towering but often rather ramshackle edifice constructed on the top. It takes hundreds of devotees to tow the main chariot and the Nepali army is often called in to help in the Patan Rato Machhendranath festival. This happens despite the intense local enthusiasm to take part in pulling the chariot. The long procession is often halted to await an auspicious occasion for the next leg, or just to make important roadside repairs to the chariot.

Similar temple chariot processions take place in India including the largest of them all, the great Jagannath procession at Puri in the state of Orissa.

Mata Tirtha Puja The last day of the dark fortnight of Baisakh is Mata Tirtha Puja. It's the Nepali equivalent of Mother's Day and every Nepali should go to 'look upon their mother's face'. Those whose mothers have died in the past year are supposed to bathe at the Mata Tirtha pond, 10km south-west of Kathmandu near the Thankot road.

May–June

Buddha Jayanti (Buddha's Birthday) Siddhartha Gautama (Buddha) was born at Lumbini, so it is fitting that his birthday should be celebrated in Nepal. Swayambhunath is the centre for the celebrations, although events also take place at Boudha and in Patan.

A constant procession of pilgrims makes its way around the stupa at Swayambhunath. The stupa's collection of rare *thangkas* (Tibetan paintings on cotton) and *mandalas* (geometrical representations of the world) is shown on the southern wall of the stupa courtyard on this single day each year. The stupa's lamas dress in colourful silk robes and dance around the stupa with an accompaniment provided by musicians.

Kumar Sasthi The birthday of Shiva's son Kumar or Kartikkaya, the god of war and brother of Ganesh, is also known as Sithinakha. The festival also marks the start of the rice planting season and is an annual occasion for cleaning wells. Once the god of war's birthday was commemorated by stone-throwing contests. Since these contests often turned into strictly local – but often decidedly real – 'wars' they are now confined to young boys.

July–August

Naga Panchami On the fifth day after the new moon in the month of Saaun, *nagas* (serpent deities) are honoured all over the country. Numerous legends are told about snakes, they are considered to have all sorts of magical powers including special powers over the monsoon rains. Pictures of the nagas are hung over doorways of houses, this not only appeases the snakes but also keeps harm from the household. Various foods are put out for snakes and there are interesting legends behind the offerings of milk and boiled rice, such as the following.

A farmer inadvertently killed three baby snakes with his plough and the enraged mother snake chased the farmer back to his house and killed the farmer, his wife and his two sons. The daughter was about to get the same treatment when she offered the serpent a bowl of milk. The snake was so taken by this act of kindness that it chose to spare the daughter and offered her any wish. 'Bring my parents and brothers back to life', replied the daughter and the snake duly did so. Ever since then snakes are offered a bowl of milk on Naga Panchami.

The bowl of rice is offered because of an incident at the Siddha Pokhari pond just outside Bhaktapur which, as the following legend recounts, was once inhabited by an evil naga.

A holy man determined to kill the naga himself by taking the form of a snake, and told his companion to be ready with a bowl of magic rice. If, after he entered the pond, the water turned white then the naga had won and it was all over. If, on the other hand, the water turned red then he had defeated the naga and although he would emerge from the pond in the form of a snake, the magical rice could restore his original form. Sure enough the water turned red but when the holy man in the form of a hideous serpent emerged from the water his horrified companion simply turned tail and ran, taking the rice with him. The holy man tried to catch him but failed and eventually decided to return to the pond and remain there.

To this day the inhabitants of Bhaktapur keep well clear of the Siddha Pokhari pond and on the day of Naga Panchami a bowl of rice is put out – just in case the holy man/snake turns up.

Janai Purnima On the day prior to (and on the day of) the full moon in the month of Saaun, all high-caste men (Chhetri and Brahman) must change the *janai* (sacred thread), which they wear looped over their left shoulder and tied under their right arm. The three cords of the sacred thread symbolise body, speech and mind. Young men first put on the thread in an important ritual that officially welcomes them into their religion. From that date they wear the sacred thread for the rest of their lives, changing it on this one occasion each year as and any time it has been damaged or defiled, such as coming into contact with a woman while she is menstruating.

Although only men wear the thread, anybody, including curious foreigners, can wear a *raksha bandhan* (yellow thread) around their wrist, worn on the right wrist for men, left for women. Wearing this thread on your wrist is said to bring good fortune and on this day priests tie the threads on all who come. You are supposed to wear it for at least a week, but preferably for three months until the Festival of Lights (during Tihar) in October–November.

Janai Purnima also brings crowds of pilgrims to the sacred Gosainkund Lake, across the mountains to the north of Kathmandu. There they garland a statue of Shiva and throw coins at the sacred lingam, which rises up from the lake. A direct channel is said to lead from the lake to the pond in the Kumbeshwar Temple in Patan and a silver lingam is installed in the pond for the occasion. The rituals at the temple attract *jhankris*, faith healers who perform in a trance while beating drums.

Ghanta Karna On the 14th day of the dark fortnight of Saaun. Ghanta Karna, which means 'bell ears', was a horrible demon who was so named because he wore bell earrings to drown out the name of Vishnu, his sworn enemy. The festival celebrates his destruction when a god, disguised as a frog, lured him into a deep well where the people stoned and clubbed him to death. Ghanta Karna is burnt in effigy on this night and evil is cleansed from the land for another year.

August–September

Gai Jatra This festival (Cow Festival) takes place immediately after Janai Purnima on the day after the Saaun full moon, and is dedicated to those who died during the preceding year. Newars believe that after death, cows will guide them to Yama, the god of the underworld, and finding your way on this important journey will be much easier if by chance you should be holding onto a cow's tail at the moment of death! Therefore on this day cows are lead through the streets of the valley's towns or, if a cow is not available, small boys dress up as cows.

The festival also celebrates an event during the reign of King Pratap Malla (1641–74). The king's youngest son died and the queen was grief-stricken. Nothing could cheer her up and eventually the king offered rewards to anybody who could bring a smile to her face. Crowds of people appeared before the royal palace and danced and clowned, dressed in outlandish costumes. The queen could not help laughing at this mass outbreak of merry madness and the king proclaimed that henceforward Gai Jatra would be a day for costumes and games. Many other peculiar outfits appear on the streets, apart from boys dressed up as cows. The festival is celebrated with maximum energy on the streets of Bhaktapur.

Krishna Jayanti (Krishna's Birthday) The seventh day after the full moon in the month of Bhadra is celebrated as Krishna's birthday, sometimes also known as Krishnasthami. Krishna is an incarnation of

Vishnu, and his daring exploits, good nature and general love of a good time endear him to many people. The Krishna Mandir in Patan is the centre for the celebrations and an all-night vigil is kept at the temple on the night before his birthday. Oil lamps light the temple and singing continues through the night.

Teej The Festival of Women lasts three days, from the second to the fifth day after the Bhadra new moon, and is based in Pashupatinath. Women celebrate Teej in honour of their husbands and in the hope of a long and happy married life.

The festival starts with a sumptuous meal and the women gather together and spend the rest of the day feasting and talking, right through until midnight when they must commence 24 hours of fasting.

During the day of the fast women from all over the valley converge on Pashupatinath, traditionally dressed in red and gold saris, usually the ones in which they were married. At Pashupatinath the women take ritual dips in the river and call on the gods to protect their husbands.

The following morning the women must offer their husbands small items of food which have previously been offered to the gods. The day-long fast can then be broken although some years the festival continues for an extra day (in which case this is a day of partial fasting). Another ritual bathing ceremony takes place on this day, preferably at a river confluence, such as where the Bagmati and Vishnumati Rivers meet, just south of Kathmandu. Completion of these ceremonies washes away all female sin, including the sin of a woman touching her husband during her period!

Gunla The 15 days before and after the full moon in August or early September is celebrated as a full month of Buddhist ceremonies, penance and fasting. Activities are centred on Swayambhunath, west of Kathmandu. **Pancha Dan**, the Festival of Five Offerings, is held in Patan during Gunla; there are various other festivals and ceremonies during the month.

Gokarna Aunsi The Nepali equivalent of Father's Day is celebrated by visiting living fathers at their homes and honouring deceased fathers at the Shiva Temple in Gokarna, Kathmandu Valley.

Indra Jatra This important festival runs from the end of the month of Bhadra into the beginning of Ashwin. Indra Jatra is a colourful and exciting festival, which manages to combine homage to Indra with an important annual appearance by Kumari (the living goddess), respects to Bhairab and commemoration of the conquest of the valley by Prithvi Narayan Shah. The festival also marks the end of the monsoon and the start of the fine months that follow.

Indra is the ancient Aryan god of rain and he once paid a visit to the Kathmandu Valley to pick a certain flower which his mother Dagini needed for the festival of Teej. Unfortunately for Indra he was captured in the act of stealing the flowers and imprisoned until his mother came down to rescue him. When she revealed whom they had imprisoned, his captors gladly released him (but the festival continues to celebrate this remarkable achievement – villagers don't capture a real god every day of the week!). In return for his release Dagini promised to spread morning moisture and dew over the crops for the coming months and to take back with her to heaven all those who had died in the past year.

The festival therefore honours the recently deceased and pays homage to Indra and Dagini for the coming harvests. It starts with the erection of a huge pole outside the Hanuman Dhoka in Kathmandu. The carefully selected pole has first been brought to the Tundikhel and then carried to the square. The pole is set up while images and representations of Indra, usually as a captive, are displayed and sacrifices of goats and roosters are made. At the same time the screened doors obscuring the horrific face of White Bhairab are opened and for the next three days his gruesome visage will stare out at the proceedings.

The day before all this activity, three golden temple chariots are assembled in Basantapur Square, outside the home of the Kumari. In the afternoon, with the Durbar Square packed with colourful and cheerful crowds, two boys emerge from the Kumari's house. They play the roles of Ganesh and Bhairab and will each ride in a chariot as an attendant to the goddess. Finally, the Kumari herself appears either walking on a rolled-out carpet or carried by attendants so that her feet do not touch the ground.

The chariots move off and the Kumari is greeted from the balcony of the old palace by the king. The procession then continues out of Durbar Square towards Hanuman Dhoka where it stops out in front of the huge Seto (White) Bhairab mask. The Kumari greets the image of Bhairab and then, with loud musical accompaniment, beer starts to pour from Bhairab's mouth! Getting a sip of this beer is guaranteed to bring good fortune, but one lucky individual will also get the small fish, which has been put to swim in the beer – this brings especially good luck.

The procession moves off again and for the remaining days of the festival it moves from place to place around the town, to the accompaniment of ceremonies, dances and other activities. Numerous other processions also take place around the town until the final day when the great pole is lowered and carried down to the river. It was during the Indra Jatra festival back in 1768 that Prithvi Narayan Shah conquered the valley and unified Nepal, so this important event is also commemorated in this most spectacular of Kathmandu occasions.

Ganesh Chata On the fourth day of the bright fortnight in September, offerings are made to Ganesh. The festival celebrates a bitter dispute between Ganesh and the moon goddess, and the Nepalis try to stay indoors on this night and shut out all signs of moonlight.

September–October

Pachali Bhairab Jatra The fearsome form of Bhairab, as Pachali Bhairab, is honoured on the fourth day of the bright fortnight in September or early October. The festivities for this are in line with Bhairab's bloodthirsty nature, as there are numerous sacrifices.

Dasain The pleasant post-monsoon period when the sky is clearest, the air is cleanest and the rice is ready for harvesting is also the time for Nepal's biggest annual festival. Dasain lasts for 15 days, finishing on the full-moon day of late September or early October, and there are a number of important days right through the festival. Although much of Dasain is a quiet family affair, there are colourful events for visitors to see both in Kathmandu and in the country. Dasain is also known as Durga Puja, as the festival celebrates the victory of the goddess Durga over the forces of evil in the guise of the buffalo demon Mahisasura. Since Durga is a bloodthirsty goddess, the festival is marked by wholesale blood-letting and features the biggest animal sacrifice of the year. Dasain also celebrates Rama's victory over the 10-headed demon Ravana.

Even before Dasain commences, Nepalis spring-clean their houses, while in the country, swings and primitive hand-powered Ferris wheels are erected at the entrance to villages or in the main square. For trekkers, Dasain is very much the 'Festival of Swings'. On the first day of the festival, a sacred jar of water is prepared in each house and barley seeds are planted in carefully prepared soil. Getting the seeds to sprout a few centimetres during Dasain ensures a good harvest.

Although Dasain is principally a Hindu festival it has also been adopted by Buddhists; activities also take place at Buddhist shrines in Patan and Bhaktapur. In the country the swings and Ferris wheels will be busier than ever, before finally being dismantled for another year.

Fulpati is the first really important day of Dasain and is called the 'Seventh Day' although it may not actually fall on the seventh day. Fulpati means 'Sacred Flowers', and a jar containing flowers is carried from Gorkha to Kathmandu and presented to the king at the Tundikhel parade ground. The flowers symbolise Taleju, the goddess of the royal family, whose most important image is in the Gorkha Palace. From the parade ground, the flowers are transported on a palanquin to Hanuman Dhoka (the old Royal Palace) on Durbar Square where they are inspected again by the king and his entourage.

Left: During the festival of Dasain, bamboo swings are a part of the fun, here with the backdrop of the Annapurnas, near Pokhara. (Photo: Hugh Finlay)

KRAIG LIEB

Nepali chariots – transport for the gods!

STAN ARMINGTON

Mani Rimdu – festival of the Sherpas

STAN ARMINGTON

Fierce deities add to the drama of Mani Rimdu.

RICHARD I'ANSON

Crowds gather for Bisket Jatra (Nepali New Year), the spectacular annual chariot festival of Bhaktapur.

STAN ARMINGTON

The clash of cymbals announces the second day of Losar (Tibetan and Bhotiya New Year).

KRAIG LIEB

The ever-present Dalai Lama at Boudha stupa.

GREG ELMS

Festival of Lights – an attraction to the gods.

HUGH FINLAY

Maha Shivrati celebrates Shiva's birth.

Kite Flying in the Kathmandu Valley

No visitor to the Kathmandu Valley in autumn, around the time of Dasain, can fail to notice the local penchant for kite flying – kids on rooftops, on streets, in open spaces and in parks can be seen flying kites.

To the uninitiated, this looks like, well, kids flying kites, but there is a lot more to it than meets the eye. First and foremost is the fact that kites are flown to fight other kites – whereby downing your opponent is the objective, and this is done by cutting their line.

The way to protect yourself from the ignominy of becoming a dreaded *hi-chait* (kite with a cut line) and to make your own kite as lethal as possible is to armour the line of the kite. In the past, people used to make their own *maajhaa* (line armour) and everyone had their own secret recipe, often involving crushed light bulbs, boiled slugs and gum. The trick was to make it sharp enough to cut an opponent's line, but not so sharp that it would cut itself when wound on to the *lattai* (wooden reel). These days people use ready-made threads, which cost anything from Rs 40 for 1000m up to Rs 25 per metre for pre-armed line from India.

The other hazard that may catch the unwary is the *mandali*, a stone on a string launched by a pirate on low-fliers – the idea being they cross your string, bring down your kite and then make off with said kite!

The paper kites themselves look very basic but are surprisingly manoeuvrable, the so-called Lucknow kites being the most sought after. Prices for kites start as low as Rs 5 and go to a modest Rs 50 or so. Popular places to buy kites are Asan Tole and Bhotahiti in Kathmandu's old city.

Maha Astami or the 'Great Eighth Day' and Kala Ratri, the 'Black Night', follow Fulpati and this is the start of the sacrifices and offerings to Durga. The hundreds of goats you may see contentedly grazing in the Tundikhel parkland prior to Maha Astami are destined to die for the goddess. At midnight, in a temple courtyard near Durbar Square, eight buffaloes and 108 goats are beheaded with a single stroke of the sword or knife.

The next day is **Navami** and the Kot Square near Durbar Square, the scene of the great massacre of noblemen, which led to the Rana period of Nepali history, is the scene for another great massacre. Visitors can opt to witness the bloodshed, but you'll need to arrive early to secure a place. Sacrifices continue through the day and blood is sprinkled on the wheels of cars and other vehicles to ensure a safe year on the road. At the airport, each Royal Nepal Airlines aircraft will have a goat sacrificed to it! The average Nepali does not eat much meat, but on this day almost everybody in the country will find that goat is on the menu for dinner.

The 10th day of the festival, **Vijaya Dashami**, is again a family affair as cards and greetings are exchanged, family visits are made and parents place a *tika* (red mark) on their children's foreheads.

In the evening, the conclusion of Dasain is marked by processions and masked dances in the towns of the Kathmandu Valley. The Kharga Jatra or sword processions feature priests dressed up as the various gods and carrying wooden swords, symbolic of the weapon with which Durga slew the buffalo demon. This day also celebrates the victory of Lord Rama over the evil King Ravana in the Ramayana. The barley sprouts that were planted on the first day are picked and worn as small bouquets in the hair.

Kartika Purnima, the full-moon day marking the end of the festival, is celebrated with gambling in many households, and you will see even small children avidly putting a few coins down on various local games of chance. Women fast and many of them make a pilgrimage to Pashupatinath near Kathmandu.

October–November

Tihar With its colourful Festival of Lights, Tihar (also called Diwali or Deepawali after the third day of celebrations) is the most important Hindu festival in India, and in Nepal it ranks second only to Dasain. The five days of festival activities take place in late October or early November.

The festival honours certain animals on successive days, starting with offerings of rice to the crows which are sent by Yama, the god of death, as his 'messengers of death'. On the second day, dogs are honoured with tikas and garlands of flowers. This must be a considerable surprise to most Nepali dogs, who are usually honoured with no more than the occasional kick, but the fact that in the afterworld it is dogs who guide departed souls across the river of the dead must not be forgotten. Bhairab's vehicle also happens to be a dog. On the third day it is cows who are remembered, and on this day you will often see cows with one horn painted silver, one horn painted gold. On the fourth day bullocks are honoured.

A Bad Day for Goats

After reading about Nepal's many festivals, it may sound like the pavements of the country are awash with animal blood. The fact is that animal sacrifices are mostly done in private (ie, in homes or temples, where foreigners can't enter) and there is only the slimmest chance of stumbling across such a sacrifice without warning. If animal sacrifices are something that you don't want to witness, see the earlier table 'Major Festivals of Nepal' in this special section to work out when not to go to certain spots. You will certainly not be alone if you feel upset or squeamish about such traditional practices, but a surprisingly high number of visitors to Nepal find animal sacrifices gruesomely fascinating, and go to particular temples at certain times (especially Saturday at Dakshinkali in the Kathmandu Valley) specifically to witness one.

The third day, **Deepawali**, is the most important day of the festival when Lakshmi (Vishnu's consort and the goddess of wealth) comes to visit every home that has been suitably lit for her presence. Since one can hardly turn down a surprise visit from the goddess of wealth, homes throughout the country will be brightly lit with candles and lamps for the Festival of Lights. The effect is also highlighted because Deepawali falls on the new-moon day.

The fourth day is also the start of the New Year for the Newar people of the Kathmandu Valley. The fifth day is known as **Bhai Tika** and on this day brothers and sisters are supposed to meet and place tikas on each others' foreheads. Sisters offer small gifts of fruit and sweets to their brothers while the brothers give their sisters money in return. The markets and bazaars of Kathmandu will be busy supplying the appropriate gifts.

Haribodhini Ekadashi This falls twice in every lunar month, on the 11th day after each new and full moon. Each Ekadashi is celebrated with ceremonies and activities but the Haribodhini Ekadashi, falling in late October or early November (on the 11th day after the new moon) is the most important. On this day Vishnu awakens from his four month monsoonal slumber. The best place to see the associated festivities is at Budhanilkantha, the temple of the sleeping Vishnu. Activities also take place at other Vishnu temples and many Vishnu devotees make a circuit of the important ones from Ichangu Narayan to Changu Narayan, Bishankhu Narayan and Sekh Narayan in the Kathmandu Valley.

Mahalakshmi Puja Lakshmi is the goddess of wealth, but to farmers wealth is rice. Therefore this harvest festival, following immediately after Haribodhini Ekadashi, honours the goddess with sacrifices and colourful dances.

November–December

Mani Rimdu The Sherpa festival of Mani Rimdu takes place at the monastery of Tengboche in the Solu Khumbu region. This three-day festival features masked dances and dramas, which are performed by the monastery's monks and seeks to celebrate the victory of Buddhism over the older Tibetan Bön religion.

Another Mani Rimdu festival takes place six months later in the lunar month that occurs in Jeth, the Gregorian months of May–June. This is at the Thami Monastery, which is a day's walk west of Namche Bazaar.

Right: Mani Rimdu is the biggest event of the year for the Sherpas of the Solu Khumbu region. (Photo: Stan Armington)

Bala Chaturdashi Like Ekadashi, there are two Chaturdashis each month; Bala Chaturdashi falls on the new-moon day in late November or early December. Pilgrims flock to Pashupatinath for this festival, burning oil lamps at night and bathing in the holy river on the following morning. A pilgrimage is then made along a traditional route through the woods overlooking Pashupatinath, and as they walk the devotees scatter sweets and seeds for their deceased relatives to enjoy in the afterlife.

The festival is at its most colourful during the first evening, and is best observed from the other side of the Bagmati River, looking down towards the temple at the lamp-lit singing and dancing pilgrims.

Bala, incidentally, once worked at Pashupatinath where he cremated corpses until an unfortunate incident transformed him into a demon. He then haunted the area around the temple until a means was found to dispose of him. Various legends relate how the demon was killed by one of poor Bala's former friends and the festival of Bala Chaturdashi was then instituted.

Sita Bibaha Panchami On the fifth day of the bright fortnight in late November or early December, pilgrims from all over Nepal and India flock to Janakpur to celebrate the marriage of Sita to Rama. It was in Janakpur that Sita was born, and she and Rama both have temples in the town. The wedding is re-enacted with a procession carrying Rama's image to Sita's temple by elephant. (Rama's birthday is celebrated in March in Janakpur and in Kathmandu.)

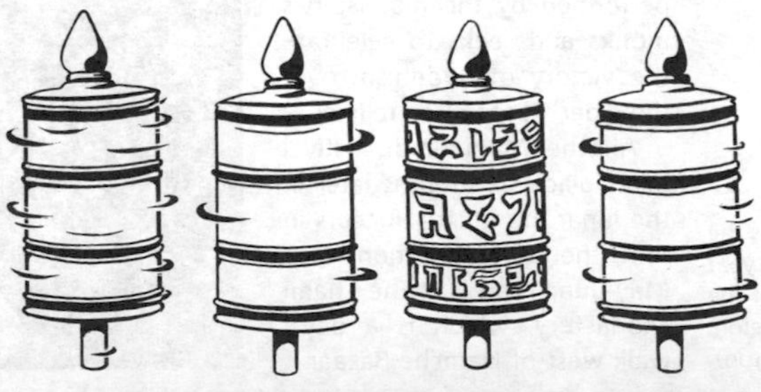

Getting There & Away

AIR

Airports

Kathmandu is the site of Nepal's only international airport, Tribhuvan Airport.

The international terminal is a modern building which was being refurbished at the time of writing. Touts are excluded from the building, so everything is fairly calm until you hit the outside world.

There's a branch of the Arab Bank before you clear immigration on the 1st floor. There's another branch on the ground floor of the departure section; both are open for flights, which normally means till around 8 pm, and both have decent exchange rates.

The small duty-free shop has a limited range of liquor and cigarettes available for purchase with US dollars.

When you leave, check in at least two hours early, preferably three in the high season, as the check-in desks can be a bit of a scrum. Also, don't forget to confirm and reconfirm your flight at least 72 hours before departure. If you are flying Singapore Airlines you can check in at the airline's city office on Durbar Marg the day before your flight, which simplifies the airport crush immeasurably.

All baggage is X-rayed and tagged as you enter the departure hall. At the airport, it is possible to re-exchange up to 15% of the Nepali rupees you have officially changed, but you must be able to show unused foreign exchange encashment receipts. If you are leaving for India, you can get between INRs 500 and INRs 2000 on presentation of your ticket.

Make sure you have clearance for anything that might be construed as an antique – metal statues show up on the baggage X-ray and are often checked. The X-ray machines that screen cargo baggage are not film-safe, and there are signs that say just that. Insist that the security officers physically inspect your film.

There is a pleasant restaurant on the top (2nd) floor, which is open to all, or go through immigration on the 1st floor, where there is a basic cafe. On the ground floor is a post office.

> **Warning**
>
> The information in this chapter is particularly vulnerable to change: Prices for international travel are volatile, routes are introduced and cancelled, schedules change, special deals come and go, and rules and visa requirements are amended. Airlines and governments seem to take a perverse pleasure in making price structures and regulations as complicated as possible. You should check directly with the airline or a travel agent to make sure you understand how a fare (and ticket you may buy) works. In addition, the travel industry is highly competitive and there are many lurks and perks.
>
> The upshot of this is that you should get opinions, quotes and advice from as many airlines and travel agents as possible before you part with your hard-earned cash. The details given in this chapter should be regarded as pointers and are not a substitute for your own careful, up-to-date research.

Airlines

The notoriously unreliable Royal Nepal Airlines Corporation (RNAC) has a limited number of international services. However, it is worth flying with any airline other than RNAC if at all possible, as its services are frequently subject to inconveniences such as delays and cancellations.

Austrian Airlines, Lauda Air and the Dutch company Transavia have direct flights between Europe and Nepal, and Aeroflot connects Nepal with Europe via Moscow. Two Middle Eastern airlines, Gulf Air and Qatar Airways, have connections between Europe and Nepal, although these involve a change of aircraft in the Middle East. Travellers arriving with other airlines from Europe or from the east coast of North America transfer to RNAC or Indian Airlines in New Delhi for

Air Travel Glossary

Alliances Many of the world's leading airlines are now intimately involved with each other, sharing everything from reservations systems and check-in to aircraft and frequent-flyer schemes. Opponents say that alliances restrict competition. Whatever the arguments, there is no doubt that big alliances are the way of the future.

Courier Fares Businesses often need to send urgent documents or freight securely and quickly. Courier companies hire people to accompany the package through customs and, in return, offer a discount ticket which is sometimes a bargain. However, you may have to surrender all your baggage allowance and take only carry-on luggage.

Fares Airlines traditionally offer 1st class (coded F), business class (coded J) and economy class (coded Y) tickets. These days there are so many promotional and discounted fares available that few passengers pay full fare.

Lost Tickets If you lose your airline ticket, an airline will usually treat it like a travellers cheque and, after inquiries, issue you with another one. Legally, however, an airline is entitled to treat it like cash and if you lose it then it's gone forever. Take very good care of your tickets.

Onward Tickets An entry requirement for many countries is that you have a ticket out of the country. If you're unsure of your next move, the easiest solution is to buy the cheapest onward ticket to a neighbouring country or a ticket from a reliable airline which can later be refunded if you do not use it.

Open-Jaw Tickets These are return tickets where you fly out to one place but return from another. If available, this can save you backtracking to your arrival point.

Overbooking Since every flight has some passengers who fail to show up, airlines often book more passengers than they have seats. Usually excess passengers make up for the no-shows, but occasionally somebody gets 'bumped' onto the next available flight. Guess who it is most likely to be? The passengers who check in late. If you do get 'bumped', you are normally offered some form of compensation.

Reconfirmation Some airlines require you to reconfirm your flight at least 72 hours prior to departure. Check your travel documents to see if this is the case

Restrictions Discounted tickets often have various restrictions on them – such as needing to be paid for in advance and incurring a penalty to be altered or cancelled. Others are restrictions on the minimum and maximum period you must be away.

Round-the-World Tickets RTW tickets give you a limited period (usually a year) in which to circumnavigate the globe. You can go anywhere the carrying airlines go, as long as you don't backtrack. The number of stopovers or total number of separate flights is decided before you set off and they usually cost a bit more than a basic return flight.

Ticketless Travel Airlines are gradually waking up to the realisation that paper tickets are unnecessary encumbrances. On simple one-way or return trips, reservations details can be held on computer and the passenger merely shows ID to claim their seat.

Transferred Tickets Airline tickets cannot be transferred from one person to another. Travellers sometimes try to sell the return half of their ticket, but officials can ask you to prove that you are the person named on the ticket. On an international flight, tickets are compared with passports.

the final short flight from New Delhi to Kathmandu.

From the west coast of North America or from Australasia, Bangkok is the usual transfer point, although there are also flights to Kathmandu from Hong Kong and Singapore. Thai Airways International and RNAC share the Bangkok to Kathmandu route.

Where to Sit

If you want to see the mountains as you fly into Kathmandu you must sit on the correct side of the aircraft. Flying in from the east – Bangkok, Kolkata (Calcutta), Hong Kong, Yangon (Rangoon) or Singapore – you want the right side. Flying in from the west – New Delhi or Varanasi – you want the left side.

Travellers with Special Needs

If you have special needs of any sort – you've broken a leg or you're vegetarian, travelling in a wheelchair, taking the baby, terrified of flying – you should let the airline know as soon as possible so that they can make arrangements accordingly. You should remind them when you reconfirm your booking (at least 72 hours before departure) and again when you check in at the airport. It may also be worth ringing round the airlines before you make your booking to find out how they can handle your particular needs.

Airports and airlines can be surprisingly helpful, but they do need advance warning. Guide dogs for the blind will often have to travel in a specially pressurised baggage compartment with other animals, away from their owner; smaller guide dogs may be admitted to the cabin. All guide dogs will be subject to the same quarantine laws (six months in isolation etc) as any other animal when entering or returning to countries currently free of rabies such as Australia.

Deaf travellers can ask for airport and inflight announcements to be written down for them.

Children under two travel for 10% of the standard fare (or free, on some airlines), as long as they don't occupy a seat. They don't get a baggage allowance either. Children between two and 12 can usually occupy a seat for half to two-thirds of the full fare and do get a baggage allowance. Push chairs can often be taken as hand luggage.

Departure Tax

A departure tax of Rs 1100 is payable in Nepalese rupees at the check-in counters in the departures terminal. The tax is Rs 660 if you are flying to South Asian Area Regional Cooperation (SAARC) countries (India, Pakistan or Bangladesh).

The UK & Europe

Ticket discounting has long been established in the UK and it's wide open – the various agencies advertise their fares and there's nothing under the counter about it at all.

Trailfinders, in west London, produces a lavishly illustrated brochure which includes air fare details. STA Travel also has branches in the UK. Look for ads in the Sunday papers and *Exchange & Mart*. Also look out for free magazines, such as *TNT*, which are widely available in London. Start by looking outside the main railway stations.

Most British travel agencies are registered with the Association of British Travel Agents (ABTA). If you buy your ticket from an ABTA-registered agent that goes out of business, ABTA will guarantee a refund or an alternative. For this reason it's best to use a registered agent, even though cheaper fares may sometimes be available from unregistered ones.

The Globetrotters Club (BCM Roving, London WC1N 3XX) publishes a newsletter called *Globe* which covers obscure destinations and can help in finding travelling companions.

London to Kathmandu on RNAC's flights costs £650 return in the high season; Gulf Air charges around £799 return. Austrian Airlines and Lauda Air charge $663 for the return flight from Vienna to Kathmandu.

Sample one-way air fares from Kathmandu include around US$400 to London (Gulf Air), US$550 to London, Munich or Paris (Qatar), US$468 to any European destination (Aeroflot) and US$555 to Amsterdam (Transavia).

The USA & Canada

Intense competition between Asian airlines on the US west coast and Vancouver has resulted in ticket discounting.

The *New York Times,* the *Chicago Tribune,* the *LA Times* and the *San Francisco Examiner* all produce weekly travel sections in which you'll find any number of travel agency ads. Student travel specialists Council Travel and STA Travel have offices in major US cities. The magazine *Travel Unlimited* (PO Box 1058, Allston, Mass 02134, USA) publishes details of the cheapest air fares and courier possibilities for destinations all over the world from the USA.

Fares to Kathmandu will often be about the same from the east or west coast – it's about as far away as you can get in either direction! Typical return fares are around US$1400 to US$2200.

From Kathmandu, a one-way ticket with Northwest and Thai to the west coast is US$673.

Australia & New Zealand

STA Travel and Flight Centres International are major dealers in cheap air fares. Check the travel agency ads in the *Yellow Pages* or the travel section in the Saturday newspapers and phone around.

Fares from Australia depend on the season and typically cost around A$1500 return. Bangkok is the most popular transit point although you can also fly via Singapore or Hong Kong.

From Kathmandu to east coast Australia, a one-way ticket with Singapore Airlines costs US$695; with Thai it's US$660.

India

RNAC and Indian Airlines share the main routes between India and Kathmandu. Both airlines give a 25% discount to those under 30 years of age on flights between Kathmandu and India; no student card is needed.

The Nepali airline Necon Air also has flights that connect Kathmandu with Lucknow and Patna.

New Delhi is the main departure point for flights between India and Kathmandu. The one-hour New Delhi to Kathmandu flight costs US$142 one way. RNAC has two flights daily, Indian Airlines has one.

Other cities in India with direct connections to Kathmandu are: Kolkata (US$96), Varanasi (US$71), Bangalore (US$265), Mumbai (US$265) and Patna (US$75).

Elsewhere in Asia

Other departure points for Kathmandu and approximate one-way fares include:

Bangkok, Thailand	US$220
Dhaka, Bangladesh	US$90
Karachi, Pakistan	US$195
Lhasa, Tibet	US$273
Singapore	US$310 (RNAC)
Singapore	US$389 (Singapore Airlines)
Hong Kong	US$321

There are also some interesting through fares; one to consider is with Biman Bangladesh Airlines, whose Kathmandu-Dhaka-Yangon-Bangkok ticket sells for US$304.

LAND

Political and weather conditions permitting, there are four main entry points into Nepal by land: three from India, one from Tibet.

A steady trickle of people drive their own vehicles overland from Europe – there are some interesting, though difficult, routes to the subcontinent through Eastern Europe and the republics that were once a part of the USSR. An international carnet is required. If you want to abandon your transport in Nepal, you must either pay a prohibitive import duty or surrender it to customs. It is not possible to import cars more than five years old.

India

The most popular crossing points from India are Sunauli (south of Pokhara); between Raxaul Bazaar and Birganj (south of Kathmandu); and Kakarbhitta (near Siliguri and Darjeeling in the far east). There are other less popular, but still viable, options.

All the options described in this section involve trains or buses or a combination of both.

To/From Delhi If you are travelling to or from Delhi or elsewhere in western India, the route through Sunauli and Bhairawa is the most convenient as it involves more train travel and less bus travel. However, the route through Mahendranagar in the far west of Nepal is another straightforward option and allows a visit to Royal Bardia National Park on the way.

Via Sunauli Delhi to Gorakhpur involves an overnight rail journey, from where frequent buses make the three-hour run to the border at Sunauli.

Buses from Sunauli to Kathmandu travel north-east along the beautiful Siddhartha Hwy as far as Mugling before joining the Kathmandu-Pokhara (Prithvi) Hwy. The journey takes around nine hours, and there are both day and night buses. Buses to Pokhara also travel via Mugling, and the trip also takes nine hours.

For more information, see Sunauli & Bhairawa in the Terai chapter.

Via Mahendranagar The border crossing at Mahendranagar in the far west of Nepal is the more interesting option as it allows a visit to Royal Bardia National Park en route.

There are daily buses from Delhi to Banbassa, the nearest Indian village to the border (nine hours). Banbassa is also connected by bus with the hill station Almora in India, as well as with Agra and Dharamsala. The nearest broad-gauge Indian railway station is Barielly, about three hours from the border by bus.

There are direct buses from Mahendranagar to Kathmandu at 2 pm, but they take a gruelling 15 hours. The countryside is beautiful and fascinating, so it's much better to do the whole trip during daylight and to break the journey at Royal Bardia National Park (four hours from Mahendranagar) or Nepalganj (six hours from Mahendranagar) or both.

For more information on the border crossing, see Mahendranagar in the Terai chapter.

To/From Varanasi Once again, it is the Sunauli crossing that is most convenient. There are direct buses here from Varanasi and the journey takes about nine hours.

From Sunauli it's another 10 hours to Kathmandu or Pokhara; there are day and night buses on both routes.

Some private companies make bookings all the way through to Kathmandu and Pokhara for around INRs 400, including Spartan accommodation at Sunauli. However, if you organise things yourself as you go, it will be cheaper, and you will have more flexibility, including a choice of bus within Nepal and of accommodation in Sunauli. Catch a bus to Sunauli, stay overnight on the Nepal side of the border (there are several reasonable hotels in Sunauli and Bhairawa), then catch a Nepali bus the next morning.

To/From Kolkata & Patna The entry point between Raxaul Bazaar (India) and Birganj (Nepal) is the most convenient option in the east of India.

In India, the trip from Kolkata to Patna takes about 10 hours, and you can do this by overnight train. It's then a five-hour journey from Patna to Raxaul Bazaar (the Indian border town).

Raxaul Bazaar is virtually a twin town with Birganj in Nepal. Both towns are dirty, unattractive transit points strung along the highway and are full of heavy traffic. The border is open from 7 am to 7 pm every day.

All direct buses between Birganj and Kathmandu or Pokhara turn west at Hetauda, then at Narayanghat turn north to Mugling, which is located on the Kathmandu-Pokhara (Prithvi) Hwy. Although it is not as spectacular as the Tribhuvan Hwy, this is nonetheless an interesting route with some beautiful views. It also means that all buses go through Tadi Bazaar, the jumping-off point for Sauraha and Royal Chitwan National Park.

Between Birganj and Kathmandu direct buses take around 10 hours; between Birganj and Pokhara they are marginally quicker. There are numerous night and day buses.

For more information on the border crossing, see Birganj in the Terai chapter.

To/From Darjeeling Kakarbhitta is the entry point in the far east of Nepal, and there are good connections to West Bengal.

There are many companies that handle bookings between Darjeeling and Kathmandu, although with all of them you have to change buses at the border and at Siliguri in India.

It's just as easy to get from Darjeeling to Kathmandu on your own – direct share 4WDs run from Darjeeling to Raniganj at the border (INRs 100, four hours), from where you take a rickshaw across the border to Kakarbhitta. This is cheaper than the package deal, and you have a choice of buses from the border; you also have the option of travelling during the day and overnighting along the way.

There are also direct share 4WDs to the border from Kalimpong (INRs 70, three hours) and Siliguri (INRs 70).

Buses from Kakarbhitta to Kathmandu travel west along the Mahendra Hwy to the Tribhuvan Hwy between Birganj and Hetauda, then head briefly north to Hetauda. They then travel west again until Narayanghat where they turn north to Mugling, on the Kathmandu-Pokhara (Prithvi) Hwy.

It's more than 600km between Kakarbhitta and Kathmandu, which means direct buses can take an exhausting 13 hours to complete the trip, and the direct buses all travel at night.

If you have time it is worth considering breaking your journey at Janakpur, which is roughly halfway, and is an interesting place in its own right. This will enable you to travel during the day and get a feel for the Terai; the flood plain of the Sapt Kosi is particularly interesting. There are day buses from Kakarbhitta that go to a number of towns on the Terai including Janakpur, and night buses direct to Pokhara. See the Kakarbhitta section in the Terai chapter for details.

Ticket Packages Many travellers have complained about scams involving ticket packages to India. The package usually involves coordination between at least three different companies so the potential for an honest cockup is at least as high as the potential for a deliberate rip-off.

Two long-standing and reliable Nepali companies handling through tickets are Wayfarers Travel Service (☎ 417176, ⓔ wayfarer@mos.com.np) in Thamel, Kathmandu; and Yeti Travels (☎ 221234, ⓔ yeti@vishnu.ccsl.com.np) in Durbar Marg, Kathmandu. Bear in mind, however, that everyone has to change buses at the border whether they book a through ticket or not, and that despite claims to the contrary, there are no 'tourist' buses on either side of the border. Buses through to Varanasi cost from Rs 650, and to Darjeeling Rs 950. Bus-and-train packages to Agra cost Rs 3275, including an air-con sleeper on the train, or Rs 1125 in a 2nd-class sleeper. Bus and train to Delhi costs Rs 3675 with air-con, Rs 1200 in 2nd class. (Note that the fares given in this section are in Nepali rupees.)

It is worth considering making advance bookings if you are in a major hurry, or if you plan to use the Indian railway system. Some trains, and especially sleeping compartments, can be heavily booked (this is apparently the case for Gorakhpur to Delhi trains). A Nepali agency will need a week to organise a booking. Beware – there's always a chance that what you pay for and what you get will be two different things. Make sure you get a receipt clearly specifying what you think you have paid for, and hang on to it.

Tibet

At the time of research the route to Tibet from Nepal (via Kodari) was closed to independent travellers, but independent travellers are entering Tibet through China and continuing, without problems, to Nepal. Only organised groups are allowed to cross from Nepal into Tibet, but this option is expensive.

On the face of it, it doesn't make much sense to allow individuals into Tibet from China, but not from Nepal. However, the package business is so lucrative, and Nepal is so full of seditious Tibetans, that the Chinese see little incentive to change. Bear in mind the road is poor and regularly closed by landslides during the monsoon.

Political disasters are even more likely than natural ones. Tibet is a volatile region with regular violent protests against Chinese rule and these upheavals are often followed by restrictions on visitors to the region. These restrictions are applied more stringently to independent visitors than to people on organised tours. The bottom line is that if you intend to enter or leave Nepal via Tibet you should come prepared with alternative plans in case travel along this route proves impossible.

Independent Travel If independent travel into Tibet is permitted you must first get a Chinese visa (see Embassies & Consulates in the Facts for the Visitor chapter for more details).

From Khasa (Zhangmu), the Tibetan town just over the border, there are infrequent buses to Lhasa, so you must plan carefully or you may be stranded for several days. Take food and drink on this trip, as there's not much available along the way. It's also possible to get a ride on a truck to Shigatse, but the 15-hour trip in the back of a truck is strictly for the hardy. From Shigatse there are local buses to Gyantse and from there to Lhasa.

This is not an easy trip by any means. Altitude sickness is a real danger as the maximum altitude along the road is 5140m, and there have been reports of deaths.

It is not possible to catch a bus direct from Kathmandu to Kodari, but daily buses run to Barabise (five hours). From Barabise there are buses to Kodari (two hours).

Organised Tours A number of agencies in Kathmandu organise fully inclusive return trips to Lhasa, with prices around US$100 per day for eight- to 12-day trips. Once in Tibet you can leave the tour in Lhasa and continue on your own. If this is your intention, make sure you state this when booking the tour in Kathmandu as a different visa is required for independent travel.

Most tours from Kathmandu take eight days and involve a flight to Lhasa and an overland return trip (or vice versa). Flights stop from the end of November to the end of March due to weather. China International Travel Service (CITS), the official state travel agency, runs the tours within China.

The following agencies in Nepal operate trips to Tibet. Most agencies advertising in Thamel are agents only; they don't actually run the trips.

Explore Nepal Richa Tours & Travel (☎ 423064, ⓔ explore@enrtt.mos.com.np) PO Box 1657, Namche Bazaar Bldg, Thamel, Kathmandu

Green Hill Tours (☎ 414968, ⓔ ghill@wlink.com.np) PO Box 5072, Thamel, Kathmandu

Natraj Tours & Travels (☎ 222906, ⓔ natraj@vishnu.ccsl.com.np) PO Box 495, Kantipath, Kathmandu

Tibet Tours & Travel (☎ 249140, ⓔ kalden@tibet.wlink.com.np) PO Box 7246, Tridevi Marg, Thamel, Kathmandu

Yeti Travels (☎ 221234, ⓔ yeti@vishnu.ccsl.com.np) PO Box 5376, Durbar Marg, Kathmandu

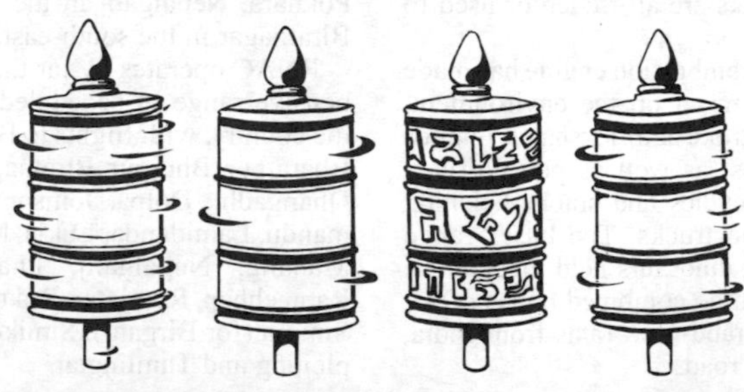

Getting Around

Getting around Nepal can be a challenging business. The impossible terrain and extreme weather conditions, plus incompetence and disorganisation, mean that trips rarely go exactly according to plan. On the other hand, Nepali ingenuity will usually get you to your destination in the end. Although travel can be frustrating, it also creates memorable moments by the score. Good humour and patience are essential prerequisites. Losing your cool will get you nowhere fast.

The whole gamut of transport options is available, with the possible exceptions of submarine and monorail. Most of the others can be found together on the average road, simultaneously competing with ducks, dogs, chickens, pigs and invincible pedestrians, and none of them have the vaguest traffic sense.

Walking is still the most important, and the most reliable, method of getting from A to B and for moving cargo; more is carried by people and porters in Nepal than by every other form of transport combined.

Bicycling is popular with visitors – local buses are so slow and uncomfortable that bicycles are often almost as quick (over short distances at least), and have the added advantage of allowing you to travel at your own speed and to stop whenever you like. There are other human-powered contraptions ranging from barrows to bicycle rickshaws, canoes, kayaks and rafts.

There are numerous forms of animal transport. Bullocks, oxen, buffaloes and ponies are all attached to carts. Elephants, donkeys and yaks are all ridden or used to carry loads.

The internal combustion engine has made an obnoxious impact on the environment. There are two-stroke autorickshaws, tempos and motorcycles, as well as petrol-driven cars and motorcycles and smoke-belching diesel buses and trucks. The buses range from lumbering dinosaurs held together by bits of wire and the combined hopes of the passengers to brand-new Tatas from India, the kings of the road.

Then there are planes of ranging sizes, a train at Janakpur in the south-east, a cableway (a kind of ski lift that carries cargo) at Hetauda, and even a cable car that carries passengers up to the temple of Manakamana near Mugling.

One of the major considerations when using any form of public transport is to avoid travelling during festival times, especially major ones such as Dasain and Tihar (Diwali). Buses and planes are booked solid for days either side of these festivals and it can be extremely difficult to get about – you will probably end up on the roof of buses, and can forget about plane travel unless you have booked weeks in advance.

AIR

A number of private companies operate alongside the long-running, government-owned and chronically inefficient Royal Nepal Airlines Corporation (RNAC). These are Necon Air, Buddha Air, Mountain Air, Skyline Airways, Shangri-La Air, Cosmic Air, Yeti Airlines and Gorkha Airlines, with seemingly more every year. These airlines operate largely on the popular (ie, economically viable, tourist-oriented) routes, although government regulations require that airlines devote 40% of their capacity to nontourist routes. The prices for the private airlines are slightly more than RNAC (by US$10 per sector), but they offer better service and are much more reliable.

The main air travel hubs are Kathmandu, Pokhara, Nepalganj in the south-west and Biratnagar in the south-east.

RNAC operates by far the most comprehensive range of scheduled flights around the country, with flights to Bajhang, Bajura, Bharatpur, Bhojpur, Biratnagar, Chaurjhari, Dhangadhi, Dolpa, Jomsom, Jumla, Kathmandu, Lamidanda, Lukla, Mahendranagar, Manang, Nepalganj, Phaplu, Pokhara, Ramechhap, Rumjatar, Rukum, Sanfebagar, Simara (for Birganj), Simikot, Surkhet, Taplejung and Tumlingtar.

Necon Air is among the largest of the private operators. It is able to service Kathmandu, Bhadrapur, Bhairawa, Biratnagar, Janakpur, Nepalganj and Pokhara.

Buddha Air and Mountain Air have fast, modern aircraft, which means that the trip to Pokhara takes just 20 minutes, compared with up to 40 minutes with RNAC. Buddha Air has daily flights servicing Kathmandu, Biratnagar, Bhadrapur, Bhairawa, Nepalganj and Pokhara.

Cosmic Air services Kathmandu, Bhadrapur, Bharatpur, Jomsom, Pokhara and Tumlingtar. Yeti Airlines flies to Kathmandu, Phaplu, Lamidanda, Pokhara, Rumjhatar and Simara (for Birganj).

Some flights, such as Kathmandu to Lukla (the main airstrip in the Everest region), are used mainly by trekkers. These flights are frequent during the trekking season, but the schedules can be extremely variable. Kathmandu to Jomsom flights, for example, are plagued by bad weather at both ends. Early-morning departures from Kathmandu are often delayed by fog, but if they don't arrive in Jomsom by around 11 am landing may be impossible due to high winds. The result is regular cancellations. Flights out of Lukla are equally unreliable – the airport can easily be closed for a week by bad weather – and there is often an enormous backlog of frustrated trekkers waiting for flights, both in Kathmandu and Lukla. For flights in and out of Jomsom, Cosmic Air is the one to choose; for Lukla, Yeti Airlines are the best bet.

It is advisable to book domestic flights a week in advance and, just as for flights out of Nepal, the most important rule is to reconfirm and reconfirm again. Names can easily 'fall off' the passenger list, particularly when there is pressure for seats. This is much more of a problem with RNAC than the private operators.

Air Fares

Residents and Nepali citizens pay approximately 35% of the tourist price for domestic airfares. Airlines will accept payment from visitors only in hard currency. See the Nepal Air Fares chart for details.

A number of the airlines have daily mountain flights that cost from US$99 to US$109. See the boxed text 'Mountain Flights' in the special section 'Mountaineering in the Himalaya' in the Trekking chapter for details.

NEPAL AIR FARES

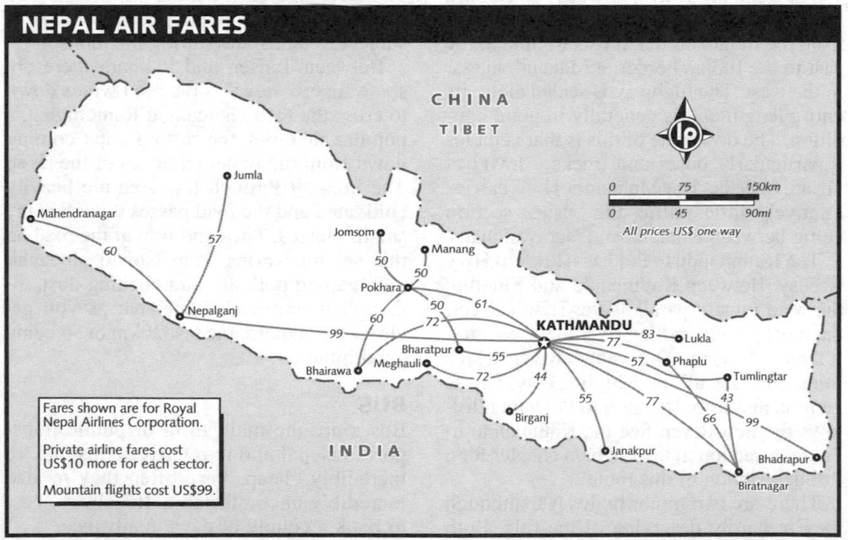

Fares shown are for Royal Nepal Airlines Corporation.

Private airline fares cost US$10 more for each sector.

Mountain flights cost US$99.

Domestic Airport

The domestic terminal is the old Kathmandu airport, and its age shows. It can be a nasty and chaotic spot, particularly when flights are cancelled and crowds of stressed tourists generate an atmosphere of fear and loathing. You can escape the worst of the crush in the fairly rundown restaurant on the 1st floor.

Check in an hour early for domestic flights; there is a Rs 110 airport tax payable at check-in. Once through security, the waiting lounge is reasonably comfortable and you can also get drinks. Don't carry pocket knives, gas cigarette lighters or matches in your carry-on luggage on any domestic flights as they will be confiscated.

It can be difficult finding a taxi into Kathmandu if you arrive late. If the worst comes to the worst, it's a 10-minute walk to the international terminal, where you are certain to find something.

See Getting Around in the Kathmandu chapter for information on transport to and from the airport.

HIGHWAY TRAVEL

There are just two main highways in Nepal, and the condition of both is generally good.

The main highway is the busy Mahendra Hwy, which runs the length of the country from the Indian border at Kakarbhitta in the east to the Indian border at Mahendranagar in the west. The highway is sealed along its entire length and is generally in good condition. The downside of this is that vehicles – particularly buses and trucks – travel at unsafe speeds. The Mahendra Hwy carries relatively little traffic, the busiest section being between Hetauda and Narayanghat.

The Kathmandu to Pokhara (Prithvi) Hwy is busy. Between Kathmandu and Mugling the road mostly parallels the Trisuli River, the most popular rafting river in the country. It then follows the Marsyangdi River (which joins the Trisuli at Mugling) as far as Dumre, and from Damauli to Pokhara it follows the Seti River. See the Kathmandu to Pokhara section in the Pokhara chapter for a full description of this route.

There are two minor highways, although they're hardly deserving of the title. Both offer spectacular views and are well worth travelling on. The Tribhuvan Hwy (or Rajpath) branches off the Prithvi Hwy at Naubise, about 30km west of Kathmandu, and heads south over the mountains to Hetauda, and on to the Indian border at Birganj. The other is the diabolically potholed Siddhartha Hwy, which joins Pokhara with Butwal on the Mahendra Hwy, going via the interesting town of Tansen (Palpa).

The Tribhuvan Hwy was the first road to link the Kathmandu Valley with the outside world; it was built by the Indian government and completed in 1956. If you have time and feel energetic, consider catching a bus over the mountains from Hetauda to Kathmandu.

If you are travelling in a group or have the funds, consider hiring a car. It won't be cheap, partly because you'll have to pay for the driver's return trip whether or not you return yourself (expect to pay around US$150). Alternatively, if you're fit and have a mountain bike, this is regarded as one of the most spectacular cycling routes in the country (see the Mountain Biking chapter for details).

From Butwal, the Siddhartha Highway snakes 36km through the picturesque Mahabharat Range to the historic town of Tansen (Palpa). It is a narrow, winding road which is generally in poor condition, and is subject to landslides during the monsoon.

Between Tansen and Pokhara there are some superb views as the road winds down to cross the Kali Gandaki at Ramdhighat, a popular take-out for rafting trips coming down from the upper stretches of the river. The hills all through this area are heavily cultivated and the road passes though many small villages. The condition of the road on this section varies from bad to abysmal, with gaping potholes and choking dust, although it improves somewhat as you get closer to Pokhara, the last 20km or so being good bitumen.

BUS

Buses are the main form of public transport in Nepal and in relative terms they're incredibly cheap. Very often they're also incredibly uncomfortable. It's always best to book a couple of days in advance.

There are numerous services with buses and smaller minibuses around the Kathmandu Valley, out from Kathmandu towards the Tibetan border, down to the Indian border or to Pokhara. As well as the regular public buses between Kathmandu and Pokhara there are a number of services aimed particularly at the tourist market. Buses also run from Pokhara to the Indian border as well as along the length of the country from Kakarbhitta in the east to Mahendranagar in the west. This road, called the Mahendra Hwy, runs through the Inner Terai, which is parallel to the Indian border.

Many people – locals and Westerners – prefer to ride on bus roofs. While this is officially banned in the Kathmandu Valley, it is not uncommon elsewhere, particularly during Dasain when pressure for seats is greatest. The arguments in favour are that you get an exhilarating ride with great views, the opportunity to watch your bags and, sometimes, room to stretch your legs. Some people argue it is also safer, because you can jump off before the bus goes over the side into a gorge! This latter point is debatable. If you are on top, make sure you're well wedged in, so you don't catapult off when the bus swerves, brakes, or lurches. It's also best to sit facing forwards – that way you can see low-hanging wires and branches before you get swatted. Make sure you have sunscreen and appropriate clothing too.

Bus Services

There are both government and private buses. The government bus company, known as Sajha Yatayat, has distinctive blue and white buses that service all the main routes except the far east and far west. Although marginally cheaper than private buses, these buses are generally very shabby, poorly maintained and rarely run to schedule; overall they are best avoided. Each major town has a Sajha office where you can make advance reservations.

There are literally dozens of private bus companies – it seems all you need is one bus and you've got yourself a company. The vehicles are mostly Indian Tata buses, and range from new and reasonably comfortable to unbelievably shabby, poorly maintained death-traps. As with the Sajha buses, there is a booking office in each town where you can buy tickets in advance on the long-distance routes.

Private buses run on all routes, and on the longer routes there are 'express' buses scheduled both by day and night. Fares are cheap, but day buses are marginally cheaper than night buses. Day travel is generally preferable because you get to see the countryside (and there are some spectacular roads) and it's safer. Express bus drivers have mastered the art of maniacal driving, and accidents are not at all uncommon. However, day travel is slower than night travel simply because there are more people getting on and off, and yet the danger posed by express night buses should not be underestimated.

There's nothing very express about the express buses, but they are lightning fast in comparison to local buses that run shorter routes, carry people, their luggage and often animals, and seem to stop more than they go. Travelling by local bus is no fun and should be kept to a minimum, although to get to many of the trekking road-heads there is little alternative.

TRAIN

There are two train lines from Janakpur, one runs east to Jaynagar over the Indian border, and the other which runs north-west to Bijalpur, although only the former route carries passenger traffic. They're narrow-gauge trains and very slow, so they offer an interesting if somewhat crowded method of seeing the countryside. Note that tourists are not allowed to cross the border using the passenger train. See the Around Janakpur section in the Terai chapter for more details.

CAR & MOTORCYCLE

There are no drive-yourself rental cars available in Nepal but you can easily hire cars with drivers. Expect to pay around US$40 a day, plus fuel, which at the time of research was set at Rs 47 per litre across the country.

It is quite popular to hire cars for return trips to both Pokhara and Royal Chitwan National Park from Kathmandu. A car to

Pokhara should cost around US$30 one way, although this can rise at peak times. A car to Chitwan should cost around US$60, but could also rise at peak times.

Motorcycles can be rented in Kathmandu and Pokhara. See the Getting Around sections in those chapters for more details about car and motorcycle rental.

BICYCLE

In Kathmandu and Pokhara there are many bicycle-rental outlets and this is a cheap and convenient way of getting around. Virtually the entire Kathmandu Valley is accessible by bicycle, though if you are venturing far outside the Kathmandu and Patan area, a mountain bike is definitely worthwhile. A regular bicycle only costs around Rs 50 per day to rent, and a mountain bike costs from Rs 100 to Rs 200. Children's bicycles can also be hired. See the Mountain Biking chapter for more information on cycling in Nepal.

HITCHING

Hitching is not possible in Nepal – don't bother trying to hitch here. Those people waiting by the roadside are waiting for local buses.

LOCAL TRANSPORT

Taxi

Larger towns such as Kathmandu and Pokhara have taxis which, between a group of people, can be a good way to explore the Kathmandu Valley. Metered taxis have black licence plates; private cars often operate as taxis, particularly on long-distance routes or for extended periods, and have red plates.

Taxi rates often rise faster than meters can be recalibrated, so frequently there is a surcharge on top of the meter reading. If the meters are out of date (at the time of research they were OK) tourists will be hard pushed to convince drivers to use their meters (with or without a surcharge) and will almost certainly have to negotiate the fare in advance.

Tempo

Three-wheeled tempos are a common form of local transport throughout the country. Tempos are designed to seat about eight people; in practice they seat anything up to 15. They run on set routes and can be very useful for travelling short distances; the fare is rarely more than Rs 10. Drivers pick up and drop off anywhere along the route; tap on the roof when you want to stop.

The despised smoke-belching, diesel-fuelled Vikram tempo was ubiquitous until recently – in 2000 all diesel tempos were banned in the Kathmandu Valley, and have been replaced by electric and gas powered tempos and conventional petrol minibuses. This has made a noticeable difference to the levels of air pollution in the valley; the Vikram tempos have all been relocated and can now be seen doing their smoke-belching best to clog the air of Terai towns.

Three-wheeled tempos operate like minibuses – they leave when full and have fixed fares.

Autorickshaw & Cycle-Rickshaw

Autorickshaws, those curious and noxious three-wheeled, two-stroke-engine devices, are found in Kathmandu.

Cycle-rickshaws are common in the old part of Kathmandu and can be a good way of making short trips through the crowded and narrow streets. They are also the most common form of short-distance public transport in towns throughout the Terai.

Note that autorickshaws as well as cycle-rickshaws operate much like taxis – they do not wait for other passengers and prices are negotiable.

ORGANISED TOURS

There are few organised tours available in Kathmandu or to places of interest around the valley and farther afield. It's usually a matter of organising something through a travel agent. If your stay in Nepal is too short to allow decent exploration on your own, then you could organise a tour. For information on tours around Kathmandu, see Organised Tours in the Kathmandu chapter. If you're into activities, see Organised Tours in the Trekking and Rafting & Kayaking chapters.

MARK KIRBY

Seeking inner peace.

RICHARD I'ANSON

Novice monk at prayer.

KRAIG LIEB

Just chillin', been joggin'!

KRAIG LIEB

In attendance at New Year's proceedings, Boudha (Bodhnath) stupa.

RICHARD I'ANSON

'Namaste!'

RICHARD I'ANSON

The frozen peak of Mt Nuptse (7879m) in the Solu Khumbu region reaches to the heavens.

GARETH McCORMACK

Mustard crops colour gold the fields of western Nepal.

GARETH McCORMACK

Pokhara offers fine vistas over the glassy waters of Phewa Tal.

Kathmandu

☎ 01 • pop 500,000 • elevation 1300m

For most visitors to Nepal, Kathmandu is their arrival point and the centre of their visit. It is the capital of Nepal, the largest city in the country and the main centre for hotels and restaurants. This amazing city seems, in places, unchanged since the Middle Ages; at other times it is just another developing-world capital rushing into the modern era. Along with the two other major cities in the Kathmandu Valley – Patan and Bhaktapur – Kathmandu has an artistic and architectural tradition that rivals anything you'll find in the great cities of Europe.

For many people, arriving in Kathmandu is a shock – the sights, sounds and smells can lead to sensory overload: There are narrow streets and lanes with carved wooden balconies perched above tiny hole-in-the-wall shops; town squares packed with extraordinary temples and monuments; and fruit and vegetable markets alive with a constant throng of humanity. And then there are the choking dust and fumes and stinking gutters; the concrete monstrosities and Coca-Cola billboards; and the touts and maimed beggars.

The gap between rich and poor is a chasm, but despite the pressures of extreme overcrowding and poverty, people retain a good-humoured self-respect and integrity. It is probably safer to walk the streets of Kathmandu than it is to walk those in your home town – and certainly it's more interesting.

Like Patan and Bhaktapur, Kathmandu's historic centre is concentrated around Durbar Square (*durbar* is Nepali for 'palace'). There's a distinct difference between the tightly packed old city area and the more spacious newer parts of town.

Kathmandu is the administrative and educational centre for the country. Many of the Ranas' grand palaces now house bureaucracies that are, arguably, of greater benefit to the general populace. Kathmandu is also the main focus for visiting tourists, so there has been a large investment in the necessary infrastructure, and many local people are dependent on the tourist dollar.

Highlights

- Strolling around the history-rich capital city and soaking up its atmosphere
- Whiling away an hour or two on the steps of the Maju Deval, watching the passing parade of humanity in Durbar Square
- Dining in one of the city's superb Newari restaurants, with the accompaniment of traditional dances
- Walking in the medieval-like marketplaces

HISTORY

The history of Kathmandu is really a history of the Newar people, the main inhabitants of the valley. The Newar people are covered with other general facts about the valley under History in the Around the Kathmandu Valley chapter.

While the documented history of the Kathmandu Valley goes back to the Kiratis, around the 7th century BC, the foundation of Kathmandu itself dates from the 12th century AD, during the time of the Malla dynasty.

Originally known as Kantipur, the city flourished during the Malla reign, and its superb temples, buildings and other monuments date from this time. Initially, Kathmandu was an independent city within the valley, but in the 14th century the valley was united under the rule of the Malla king of Bhaktapur. The 15th century saw the valley divided once again, this time into the three independent kingdoms of Kathmandu, Patan and Bhaktapur. Rivalry between the three city-states led to a series wars that left each state weakened and paved the way for the 1768 invasion of the valley by Prithvi Narayan Shah of the kingdom of Gorkha.

The Shah dynasty unified Nepal and made Kathmandu the new capital – a position the city has held ever since. The Shahs

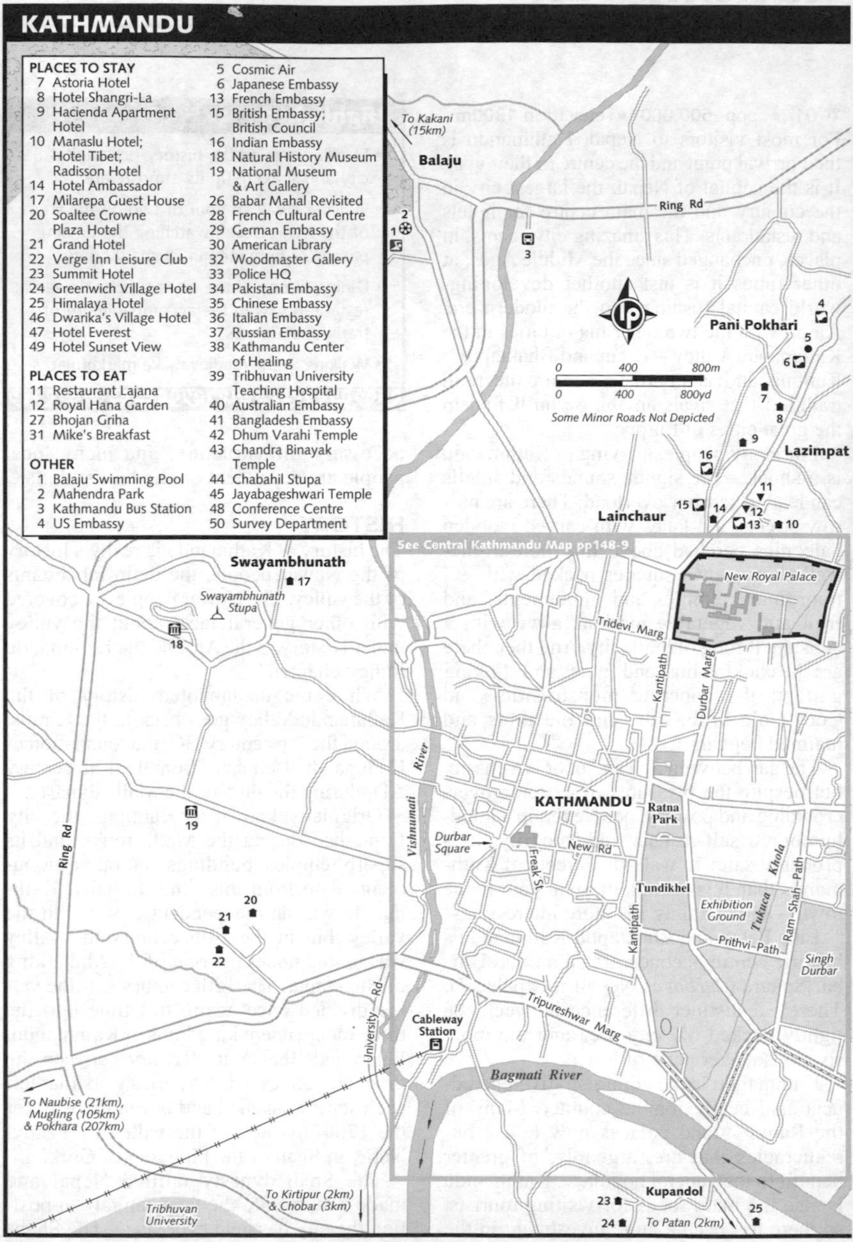

KATHMANDU

PLACES TO STAY
7 Astoria Hotel
8 Hotel Shangri-La
9 Hacienda Apartment Hotel
10 Manaslu Hotel; Hotel Tibet; Radisson Hotel
14 Hotel Ambassador
17 Milarepa Guest House
20 Soaltee Crowne Plaza Hotel
21 Grand Hotel
22 Verge Inn Leisure Club
23 Summit Hotel
24 Greenwich Village Hotel
25 Himalaya Hotel
46 Dwarika's Village Hotel
47 Hotel Everest
49 Hotel Sunset View

PLACES TO EAT
11 Restaurant Lajana
12 Royal Hana Garden
27 Bhojan Griha
31 Mike's Breakfast

OTHER
1 Balaju Swimming Pool
2 Mahendra Park
3 Kathmandu Bus Station
4 US Embassy
5 Cosmic Air
6 Japanese Embassy
13 French Embassy
15 British Embassy; British Council
16 Indian Embassy
18 Natural History Museum
19 National Museum & Art Gallery
26 Babar Mahal Revisited
28 French Cultural Centre
29 German Embassy
30 American Library
32 Woodmaster Gallery
33 Police HQ
34 Pakistani Embassy
35 Chinese Embassy
36 Italian Embassy
37 Russian Embassy
38 Kathmandu Center of Healing
39 Tribhuvan University Teaching Hospital
40 Australian Embassy
41 Bangladesh Embassy
42 Dhum Varahi Temple
43 Chandra Binayak Temple
44 Chabahil Stupa
45 Jayabageshwari Temple
48 Conference Centre
50 Survey Department

To Kakani (15km)
Balaju
Ring Rd
Pani Pokhari
Lazimpat
Lainchaur
0 400 800m
0 400 800yd
Some Minor Roads Not Depicted
See Central Kathmandu Map pp148-9
New Royal Palace
Swayambhunath
Swayambhunath Stupa
Tridevi Marg
Kantipath
Durbar Marg
Vishnumati River
KATHMANDU
Ratna Park
Durbar Square
New Rd
Freak St
Tundikhel
Exhibition Ground
Tukuca Khola
Ram-Shah-Path
Prithvi-Path
Singh Durbar
Tripureshwar Marg
University Rd
Cableway Station
Bagmati River
To Naubise (21km), Mugling (105km) & Pokhara (207km)
Tribhuvan University
To Kirtipur (2km) & Chobar (3km)
Kupandol
To Patan (2km)

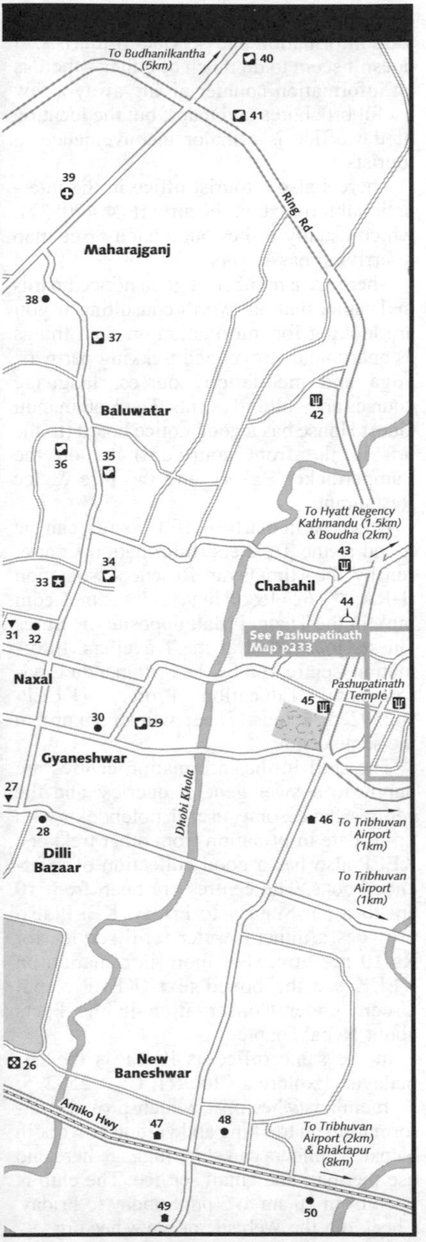

also retain their position, however, these days the political landscape has changed drastically.

ORIENTATION

Most of the interesting things to see in Kathmandu are clustered in the old part of town from Kantipath (the main north–south road) west towards the Vishnumati River. New Rd, constructed after the great earthquake of 1934, starts from the ugly ornamental gateway (where New Rd intersects with Kantipath) and goes straight into the heart of old Kathmandu, changing its name to Ganga Path before it comes to Durbar Square.

The offices of Royal Nepal Airlines (RNAC) are at the Kantipath end of New Rd, and along New Rd are banks, shops and the modern shopping area of the city. Continue farther west along New Rd to Ganga Path and you reach the large Basantapur Square, then Durbar Square where Hanuman Dhoka (the old Royal Palace) is located. Freak St, Kathmandu's famous street from the hippie overland era, runs south off Basantapur Square.

Running north-east from Durbar Square is the thoroughfare that was once the main trading artery of the city and is still the busiest street in old Kathmandu. This narrow road, usually thronging with people, cuts through the heart of old Kathmandu from Indra Chowk through Kel Tole to Asan Tole.

Kantipath forms the boundary between the older and newer parts of the city. South of the junction with New Rd is the main post office, easily located by the nearby Bhimsen Tower (or Sundhara). On the east side of Kantipath is a large, open parade ground known as Tundikhel, and on the eastern edge of this is the city bus station, for buses around the Kathmandu Valley.

North along Kantipath from New Rd is the government-run Bir Hospital on the left – look for Hanuman the monkey god on the wall carrying a Himalayan mountain complete with medicinal herbs. On the right is Ratna Park and just north of this Rani Pokhari, the artificial lake. As Kantipath crosses Tridevi Marg the new Royal Palace compound is on the right; Kantipath continues into Maharajganj, the embassy sector.

Running parallel to and east of Kantipath is Durbar Marg, a wide street flanked by travel agencies, airline offices and a number of restaurants and expensive hotels. Its northern end is at the main entrance to the new Royal Palace. East from this intersection, Tridevi Marg passes the South Asian Association for Regional Cooperation (SAARC) and a couple of blocks later enters the Thamel area, the popular cheap tourist accommodation and restaurant centre of the city. Thamel is a 15- to 20-minute walk north from Durbar Square, the centre of Kathmandu.

The city is encircled by the Ring Rd. On this road in the north of the city is the main Kathmandu bus station and on the eastern edge is Tribhuvan Airport.

Addresses

In old Kathmandu streets were not given names, and although some of the major thoroughfares now have names, most still don't – smaller streets and laneways never do. Kathmandu grew as a series of interlocking squares that gradually swallowed neighbouring villages. The names of these squares, villages and other landmarks (perhaps a monastery or temple) have come to be used as addresses of sorts.

For example, the address of everyone living within a 100m radius of Thahiti Tole is Thahiti Tole, and if you want to find a resident you go to Thahiti Tole and ask around – simple if you can speak Nepali and can find your way around the warren of laneways and courtyards. Thamel is now used to describe a sprawling area with at least a dozen roads and several hundred hotels and restaurants. They all have the same address: Thamel.

Given this anarchic approach it is amazing that any mail gets delivered – it does, but slowly. Most businesses have post office boxes. If you're trying to find a particular house, shop or business, make sure you get detailed directions.

INFORMATION

Tourist Information

The Tourist Service Centre (☎ 247041) on Bhrikutimandap Marg, on the eastern side of Tundikhel parade ground, is a government centre that supposedly exists to provide information and service to tourists. It doesn't seem to do much of either – there is an information counter giving away a few useful brochures and maps, but the location of the office is a major inconvenience to tourists.

There's also a tourist office in the international terminal at the airport (☎ 470537), which usually dishes out a handy free map to arriving passengers.

There are a number of good notice boards in Thamel that are worth consulting if you are looking for information on such things as apartments, travel and trekking partners, yoga and meditation courses, language courses and cultural events. The Kathmandu Guest House has a good notice board (to the left in the front courtyard), as do the Pumpernickel Bakery and the Fire & Ice Restaurant.

Other particularly useful boards can be found at the Trekkers' Information Centre, run by the Himalayan Rescue Association (HRA; ☎ 262746, ⓔ hra@aidpost.mos.com.np), in the Thamel Mall opposite the Shree Guest House; and at the Travellers' Information Centre, run by the Kathmandu Environmental Education Project (KEEP; ☎ 259275, ⓔ tours@keep.wlink.com.np), in the same centre.

The staff in the information centres are happy to answer general queries, and the centres have some useful notebooks with up-to-date information from other trekkers. KEEP also has a good collection of reference books. The centres are open from 10 am to 5 pm Sunday to Friday. KEEP also provides a mineral-water refill service for Rs 10 per litre. (For more information on KEEP, see the boxed text 'KEEP Nepal Green' under Conservation in the Facts about Nepal chapter.)

In the same office as KEEP is the Himalayan Explorers Club (HEC; ☎ 259275, ⓔ members@hec.org), which provides information on trekking and volunteer work in Nepal. Members can store luggage here and use the mail and email service. The club is open from 10 am to 5 pm Sunday to Friday. Check out the Web site at www.hec.org.

The Annapurna Conservation Area Project (ACAP; ☎ 225393, ext 363) has its office in the basement of the Sanchaya Kosh Bhawan shopping centre, on Tridevi Marg on the edge of Thamel. In addition to issuing ACAP permits, the office also provides information on trekking in the Annapurna region. It is open from 9 am to 4 pm Monday to Saturday and 10 am to 3 pm Sunday. There is another ACAP office in Patan (☎ 526571, fax 526570), PO Box 3712, Jawlakhel, and one in Pokhara (see under Information in the Pokhara chapter).

Travellers' Nepal and *Nepal Traveller* are similar, good-quality, free monthly magazines that cover a broad range of topics and have a section of practical information.

Money

It is worth checking the exchange rate that banks and moneychangers offer and the commission they charge – both vary. There are dozens of licensed moneychangers in Thamel. Their hours are much longer than those of the banks, but rates vary considerably so shop around. Some charge commission, others don't. See under Money in the Facts for the Visitor chapter for information on exchange rates, commissions and Western Union transfers.

The most convenient bank for travellers staying in the Thamel region is the small branch of the Nepal Grindlays Bank on Tridevi Marg (opposite the Three Goddesses Temples). It is open from 9.30 am to 7.30 pm Monday to Friday and 10 am to 5 pm Sunday.

There's another branch of Nepal Grindlays Bank around the corner on Kantipath, and this one has an ATM for credit-card withdrawals. There are two more Nepal Grindlays ATMs in Thamel: one opposite the Third Eye Restaurant and one in the compound of the Kathmandu Guest House.

Citibank (☎ 228884), GPO Box 2826, has an office in the Yak & Yeti Hotel (see the Central Kathmandu map), and the main Nepal Bank (☎ 221185, fax 222381) is in Dharma Path near New Rd. The latter is handy if you're staying in Freak St, and it has the important advantage of being open from 7 am to 7 pm seven days a week.

The American Express (AmEx) agent is Yeti Travels (☎ 221234, fax 226152/3, ⓔ yeti@vishnu.ccsl.com.np), which has its office off the forecourt of the Hotel Mayalu on Jamal Tole, which is just off the southern end of Durbar Marg. It's open from 10 am to 5 pm Sunday to Friday, and provides cash advances between 10 am and 1 pm.

Sita World Travel (☎ 418363, ⓔ sita ktm@sitanep.mos.com.np), up the laneway opposite the Three Goddesses Temples in Thamel, is the agent for Western Union money transfers.

Post

The main Kathmandu post office is on the corner of Kantipath and Khichapokhari, close to Bhimsen Tower (see the Central Kathmandu map). Theoretically, the stamp counter is open from 8 am to 7 pm Sunday to Friday and from 11 am to 3 pm Saturday, but regardless it can mean queuing and frustration. Unless you have a *lot* of mail, you are better off taking advantage of the hotels, bookshops and communication centres, which will tackle the bureaucracy for you for a nominal charge.

The poste restante section at the main post office is quite efficient: The staff sort mail into alphabetised boxes and you simply sit down and go through the appropriate box yourself. You are required to show your passport before you take anything away. Ask your correspondents print and underline your surname; if in doubt check under your first name as well. Poste restante (inside to the left, behind the main counter) is open from 10.15 am to 4 pm Sunday to Thursday (closing 3 pm from mid-November to mid-February) and 10.15 am to 2 pm on Friday, closed Saturday.

The most convenient post office to Thamel is in the basement of the Sanchaya Kosh Bhawan shopping centre on Tridevi Marg, on the eastern side of Thamel.

Parcels can be sent from the foreign post office, just north of the main post office. It's open from 10 am to 5 pm Sunday to Thursday and 10 am to 2 pm Friday, closed Saturday. Parcels have to be examined and sealed by a customs officer and then packed in an approved manner. It's something of a procedure, so if you're short of time you're best off using one of the many cargo agencies. Diki Continental Exports (☎ 417681), opposite the Hotel Mandap in Thamel, and Sharmasons Movers (☎ 222709) are two agencies that have been recommended.

AmEx has a clients' mail service at its offices off the forecourt of the Hotel Mayalu in Jamal Tole (see the Durbar Marg map). Address letters to: American Express, Yeti Travels Pty Ltd, Hotel Mayalu, Jamal Tole, PO Box 5376, Durbar Marg, Kathmandu.

Telephone & Fax

International telephone calls can be made and faxes can be sent from any of the dozens of 'communication centres' in Thamel and elsewhere throughout the city. They are no more expensive, and are certainly more convenient, than the central telegraph office about 500m south of the post office, opposite the National Stadium. However, the central telegraph office is open 24 hours.

Many of the communication centres offer Internet phone calls, where computers are used to make phone calls to phones anywhere in the world. The cost varies considerably, from Rs 10 to Rs 50 per minute, depending on the destination. See under Telephone & Fax in the Facts for the Visitor chapter for more information.

For domestic telephone information call ☎ 197.

Email & Internet Access

Email services are widely available in Thamel and elsewhere in Kathmandu. Providers range from a hotel or travel agency with one computer to cybercafes with a dozen or more terminals. Connection speeds are fast and the rates are a fairly standard – and very cheap – Rs 1 per minute.

Travel Agencies

Kathmandu has a great number of travel agencies, particularly along Durbar Marg, Kantipath and in Thamel. See under Organised Tours in the Trekking chapter for details of trekking agencies.

For straightforward travel and ticketing matters, try Wayfarers Travel Service (☎ 417176, ⓔ wayfarer@mos.com.np) in Thamel, not far from the Kathmandu Guest House.

Bookshops

Kathmandu has a large number of very good bookshops. Many have particularly interesting selections of books on Nepal, including books that are not usually available outside the country. Prices for British and US books are surprisingly competitive with their home-market prices. There are many shops with second-hand books for sale and trade. Most dealers will buy back books for 50% of what you paid.

Pilgrims Book House is a couple of doors north of the Kathmandu Guest House and has an extensive collection of books on Nepal and other Himalayan regions. Kailash Bookshop, on the road from Durbar Marg to the Yak & Yeti Hotel, is owned by the same company and it has an antiquarian section. There's also a branch of Pilgrims opposite the Hotel Himalaya on the road to Patan.

Walden Book House, at Chhetrapati in greater Thamel, is another place with a very good range, as is the Barnes & Noble Bookhouse, just south of the Kathmandu Guest House.

There are many other good bookshops around Thamel, including Bookworld on Tridevi Marg. Mandala Bookpoint on Kantipath in greater Thamel has an excellent selection of books, with a good range in French and German.

Libraries & Cultural Centres

Following is a selection of the libraries and cultural centres in Kathmandu:

American Library (☎ 410041) Gyaneshwar, east of the city centre. Only Nepalis and foreign residents of Nepal are allowed to use this library. It's open from 11 am to 6 pm Monday to Friday.

British Council Library (☎ 222698) British Council, Lainchhaur. This library has a good selection of books on Nepal, as well as British newspapers and magazines. It's open from 11 am to 6 pm Monday and Friday, and 11 am to 5 pm Tuesday, Wednesday and Thursday.

French Cultural Centre (☎ 224326) Dilli Bazaar, east of the city centre. This place has French publications and French film screenings (with a small entry charge).

Goethe Institut (☎ 250871) in Ganabahal, near Bhimsen Tower. This place has German film screenings, occasional exhibitions and a library.

Kaiser Library (☎ 411318) in the Department of Education compound, on the corner of Kantipath and Tridevi Marg. Also known as Kesar Library, this place is worth a visit just to see the building and gardens. It has an incredible collection of books on Buddhism, Tibet and Nepal. Kaiser Shamsher Jung Bahadur Rana was a Rana aristocrat, scholar, scientist and gourmet. He built up a superb collection of books, all of which, it is said, he read in their original language. Most of his palace is now used as government offices, but his library is kept as he left it and can be visited.

Nepal National Library (☎ 521132) Pulchowki, Patan. Also known as Rastriya Pustakalaya, this place has books in English and Hindi.

Tribhuvan University Library, Kirtipur. This library has a good collection; it is open from 9 am to 6 pm Sunday to Friday. See under the Kirtipur, Chobar & Dakshinkali Route section in the Around the Kathmandu Valley chapter for more details.

Photo Shops

There are numerous places offering a same-day service for print film. Hicola (☎ 410200) in Lazimpat, Das Photo (☎ 213621), Nepal Colour Lab (☎ 211290) and Photo Concern (☎ 223275) are fairly reliable and can handle colour prints and E-6 or Ektachrome slides. Several of these companies have branches in Thamel and throughout Kathmandu. Colour enlargements are produced at reasonable prices. Ganesh Photo Lab (☎ 216898), in an alley behind Hanuman Dhoka in Durbar Square, and Print Maker (☎ 416971), in Lazimpat, are the places to go for black-and-white processing.

Immigration Office

To get a visa extension in Kathmandu, go to the Central Immigration Office (☎ 222453, 223590) next to the Tourist Service Centre on Bhrikutimandap Marg, across the Tundikhel parade ground from the main post office. It's open from 10 am to 1 pm Sunday to Thursday and 10 am to noon Friday for applications; you will need to go back between 4 and 5 pm (2 to 3 pm Friday) to retrieve your passport. It's wise to start the process early as renewing a visa can be time-consuming. Any transaction with the immigration office requires two trips or a wait of several hours. See Visas in the Facts for the Visitor chapter for more details.

Medical Services

The centrally located, government-operated Bir Hospital (☎ 221119) is not recommended. The best bet in the Kathmandu Valley is the Patan Hospital (☎ 521034), which is partly staffed by Western missionaries and is in the Lagankhel district of Patan, near the last stop of the Lagankhel bus. The hospital also has an ambulance service (☎ 521048).

Reasonably well equipped (and carrying a ventilator) is the Tribhuvan University Teaching Hospital (☎ 412363) north-east of the centre in Maharajganj.

The Clinic Travel Medicine Center (CIWEC; ☎ 228531, ⓔ advice@ciwec-clinic.com), just off Durbar Marg, is used by many foreign residents of Kathmandu. It has operated since 1982 and has developed an international reputation for research into travellers' medical problems. It's open from 9 am to 4 pm Monday to Friday, and a doctor is on call around the clock. The clinic is staffed mostly by foreigners. With a single visit costing around US$45, it is hardly surprising that the clientele is made up almost exclusively of foreigners. See under Health in the Facts for the Visitor chapter for the Web site.

The Nepal International Clinic (☎ 434642, ⓔ nic@naxal.wlink.com.np) is just south of the new Royal Palace, east of Thamel. It has an excellent reputation and is cheaper than the CIWEC clinic. It's opening hours are from 9 am to 5 pm every day; a consultation costs about US$35.

Emergency

Fire Brigade	☎ 101, 221177
Police, Durbar Square	☎ 100, 223011
Red Cross Ambulance	☎ 228094

[Continued on page 147]

WALKING TOURS

A stroll around Kathmandu will lead the casual wanderer to many intriguing sights, especially in the crowded maze of streets, courtyards and alleys in the market area north of Durbar Square. There are temples, shrines and many individual statues and sculptures hidden away in the most unlikely places. You can really appreciate Kathmandu's museum-like quality when you stumble upon a 1000-year-old statue – something that would be a prize possession in many Western museums – here being used as a children's plaything or a washing line. The walks described in this section can be done whenever you have an hour or two to spare. Walking Tours 1 and 2 can be used as routes from the accommodation centre of Thamel to the central Durbar Square area.

Each of the three walks will take you to a number of markets, temples and *chowks* (courtyard or marketplace), which are the centre of Nepali life. A number of chowks are surrounded by *bahils* or *bahals* (dwellings for monastic Buddhist communities), although none are used for that purpose today – they have been taken over by families and sometimes by schools. The courtyards may be large and open, dotted with *chaityas* (small *stupas* or hemispherical Buddhist religious structures) and shrines, or they may be enclosed within a single building. A bahil is distinguished from a bahal because it includes accommodation for nonmonastic visitors, is generally simpler than a bahal and the main shrine is not necessarily in the centre of the courtyard.

The walks can be made as individual strolls or linked together into one longer walk. Walking Tour 1 gives you a taste of the crowded and fascinating shopping streets in the oldest part of Kathmandu and takes you to some of the city's most important temples. Walking Tour 2 visits some very old bahals and an important Buddhist stupa, and it passes by a number of ancient and important stoneworks and introduces you to a toothache god. Walking Tour 3 takes you to a lesser known section of Kathmandu, without spectacular attractions but where the everyday life of city dwellers goes on and tourists are fairly rare.

Inset: Seto (White) Bhairab in Durbar Square, Kathmandu (Photo: Richard I'Anson)

Walking Tour 1 – North from Durbar Square

The road angling across the city from Durbar Square to the artificial lake Rani Pokhari (see Walking Tour 2 map) is the most interesting street in old Kathmandu. Modern roads such as Durbar Marg are no match for this narrow artery's varied and colourful shops, temples and people. The road was at one time the main street in Kathmandu, and it was the start of the route to Tibet. It was not replaced as Kathmandu's most important street until the construction of New Rd after the great earthquake of 1934, and it was not paved until the 1960s.

Walking Tour 1

1 Garuda Statue
2 Tana Deval Temple
3 Akash Bhairab Temple
4 Ganesh Shrine
5 Shiva Temple
6 Seto (White) Machhendranath Temple
7 Lunchun Lunbun Ajima
8 Krishna Temple
9 Jana Bahal Temple
10 Pagoda Platform
11 Yitum Bahal
12 Stupa
13 Kichandra Bahal
14 Chaitya
15 Nara Devi Temple
16 Dance Platform
17 Wooden Window
18 Yatkha Bahal
19 Kathmandu Lodge

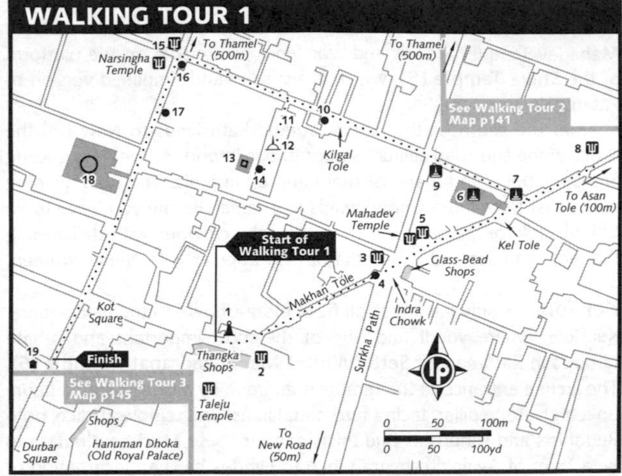

Makhan Tole The crowded street that is known as Makhan Tole (*makhan* is the Nepali word for butter) starts from the north-eastern corner of Durbar Square, by the Taleju Temple, and then runs towards the busy marketplace of Indra Chowk. Many worthwhile shops along this stretch of the street sell *thangkas* (religious paintings) and paintings as well as clothes.

Garuda Statue

Tana Deval Temple

Directly across from the Taleju Temple is a 10th-century kneeling **Garuda statue (1)**. It faces a small Vishnu Temple. To your right, in a walled courtyard just past the long row of stalls, is the **Tana Deval Temple (2)**, with three carved doorways and struts, which show the multi-armed Ashta Matrikas (Mother Goddesses).

Indra Chowk The busy shopping street of Makhan Tole spills into Indra Chowk, the courtyard named after the ancient Vedic deity, Indra. On the left of the square is a notable building covered in brightly coloured modern ceramic tiles. From the balcony four metal lions rear out over the street. This is the **Akash Bhairab Temple (3)**, or Bhairab of the Sky Temple. To get to the temple – the ground floor is occupied by shop stalls – you have to climb a flight of steps at the right-hand side of the building, guarded by two more metal lions. A sign at the entrance announces that non-Hindus cannot enter, although there's not much to see here anyway. The silver image inside is visible through the open windows from out in the street, and during important festivals, particularly Indra Jatra (September), the image is displayed in the square. A large *lingam* (phallic symbol) is also erected in the centre of the square at that time.

Akash Bhairab Temple

Ganesh Shrine

In a small niche just near the Akash Bhairab Temple is a very small but much-visited brass **Ganesh shrine (4)**.

Indra Chowk is traditionally a centre for the sale of blankets and cloth, and there are often many merchants on the platforms of the Mahadev Temple. Shawls and woollen rugs are sold on the platform of the **Shiva Temple (5)**, which is a smaller and simplified version of Patan's Krishna Temple.

- Shiva Temple

From the south of the square Surkha Path leads to New Rd; the shops along this road sell consumer goods imported from Hong Kong and Singapore, and many of them end up in India. The road heading north-east from Indra Chowk leads to Thamel. Before you leave Indra Chowk look for the narrow alley to the right, crowded with stalls selling the glass bangles and beads that are so popular with Nepali women.

Kel Tole It's only a short stroll from Indra Chowk to the next square, Kel Tole, where you'll find one of the most important and ornate temples in Kathmandu, **Seto (White) Machhendranath Temple (6)**. The arched entrance to the temple is guarded by a small Buddha figure on a high stone pillar, facing two metal lions. The temple attracts both Buddhists and Hindus as Buddhists consider Seto Machhendranath to be a form of Avalokiteshvara while to Hindus he is an incarnation of Shiva who can bring rain. Although the temple's age is not known, it was restored during the 17th century.

- Seto (White) Machhendranath Temple

In the courtyard there are numerous small shrines, chaityas and statues, including a mysteriously European-looking figure facing the temple. It may well have been an import from Europe, which has simply been accepted into the pantheon of gods. Facing the other way, just in front of the temple, are two graceful bronze figures of the Taras seated on top of tall pillars.

Inside the temple you can see the white-faced image of the god, sitting rather like a seated Buddha. The image is taken out of the temple during the Seto Machhendranath festival in March/April each year and paraded around the city in a chariot. The procession ends at the Machhendranath Temple in the south of the city (visited on Walking Tour 3).

During the day, Kel Tole is busy with worshippers, children playing and with the activities of the people whose homes surround it.

As you leave the temple, to the right is the small, triple-roofed **Lunchun Lunbun Ajima (7)**, a Tantric temple, white-tiled around the lower level and with some erotic carvings on the struts at the back.

- Lunchun Lunbun Ajima

The diagonal street continues to Asan Tole, the busiest of the junctions along the old street (covered in Walking Tour 2). Walk partway towards Asan Tole to see the three-, four- and five-storey houses, tightly squeezed together on the right-hand side of this stretch of the street. On the left, the polygonal **Krishna Temple (8)** is jammed between other buildings, with the ground floor occupied by shops. The woodcarvings on this temple are very elaborate.

- Krishna Temple

Return to Kel Tole and turn right (west). The shops along this stretch specialise in *topis* (Nepali caps). At the next junction the large **Jana Bahal Temple (9)** is on your left. The domed temple is of little interest.

- Jana Bahal Temple

Pagoda Platform
Yitum Bahal
Stupa
Kichandra Bahal
Chaitya

Kilgal Tole to Yitam Bahal Continue across the junction and on the left you pass the small **Kilgal Tole** beside the road. It's a grubby little square with a decaying **pagoda platform (10)** and, in the middle, a fine chaitya with faces on each side.

An opening on the left leads into the long, rectangular courtyard of **Yitum Bahal (11)**. A small, white-painted **stupa (12)** stands in the centre of the courtyard. Opposite it, on the western side of the courtyard, is one of the oldest bahals in the city, its entrance flanked by the usual stone lions. This is the **Kichandra Bahal (13)**, dating from 1381. A **chaitya (14)** in front of the entrance is completely shattered by a bodhi tree, which has grown right up through its centre.

Inside the Kichandra Bahal is a pagoda-like sanctuary in the centre, to the south is a small chaitya decorated with Bodhisattvas in a standing, rather than the usual sitting, position. On the northern side of the courtyard are four brass plaques mounted on the upper-storey wall. The one on the extreme left shows a demon known as Guru Mapa taking a child from a woman and stuffing it greedily into his mouth. The demon had an appetite for bad children and the two central plaques show two more children, presumably lining up to be consumed! Eventually the demon was bought off with the promise of an annual feast of buffalo meat, and the plaque to the right shows him sitting down and dipping into a pot of food.

To this day Guru Mapa is said to live in a tree in the Tundikhel parade ground; a buffalo is sacrificed to him every year. With such a clear message on juvenile misbehaviour it is probably fitting that the courtyard houses a primary school – right under the Guru Mapa plaques!

Nara Devi Temple

Nara Devi Temple From Kichandra Bahal go back into the large courtyard, exit at the north and turn left (west). On your right at the next junction is the **Nara Devi Temple (15)**. The temple is dedicated to Kali, Shiva's consort in her destructive incarnation, and is also known as the Seto Kali (White Kali) Temple.

Although the temple, with its three tiers, golden roof and red and white guardian lions, is quite old, some of the decorations (including the black-and-white chequered paintwork) are clearly more recent additions. It is said that Kali's powers protected the temple from the 1934 earthquake, which destroyed so many other temples in the valley. A Malla king once stipulated that a dancing ceremony should be held for the goddess every 12 years, and dances are still performed on the small **dance platform (16)** that is across the road from the temple. Also across the road is a three-roofed **Narsingha temple** to Vishnu as the demon-destroying man-lion. You have to find your way to it through a maze of small courtyards.

Dance Platform

Postage-Stamp Window At the Nara Devi corner turn left (south) and you soon come to a nondescript modern building on your left with an utterly magnificent **wooden window (17)**. It has been called *deshay madu* in Nepali, which means 'there is not another one like it'.

Wooden Window

A postage stamp worth Rs 0.50 was issued in 1978, which showed the window. Next to the building is a recently restored triple-roofed pagoda, which serves as a landmark.

A little farther south and on your right is the entrance to the **Yatkha Bahal (18)**, a huge open courtyard with an unremarkable stupa in the centre. Directly behind it is an old building, which used to have its projecting upper storey supported by four superb carved-wood struts. Dating from the 14th century, they were carved in the form of *yakshas* (attendant deities or nymphs), one of them gracefully balancing a baby on her hip. Unfortunately, the struts have been removed, hopefully just for refurbishment.

Yatkha Bahal

Back on the road and heading south you soon pass Kot Square, scene of the great massacre that brought the Ranas to power in 1846. The ***New Kathmandu Lodge*** **(19)** is on your right and you soon see Durbar Square ahead.

New Kathmandu Lodge

Finish

Walking Tour 2 – South of Thamel

This walk can be started from the southern end of Thamel or it can easily be linked to Walking Tour 1 to make a 'figure eight' starting from either Thamel or Durbar Square. This walk can be started from the bustling Thahiti Tole or, if that's hard to find, from the Hotel Gautam on Kantipath. To get to Thahiti Tole walk south from Thamel on the road from the main Thamel Chowk; the first open square you will come to is Thahiti.

Thahiti Tole In the **stupa (1)** in the centre of the square is a stone inscription indicating it was constructed in the 15th century. Legends relate that it was built over a pond plated with gold and that the stupa served to keep thieves at bay. Or perhaps the pond was full of dangerous snakes and the stupa kept the snakes in their place – the legends vary!

Stupa

Nateshwar Temple (2), on the northern side of the square, is dedicated to Shiva; the metal plates that surround the doors show creatures busily playing a variety of musical instruments. Above the door are somewhat crudely painted pictures of Shiva's *ganas* (companions), in this case a skeleton-like creature and what looks like a yeti.

Nateshwar Temple

Two Ancient Bahals Leave the north-eastern corner of the square taking the narrow road running east. You soon come to the entrance of the **Musya Bahal (3)** on your right, with a modern facade and guarded by stone lions. The road continues east and then takes a right then left bend, at the corner of which is a second old monastery, the recently restored **Chusya Bahal (4)**.

Musya Bahal

Chusya Bahal

This stretch of street is popular with potters, and you often see them working on the roadside outside the bahals or see their products piled up inside. Often these are just the simple little disposable cups used by *chia* (milk tea) sellers.

Walking Tour 2

1 Stupa
2 Nateshwar Temple
3 Musya Bahal
4 Chusya Bahal
5 Shiva Temple
6 Annapurna Temple
7 Ganesh Pagoda
8 Narayan Temple
9 Haku Bahal
10 Ugratara Temple
11 Sunken Shrine
12 Wood with Coins
13 Ikha Narayan Temple
14 Saraswati Shrine
15 Buddha Statue
16 Stone Relief
17 Nag Bahal
18 Kathesimbhu Stupa
19 Avalokiteshvara Statue

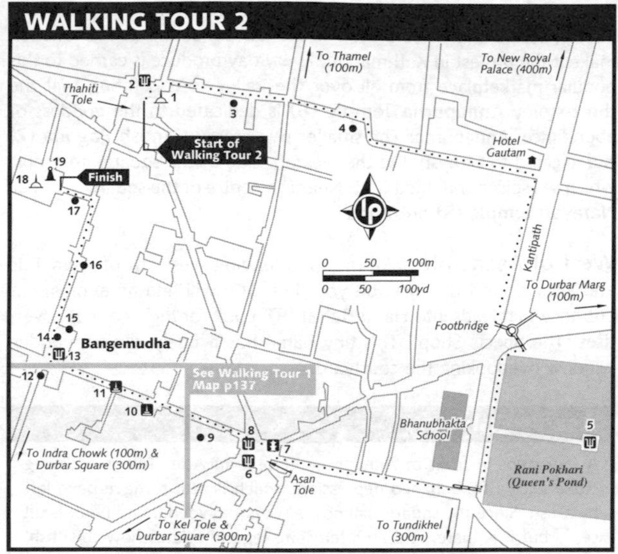

Beyond the second bahal there is a string of upper-level budget hotels, and just before the road joins the busy Kantipath is the Hotel Gautam. Turn right (south) and then cross the road via the footbridge to Rani Pokhari (Queen's Pond). The bridge itself offers a decent view over Rani Pokhari, although it is somewhat obscured by the tangle of electric wires.

Rani Pokhari The large fenced tank (or small lake) called Rani Pokhari (Queen's Pond) was built by King Pratap Malla in 1667 to console his queen over the death of their son. Various legends and tales are connected with the tank and it's believed that it may have been built by Pratap Malla at an earlier date and renamed for his queen only after their son died; according to records the son was trampled by an elephant.

Unfortunately, the gate to the tank is unlocked only one day each year, during the festival of Tihar, so you will have to be content with peering through the fence. A causeway leads across the tank to a small and undistinguished **Shiva temple (5)**.

Shiva Temple

Across Kantipath from the tank is a long building originally known as the Durbar School, which was the first school in Nepal. It has since been renamed the **Bhanubhakta School**, after the Nepali poet of that name. Walk south along Kantipath to the footbridge at the southern end of Rani Pokhari, and cross Kantipath. This footbridge affords the best views of Rani Pokhari. From here head straight into the old part of the city to Asan Tole.

Asan Tole From dawn until late at night Asan Tole is jammed with buyers, sellers and passers-by. The six roads meeting at this junction make it the busiest in Kathmandu. Every day produce is carried to this popular marketplace from all over the valley so it is fitting that the three-storey **Annapurna Temple (6)** is dedicated to the goddess of abundance, Annapurna. The smaller two-storey **Ganesh Pagoda (7)** is dedicated to Ganesh. On the western side of the square are shops, which sell spices and dried fruit. Near the centre of the square is a small **Narayan temple (8)** or Vishnu.

West of Asan Tole Take the road leading west out of Asan Tole and after a short distance, on your left, you will find an anonymous entrance that leads into **Haku Bahal (9)**. Look for the sign that advertises 'The Spects Shop'. This tiny bahal has a finely carved wooden window overlooking the courtyard.

- Annapurna Temple
- Ganesh Pagoda
- Narayan Temple
- Haku Bahal

Asan's Fish

A few steps in front of Annapurna Temple in Asan Tole is a paving stone with a foot-shaped depression, which is said to have been left by a fish. Since the square is almost always crowded it can be difficult see – but it is there, and an interesting legend relates how this 'fish' fell out of the sky.

Once upon a time a famous astrologer named Barami was about to become a father. A bell would be rung to announce the birth of his child so he waited expectantly in his study. At the instant he heard the sound of the bell across the rooftops, he cast his newborn son's horoscope and discovered to his horror that he was not the father. In anger and disgust he abandoned his wife and child and fled from the kingdom.

Many years later he returned to Kathmandu and became the pupil of a younger and more brilliant astrologer named Dak. As a final test Dak asked Barami to foretell the miraculous event that would shortly occur in Asan Tole. Barami correctly predicted that a fish would fall from the heavens, and he correctly predicted the exact time this strange event would occur, but he missed by several steps the exact place where the fish would crash to earth. His teacher suggested that he had forgotten to take account of the wind. Sure enough this was the case.

Barami realised he had forgotten to take account of the wind once before: On the occasion that the sound of a bell carried to his ears the news of his son's birth. Accounting for the wind factor, Barami once again cast the child's horoscope. To his delight he discovered that the child was indeed his son, and to his amazement the boy's name was Dak!

This left Dak and Barami with a peculiar problem: A son must revere his father and a pupil must revere his teacher, yet here the son had been teaching the father. Eventually the decision was reached that father and son should jointly erect a monument to the event that had brought them together. And there it is in Asan Tole, a small memorial to a fish that fell from the sky.

Ugratara Temple
Sunken Shrine
Wood with Coins

A few strides farther west you'll come to the triple-roofed **Ugratara Temple (10)** at a small square known as Nhhakantalla. Come here if your eyes are sore; a prayer at the shrine is said to work wonders for the eyes. A little farther along is a small, **sunken shrine (11)** on the left and a Ganesh shrine set into the wall on the right. Soon after you'll arrive at a crossroads with an open square to the north. Turn left (south) and on your left you will see a lump of **wood with coins (12)** into which thousands of coins have been nailed. A coin and nail embedded in the wood is supposed to cure toothache, and the deity who looks after this ailment is represented by a tiny image in the ugly lump of wood. The square at the junction is known as Bangemudha, which means 'Twisted Wood'.

Ikha Narayan Temple
Saraswati Shrine

Ancient Buddha Turn north into the open square and you'll see a small, double-roofed **Ikha Narayan temple (13)**, easily identified by the kneeling Garuda figure in front of it. The temple houses a beautiful 10th- or 11th-century four-armed Vishnu figure. The square also has a fine image of the goddess Saraswati playing her lute at the **Saraswati Shrine (14)**.

Buddha Statue

The northern side of the square is closed off by a modern building with shops on the ground floor. In the middle of this nondescript frontage, directly beneath the Cyrus Electronics shop, is a standing **Buddha statue (15)** framed by modern blue and white tilework. The image is only about 60cm high but it dates from the 5th or 6th century. A very similar Buddha figure stands on the riverbank near the temple of Pashupatinath.

Stone Relief

If the toothache god hasn't done his duty, as you take the road north from the square you'll pass a string of dentists shops – proclaimed by the standard signs showing a smiling mouthful of teeth. On the right is a small open area surrounded by concrete with a red-coloured Ganesh head and a small but intricate **stone relief (16)** dating from the 9th century. It shows Shiva sitting with Parvati on Mt Kailash, her hand resting proprietorially on his knee in the pose known as Uma Maheshwar. Various deities and creatures, including Shiva's bull Nandi, stand around them.

Nag Bahal

There's an impressive wooden balcony across the road, which is said to have had the first glass windows in Kathmandu. Nearby is a rather worn out, and bricked-in, stone trough. A little farther on your left a single broken stone lion (his partner has disappeared) guards a passageway, above which hangs a carved wooden *torana* (pediment above temple doors that can indicate the god to whom the temple is dedicated). Inside is the small enclosed courtyard of **Nag Bahal (17)**, with painted murals above the shrine, which is flanked by banners with double-triangle flags.

Kathesimbhu Stupa

Kathesimbhu Stupa Just a couple of steps beyond the Nag Bahal entrance is the entrance to the **Kathesimbhu Stupa (18)**, just southwest of Thahiti Tole. The entrance is flanked by beheaded stone lions and more-recent metal lions atop tall concrete pillars.

In the courtyard is a small copy (dating from around 1650) of the great Swayambhunath complex outside Kathmandu. If a devotee is unable to make the ascent to Swayambhunath then a circuit of this miniature is said to be a good substitute. Just as at Swayambhunath, there is a small pagoda to Harti, the goddess of smallpox, right behind the main stupa.

Various statues and smaller chaityas stand around the temple, including a fine standing **Avalokiteshvara statue (19)** enclosed in a glass case and protective metal cage. Avalokiteshvara carries a lotus flower in his left hand, and the Dhyani Buddha Amitabha is seen in the centre of his crown with downcast eyes.

• Avalokiteshvara Statue

From Kathesimbhu Stupa it's only a short walk north to Thahiti Tole, the starting point of the walking tour.

Finish

Walking Tour 3 – South from Durbar Square

Walking Tour 3

Starting from beside the Kasthamandap in Durbar Square a circular walk can be made to the older parts in the south of the city. This area is not as packed with historical interest as the walks north of Durbar Square, but the streets are less crowded and you are far less likely to run into other tourists.

Bhimsen Temple Starting from the **Kasthamandap (1)** in the south-western corner of Durbar Square, the road out of the square forks almost immediately around the **Singh Sattal (2)**, a squat building with small shop stalls around the ground floor and golden-winged lions guarding each corner of the upper floor. Take the road running to the right of this building and you soon come to a square tank-like **hiti (3)**, or water conduit, where men will usually be washing clothes.

• Kasthamandap
• Singh Sattal
• Hiti

Immediately beyond is the highly decorated **Bhimsen Temple (4)**, which is fronted by a brass lion on a pillar and has white-painted lions guarding the two front corners. Bhimsen is supposed to watch over traders and artisans so it's quite appropriate that the ground floor of this well-kept temple should be devoted to shop stalls.

• Bhimsen Temple

Jaisi Deval Temple Continue south beyond the Bhimsen Temple then turn sharp left (uphill) where the road ends. At the top of the hill you'll come out by the tall, triple-roofed, 17th-century **Jaisi Deval Temple (5)**, which stands on a seven-level base. This is a Shiva temple, which is indicated by the bull on the first few steps and the mildly erotic carvings on some of the temple struts. Right across the road from the temple is a **stone lingam (6)** rising a good two metres from a *yoni* (female equivalent of a phallic symbol). This is definitely a god-sized phallic symbol and a prayer here is said to aid fertility.

• Jaisi Deval Temple
• Stone Lingam

In its procession around the town during the Indra Jatra festival, the Kumari Devi's chariot pauses here. During its stop, dances are held on the small **dance platform (7)** across the road from the temple.

• Dance Platform

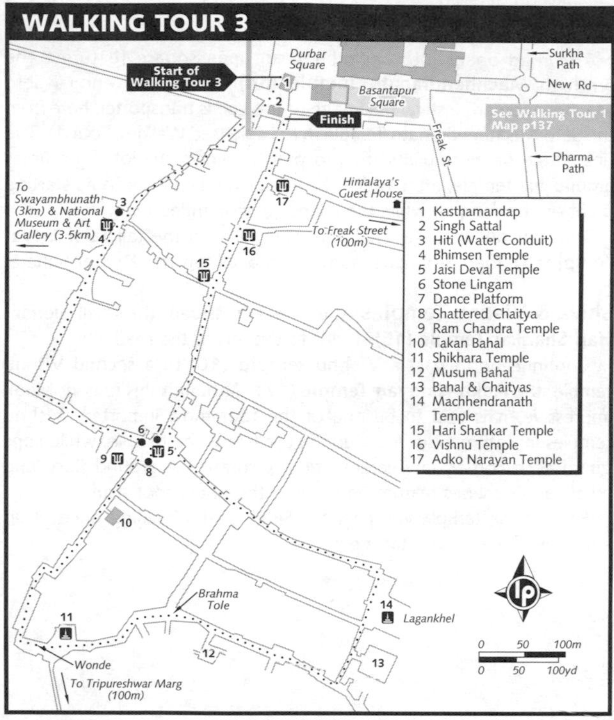

Chaitya

Ram Chandra Temple

Cross the road from the **shattered chaitya (8)** and enter the courtyard of the **Ram Chandra Temple (9)**. This small temple is notable for the tiny erotic scenes on its roof struts. This is straightforward sex and no funny business; it looks as if the carver set out to illustrate 16 different positions, starting with the missionary position, and just about made it before running out of ideas.

Takan Bahal

Machhendranath Temple There is a series of bahals on the next stretch of the walk but most are of little interest. Cross the road from the Ram Chandra Temple and enter the small courtyard of the **Takan Bahal (10)**. The surprisingly large 14th-century stupa in the centre has recently been restored and is now in fine condition.

Shikhara Temple

Musum Bahal

The road continues with a few slight bends then turns sharply left (east) at Wonde junction, which is marked by several temples, including a taller **shikhara temple (11)**. If you take the downhill road leading from this junction (and off the Walking Tour 3 map) you merge on to Tripureshwar Marg, just beyond the Vishnumati River bridge. The walk continues past Bramha Tole to the **Musum Bahal (12)**, with its four ancient Licchavi chaityas and a caged-in well. Turn sharp left (north) at the next main junction and look out for a large, open **bahal** and many **chaityas (13)**.

The road opens into Lagankhel, an open square featuring the 5m-high **Machhendranath Temple (14)**. During the annual Seto Machhendranath festival the image of the god is transported here from the Seto Machhendranath Temple in Kel Tole (see Walking Tour 1). The final stage of the procession is to pull the god's chariot three times around the temple, after which the image is taken back to its starting point on a palanquin while the chariot is dismantled here.

Turn left out of Lagankhel and walk back to the tall **Jaisi Deval Temple (5)**, then turn right (north-east) back towards Durbar Square.

Shiva & Vishnu Temples At the next crossroads the small, slender **Hari Shankar Temple (15)** stands to the left of the road.

Continue north past a **Vishnu temple (16)** to a second Vishnu temple, the **Adko Narayan Temple (17)**. Although this may not look impressive, it is said to be one of the four most important Vishnu temples in Kathmandu. A Garuda figure fronts the temple, while lions guard each corner, tiny ceramic tiles decorate the ground floor and mildly erotic scenes feature on some of the upper roof struts.

Beyond the temple you pass the Singh Sattal building once again and arrive back at the starting point.

- Chaityas
- Machhendranath Temple
- Jaisi Deval Temple
- Hari Shankar Temple
- Vishnu Temple
- Adko Narayan Temple

Finish

[Continued from page 135]

FREAK STREET (JOCHNE)

Freak St, Kathmandu's famous street from the old hippie days of the late 1960s and early 1970s, runs south from Basantapur Square. Its real name is Jochne, and it is better known by that name these days. In its hippie prime this was the place for cheap hotels, colourful restaurants, hashish shops, moneychangers and, of course, the weird and wonderful 'freaks' who gave the street its name. In those days Freak St was one of the great gathering places on 'the road east'.

Times change and Freak St today is a pale shadow of its former self, and while there are still cheap hotels and restaurants, it's the Thamel area in the north of the city

Kumari Devi

Not only does Nepal have countless gods, goddesses, deities, Bodhisattvas (near Buddhas), avatars and manifestations, which are worshipped and revered as statues, images, paintings and symbols, but it also has a real living goddess. The Kumari Devi is a young girl who lives in the building known as the Kumari Bahal, right beside Kathmandu's Durbar Square.

The practice of having a living goddess probably came about during the reign of Jaya Prakash Malla, the last of the Malla kings of Kathmandu, whose reign abruptly ended with the conquest of the valley by Prithvi Narayan Shah in 1768. As usual in Nepal, where there is never one simple answer to any question, there are a number of legends about the Kumari.

One such legend relates that a Malla king had intercourse with a pre-pubescent girl. She died as a result of this and in penance he started the practice of venerating a young girl as a living goddess. Another tells of a Malla king who regularly played dice with the goddess Taleju, the protective deity of the valley. When he made an unseemly advance she threatened to withdraw her protection, but relented and promised to return in the form of a young girl. Yet another tells of a young girl who was possessed by the goddess Durga and banished from the kingdom. When the furious queen heard of this she ordered her husband to bring the young girl back and keep her as a real goddess.

Whatever the background, in reality there are a number of living goddesses around the Kathmandu Valley, although the Kumari Devi, or Royal Kumari, is the most important. The Kumari is selected from a particular caste of Newari gold and silversmiths. Customarily, she is somewhere between four years old and puberty and must meet 32 strict physical requirements ranging from the colour of her eyes and shape of her teeth to the sound of her voice. Her horoscope must also be appropriate, of course.

Once suitable candidates have been found they are gathered together in a darkened room where terrifying noises are made, while men dance by in horrific masks and gruesome buffalo heads are on display. Naturally these goings-on are unlikely to frighten a real goddess, particularly one who is an incarnation of Durga, so the young girl who remains calm and collected throughout this ordeal is clearly the new Kumari. In a process similar to the selection of the Dalai Lama, the Kumari then chooses items of clothing and decoration worn by her predecessor as a final test.

Once chosen as the Kumari, the young girl moves in to the Kumari Bahal with her family and makes only a half-dozen ceremonial forays into the outside world each year. The most spectacular of these occasions is the September Indra Jatra festival, when she travels through the city on a huge temple chariot over a three-day period. During this festival the Kumari customarily blesses the king of Nepal, and it is curious that Prithvi Narayan Shah's defeat of the Malla kingdoms took place at this time, just as if the goddess Taleju had indeed withdrawn her protection over the valley. The new king was blessed by the Kumari and the custom continued without skipping a beat!

The Kumari's reign ends with her first period, or any serious accidental loss of blood. Once this first sign of puberty is reached she reverts to the status of a normal mortal, and the search must start for a new Kumari. During her time as a goddess the Kumari is supported by the temple income and on retirement she is paid a handsome dowry. It is said that marrying an ex-Kumari is unlucky, but it's more likely believed that taking on a spoilt ex-goddess is likely to be hard work!

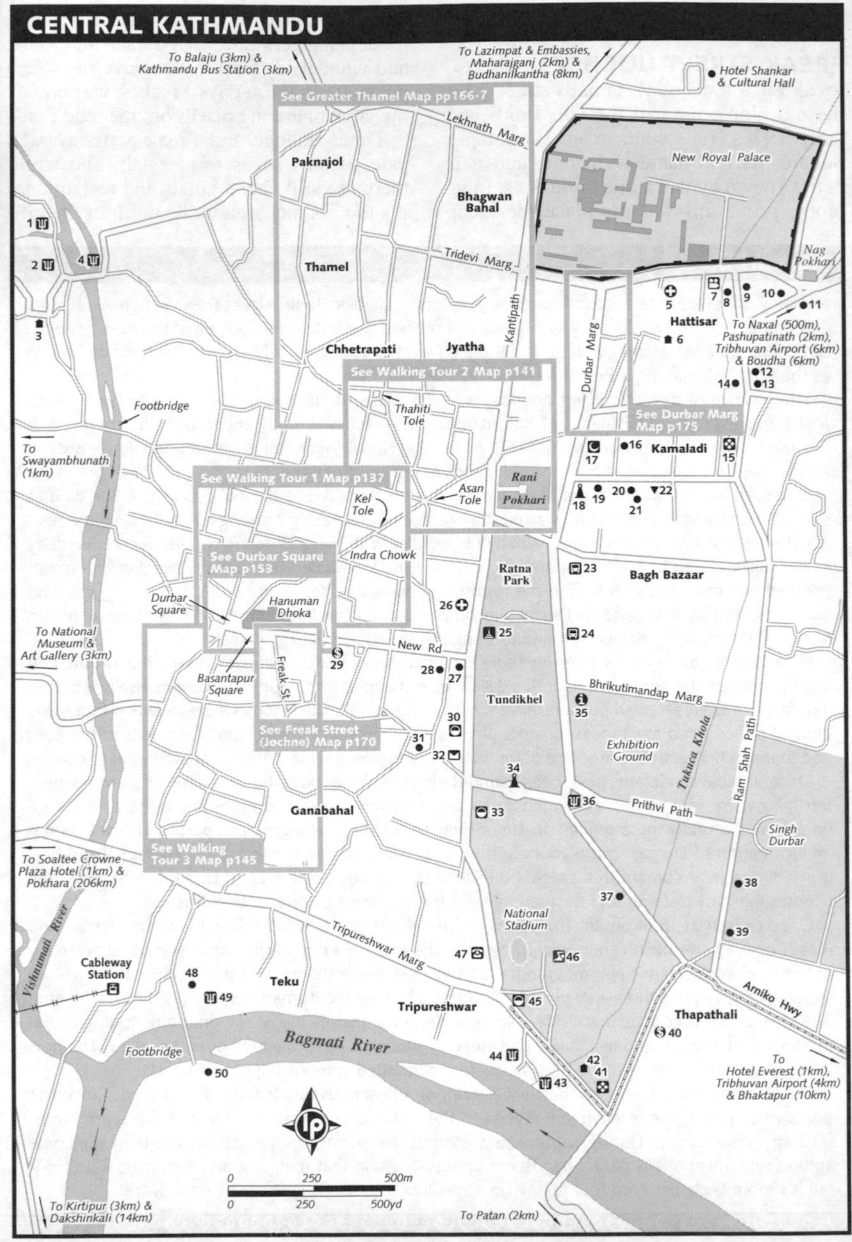
CENTRAL KATHMANDU
To Balaju (3km) & Kathmandu Bus Station (3km)
To Lazimpat & Embassies, Maharajganj (2km) & Budhanilkantha (8km)
Hotel Shankar & Cultural Hall
See Greater Thamel Map pp166-7
Lekhnath Marg
New Royal Palace
Paknajol
Bhagwan Bahal
Thamel
Tridevi Marg
Nag Pokhari
Kantipath
Durbar Marg
Hattisar
To Naxal (500m), Pashupatinath (2km), Tribhuvan Airport (6km) & Boudha (6km)
Chhetrapati
Jyatha
See Walking Tour 2 Map p141
Thahiti Tole
Footbridge
See Durbar Marg Map p175
To Swayambhunath (1km)
Kamaladi
Rani Pokhari
See Walking Tour 1 Map p137
Kel Tole
Asan Tole
Indra Chowk
See Durbar Square Map p153
Ratna Park
Bagh Bazaar
Hanuman Dhoka
Durbar Square
To National Museum & Art Gallery (3km)
New Rd
Freak St
Basantapur Square
Bhrikutimandap Marg
Tundikhel
See Freak Street (Jochne) Map p170
Exhibition Ground
Tukuca Khola
Ram Shah Path
Prithvi Path
Ganabahal
Singh Durbar
To Soaltee Crowne Plaza Hotel (1km) & Pokhara (206km)
See Walking Tour 3 Map p145
National Stadium
Tripureshwar Marg
Vishnumati River
Cableway Station
Teku
Tripureshwar
Arniko Hwy
Thapathali
Bagmati River
Footbridge
To Hotel Everest (1km), Tribhuvan Airport (4km) & Bhaktapur (10km)
0 250 500m
0 250 500yd
To Kirtipur (3km) & Dakshinkali (14km)
To Patan (2km)

CENTRAL KATHMANDU

PLACES TO STAY
3 Hotel Vajra
6 Yak & Yeti Hotel; Citibank Office
42 Blue Star Hotel

PLACES TO EAT
22 Bhanchha Ghar Restaurant

OTHER
1 Shobabaghwati Temple
2 Bijeshwari Temple
4 Indrani Temple
5 Nepal International Clinic
7 Jaya Nepal Cinema
8 PIA; Gulf Air; Buddha Air
9 Mountain Air
10 Nepal Mountaineering Association
11 Biman Bangladesh Airlines
12 China Airlines
13 Shangri-La Air
14 Air India; Indian Airlines; Gorkha Airlines; Skyline Airways
15 Kathmandu Plaza; Kathmandu Mini Vision
16 Heritage Plaza; Moon Sun Disco; Transavia
17 Mosque
18 Clocktower
19 Austrian Airlines; Lauda Airlines
20 DHL; Aeroflot
21 Himalayan Buddhist Meditation Centre
23 Minibuses for Bhaktapur
24 City Bus Station
25 Mahakala Temple
26 Bir Hospital
27 RNAC (International & Domestic Tourist Flights)
28 RNAC (Other Domestic Flights)
29 Nepal Bank
30 Tempos to Patan & Boudha
31 Bhimsen Tower
32 Main Post Office
33 Buses for Pharping & Dakshinkali
34 Martyr's Memorial Gate
35 Tourist Service Centre; Immigration Office
36 Bhadrakali Temple
37 Army Headquarters
38 Supreme Court
39 National Archives
40 Nepal Rastra Bank
41 Bluebird Supermarket
43 Kalmochan Temple
44 Tripureshwar Mahadev Temple
45 Bhaktapur Trolleybus Terminus
46 Swimming Pool
47 Central Telegraph Office
48 Pachali Bhairab
49 Tindeval Temple
50 Raj Ghat

that is the main gathering place for travellers. However, for those people who find Thamel altogether too much of a scene, Freak St offers a quiet and interesting alternative. Its recent historical connections are interesting, and it is right in the heart of old Kathmandu where real life continues.

THREE GODDESSES TEMPLES

Next to the modern Sanchaya Kosh Bhawan shopping centre in Thamel are the Three Goddesses Temples. The street on which the temples are located is named Tridevi Marg – *tri* means 'three' and *devi* means 'goddesses'. The goddesses are Dakshinkali, Mankamna and Jawalamai, and the temples are most interesting for the roof struts, on which erotic carvings illustrate some interesting positions.

MAHAKALA TEMPLE

On the eastern side of Kantipath, just north of New Rd, Mahakala Temple was very badly damaged in the 1934 earthquake and is of little architectural merit following its reconstruction. If you can see inside the darkened shrine you may be able to make out the 1.5m-high figure of Mahakala, the Great Black One, a particularly ferocious form of Shiva. *Kal* means 'death' as well as 'black' in Nepali so it can also be described as the Temple of Great Death. The Tantric god has Buddhist as well as Hindu followers.

You can climb to the top of one of the buildings around the courtyard to look over the Tundikhel parade ground.

BHIMSEN TOWER

This white, minaret-like watchtower is also known as Sundhara and is a useful landmark although it's of no importance. It stands near the main post office and was originally built by a Rana prime minister. It was rebuilt after being severely damaged in the 1934 earthquake.

PACHALI BHAIRAB

Between Tripureshwar Marg and the Bagmati River is a huge and ancient pipal tree. The tree forms a sanctuary for the image of Pachali, which is surrounded by tridents. Nearby lies what some believe to be the brass body of Baital, another of Shiva's manifestations. Others believe it is Surya, the sun god. Worshippers gather here on Tuesday and Saturday, and it is particularly busy here during the festival of Pachali Bhairab Jatra (see the Festivals of Nepal special section in the Facts for the Visitor chapter).

NATIONAL MUSEUM & ART GALLERY

West of Thamel and not far from Swayambhunath, the National Museum is a bit disappointing, but the Art Gallery has a fine collection of religious art. A visit can easily be combined with a trip to Swayambhunath.

The museum has a rather eccentric collection that includes some moon rock, a number of moth-eaten, stuffed animals, a vast number of uniforms and military decorations, swords and guns, and a portrait gallery. The most interesting museum exhibit is a leather Tibetan cannon; the most eccentric is an electrical contraption that fires a normal rifle.

The gallery displays a number of treasures. There's a superb collection of statues and carvings (stone, wood, bronze and terracotta) – some pieces date to the 1st century BC. A visit is a must.

Also worth a look is the new gallery of Buddhist art, which has separate sections on Terai and Kathmandu art.

The museum is open from 9.30 am to 4 pm Tuesday to Saturday from May to September, and 9.30 am to 3 pm from October to April. Ticket sales stop an hour before closing time; entry is Rs 50, plus Rs 50 for a camera. Bags must be deposited at the gate.

ACTIVITIES

Pools & Fitness Centres

Generally, pools in the major hotels can be used by friends of hotel guests, or at some hotels (such as Hotel de l'Annapurna) by outsiders, for a US$2 to US$3 charge.

There are public pools at Balaju, northwest of Thamel, and at the National Stadium, in the south of Kathmandu, although they close from October to February. A swim at the National Stadium pool costs Rs 15; it is

Erotic Art

The most interesting woodcarving on Nepali temples is on the roof struts, and on many temples these carvings include erotic scenes. These scenes are rarely the central carving on the strut, they're usually the smaller carving at the bottom of the strut, like a footnote to the larger image. Nor are the carvings sensuous and finely sculptured like those at Khajuraho and Konark in India. In Nepal the figures are often smaller and cruder, even quite cartoon-like.

The themes have a Tantric element, a clear connection to the intermingling of Tibetan Buddhist and Hindu beliefs in Nepal, but their real purpose is unclear. Are they simply a celebration of an important part of the lifecycle? Are they simply a more explicit reference to Shiva's and Parvati's creative roles than the enigmatic lingams and yonis scattered around so many temples? Or are they supposed to play some sort of protective role for the temple? It's popularly rumoured that the goddess of lightning is a shy virgin who wouldn't dream of striking a temple with such goings-on, although that's probably more a tourist-guide tale than anything else.

Whatever the reason for their existence, the Tantric elements can be found on temples in all three of the major towns of the valley. Some temples may reveal just the odd depiction while on others something will be depicted on every roof strut. The activities range from straightforward exhibitionism to scenes of couples engaged in often quite athletic acts of intercourse. More exotic carvings include *ménages à trois* scenes of oral or anal intercourse or couplings with demons or animals. Temples in Kathmandu Valley with some of the more interesting erotic carvings include the following.

Kathmandu

In Durbar Square there are carvings on many of the roof struts of the Jagannath Temple, just outside the entrance to Hanuman Dhoka (the old Royal Palace). The palace's lofty Basantapur Tower, overlooking Basantapur Square, has some of the finest erotic carvings on its roof struts. The large Shiva temple, Maju Deval Temple (also known as Mahadev Temple), in the middle of the square, has some erotic carved struts.

open from 10 am to 5 pm daily and Monday is reserved for women. The Balaju pool only costs Rs 10, but it can get very crowded.

A recommended health club for aerobic classes is Banu's Total Fitness (☎ 434024, ⓔ ahmed@wlink.com.np), in Kamal Pokhari. A number of the five-star hotels, such as the Radisson, north of the new Royal Palace, have fitness centres.

Hot-Air Ballooning

On a clear day hot-air ballooning is a breathtaking way to view the vast expanse of the Himalaya – from over 2000m up – and it's a chance to get some clean air!

Flights take place daily during the main tourist season (October to November), and, depending on the wind, fly either east to west or vice versa over the city. It's an amazing experience, although crossing right over the international airport is a little unnerving. The rice field landings usually attract a huge, excited and curious crowd of local villagers.

The cost of a one-hour flight is US$195 per person, which includes transport to and from your hotel and a buffet breakfast at a Thamel restaurant. For bookings contact a travel agent or Balloon Sunrise Nepal (☎ 424131, ⓔ balloon@sunrise.mos.com.np).

Golf

At Gokarna, east of Boudha (Bodhnath), the nine-hole Gokarna Forest Gold Resort (☎ 450444, ⓔ gokarna@mos.com.np) has a beautiful setting in one of the valley's few remaining forested areas. The course is mainly for members, but it is open to the public at a price: US$40/50 weekdays/weekends; there are clubs, shoes and caddies for hire.

[Continued on page 163]

Erotic Art

North of the centre, near the restaurant and guesthouse centre of Thamel, the Three Goddesses Temples – dedicated to Dakshinkali, Mankamna and Jawalamai – have a number of interesting roof struts. The Indrani Temple (see the Central Kathmandu map), on the east bank of the Vishnumati River (when crossing from Thamel to Swayambhunath) is also has interesting scenes. South of Durbar Square the small Ram Chandra Temple (see Walking Tour 3 map) has some tiny carvings.

Patan

In Patan's Durbar Square, the Jagannarayan (or Charnarayan) Temple is the most interesting temple in the town for erotic carvings.

Bhaktapur

Several temples in Bhaktapur have erotic scenes, including the Pashupatinath Temple in Durbar Square. There are also some carvings in the Cafe Nyatapola, in Taumadhi Tole, where the soaring five-storey Nyatapola Temple is located. The Dattatraya Temple, near the Pujari Math monastery in the eastern part of town, also has relief figures around its base.

Elsewhere in the Valley

There are many other temples with erotic artwork around the valley. Dedicated to Ganesh, the Jal Binayak Temple at Chobar Gorge just south of Patan has many interesting roof struts, as does the Gokarna Mahadev Temple, north-east of Boudha (Bodhnath). Other temples worth inspecting include the small Ajima, or Shitala Mai Temple in Balaju's Mahendra Park near the sleeping Vishnu figure and the Bagh Bhairab Temple in Kirtipur, west of Patan.

Several temples in and around Pashupatinath are ornamented with erotic scenes but non-Hindus aren't permitted to enter the temple courtyards to see them. En route to Pashupatinath, however, you can visit the Mahadev Gyaneshwar in Deopatan, the village by Pashupatinath.

DURBAR SQUARE (KATHMANDU)

Inset: Hanuman Dhoka (Old Royal Palace) in Durbar Square, Kathmandu (Photo: Sara-Jane Cleland)

In Nepali *durbar* means 'palace', and in Kathmandu, as well as Patan and Bhaktapur, there are durbar squares in front of the old palaces. The king no longer lives in the Hanuman Dhoka (old Royal Palace) in Kathmandu – the palace was moved north to Narayanhiti about a century ago. At that time it was on the edge of the city, now it's close to the popular tourist area of Thamel. Clustered around the central Durbar Square are the Hanuman Dhoka, numerous interesting temples, the Kumari Bahal (House of the Living Goddess) along with Kumari Chowk, and the Kasthamandap (House of Wood).

It's easy to spend hours wandering around the often crowded Durbar Square and the adjoining Basantapur Square. This is very much the centre of old Kathmandu and watching the world go by from the terraced platforms of the towering Maju Deval is a wonderful way to get a feel for the city. Although many of the buildings around the square are very old, a great deal of damage was caused by the great earthquake of 1934 and many were rebuilt, not always in their original form.

The Durbar Square area is actually made up of three loosely linked squares. To the south is the open Basantapur Square area, off which runs Freak St. The main Durbar Square area, with its popular watch-the-world-go-by temples, is to the west. Running north-east is a second part of Durbar Square, which contains the entrance to the Hanuman Dhoka and an assortment of temples. From this open area Makhan Tole, at one time the main road in Kathmandu and still the most interesting street to walk down, continues north-east.

A good place to start an exploration of the square is with what may well be the oldest building in the valley, the unprepossessing Kasthamandap. Note that the numbers in the following section correspond to item numbers on the key for the Durbar Square (Kathmandu) map.

Kasthamandap (35) In the south-western corner of the square, the Kasthamandap is the building that gave Kathmandu its name. Although its history is uncertain, it was possibly constructed around the 12th century. A legend relates that the whole building was constructed with the wood from a single sal tree. At first it was a community centre where visitors gathered before major ceremonies, but later it was converted to a temple dedicated to Gorakhnath.

Kasthamandap

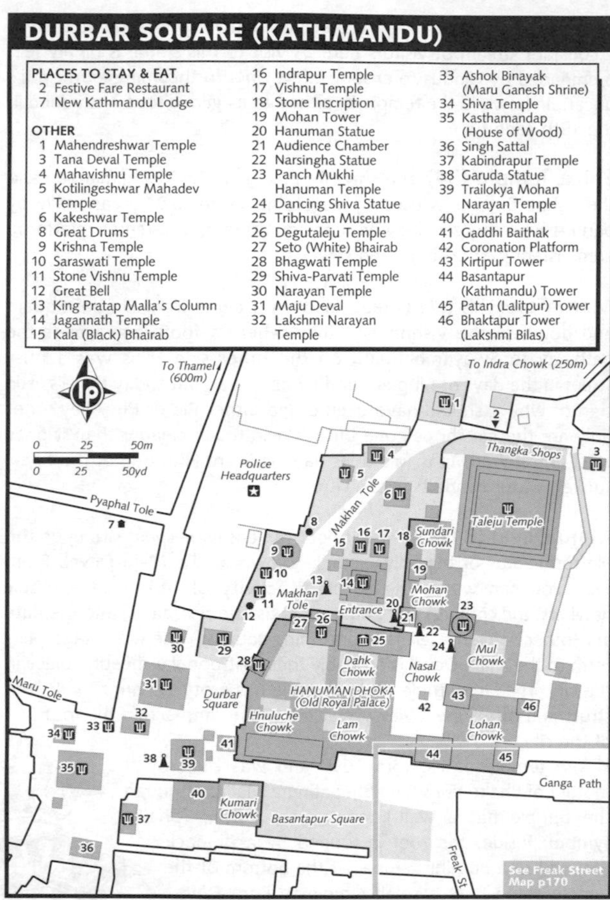

A small wooden enclosure in the centre of the building houses the image of the god. Images of Ganesh can be found at each corner of the building, and there are also shrines to a number of other gods. Bronze lions guard the entrance and Hindu epics are illustrated around the 1st-floor cornices of the three-storey building.

The squat, medieval-looking building is busy in the early-morning hours when porters sit here waiting for customers.

Ashok Binayak (33) On the northern side of the Kasthamandap, at the top of Maru Tole (the laneway down to the river), stands the tiny Ashok Binayak, or Maru Ganesh Shrine. The small size of this shrine belies its importance, as this is one of the four most important

Ganesh shrines in the valley. Ganesh is a much-loved god and there is a constant stream of visitors here. A visit to this shrine is highly recommended by Hindus to ensure safety on a forthcoming journey. It's uncertain how old the temple is, although its gilded roof was added in the 19th century.

Shiva Temple (34) The Shiva Temple near the Kasthamandap and the Ashok Binayak is used by vegetable sellers, and occasionally by barbers who can generally be seen squatting on the temple platform, administering 'short back and sides'.

Maru Tole This *tole* (street) leads you away from Durbar Square and down to the Vishnumati River where a footbridge meets the pathway to Swayambhunath on the other side. This was a busy street in the days of hippies and flower power, but today there's little sign of why it should have been called either Pie or Pig Alley – not only are the pie shops gone but it's also much cleaner than it once was. One thing Maru Tole does have is Maru Hiti, one of the finest sunken water conduits in the city.

Maju Deval (31) A pleasant hour can easily be spent sitting on the platform steps of the Shiva temple known as the Maju Deval. From here you can watch the constant activity of fruit-and-vegetable hawkers, the comings and goings of taxis and rickshaws, and the flute and other souvenir sellers importuning tourists. The nine-stage platform of the Maju Deval is probably the most popular meeting place in the city. The large, triple-roofed temple has erotic carvings on its roof struts and offers great views over the square and across the roofs of the city.

The temple dates from 1690 and was built by the mother of Bhaktapur's King Bhupatindra Malla. Although the temple has a well-known Shiva *lingam* (phallic symbol) inside, the roof is topped by a pinnacle shaped like a Buddhist stupa. At the bottom of the temple stairway is a small temple to Kam Dev, a 'companion' of Shiva. It was built in the Indian *shikhara* style, with a tall corncob-like spire.

Trailokya Mohan Narayan Temple (39) The other temple standing in the open area of the square is the smaller Trailokya Mohan Narayan. This temple has five-tiers and was built by Prithvibendra Malla in 1680. It is easily identified as a temple to Narayan, or Vishnu, by the fine Garuda kneeling before it. The Garuda figure was a later addition, erected by the king's widow soon after his death. Look for the

Maju Deval

Vaishnavite images on the carved roof struts and the window screens with their decoratively carved medallions.

Shiva-Parvati Temple (29) From the steps of the Maju Deval you can look across the square to the Shiva-Parvati Temple, where images of Shiva and his consort look out from the upstairs window on the comings and goings below them. The temple was built in the late 1700s by Bahadur Shah, the son of Prithvi Narayan Shah. Although the temple is not very old by Kathmandu standards, it stands on a two-stage platform, which may have been an open dancing stage hundreds of years earlier. A Narayan (Vishnu) temple stands to one side of it.

Kumari Bahal (40) At the junction of Durbar and Basantapur Squares is a white, three-storey building with intricately carved windows. The Kumari Bahal (House of the Living Goddess) faces Durbar Square, its door guarded by stone lions. The building, in the style of the courtyarded Buddhist *viharas* (abodes) of the valley, was built in 1757 by Jaya Prakash Malla. Inside lives the young girl (the Kumari), who is selected to be the town's living goddess until she reaches puberty and reverts to being a normal mortal! (See the boxed text 'Kumari Devi' in the Kathmandu chapter.)

Inside the building the three-storey courtyard, or Kumari Chowk, is enclosed by magnificently carved wooden balconies and windows. Photographing the goddess is forbidden, but you are quite free to photograph the courtyard when she is not present. Westerners, however are not allowed to go beyond this area. The courtyard contains a miniature stupa carrying the symbols of Saraswati, the goddess of learning.

Miniature stupa within the Kumari Bahal

The big gate beside the Kumari Bahal serves to conceals the huge chariot that takes the Kumari around the city of Kathmandu once a year, an annual festival that was begun during the rule of Jaya Prakash Malla.

Gaddhi Baithak (41) The eastern side of Durbar Square is closed off by this white neoclassical building. The Gaddi Baithak, with its imported European style, was built as part of the palace during the Rana period and it makes a strange contrast to the traditional Nepali architecture that dominates the square.

Bhagwati Temple (28) Next to the Gaddi Baithak, this triple-storey, triple-roofed temple is easily missed since it surmounts the building below it, which has *thangka* (religious Tibetan painting in cloth) shops along its front. The best view of the temple with its golden roofs is probably from the Maju Deval, across the square. The temple was built by Jagat Jaya Malla and originally had an image of Narayan. This image was stolen in 1766, so when Prithvi Narayan Shah conquered the valley two years later he simply substituted it with an image of the goddess Bhagwati, which he just happened to be toting around with him. In April each year the image of the goddess is conveyed to the village of Nuwakot, 65km to the north, then returned a few days later.

Notice the succession of interesting buildings and statues that stand to the north-east of Bhagwati Temple.

Great Bell (12) On your left as you leave the main square along Makhan Tole is the Great Bell, erected by Rana Bahadur Shah (son of Prithvi Narayan Shah) in 1797. During the Malla era a novel addition to one of the valley's durbar squares would almost immediately be imitated in another. Curiously, Patan and Bhaktapur got their bells in 1736, while the Kathmandu version did not follow until long after the fall of the Mallas. The bell's ring will drive off evil spirits, but it is only rung during *puja* (worship) at the Degutaleju Temple (26).

Stone Vishnu Temple (11) Next to the bell is a small stone Vishnu temple about which very little is known. It was badly damaged by the earthquake of 1934 and has only recently been restored.

Saraswati Temple (10) Next is the Saraswati Temple, which also suffered badly in the great earthquake. Prior to the quake it was over 14m high, but now is only half that height. Like the adjoining Vishnu temple, little is known about its history.

Krishna Temple (9) The history of the octagonal Krishna Temple is well documented. It was built in 1648 by Pratap Malla, perhaps as a response to Siddhinarsingh's magnificent Krishna Temple in Patan. Inside there are images of Krishna and two goddesses, which, according to a Sanskrit inscription, are modelled on the king and his two wives! The temple also has a Newari inscription, but this neglects to mention the king's little act of vanity.

Great Drums (8) & Kot Square Just beyond the temple are the Great Drums, to which a goat and a buffalo must be sacrificed twice a year. Then there is the police headquarters building, beyond which is Kot Square.

Krishna Temple

It was here that Jung Bahadur Rana perpetrated the famous 1846 massacre that led to a hundred years of Rana rule. Kot means 'armoury' or 'fort'. During the Dasain festival each year, blood again flows in Kot Square as hundreds of buffaloes and goats are sacrificed. Young soldiers are supposed to lop off each head with a single blow. The square is closed off to the public.

King Pratap Malla's Column (13) Across from the Krishna Temple is a host of smaller temples and other structures, all standing on a raised platform in front of the Hanuman Dhoka and the towering Taleju Temple. The square stone pillar, known as the Pratap Dhvaja, is topped by a statue of the famous King Pratap Malla, seated with folded hands and surrounded by his two wives and his five (including an infant) sons. He looks towards his private prayer room on the third floor of the Degutaleju Temple (26). The column was erected in 1670 by Pratap Malla and preceded the similar columns in Patan and Bhaktapur.

This area and its monuments are usually covered in hundreds if not thousands of pigeons, and you can buy packets of grain to feed them. This is Kathmandu's answer to Trafalgar Square.

Seto (White) Bhairab (27) Seto (White) Bhairab's horrible face is hidden away behind a grille opposite King Pratap Malla's column. The huge mask dates from 1794, during the reign of Rana Bahadur Shah, the third Shah dynasty king. Each September during the Indra Jatra festival the gates are swung back to reveal the mask for a few days. At that time the face is covered in flowers and rice and at the start of the festivities beer is poured through the horrific mouth. Crowds of men fight to get a drink of this blessed beer! At other times of year you can peek through the lattice to see the mask, which is used as the symbol of Royal Nepal Airlines.

Jagannath Temple (14) This temple, noted for the erotic carvings on its roof struts, is the oldest structure in this part of the square. Pratap Malla claimed to have constructed the temple during his reign, but it may actually date back to 1563, during the rule of Mahendra Malla. The temple has a three-tiered platform and two storeys. There are three doors on each side of the temple but only the centre door opens.

Kala (Black) Bhairab (15) Behind the Jagannath Temple is the large figure of Kala (Black) Bhairab. Bhairab is Shiva in his most fearsome aspect, and this huge stone image of the terrifying Kala Bhairab has six arms, wears a garland of skulls and tramples a corpse, symbolic of human ignorance. The figure is said to have been brought here by Pratap Malla, having been found in a field to the north of the city. The image was originally cut from a single stone, but the upper right-hand side has been repaired with another stone, and the sun and moon to the left and the lions at the top are later additions. It is said that telling a lie while standing before Kala Bhairab will bring instant death and it was once used as a form of trial by ordeal!

Indrapur Temple (16) Immediately to the east of horrific Bhairab stands the mysterious Indrapur Temple. This curious temple may be of great antiquity but little is known of its history. Even the god to which it is dedicated is controversial – inside there is a lingam indicating that it is a Shiva temple. However, half-buried on the southern side of the temple is a Garuda image, indicating that the temple is dedicated to Vishnu. To compound the puzzle, however, the temple's name clearly indicates it is dedicated to Indra! The temple's simple design and plain roof struts together with the lack of an identifying *torana* (pediment above the temple doors indicating the deity to which it is dedicated) give no further clues.

Vishnu Temple (17) Little is known about the adjoining Vishnu Temple. This triple-roofed temple stands on a four-level base. The roof-strut carvings and the golden image of Vishnu inside show that it is a Vishnu temple, but it is not known how old the temple is, although it was in existence during Pratap Malla's reign.

Kakeshwar Temple (6) This temple was originally built in 1681 but rebuilt after it was badly damaged in the 1934 earthquake. It may have been considerably altered at that time as the temple is a strange combination of styles. It starts with a two-level base from that rises from a lower floor (in typical Nepali style). Above the first floor, however, the temple is in the Indian shikhara style, topped by a spire shaped like a *kalasa* (water vase), indicative of a female deity.

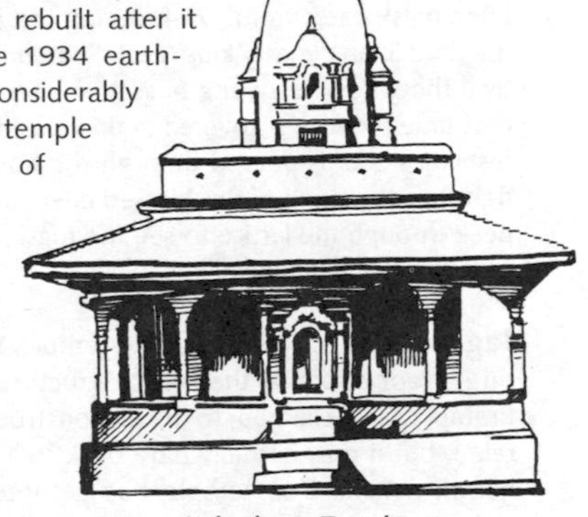

Kakeshwar Temple

Stone Inscription (18) On the outside of the palace wall, opposite the Vishnu Temple (17) is a stone inscription to the goddess Kalika written in 15 languages, including French. King Pratap Malla, renowned for his scholastic abilities, set up this inscription in 1664 and a Nepali legend relates that milk will flow from the spout in the middle if somebody is able to read all 15 languages!

Kotilingeshwar Mahadev Temple (5) This early Malla temple dates from the reign of Mahendra Malla in the 16th century. The three-stage plinth is topped by a temple in the *gumbhaj* style, which basically means a square structure topped by a dome. The bull facing the temple indicates that it is a Shiva temple.

Mahavishnu Temple (4) Built by Jagat Jaya Malla, this double-roofed temple on a four-level plinth was badly damaged in the 1934 earthquake and was not restored. Only the golden spire, topped by a golden umbrella, hints at its prior appearance.

Mahendreshwar Temple (1) At the extreme northern end of the square, this temple dates from 1561, during Mahendra Malla's reign. The temple was restored in 1963 and is dedicated to Shiva. A small image of Shiva's bull Nandi fronts the temple and at the north-eastern corner there is an image of Kam Dev. The temple has a wide, two-level plinth and a spire topped by a golden umbrella.

Taleju Temple The square's most magnificent temple stands at its north-eastern extremity but it is not open to the public. Even for Nepalis entry is restricted; they only visit the temple during the annual Dasain festival.

The Taleju Temple was built in 1564 by Mahendra Malla. Taleju Bhawani was originally a goddess from the south of India, but she became the titular deity or royal goddess of the Malla kings in the 14th century. Taleju temples were erected in her honour in Patan and Bhaktapur as well as in Kathmandu.

The temple stands on a 12-stage plinth and reaches over 35m high, not surprisingly dominating the Durbar Square area. The eighth stage of the plinth has a wall around the temple, in front of which are 12 miniature temples; four more miniature temples stand inside the wall, which has four beautifully carved wide gates. If entry to the temple were permitted it could be reached from within the Hanuman Dhoka or from the Singh Dhoka (Lion Gate) from the square.

Taleju Temple

Hanuman Dhoka Hanuman's very brave assistance to the noble Rama during the exciting events of the Ramayana has led to the monkey god's appearance guarding many important entrances. Here, cloaked in red and sheltered by an umbrella, a **Hanuman statue (20)** marks the *dhoka* (entrance) to Kathmandu's Hanuman Dhoka and has even given the palace its name. The statue dates from 1672 but the god's face has disappeared under a coating of red paste applied by faithful visitors.

Standards bearing the double-triangle flag of Nepal flank the statue, while on each side of the palace gate are stone lions, one ridden by Shiva, the other by his wife Parvati. Above the gate a brightly painted niche is illustrated, with a figure of a ferocious Tantric version of Krishna in the centre. On one side is the gentler Hindu Krishna in his traditional blue colour accompanied by two of his comely *gopis* (milkmaids). On the other side is King Pratap Malla and his queen.

The palace was originally founded during the Licchavi period, but as it stands today most of it was constructed by King Pratap Malla in the 17th century. The palace was renovated many times in later years. The oldest parts are the smaller Sundari Chowk and Mohan Chowk at the northern part of the palace (both closed). From here construction moved south and in all there are 10 *chowks* (courtyards) in the palace.

Entrance to the palace costs Rs 250 and it is open from 10.30 am to 3 pm daily (except Tuesday); from 10.30 am to 4 pm in summer.

Nasal Chowk From the entrance gate of the Hanuman Dhoka you immediately enter the most famous *chowk* (courtyard). In Nepali *nasal* means 'dancing one', and the courtyard takes its name from the **dancing Shiva statue (24)** inside the whitewashed chamber on the eastern side of the square. Although the courtyard was constructed in the Malla period many of the buildings around the square are Rana constructions. During that time Nasal Chowk became the square used for coronations, a practice that continues to this day. King Birendra was crowned in the 1975 ceremony on the **coronation platform (42)** in the centre of the courtyard. The nine-storey **Basantapur (Kathmandu) Tower (44)** looms over the southern end of the courtyard.

The rectangular courtyard is aligned north–south and the entrance is at the north-western corner. Near the entrance there is a surprisingly small and beautifully carved doorway, which once led to the Malla kings' private quarters. The panels feature images of four gods.

Beyond the door is the large **Narsingha Statue (22)**, Vishnu in his man-lion incarnation, in the act of killing a demon. The stone image was erected by Pratap Malla in 1673 and the inscription on the pedestal explains that he placed it here in

Left: Narsingha, or Vishnu, in his man-lion incarnation. The statue of this fearsome character is in the Nasal Chowk of Hanuman Dhoka (Old Royal Palace). (Photo: Paul Beinssen)

fear that he had offended Vishnu by dancing in a Narsingha costume. The Kabindrapur Temple (37) in Durbar Square was built for the same reason.

Next there is the **Audience Chamber (21)** of the Malla kings. The open verandah houses the Malla throne and portraits of the Shah kings. A golden image of Mahavishnu is set into an open verandah on the eastern wall. This image was originally in the **Mahavishnu Temple (4)** in the square, but was moved here after the 1934 earthquake.

Panch Mukhi Hanuman Temple (23) At the north-eastern corner of the Nasal Chowk stands the Panch Mukhi Hanuman with its five circular roofs. Each of the valley towns has a five-storey temple, although it is the great Nyatapola Temple of Bhaktapur that is by far the best known. Hanuman is worshipped in the temple in Kathmandu, but only the priests of the temple may enter it.

Lohan Chowk King Prithvi Narayan Shah was involved in the construction of the four red-coloured towers around the Lohan Chowk. The towers represent the four ancient cities of the valley, the towers include the **Kathmandu** or **Basantapur Tower (44)**, the **Kirtipur Tower (43)**, the **Bhaktapur Tower** or **Lakshmi Bilas (46)** and the **Patan** or **Lalitpur Tower (45)**.

The dominant nine-storey Basantapur Tower was extensively restored prior to King Birendra's coronation. A series of steep stairways climb to the top from where there are superb views over the palace and the city. The struts along the facade of the Basantapur Tower, particularly those facing out to Basantapur Square, are decorated with erotic carvings.

Mul Chowk This courtyard was completely dedicated to religious functions within the palace and is configured like a *vihara* (a dwelling place for Buddhist monks), with a two-storey building surrounding the courtyard. Mul Chowk is dedicated to Taleju Bhawani, the royal goddess of the Mallas, and sacrifices are made to her in the centre of the courtyard during the Dasain festival. A smaller Taleju temple stands in the southern wing of the square and the image of the goddess is moved here from the main temple during the Dasain festival. Images of the river goddesses, Ganga and Jamuna, guard the golden temple doorway, which is topped by a golden torana. Unfortunately, from the **Bhaktapur Tower (46)**, where visitors normally observe the courtyard, the view is less than inspiring and the temple itself cannot be seen at all.

Degutaleju Temple (26) Degutaleju is another manifestation of the Malla's personal goddess Taleju. This temple was built by Shiva Singh Malla and is integrated into the palace structure itself. The triple-roofed temple actually starts from above the common buildings it surmounts.

Mohan Chowk North of the Nasal Chowk is the residential courtyard of the Malla kings. It dates from 1649 and at one time a Malla king had to be born here to be eligible to wear the crown. The last Malla king, Jaya Prakash Malla, had great difficulties during his reign, even though he was the legitimate heir, because he was born elsewhere. The golden waterspout, known as Sun Dhara, in the centre of the courtyard delivers water from Budhanilkantha in the north of the valley. The richly sculptured spout is actually several metres below the courtyard level. The Malla kings would ritually bathe here each morning.

The courtyard is surrounded by towers at its four corners, and north of the Mohan Chowk is the small Sundari Chowk.

Tribhuvan Museum (25) The part of the palace west of Nasal Chowk, overlooking the main Durbar Square area, was principally constructed by the Ranas in the middle to late part of the 19th century. Ironically, it is now home to an interesting museum that celebrates King Tribhuvan's successful revolt against their regime. If you are interested in Nepal's modern history a visit is a must. There are some fascinating re-creations of the king's bedroom and study with genuine personal effects that give quite an eerie insight into his life. There are also lots of photos and newspaper clippings that catch the drama of his escape and his triumphant return. There are several magnificent thrones, some superb stone carvings and, oddly, a coin collection.

Entry is from Nasal Chowk, and cameras have to be deposited in lockers at the door.

[Continued from page 151]

ORGANISED TOURS

There are limited organised tours of Kathmandu and these are mostly geared towards group tours.

Grayline (☎ 413188) Operating through Nepal Travel, Grayline is the only operator with scheduled trips, and these only operate on certain days of the week, and only during the tourist season. A three-hour tour of Bhaktapur, Boudha and Pashupatinath operates on Monday, Wednesday and Friday mornings (Rs 250); three-hour tours go to Patan and Swayambhunath on Tuesday, Thursday and Sunday mornings (Rs 200); tours to Dakshinkali and Chobar Gorge go on Saturday morning (Rs 300); and four-hour afternoon tours go to Nagarkot (Rs 400) and Dhulikhel (Rs 300) daily. If there's a group of you, it's just as easy to hire a taxi for half a day.

Wayfarers Travel Service (☎ 264245, ⓔ info@wayfarers.com.np) This place offers twice-weekly, one-day guided walks of the settlements of the southern valley rim: Kirtipur, Khokana, Bungamati and Chapagaon.

PLACES TO STAY

Kathmandu has an excellent range of places to stay, from expensive international-style hotels to cheap and comfortable lodges.

This section is divided by price into budget, mid-range and top-end options, and then by location. A budget hotel or guesthouse is a place where you can get a double room for less than Rs 500, say US$7. There are quite a few where you can get a room for less than Rs 200 (US$3) and some where you can pay less than Rs 140 (US$2). Mid-range means from US$10 to US$50 a night and the top end is from US$50 up. Double rooms in the most expensive hotels in Kathmandu will cost more than US$150 a night, getting close to the nation's average annual per capita income! Quite a few hotels bridge the budget and mid-range categories by having a range of room standards – these places have been grouped according to their lowest price.

All mid-range and top-end hotels charge a VAT tax of 10% plus a tourism service charge of 2%. Almost all quote their prices in US dollars. However, at all but the most expensive places you can pay the equivalent in local currency. Where you are required to pay in hard currency (see Money in the Facts for the Visitor chapter), this means payment by either cash, travellers cheque, credit card or rupees accompanied by a foreign exchange encashment receipt. Budget places usually quote prices in rupees and rarely bung on a tax.

It is definitely worth looking around if you plan to stay for any length of time. It's difficult to recommend particular hotels, especially in the budget and middle brackets, because rooms in each hotel can vary widely. Many of these hotels have additions to additions, and while some rooms may be very gloomy and run-down others might be very pleasant. A friendly crowd of fellow travellers can also make all the difference.

For budget and mid-range places the Thamel area is the main locale, and it is something of a tourist ghetto. Its development has been rapid and uncontrolled, with ugly multistorey hotels and signboards taking the place of beautiful Newari houses. The introduction of a one-way traffic system and daily garbage collection have gone a long way to halting what seemed like an unstoppable slide into chaos and squalor, but it's still a very busy place during the high season.

The Thamel area is where the largest number of independent travellers stay. There are dozens and dozens of lodges, restaurants, Internet cafes, travel agencies and shops, and a bustling cosmopolitan atmosphere. It's still a convenient and enjoyable area to stay for a short time, especially if you want to meet fellow travellers. It can also be a welcome relief to find Western-style menus, people who speak English and hot showers at budget prices.

The name Thamel is used to describe a sprawling area with at least a dozen roads and several hundred hotels and restaurants. It is so well known and has such cachet that many places now claim Thamel as their address, even though they are in bordering areas that have traditionally had different names. The problem is partly due to the fact that these areas never had strictly defined boundaries anyway.

Despite what the hotel owners might think, many people prefer to be a bit removed from the crowded centre of Thamel. There are several places on its periphery that are close enough to be reasonably convenient but that aren't in the centre of the maelstrom.

In an attempt to establish some order, we have somewhat arbitrarily divided the greater Thamel area (see the Greater Thamel map) into: Thamel, around the two main intersections; Paknajol, to the north; Bhagwan Bahal, to the north-east; Jyatha, to the south-east; and Chhetrapati, to the south-west.

There is still a scattering of really rock-bottom places along Freak St, close to Durbar Square, and these offer the impecunious an escape from the Thamel crowds. The Freak St location is excellent, and real Newari city life continues in the surrounding side streets. Most of the accommodation options are *very* basic, but they are also among the cheapest in Kathmandu.

Mid-range places are widely scattered, with a majority in and around Thamel. Kathmandu's limited number of international-standard hotels are also widely spread, some of them quite a distance from the city centre. There's also an increasing number of mostly top-end resorts springing up around the valley. These usually offer great views and a peaceful rural atmosphere, and are less than an hour from the centre of Kathmandu. For those with the funds, they offer an alternative to being right in the city.

There is a hotel reservations' counter as soon as you get out of customs at the airport. Most of the hotels it represents are reasonably expensive, but it has a few in the US$5 to US$10 bracket, and the staff arrange free transport. If you don't feel like tackling the touts and taxis outside the main doors, this service can be useful.

Taxi drivers and hotel touts (they are often one and the same) lie in wait outside the airport terminal and around bus stations. If you ask to be taken to one of the hotels recommended in this book, you may well be told that the place in question has closed or become ridiculously expensive. Although this may be possible, it is considerably more likely that they want you to go to the hotel where they get the best commission – often more than 50% of the room price. The best solution is to take a taxi to Thamel or Freak St (Rs 200, about US$3, from the airport) and look for yourself.

During the peak times (October to November and February to April) rooms in the most popular hotels can be in short supply. Otherwise, there are so many fiercely competitive mid-range and budget places that only the really popular hotels are likely to be full. The prices given here are the high-season prices shown on hotel tariff cards. At all but the top-end hotels these prices are pure fiction, shown to you more in the hope that you might be silly enough to pay them. In reality prices are highly negotiable; 50% discounts are par for the course.

PLACES TO STAY – BUDGET

Intense competition between Kathmandu's enormous number of low-priced hostels means that you can find hot showers in even the cheapest places, although they are usually solar-heated and are only hot in the late afternoon.

Hotels in this category do not have heating, and Kathmandu in winter is a rather chilly place. In winter you'll appreciate places with a garden as it's always pleasant to sit outside during the cool, but invariably sunny, autumn and winter days. A south-facing room will mean you get some sunlight in your room. In general, the top-floor rooms are the best, as you stand a chance of getting a view and have easy access to the roof (often a nice place to relax).

Thamel

Any mention of Thamel accommodation has to start with ***Kathmandu Guest House*** *(☎ 413632, ⓔ kgh@wlink.com.np)*, the first hotel to open in the area and still one of the most popular. It also serves as the central landmark – everything is 'near the Kathmandu Guest House'. In strictly dollar terms you can get better rooms elsewhere, but most people enjoy the atmosphere and it's usually booked out weeks in advance during high season. The position is excellent and you definitely feel you're at the nerve centre, with various expeditions coming and going, trekkers looking for partners and the place a hive of activity. There's parking space for cars out the front, a very pleasant front courtyard and rear garden, a money-change desk (guests only), a storage facility for luggage and valuables, a travel desk, a hairdresser and even an art gallery upstairs – this is budget travel in the deluxe category! The cheapest rooms form part of the original 13-room guesthouse, and singles/doubles range from US$2/3 to US$10/12 with washbasin. In the newer wing, pleasant, small rooms with bathroom are US$17/20, and US$25/30 with a garden outlook. At the top of the scale are very large, modern rooms with air-con for US$50/60. There's a 12% tax on top of all these prices, and discounts are available for weekly and monthly stays.

If this is too extravagant for your budget you don't have to go far for something cheaper – there are a dozen or more places within a stone's throw. Turning south from the Kathmandu Guest House there's a cluster of hotels, starting with the ***Hotel Star*** *(☎ 414000)*, right next door, which features prominently in Kim Stanley Robinson's book *Escape from Kathmandu*. It has long been a popular alternative to the Kathmandu Guest House. The rooms are nothing special but it is quiet and quite OK. Rooms start at Rs 200/250 with shared bathroom, and Rs 350/450 with private bathroom.

The basic but good-value ***Cosy Corner Lodge*** *(☎ 428025, ⓔ stupa@wlink.com.np)* is adjacent to the Hotel Star, and has OK rooms, all with shared bathroom, at Rs 150/250.

Pheasant Lodge *(☎ 417415)* is tucked farther around the laneway, so it feels quite removed from the Thamel bustle even though it is as central as you can get. There's an atmospheric courtyard, and although the rooms are basic they're good value – which is why it's often full. Rooms are Rs 200/250.

Also close to the heart of Thamel is ***Hotel Potala*** *(☎ 419159, fax 416680)*, almost opposite KC's Restaurant. This small and friendly Tibetan-run place is cheap and cheerful, with rooms at Rs 200 and Rs 250, all with shared bathroom.

A good choice off the main street, the ***Hotel Horizon*** *(☎ 220904, ⓔ horizon@hons.com.np)* down near the bank of tapestry shops, has a range of rooms at reasonable prices, starting at Rs200/250 for fairly spartan rooms with bathroom and up to US$10 for good luxury rooms.

The very cheap ***Hotel California*** *(☎ 242076, ⓔ glocom@mos.com.np)* in the same lane, offers spartan but clean enough rooms; many have a balcony. Rooms cost Rs 200 and Rs 250 with private bathroom. Unusually for Thamel, there is also a dorm (Rs75). It's a good, friendly place.

Tucked away in the lane behind the Pumpernickel Bakery, ***Memorable Guest House*** *(☎ 419288)* hardly lives up to the name, but it's clean and convenient. Rooms are a bargain at Rs 100/125 with shared bathroom; Rs 150/200 with private bathroom.

In this same quiet back lane is ***Hotel Pacifist*** *(☎ 258320)*, which has good-sized rooms at Rs 165/220 (Rs 250 for something slightly bigger). All have private bathroom.

The main road from the centre of Kathmandu to Thamel runs into the main Thamel Chowk. Cheapies in this area include ***Hotel Puska*** *(☎ 228997, fax 250200)*, which is not great but is decent value for US$3/4 with shared bathroom or US$4/6 with private bathroom.

Closer to the centre of Thamel on the traffic-choked extension of Tridevi Marg, ***Marco Polo Guest House*** *(☎ 251914)* is popular. The rooms at the back are particularly good and there are some surprisingly pleasant rooftop patios. Doubles cost US$4; US$6 with bathroom.

The ***Student Guest House*** *(☎ 251551, ⓔ krishna@student.wlink.com.np)* is right next door, it's quiet and clean with decent-sized but somewhat dark rooms for US$5/8.

Tucked away just north of Kathmandu Guest House is ***Hotel Red Planet*** *(☎ 432879, ⓔ telstar@wlink.com.np)*, a good Thamel cheapie, and far enough off the main strip not to be noisy. Rooms are quite good value at Rs 350/450.

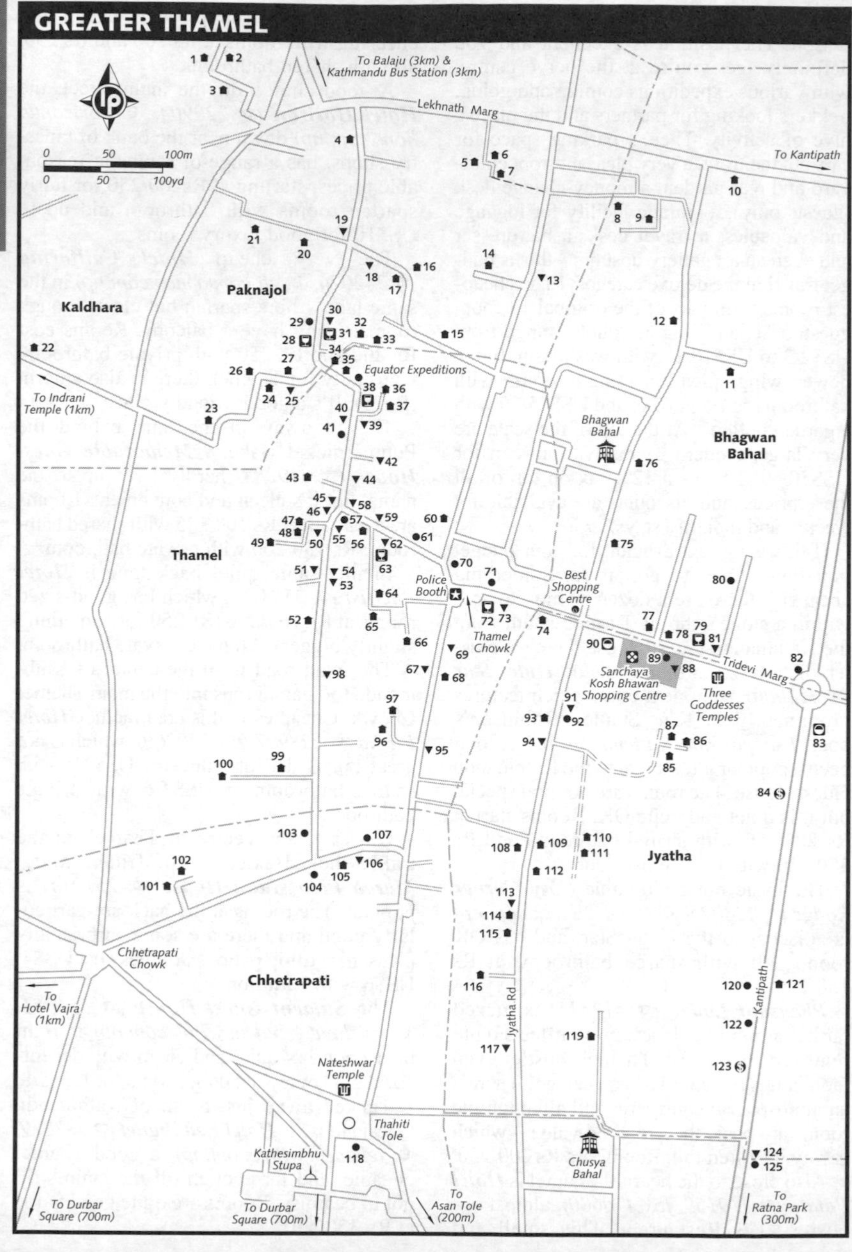
GREATER THAMEL
To Balaju (3km) & Kathmandu Bus Station (3km)
Lekhnath Marg
To Kantipath
0 50 100m
0 50 100yd
Paknajol
Kaldhara
Equator Expeditions
To Indrani Temple (1km)
Bhagwan Bahal
Bhagwan Bahal
Thamel
Police Booth
Thamel Chowk
Best Shopping Centre
Sanchaya Kosh Bhawan Shopping Centre
Tridevi Marg
Three Goddesses Temples
Jyatha
Chhetrapati Chowk
Chhetrapati
To Hotel Vajra (1km)
Jyatha Rd
Kantipath
Nateshwar Temple
Thahiti Tole
Kathesimbhu Stupa
Chusya Bahal
To Durbar Square (700m)
To Durbar Square (700m)
To Asan Tole (200m)
To Ratna Park (300m)

GREATER THAMEL

PLACES TO STAY

1 Kathmandu Garden House
2 Kathmandu Peace Guest House
3 Tibet Peace Guest House
4 Hotel Manang; Hotel Marshyangdi
5 Hotel Gauri Shankar
6 Hotel Greeting Palace
7 Hotel Pilgrims
8 Hotel Crown
9 Hotel Norbhu Linka
10 Hotel Malla
11 Hotel Yeti
12 Souvenir Guest House
14 Hotel Thamel
15 Namaskar Guest House
16 Hotel Vaishali
17 Hotel Shree Tibet
20 Hotel Lily
21 Hotel Florid
22 International Guest House
23 Hotel Tradition
24 Prince Guest House
26 Hotel Down Town
27 Holy Lodge
32 Mustang Guest House
33 Hotel Tashi Dhargey
34 Hotel Surya Central
35 Hotel Garuda
36 Acme Guest House
37 Hotel Red Planet
43 Kathmandu Guest House; Las Kus Restaurant; Dawn Till Dusk; Nepal Grindlays Bank (ATM only)
47 Hotel Star; Pub Maya
48 Cosy Corner Lodge
49 Pheasant Lodge
52 Hotel The Earth
56 Hotel Potala
60 Hotel Centre Point
64 Hotel Excelsior
65 Memorable Guest House
66 Hotel Pacifist
68 Hotel Puska
74 Marco Polo Guest House; Student Guest House
75 Hotel Earth House
76 Panda Hotel
77 Tibet Holiday Inn
78 Hotel Tilicho; Yeti Airlines
85 Hotel White Lotus
86 Mustang Holiday Inn
87 Imperial Guest House
93 Shree Guest House
96 Thorong Peak Guest House
97 Hotel Tashi Dhelek
99 Hotel California
100 Hotel Horizon
101 Tibet Guest House
102 Nirvana Hotel
105 Potala Guest House
108 Hotel Blue Diamond
109 Hotel Norling
110 Hotel Dynasty
111 Fuji Guest House
112 Hotel Utse
114 New Tibet Rest House
115 Siddhartha Guest House
116 Mt Annapurna Guest House
119 Kantipur Temple House
121 Hotel Mountain

PLACES TO EAT

13 Thamel House Restaurant
18 BK's Place
19 Thakali Banchha
25 Rum Doodle Restaurant & Bar
30 Krua Thai Restaurant
39 Nargila Restaurant; Tom & Jerry Pub
40 Northfield Cafe; Adventure Centre Nepal
42 New Orleans Cafe
44 Brezel Bakery
45 Hot Bread Outlet
46 Le Bistro Restaurant
50 Restaurant Casa Della Pasta; Paddy Foley's Irish Bar; Barnes & Noble Bookhouse
51 Third Eye Restaurant; Yin Yang Restaurant
53 Roadhouse Café; Roadhouse Inn Apartments; Wayfarers Travel Service; Nepal Grindlays Bank (ATM only); Baskin & Robbins
54 K-Too Beer & Steakhouse
55 Alice's Restaurant; Café Jalapeno
58 La Dolce Vita
59 KC's Restaurant
62 Pumpernickel Bakery
67 Cinderella Restaurant
69 Sandwich Point
73 Botega; Necon Airlines
81 Himlayan Java; Nanglo Deli; Nepal Grindlays Bank
88 Dechenling Restaurant
91 Kilroy's of Kathmandu
94 Omei Japanese Restaurant
95 Himalatte Café
98 Wiesel Bakery
106 Narayan's Steak House Restaurant
113 Chikusa
117 Dolma Momo Restaurant
124 Delicatessen Center

OTHER

28 Tunnel Club
29 Hotel Mandap
31 Sam's Bar
38 Jump Club
41 Pilgrims Book House; Pilgrims Feed N Read
57 Namche Bazaar Building
61 The Last Resort office; Himalayan Bank
63 Maya Cocktail Bar
70 Bicycle Hire & Souvenir Stalls
71 Himalayan Holistic Healing Centre
72 Underground Bar
79 Studio 54
80 Sita World Travel; Western Union
82 Kaiser Library
83 Bus Stop for Pokhara Tourist Buses
84 Nepal Grindlays Bank
89 Bookworld
90 Taxi & Autorickshaw Stand
92 KEEP; Trekkers' Information Centre; Travellers' Information Centre; Himalayan Rescue Association; Himalayan Explorers Club
103 Amrita Craft Collection
104 Walden Book House
107 Nepal Colour Lab
118 Lucky Traveller Service
120 Jyoti Bhawan
122 Qatar Airlines
123 Nepal Arab Bank
125 Mandala Bookpoint

Paknajol

This area lies to the north of Thamel and can be reached by continuing north from the Kathmandu Guest House, or by approaching on Lekhnath Marg.

Tucked away down an inconspicuous laneway, ***Mustang Guest House*** *(☎ 426053, ⓔ chitaure@mos.com.np)* is good value, with pleasant, quiet rooms. Singles/doubles are Rs 140/180 with shared bathroom; Rs 200/250 with private bathroom.

The ***Hotel Surya Central*** *(☎ 439246, ⓔ intelcom@vishnu.ccsl.com.np)*, nearby is a surprisingly quiet hotel given its location overlooking one of the main Thamel thoroughfares. Rooms start at Rs 400 with private bathroom and go right up to US$25.

Down a lane to the west is ***Hotel Florid*** *(☎ 416155, ⓔ florid@wlink.com.np)*. There is a small garden at the rear and no buildings behind so there's a feeling of space that is often lacking in Thamel. The rooms are small but OK, and cost US$5/7 with shared bathroom; US$8/12 with private bathroom.

Nearby is the pleasant ***Hotel Lily*** *(☎ 426264, ⓔ lily@ccsl.com.np)* with the obligatory rooftop garden and furnished rooms. Rates are US$15/20 with private bathroom, but discounts bring this price down considerably.

The ***Namaskar Guest House*** *(☎ 420160, ⓔ madu18@hotmail.com)* in the same lane, on the other side of Hotel Vaishali, is another good place. This clean and comfortable place offers good value at Rs 200/250 with private bathroom.

Not far from the steep Paknajol intersection with Lekhnath Marg (north-west of Thamel) there are a few pleasant guesthouses. They're away from traffic, a short walk from Thamel (but it could be a million miles), and they have beautiful views across the valley towards Balaju and Swayambhunath.

Tibet Peace Guest House *(☎ 415026, ⓔ tpghouse@wlink.com.np)* is friendly, small and family-run. This place offers well-equipped rooms with lockers, bathrooms and phones. Rooms cost from Rs 350 to Rs 500, and there's a small restaurant.

The ***Kathmandu Peace Guest House*** *(☎ 439369, ⓔ ktmpeacegh@visitnepal.com)* at the end of the road, has rooms starting at US$8/12 with shared bathroom; US$12/16 with private bathroom, TV, fan and phone – this represents not bad value in this range.

The new, popular ***Kathmandu Garden House*** *(☎ 415239, ⓔ hmtql@ccsl.com.np)*, opposite, offers excellent-value doubles at the cost of Rs 200 with shared bathroom and Rs 400 with private bathroom. The views are excellent and the garden is good for relaxing.

Back in Paknajol, head south-west from the Hotel Garuda to find several reasonable cheapies. Neat, clean rooms at ***Holy Lodge*** *(☎ 416265, ⓔ holylodge@wlink.com.np)* cost from Rs 200/300 without bathroom to Rs 500/700 with bathroom.

One door down, the ***Hotel Down Town*** *(☎ 430471, ⓔ downtown@wlink.com.np)* is a new but fairly standard Thamel hotel, with good-sized rooms ranging from US$5/7 with shared bathroom up to US$13/15 for deluxe rooms.

Across the road is ***Prince Guest House*** *(☎ 414456, ⓔ glocom@mos.com.np)*, which is a very decent budget place, with pleasant rooftop and rear gardens. Rooms cost US$6/8 with bathroom and phone.

There's a small group of hotels built around a cul de sac south off Lekhnath Marg. The clean ***Hotel Pilgrims*** *(☎ 416910, ⓔ hotel@pilgrims.wlink.com.np)* is undistinguished (especially some of the dark single rooms), but the place is well managed and provides pretty good value for money. Rooms are US$10/15 with shared bathroom; US$20/25 with private bathroom. As ever, the prices are highly negotiable.

In the same group is the popular ***Hotel Greeting Palace*** *(☎ 417212, fax 426597)*, which offers good-sized carpeted rooms for US$10/15 and deluxe (meaning with TV and slightly larger) for US$15/25, but nobody pays that much. With smallish rooms the ***Hotel Gauri Shankar*** *(☎ 417181, ⓔ hgshankar@wlink.com.np)* is otherwise OK with rooms for US$15/20; US$2 more with breakfast included.

Bhagwan Bahal

This area to the north-east of Thamel takes its name from a Buddhist monastery. Some travellers like the area because it is much quieter than Thamel proper, and has not yet been completely taken over by restaurants, souvenir shops and travel agencies. For a mid-range place with budget prices (after the discount) see Hotel Crown under Places to Stay – Mid-Range following.

Hotel Earth House *(☎ 418197, fax 41635)*, just off Tridevi Marg, is a good budget hotel that is already starting to show its age. However, it does have friendly staff, a nice rooftop garden and a variety of clean and decent rooms. Singles/doubles start at US$4/6 and can go as high as US$10/16. The rooms at the back are best.

Panda Hotel *(☎ 424683, fax 425657)* is a little beyond the Earth House. The front rooms with balconies are good value; others can be dark so check first. Rooms with shared bathroom are US$4/8; US$8/10 with private bathroom.

A little farther north is the ***Souvenir Guest House*** *(☎ 410277)*, on the way to Hotel Malla, which is small but has a nice garden. Rooms are US$3/4 with shared bathroom and US$4/5 with private bathroom, but in the high season the prices are US$5/8 and US$8/15 respectively.

As you head north, turn right (east) just before the Souvenir to find the ***Hotel Yeti*** *(☎ 414858, ⓔ adventure@mos.com.np)*, which is a reasonable place with a garden and sunny rooms. Rooms with shared bathroom are US$8/10, US$12/16 with private bathroom, but unless things are really busy you should get a room for less.

Jyatha

The neighbourhood to the south-east of Thamel has traditionally been known as Jyatha, but the word is increasingly used to describe the main north–south road that runs into the western end of Tridevi Marg. For a mid-range hotel at budget prices see Hotel White Lotus under this heading in Places to Stay – Mid-Range following.

Head south along Jyatha Rd for the basic, cheap and friendly ***Shree Guest House*** *(☎ 256105, ⓔ joshi@vishnu.ccsl.com.np)*. Singles/doubles cost Rs 200/250 with private bathroom.

Farther south is ***Hotel Blue Diamond*** *(☎ 226320, fax 226392)*, which has rooms with fan and bathroom for US$12/15; US$18/22 with air-con. It's a fairly modern place, set well back from the street. It's popular with tour groups.

The ***New Tibet Rest House*** *(☎ 225319, ⓔ sunny@sunnytrv.mos.com.np)* is run by the same people that run the popular Tibet Guest House in Chhetrapati. Rooms are US$6/10 with shared bathroom; US$10/15 with private bathroom.

A bit farther south is ***Siddhartha Guest House*** *(☎ 227119)*, with a small garden with fruit trees. Rooms are standard for Thamel and cost US$5 for a double with shared bathroom; US$8/12 for singles/doubles with private bathroom.

Mt Annapurna Guest House *(☎ 225462, ⓔ sandipkumar60@hotmail.com)* is farther south, down a short alley and is therefore insulated from the worst of the street noise. The upper-floor rooms are best as they are a bit brighter. Rooms cost around US$8 for a double with private bathroom.

Chhetrapati

This area is named after the important five-way intersection (notable by its distinctive bandstand) to the south-west of Thamel. The farther you are from Thamel, the more traditional the surroundings become.

South of the Kathmandu Guest House and left at the junction (Narayan's Restaurant is a good landmark) you'll see the popular ***Potala Guest House*** *(☎ 220467, fax 223256)* where singles/doubles start at about US$10/15. There's hot water and a small, quiet garden.

Freak Street (Jochne) & Durbar Square Area

Although Freak St's glory days have passed, a few determined restaurants and lodges have hung on. Staying here offers two big pluses – you won't find anything cheaper and you're right in the heart of the old city. Thamel is so crowded and hectic that Freak

St offers a good alternative, although the choices are much fewer.

Freak St's real name is Jochne and it runs south from Basantapur Square, the open square full of souvenir sellers adjoining Durbar Square.

Overlooking the square, the ***Hotel Sugat*** *(☎ 245824, e maryman@mos.com.np)* is one of the best options in the area. Rooms tend to be dark, but they're large and decent. Singles/doubles with shared bathroom start at Rs 110/300; Rs 300/350 with private bathroom. Single women may do better looking elsewhere.

Almost next door to Hotel Sugat is ***Park Guest House*** *(☎ 247487)*, which has small rooms with fan and TV, some rooms overlooking Basantapur Square. It's modern and consequently a bit more expensive than some places in this area, at Rs 250/400 with shared bathroom; Rs 400/500 with private bathroom.

Just off Freak St proper is the excellent ***Annapurna Lodge & Diyalo Restaurant*** *(☎ 247684)*. The place is well kept and cheerful. A room is Rs 150/200 with a shared bathroom; Rs 250/280 with a private bathroom.

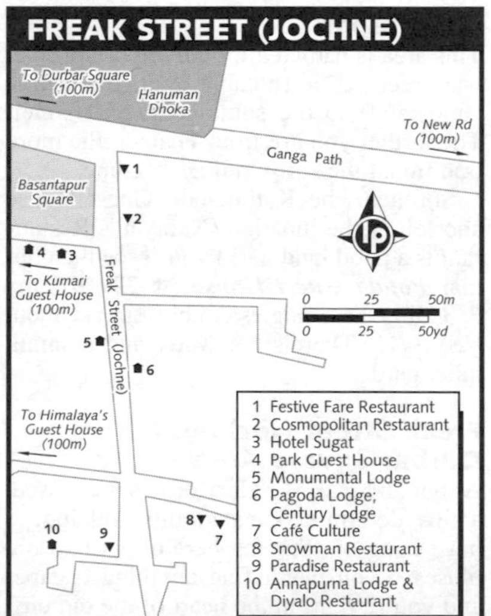

Century Lodge *(☎ 247641)* is one of Freak St's long-term survivors and it remains a popular, atmospheric place offering excellent value for money. Rooms cost just Rs 100/200 with shared bathroom; small doubles with private bathroom are Rs 250.

Pagoda Lodge *(☎ 247629)* is reached from the same courtyard as Century Lodge in the heart of Freak St. It's about as basic as they get, and rooms cost just Rs 100/180 (all with shared bathroom), although even this price is negotiable.

Monumental Lodge *(☎ 247864)* is across the road, with rooms for Rs 80/150; Rs 250 with private bathroom. Conditions are as spartan and straightforward as the price indicates, but if you're travelling on a very tight budget they offer all you can expect!

Himalaya's Guest House *(☎ 246555)*, a couple of short blocks west of Freak St, is excellent. This modern place has clean and comfortable rooms starting at Rs 150/250 with shared bathroom; Rs 400 for a double with private bathroom. There's a good cafe here, and the rooftop views are great.

Only a few steps north of Durbar Square, then to your left on Pyaphal Tole, the popular ***New Kathmandu Lodge*** *(☎ 254173, e smsb@enet.com.np)* offers a little more comfort than the Freak St places do. It's clean, well kept and very good value. Rooms with fan cost Rs 150/175 with shared bathroom; Rs 200/275 with private bathroom.

Elsewhere

Those with a campervan might like to head for the ***Verge Inn Leisure Club*** (true!) *(☎ 271768, e vergie@vigi.wlink.com.np)*, out near the Soaltee Crowne Plaza Hotel west of the city (see Places to Stay – Top End). This is a mid-range hotel with some sporting facilities, but they allow people with campervans to park in the shady, secluded car park as well as use the showers, toilets and pool for Rs 150 per night.

PLACES TO STAY – MID-RANGE

Mid-range in Kathmandu means from around US$10 to US$50 for a double. The borderlines are fuzzy. The Kathmandu

Guest House is partly a mid-range hotel as many of its rooms are over US$10, but it does offer cheaper ones as well.

Thamel

Thorong Peak Guest House *(☎ 253458, fax 251008)* is in the centre of things but is off the main street in a small cul de sac. It has a rather garish Tibetan-moderne decor. Some of the rooms are a bit dark, although most are large and airy. Full single/double prices are US$14/18 with private bathroom and US$8/12 with shared bathroom, but the discounted rates are 30% less.

The ***Hotel Tashi Dhelek*** *(☎ 250189, fax 259795)*, next door, is a comfortable, modern hotel with rooms for US$12/20, or with TV for US$15/18 (discounted by 50% much of the time).

Close to Kathmandu Guest House is ***Hotel The Earth*** *(☎ 229039, fax 223194)*, another modern and rather nondescript place. It charges US$12/15 for rooms with private bathroom.

In the thick of things, the ***Hotel Excelsior*** *(☎ 411566, ⓔ excel@wlink.com.np)* is a large place with standard rooms for US$20/25; and deluxe rooms with TV for US$25/32. There's even a lift in case you can't stagger to the 4th floor.

In a cramped area of Thamel, and about 100m north of the Kathmandu Guest House you will find the ***Hotel Garuda*** *(☎ 416340, ⓔ garuda@mos.com.np)*. It is well run, clean and good value. There's a great view over the Thamel area from the rooftop of this friendly place. Rooms are from US$9/13 to US$29/36, for a heated room with TV and balcony, plus 12% tax.

Tucked away close by is the ***Acme Guest House*** *(☎ 414811, ⓔ amc@wlink.com.np)*. The rooms are quite large and there is an open lawn area, which is something of a rarity in crowded Thamel. It's not bad value at US$14/18 with bathroom rising in price to US$20/ 25 with balcony and heating. Large discounts are available.

Paknajol

North from the Kathmandu Guest House is the Tibetan-run ***Hotel Shree Tibet*** *(☎ 419902, ⓔ sritibet@ccsl.com.np)*, which is a clean place with good rooms, although many are dark due to the buildings being very close together. Singles/doubles go for US$10/15, although there is room to negotiate here. The small restaurant serves decent food.

Hotel Tashi Dhargey *(☎ 417030, fax 423543)*; good rooms are US$10/12 (fan and phone); US$15/18 (air-con and TV).

Follow the double bend north of Kathmandu Guest House and turn left towards the Holy Lodge, continuing through several more sharp bends (known as Satghumti, or 'Seven Bends'), and you'll find one of a new breed of Thamel hotels. At seven storeys the ***Hotel Tradition*** *(☎ 428217, ⓔ hotel@tradition.wlink.com.np)* is probably the tallest in the area. The rooms are comfortable and well-furnished and discounts are available on the standard rates of US$30/40. The views from the top-floor terrace restaurant are sensational.

Farther west along the same road in an area known as Kaldhara is the nicely decorated and furnished ***International Guest House*** *(☎ 252299, ⓔ igh@wlink.com.np)* with rooms starting at US$16/20 with private bathroom, but substantial discounts are offered. It's a pleasant hotel with one of the best rooftop views in the city. This area is quieter and less of a scene than Thamel but not too far away from the restaurants.

Down a lane, ***Hotel Thamel*** *(☎ 417643, ⓔ hotelthamel@visitnepal.com)* is almost opposite the Thamel House Restaurant. It's one of the modern breed of comfortable, concrete monstrosities, with deluxe air-con rooms starting at US$45/55, and rooms with private balconies looking back to the city for US$30/40 (all with TV and phone). A discount of 50% is offered outside the high season.

Bhagwan Bahal

For a clean and rather characterless place on Tridevi Marg try ***Hotel Tilicho*** *(☎ 410132, ⓔ bishnudhamala@hotmail.com)* which offers pretty high standards. Singles/doubles start at US$10/15, but it's worth negotiating the price and checking a number of rooms before you pick one.

Nearby is ***Tibet Holiday Inn*** *(☎ 423530, e hotelgnr@col.com.np)*, a similar place but set back from the somewhat noisy street. Large, clean rooms here cost from US$25/30, but discounts of more than 50% are a matter of course and make it good value.

The ***Hotel Norbhu Linka*** *(☎ 414799, e ggclama@vishnu.ccsl.com.np)* is a large, modern place with good rooftop views. At the discounted rates of US$20/25, this place is good value as the rooms are large and have TV and private bathroom. The full tariff is US$35/45, plus 12% tax.

In the same area, down a somewhat scruffy side alley, is the new ***Hotel Crown*** *(☎ 416285)*. The rooms are clean and comfortable, and some have views over the busy Thamel Gaa Hiti (tank) nearby. With discounts it's excellent value with rooms for US$6/8.

Jyatha

Turn left (east) off Tridevi Marg, walk only a short distance down the Jyatha Rd and a couple of twists and turns will bring you to a neat little cluster of modern guesthouses, directly behind the Sanchaya Kosh Bhawan shopping centre. This is a central but quiet location.

Mustang Holiday Inn *(☎ 249041, fax 249016)* has pleasant rooms and is well run. Singles/doubles are US$8/10 with private bathroom and slightly more deluxe rooms are US$15/20, also with private bathroom, although these are negotiable, even in high season.

Also in this quiet little enclave is the popular ***Imperial Guest House*** *(☎ 249339, fax 249733)*, which charges US$12/15. ***Hotel White Lotus*** *(☎ 249842)* is much cheaper, with rooms for US$4/5 with shared bathroom; US$6/8 with private bathroom.

Hotel Utse *(☎ 226946, e utse@wlink.com.np)* is a comfortable Tibetan hotel owned by Ugen Tsering, one of the original Thamel pioneers with his long-running and popular Utse Restaurant. The rooms are spotlessly clean and very comfortable – putting some of the more expensive hotels to shame. Rooms cost start at US$15/22; deluxe rooms with carpet and TV are US$17/24. It's a very well-run hotel, with a good rooftop area, and it is often full in the high season.

Right next door, ***Hotel Norling*** *(☎ 240734, fax 226735)*, also Tibetan-run, has good-sized rooms for US$10/18 and US$18/20 for rooms with a bit more comfort.

Tucked away in a lane behind the Utse, ***Hotel Dynasty*** *(☎ 263172, e hoteldyn@wlink.com.np)* is a good find. It's a modern, upmarket place that even has a lift. The rooms are a good size and have air-con, TV and phone, and cost US$50/60, US$40/50 without air-con, plus 12% taxes. Discounts of 30% are offered.

In the same lane is the multistorey ***Fuji Guest House*** *(☎ 250435, e fujighouse@wlink.com.np)*, with straightforward, carpeted rooms with private bathroom and balcony for US$15/20; US$6/10 with shared bathroom. Discounts are available.

Chhetrapati

Two popular mid-range hotels can be found in Chhetrapati. Coming from the Kathmandu Guest House in Thamel turn right at the junction by Narayan's Restaurant and you pass a string of restaurants, bookshops and guesthouses on your way to Chhetrapati Chowk. ***Tibet Guest House*** *(☎ 254888, e tibet@guesths.mos.com.np)* is in the lower-middle bracket. It has good-sized and well-maintained rooms with bathroom starting at US$24/27, plus 12% tax, but a 20% discount is standard. It has a restaurant and pleasant garden, and offers good views from the rooftop garden.

Nirvana Hotel *(☎ 256200, e nirvana@wlink.com.np)* has smallish but pleasant rooms, each with balcony, TV, phone and private bathroom. There's a small garden, and at the discounted rate of US$15/20 Nirvana is good value. Full rates are US$30/40, plus 12% tax.

Lazimpat

North of Thamel is the Lazimpat embassy area. There are a few options in this area, and it's much less frenetic than Thamel.

Hotel Ambassador *(☎ 410432, e kgh@wlink.com.np)* is run by the people who run

Kathmandu Guest House. There's a good restaurant and a small garden, but it is on a rather noisy intersection. The hotel is within walking distance of Thamel and Durbar Marg. Singles/doubles start at US$33/44; US$44/55 with air-con.

Nearby, and just off the road to the right, is ***Manaslu Hotel*** *(☎ 410071, ⓔ postfax@mos.com.np)*, a very nice modern hotel with a pleasant garden area. The slightly inconvenient location explains the cheap price of US$28/32.

In the same area, just in front of the Radisson Hotel, is the comfortable ***Hotel Tibet*** *(☎ 429085, ⓔ hotel@tibet.mos.com.np)*. It's a friendly little place, with rooms with TV and private bathroom for US$70/80, although these are automatically discounted to US$42/48, plus 12% taxes.

A little farther north in Lazimpat, signposted to the side of the Shangri-La Hotel, is the excellent ***Astoria Hotel*** *(☎ 428810, ⓔ nepcraft@mos.com.np)*. This hotel is tucked away in a quiet area and it has pleasant gardens, including a vegetable garden, which supplies the small restaurant with fresh produce. The light and airy rooms are spotlessly clean, and have TV, carpet and private bathroom and cost US$28/35. Deluxe rooms are slightly bigger, have air-con and a minibar, and cost US$50/60.

Elsewhere

Across the Vishnumati River in the Bijeshwari area, on the way from Thamel to Swayambhunath (see the Central Kathmandu map), ***Hotel Vajra*** *(☎ 272719, ⓔ vajra@mos.com.np)* is one of Kathmandu's most interesting hotels in any price category. It has a distinct style and a superb location looking across the river to Kathmandu. The hotel has an art gallery, a theatre where classical Nepali dances are performed (7 pm Tuesday), a library of books on Tibet and Buddhism, a rooftop garden and the Explorer's Restaurant. Singles/doubles start at a bargain US$14/16 with shared bathroom, US$33/38 with private bathroom and US$53/61 in the much swankier new wing, all plus 12% tax. However, the one catch to staying at Hotel Vajra is its location, which makes it terrible for getting a taxi. If you're staying here it's wise to have transport at the ready.

Closer again to Swayambhunath is ***Milarepa Guest House*** *(☎ 275544, ⓔ nya@phel.wlink.com.np)*. It's owned by the Nyanang Phelgyeling Monastery next door and is not far from the eastern steps of Swayambhunath. It's a large, modern place and many of the rooms have views of either Swayambhunath or the city. Straightforward rooms cost US$10/15 with private bathroom; discounts may be possible.

Increasingly, people are looking to escape the pollution and bustle of central Kathmandu, and one of the nicest alternatives, which is not too far removed, is ***Hotel Sunset View*** *(☎ 480057, ⓔ sunset@wlink.com.np)* at New Baneswar. To reach it continue along the Arniko Hwy and take the first right past the Hotel Everest, opposite the huge conference centre. There's a beautiful garden with great views, as well as 12 comfortable rooms and an excellent restaurant that serves good Nepali food. Rooms are US$55/70 with garden views and US$65/80 with valley views. A 15% discount is usually available.

PLACES TO STAY – TOP END

Top-end hotels in Kathmandu start at US$50 for a double room; the most expensive hotels are around US$200 for a double. Only a handful of these hotels are centrally located, although the less conveniently positioned hotels usually offer a free bus service into town. All offer 24-hour room service, 24-hour satellite TV and the best available communications. You can also pay by credit card.

The rates below are the standard individual rates for the high season; they're certainly negotiable for groups and are also likely to be flexible during the monsoon (June to September).

Thamel

Hotel Manang *(☎ 410993, ⓔ htlmnang@vishnu.ccsl.com.np)* in Paknajol is a modern three-star hotel with everything you could possibly need. Many of the rooms have magnificent views and all have TV, air-con, phone and minibar. Facilities include a restaurant, room service and a parking area. Standard singles/doubles are US$55/65 (often discounted to US$40/55) and deluxe rooms are US$80/90, plus 10% tax.

Hotel Marshyangdi *(☎ 414105, ⓔ htlgold@mos.com.np)*, next door, has been established longer and offers a similarly high standard. The rooms are large and well furnished and have writing desks and chairs. Standard rooms cost US$60/70 and deluxe rooms US$75/80, plus 10% tax, but discounts of up to 30% are available depending on occupancy levels.

Hotel Vaishali *(☎ 413968, ⓔ vaishali@vishnu.ccsl.com.np)* is well located and has pleasantly furnished but small rooms with air-con, TV and minibar. Rooms are US$90/110, but they seem to be on offer at a more realistic US$45/55 much of the time. A bonus here in summer is the small swimming pool.

Just around the corner is the modern ***Hotel Centre Point*** *(☎ 424522, ⓔ cenpoint@wlink.com.np)*. It is set back slightly from the street, but has no garden or other open space. The rooms are a decent size, however, and the price is US$55/65.

The small and modern ***Hotel Mountain*** *(☎ 246744, fax 249736)*, on busy Kantipath, has small but pleasant rooms with air-con, TV and phone for US$80/90, but discounts of 40% shouldn't be too hard to get.

Hotel Malla *(☎ 418383, ⓔ malla@htgrp.mos.com.np)* is on the northern edge of Thamel, west of the new Royal Palace in Bhagwan Bahal, but is still only a five-minute walk to all the Thamel restaurants. The recently refurbished rooms have air-con, TV, phone and minibar. There's a restaurant and bar, a swimming pool and a superb garden, complete with a ministupa topping a minihill in the centre. It's one of the nicest top-end places. Rooms are US$130/156 and deluxe rooms are US$150/182, all plus 12% tax. In the low season a 20% discount is offered.

One of the more interesting top-end places is ***Kantipur Temple House*** *(☎ 250131, ⓔ kantipur@tmplhouse.wlink.com.np)*, along an alley at the southern end of Jyatha. It's a new hotel that has been built in old Newari temple style, and has been very well done. The tastefully decorated rooms cost US$50/60, plus 12% tax. This place is doing its best to be eco-friendly – guests are given cloth bags to use when shopping and bulk mineral water is available free of charge, so you don't need to buy plastic bottles. In fact, the use of plastic anywhere in the establishment has been banned by the owner.

Durbar Marg

Entered from Durbar Marg, but set well back from the road (see the Central Kathmandu map), ***Yak & Yeti Hotel*** *(☎ 248999, ⓔ reservation@yakandyeti.com)* boasts probably the best-known hotel in Nepal, due to its connections with the legendary Boris Lissanevitch, its original owner. The oldest section of the hotel is part of a Rana palace, and it houses the hotel's restaurants and casino; these retain an overblown but spectacular Rana-baroque decor. The rooms are in two modern wings; the Newari Wing is the older of the two and the rooms incorporate elements of carved wood and local textiles without being kitsch. Rooms are very comfortable and well maintained, and cost US$175/185 for singles/doubles . The newer Durbar Wing has conventional 'international standard' rooms for US$195/205. There are also executive rooms in this wing (with fax machine) for US$250. Business people will find a well-equipped business centre with secretarial, translation and interpretation facilities. There's also a beautiful garden, two swimming pools, tennis courts and a fitness centre.

Just off Durbar Marg, ***Hotel de l'Annapurna*** *(☎ 221711, ⓔ apurna@taj.wlink.com.np)* is one of Kathmandu's longest established hotels, and is architecturally an undistinguished example of a 1960s international hotel – it is really showing its age these days. Its central location on Durbar Marg is convenient, and apart from the usual five-star facilities, including bars and restaurants, it has a casino and nightly dance shows (see Entertainment later in this chapter), plus the largest hotel swimming pool in Kathmandu (about 25m). The rooms

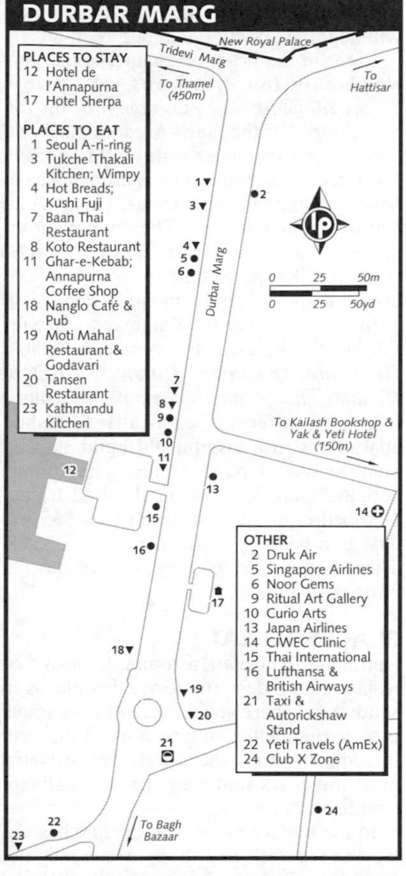

are comfortable; standard rooms are US$120/130 and the much plusher deluxe rooms are US$160/170, all plus 12% tax.

Hotel Sherpa *(☎ 227000, ⓔ sherpa@mos.com.np)*, opposite the Hotel de l'Annapurna on Durbar Marg, is cheaper and rates four stars, although it is a bit gloomy and dull. It has a pleasant rooftop swimming pool, but lacks much in the way of a garden (a garden oasis can be a much-appreciated escape in Kathmandu). The rooms are well equipped and quite pleasant, and cost US$105/115, but discounts of up to 40% can make this place a bargain.

Lazimpat

North of the city in the Lazimpat embassy area (see the Kathmandu map), is the ***Radisson Hotel*** *(☎ 411818, ⓔ radisson@radkat.com.np)*. It's a very modern, well-maintained and pleasantly decorated hotel with excellent facilities, including a 5th-floor pool with great views and a fully equipped gymnasium. Standard rooms are US$175 and larger deluxe rooms, complete with nice touches such as data ports for laptop computers, are US$185.

Farther north again, ***Hotel Shangri-La*** *(☎ 412999, ⓔ hosang@info.com.np)* is one of Kathmandu's best hotels. The rooms are attractive and well maintained, the service is swift and professional, and best of all, there's a beautiful garden with an adjoining restaurant and a swimming pool. Rooms are not especially cheap for US$120/130, but are very good value in this range.

Elsewhere

See the Kathmandu map for all of the following. Kathmandu's original luxury hotel, ***Soaltee Crowne Plaza Hotel*** *(☎ 273999, ⓔ crowneplaza@shicp.com.np)*, is on the western edge of town, but it operates a bus service into town for its guests. It's one of the largest hotels in Nepal and apart from good restaurants, spacious grounds, bars, a health club, swimming pool and other facilities it also has a casino. Singles/doubles are US$180/190; deluxe rooms are US$200/210, plus 12% tax. There are also more expensive suites.

Very close by is the new ***Grand Hotel*** *(☎ 282482, ⓔ grandhotel@wlink.com.np)*, a large multistorey, which has decent facilities but lacks any real atmosphere. Rooms start at US$95/105, discounts of 40% are available.

Hotel Everest *(☎ 488100, fax 490288)* is on the eastern edge of town, beside the main road to the airport and Bhaktapur. The modern building is eight storeys high, making it one of the tallest buildings in Nepal, and the views, especially on the northern side, are spectacular. The standards are reasonably high and the facilities are good, but it's still probably overpriced at US$150/160.

Closer to Pashupatinath, ***Dwarika's Village Hotel*** *(☎ 470770, ⓔ dwarika@mos.com.np)*, built in traditional style and featuring superb examples of antique woodwork, is an outstanding and unusual hotel. The owners have rescued thousands of carvings from around the valley (from buildings facing demolition or collapse) and many have been incorporated into the complex, which consists of a small cluster of buildings separated by pleasant brick-paved courtyards. A large workshop is funded by the hotel and craftspeople patiently repair and restore lattice windows and carvings that would otherwise almost certainly be lost in Kathmandu's rush to survive and modernise. The same craftsmen also manufacture all of the furniture on the premises. The end result is a beautiful hybrid – a cross between a museum and a boutique hotel. The hotel is near the airport and Pashupatinath – its only disadvantage is that it's a bit of a distance to the eating places in Thamel and Durbar Marg; taxis are not a problem, however. The hotel has won a Heritage Award from the Pacific Asia Travel Association (PATA), and has excellent rooms for US$135/155; deluxe (larger) rooms are an extra US$40, plus tax. The rooms are large, atmospheric and very comfortable, but do not have air-con or TV (the latter is available on request).

The latest addition to the scene is the superb Hyatt Regency Kathmandu *(☎ 491234, ⓔ info@hyatt.com.np)* a few kilometres from the centre near the Boudha stupa. No expense has been spared on this place, and the architecture is very much in keeping with the older buildings in the valley. It's worth coming here just to admire the sculptures in the lobby. As you'd expect, the rooms are tastefully furnished and many have views over Boudha. If you like this level of comfort you won't find any better place in the valley. There's also a swimming pool, fitness centre, business centre, a cafe and restaurant. Doubles start at US$210, plus 12% tax.

Long-Stay Accommodation

If you are in and around the valley for some time, it's worth looking into something other than a regular hotel, although most hotels will negotiate pretty good long-term rates.

Right in the heart of Thamel is the new ***Roadhouse Inn Apartments*** *(☎ 260187, ⓔ arcadia@ladolce.mos.com.np)*, on the top floors of the new Arcadia building (above the Roadhouse Café) right opposite Third Eye Restaurant. The apartments have basic cooking facilities, fridge, TV, separate bedroom and a balcony. They're not cheap, however, with rates of US$245 per week and US$1000 per month, although a 30% discount applies on the monthly rate.

In Lazimpat (see the Kathmandu map for the location) there's the very comfortable ***Hacienda Apartment Hotel*** *(☎ 410216, ⓔ hah@hacienda.mos.com.np)*. This place is luxury, offering beautifully furnished apartments in a tasteful old building. The apartments all have separate bedrooms, cooking facilities, air-con, TV and fridge. One-bedroom apartments cost US$65 per day, two-bedroom apartments are US$95. These rates are reduced by 30% for stays of more than a month.

PLACES TO EAT

Kathmandu has an astounding array of restaurants. Indeed, there are few places in south Asia where your choice of restaurants is so varied. After long months on the road in India or long weeks trekking in Nepal most travellers find Kathmandu a culinary paradise.

In the budget range, Kathmandu has numerous tea stalls and shops. Many may not even have a name but at these stalls *dal bhaat tarkari* (the lentil soup, rice and vegetable everyday meal of most Nepalis) will be the main dish on offer. If you are going by up-country standards these places aren't cheap: Dal bhaat tarkari will set you back around Rs 50.

In Thamel, if you stay away from beer, you can eat until you burst for less than Rs 200. A bottle of beer can cost anything from Rs 90 to Rs 130 and nearly double your bill.

As you might expect, the top restaurants have prices to match, but they're still reasonable by Western standards. More expensive restaurants slap a 12% government tax

HUGH FINLAY

Street shrines honour Ganesh.

OLIVIER CIRENDINI

Hindu goddess cast in bronze

MARTIN FOJTEK

A holy man and follower of Vishnu in contemplation.

ANDERS BLOMQVIST

Silk saris and gilted gods colour the festivals of the valley.

DUSHAN COORAY

Watching over Kathmandu Valley from Swayambhunath stupa.

RICHARD I'ANSON

Illumination, Boudha stupa

GREG ELMS

Buddha – sculpted serenity

KRAIG LIEB

Monks gather at the Tibetan religious centre of Boudha (Bodhnath) stupa.

on top of the bill, but you'll still probably pay less than US$20 per person. Kathmandu's big hotels have some interesting restaurant options and there's an ever-growing number of high-class restaurants dotted around the city.

Tipping is accepted (and appreciated) in Nepal, but your loose change (or 5%) is fine in cheaper places; a bit more will be expected in the expensive restaurants.

Thamel

Thamel restaurants spill into Paknajol, Jyatha and Chhetrapati, just like the Thamel hotels do. The junction outside the Kathmandu Guest House is the centre of Thamel dining and you can find numerous budget-priced restaurants within a minute's walk in either direction.

While there are literally dozens of budget restaurants here, there is often little between them in what they offer. A standard menu has pretty well everything on it, and after eating in a few places you may well come to the conclusion that the chefs were all taught by the same person, or perhaps there is only one chef who runs around and cooks at all of them! The food tends to be remarkably similar and often very bland. What marks the difference between these places is the atmosphere, music, service and who happens to be there on the night. Terraces are *de rigueur*. These days there are quite a number of restaurants in Thamel serving really top-class food at affordable prices.

The central Thamel restaurants include the best known of the lot, ***KC's Restaurant***. KC himself no longer presides (it's run by his nephew these days), but he hit the magic travellers' restaurant formula spot-on. Although the food is still good, the restaurant has become a bit expensive by Thamel standards. A delicious breakfast starts at around Rs 100 (which isn't bad), but a vegetarian lasagne is Rs 200, and one of KC's famous steaks is around Rs 230.

On this same stretch of Thamel's restaurant centre you can try the ***Pumpernickel Bakery*** for freshly baked bread. In the morning, tourists crowd in for fresh croissants, rolls, pastries and filter coffee in the pleasant garden area at the back. It is uncomfortably crowded at the height of the season.

The ***Café Jalapeno*** on the 1st floor of the Namche Bazaar building on the intersection near Kathmandu Guest House is most popular for its window seats, which offer a great view of the passing parade. The food itself is nothing remarkable, but the pleasant decor, top location and attentive service make it worth a visit. Oh, and it has about the cheapest beer in Thamel.

On the floor above is the popular ***Alice's Restaurant***, a decent place and a cut above the cheapies, but still very reasonable and it has great views. Pizza is Rs 130 and pancakes Rs 45.

Opposite is a ***Hot Bread*** outlet, which does a roaring trade in sandwiches, bread rolls, pizza slices and pastries. These are very popular at lunchtime, and the ham and cheese rolls (Rs 65) make a great lunch on the run.

Yin Yang Restaurant, just south of the intersection, is one of Thamel's most highly regarded restaurants. It serves authentic Thai food cooked by an authentic Thai chef. It's not particularly cheap, with starters around Rs 90 and main meals from Rs 200 to Rs 300, but the food is a definite cut above the imitation Thai food found elsewhere. You won't get in here without a booking in the high season.

Third Eye Restaurant, next door to Yin Yang, is a long-running favourite that retains something of the old Kathmandu atmosphere. There's a sit-down section at the front, and a more informal section with low tables and cushions at the back and a rooftop terrace. Indian food is the speciality, but there are also a small number of continental offerings. The tandoori dishes here are especially good. It's wise to book a table at this popular place in the high season.

Across the road is ***Roadhouse Café***. The big attraction here is the pizzas from the wood-fired oven (we have been assured the wood is offcuts from a Terai timbermill). The pizzas are pretty darn good, and the courtyard out back is very pleasant.

In this same congested area is the ***K-Too Beer & Steakhouse***, run by the same people who run Kilroy's (see later). The decor and furnishings are deliberately rough and ready, and the atmosphere is good – as is the food. Steaks start at Rs 185, but the snack menu is also worth a browse – homesick Poms might like to reacquaint themselves with that great English delicacy: the chip butty.

Down the road from the Yin Yang, the ***Wiesel Bakery*** serves good vegetarian food. It has a pleasant garden and is a nice quiet place for breakfast, with newspapers to read and music playing in the background. This is another place with a good range of cakes, breads and pastries.

Many Thamel restaurants have a go at some Italian dishes, but ***La Dolce Vita***, with the movie motifs, makes the best attempt at true Italian cuisine and the menu is a bit more imaginative than the standard Thamel offering, with delights such as *tiramisu*. There are both indoor and open-air sections, and the food is pretty good. Prices are a little higher than the rock-bottom Thamel average – vegetarian dishes cost Rs 130 to Rs 160, pizzas Rs 180 to Rs 200, pasta Rs 150 to 190 – but so is the quality. It's right on the corner opposite Kathmandu Guest House.

Continue a little north and you come to Pilgrims Book House. Out through the rear of the shop is ***Pilgrims Feed N Read***, but it is also accessible from the compound next to Kathmandu Guest House. It's a relaxed place, with indoor and outdoor areas. The focus is on Indian food – the ginger chicken is worth trying, and *tungba* (Tibetan millet beer) is available (Rs 70).

Next door is the open-air ***Northfield Cafe***. This is the place for serious breakfast devotees – eggs any way you like and a bottomless ground coffee (Rs 45) – and the Mexican lunch dishes are also good, although prices are a bit higher than elsewhere.

The Kathmandu Guest House's ***Las Kus Restaurant*** serves straightforward, well-prepared food; the outdoor breakfast buffet is also popular. This is a good place to try traditional Newari dishes such as *chhoyla* (marinated roast buff) and *chatamari* (small rice-flour pancakes). The courtyard also has a ***New York Pizza*** outlet (there's another in Patan), which turns out pretty decent pizzas.

Directly across the road and upstairs is the ***Brezel Bakery***, a pleasant rooftop spot overlooking the Thamel activity below. This is another good breakfast place, with fresh brown bread.

Almost next door and tucked away off the street, is the popular ***New Orleans Cafe***. It's a good spot for a meal or a drink, and there's live music on weekends. The menu ranges far and wide, from Nepali dishes to jambalaya, a New Orleans chicken and rice dish (Rs 180). It's also a popular spot for breakfast.

A few doors along on the 1st floor is the ***Nargila Restaurant***, one of the very few places to offer Middle Eastern food. It does a pretty reasonable job of it too. Felafel and pitta is Rs 95, couscous (Rs 75) and dips such as baba ghanoush or hummus served with pitta is Rs 60.

The ***Rum Doodle Restaurant & Bar*** was named, of course, after the world's highest mountain, the 40,000½ foot Mt Rum Doodle. The heroic conquest of Rum Doodle was dramatically described in that spoof on heroic mountaineering books by WE Bowman in *The Ascent of Rum Doodle*. The restaurant is in the same side street as the Holy Lodge, and specialises in steak and pasta. It's a favourite meeting place for mountaineering expeditions – many have left their mark on the walls, particularly in the upstairs 40,000½ Foot Bar. You can eat here free for life – the only catch is that you have to conquer Everest first!

Farther north, opposite the Hotel Mandap, is another good open-air Thai place, the ***Krua Thai Restaurant***. The food is reasonably authentic (ie, spicy) although not that cheap: soups are Rs 180 to Rs 210 and main courses Rs 210 to Rs 440.

A little farther north again, and down a side street, is the diminutive ***BK's Place***, which has a growing reputation for good old-fashioned chips (French fries).

Back at the main Thamel Chowk, the tiny ***Sandwich Point*** is a good little place with small (from Rs 50) and large (from Rs 70) rolls, which they stuff full with a variety of fillings. It's just the place for late night ragers – it's open 24 hours.

Close to the Thamel Chowk is the ***Botega***, a Mexican place that does good food (Rs 250 to Rs 300 for main dishes), has authentic music and a bar with a fine repertoire of tequila cocktails.

South from Thamel Chowk is the modern ***Himalatte Café***, which has an impressive array of coffees and teas. It does decent food (good burgers cost Rs 150) and there's live music in the evenings during the high season.

In this same area is ***Cinderella Restaurant***, a rooftop restaurant with live bands on some evenings.

In the modern Sanchaya Kosh Bhawan shopping centre on Tridevi Marg there are a couple of places worth mentioning. ***Fire & Ice Restaurant*** is an excellent open-air Italian place serving some of the best pizzas in Kathmandu (Rs 200 to Rs 300), imported Italian soft-serve ice cream and seriously good coffee and rousing opera – Italian, of course. It's deservedly popular and you'll need a reservation in the high season, or eat early. Next door is the ***Dechenling Restaurant***, a good little Tibetan place with very reasonable prices.

Just across the road is the ***Nanglo Deli***, a modern place that is a good choice for a croissant breakfast. On the 1st floor here is the ***Himalayan Java***, one of the new breed of upmarket cafes. The coffee here is good (the iced coffee great) and the menu varied, although no alcohol is served.

Jyatha

Ireland meets Nepal at ***Kilroy's of Kathmandu***, named after the Irish owner and head chef. You can sit inside, or outside in the shady garden complete with waterfall. The prices are definitely a cut above your average Thamel restaurant, but then again, so is the food. The menu ranges from a Royal dal bhaat (Rs 250) to beef and Guinness hot pot (Rs 345). Vegetarians also get a look in with dishes such as saffron and mushroom risotto (Rs 240). If you're still keen take a look at the dessert menu: caramelised bananas, apple crumble with custard – enough said!

The ***Utse Restaurant***, in the hotel of the same name in Jyatha, is one of the longest-running restaurants in Thamel and it turns out excellent Tibetan dishes, such as *momo* and *kothe* (fried pasta stuffed with meat/vegetables). *Talumein* (egg noodle) soup costs Rs 60, and the traditional Tibetan-style meals are also worth a try. *Gacok* (also spelt *gyakok*) is a meal named after the brass tureen that is heated at the table and from which various meats and vegetables are served (Rs 1300 for four).

An excellent spot for tasty *momos* (meat/veg-filled pasta) is the tiny ***Dolma Momo Restaurant***, a bit farther south from the Utse. This place is typical of the Tibetan eateries dotted around town – it's just a hole in the wall, and momos are the only thing on the menu, but they are excellent and, at Rs 15 for a plate, top value.

In this same street, the ***Omei Japanese Restaurant*** is not a bad Japanese place, and the ***Chikusa*** is a Japanese coffee shop, which serves excellent coffee.

A good place for deli items is the glossy ***Delicatessen Center***, this place is prominently signposted on Kantipath and with a mind-boggling array of imported cheeses.

Chhetrapati

Head south from Thamel into Chhetrapati to find more popular travellers' restaurants, including ***Narayan's Steak House Restaurant***, another of the long-term survivors in this area. It's very popular, competent and low-priced with a wide range of breakfast dishes, pasta (Rs 90 to Rs 110) and pizza (Rs 100 to Rs 125). Narayan's also produces delicious ice cream in half a dozen different flavours, and offers a great selection of pies and cakes.

Freak Street (Jochne) & Durbar Square Area

Freak St has a number of restaurants where you can find good food at low prices, although the choice is fairly limited. Even if you're staying in other areas of the city it's nice to know there are some good places for lunch if you're sightseeing around Durbar Square.

The popular ***Diyalo Restaurant*** at the Annapurna Lodge is a good little place with

Nepali Restaurants

There is a growing number of restaurants around town that specialise in Nepali (mostly Newari) food. These run the gamut from unobtrusive little places in Thamel, where Rs 80 will get you a good meal, up to fancy places with cultural shows, which cost 10 times that but are still good value. Most places offer a set meal, either veg or nonveg, and you dine on cushions at low tables. The 'cultural shows' consist of musicians and dancers performing 'traditional' items. The whole thing is generally pretty touristy, but popular nonetheless. At most places it's a good idea to make a reservation during the high season.

In Paknajol, in greater Thamel, the ***Thamel House Restaurant*** *(☎ 410388)* is set in a traditional old Newari building and has bags of atmosphere. The food is traditional Nepali, although they may try to lumber you with the set menu at Rs 550. Ask for the a la carte menu and choose individual dishes (Rs 70 to Rs 180); there are a few unusual ones, such as wild boar. It's a good night out, although the service can be patchy. It's also open for lunch, and the Rs 250 set menu is not bad value.

Also in Thamel is the ***Thakali Banchha***, a modern place popular with local people working in Thamel. A good dal bhaat here is only Rs 90.

On Durbar Marg there's the small and cosy ***Tukche Thakali Kitchen***, which also serves Tibetan dishes. This is not really a tourist place, the interior is authentically gloomy but the food is good and reasonably priced at Rs 150 for a veg set lunch and Rs 195 with meat. In the evenings it's Rs 450 for a fixed menu of around 10 dishes.

Near the entrance to the Radisson Hotel in Lazimpat (see the Kathmandu map) is the new ***Restaurant Lajana*** *(☎ 413874)*. The building is done in traditional Newari style, the food is the usual multicourse set meal and the Rs 700 price includes a dance show.

Bhanchha Ghar Restaurant *(☎ 225172)* is in a traditional three-storey Newari house in Kamaladi, just east of Durbar Marg from the turn-off by the clock tower (see the Central Kathmandu map). Unfortunately this fine old building has been overshadowed somewhat by the ugly modern

a large menu, which includes crepes (Rs 85), burgers (Rs 85) and a few Chinese and Indian dishes, all for less than Rs 90.

The ***Paradise Restaurant*** is a good vegetarian place, with generous dishes such as lasagne (Rs 80) and vegetarian schnitzel burgers (Rs 85).

Café Culture is a cosy place to hang out with a good atmosphere, good music and board games to help while away the time. The menu features vegetarian dishes (Rs 70 to Rs 85) and there's a great range of lassis and juices.

Next door, the long-running ***Snowman Restaurant*** is a bit old fashioned these days but it still has the best range of cakes in this area.

At the Basantapur Square end of Freak St, the ***Cosmopolitan*** is a pleasant place with friendly staff. Right next door, also overlooking the square, and with a great top-floor terrace is ***Festive Fare Restaurant***.

At the other end of Durbar Square is another ***Festive Fare***, a reasonable rooftop place right opposite the Taleju Temple. It offers great views over the Hanuman Dhoka rooftops, and the food and service aren't too bad either.

Central Kathmandu

The restaurants in the Kantipath and Durbar Marg areas are generally more expensive than around Thamel although there are a few lower-priced exceptions. See the last few listings in this section for some of Kathmandu's real night-out possibilities.

Several places on Durbar Marg have good food. The ***Nanglo Café & Pub*** has a popular open-air terrace dining area and an international menu. There's quite a lively atmosphere and there's a 'cybercorner' for net surfers. A large pizza costs Rs 200, burgers Rs 75 to Rs 100, pasta Rs 90 to Rs 120 and a fixed Nepali lunch with rice, dal,

Nepali Restaurants

monstrosities either side of it. There is an upstairs loft where you can stretch out on handmade carpets and cushions for a drink, snacks and a brief 'cultural show' featuring the various ethnic costumes of Nepal. You can then move downstairs to take advantage of an excellent menu of traditional Nepali dishes and delicacies. Musicians stroll between the tables playing traditional Nepali folk songs. It's not all that cheap (US$12 per person, plus drinks and tax) but the food is very good. It's open from 11 am to 10.30 pm daily.

See the Kathmandu map for the locations of following restaurants. In the same vein as Bhanchha Ghar, but perhaps more ambitious, is ***Bhojan Griha*** *(☎ 416423)* in a recently restored 150-year-old mansion in Dilli Bazaar, just east of the city centre. It's worth eating here just to see the imaginative renovation of this beautiful old building. Again, dancers and musicians stroll through the various rooms throughout the evening. Most of the seating is traditional (ie, on cushions on the floor, although these are actually legless chairs, which saves your back and knees), but there are a couple of rooms with conventional tables for those who prefer them. The set menu is Rs 997, plus tax and drinks, or you can order a la carte – it's a worthwhile night out. In an effort to reduce waste, plastic is not used in the restaurant and mineral water is bought in bulk and sold by the glass.

One of the best places for Nepali food is the ***Krishnarpan Restaurant*** *(☎ 470770)* at Dwarika's Village Hotel, east of the centre near the Ring Rd. The atmosphere is superb and the food gets consistent praise from diners. Prices range from US$19 for a six-course meal up to US$28 for a full 16-course extravaganza. Bookings are advisable.

At Babar Mahal Revisited, east of the centre (see the boxed text 'Babar Mahal Revisited' later), ***Baithak Restaurant*** has a dramatic setting where diners are watched over by huge portraits of various Ranas. This is probably the most memorable part of the restaurant; the food is good but not remarkable. The multicourse set menu is Rs 945.

meat, vegetable curry, pickle and green salad is Rs 185.

There is a ***Wimpy*** outlet on Durbar Marg, and close by is a ***Hot Breads*** outlet, with good bakery items.

Beside the entrance to the Hotel de l'Annapurna, ***Annapurna Coffee Shop*** offers a standard 'big hotel' menu, with burgers starting at Rs 250, pizza at Rs 275, Nepali dishes from Rs 100 to Rs 275 and milkshakes and lassi (yogurt with sugar and fruit) at Rs 120. It's popular but the food is average.

Other Durbar Marg options include the moderately priced ***Koto Restaurant***, which some say prepares the best Japanese food in town. A set menu is Rs 330, but there are plenty of dishes for around Rs 160. ***Baan Thai Restaurant*** serves excellent Thai food, and the service is very attentive. Expect to pay around Rs 450, plus service and drinks.

Close by is the ***Kushi Fuji***, a Japanese place with both traditional and table seating. You can order a la carte from the extensive menu, or there is a variety of set meals from Rs 530 to Rs 630.

Heading south, ***Moti Mahal Restaurant*** serves pretty decent Indian food. Most main dishes are around Rs 150 to Rs 230. Upstairs is a vegetarian section, ***Godavari***, which serves *dosas* for Rs 70 and a *thali* lunch for Rs 150 or dinner at Rs 190. Just a few doors along is the more expensive ***Tansen Restaurant***, which has a very good reputation for Indian food.

At the northern end of Durbar Marg ***Seoul A-ri-ring*** has a pleasant rooftop area and serves dishes barbecued at your table for Rs 440. Other main dishes cost Rs 250 to Rs 450 and there's a set meal at Rs 550 (Rs 750 seafood). It's open daily for lunch and dinner.

One of the most famous restaurants is the Yak & Yeti Hotel's ***Chimney Room*** *(☎ 248999)* north-west of the centre and across the Vishnumati River (see the Kathmandu map). It retains a tenuous historical link with Russian-born Boris Lissanevitch, who was the founder of the Royal Hotel, Kathmandu's first hotel for Western visitors. The central, open fireplace gives it plenty of atmosphere, but apart from the borsch (beetroot soup), which is still excellent, there are few reminders of Boris' days. The mostly Russian food is well prepared, if somewhat bland. The borsch is Rs 150; main dishes are from Rs 550 to Rs 1100.

Also in the Yak & Yeti is the ***Naachghar Restaurant*** *(☎ 248999)*. It's a grand, baroque room with high ceilings, gilt mirrors, marble features and ornate plasterwork. Performances of Nepali music and dance are given, but ring ahead to check what nights they are on. The menu is strong on both Indian and Nepali dishes – those from the tandoor oven are said to be good – but there are also some Continental options. Vegetarian dishes are around Rs 170 to Rs 360, nonveg from Rs 370 to Rs 450.

Ghar-e-Kebab, on Durbar Marg outside the Hotel de l'Annapurna, has some of the best tandoori and other Indian food in the city. Indian miniatures hang on the walls and in the evenings classical Indian music is played and traditional Urdu *ghazals* (love songs) are sung. A complete meal for two, including drinks, costs about Rs 2000.

Elsewhere

See the Kathmandu map for the following listings. You can start the day at one of the best and most popular breakfast places in the city. As the name suggests, ***Mike's Breakfast*** specialises in breakfasts, and they do them well. The restaurant is in the suburb of Naxal, about a 15-minute walk from the top end of Durbar Marg, and Mike presides over the whole operation. Meals are served in the attractive, leafy garden of an old Rana house, and are accompanied by soothing classical music. Mike's is open from 7 am to 9 pm daily, and does pizza on Tuesday and Friday nights only. It's not cheap, but is certainly a laid-back way to start the day. The breakfast menu includes excellent waffles with yogurt, fruit and syrup for Rs 190 and great eggs Florentine for Rs 250. Lunch is also good, with dishes such as quiche and salad costing around Rs 160. While you're here take a look at the excellent Indigo Gallery.

In Lazimpat, just north along the main road from the Ambassador Hotel, is ***Royal Hana Garden*** *(☎ 416200)*. This place is a bit of a find – there are two outdoor hot-spring baths where you can luxuriate for as long as you like before heading inside for a Japanese meal. The baths cost Rs 250 (towels and bathing wear provided) and are open daily from 3 to 8 pm. The restaurant (open from 10 am to 10 pm daily) serves very reasonably priced Japanese food for Rs 200 to Rs 300 for a main course. It is worth ringing ahead to book a spring bathroom.

The trek out to the Soaltee Crowne, Plaza Hotel on the western side of town, may be worthwhile to try the excellent Indian and Nepali dishes at the ***Himalchuli Restaurant***. The restaurant features woodcarvings from Bhaktapur and traditional Nepali music, but it's only open in the evenings. Local dishes cost around Rs 300, while Indian dishes are Rs 150 to Rs 350.

Also out of town, south-east on the Bhaktapur road, ***Far Pavilions Restaurant*** at Hotel Everest offers great views over Kathmandu from its 7th-floor vantage point and serves tandoori (Rs 350 to Rs 750) and other Indian dishes. Main courses are around Rs 350 and a set thali meal is Rs 580 nonveg or Rs 550 veg. It's a good place, but is open in the evenings only.

In the same direction, out at the Babar Mahal Revisited complex (see the boxed text 'Babar Mahal Revisited' later) near Singh Durbar government offices, is ***Simply Shutters Bistrot***. It offers excellent French-influenced food in very pleasant surroundings, particularly in the evenings when the courtyard is illuminated. Entrees are Rs 120 to Rs 200, main courses, such as quail or mackerel fillets, are Rs 300 to Rs 500. The restaurant is open from noon to 11 pm daily.

Also here is ***Chez Caroline***, a very swanky (pretentious even?) outdoor restaurant popular with many expats. French-influenced main courses are in the Rs 300 to Rs 500 range.

Self-Catering

In Thamel, for trekking food such as noodles, nuts, dried fruit and cheese, there are a number of small supermarkets, such as the ***Best Shopping Centre*** at the end of Tridevi Marg, at the corner where the road narrows and enters Thamel proper.

The ***Bluebird supermarkets*** have a wide variety of goods. There's a branch near the Blue Star Hotel (see the Central Kathmandu map), by the main bridge across the Bagmati River to Patan. You'll find branch in Lazimpat, near the French embassy (see the Kathmandu map), on the continuation of Kantipath about 1km from Thamel.

ENTERTAINMENT

Nepal is an early-to-bed country and even in Kathmandu you'll find few people on the streets after 10 pm. The exception to this is Thamel, which is not surprising, as Thamel is not really Nepal. Restaurants in Thamel generally don't close until after 10 pm and there are a number of bars that stay open until well after midnight. Bands play at various places in Thamel in the high season – just follow your ears. Kathmandu also has a couple of discos, and there are cultural shows and four of west Asia's very few casinos.

Bars

There are half a dozen bars scattered around Thamel, all within a short walk of each other. Each has quite a distinctive atmosphere, so it's worth poking your nose in to see which has the crowd and style that appeals to you.

Tom & Jerry Pub is upstairs opposite Pilgrims Book House. It is a long-running, rowdy place with pool tables. Close by is the ***New Orleans Cafe***, a popular place which often has live music. It's also not a bad place to eat. In the same area is the ***Jump Club***, a popular bar with a DJ and small dance floor.

A little farther north is the popular ***Tunnel Club***, a big top-floor place with loud music and late hours. Almost opposite is ***Sam's Bar***, a very cosy little place with good music. It opens after 5 pm.

One of the most well-known bars is the ***Rum Doodle Restaurant & Bar***, which attracts an interesting crowd of adventurers (see Places to Eat earlier).

The ***Pub Maya***, near the Hotel Star and Kathmandu Guest House, is another long-running favourite that remains popular, as is the associated ***Maya Cocktail Bar***.

Close to Thamel Chowk is ***Underground Bar***, which always has the music cranked up pretty high. On Tridevi Marg, ***Studio 54*** is also currently popular.

On the top floor of the new building between the Kathmandu Guest House and the Yin Yang Restaurant is ***Paddy Foley's Irish Bar***. This place has an outdoor terrace and often has live music.

Discos

Kathmandu has a couple of discos, popular with well-to-do Nepalis. The ***Moon Sun Disco***, at the Heritage Plaza in Kamaladi, and just along the street, the ***Club X Zone***, in the Durbar Marg area. Both are open until late nightly and are probably not ideal for visiting tourists. If you want to dance, Thamel bars such as the ***Jump Club*** are a better bet.

Casinos

Kathmandu has four casinos, these are all at the upmarket hotels: the Soaltee Crowne Plaza Hotel, Everest Hotel (both on the Kathmandu map), Hotel de l'Annapurna (see the Durbar Marg map) and the Yak & Yeti Hotel (see the Central Kathmandu map).

If you turn up at any of them within a week of arrival with your onward airline ticket and passport you can get Indian Rs (INRs) 200 of free coupons. You can play in either INRs (almost a hard currency in Nepali terms) or US dollars, and winnings (in the same currency) can be taken out of the country when you leave. The casinos are open 24 hours a day, and they'll ply you with free beer and food if you're actually playing at the tables. The main games offered are roulette and blackjack, and the main clients are Indians. Nepalis are officially forbidden from entering.

Nepali Music & Dance

There are regular performances of Nepali music and dancing in Kathmandu, including at the ***National Theatre***. All the big hotels have nightly cultural shows, usually in their main restaurant at around 7 pm, and these typically cost around Rs 200.

The Himalchuli Cultural Group is a dance troupe, which performs nightly at the ***Cultural Hall*** attached to the Hotel Shankar in Lazimpat, north of the new Royal Palace. The hour-long show costs Rs 350 and starts at 7 pm in summer (October to April) and 6.30 pm in winter (May to September).

Cinemas

Video Night in Kathmandu (see under Books in the Facts for the Visitor chapter) has certainly had an impact on the city – there are video shops everywhere and cinemas are having a hard time of it. Indian films, mostly without subtitles, are the usual cinematic fare, although there are occasional English-language films. Entry charges are minimal and catching a Hindi movie is well worthwhile since understanding the language is not essential to enjoying these comedy-musical spectaculars. Indians call them 'masala movies' as they have a little bit of everything in them.

In a number of the restaurants in Thamel popular Western movies appear on pirated videos or laser discs almost as soon as they hit the cinemas in the West. You'll see the movies chalked up on pavement blackboards.

In the Kathmandu Plaza in Kamaladi is the Kathmandu Mini Vision, the only cinema in Kathmandu showing Western films. Although it was closed at the time of research, it is supposedly reopening; call ☎ 245817 for details.

SHOPPING

Everything that is turned out in the various centres around the valley can be found in Kathmandu, although you can often find a better choice, or more unusual items, in the centres that produce the items – eg, Jawlakhel, south of Patan, for Tibetan carpets; Patan for cast metal statues and other craftwork; Bhaktapur for the finest woodcarvings and pottery; and Thimi for more pottery and masks. See Shopping in the Patan and Bhaktapur sections of the Around the Kathmandu Valley chapter for more details.

Crafts of various kinds are on sale all around Kathmandu, and the money that tourists spend on craft items makes an important contribution to Nepal's economy.

The most important rules when buying anything worth a reasonable amount of money are: first, put in some legwork and second, buy just before you leave, not just after you arrive. Prices vary hugely and until you have done some research, you'll have no idea whether you're being ripped off (to an acceptable degree) or not.

All serious shoppers should read Jeff Greenwald's amusing *Shopping for Buddhas* (a title in Lonely Planet's Journeys series), which gives fair warning of the fate that can befall obsessive types.

Bronze Statues

The best place to start is on Durbar Marg, but there are also some shops worth visiting on New Rd. This is one area where research is vitally important, as quality and prices do not necessarily correlate. Curio Arts on Durbar Marg is a good place to start.

Curios

An endless supply of curios, stuff, knick-knacks, pieces, thingos and plain junk is turned out for tourists. Most does not come from Tibet (but from the local Tamang community) and most are not more than six weeks old, but none of this matters. If you shop around you can find creations that are beautifully made by craftspeople whose time is obviously not worth a lot of money. Basantapur Square is the headquarters for this trade, but before you match wits with these operators, visit the Amrita Craft Collection in greater Thamel. This relatively small shop has a wide collection, all with marked prices that are reasonably fair.

Thangkas

The main centre for thangkas is just off Durbar Square, and this is where you'll find the best salespeople (not necessarily the best thangkas). For modern work in Thamel, visit the Tibetan Thangka Treasure, near KC's Restaurant in Thamel.

The Indigo Gallery, at Mike's Breakfast in Naxal, has some excellent pieces. Another good little place is the Tibetan Thangka Gallery in Lazimpat, just past the Ambassador Hotel. Thangkas are painted on the spot (you can watch the artists at work) and many pieces from here end up in the Durbar Square shops with higher price tags. (See the Kathmandu map for both of these.)

Clothing

Kathmandu is the best place in the valley for clothes and many places have good-quality ready-to-wear Western fashions, particularly shirts. Amusing embroidered T-shirts are a popular speciality. There are lots of good tailors around Thamel and, apart from embroidered T-shirts, they'll also embroider just about anything you want on your own jacket or jeans. Tara Boutique, with shops on Tridevi Marg near Thamel and on Durbar Marg, makes wonderful hand-painted pure silk women's fashions at prices very favourable compared with what you'd pay at home.

Handicrafts

For general handicrafts such as handmade paper, ceramics and woodwork – much of it made by disadvantaged or minority groups – one of the best places to start looking is Kupandol, the road that runs from Bagmati Bridge up to Patan. Here there are a number of shops, such as Dhankuta Sisters Handicrafts, Mahaguthi (also with an outlet in Lazimpat) and Women Entrepreneurs Association of Nepal (WEAN), each with a wide range of goods at reasonable prices.

The Woodmaster Gallery, in Naxal opposite the police headquarters (see the Kathmandu map), displays beautiful pieces made by Newar woodcarvers of the valley. Prices are generally high but so is the quality of what's on offer. You can also arrange for a visit to the workshop in Jawlakhel.

Babar Mahal Revisited

This shopping complex at Babar Mahal, near the Singh Durbar government offices, is an example of what can be done with a bit of imagination – oh, and plenty of money. The building consists of old Rana palace outbuildings that have been redeveloped to house a dozen or so upmarket shops and a couple of good restaurants. Although aimed at the tour groups, it's worth coming for a look as the shops sell top-quality merchandise.

Gems & Jewellery

Buying gems is always a risky business unless you know what you're doing. Be immediately suspicious of anyone who tells you that you will be able to make an enormous profit – if this was possible and legal they would do it themselves. Noor Gems on Durbar Marg is a long-running and reputable place.

There are dozens of jewellery shops in Thamel and elsewhere in the city, including on New Rd and Durbar Marg. Much of the merchandise comes from India, but a lot is also produced locally. When walking between Thamel and Durbar Square you'll often come across small shops with a few craftspeople working with silver.

The prices for silver jewellery are very low compared with what you'd pay at home, and many people have jewellery made to order. You buy the stones or draw the design and they'll make it up, usually in just a day or two. The quality is usually excellent, but be sure to agree on a price before giving the go-ahead to have anything made.

Tibetan Antiques

Kathmandu seems to be the world clearing house for a continual stream of antiques from Tibet, including everything from thangkas to carpets, jewellery, storage chests, carvings, religious objects, saddles and clothing. Since the Chinese have done their utmost to destroy Tibetan culture, removing some of what remains to safety is perhaps more morally acceptable than some other 'collecting' that goes on in Nepal.

There are a number of good shops on Durbar Marg, but don't go without a very healthy wallet. The Ritual Art Gallery and Potala Art Gallery are both worth a look.

Kashmiri Goods

Since the war in Kashmir killed the tourist trade there, many Kashmiris have migrated to Nepal to sell traditional crafts such as carpets, tapestry, woollen shawls and papier-mâché. These guys are excellent salespeople, so buy with caution. Prices are pretty good; they would be cheaper in Kashmir of course, but might well come with a bonus bullet. Cottage Crafts on the ground floor of the Sanchaya Kosh Bhawan shopping centre in Jyatha has a good selection and reliable prices.

Indian Goods

With the resurgence of popularity for Gujarat's and Rajasthan's embroidered clothing and manchester, a number of shops have opened in Kathmandu. Prices are, needless to say, considerably higher than if you buy in India, but considerably less than if you buy in the West.

GETTING THERE & AWAY

See the Getting There & Away chapter for details of getting to Kathmandu both by air and by land.

Air

Kathmandu is the only international arrival point for flights to Nepal and is also the main centre for domestic flights.

International Airlines See the Central Kathmandu map for the location of many of the following international airlines offices:

Aeroflot (☎ 227399) Kamaladi
Air India (☎ 415637) Hattisar
Austrian Airlines/Lauda Airlines (☎ 241506) Kamaladi
Bangladesh Biman (☎ 434740) Naxal
British Airways (☎ 222266) Durbar Marg
China Airlines (☎ 411302) Hattisar
Druk Air (☎ 225166) Durbar Marg
Gulf Air (☎ 430456) Hattisar
Indian Airlines (☎ 410906) Hattisar
Japan Airlines (☎ 224854) Durbar Marg
Lufthansa (☎ 223052) Durbar Marg
Necon Air (☎ 473860) Sina Mangal; (☎ 258664, e reservation@necon.mos.com.np) Tridevi Marg, Thamel
Pakistan International Airlines (PIA; ☎ 439234) Hattisar
Qatar Airlines (☎ 256579) Kantipath
Royal Nepal Airlines (RNAC; ☎ 220757) Kantipath
Singapore Airlines (☎ 220759) Durbar Marg
Thai International (☎ 223565) Durbar Marg
Transavia (☎ 247215) Kamaladi

There are three important rules with flights out of Kathmandu: reconfirm, reconfirm and reconfirm! This particularly applies to Royal Nepal Airlines; at peak times when flights are heavily booked you should reconfirm when you first arrive in Nepal and reconfirm again towards the end of your stay. Even this may not guarantee you a seat – make sure you get to the airport very early as people at the end of the queue can still be left behind.

Domestic Airlines The various domestic airlines have offices around the city. However, these companies, their offices and their phone numbers seem to change with the weather; it is far less hassle to buy tickets through a travel agency or your hotel. See the Getting Around chapter for more on getting to and from Kathmandu by air.

Domestic airlines with offices in Kathmandu include:

Buddha Air (☎ 437025, e buddhaair@buddhaair.com) Hattisar
Cosmic Air (☎ 427150, e soi@wlink.com.np) Maharajganj
Gorkha Airlines (☎ 435121, e gorkha@mos.com.np) Hattisar
Mountain Air (☎ 489065, e mountainair@sbbs.wlink.com.np) Hattisar
Necon Air (☎ 480565) Sina Mangal; (☎ 258664, e reservation@necon.mos.com.np) Tridevi Marg, Thamel
Royal Nepal Airlines (RNAC; ☎ 225347, fax 225348) RNAC Bldg, corner New Rd & Kantipath
Shangri-La Air (☎ 439692) Hattisar
Skyline Airways (☎ 488657, e res@skyair.com.np) Hattisar
Yeti Airlines Lazimpat; Tridevi Marg, Thamel

Buses from Kathmandu Bus Station

destination	km	duration (hrs)	cost (Rs) night/day	ticket window
Bhairawa/Sunauli	282	10	230/189	23 & 24
Biratnagar	541	12	374/–	14
Birganj	298	10	207/190	13
Butwal	237	8	208/167	23 & 24
Dharan Bazaar	539	14	369/–	11
Gorkha	141	5	92/82	17 & 18
Hile	635	14	420/–	10
Ilam	697	15	466/–	3
Janakpur	375	9	260/–	13
Kakarbhitta	610	13	408/–	1 & 2
Mahendranagar	695	15	552/–	6
Narayanghat	146	3	117/104	13
Nepalganj	531	12	421/–	19
Pokhara	202	8	–/180	17 & 18
Tansen	302	12	244/187	17

The RNAC has computerised booking only on five routes: Pokhara, Jomsom, Lukla, Bharatpur and mountain flights. These can be booked at the main RNAC office; open 9 am to 4 pm daily.

All other domestic flights are booked in an utterly haphazard manner at a small office just around the corner. Here it seems the booking clerk keeps issuing tickets as long as people keep fronting up with money. With no apparent reservation charts to speak of, the potential for overbooking is high. Confirm more than once, and get to the airport early. The other domestic carriers seem to be well organised.

Bus

The main bus station is on the Ring Rd at Balaju, north of the city centre. It is officially called the Gongbu Bus Park, but is generally known as the Kathmandu bus terminal, or simply 'bus park'. This bus station is basically for all long-distance buses to Pokhara and destinations in the Terai. It's a huge and busy place, and there are no signs in English, so unless you read Nepali it can be thoroughly confusing. There's at least one reservation counter for each destination and bookings for long trips should be made a day in advance.

Buses for destinations within the Kathmandu Valley, and for those on or accessed from the Arniko Hwy (Jiri, Barabise, and Kodari on the Tibetan border) operate from the city bus station, in the centre of the city on the eastern edge of Tundikhel parade ground.

The exceptions to this are the more expensive tourist buses – heavily promoted in Thamel – which depart from the Thamel end of Kantipath. See Getting There & Away in the Pokhara chapter and in the Royal Chitwan National Park section in The Terai chapter for more details.

See the table 'Buses from Kathmandu Bus Station' for a list of destinations served from Kathmandu.

GETTING AROUND

The best way to see Kathmandu and the valley is to walk or ride a bicycle. Most of the sights in Kathmandu can easily be covered on foot, and this is by far the best way to appreciate the city. If and when you run out of steam, there are plenty of reasonably priced taxis and autorickshaws available. There are also limitless opportunities for

Tribhuvan Airport – International Airport or Wildlife Sanctuary?

Imagine this – the pilot of an international jet one minute from landing at Kathmandu's Tribhuvan Airport gets the following radio message from the control tower: 'Caution, cow on the runway. Request your intention'. Well, this was exactly the scenario that occurred on a flight in October 2000. Less than a week later another flight preparing for take-off received the following message: 'Stand-by for take-off. Four dogs on runway'.

Around the same time there were a number of 'bird-scares' at the airport, when approaching or departing planes made contact with some of the (feathered) kites flying in the vicinity of the airport. There were a couple of very near misses, with at least two large jets having to abort take-off after they'd started barrelling down the runway.

The bird-scare problem arose due to the siting of a temporary garbage dump within 100m of the airport. It seems the city's municipal chiefs, in their wisdom, decided that the Bagmati River, which runs close to the northern end of the runway, would make a suitable spot for a temporary garbage tip. The rotting garbage, which included carcasses of animals sacrificed during the Dasain festival, was a magnet for all manner of birds.

While the planes sport the latest in navigation equipment and electronic wizardry, and the airport itself is well equipped, it seems the perimeter fence is state of the art circa 40 years ago. Animals (and humans, using the airport as a short-cut) are free to wander at random through the gaping holes and unlocked gates, and the airport authorities simply don't have the will to do anything about it.

As long as such mismanagement and neglect is allowed to continue, the problems at Tribhuvan airport are only going to get worse, until one day...

short walks around the valley. A number are described in the Around the Kathmandu Valley chapter.

The valley is the perfect size and shape for cycling. A single-speed bicycle is fine for around the three main cities, but if you want to get into the countryside consider hiring a multigeared machine. Since the farthest point in the valley is never more than about 20km from Kathmandu, you can ride out (uphill) and return (downhill) easily within a day. Bicycle speed allows you to appreciate your surroundings and stop whenever you like.

To/From the Airport

Kathmandu's international airport is named Tribhuvan Airport after the late king, although it once rejoiced in the name Gaucher (literally 'cow pasture'!).

Getting into town is quite straightforward. There is an organised taxi service on the ground-floor foyer immediately after you leave the baggage collection and customs section. The taxis have a fixed fare of Rs 250 to Thamel or Rs 200 to Durbar Marg.

Once outside the international terminal you are confronted by hordes of hotel touts, who are often taxi drivers making commission on taking you to a particular hotel. Many hold up a signboard of the particular hotel they are connected with, and if the one you want is there, you can get a free lift. The only drawback is that the hotel is then much less likely to offer you a discount as they will be paying a hefty commission to the taxi driver.

If you don't want to be taken to a hotel of their choice, a ride to Thamel or the city centre should cost no more than Rs 200, although in the opposite direction you should be able to get a taxi for Rs 100.

There are public buses that leave from the main road – about 300m from the terminal – but they're only really useable if you have very little luggage and know exactly how to get to where you want to go.

Bus

While bus travel is very cheap, it is often unbelievably crowded. The primary disadvantage, apart from severe discomfort, is that you cannot see the views or stop when you want. Still, if you're short of cash and want to get from point A to B *reasonably* quickly, the buses will do the trick. Over a short distance – say from Thamel to Boudha – you'll probably be just as quick on a bicycle. The smaller minibuses and curious little *tempos* (automated three-wheeled vans) are generally quicker than the full-sized buses and are slightly more expensive.

Nearly all buses to points around the valley operate from the city bus station. As with anything in Nepal, however, there are exceptions to the rule.

The incredibly dilapidated electric trolleybuses that go to Bhaktapur leave from the southern end of Kantipath near the National Stadium. These trolleybuses cost Rs 4 and drop you off a 10-minute walk from the centre of Bhaktapur. Buses to Pharping (Dakshinkali) leave from Martyr's Memorial Gate at the southern end of Tundikhel parade ground.

Buses to Bungamati, Godavari and Chapagaon leave from Patan. See the Patan section in the Around the Kathmandu Valley for more details.

Taxi

Taxis are quite reasonably priced. The current charge for a metered taxi is Rs 7 flagfall and Rs 2 for every 200m; drivers don't usually take too much convincing to use the meter for short trips, although in the evenings you may have to negotiate. Shorter rides around town rarely come to more than Rs 50.

Many so-called taxis are in fact private vehicles operating as taxis. Consequently they don't have meters, in which case it's a matter of negotiating the fare in advance. Licensed taxis have black licence plates while private cars have red plates. Taxis can be booked in advance on ☎ 420987; at night call ☎ 224374.

Between several people, longer trips around the valley, or even outside it, are affordable. A half-day sightseeing trip within the valley should cost around Rs 800, and a full-day trip, Rs 1500.

Other approximate taxi fares (from Thamel) include:

Pashupatinath	Rs 80
Boudha	Rs 100
Patan	Rs 100
Bhaktapur	Rs 250
Changu Narayan	Rs 600
Dhulikhel/Nagarkot	Rs 800

For longer journeys outside the valley count on about Rs 2500 per day plus fuel, for which prices are set by the government. At the time of research, it was Rs 47 per litre.

Car

Although you cannot rent cars on a drive-yourself basis they can be readily rented with a driver from a number of operators. Try Gorkha Travels (☎ 224896) or Yeti Travels (☎ 221234) off Durbar Marg, or one of the many travel agencies in Thamel.

The rental cost is fairly high, both in terms of the initial hiring charge and fuel. Charges are as high as Rs 3000 a day, although they can be lower, especially if you are not covering a huge distance. Around the valley expect to pay about Rs 2500, plus fuel.

Motorcycle

There are a number of motorcycle rental operators around Freak St and Thamel. Officially, you need an international driving licence, but no-one ever checks. You are also required to leave a substantial deposit or your passport. For Rs 400 per day you'll get a 100cc Indian-made Honda road bike, and will basically be restricted to the Kathmandu Valley (but also including Daman and Kakani – neither in the valley – and Nagarkot and Dhulikhel). A 250cc trail bike costs around Rs 1000 per day.

Motorcycles can be great fun, once you master the traffic. However, think carefully before you do hire a motorcycle, as you will be encouraging the proliferation of noisy, polluting machines and adding to Nepal's trade imbalance. Most reasonably fit people will find that a mountain bike is a better option, especially as you can get to more places.

Autorickshaw & Cycle-Rickshaw

Three-wheeled metered autorickshaws are quite common in Kathmandu and cost as little as half of what you would pay for a cab. Flagfall is Rs 2, plus Rs 6 per kilometre. They're still a bit of a lottery – most will blankly refuse to use the meter, and if this is the case make sure you establish a price. Most rides around town should cost less than Rs 40.

Cycle-rickshaws cost Rs 30 to Rs 50 for most rides around town – they can be more expensive than going by autorickshaw or taxi. The tourist rate from Thamel to Durbar Square is Rs 40, from Thamel to the Hotel de l'Annapurna is Rs 25. You must agree on a price before you start.

Bicycle

Once you get away from the crowded streets of central Kathmandu, cycling is a pleasure, and if you're in reasonable shape this is the ideal way to explore the valley. It costs around Rs 50 a day for a regular single-speed Indian or Chinese-made bicycle. Check the brakes before taking it out and be certain to lock it whenever you leave it.

Multigeared mountain bikes have become the rage in Kathmandu, and many places around Thamel rent them out. Most are Chinese- or Indian-made bicycles that are not all that strong, but should be fine for light use around the valley. Imported bicycles are available for rent but these cost considerably more. Count on Rs 150 a day, which, if you are planning to really explore the valley, is money well spent. It's a real pleasure to surge up the long hill into Patan, sweeping by all the riders of regular bicycles who have to get off and push.

For rental of high quality equipment, check out Dawn Till Dusk in the Kathmandu Guest House compound.

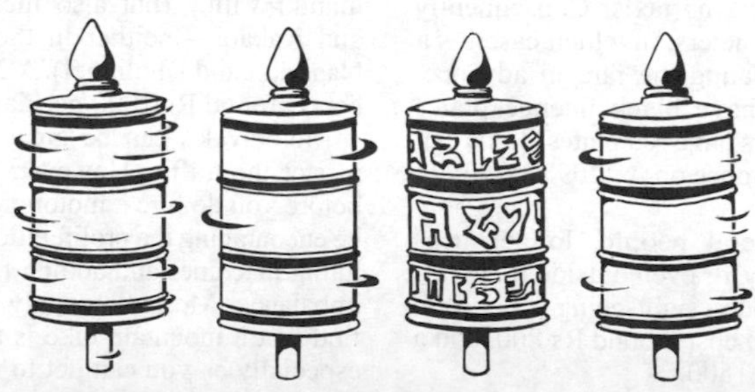

Nepal
5th edition – August 2001
6-monthly updates of this title available free on
www.lonelyplanet.com/upgrades
First published – October 1990

Published by
Lonely Planet Publications Pty Ltd ABN 36 005 607 983
90 Maribyrnong St, Footscray, Victoria 3011, Australia

Lonely Planet Offices
Australia Locked Bag 1, Footscray, Victoria 3011
USA 150 Linden St, Oakland, CA 94607
UK 10a Spring Place, London NW5 3BH
France 1 rue du Dahomey, 75011 Paris

Photographs
Many of the images in this guide are available for licensing from Lonely Planet Images.
email: lpi@lonelyplanet.com.au

Front cover photograph
Kathmandu Valley – Swayambhunath (Hannah Levy)

ISBN 1 86450 247 9

Printed by The Bookmaker International Ltd
Printed in China

Although the authors and Lonely Planet try to make the information as accurate as possible, we accept no responsibility for any loss, injury or inconvenience sustained by anyone using this book.

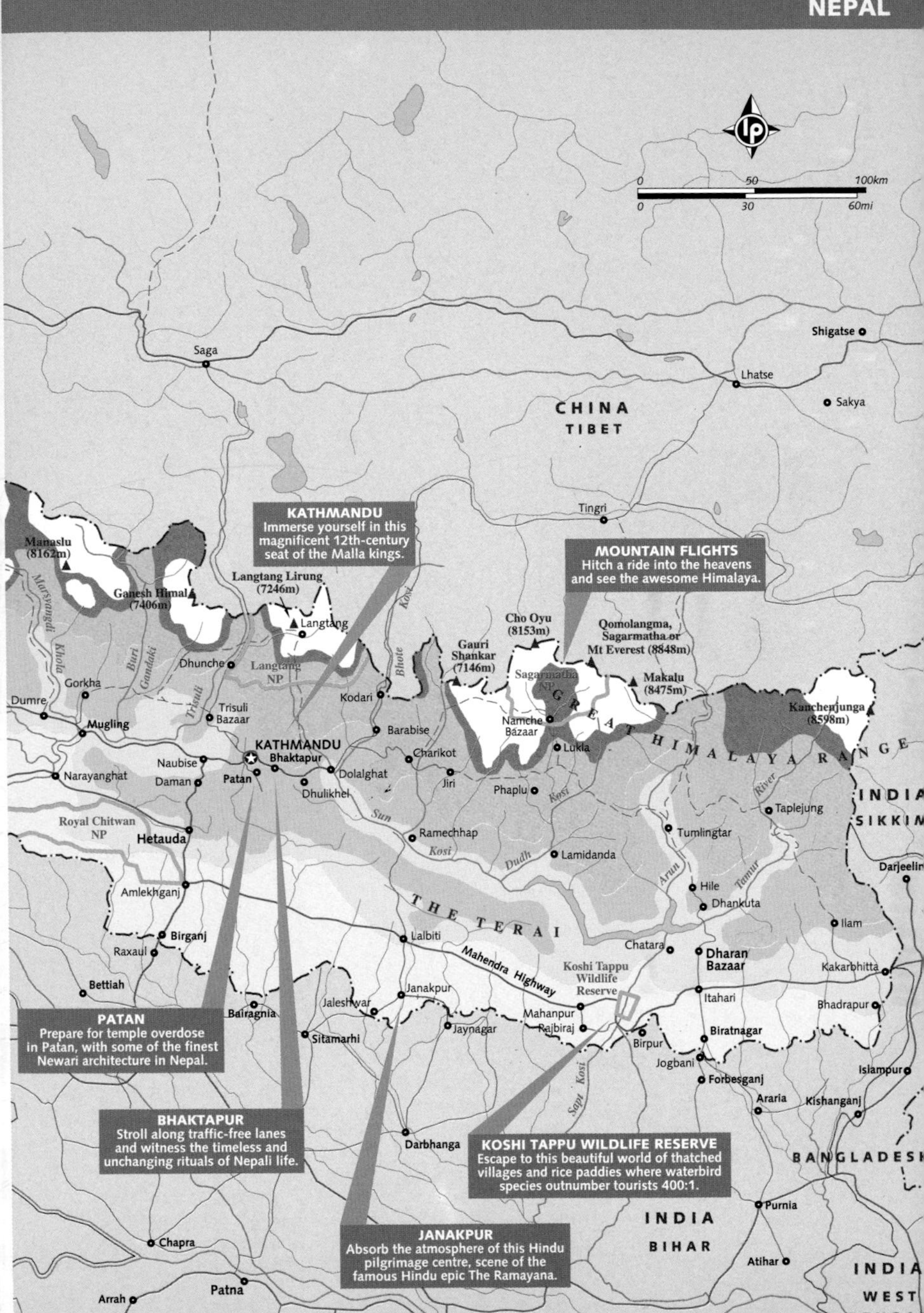
0
50
100km
0
30
60mi
Shigatse
Saga
Lhatse
Sakya
CHINA
TIBET
Tingri
KATHMANDU
Immerse yourself in this magnificent 12th-century seat of the Malla kings.
MOUNTAIN FLIGHTS
Hitch a ride into the heavens and see the awesome Himalaya.
Manaslu (8162m)
Ganesh Himal (7406m)
Langtang Lirung (7246m)
Langtang
Cho Oyu (8153m)
Qomolangma, Sagarmatha or Mt Everest (8848m)
Gauri Shankar (7146m)
Makalu (8475m)
Kanchenjunga (8598m)
Sagarmatha NP
Langtang NP
Marsyangdi
Khola
Buri
Gandaki
Trisuli
Bhote
Kosi
Dhunche
Gorkha
Dumre
Mugling
Trisuli Bazaar
Kodari
Barabise
Namche Bazaar
Lukla
GREAT HIMALAYA RANGE
KATHMANDU
Bhaktapur
Naubise
Charikot
Narayanghat
Daman
Patan
Dolalghat
Jiri
Dhulikhel
Phaplu
Sun
Kosi
Royal Chitwan NP
Hetauda
Ramechhap
Kosi
Dudh
Lamidanda
Taplejung
Tumlingtar
River
INDIA
SIKKIM
Arun
Tamur
Darjeeling
Amlekhganj
Hile
Dhankuta
THE TERAI
Ilam
Birganj
Lalbiti
Raxaul
Chatara
Dharan Bazaar
Mahendra Highway
Koshi Tappu Wildlife Reserve
Kakarbhitta
Bettiah
Janakpur
Itahari
Jaleshwar
Bhadrapur
Bairagnia
Mahanpur
Rajbiraj
Jaynagar
Biratnagar
Sitamarhi
Birpur
Jogbani
Islampur
PATAN
Prepare for temple overdose in Patan, with some of the finest Newari architecture in Nepal.
Sapt Kosi
Forbesganj
Araria
Kishanganj
BHAKTAPUR
Stroll along traffic-free lanes and witness the timeless and unchanging rituals of Nepali life.
Darbhanga
KOSHI TAPPU WILDLIFE RESERVE
Escape to this beautiful world of thatched villages and rice paddies where waterbird species outnumber tourists 400:1.
BANGLADESH
Purnia
INDIA
BIHAR
Chapra
JANAKPUR
Absorb the atmosphere of this Hindu pilgrimage centre, scene of the famous Hindu epic The Ramayana.
Atihar
INDIA
WEST BENGAL
Patna
Arrah

Contents – Text

AROUND THE KATHMANDU VALLEY 191

POKHARA 265

THE TERAI 292

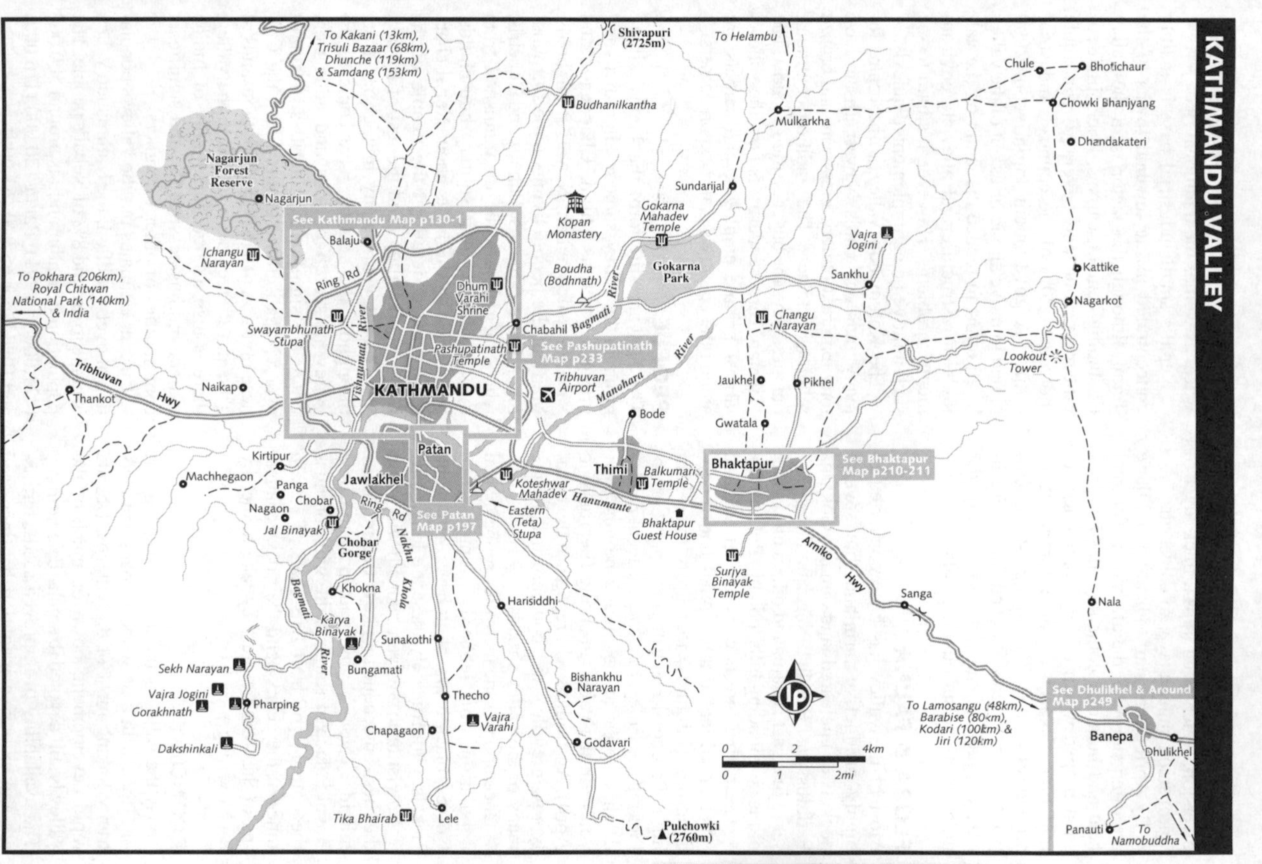

KATHMANDU VALLEY
To Kakani (13km), Trisuli Bazaar (68km), Dhunche (119km) & Samdang (153km)
Shivapuri (2725m)
To Helambu
Chule
Bhotichaur
Budhanilkantha
Mulkarkha
Chowki Bhanjyang
Dhandakateri
Nagarjun Forest Reserve
Nagarjun
Sundarijal
See Kathmandu Map p130-1
Kopan Monastery
Gokarna Mahadev Temple
Balaju
Vajra Jogini
Ichangu Narayan
Gokarna Park
Boudha (Bodhnath)
Kattike
Sankhu
To Pokhara (206km), Royal Chitwan National Park (140km) & India
Ring Rd
Dhum Varahi Shrine
Bagmati River
Nagarkot
Changu Narayan
Chabahil
Swayambhunath Stupa
Vishnumati River
Pashupatinath Temple
See Pashupatinath Map p233
Manohara River
Lookout Tower
Tribhuvan Hwy
Tribhuvan Airport
Jaukhel
Pikhel
Thankot
Naikap
KATHMANDU
Bode
Gwatala
Kirtipur
Patan
Bhaktapur
See Bhaktapur Map p210-211
Machhegaon
Jawlakhel
Thimi
Balkumari Temple
Panga
Koteshwar Mahadev
Hanumante
Chobar
Nagaon
Ring Rd
See Patan Map p197
Eastern (Teta) Stupa
Bhaktapur Guest House
Jal Binayak
Chobar Gorge
Arniko Hwy
Nakhu Khola
Surjya Binayak Temple
Bagmati River
Khokna
Sanga
Harisiddhi
Nala
Karya Binayak
Sunakothi
Sekh Narayan
Bungamati
Bishankhu Narayan
Vajra Jogini
Pharping
Gorakhnath
Thecho
See Dhulikhel & Around Map p249
To Lamosangu (48km), Barabise (80km), Kodari (100km) & Jiri (120km)
Vajra Varahi
Chapagaon
Banepa
Godavari
Dakshinkali
0 2 4km
Dhulikhel
0 1 2mi
Tika Bhairab
Lele
Pulchowki (2760m)
Panauti
To Namobuddha

with airline schedules; and the temperature inversion, which often traps a thick layer of warm smog under a layer of colder air.

By April things start to heat up and there are often storms in the afternoon. The real heat and humidity coincide with the monsoon proper, which usually commences in mid-June. Expect daytime temperatures around 30°C to 35°C, and night-time temperatures between 15°C and 20°C. Fortunately, much of the rain falls during the night or on the surrounding hills.

FLORA & FAUNA

Most of the valley has been converted to highly productive farmland, but several pockets of uncleared land remain: Gokarna Park just past Boudha; Nagarjun Forest Reserve just past Balaju; and others on several of the surrounding hills, notably Pulchowki.

The native forests consisted of oak and other broad-leafed trees, pines and rhododendrons (laliguras) that grow over 15m high. Pulchowki, the highest point overlooking the valley, has a magnificent rhododendron forest and shouldn't be missed if you're in the valley in spring (February to April). Australians will recognise the eucalyptus, grevillea and bottlebrush that line many of the valley's roads.

Once upon a time the valley probably had populations of leopards, jungle cats, wolves, black bears, sloth bears, otters and jackals. Unfortunately these are long gone.

No visitor to Swayambhunath will avoid the rhesus macaque monkeys that infest the hillside. (Nor, if you walk past the new Royal Palace in Kathmandu, will you miss the colonies of fruit bats that, at certain times of the year, spend their days chattering in the trees before they take to the sky each evening.)

ECONOMY

Today the valley is the most developed part of Nepal, with a network of roads and electricity linking most of the villages. Despite rapid development, however, much of the valley is still devoted to small-scale farming. The availability of improved seeds, fertilisers and extensive irrigation has increased productivity and made it possible to grow wheat as well as the traditional rice.

Nepal's small industrial base is mainly concentrated in the lowland towns of the Terai, although the factories in the valley (including cement, carpets, brick, light engineering, food and beverage) contribute more than 20% of the country's industrial output. A government initiative in 2000 aimed to move all factories out of the valley in an effort to reduce the strain on the valley's infrastructure and alleviate environmental problems. However, it's hard to see such a move being implemented quickly.

The Kathmandu Valley is the centre for many traditional crafts. Newari artisans have long exported pottery, brassware and bronze religious artefacts. The tradition continues, but these days the buyer is often a tourist. The 'Tibetan' carpet industry is now the valley's largest private employer, and carpets are among the country's major export earners.

PEOPLE

The Newars still form the largest single group in the valley, some smaller towns and villages, such as Thimi, Chapagaon and Sankhu, which remain Newari strongholds. Many of the people living on the surrounding hills are Tamangs, Bahuns and Chhetris, who can generally be distinguished from the Newars by their solitary households. See People in the Facts about Nepal chapter for more detail on the people of the Kathmandu Valley (and the rest of Nepal).

In recent years many immigrants from throughout the country have come to the valley in search of jobs and education. There are significant minorities of almost every Nepali ethnic group. Since the Chinese invasion of Tibet in 1959, thousands of Tibetan refugees have settled in the valley; there is also a large community of Indian traders and businesspeople, and significant communities of other foreigners.

Current estimates put the valley's population at over 1 million; the Kathmandu Valley is home to around 8% of Nepal's people. The population of Kathmandu is around 500,000 (421,000 in 1991), Patan 120,000 (116,000) and Bhaktapur 65,000 (61,000).

CULTURAL CONSIDERATIONS

You do not have to go far to escape the hordes of camera-clutching tourists, but you will nonetheless be unable to escape their legacy: suspicious people and the cries of 'one rupee, one rupee' from children. If you do venture off the beaten track, your responsibility as a visitor is greater than ever.

Whatever the temptation, do not give gifts to begging children. Do not intrude with a camera, unless it is clearly OK with the people you are photographing. Ask before entering a temple compound, although unless otherwise noted it is permissible to enter and photograph the temples described in this chapter. See Society & Conduct in the Facts about Nepal chapter for further details on cultural considerations.

ACCOMMODATION

In recent years there's been an increase in the number of accommodation options outside Kathmandu. If you don't need the bright lights and bustle of Thamel or the city, staying elsewhere in the valley can make a lot of sense. Unfortunately most of the options are not all that cheap, although places such as Dhulikhel and Nagarkot have a fair range. Some of the other options include Pharping, Dakshinkali, Lele, Godavari and Kakani (see all of these later in this chapter for details).

GETTING AROUND

Bicycle, Bus & Motorcycle

Swayambhunath and Pashupatinath can be reached on foot from Kathmandu, but by far the easiest and most economical way of getting around the valley is by bicycle. If you are aiming for somewhere on the rim of the valley, make sure you have a mountain bike. A reasonably fit person can go anywhere in the valley and return to Kathmandu within daylight on such a bicycle.

Buses and minibuses service all of the roads, but although cheap, they are uncomfortable and limiting. If you are part of a group or if the budget allows, you could consider hiring a car or taxi for the day. Motorcycles also offer a way of accessing most parts of the valley.

Organised Tours

There is one company in Kathmandu that offers limited vehicle tours around the valley for around Rs 300 for half a day. (See Organised Tours in the Kathmandu chapter for details.) If you have limited time or want a speedy introduction to the area, they're worth considering. On the other hand, taxis can be hired for about Rs 800 per half day, Rs 1500 per full day. With a taxi you aren't stuck to a schedule, and if you have this book who needs a guide?

Valley Walks

There are many interesting walks around the valley, which can take you between traditional villages and temples, and along ridge tops to mountain viewpoints; many of them make pleasant alternatives to travelling by vehicle or bicycle. You can, for example, follow a trail from Kirtipur to Chobar and from there into Patan, or walk from the Gokarna Mahadev Temple to the Boudha Stupa. These walks, among others, are detailed throughout this chapter.

In addition, there are a number of interesting walks down from Nagarkot on the valley rim to various points in and outside the valley, including a pleasant short stroll down to the beautiful temple of Changu Narayan.

For more details on walks on the edge of the Kathmandu Valley, look for Alton C Byers' *Treks on the Kathmandu Valley Rim*, or James Giambrone's *Kathmandu: Bikes & Hikes*, which are available in Kathmandu bookshops.

Patan

☎ 01

Patan is separated from Kathmandu only by the Bagmati River and is the second-largest town in the valley. It is often referred to as Lalitpur, which means 'City of Beauty'. Patan has a long Buddhist history and the four corners of the city are marked by stupas said to have been erected by the great Buddhist emperor Ashoka around 250 BC. Later inscriptions refer to palaces in the city in the 5th century AD, although Patan's great building boom took place under the Mallas in the 16th, 17th and 18th centuries.

Patan's central Durbar Square is packed with temples; it has a far greater concentration of temples per square metre than in Kathmandu or Bhaktapur. Numerous other temples of widely diverse style, as well as many *bahals* (Buddhist monasteries), are scattered around this fascinating town.

It is possible to stay in Patan, although it's so close to Kathmandu that it scarcely seems worthwhile – the choice of accommodation and restaurants is far more limited.

ORIENTATION & INFORMATION

Durbar Square is the centre of Patan. From here, four main roads lead to the four Ashoka stupas (see later in this section). Jawlakhel, to the south of the city, has a major Tibetan population and is the centre for carpet-weaving in the valley.

Buses from Kathmandu drop you at the Patan Dhoka city gate bus stop, about a 15-minute walk from Durbar Square. There's the larger Lagankhel bus stop directly south of Durbar Square, near the Southern (Lagan) Stupa. Taxis normally drop you at Patan Dhoka, the original entrance to the city. An entry fee of Rs 200 is payable at Durbar Square. Fee collection seems pretty random, and basically if you don't walk past the ticket desk (at the southern end of the square) chances are that no-one will ask you to pay.

The Nepal National Library is in Patan and Patan Hospital is the best bet in the Kathmandu Valley (see under Information in the Kathmandu chapter for details on these and all other tourist facilities).

Patan Walk

The Patan Tourist Development Organisation has developed a fascinating walk that traverses some of the most interesting sections of the old city. Unnoticed by many visitors, much of the traditional heart of the city still survives, and a complex structure of interlinked courtyards, laneways and squares can be explored.

While exploring at random is quite feasible, the walk that has been developed (and is erratically signposted throughout) takes you through the northern and north-western parts of the city, from Patan Dhoka to Durbar Square. It offers a fascinating insight into the traditional rules, regulations and cultural institutions that lay behind the creation of Newari towns and the way in which modern developments are bringing about change.

The walk is described in a small booklet entitled *Patan Walkabout*, which is available from the bookshop at Patan Dhoka.

GOLDEN TEMPLE

Also sometimes known as the Kwa Bahal or the Suwarna Mahavihara (Golden Temple), this unique Buddhist monastery is just north of Durbar Square. Legends relate that the monastery was founded in the 12th century, although the earliest record of its existence is 1409. From the street, a sign points to the monastery, entered through a doorway flanked by painted guardian lion figures, giving no hint of the magnificent structure within.

The large rectangular building has three roofs and a copper-gilded facade. Inside the shrine are images of Buddha and Avalokiteshvara; a stairway leads to the 1st floor, where monks will show you the various Buddha images and frescoes that illustrate the walls. The life of Buddha is illustrated in a frieze in front of the main shrine.

The inner courtyard has a railed walkway around three sides. Shoes and other leather articles must be removed if you leave the walkway and enter the inner courtyard itself. In the centre of the courtyard is a small but richly decorated temple crowned with a golden roof that has an extremely ornate *gajur* (a bell-shaped top). Look for the sacred tortoises pottering around in the courtyard – they are temple guardians. The monastery was dedicated by a Patan merchant grown rich from trade with Tibet. There is a small entry charge for entry to the temple.

KUMBESHWAR TEMPLE

Directly north of Durbar Square is Kumbeshwar Temple, one of the valley's three five-storey temples. The others are the towering

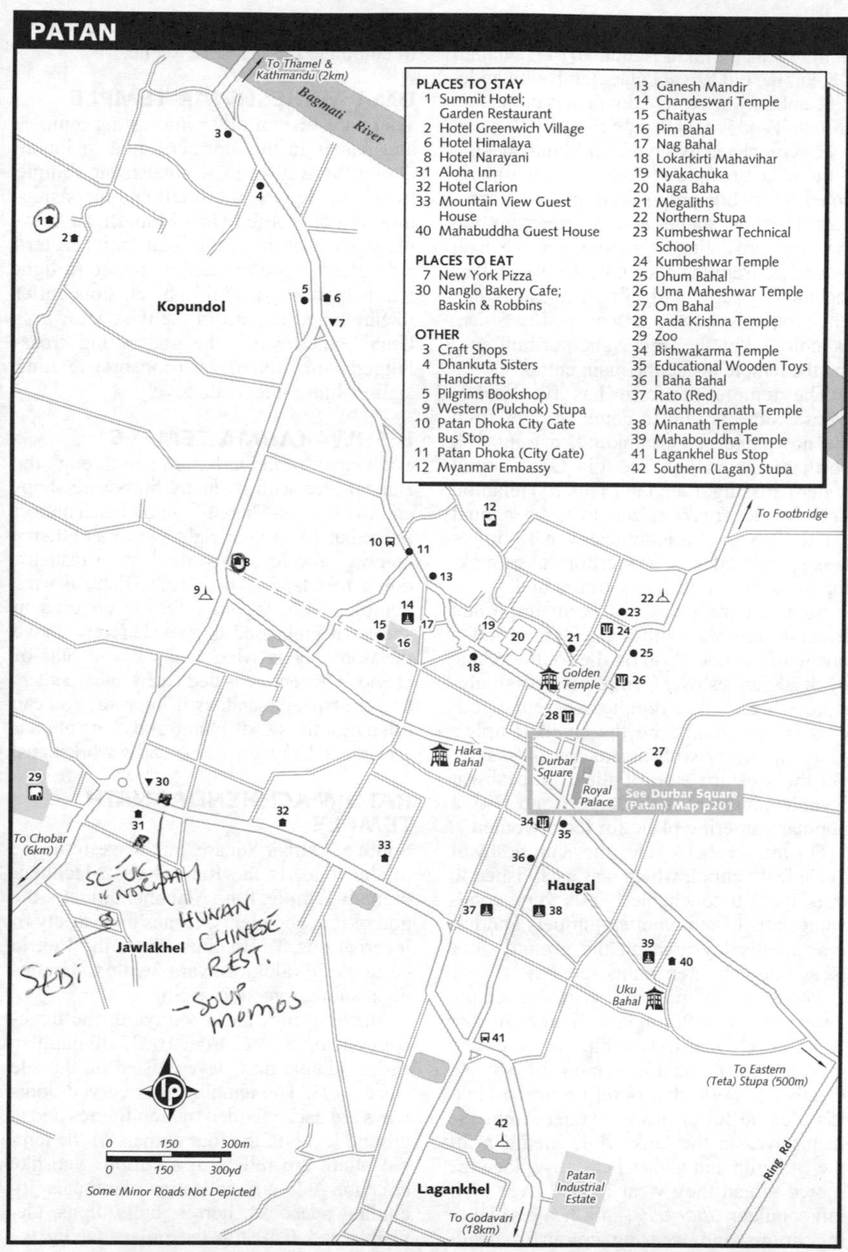
PATAN
To Thamel & Kathmandu (2km)
Bagmati River
PLACES TO STAY
1 Summit Hotel; Garden Restaurant
2 Hotel Greenwich Village
6 Hotel Himalaya
8 Hotel Narayani
31 Aloha Inn
32 Hotel Clarion
33 Mountain View Guest House
40 Mahabuddha Guest House
PLACES TO EAT
7 New York Pizza
30 Nanglo Bakery Cafe; Baskin & Robbins
OTHER
3 Craft Shops
4 Dhankuta Sisters Handicrafts
5 Pilgrims Bookshop
9 Western (Pulchok) Stupa
10 Patan Dhoka City Gate Bus Stop
11 Patan Dhoka (City Gate)
12 Myanmar Embassy
13 Ganesh Mandir
14 Chandeswari Temple
15 Chaityas
16 Pim Bahal
17 Nag Bahal
18 Lokarkirti Mahavihar
19 Nyakachuka
20 Naga Baha
21 Megaliths
22 Northern Stupa
23 Kumbeshwar Technical School
24 Kumbeshwar Temple
25 Dhum Bahal
26 Uma Maheshwar Temple
27 Om Bahal
28 Rada Krishna Temple
29 Zoo
34 Bishwakarma Temple
35 Educational Wooden Toys
36 I Baha Bahal
37 Rato (Red) Machhendranath Temple
38 Minanath Temple
39 Mahabouddha Temple
41 Lagankhel Bus Stop
42 Southern (Lagan) Stupa
Kopundol
To Footbridge
Golden Temple
Haka Bahal
Durbar Square
Royal Palace
See Durbar Square (Patan) Map p201
To Chobar (6km)
Haugal
Jawlakhel
Uku Bahal
To Eastern (Teta) Stupa (500m)
Ring Rd
0 150 300m
0 150 300yd
Some Minor Roads Not Depicted
Lagankhel
Patan Industrial Estate
To Godavari (18km)
SC-UK
HUNAN CHINESE REST.
SEDI
-SOUP MOMOS

Nyatapola Temple of Bhaktapur and the smaller Panch Mukhi Hanuman of Hanuman Dhoka (the old Royal Palace) in Kathmandu.

Kumbeshwar Temple dominates the streets around it and is said to date from 1392, when it was completed by Jayasthiti Malla, making it the oldest temple in Patan. The temple is noted for its fine proportions and woodcarvings. There are statues and sculptures around the courtyard dating from a number of Nepali dynasties, from the Licchavis to the Mallas, including a particularly fine Ganesh figure. The temple is, however, dedicated to Shiva, as indicated by the large Nandi, or bull, facing the temple inside the main entrance.

The temple platform has two ponds whose water is said to come straight from the holy lake at Gosainkund, a long trek north of the valley (see Via Gosainkund under Crossing: Langtang Trek to Helambu Trek in the Trekking chapter). An annual ritual bath in the Kumbeshwar Temple's tank is claimed to be as meritorious as making the arduous walk to Gosainkund.

South of the courtyard is an important Bhairab Temple, with a life-size wooden image of the god. Also on the southern side of the Kumbeshwar Temple is the single-storey Baglamukhi Temple, where the goddess is represented by the small temple's gilded archway with its canopy of snakes. On the western side of the Kumbeshwar Temple courtyard is the large Konti Hiti, a popular gathering place for local women.

On the northern side, the Kumbeshwar Technical School, which was established to train local untouchables, sells very good-value carpets and woollen jumpers and has a small display area on the ground floor (see Shopping later in this section).

Thousands of pilgrims visit the temple during the Janai Purnima festival in July or August each year to worship the silver and gold *lingam* (a phallic symbol of Shiva's creative powers) that is set up in the tank. It's a colourful occasion: bathers immerse themselves in the tank while members of the Brahmin and Chhetri castes replace the sacred thread they wear looped over their left shoulder. *Jhankris* (faith healers) beating drums and wearing colourful head-dresses and skirts dance around the temple to complete the dramatic scene.

UMA MAHESHWAR TEMPLE

There are several other interesting temples and bahals in this northern area of Patan. Along the way from Kumbeshwar Temple to Durbar Square, the small and inconspicuous double-roofed Uma Maheshwar Temple is set back from the road on its eastern side. Peer inside the temple to see (a light will help) a very beautiful black-stone relief of Shiva and Parvati in the pose known as Uma Maheshwar – the god sitting cross-legged with his *shakti* (consort) leaning against him rather seductively.

BISHWAKARMA TEMPLE

Walk south from Durbar Square through the Haugal area with its many brassware shops and workshops. There is a small bahal almost immediately on your right (west) and then a laneway also leading west. A short distance down this lane is the brick Bishwakarma Temple, with its entire facade covered in sheets of embossed copper. Directly above the doorway is what looks like a Star of David. The temple is dedicated to carpenters and craftspeople and, as if in proof, you can often hear the steady clump and clang of metalworkers' hammers from nearby workshops.

RATO MACHHENDRANATH TEMPLE

South of Durbar Square, on the western side of the road, is the Rato (Red) Machhendranath Temple. Rato Machhendranath, the god of rain and plenty, comes in a variety of incarnations. To Buddhists he is the Tantric edition of Avalokiteshvara, while to Hindus he is another version of Shiva.

Standing in a large courtyard, the three-storey temple dates from 1673, although an earlier temple may have existed on the site since 1408. The temple's four carved doorways are each guarded by lion figures and at ground level on the four corners of the temple plinth are reliefs of a curious yeti-like creature. A diverse collection of animals (including peacocks, horses, bulls, lions, elephants and fish) top the pillars facing the northern side of the temple; they are the Tibetan symbols for the months of the year. The metal roof is supported by struts, each showing Avalokiteshvara standing above figures being tortured in hell. Prayer wheels are set into the base of the temple.

The Machhendranath image is a crudely carved piece of red-painted wood, but each year during the Rato Machhendranath celebrations it is paraded around the town on a temple chariot. The celebration moves the image from place to place over several weeks in the month of Baisakh (April–May), ending at Jawlakhel, where the chariot is dismantled.

Occurring on a 12-year-cycle (the next time will be in 2003), the procession continues out of Patan to the village of Bungamati, 5km to the south. Dragging the heavy chariot along this bumpy and often uphill track is no easy feat. In the village the god has another temple, where, since 1593, it has been the custom for the image to spend six months of each year.

MINANATH TEMPLE

South of Durbar Square is a two-storey temple dedicated to a Buddhist Bodhisattva who is considered to be the brother of Rato Machhendranath. The Minanath image is towed around town during the Rato Machhendranath festival, but in a much smaller chariot. The temple dates from the Licchavi period but has undergone several recent restorations and 'improvements' and has roof struts carved with figures of multi-armed goddesses, all brightly painted. A large prayer wheel stands in a cage beside the temple.

MAHABOUDDHA TEMPLE

Despite its height, the Mahabouddha Temple (Temple of a Thousand Buddhas) is obscured because it is surrounded by other buildings. It's a *shikhara* (Indian-style) temple, modelled on the Mahabouddha Temple at Bodhgaya in India, where Buddha gained enlightenment. The temple takes its name from the terracotta tiles with which it is covered, each bearing an image of Buddha. It is believed to have been built in 1585, although some sources suggest an earlier date. It suffered severe damage in the 1934 earthquake and was totally rebuilt. Unfortunately, without plans to work from, the builders ended up with a different-looking temple and there were enough bricks left over to construct a shikhara-style shrine to Maya Devi, Buddha's mother, which stands to the south-west of the Mahabouddha.

The Mahabouddha Temple is about 10 minutes' walk south-east of Durbar Square. A signpost points down a lane full of curio shops leading to the temple; if you have trouble finding it, simply ask directions. The roof terrace of the shops at the back of the courtyard has a good view of the temple.

RUDRA VARNA MAHAVIHARA

Also known as Uku Bahal, this Buddhist monastery near the Mahabouddha Temple is one of the best known in Patan. A large rectangular structure with two-storey gilded roofs encloses a courtyard absolutely packed with interesting bits and pieces. There are *dorjes* (thunderbolt symbols of Bhuddist power), bells, peacocks, elephants, Garudas, rampant goats, kneeling devotees and a regal-looking statue of a Rana general. The lions are curious, seated on pillars with one paw raised in salute, there are also a couple with a decidedly British appearance, looking as if they should be guarding a statue of Queen Victoria in her 'not-amused' incarnation, rather than a colourful Nepali monastery.

As you enter the courtyard look for the finely carved wooden struts on the right. They are said to be among the oldest of this type in the valley and prior to restoration they were actually behind the monastery, but were moved to this safer location inside the courtyard. The monastery in its present form probably dates from the 19th century, but certain features and the actual site are much older.

HAKA BAHAL

Take the road west from the southern end of Durbar Square, past Café de Patan, and you come to the Haka Bahal, a rectangular building with an internal courtyard. Traditionally, Patan's Kumari (living goddess) is a daughter of one of the priests of this monastery.

[Continued on page 205]

DURBAR SQUARE (PATAN)

As in Kathmandu, the ancient Royal Palace of Patan faces on to the square, but it is a concentrated mass of temples, undoubtedly the most visually stunning display of Newari architecture to be seen in Nepal. The rectangular square has its longer axis running approximately north–south and the palace forms the eastern side of the square. A continuous row of temples in widely diverse styles faces the palace on the western side.

The square rose to its full glory during the Malla period, and particularly during the reign of King Siddhinarsingh Malla. Patan's major market, the Mangal Bazaar, is beside the square. See also the boxed text 'Erotic Art' in the Kathmandu chapter for details on erotic temple carvings in Patan.

Bhimsen Temple (9) At the northern end of Durbar Square, the Bhimsen Temple is dedicated to the god of trade and business, which possibly explains its well-kept and prosperous look. Bhimsen, a hero of the *Mahabharata*, was said to be extraordinarily strong.

The three-storey temple has had a chequered history. Although it is not known when it was first built, an inscription records that it was rebuilt in 1682 after a fire. Restorations also took place after the great 1934 earthquake, and again in 1967. A lion tops a pillar in front of the temple, while the brick building has an artificial marble facade and a gilded facade on the first floor.

Inset: Krishna Temple surrounded by Newari pagoda temples. (Photo: Chris Klep)

Manga Hiti (7) Immediately north of the palace is the sunken Manga Hiti, one of the water conduits with which Patan, and even more so Bhaktapur, are so liberally endowed. This one has a lotus-shaped pool and three wonderfully carved stone crocodile-head waterspouts. Next to it is the **Mani Mandap (8)**, a pavilion built in 1700 and used for royal crownings.

Vishwanath Temple (10) Next to the Bhimsen Temple stands the Vishwanath (Shiva) Temple. This elaborately decorated two-storey temple was built in 1627 and has two large stone elephants guarding the front entrance. Shiva's vehicle, the bull, is on the other side of the temple, while inside is a large *lingam* (phallic symbol). As yet further proof of Shiva's influence, the roof struts have been decorated with erotic themes. The temple has been restored in recent years.

Krishna Mandir (11) Continuing into the square, the third temple you reach is the Krishna Mandir, which is dedicated to Krishna

Krishna Mandir

DURBAR SQUARE (PATAN)

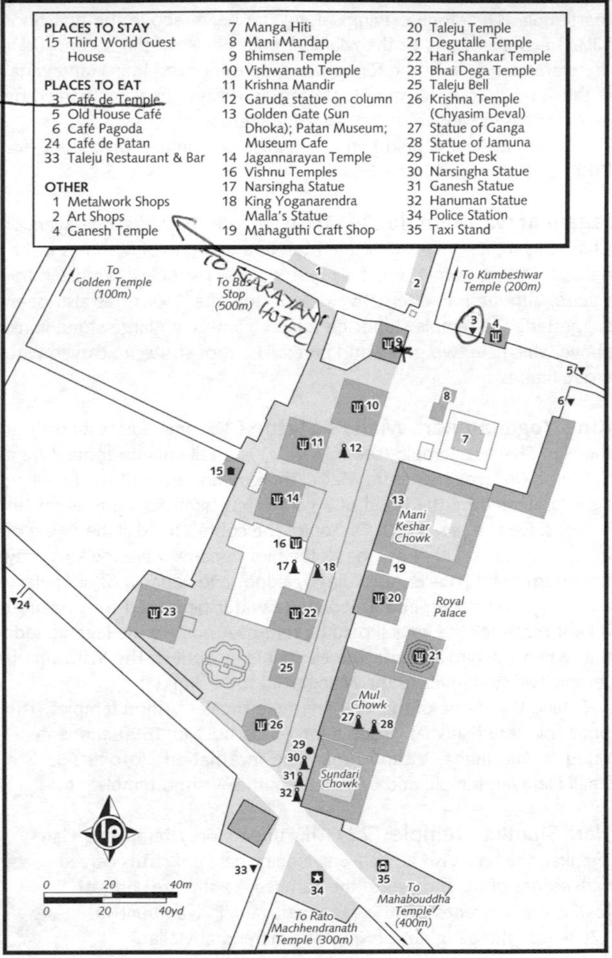
PLACES TO STAY
15 Third World Guest House
PLACES TO EAT
3 Café de Temple
5 Old House Café
6 Café Pagoda
24 Café de Patan
33 Taleju Restaurant & Bar
OTHER
1 Metalwork Shops
2 Art Shops
4 Ganesh Temple
7 Manga Hiti
8 Mani Mandap
9 Bhimsen Temple
10 Vishwanath Temple
11 Krishna Mandir
12 Garuda statue on column
13 Golden Gate (Sun Dhoka); Patan Museum; Museum Cafe
14 Jagannarayan Temple
16 Vishnu Temples
17 Narsingha Statue
18 King Yoganarendra Malla's Statue
19 Mahaguthi Craft Shop
20 Taleju Temple
21 Degutalle Temple
22 Hari Shankar Temple
23 Bhai Dega Temple
25 Taleju Bell
26 Krishna Temple (Chyasim Deval)
27 Statue of Ganga
28 Statue of Jamuna
29 Ticket Desk
30 Narsingha Statue
31 Ganesh Statue
32 Hanuman Statue
34 Police Station
35 Taxi Stand
To Golden Temple (100m)
To Bus Stop (500m)
To Kumbeshwar Temple (200m)
Mani Keshar Chowk
Royal Palace
Mul Chowk
Sundari Chowk
0 20 40m
0 20 40yd
To Rato Machhendranath Temple (300m)
To Mahabouddha Temple (400m)

and was built by King Siddhinarsingh Malla. Records indicate that the temple was completed with the installation of the image on the first floor in 1637. With its strong Mughal influences, this stone temple is clearly of Indian design, unlike the nearby brick and timber, multiroofed Newari temples. The first and second floors of this temple are made up of a line of pavilions, from the top of which rises a corncob-like spire. Musicians can often be heard playing upstairs.

Krishna is an incarnation of Vishnu, so the god's vehicle, the man-bird Garuda, kneels with folded arms on top of a **column (12)** facing the temple. The stone carvings along the beam above the first-floor pillars recount events of the *Mahabharata* while on the second floor there are scenes from the *Ramayana* (see the boxed text 'Ramayana' in the Terai chapter for more). These fine friezes are accompanied by explanations in Newari of the narrative scenes.

A major festival is held here in August–September, or Bhadra, for Krishna's birthday, Krishnasthami.

Jagannarayan Temple (14) The two-storey brick Jagannarayan, or Charnarayan, Temple is dedicated to Narayan, one of Vishnu's incarnations. Dating from 1565, it is reputed to be the oldest temple in the square, although an alternative date in the late 1600s has also been suggested. The temple stands on a brick plinth with large stone lions, above which are two guardian figures. The roof struts are carved with erotic figures.

King Yoganarendra Malla's Statue (18) Immediately north of the Hari Shankar Temple (see following) is a tall column topped by a figure of King Yoganarendra Malla. The golden figure of the kneeling king, protected by the hood of a cobra, has been facing towards his palace since the year 1700. On top of the cobra's head is the figure of a bird; legends say that as long as the bird remains there the king may still return to his palace. Accordingly, a door and window of the palace are always kept open and a *hookah* (a water pipe used for smoking) is kept ready for the king should he return. A rider to the legend adds that when the bird flies off, the elephants in front of the Vishwanath Temple will stroll over to the Manga Hiti for a drink!

Behind the statue of the king are three smaller Vishnu temples. The small, plastered shikhara-style temple was built in 1590 and is dedicated to Narsingha, Vishnu's man-lion incarnation. To one side is a small Narayan temple and behind it another Vishnu temple.

Hari Shankar Temple (22) This three-storey temple to Hari Shankar, the half-Vishnu, half-Shiva deity, has roof struts carved with scenes of the tortures of the damned – a strange contrast to the erotic scenes on the Jagannarayan. It was built in 1704–5 by the daughter of King Yoganarendra Malla.

Taleju Bell (25) Diagonally opposite Taleju Temple in the palace complex, the large bell, hanging between two stout pillars, was erected by King Vishnu Malla in 1736. An earlier bell, erected in 1703, was then moved to the Rato Machhendranath Temple. Petitioners could ring the bell to alert the king to their grievances. Shop stalls are in the building under the bell platform, and behind it is a lotus-shaped pool with a bridge over it.

Hari Shankar Temple

Krishna Temple (26) This attractive, octagonal stone temple, also known as the Chyasim Deval, completes the 'front line' of temples in the square. The stairway to the temple, which faces the palace's Sundari Chowk, is guarded by two stone lions. The temple was built in 1723 and, like the square's Krishna Mandir (see earlier), is a stark contrast to the usual Newari pagoda temple designs.

Bhai Dega Temple (23) Behind the Krishna Temple stands the squat Bhai Dega, or Biseshvar, dedicated to Shiva. It's a singularly unattractive temple, although it is said to contain an impressive lingam. A few steps back from the square is another stone shikhara-style temple, clearly owing inspiration to the important Krishna Mandir of the square. This same design pops up in several other temples around Patan. The popular Café de Patan is just behind this temple.

Royal Palace Forming the whole eastern side of the Durbar Square is the Royal Palace of Patan. Parts of the palace were built in the 14th century, but the main construction was during the 17th and 18th centuries by Siddhinarsingh Malla, Srinivasa Malla and Vishnu Malla. The Patan palace predates the palaces of Kathmandu and Bhaktapur. It was severely damaged during the conquest of the valley by Prithvi Narayan Shah in 1768 and also by the great earthquake of 1934, but it remains one of the architectural highlights of the valley, with a series of connecting courtyards and three temples dedicated to the valley's main deity, the goddess Taleju.

Mani Keshar Chowk The northern courtyard of the Royal Palace and museum are entered from the square by the **Golden Gate (13)**, or Sun Dhoka. Completed in 1734, this is the newest part of the palace. The courtyard is entered through a magnificent gilded door topped by a golden *torana* (portico above the door indicating whom the temple is dedicated to) showing Shiva, Parvati, Ganesh and Kumar. Directly above the golden door is a golden window, at which the king would make public appearances.

The rear courtyard here is reached by a passage between the Mani Keshar Chowk and the Taleju Temple. It was used for dance and drama performances during the Malla period and one wall is decorated with erotic figures. Today it houses the excellent Museum Cafe (see Places to Eat in the Patan section).

Patan Museum (13) This part of the palace has been superbly renovated and houses one of the finest museums on the subcontinent. There have been some modern elements added to the building as part of the renovations, and the result is a beautiful synthesis of old and new.

The main feature of the museum is an outstanding collection of cast-bronze and gilt-copper work, mostly of Hindu and Buddhist deities. Three galleries are devoted to Hinduism and two to Buddhism. Another gallery shows the stages involved in the production of hammered sheet-metal relief designs (known as repoussé) and the 'lost-wax' method of casting. In yet another there are also some fascinating photos of Patan at the turn of the 19th and 20th centuries.

The museum is open from 10.30 am to 4.30 pm daily (except Tuesday); entry is Rs 20. You need at least an hour or so to do this place justice. For a sneak preview of the museum check out its Web site at www.asianart.com/patan-museum.

Mul Chowk The central courtyard is the largest and oldest of the palace's three main *chowks* (squares). Two stone lions guard the entrance to the courtyard, which was built by Siddhinarsingh Malla, destroyed in a fire in 1662 and rebuilt by Srinivasa Malla in 1665–6. At the centre of the courtyard stands the small, gilded Bidya Temple.

The palace's three Taleju temples stand around the courtyard. The doorway to the Shrine of Taleju or Taleju Bhawani, on the southern side of the courtyard, is flanked by the statues of the river goddesses **Ganga (27)** on a tortoise and **Jamuna (28)** on a nice mythical *makara* (crocodile).

The five-storey **Degutalle Temple (21)**, topped by its circular triple-roofed tower, is on the north-eastern corner of the square. The larger, square, triple-roofed **Taleju Temple (20)** is directly north, looking out over Durbar Square. It was built by Siddhinarsingh Malla in 1640, rebuilt after a fire and rebuilt after the 1934 earthquake, which completely demolished it. The goddess Taleju was the personal deity of the Malla kings from the 14th century, and Tantric rites were performed to her in this temple.

Taleju Temple

Sundari Chowk South of the larger Mul Chowk is the Sundari Chowk, with its sunken tank known as the Tusha Hiti. The superbly carved stonework in the tank depicts the eight Ashta Matrikas, the eight Bhairabs and the eight Nagas. The tank was originally built in about 1670 and restored in 1960. A toy-size replica of the Krishna Mandir in the main square sits above the tank.

The courtyard is surrounded by a three-storey building with finely carved struts and windows. The entrance to the courtyard from the main square is guarded by stone statues of **Hanuman (32)**, **Ganesh (31)**, and Vishnu as **Narsingha (30)**, the man-lion. The gilded metal window over the entrance from the square is flanked by windows of carved ivory.

Behind the Sundari Chowk, but unfortunately not open to the public, is the Royal Garden, with a water tank known as the Kamal Pokhari.

[Continued from page 199]

ASHOKA STUPAS

The four stupas marking the boundaries of Patan are said to have been built when the great Buddhist emperor Ashoka visited the valley 2500 years ago. Although remains of all four can still be seen today, they probably bear little similarity to the original stupas. The northern stupa is just beyond the Kumbeshwar Temple, not far from Durbar Square. It's well preserved and whitewashed. The other three are all grassed over. The Southern, or Lagan, Stupa is just south of the Lagankhel bus stop and is the largest of the four. The smaller western, or Pulchok Stupa is beside the main road from Kathmandu that runs through to Jawlakhel and across from the Hotel Narayani. Finally, the small Eastern, or Teta, Stupa is well to the east of centre, across Kathmandu's Ring Rd and just beyond a small river.

ZOO

Nepal's only zoo is in the south-western part of Patan, just north of Jawlakhel. It includes a reasonably extensive collection of Nepali wildlife, including rhinos, tigers, leopards, monkeys and birds. While it is yet another depressing animal prison, it is a quiet, shady place and you can hire pedal boats for a paddle around the lake. There's also a small aquarium here.

Keen naturalists, as well as students of the grotesque and young kids may still enjoy a visit. Entry is Rs 60/30 for adults/children. The zoo is open 10 am to 6 pm (last entry 5 pm) daily except Monday.

JAWLAKHEL

The 'Tibetan refugee camp' of Jawlakhel is no longer really a camp at all, but a large centre for carpet production. It was established in 1960 with help from the International Red Cross and the Swiss government and employs 1000 refugees in the production of Tibetan carpets. This is where the enormous carpet industry of today got its start; it's still the place to begin if you want to buy a carpet.

You may well be able to buy cheaper carpets outside the camp, but those in the shops by the entrance have marked prices, so you can get a good idea of values (other Tibetan crafts are also on sale). You can go inside to the workshop area and actually see the carpets being made (see Shopping later in this section).

KOTESHWAR MAHADEV TEMPLE

East of the city, outside the Patan city limits, the important temple of Koteshwar Mahadev is just north of the confluence of the Manohara and Hanumante Rivers, which in turn joins the Bagmati River. Mahadev means 'Great God', the usual term for Shiva, but Koteshwar can also be translated as 'Millions of Gods', so this is a temple of Shiva with many faces, a particularly powerful form of Lord Shiva. The shrine's Shiva lingam is said to date from the 8th century.

A little south of the temple is the Kuti Bahal, where travellers bound for Tibet were customarily farewelled. The monastery has a 15th-century chaitya (small stupa).

PLACES TO STAY

Patan's accommodation consists mainly of mid-range and top-end places. Some overseas aid agencies are in Patan, particularly around Jawlakhel, and many of the long-term foreign residents live here.

PLACES TO STAY – BUDGET & MID-RANGE

Close to the Mahabouddha Temple south-east of Durbar Square, the ***Mahabuddha Guest House*** *(☎ 540575, ⓔ nfosterm@wlink.com.np)* is a comfortable little place in a very handy location. Rooms with shared bathroom (there is one bathroom for every three rooms) are a bargain at Rs 180, with private bathroom they are Rs 300.

Between Jawlakhel and Durbar Square is the district of Kumaripati, and here you'll find the ***Mountain View Guest House*** *(☎ 538168)*, down a side street off the main road. It's nothing flash, but is clean and comfortable. Singles/doubles with shared bathroom cost Rs 200/300, or there are a few doubles with bathroom for Rs 350.

The ***Third World Guest House*** *(☎ 522187, ⓔ dsdp@wlink.com.np)* has a top location on the west side of Durbar Square, with all rooms having views over the square. It's a privilege you pay for, however, as the doubles cost US$15 with shared bathroom, and US$20 with private bathroom, although there appears to be some room to negotiate. The Summit Hotel also has rooms in this price range (see Places to Stay – Top End later in this section).

Patan has a popular mid-range hotel if you'd like a complete break from frantic Kathmandu. The ***Aloha Inn*** *(☎ 522796, ⓔ aloha@ati.mos.com.np)* is located in the Jawlakhel area, not too far from the southern edge of the old city. Singles/doubles cost US$30/40 plus 12% tax. It's a friendly place, clean, well kept and quiet, and there's a very pleasant garden.

Close by and a little closer to the old city is the ***Hotel Clarion*** *(☎ 524512, ⓔ clarion@wlink.com.np)*, which is set in a pleasant garden but is still uncomfortably close to the noisy road – ask for a room at the back. Comfortable, well-kept rooms with TV, phone and private bathroom cost US$50/60 plus taxes, but discounts of 20% are easy to negotiate.

PLACES TO STAY – TOP END

Patan also has a number of top-end hotels, although none of them are close enough to the interesting centre of the old city to be particularly convenient.

The ***Summit Hotel*** *(☎ 521810, ⓔ summit@wlink.com.np)* tops a hillock in the Kopundol area and has great views across the river to Kathmandu and the distant mountains. There's a very beautiful garden with a swimming pool – a real pleasure in hot weather. This relaxed, low-key hotel's inconvenient location is its only drawback; finding taxis can sometimes be difficult. Standard singles/doubles cost US$75/85, and US$10 more for balconies with mountain views, dropping to US$55/70 in summer. There are some budget rooms with shared bathroom and no views for US$25/35 (US$15/25 in summer). There's a pleasant bar and the ***Garden Restaurant*** turns out superb food.

Also topping the Kopundol hill is the nearby ***Hotel Greenwich Village*** *(☎ 521780)*, with rooms at US$60/70, but discounts of up to 30% are offered. There's also a swimming pool, and a top-floor restaurant so you can take advantage of the view.

Two other Patan hotels are more distinctly in the top-end price bracket. The ***Hotel Narayani*** *(☎ 525015, ⓔ travel@go-nepal.com)* has a garden, a swimming pool and rooms at US$70/85, plus 12% tax, although discounts of 30% or more seem to be par for the course.

The modern ***Hotel Himalaya*** *(☎ 523900, ⓔ himalaya@lalitpur.mos.com.np)* has terrific views, a swimming pool, tennis and badminton courts and is at the top of the Kathmandu Valley price range, with comfortable rooms from US$110/120 plus 12% tax. The hotel has a shuttle bus to the city centre.

PLACES TO EAT

Just a few steps from the south-western corner of Durbar Square, the small ***Café de Patan*** is a long-running favourite, with two pleasant open-air dining areas: a small courtyard and a rooftop garden. It's a good place for a drink, snack or even a meal. It turns out a superb lassi and a number of good-value dishes, such as pizza and chicken, from Rs 50 to Rs 135.

Overlooking the square, the nicely decorated ***Third World Restaurant*** (attached to the Third World Guest House) has a brilliant rooftop area with views over Patan and, on a clear day, pagodas with a Himalayan backdrop. Snacks are around Rs 80, burgers, nice pastas and sandwiches around Rs 90.

Café de Temple, on the northern edge of the square, has excellent views from the roof, and an ambitious menu, with snacks for Rs 50 to Rs 150 and main meals (continental, Indian and Chinese) for Rs 80 to Rs 180. The ***Café Pagoda*** also looks directly onto this northern part of the square and has a similar menu, but is tucked off the least interesting corner.

Also in this corner of the square is the ***Old House Café***, which, true to its name, is set in an old Newari house. The building is probably of more interest than the food, however.

In the rear courtyard of the museum is the excellent open-air ***Museum Cafe***, which is operated by the Summit Hotel. Light meals cost Rs 100 to Rs 190, which is a bit more than elsewhere, but the setting more than compensates.

At the opposite end of the square is the ***Taleju Restaurant & Bar***. Head for the 5th-floor terrace, as the views from here are outstanding, especially on a clear day when you have the snow-capped Ganesh *himal* (range with permanent snow) as a great backdrop. The food comes a distant second.

Near the zoo roundabout at Jawlakhel is another in the chain of Nanglo ***Bakery Cafés***. It's a good place to drop in for a snack. A number of the waiters here are deaf (literally).

SHOPPING

Patan has many small handicraft shops and for certain crafts it is the best place in the valley. The Tibetan Jawlakhel area in the south of Patan is the place for Tibetan crafts and carpets. There is a string of carpet shops as you enter Jawlakhel, and a shop front, Khukuri House, is the official supplier of khukuri knives to the renown British Gurkha regiments.

The Patan Industrial Estate, in the south of Patan, doesn't sound like a very promising place to shop for handicrafts. It is, however, more like a large compound, containing a number of handicraft factory-cum-showroom places. While these places are definitely aimed at the group tourist, there is nothing to stop individuals having a wander around. Generally there is no pressure to buy and you can often see craftspeople at work. Places here manufacture carpets, woodwork and metalwork.

Fair Trade Shops

Those interested in crafts should definitely visit the string of interesting shops at Kopundol, just to the south of the main Patan bridge. A number are run as part of non-profit development organisations, so their prices are fair, and the money actually goes to the craftspeople, sometimes as training and product development.

One of the best of these organisations is Mahaguthi, which was established with the help of Oxfam. It has three shops and sells a wide range of crafts produced by thousands of people. Among other things, it sells beautiful hand-woven *dhaki* (cotton cloth), rice paper, pottery, block prints, woven bamboo, woodcrafts, jewellery, knitwear, embroidery and Mithila paintings (see the boxed text 'Mithila Painting' in the Terai chapter). The Kopundol shop is on the right as you go up the hill (the main street) approaching from Kathmandu, but there are also shops on Durbar Square (Patan), and in Lazimpat, north of the new Royal Palace in Kathmandu.

Tigers & Goats

Nepal's national board game is *bagh chal*, which literally means 'move *(chal)* the tigers *(bagh)*'. The game is played on a lined board with 25 intersecting points. One player has four tigers, the other has 20 goats, and the aim is for the tiger player to 'eat' five goats by jumping over them before the goat player can encircle a single tiger and prevent it moving.

The game starts with the four tigers at the four corners of the board. Play alternates between the goats and the tigers and the goat player places their goats on the board one at a time. No goat can be moved from its initial position until every goat has been placed on the board. By backing up one goat with another so that the tiger cannot jump them the goats can soon clutter up the board so effectively that the tigers cannot move. That is, if the tigers haven't done a good job of eating the goats!

All you need to play is a board scratched out on the dirt and 24 bottle caps or stones as markers, but you can also buy attractive brass bagh chal sets in Kathmandu, and in Patan where they are made.

Near the Kumbeshwar Temple, the Kumbeshwar Technical School provides the untouchable community of Patan with skills; they produce excellent carpets, jumpers and woodwork. You can buy direct, and they have a small showroom and shop on the ground floor of the school.

Metalwork

Patan is the centre for bronze-casting and other metalwork. The statues you see on sale in Kathmandu will most probably have been made in Patan and there are a number of excellent metalwork shops just to the north of Durbar Square. They have fine images of Buddha, the Green and White Taras (*taras* are consorts) and other figures from the Tantric Buddhist pantheon. Good-quality gold-plated and painted bronze figures will cost Rs 2000 to Rs 5000 for smaller ones, up to more than Rs 10,000 for large images.

Paintings

In the north of Durbar Square, just beyond the Bhimsen Temple, are a number of interesting art shops selling paintings. Some sell Sherpa-style paintings rather like the naive art of the Balinese 'young artist'. It's clearly something developed for the tourist trade, but never mind – they're nicely done and you can have all of the Kathmandu Valley, or even all of Nepal, in one painting. Prices start at Rs 2000.

Carpets

Those interested in carpets must visit Jawlakhel and Boudha. The Tibetan refugee camp at Jawlakhel has numerous shops on the approach road, past the zoo. The carpets at the Kumbeshwar Technical School are fairly priced, and this is possibly the only place where you can buy carpets made from 100% pure Tibetan wool.

Toys

Just south of Durbar Square is Educational Wooden Toys, which sells wonderful wooden toys including authentic Nepali trucks from Rs 300 to Rs 600, autorickshaws for Rs 500 and rickshaws for Rs 400. You can find these toys on sale in Kathmandu (including at some of the craft shops), but they're cheaper here where they're made. The factory is only a stone's throw from the shop and it's fascinating to see the parts being cut out with pedal-operated jigsaws.

GETTING THERE & AWAY

You can get to Patan from Kathmandu easily, whether by bicycle, taxi, bus or *tempo* (three-wheeled minivan). It's an easy 5km ride from Thamel to Patan's Durbar Square. The same trip costs around Rs 100 by taxi. Buses (Rs 3) leave regularly from Kathmandu's City bus station and drop you at the Patan city gate bus stop, a short walk from Durbar Square. Tempos (Rs 6, route 14) also leave from the Kathmandu main post office as soon as they have 10 passengers. Some buses for more distant destinations leave from Patan: Buses to Godavari and Chapagaon leave from the Lagankhel bus stop and buses to Bungamati from Jawlakhel.

If you come to Patan by bicycle, an interesting route from Kathmandu is to take the track down to the river from opposite the big convention centre on the Bhaktapur road. A footbridge crosses the river here and you enter Patan by the Northern Stupa near the Kumbeshwar Temple.

Bhaktapur

☎ 01

Bhaktapur, also known as Bhadgaon (pronounced bud-gown), Khwopa in Newari, or the City of Devotees, is the third major town of the valley and in many ways it is the most medieval. Since the big German-funded Bhaktapur Development Project in the 1970s, it has been a much cleaner and tidier town, but there's still a distinctly timeless air to the place. The project workers restored buildings, paved dirt streets and established sewerage and waste water management facilities.

The oldest part of the town is around Tachupal Tole, to the east. Bhaktapur was the capital of the whole valley during the 14th to 16th centuries and during that time the focus of the town shifted west, to the

CRAIG PERSHOUSE

Weighing it up in Patan.

HUGH FINLAY

Patan, Nepal's metalwork centre

CHRIS IVIN

Valley produce maketh the market.

GREG ELMS

Flower power along Asan Tole, Kathmandu.

CHRIS MELLOR

The warp and weft of tradition

ANDERS BLOMQVIST

The wheels spin and clay is thrown at Potters' Square, Bhaktapur.

LINDSAY BROWN

The symmetry of everyday life in Nepal

ANDERS BLOMQVIST

Dhoko (basket) weaving, Surkhet

DUSHAN COORAY

Cycle-rickshaws are a great way to navigate the streets of old Kathmandu.

Durbar Square area. Much of the town's great architecture dates from the end of the 17th century, which was during the rule of King Bhupatindra Malla.

ORIENTATION

Bhaktapur rises up on the northern bank of the Hanumante River. It's basically a pedestrian's city, and much better for it. Taxis and tour buses stop at the tourist bus and taxi park on the northern edge of Bhaktapur, a short walk from the heart of the city; public buses stop at Navpokhu Pokhari on the western edge of town. If you come to Bhaktapur from Kathmandu by trolleybus, the stop is on the main road bypassing Bhaktapur, a 10- to 15-minute walk south-west of Taumadhi Tole.

For the visitor, Bhaktapur is really a town of one curving road, punctuated by several squares. From the bus stop at Navpokhu Pokhari you come first to Durbar Square, then Taumadhi Tole with the famous five-storey Nyatapola Temple, then to Tachupal Tole.

INFORMATION

Foreigners visiting Bhaktapur are charged a hefty fee of Rs 750. This is collected at the various entrances to the city; On the larger streets there is a ticket booth; smaller streets have roaming ticket collectors who pop up out of the woodwork when someone tries to enter by this way. If you are staying in Bhaktapur for up to a week, you only need to pay the entrance fee once, but you must state this at the time of buying the ticket. For longer stays (up to one year), a Bhaktapur Visitor Pass is available. These are issued by the Bhaktapur Municipality (on the eastern end of Durbar Square) and require you to supply one photo and a photocopy of your visa and passport details.

WALKING TOURS

Bhaktapur is a fascinating town to wander in, and the lack of traffic makes walking a real pleasure, particularly compared with the busy streets of Kathmandu, where walking would be so much more enjoyable without those motor vehicles to dodge!

These walks take you by a number of interesting temples and shrines, but in Bhaktapur it's simply observing the timeless and seemingly unchanging rituals of life that is most interesting. Look for grain laid out to dry in the sun, people collecting water or washing under the communal taps, dyed yarns hung out to dry, children's games, fascinating shops, potters at work and women pounding grain – there's plenty to see. Perhaps most entrancing of all is Bhaktapur's medieval atmosphere.

For the walking tour that is marked on the Bhaktapur map see Circular Tour last in this section.

Navpokhu Pokhari to Potters' Square

If you feel like a guided walk into the heart of the city from the western edge of Bhaktapur (on the approach from Kathmandu) then read on.

The main road heading through Bhaktapur from the west forks at Siddha Pokhari. The southern road in this fork is much more interesting, as it is the main road through Bhaktapur connecting Taumadhi Tole and Tachupal Tole. To get onto this road from Navpokhu Pokhari turn south from the corner of the *pokhari* (large water tank) and then left on the road, immediately before the town's **Lion Gate**. You pass a small tank on your right and then the much larger **Teka Pokhari**. Just before the next major junction, to your left, is the constricted, tunnel-like entrance to the tiny **Ni Bahal**, dedicated to the Maitreya Buddha, the Buddha yet to come.

Cross the junction, where the road runs downhill to the **Mangal Tirtha Ghat**, and you will see on your left is the red-brick **Jaya Varahi Temple**. There are elaborately carved wooden *toranas* (porticos that can indicate the god to whom the temple is dedicated) over the central door and the window above it. At the western end of the temple is the entrance to the upper floor, flanked by stone lions and banners. Two ornate windows, on either side of the upper torana, were at one time coloured gold and some traces remain.

A few more steps brings you to a small **Ganesh shrine** that juts out into the street. Continue to **Nasamana Square**, which is somewhat decrepit but has a Garuda statue without a temple. Almost immediately after this is a second square with the Jyotirlingeshwar, a shikhara-style temple that houses an important lingam. Behind the shrine is an attractive *hiti*, one of the many sunken water conduits in Bhaktapur. Walk a few more steps and you will arrive at the turn-off to Potters' Square. Walk a little farther on and you will come to Taumadhi Tole.

Potters' Square

Potters' Square can be approached from Durbar Square, Taumadhi Tole or along the western road into town from Siddha Pokhari and Navpokhu Pokhari. You also pass right by the square when walking into town from the trolleybus stop on the Arniko Hwy to the south of the centre.

On the northern side of the square a small hillock is topped by a Ganesh shrine and a shady pipal tree. There are fine views over the river to the hills south of Bhaktapur. The square itself has two small temples: a solid-brick **Vishnu Temple** and the double-

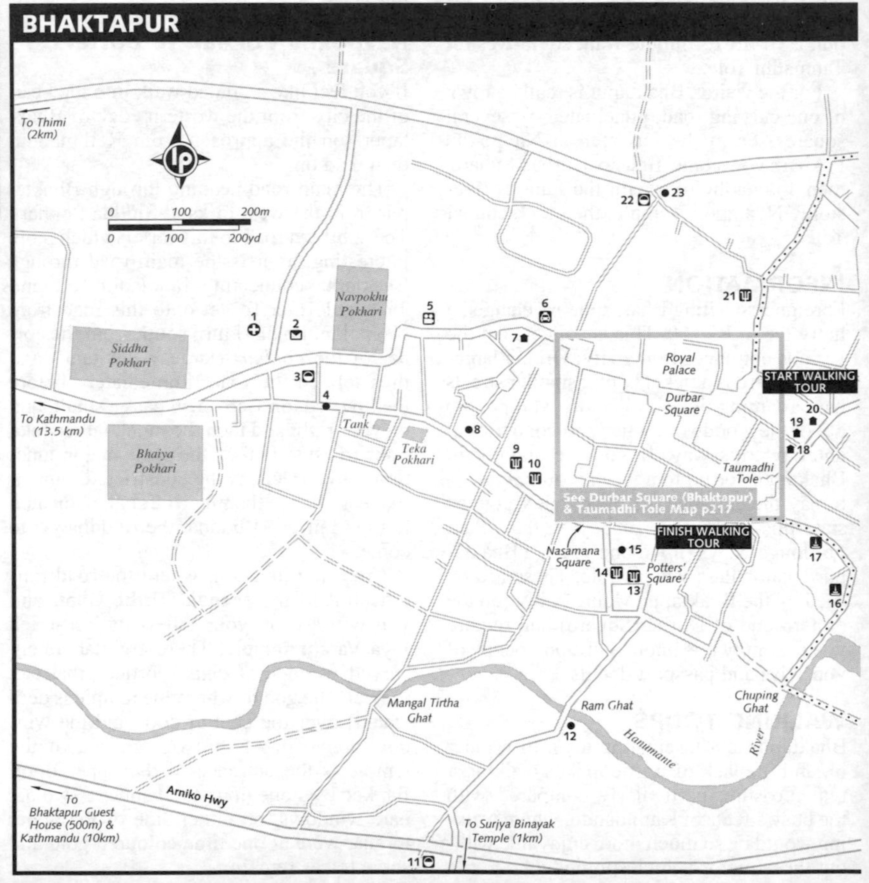

roofed **Jeth Ganesh Temple**. The latter is an indicator of how long the activity all around the square has been going on – the temple was donated by a wealthy potter in 1646 and to this day its priest is a potter. Pottery is very clearly what this square is all about. Under the shady, open verandahs and tin-roofed sheds located all around the square, the potters' wheels spin and clay is thrown. In the square itself, literally thousands of finished pots sit out in the sun to dry, and are sold in the stalls around the square and also between the square and Taumadhi Tole.

Taumadhi Tole to Tachupal Tole

The curving main road through Bhaktapur runs from beside the Bhairabnath Temple in Taumadhi Tole to Tachupal Tole, the old centre of town. The first stretch of the street is a busy shopping thoroughfare with a constant hum of activity – everything is on sale, from brass pots to video cassettes, from porters' *tumplines* (the leather or cloth strips across the forehead or chest used to support a load carried on the back) to mineral water.

At the first bend there are two interesting old buildings on the right-hand (southern) side. The **Sukul Dhoka** is a *math* (Hindu

priest's house), with superb woodcarving both on its facade and inside in the courtyard. Almost next door is the **Lun Bahal**, originally a 16th-century Buddhist monastery that was converted into a Hindu shrine with the addition of a stone statue of Bhimsen. If you look into the sanctum, in the inner courtyard, you can see the statue, dating from 1592, complete with a ferocious-looking brass mask.

A little farther along, the road opens into the **Golmadhi Square** with a deep hiti, the small, triple-roofed Golmadhi Ganesh Temple and adjacent to it a white chaitya. Another short stretch of road brings you to another small open area with a *path* (pilgrim's shelter) on your right. Behind it is a tank and the Inacho Bahal (described in the Circular Tour later in this section). A few more steps brings you to Tachupal Tole.

Tachupal Tole

Tachupal Tole was probably the original central square of Bhaktapur, so this is most likely the oldest part of the town. It's only about a 10-minute walk from the Nyatapola Temple in Taumadhi Tole to this square (also called Dattatraya Square) containing the Dattatraya Temple and the Pujari Math. As a result of the major 'renovation' Bhaktapur underwent in the late 1970s, today you stroll down a well-paved street. These brick-paved streets are a real contrast to some of the muddy, potholed alleys reminiscent of the past, which you can still find in the back blocks of town.

South from this square a maze of narrow laneways, passageways and courtyards runs down to the *ghats* (steps) on the river.

Dattatraya Temple This tall, square temple was originally built in 1427, but alterations were made in 1458. Like some other important structures in the valley it is said to have been built using the timber from a single tree. The temple is dedicated to Dattatraya, although the Garuda-topped pillar

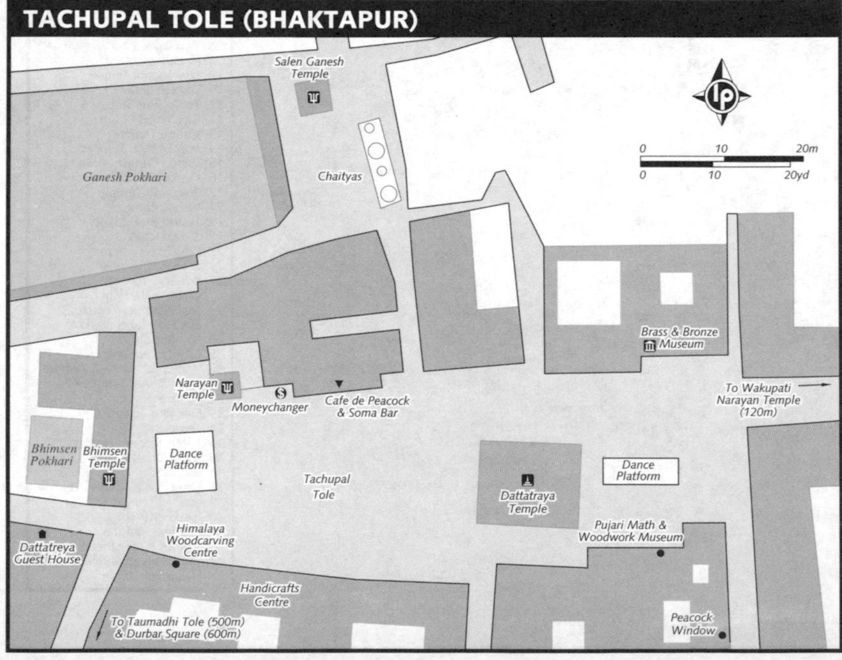

and the traditional weapons of Vishnu indicate that Dattatraya is actually another of Vishnu's many incarnations. He is also said to have been Shiva's teacher and is even claimed to have been a cousin of Buddha so the temple is important to Shaivites as well as Vaishnavites and Buddhists.

The three-storey temple is raised well above the ground on its base, around which are carved some erotic scenes. The front section, which was a later addition to the temple, stands almost separate and the temple entrance is guarded by the same two Malla wrestlers who watch over the first plinth of the Nyatapola Temple.

Bhimsen Temple At the other end of the square is the two-storey Bhimsen Temple, variously dated to 1605, 1645 and 1655. The temple is squat, rectangular and open on the ground floor. It's fronted by a platform with a small double-roofed Vishnu Temple and a pillar topped by a brass lion. Behind it is the deeply sunken and rather pretty Bhimsen Pokhari.

Pujari Math & Woodwork Museum There are 10 buildings around the square that were originally used as maths. The best known was the Pujari Math, which has been restored by the same German aid project which has done so much work in Bhaktapur. The Pujari Math was originally constructed in the 15th century during the reign of King Yaksha Malla, but was restored in 1763. Until the 20th century, an annual caravan brought tributes to the monastery from Tibet.

The Pujari Math is principally famed for the superb peacock window in the small alley beside the monastery, on its left-hand side if you face it from the square. The window is reputed to be the finest carved window in the valley and is the subject of countless postcards and photographs. There are some extraordinarily rich woodcarvings inside the building's courtyard.

The building now houses a **Woodwork Museum**, which has some fine examples of the woodcarving for which Bhaktapur, and indeed the whole Kathmandu Valley, has long been famous. It is open from 10 am to 5 pm daily except Friday (closes at 3 pm) and Tuesday (closed all day). Entry is Rs 20 plus Rs 20 to use a camera.

Other Things to See Directly across the square from the Pujari Math is the **Brass & Bronze Museum**, with fine examples of metalwork from the valley. Its opening hours and entry price are the same as those of the Woodwork Museum.

At the other end of the square, near the Bhimsen Temple, is a **Handicrafts Centre** selling woodcarvings and other examples of Bhaktapur crafts.

In the north of Tachupal Tole is another open area, with the small **Salan Ganesh Temple**, dating from 1654. The open temple is ornately decorated, but the image is just a rock with only the vaguest elephant-head shape. To one side of the temple is the Ganesh Pokhari, a large tank.

Circular Tour

See the Bhaktapur map for this circular walking tour.

North of Durbar Square Starting from the north-eastern corner of Durbar Square, walk to the east of the high Fasidega Temple, and continue a little farther up the road to a walled-in **Vishnu Temple (21)**. Cross the junction and walk uphill past a large tank surrounded by fine old houses. Turn right (east) on the road towards Nagarkot and you soon come to the **Mahakali Temple (24)**, where the shrine tops a small hill and is reached by a steep flight of steps.

Just beyond this temple, turn right, walk downhill and then turn left. Continue walking until you reach the tiny, open, double-roofed **Mahalakshmi Temple (26)**. Turn right (south) here and continue down to another large tank, the Naga (Snake) Pokhari. Here the typically green water contrasts nicely with the dyed yarns hung out to dry alongside the tank. On the western side of the tank, two temples flank a central white shikhara, while a cobra rears up from a small island in the middle of the tank.

Turn left around the tank, continue to a second tank and then to the Salan Ganesh

Temple, described under Other Things to See in the Tachupal Tole section. A little farther on, take a short detour north to the **Nava Durga Temple (31)**. This Tantric temple is said to be the site for strange sacrificial rites. The golden door is surmounted by a golden window and is guarded by metal lions. It all contrasts nicely with the red-painted brick frontage. There's another large tank, the Quathandau Pokhari, just north of the temple.

Back on this circular walking tour you soon return to the main east-west road, which runs through Tachupal Tole and Taumadhi Tole. Around this area there are more potters at work. Turn right and immediately on your left is the entrance to the **Wakupati Narayan Temple (30)**. The ornate, golden temple is double-roofed and is fronted by a line-up of no less than four Garudas. See Tachupal Tole earlier under Walking Tours if you want to check out the tole at this point.

South of Tachupal Tole Continue on to Tachupal Tole, turn left down the side of the Pujari Math; directions to its famous peacock window are well signposted. Jog right, left, right and left again, then immediately on your left is the ornate little **Inacho Bahal (40)** with prayer wheels, Buddha figures and a strange miniature pagoda roof rising up on a pillar above the courtyard.

From here the road drops down to the Hanumante River, leaving urban surroundings for rural ones and passing by a curious collection of **chaityas, statues, shrines and lingams (41)**, including a bas-relief of a well-endowed nude Shiva. Just to the left of the bridge on the Hanuman Ghat is a Shiva-Parvati shrine with a bas-relief of Rama and Sita, guarded by a statue of their faithful ally **Hanuman (42)**. On the nearby building are four paintings, including one showing Hanuman returning to Rama from his Himalayan medicinal herb foray, clutching a whole mountain in his hand. It's said that he paused here for a rest.

Cross the bridge and then take a hairpin turn back from the road onto a pleasant, paved footpath. This rural stroll ends by another temple complex, where you cross the river by the **Chuping Ghat**. Here, as at the Hanuman Ghat or the Ram Ghat by the bridge to the trolleybus stop, there are areas for ritual bathing and cremations.

Bisket Jatra at Khalna Tole

Bisket Jatra heralds the start of the Nepali New Year and is one of the most exciting annual events in the valley. In preparation Bhairab's huge triple-roofed chariot is assembled from the parts scattered beside the Bhairabnath Temple and behind the Nyatapola Temple in Taumadhi Tole. The chariot is hauled to Khalna Tole with Betal, Bhairab's sidekick from the tiny temple behind the Bhairabnath Temple, riding out front like a ship's figurehead, while Bhadrakali, his consort, accompanies them in her own chariot. The images of the gods shelter in the octagonal *path* (pilgrims' shelter) during the festival, and a towering 25m-high lingam is erected in the stone *yoni* (female genital symbol) base. Bisket Jatra ends and the Nepali New Year starts when the lingam is taken down. Bhairab and Betal return to Taumadhi Tole, while Bhadrakali goes back to her shrine by the river.

Above the river is the open area of **Khalna Tole**, the centre for the spectacular activities during the annual mid-April Bisket Jatra (see the boxed text 'Bisket Jatra at Khalna Tole' above).

The circular walk ends with a gentle climb back into the town, emerging at the southern side of Taumadhi Tole.

Taumadhi Tole to Surjyya Binayak Temple

About 1km south of town, this 17th-century Ganesh Temple is said to be a good place to visit if you're worried about your children being late speakers! It's also popular with Nepali marriage parties. To get there, take the road down past Potters' Square to Ram Ghat, cross the river and continue to the main road by the trolleybus stop. The road continues across the other side and rises gently uphill, with some fine views back over the rice paddies to Bhaktapur.

Where the road turns sharp right, a steep stairway climbs up to the temple on a forested hilltop. As you step inside the temple enclosure the very realistic-looking long-tailed rat, sitting on top of a tall pillar, immediately indicates that this temple belongs to Ganesh. The image of the god sits in an enclosure in the bottom of a shikhara and there's a second golden image on the shikhara spire. Statues of kneeling devotees face the image and the shikhara is flanked by large bells.

PLACES TO STAY

A growing number of visitors to Bhaktapur are staying overnight. There's plenty to see and one of the pleasures is that once evening falls all the day-trippers from Kathmandu disappear, and they don't return until after breakfast the next day. There are a number of small guesthouses, but you don't get all that much for your money in Bhaktapur. There are several guesthouses of varying standards around the centre of town and it's a fascinating place to stay overnight.

Entered from behind the Pashupatinath Temple on Durbar Square, the ***Shiva Guest House*** *(☎ 613912, ⓔ bisket@wlink.com.np)* has singles/doubles at US$6/8 with shared bathroom, US$15/20 with private bathroom. Some of the rooms have good views over Durbar Square, but even this hardly justifies the price. There's a decent restaurant on the ground floor, and the hotel also has a travel desk and Internet access.

The friendly ***Golden Gate Guest House*** *(☎ 610534, ⓔ bcci@wlink.com.np)* is entered by a passageway from Durbar Square or from the laneway between Durbar Square and Taumadhi Tole. The owners are friendly, there are fine views from the roof and rooms cost US$3/5 with shared bathroom or US$10 for a double with bathroom. Some of the rooms have balconies and there's also a restaurant downstairs.

The ***New Nyatapola Inn*** *(☎ 611852, ⓔ dhaubel@craft.mos.com.np)* is off the same laneway and is not bad value at Rs 600 for a double with private bathroom, though some of the rooms are a bit spartan.

Just off Durbar Square, the ***Traditional Guest House*** *(☎ 611057)* has fairly plain but adequate rooms. The position is excellent and the views from the roof of this nice old building are simply stupendous. Doubles (all with bathroom) cost from Rs 300 to Rs 500, depending on size.

There are a few newer places just off Taumadhi Tole. The ***Bhadgaon Guest House*** *(☎ 610488, ⓔ bhadgaon@mos.com.np)* is near the south-western corner of the square, and again, has excellent rooftop views. The rooms are large, clean and comfortable, and cost US$10/20 (up to US$20/25), all with private bathroom.

On the lane that heads off from the north-western edge of the square is the squeaky-clean ***Pagoda Guest House*** *(☎ 613248, ⓔ pagoda@col.com.np)*. This place has very comfortable rooms and pleasant management. There's a variety of rooms, all clean and well maintained, from US$5/6 with shared bathroom up to US$15/20 with private bathroom. There's also a rooftop restaurant but the views are pretty limited.

On the north-eastern corner of Taumadhi Tole is the new ***Pahan Chhen Guest House*** *(☎ 612887, ⓔ srp@mos.com.np)*, which has very comfortable rooms, although they are a bit on the small side. The views from the roof are as good as you'll get. Rooms cost US$20/30 with private bathroom.

For some real shoestring accommodation there's the cheap ***Nyatapola Guest House*** *(☎ 612415)* close by, which has basic rooms with shared bathroom at Rs 200/250, and a nice terrace restaurant. This is about as cheap as you'll find.

Close by and east of the square, the modern ***Namaste Guest House*** *(☎ 610500, ⓔ travels@kumari.mos.com.np)* has smallish rooms at US$4/6 with shared bathroom, and from US$7/10 with bathroom.

Around the corner, on the road that connects the two main squares, is the ***Himalaya Guest House*** *(☎ 611908, fax 258222)*, run by the same people who have a hotel of the same name in Kathmandu's Freak St. The rooms are a good size, modern and comfortable, and there's a small courtyard. Rooms cost from US$4 to US$15, all with private bathroom.

[Continued on page 222]

AROUND THE KATHMANDU VALLEY

DURBAR SQUARE (BHAKTAPUR)

Bhaktapur's Durbar Square is much larger and more spacious than Kathmandu's and much less crowded with temples than Patan's. It wasn't planned that way: Victorian illustrations show the square packed with temples and buildings, but the disastrous earthquake of 1934 destroyed many of them and today empty plinths show where some once stood. See also the boxed text 'Erotic Art' in the Kathmandu chapter for details of such imagery on buildings in Bhaktapur.

Erotic Elephants Temple (3) Just before you enter the square, coming from the minibus and bus stop, pause for a little bit of Newari humour. On your left just before the old town entrance gate to the square is a *hiti* (tank). A few steps before that, perhaps 100m before the entrance gate, is a tiny double-roofed Shiva Parvati temple with some erotic carvings on its temple struts. One of these shows a pair of copulating elephants, in the missionary position! It's a *hathi* (elephant) Kamasutra.

Inset: The 55 Window Palace, Durbar Square (Photo: Anders Blomqvist)

Ugrachandi & Bhairab Statues (7) When entering Durbar square from the west you will pass by an entry gate (to a school) with two large stone lions built by King Bhupatindra Malla. On the northern wall are statues of the terrible Bhairab and the equally terrible Ugrachandi, or Durga, the fearsome manifestation of Shiva's consort Parvati. The statues date from 1701 and it's said that the unfortunate sculptor had his hands cut off afterwards, to prevent him from duplicating his masterpieces.

Ugrachandi has 18 arms holding various weapons and symbols and she is in the act of very casually killing a demon with a trident. Bhairab has to make do with just 12 arms but the god and goddess are both garlanded with necklaces of human heads! The gates and courtyard that these powerful figures guard are not of any particular importance.

Western End Temples A number of less significant temples crowd the western end of Durbar Square. They include the **Rameshwar Temple (8)** to Shiva and the **Bhadri Temple (9)** to Vishnu as Narayan. In front of them is an impressive, larger **Krishna temple (10)** and just beyond that is a shikhara-style **Shiva temple (11)** erected by King Jitamitra Malla in 1674.

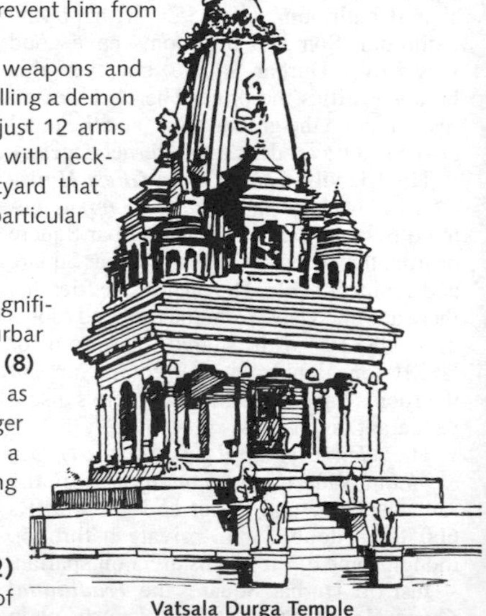

Vatsala Durga Temple

King Bhupatindra Malla's Column (22) King Bhupatindra Malla was the best known of

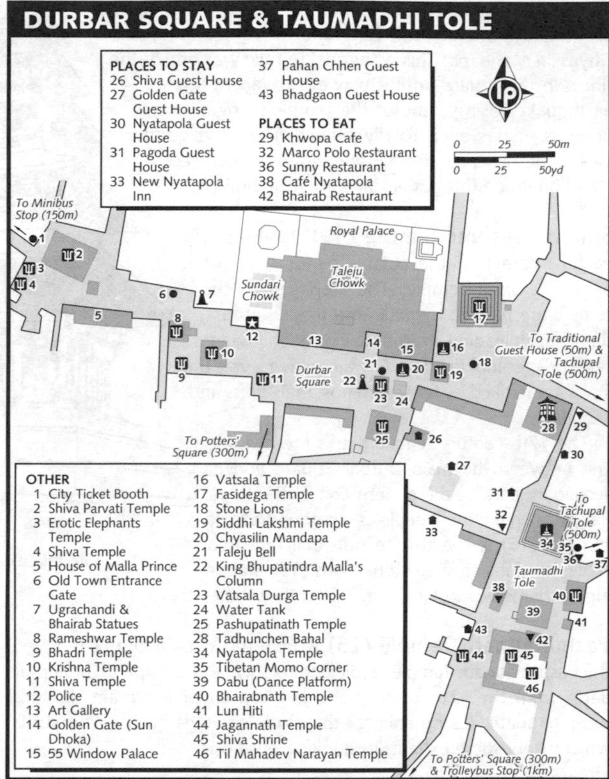

the Malla kings of Bhaktapur and had a great influence on the art and architecture of the town. Like the similar column in Patan's Durbar Square, this one was a copy of the original in Kathmandu. The king sits with folded arms, studying the magnificent entrance gate to his palace.

Vatsala Durga Temple (23) & Taleju Bell (21) Beside the king's statue and directly in front of the Royal Palace is the stone Vatsala Durga Temple, which was built by King Jagat Prakash Malla in 1672. The shikhara-style temple has some similarities to the Krishna Mandir in Patan. In front of the temple is the large Taleju Bell, which was erected by King Jaya Ranjit Malla in 1737 to call the faithful to prayer at the Taleju Temple.

A second, smaller bell stands on the temple's plinth and is popularly known as 'the barking bell'. It was erected by King Bhupatindra Malla in 1721, supposedly to counteract a vision he had in a dream, and to this day dogs are said to bark and whine if the bell is rung.

Chyasilin Mandapa (20) Beside Vatsala Durga Temple is an attractive **water tank (24)** and in front of that is the Chyasilin Mandapa. This octagonal temple was one of the finest in the square until it was destroyed by the 1934 earthquake. Using some of the temple's original components, it has been totally rebuilt. There's a good view over the square from inside; note the metal construction inside this outwardly authentic building.

Siddhi Lakshmi Temple

Siddhi Lakshmi Temple (19) By the south-eastern corner of the palace stands the stone Siddhi Lakshmi Temple. The steps up to the temple are flanked by male and female attendants, each leading a rather reluctant child and a rather eager-looking dog. On successive levels the stairs are flanked by horses, rhinos, man-lions and camels.

The 17th-century temple marks the dividing line between the main Durbar Square and its secondary part, at the eastern end of the Royal Palace. Behind the temple is another **Vatsala temple (16)**, while to one side of it are two rather lost-looking large **stone lions (18)**, standing by themselves out in the middle of the square.

Pashupatinath Temple (25) Behind the Vatsala Durga Temple is the Pashupatinath Temple, dedicated to Shiva as Pashupati. The temple dates from the 17th century and is a replica of the main shrine at Pashupatinath. It's notable for the erotic carvings on the roof struts, which show some exhausting-looking positions.

Fasidega Temple (17) The large, white, rather ugly Fasidega Temple is dedicated to Shiva and stands in the centre of the secondary part of Durbar Square. There are various viewpoints around the valley – the Changu Narayan Temple is one of them – from where you can study Bhaktapur at a distance. In each case the white bulk of the Fasidega is always an easy landmark to pick out. The temple sits on a six-level plinth with elephant guardians at the bottom of the steps, and with lions and cows above them.

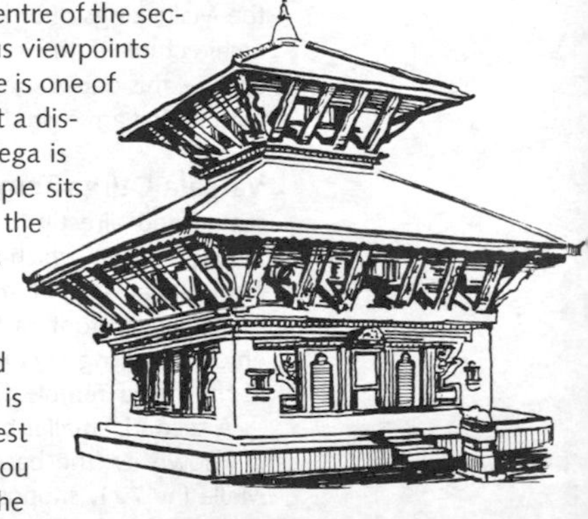

Pashupatinath Temple

Tadhunchen Bahal (28) The southern and eastern side of the secondary part of the square is made up of double-storey *dharamsalas* (rest houses for pilgrims), now used as shops. As you enter the street leading east from the square, the Tadhunchen Bahal, or Chatur Varna Mahavihara, is an ancient-looking monastery on the southern side. In the inner courtyard the roof struts on the eastern side have some highly unusual carvings showing the tortures of the damned. In one a snake is wrapped around a man, another shows two rams butting an unfortunate's head from opposite sides, while a third strut shows a nasty tooth extraction being performed with a large pair of pliers! The monastery dates from the 15th century.

Royal Palace Bhaktapur's Royal Palace was founded by Yaksha Malla and was added to by successive kings, particularly Bhupatindra Malla. As with the old palaces of Kathmandu and Patan, visitors are restricted to certain areas, but only seven courtyards remain of the 99 the palace was once claimed to have. Unfortunately, the palace suffered great damage in the terrible 1934 earthquake and its subsequent reconstruction did not match its original artistry.

Art Gallery (13) The western end of the palace has been made into an art gallery. The entrance to the gallery is flanked by figures of Hanuman the monkey god and Vishnu as Narsingha, his man-lion incarnation. These guardian figures date from 1698 and Hanuman appears in Tantric form as the four-armed Hanuman-Bhairab. This part of the palace was once known as the Malati Chowk.

The gallery has a fine collection of Hindu and Buddhist paintings, palm-leaf manuscripts, *thangkas* (paintings on cloth) and metal, stone and woodcrafts.

The gallery is open from 10.15 am to 4 pm (closes 2.30 pm Friday) Wednesday to Monday; entry is Rs 20.

Golden Gate (14) & 55 Window Palace (15) Adjoining the gallery, the magnificent Golden Gate, or Sun Dhoka, is the entrance to the 55 Window Palace. The Golden Gate is generally agreed to be the single most important piece of art in the whole valley. The gate and palace were built by King Bhupatindra Malla but were not completed until 1754, during the reign of Jaya Ranjit Malla.

A Garuda, the vehicle of Vishnu, tops the gate and is shown here disposing of a number of serpents, which are the Garuda's sworn enemies. The four-headed and 16-armed figure of the goddess Taleju Bhawani is featured below the Garuda and also directly over the door. Taleju Bhawani is the family deity of the Malla dynasty and there are temples to her in the royal palaces in Kathmandu and Patan as well as Bhaktapur.

The Golden Gate opens to the inner courtyards of the palace. First you will enter a small entrance courtyard, then move into the larger Mul Chowk, which leads around to the **Taleju Chowk** entrance. Unfortunately, only Hindus can officially enter Taleju Chowk, although non-Hindus can peer in from the doorway. Beyond Taleju Chowk is the Kumari Chowk and the **Sundari Chowk**, with its bathing tank, the Kamal Pokhari.

TAUMADHI TOLE (BHAKTAPUR)

A short street lined with tourist shops leads downhill from behind the Pashupatinath Temple in Durbar Square to the second great square of Bhaktapur, the Taumadhi Tole. Here you'll find Nyatapola Temple, the highest temple in the valley and also the Café Nyatapola, whose balconies provide a great view over the square. The building was renovated for its new purpose in 1977 and it has some finely carved roof struts.

Nyatapola Temple (34) The five-storey, 30m-high Nyatapola Temple is not only the highest temple in the whole Kathmandu Valley, but also one of the best examples of traditional Newari temple architecture. The towering temple is visible from Durbar Square, but some of the finest views of the temple are from farther away. If you take the road running out of the valley east to Banepa and Dhulikhel or walk up towards the Surjya Binayak Temple south of Bhaktapur, you can see the temple soaring up above the other buildings, with the hills at the edge of the valley as a backdrop.

The elegant temple was built during the reign of King Bhupatindra Malla in 1702, and its design and construction were so solid that the 1934 earthquake caused only minor damage. The stairway leading up to the temple is flanked by guardian figures at each plinth level. The bottom plinth has the legendary wrestlers Jayamel and Phattu, said to have the strength of 10 men. On the plinths above are two elephants, then two lions, then two griffins and finally two goddesses – Baghini in the form of a tiger and Singhini in the form of a lion. Each figure is said to be 10 times as strong as the figure on the level below; presiding over all of them, but hidden away inside the temple, is the mysterious Tantric goddess Siddhi Lakshmi, to whom the temple is dedicated.

KELLI HAMBLET

Only the temple's priests are allowed to see the image of the goddess, but the temple's 108 carved and painted roof struts depict her in her various forms. Various legends and tales relate to the temple and its enigmatic inhabitant. One is that she maintains a balance with the powers of the terrifying Bhairab, comfortably ensconced in his own temple just across the square.

Bhairabnath Temple (40) The recently restored, triple-roofed Bhairabnath Temple (also known as the Kasi Vishwanath or Akash Bhairab) has an unusual rectangular plan and has had a somewhat chequered history. It was originally built as a one-storey temple in the early 17th century but was rebuilt with two storeys by King Bhupatindra Malla in 1717. The 1934 earthquake caused great damage to the temple and it was completely rebuilt and a third floor added.

Casually stacked beside the temple are the enormous wheels and other parts of the temple chariot on which the image of Bhairab is conveyed around town during the Bisket festival in mid-April (see the special section 'Festivals of Nepal', following the Facts for the Visitor chapter). Curiously, despite Bhairab's fearsome powers and his massive temple, his image is only about 30cm high! A small hole in the central door is used to push offerings into the temple's interior, but the actual entrance to the Bhairabnath Temple is through the small Betal Temple, behind the main temple. The temple is guarded by two brass lions and there's a host of interesting details on the front.

Til Mahadev Narayan Temple (46) It's easy to miss the square's third interesting temple, the Til Mahadev Narayan, as it is hidden away behind the buildings on the southern side of the square. You can enter the temple's courtyard through a narrow entrance through those buildings, or through an arched entrance facing west, just to the south of the square.

This double-roofed Vishnu Temple has a Garuda kneeling on a high pillar in front, flanked by pillars bearing Vishnu's *sankha* (conch shell) and *chakra* (disc-shaped weapon) symbols. Some of the temple's struts also have Garudas. A *lingam* (phallic symbol) in a *yoni* (female equivalent of the phallic symbol) stands inside a wooden cage in front and to one side of the temple. Despite the temple's neglected setting it is actually an important place of pilgrimage as well as one of the oldest temple sites in the town: An inscription indicates that the site has been in use since 1080. Yet another inscription states that the image of Til Mahadev installed inside the temple dates from 1170.

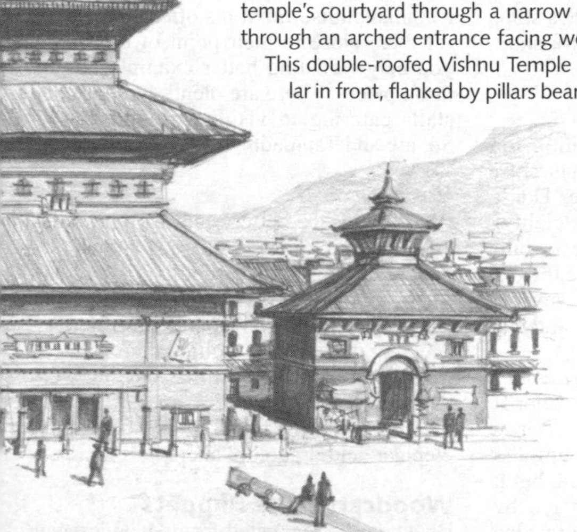

The Nyatapola and Bhairabnath Temples of Taumadhi Tole

[Continued from page 215]

Tucked away off a corner of Tachupal Tole is the economical ***Dattatreya Guest House*** *(☎ 613998)*, the only place in this part of the city. The rooftop is one of the highest in the city and has excellent 360° views. The rooms are less spectacular, but they are large, clean and good value at Rs 150/250 with shared bathroom.

Just east of the main entrance to Durbar Square is the ***Taleju Guest House*** *(☎ 611078, ⓔ taleju_ghr@hotmail.com)*. It's a modern, multistorey building, with the requisite rooftop. The price of US$15 for a double with shared bathroom and US$25 with private bathroom is a bit steep, but there may be room to negotiate.

A really pleasant option west of Bhaktapur itself is the ***Bhaktapur Guest House*** *(☎ 610670)*, perched on the edge of the valley with great views back to Kathmandu. The setting is very peaceful and quiet, and it offers an excellent retreat from Kathmandu. The rooms are comfortable, and cost US$20/25, although at quiet times this can come down as low as US$10/15. There's also a restaurant and bar. The guesthouse is signposted off to the south of the Arniko Hwy, about 1km before the trolleybus stop, and is then a steep 10-minute walk (or short drive) up a rocky path.

PLACES TO EAT

Bhaktapur is certainly no competition for Kathmandu when it comes to restaurants, but don't worry, you won't starve. Don't forget to try Bhaktapur's famous speciality: *jujudhau*, 'the king of curds' (yogurt) while you are here. You can have it in the town's main restaurants, and there are several places selling curd near the minibus and bus stop by Navpokhu Pokhari.

Right in Taumadhi Tole, ***Café Nyatapola*** is in a building that was once a traditional pagoda temple – it even has erotic carvings on some of the roof struts. From upstairs there are good views over the square, but it is very cramped and often dominated by large groups of tourists. Prices are also comparatively high.

On the corner of the square and beside the Nyatapola Temple, the ***Marco Polo Restaurant*** is a better bet than Café Nyatapola if you want a substantial meal. Pizzas are Rs 120, and there's a range of Chinese, Indian and continental dishes for around Rs 120. There's a small balcony with limited views over Taumadhi Tole.

In the opposite corner of the square is the small ***Sunny Restaurant***, which has a terrace, great views over the square and no crowds.

On Tachupal Tole, opposite the Dattatraya Temple, the ***Cafe de Peacock & Soma Bar*** is one of the best spots in the valley to while away an afternoon. The food is good and the views of the beautiful square mesmerising. The best tables are often reserved by tour groups at lunch time. The full international menu includes pizza and pasta for around Rs 150, Mexican and Western dishes at Rs 180, and there is also a set Nepali meal for Rs 220 (veg), or Rs 330 (nonveg). The cafe is open from 9 am to 9 pm.

SHOPPING

As in Patan, there are a number of crafts for which Bhaktapur is the centre. You'll find all the Kathmandu Valley crafts on sale in Kathmandu itself, but it's often fun to shop for them close to their point of origin and you may well find better examples or unusual pieces. There are plenty of shops and stalls catering to visitors around Durbar Square and Taumadhi Tole.

Pottery

Bhaktapur is the pottery centre of the valley and a visit to Potters' Square is a must (see under Walking Tours earlier in this section). There are many stalls around the square and just below Taumadhi Tole selling pottery. Much of the work is traditional pots for use in Nepali households (nice but not very transportable), but there are also items catering to tourist tastes, such as attractive elephant and dragon planters.

Woodcarving & Puppets

Bhaktapur is renowned for its woodcarving and you'll see good examples in the Handi-

PAUL HARDING

The gods of Nepal often feature in the tradition of Nepali puppet making.

crafts Centre on Tachupal Tole. There are other shops around the squares and you will find unusual pieces in the alley beside the Pujari Math, right under the peacock window in fact. If you buy anything that looks like it might be old, make sure you get a descriptive receipt for it, as it's likely to be checked on departure from Kathmandu. If it really is very old you will not be allowed to take it out of the country (see Antiques under Customs in the Facts for the Visitor chapter).

Some of the best puppets, on sale in their thousands in all the valley towns, come from Bhaktapur.

GETTING THERE & AWAY

Bus, Minibus & Trolleybus

Travelling by public bus or minibus to Bhaktapur, you disembark near the walled water tank called Navpokhu Pokhari, just beyond the even larger Siddha Pokhari and a short walk from Durbar Square. The minibuses from Kathmandu's City bus station are strictly for masochists and the poverty-stricken – they are nearly always crowded and can take over an hour, although they only cost Rs 6. The last minibus back to Kathmandu leaves at about 6 pm.

The Chinese-built trolleybuses are preferable, even though they are in an advanced state of decay and tend to get crowded around peak hours (7 am to 9 am and 4 pm to 6 pm). At the Bhaktapur end, you have to walk 10 minutes to get to the town centre (via Ram Ghat and up into the town by Potters' Square). The trolleybuses leave Kathmandu from Tripureshwar Marg, cost Rs 4, and take around 35 minutes, unless you get caught in a traffic jam. The trolleybuses run until about 9 pm.

Buses for Nagarkot leave regularly from the north-eastern corner of the city and cost Rs 15. Buses north to Changu Narayan leave from the northern edge of the city where the road to Changu Narayan leaves the main road.

Bicycle

The main road to Bhaktapur runs through to Dhulikhel, Barabise and finally to Tibet, so it carries a lot of bellowing, belching buses and trucks. Avoid peak hours. A better alternative for cyclists who want to ride from Kathamandu to Bhaktapur is to ride via Thimi. Take the Thimi turn-off, which is left at a T-junction on the Bhaktapur road.

Taxi

Taxis cost around Rs 250 one way, and they drop you at the tourist bus station and taxi rank on the northern edge of the city, just a short walk from Durbar Square.

Swayambhunath Route

SWAYAMBHUNATH (2KM)

The Buddhist temple of Swayambhunath, on the top of a hill west of Kathmandu, is one of the most popular and instantly recognisable symbols of Nepal. The temple is colloquially known as the 'monkey temple', after the large tribe of handsome monkeys that guards the hill and amuses visitors and devotees with tricks, including sliding gracefully down the double banisters of the main stairway to the temple. The roving monkeys quickly snatch up any offerings of food made by devotees and will just as quickly grab anything you may be carrying.

Geologists believe that the Kathmandu Valley was once a lake, and legends relate that the hill on which Swayambhunath stands was an island in that lake. It is said that Emperor Ashoka paid a visit to the site more than 2000 years ago. An inscription indicates that King Manadeva ordered work done on the site in 460 AD and by the 13th century it was an important Buddhist centre. In 1346 Mughal invaders from Bengal broke open the stupa to search for gold. Under the Mallas, various improvements were made and the great stairway to the stupa was constructed by King Pratap Malla in the 17th century.

An entry fee of Rs 50 is payable if you enter the site from the car park on the western side, but not if you climb the stairway from the east – maybe the thinking here is that if you've slogged it up the steps you have already earned your admission!

From its hilltop setting, Swayambhunath offers fine views over Kathmandu and the valley. It's particularly striking in the early evening when the city is illuminated, and the site is also very attractive under the soft glow of moonlight. There are numerous little shops and stalls around the stupa that sell jewellery and curios.

Eastern Stairway

Although you can get to the temple by vehicle, and save yourself the long climb up the stairs, the eastern stairway is by far the best way of approaching Swayambhunath. Look for the yellow-and-red stone seated Buddha figures at the base of the hill. The bottom end of the steps is guarded by figures of Ganesh and Kumar on their vehicles. Near the start of the steps is a huge 'footprint' on a stone, said to be either that of Buddha or Manjushri. Halfway up the steps there is another small collection of stonework, including a scene showing the birth of Buddha, his mother holding a tree branch and Buddha taking seven miraculous steps immediately after his birth.

As you climb the final stretch, look for the pairs of animals – Garudas, lions, elephants, horses and peacocks – which are the

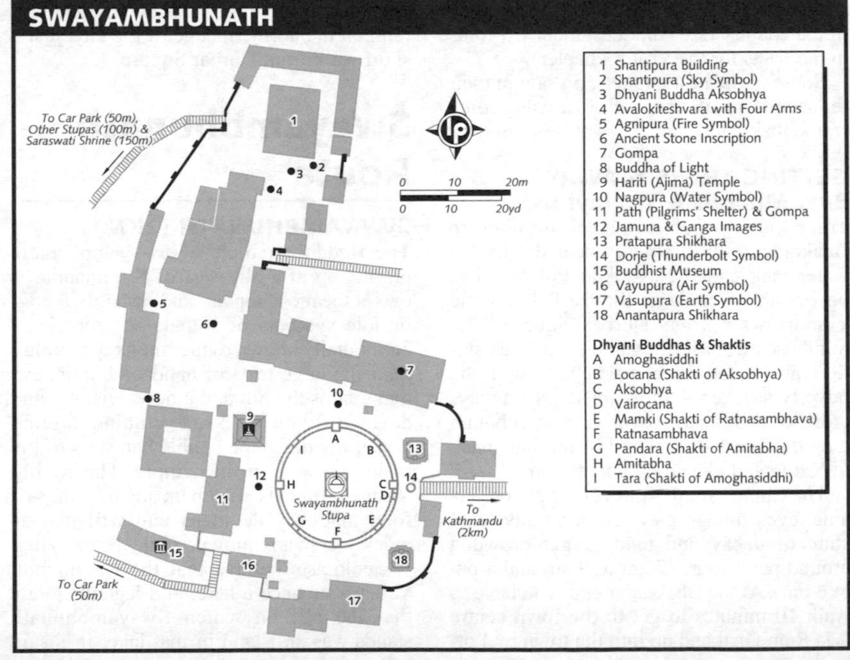

The Tibetan Calendar

Around the base of the great *dorje* (the Tibetan word for the 'thunderbolt'; symbol of Buddhist power in Nepal) at the top of the stairway to Swayambhunath are the symbols of the 12 animals of the Tibetan calendar. The animals are similar to those of the Chinese calendar; find out just what kind of animal you are by finding your birth year below.

Snake	1929	1941	1953	1965	1977	1989	2001
Horse	1930	1942	1954	1966	1978	1990	2002
Sheep	1931	1943	1955	1967	1979	1991	2003
Monkey	1932	1944	1956	1968	1980	1992	2004
Goose	1933	1945	1957	1969	1981	1993	2005
Dog	1934	1946	1958	1970	1982	1994	2006
Pig	1935	1947	1959	1971	1983	1995	2007
Rat	1936	1948	1960	1972	1984	1996	2008
Bull	1937	1949	1961	1973	1985	1997	2009
Tiger	1938	1950	1962	1974	1986	1998	2010
Hare	1939	1951	1963	1975	1987	1999	2011
Dragon	1940	1952	1964	1976	1988	2000	2012

'vehicles' of the Dhyani Buddhas. If you tire on the ascent, pause to watch the monkeys' antics, or check out the trinkets on sale from the numerous hawkers. When you reach the top remember that you should always walk around a stupa in a clockwise direction.

Great Thunderbolt

As well as building the great stairway, Pratap Malla also added a pair of shikharas and the stone lions and dorje, which visitors see immediately upon reaching the top of the stairs. Dorje is the Tibetan word for this thunderbolt symbol; in Sanskrit it is called a vajra. Dorjes are often accompanied by a bell; the thunderbolt symbolises male force and the bell symbolises female wisdom. Around the pedestal supporting Swayambhunath's mighty dorje are the animals of the Tibetan calendar.

Stupa

From the flattened top of the hill, the soaring central stupa is topped by a gold-coloured square block from which the watchful eyes of Buddha gaze out across the valley in each direction. The question mark–like 'nose' is actually the Nepali number *ek* (one) and is a symbol of unity. Between and above the two eyes is a third eye, which symbolises Buddha's clairvoyant powers.

Set around the base of the central stupa is a continuous series of prayer wheels, which pilgrims, circumambulating the stupa, spin as they pass by. Each prayer wheel carries the sacred mantra *'om mani padme hum'*. The prayer flags fluttering from the lines leading to the stupa's spire also carry mantras and each wave in the breeze carries the words away. The stupa's white-painted base represents the four elements – earth, fire, air and water – while the 13 concentric rings on the spire symbolise the 13 degrees of knowledge and the 13 steps that must be taken to reach *nirvana* (final escape from the continuous cycles of existence), which in turn is represented by the umbrella on the top of the stupa.

Stupa Platform

The great stupa is only one of many points of interest at Swayambhunath. Starting at the massive dorje at the top of the stairs, turn right to the *gompa* (Tibetan Bhuddist monastery) where, with a great deal of crashing, chanting and trumpeting, a service takes place every day at around 4 pm.

Inside the gompa there's a 6m-high figure of Avalokiteshvara. Behind the stupa, adjacent to the International Buddhist Library, is a *path* (pilgrims' shelter) with an open ground floor and a gompa above it.

The dorje at the top of the stairs is flanked by two white temples in the Indian shikhara style, both dating from 1646. The one to the right, in front of the gompa, is the Pratapura shikhara, while to the left is the identical Anantapura shikhara. Behind the stupa is the pagoda-style **Hariti (Ajima) Temple**, with a beautiful image of Hariti, the goddess of smallpox. This Hindu goddess (to the Newars she is Ajima), who is also responsible for fertility, indicates the constant interweaving of Hinduism and Buddhism in Nepal.

Near the Hariti Temple there are pillars on which figures of various gods and goddesses are seated. Look for the figure of Tara making the gesture of charity. Actually, there are two Taras, Green Tara and White Tara, who are sometimes believed to be the two wives of King Songtsen Gampo, the first royal patron of Buddhism in Tibet. The Taras are two of the female consorts to the Dhyani Buddhas.

Behind the stupa, bronze images of the river goddesses **Jamuna** and **Ganga** guard an eternal flame in a cage.

The symbols of the four elements – earth, air, water and fire – can be found around the hilltop. Behind the Anantapura shikhara are Vasupura, the earth symbol, and Vayupura, the symbol for air. Nagpura, the symbol for water, is just north of the stupa, while Agnipura, the symbol for fire, is at the northwestern corner of the platform. Shantipura, which is the symbol for the sky, is at the extreme north of the platform, in front of the Shantipura building.

In this same northern area of the platform you will find an ancient stone inscription, dating from 1372, and a large image of Buddha, next to the Agnipura symbol.

The Dhyani Buddhas

There are five Dhyani Buddhas, or 'Buddhas in Meditation', who represent various aspects of Buddhahood, unlike the mortal flesh-and-blood Buddha, Gautama Buddha. Around many stupas the figures of the five Dhyani Buddhas in different meditative postures face out from the stupa in niches, four of them facing the four cardinal directions. Once you know the hand positions you can use a stupa like a compass. The Swayambhunath stupa is a good place to study the Dhyani Buddhas, and the description that follows is from that stupa.

Amoghasiddhi faces north and raises his right hand, palm out to shoulder height in what is known as a protective position. His animal, or 'vehicle', is the Garuda. You can see the animals in niches below Buddhas' shrines. As you move around the stupa clockwise you'll come to **Aksobhya**, the lord of the east; one of his hands touches the earth. This is known as the position of subduing the devil, Mara. Buddha reaches down to touch the earth in order that it witness his resistance to temptation. His vehicle is the elephant.

Facing south is **Ratnasambhava**, who rides a horse and turns his palm outwards. **Amitabha** faces the west and his hands rest on his lap, palms-up in a meditative position. His vehicle is the peacock. The fifth of Buddhas is **Vairocana** who usually appears in the centre of the stupa and therefore is not so easily seen. If he is shown he normally faces the south-east, and at Swayambhunath you can see his figure standing beside Aksobhya in the eastern niche. His animal is the lion; his hands are held up to his chest and he makes two circles with his fingers, rather like a scuba diver's 'OK' sign!

Each Dhyani Buddha is identifiable by his colour, his hand positions, his direction and his vehicle, but each also has a *shakti* or female companion and a Bodhisattva or spiritual follower. Their shaktis or consorts are shown at the subcardinal points around the stupa. Amitabha is the Dhyani Buddha of our era and his Bodhisattva is none other than Avalokiteshvara or, as he is often known in the valley, Manjushri or Machhendranath.

Getting There & Away

You can approach Swayambhunath by taxi or under your own power – either on foot or by bicycle. See also the Kathmandu map in the Kathmandu chapter for routes to and from Swayambhunath.

Taxi Unless you ask to be taken to the stairway on the eastern side, taxis will take you on the road via the National Museum and Art Gallery and deposit you at the car park on the western side, from where it's an easy climb to the top of the hill. The other taxi routes end with the long steep climb up the eastern stairway to the stupa – this is a far more interesting way to approach Swayambhunath (but the easy stroll from Kathmandu to the base of the climb is a pleasure in itself). From Thamel, taxis to the car park cost around Rs 80, and Rs 60 to the bottom of the stairway.

Walking & Cycling There are two popular foot or bicycle routes to Swayambhunath – using both makes the trip into a pleasant circuit. Starting at Durbar Square, take Maru Tole (Pie Alley) down to the Vishnumati River, where a footbridge crosses to the western side. Flat, stone cremation ghats can be seen by the riverside. From there the path passes houses and shops to the open green at the base of the hill. Along the way you'll see people working in vegetable gardens and preparing wool for Tibetan carpets. There's quite a large Tibetan community in this area.

If you go there by bicycle you are likely to find a number of small boys offering to 'look after' your bicycle. It's probably wise to pay a rupee or two of 'protection money', otherwise you may find your tyres have gone mysteriously flat and a pump will then have to be rented from one of the nearby shops!

The alternative route starts from Chhetrapati, near Thamel. Starting at the Chhetrapati Tole junction, the road then descends to the river, with the Swayambhunath Stupa clearly visible in the distance, and passes the three riverside temples, which were mentioned earlier.

AROUND SWAYAMBHUNATH

Ichangu Narayan (5KM)

At the edge of the valley floor, and about 3km north-west of Swayambhunath, the shrine of Ichangu Narayan (not to be confused with Changu Narayan east of Kathmandu) is one of the Kathmandu Valley's important Vishnu shrines. This two-storey, 18th-century temple is fronted by two square stone pillars bearing Vishnu's sankha and chakra symbols. Various statuary can be found around the courtyard. The site was actually consecrated in 1200 and an earlier temple was built here after a famine in 1512. There's a small temple to Bhagwati on a hill overlooking Ichangu Narayan.

Getting There & Away The road to Ichangu Narayan starts beyond Kathmandu's Ring Rd, situated on the western side of the Swayambhunath hill. It quickly changes from a road to a track and as it climbs a steep hill (look back for the views over the valley), the track soon becomes a footpath. From the top of the hill, marked by a small temple, the trail descends slightly and then continues to climb gradually, leaving the valley proper. Finally, at the end of a little village is the temple compound. Going back to Kathmandu by bicycle is one long downhill breeze, but you'll certainly work up a sweat getting to the temple.

An alternative route to Ichangu Narayan is a day walk from Balaju (to the north-west of Kathmandu). The trail climbs from Balaju to the top of Nagarjun hill and skirts around the valley edge through the Jamacho Forest Reserve and the Nagarjun Forest Reserve, descending to the Ichangu Narayan trail to the west of the village and temple.

Other Things to See

There are many small buildings and shrines down the hillside behind Swayambhunath. A smaller stupa stands on a hillock, with an adjacent gompa and an important **shrine** to Saraswati, the goddess of learning. At exam time, many scholars come here to improve their chances and schoolchildren come here during Basant Panchami, the Festival of Knowledge.

There are various Tibetan settlements and gompas around the base of the Swayambhunath hill. The 2km- or 3km-walk northwest of Swayambhunath will take you to **Ichangu Narayan**, an interesting Hindu temple (see previous). The **National Museum & Art Gallery** (see the Kathmandu chapter) is on the road from Kathmandu to the stupa.

The **Natural History Museum**, west of Swayambhunath, has a large collection of butterflies, fish, reptiles, birds and animals. It's open daily from 10 am to 5 pm except Saturday and government holidays, and entry is free.

There are several routes to Swayambhunath from Kathmandu. If you take the route from Thamel, via Chhetrapati Square and down to the Vishnumati River, there are three interesting temples to look at. **Indrani Temple** just beside the river on the Kathmandu side is chiefly notable for the brightly coloured erotic scenes on its roof struts. There are cremation ghats beside the river; in 1989 the bridge here collapsed during a heavy monsoon. Across the river and just upstream is the **Shobabaghwati Temple**. A footpath runs from here up the steep hill to the **Bijeshwari Temple**, from where the road continues to the Swayambhunath hill.

Kakani & Trisuli Bazaar Route

Kakani is a viewpoint with spectacular views of the Ganesh himal. A narrow, winding tarmac road, in reasonable though not great condition, continues to Trisuli Bazaar. From Trisuli Bazaar to Dhunche the road deteriorates to very rough gravel, but the views are spectacular. Dhunche is the starting point for a number of treks in the Langtang region. A 4WD is essential. Trisuli Bazaar and destinations farther on are beyond the Kathmandu Valley itself but are accessible from Kathmandu.

Just before Malekhu, on the Kathmandu-Pokhara (Prithvi) Hwy, there's a bridge over the Trisuli River. This is the new road to Trisuli Bazaar, superseding the road that leaves the valley at Kakani. This makes an interesting circular bicycle ride a possibility, taking in Kakani, Trisuli Bazaar, Dhading and Malekhu. See the Kathmandu to Pokhara map in the Pokhara chapter for this route.

BALAJU (3KM)

The industrial centre of Balaju is less than 2km north of Thamel, just beyond Kathmandu's Ring Rd, and the expansion of the capital has virtually swallowed up this nearby suburb. Despite this, Balaju's Mahendra Park is still a peaceful retreat and its image of the sleeping Vishnu makes an interesting contrast with the larger Vishnu image at Budhanilkantha.

Mahendra Park

The gardens at Balaju were originally constructed in the 18th century and are now known as Mahendra Park. They are something of a disappointment – there's a lot of concrete and litter, and numerous ineffectual gardeners. Apart from the Vishnu image, there are a couple of small temples, an interesting group of *chortens* (Tibetan Bhuddist stupas) and lingams (for the aficionado) and the 22 waterspouts from which the park takes its local name, Bais Dhara Balaju.

Officially, the Balaju Vishnu image is said to be a copy of the older image at Budhanilkantha, but there is no positive proof of which one is actually older. Certainly the Balaju image is in more pleasant surroundings than its better-known relation. Although the king of Nepal cannot visit Budhanilkantha (since he is an incarnation of Vishnu and to gaze on his own image could be disastrous), no such injunction applies to Balaju, where the Vishnu image is just a copy of the real thing!

The park is open daily 7 am to 7.30 pm. Entry costs Rs 3, plus another Rs 2 if you take in a camera. The pool, which can often be very crowded, is open between March and September; entry is Rs 40.

Shitala Mai Temple

The double-roofed 19th-century Shitala Mai Temple stands in front of the Vishnu image and around it is a curious assembly of gods. They include a 16th-century image of Hari Shankar (the half-Shiva, half-Vishnu deity) and a 14th-century figure of the multi-armed goddess of smallpox, Shitala Mai. Others include Bhagwati, Ganesh and, in the usual clash of Hindu and Buddhist imagery, a statue of Buddha protected by the hood of a snake.

Getting There & Away

Tempos go to Balaju from the National Theatre corner of Kathmandu's Rani Pokhari (on Kantipath), or you can walk from Thamel. It's an interesting day walk from Balaju to Ichangu Narayan, west of Swayambhunath, skirting the edge of the valley.

NAGARJUN FOREST RESERVE (5KM)

On the hill behind Balaju is the walled Nagarjun Forest Reserve, which has pheasants, deer and other animals. This, along with the former Gokarna Park and Pulchowki, is one of the last significant areas of untouched forest in the valley.

You can continue up the hill to Jamacho, a popular Buddhist pilgrimage site. There are excellent views to the north, stretching, on a clear day, all the way from the Annapurnas to Langtang Lirung, while the whole of the Kathmandu Valley is laid at your feet to the south.

There is a steep, 30km unpaved road to Nagarjun at the top, or you can walk up a wide, easy-to-follow and considerably shorter trail in about two hours. There are a number of picnic shelters around a stupa and a viewing tower.

The reserve is officially open from 10 am to 5 pm daily. Entry is Rs 10 per person, plus Rs 100 per car and Rs 30 for a motorcycle.

Getting There & Away

The main entrance to the reserve is about a 20-minute bicycle ride from Thamel. The walking trail to the top begins just past the gate on the right. It's steep for the first hour, and there is no water along the way or at the top. There are several routes you can take on the way down. Don't take the road if you're on foot – it's 30km long.

KAKANI (23KM)

Standing at 2073m on a ridge north-west of Kathmandu, Kakani is nowhere near as popular as Nagarkot, but it does offer magnificent views of the Ganesh himal and the central and western Himalaya.

Apart from looking at the view (one could argue this is enough), there's not much to do. There is a century-old summer villa used by the UK embassy and a large police training college, although this does not seriously impinge on the tranquillity of the surroundings.

The road to Kakani also offers beautiful views. Once you're through the pass and out of the valley, Kathmandu seems light years away. Although the valley is terraced 1000m from top to bottom, many trees have been left behind and prosperous-looking houses dot the hillsides.

Although it's easy to get to Kakani on a day trip, it's worth staying overnight if you want to see the view (you stand a much better chance if you are there early in the morning before the clouds roll in).

Places to Stay & Eat

There's only a few accommodation options in Kakani. The government-owned ***Tara Gaon Kakani Hotel*** *(☎ 290812, ⓔ taragaon@enet.com.np)* is an old-fashioned place that has some wonderful views. Although it is small, it's also quite comfortable, and on a clear day the views from the front lawn are superb. Singles/doubles with bathroom, and some with views, cost US$20/25. The hotel also serves reasonably priced meals.

The ***Kakani Guest House***, just before the Tara Gaon Kakani Hotel, is one of a couple of typical village lodges, and is about as basic as they come. It's friendly, however, and doubles cost Rs 250. *Dal bhaat* (lentils and vegetables) is available, but there's very little else to eat. With advance notice you may be able to eat at the Tara Gaon Kakani Hotel.

Getting There & Away

Kakani is an hour by car or motorcycle from Kathmandu, so it would be a long, though rewarding, bicycle trip. There are a number of restaurants along the way, so drinks and food are not a problem. The road is sealed almost all the way and it is a fairly gentle climb – although consistent. It is downhill all the way home! See the Mountain Biking chapter for details of a route (the Scar Road from Kathmandu) that takes in Kakani.

Kakani is 3km from the main Dhunche road. Turn onto the broken bitumen road just before the Kaulithana police checkpoint (the first outside Kathmandu) and there is a signpost for the Tara Gaon Kakani Hotel and the police training college.

Buses for Kakani, Trisuli Bazaar and Dhunche leave from the Kathmandu bus station on Kathmandu's Ring Rd. You can catch a Trisuli Bazaar or Dhunche bus, get off at Kaulithana (about Rs 25) and walk the 3km to Kakani.

TRISULI BAZAAR (68KM)

Trisuli Bazaar is a classically unattractive roadside town that owes its development to a large hydroelectric project on the Trisuli River, and the fact that it was once a trail head for treks into the Langtang region. These days trekkers head straight through to Dhunche, and there are very few persuasive reasons to stop.

Nawakot, a small village a few kilometres south-east of Trisuli Bazaar, has the ruins of a fortress that was built by Prithvi Narayan Shah when he was planning his campaign to take the Kathmandu Valley. It can be reached by bicycle or foot and is an interesting spot.

Places to Stay & Eat

There are several thoroughly unimpressive places on the eastern side of the bridge, which you reach when you enter town, before the turn-off to Dhunche. If you continue over the bridge, there are a few dal bhaat restaurants and a couple of reasonable options. The ***Trishuli Rest House*** is the best of a bad lot, although the ***Ranjit Hotel*** is also OK.

Getting There & Away

It is a spectacular drive from Kakani along a narrow, twisting road with great views, and would be an excellent long descent by bicycle. Buses leave from the Kathmandu bus station between 6.30 am and about 2.30 pm (Rs 60, 5 hours).

DHUNCHE (119KM)

By the time you reach Dhunche you will have been inspected by countless redundant police and army checkpoints, plus paid Rs 1000 to enter the Langtang National Park. Irritation evaporates quickly, however, because there are great views of the Langtang Valley, and although the modern section of Dhunche is pretty tacky, it's definitely a Tamang town, and the old section is virtually unchanged. Many people start trekking from Dhunche, although there is a bus to Syabrubesi as well. (See under Langtang Trek in the Trekking chapter.)

Places to Stay & Eat

There are a number of decent trekking-style hotel restaurants. ***Hotel Namaste*** is clean, serves good food, and costs Rs 80 a double, Rs 30 for a dorm bed. The ***Hotel Langtang View*** has similar prices and is also OK.

Getting There & Away

The road to Dhunche is bad, but it deteriorates further if you continue to Syabru. The views on both stretches are spectacular. A bus leaves from the Kathmandu bus station at 7 am, and arrives in Dhunche at about 3.30 pm.

Budhanilkantha Route

DHUM VARAHI SHRINE (5KM)

Lying in an unprepossessing schoolyard just inside Kathmandu's Ring Rd to the north-east of Kathmandu city proper, a huge pipal tree encloses a small shrine and a dramatic 5th-century sculpture of Vishnu. Vishnu is shown reincarnated as a wild boar with a stocky human body, holding Prithvi, the earth goddess, on his left elbow.

From a historical point of view, the statue is interesting because it is an original depiction of an animal-human, created before iconographic rules were established, which perhaps contributes to the unusual sense of movement and vitality that the statue possesses. The statue shows Vishnu rescuing Prithvi from the clutches of a demon.

Getting There & Away

A visit to Dhum Varahi could be combined with a visit to Budhanilkantha, especially if you are approaching the Budhanilkantha intersection on Kathmandu's Ring Rd from Pashupatinath. If you are coming from Pashupatinath, take the third dirt road on your left after crossing the Dhobi River. The statue lies under a huge pipal tree in the grounds of the Shridhumrabarah Primary School.

If you are coming from the intersection of the Budhanilkantha road with Kathmandu's Ring Rd, take the second dirt road on the right after the Panchayat Silver Jubilee Garden, which features a square, black-marble column topped with a conch shell. Continue for about 1km until you see the pipal tree.

BUDHANILKANTHA (15KM)

Vishnu has many incarnations and in Nepal he often appears as Narayan, the creator of all life, the god who reclines on the cosmic sea. From his navel grew a lotus and from the lotus came Brahma, who in turn created the world. So in the end everything comes from Vishnu, and at Budhanilkantha the legend is made real. Here, a stone image of Vishnu lies serenely in a pond – the most impressive, if not the most important, Vishnu shrine in the country.

The 5m-long image of Vishnu as Narayan is believed to have been created in the 7th or 8th century. It was sculpted during the Licchavi period, probably somewhere outside the valley and laboriously dragged here. Two other similar figures of the reclining Vishnu were also carved out of stone and all three were subsequently lost for many centuries. The image here at Budhanilkantha was the first figure found and it is also the largest, but whether it was also the original (from which the others were copied) is still unresolved.

Narayan lies back peacefully on a most unusual bed: the coils of the multiheaded snake, Ananta. The snake's 11 hooded heads rise protectively around Narayan's head. Narayan's four hands hold the four symbols of Vishnu: a chakra (representing the mind), a mace (primeval knowledge), a conch shell (the four elements) and a lotus seed (the moving universe). A legend relates that the lost image was discovered when a horrified farmer saw blood coming from the ground where his plough had struck the huge buried image.

During the early Malla period, Vishnuism had gone into decline as Shiva became more popular. King Jayasthiti Malla is credited with reviving the popularity of Vishnu, he did this in part by claiming to be an incarnation of the multi-incarnated god.

To this day, the kings of Nepal make the same claim and because of this they are forbidden, on pain of death, from seeing the image at Budhanilkantha. They are allowed to look at the valley's other two reclining Vishnu images, which are said to be simply copies of the Budhanilkantha figure. One of these 'replicas' is at Balaju; the other, not on view to tourists, is in Hanuman Dhoka in Kathmandu.

The sleeping Vishnu image, which lies in a small sunken pond enclosure, attracts a constant stream of pilgrims, and prayers take place every morning at 9 am. Vishnu is supposed to sleep through the four monsoon months, waking at the end of the monsoon. A great festival takes place at Budhanilkantha each November, on the day Vishnu is supposed to awaken from his long annual slumber.

Non-Hindus are not permitted to enter the enclosure, but there are some good unobstructed views from outside the fence surrounding it.

Places to Stay & Eat

The ***Park Village Hotel*** *(☎ 415432, e kgh@mos.com.np)* is a new place run by the people who own the Kathmandu Guest House. It is set in a two-hectare garden just before Budhanilkantha, and consists of studio rooms, apartments and large rooms ranging in price from US$35 to US$70. There are ambitious plans for a recreation centre, a function centre and meditation grotto.

Getting There & Away

Buses (Rs 6) as well as tempos (Rs 8, route 5) leave from the Kathmandu City bus station and take around an hour. A taxi costs around Rs 180. The shrine is at the top of a flight of stone steps, about 100m beyond the bus and tempo terminus.

By bicycle it's a long, gradual, uphill haul – hard, sweaty work rewarded with a very pleasant return trip. You could pause at Dhum Varahi on one leg of your trip.

Pashupatinath & Boudha Route

PASHUPATINATH (5KM)

Nepal's most important Hindu temple stands on the banks of the Bagmati River, between Kathmandu and the Tribhuvan Airport and slightly south-west of Boudha. You can visit Pashupatinath en route to Boudha, as the two sites are an interesting short walk apart.

Pashupatinath Temple

Not only is Pashupatinath the most important Hindu temple in Nepal, it's one of the most important Shiva temples on the subcontinent and draws devotees from all over India, including many colourful *sadhus*, those wandering ascetic Hindu holy men.

Shiva is the destroyer and creator of the Hindu pantheon and appears in many forms. His 'terrible' forms are probably best known, particularly his appearances in Nepal as the cruel and destructive Bhairabs, but he also has peaceful incarnations including those of Mahadev and Pashupati, the lord of the beasts. As the shepherd of both animals and humans, Shiva as Pashupati shows his most pleasant and creative side.

Pashupati is considered to have a special concern for Nepal and, accordingly, he features in any message from the king. Before commencing an important journey, the king will always pay a visit to Pashupatinath to seek the god's blessing. Although Shiva is often a bloodthirsty god, he is not so in his incarnation as Pashupati, so no animal sacrifices are made here, although they are made at the nearby Guhyeshwari Temple. Nor is leather (since it comes from cows) allowed inside the temple – you will see Hindus removing their shoes before entering.

Near the entrance to the temple there are people selling flowers, incense and other offerings. Although non-Hindus are not allowed inside the temple, you may catch a glimpse inside of the mighty figure of Nandi, Shiva's bull. It dates from the 19th century but the small bull in front of the temple is about 300 years old. The black, four-headed image of Pashupati inside the temple is said to be even older; an earlier image was destroyed by Mughal invaders in the 14th century.

There is also plenty to be seen along the riverbanks and you can look down into the temple from the terraced hillside, which is on the opposite bank.

The Riverbanks of the Bagmati

The Bagmati is a holy river and, as at Varanasi on the Ganges, Pashupatinath is a popular place to be cremated. The burning ghats immediately in front of the temple, north of the footbridges, are reserved for the cremation of royalty, although you will often see ritual bathing taking place in the river here.

The four square cremation ghats just south of the bridges are for the common people and there is almost always a cremation going on. The log fires are laid, the shrouded body lifted on top and the fire lit with remarkably little ceremony.

There's often a crowd of tourists – cameras and video cameras at the ready – watching like vultures from the opposite bank. Photography is permitted, but be discreet – many tourists behave with an amazingly insensitive disregard for the funeral parties. However extraordinary the sights might seem, this is a religious ceremony, often marking a family tragedy, and the participants should be accorded respect. Behave as you would wish people to behave at a funeral in your home town.

Farther south of these cremation ghats, but still on the western bank of the river, is the ancient 6th-century **Bachhareshwari Temple**, with Tantric figures and erotic scenes. It is said that at one time Maha Shivaratri festival activities included human sacrifices at this temple. Just outside the temple entrance, right at the end of the western embankment, is a half-buried, but still quite beautiful, 7th-century standing Buddha image.

Two footbridges cross the Bagmati River, and facing the temple from across the river are 11 stone chaityas, each containing a lingam. From this bank you can watch the activities on the other bank, in front of the temple. Offerings and flowers are on sale, devotees dip in the river and there's a constant coming and going. From the northern end of the embankment you can see the cave-like shelters, which were used at one time by hermits and sadhus. These days the *yogis* (yoga masters) and sadhus head for the **Ram Temple**, farther down the river, especially during the great festival of Maha Shivaratri.

The Terraces

Climb up the steps from the eastern riverbank to the terrace, where you can look down into the Pashupatinath Temple. Unfortunately it is not a very inspiring sight: The golden roof of the central two-tiered pagoda, which dates from 1696, is now surrounded by ugly corrugated-iron roofs. Look for the enormous golden trident rising up on the right (northern) side of the temple and the golden figure of the king kneeling in prayer on the left side. Behind the temple, you can see a brightly coloured illustration of Shiva and his shakti looking out over the temple.

At the northern end of this terrace is a Shiva lingam on a circular pedestal. A finely featured face of the god has been sculptured on one side of the lingam. It is an indication of the richness of Nepal's artistic heritage that this piece of sculpture, so casually standing on the grassy terrace, is actually a masterpiece dating from the 5th or 6th century!

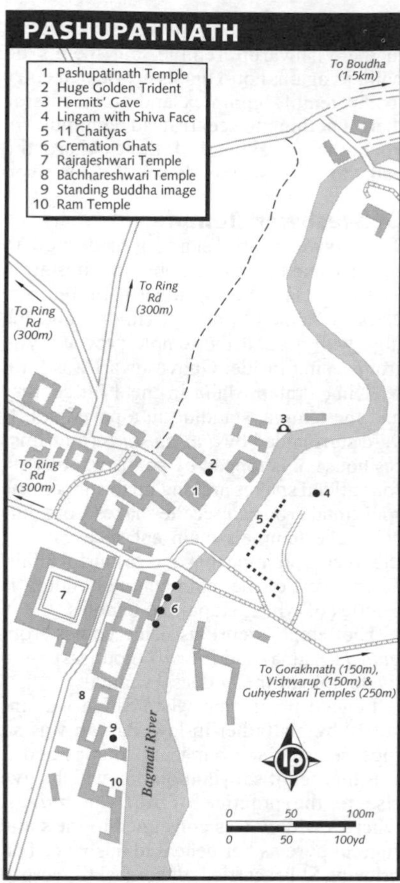

Gorakhnath & Vishwarup Temples

The steps continue up the hill from the terrace on the riverbank and, as with the steps to Swayambhunath, are a popular playground for monkeys. The Gorakhnath Temple complex is at the top of the hill. A shikhara fronted by a towering Shiva trident is the main structure, but there's a positive jungle of temples, images, sculptures and chaityas with Shiva imagery everywhere. Images of the bull Nandi stand guard, tridents are dotted around and lingams rise up on every side.

AROUND THE KATHMANDU VALLEY

You can turn right from the path and head to the Vishwarup Temple, but there's no point as again, non-Hindus are denied entry to the temple complex and from outside there's nothing to see. Instead, continue beyond the Gorakhnath Temple where the pathway turns steeply downhill to the river.

Guhyeshwari Temple

The Guhyeshwari Temple is dedicated to Shiva's shakti in her terrible manifestation as Kali. Like the Pashupatinath Temple, entry is banned to all but Hindus, and the high wall around the temple prevents you from seeing inside. Guhyeshwari was built by King Pratap Malla in the 17th century and the temple, standing in a paved courtyard surrounded by *dharamsalas* (pilgrims' resthouses), is topped by an open roof with four gilded snakes arching up to support the roof finial. You can see the snakes from outside. The temple's main entrance gate by the river is an imposing and colourful affair. To the west of the main temple building is a series of white, stupa-like temples.

The temple's curious name comes from *guhya* (vagina) and *ishwari* (goddess) – it's the temple of the goddess' vagina!

Legend has it that when Shiva was insulted by his father-in-law, Parvati was so incensed that she burst into flames and it was this act of self-immolation which gave rise to the practice of *sati* (or *suttee*), where a widow was consigned to the same funeral pyre as her deceased husband. The grieving Shiva carried off his shakti's corpse but as he wandered aimlessly, the body disintegrated and this is where her yoni fell.

Special Events

Activities take place at Pashupatinath almost all the time, but it is generally busiest (with genuine pilgrims, not tourists) from 6 to 10 am and again from 6 to 7.30 pm. The best time to visit the temple is on Haribodhini Ekadashi – 11 days after the full and new moon each month. On those days there will be many pilgrims and in the evening the ringing of bells will indicate that the *arati* (light) ceremony is to take place.

In February/March each year, the festival of Maha Shivaratri celebrates Shiva's birthday with a great fair at the temple. Pilgrims come from all over Nepal and India for this festival, and if you're in Kathmandu at the time don't miss it. Another fair takes place in November.

Getting There & Away

Buses to Boudha go via Pashupatinath from Kathmandu's City bus station; the stop for Pashupatinath is called Gosala. Pashupatinath is an easy bicycle ride from Kathmandu: Ride east from Thamel along Tridevi Marg, passing in front of the new Royal Palace. It gets more complicated after that, but you can't go wrong as long as you keep heading east. The airport is very close to Pashupatinath, so some of the roads carry a lot of traffic.

It is a pleasant and short walk between Pashupatinath and Boudha. Look from the Guhyeshwari Temple, the dome of Boudha is clearly visible to the north-east. Take the footbridge across the river right in front of Guhyeshwari and head north for a few minutes, and turn right at the first track you come across. You eventually come out on the main road, right across from the main entrance to the stupa enclosure.

CHABAHIL (6KM)

The Chabahil Stupa is like a small replica of Boudha, about 1.5km west of Boudha, back towards Kathmandu. The small village of Chabahil has been virtually swallowed up by the expansion of Kathmandu, but the site is very old and the original stupa was said to have been built by Ashoka's daughter, Charumati. It certainly predates Boudha and around the main stupa are a number of small chaityas from the Licchavi period, dating back to some time between the 5th and 8th centuries. The site includes a 1m-high, 9th-century statue of a Bodhisattva, which is claimed to be one of the finest pieces of sculpture in the valley.

Nearby is the small **Chandra Binayak Ganesh Temple**, with a double roof in brass. Ganesh's shrew stands on a pillar in front of the shrine, waiting for the tiny image of the god inside. A short distance south, but still on the Kathmandu side of the main road, is the well-designed **Jayabageshwari Temple**, dating from the late 17th century.

BOUDHA (6KM)

On the eastern side of Kathmandu, just north of the airport and an interesting walk from Pashupatinath, is the huge stupa of Boudha (also known as Bodhnath), the largest stupa in Nepal and one of the largest in the world. It is the religious centre for Nepal's considerable population of Tibetans and there are a number of thriving monasteries and many small shops selling Tibetan artefacts (beware: Prices are high and bargaining is essential).

Many of these Tibetans are refugees who fled their country following the unsuccessful uprising against the Chinese invaders in 1959. They have been both energetic and successful in the intervening years, as the large houses surrounding Boudha testify. While political and religious oppression continues in Tibet, this is one of the few places in the world where Tibetan culture is both accessible and unhindered.

Late afternoon is a good time to visit, when the group tours depart and the place once again becomes a Tibetan town. Prayer services are held in the surrounding gompas and as the sun sets the community turns out to circumambulate the stupa – a ritual that combines religious observance with a social event. Be sure to walk around the stupa in a clockwise direction.

Boudha has always been associated with Lhasa and Tibetan Buddhism. One of the major trade routes coming from Lhasa went through Sankhu, and Boudha therefore lies at the Tibetan traders' entry to Kathmandu. One can easily imagine the traders giving thanks for their successful journey across the Himalaya, or praying for a safe return. People still come here to pray before undertaking a journey in the Himalaya.

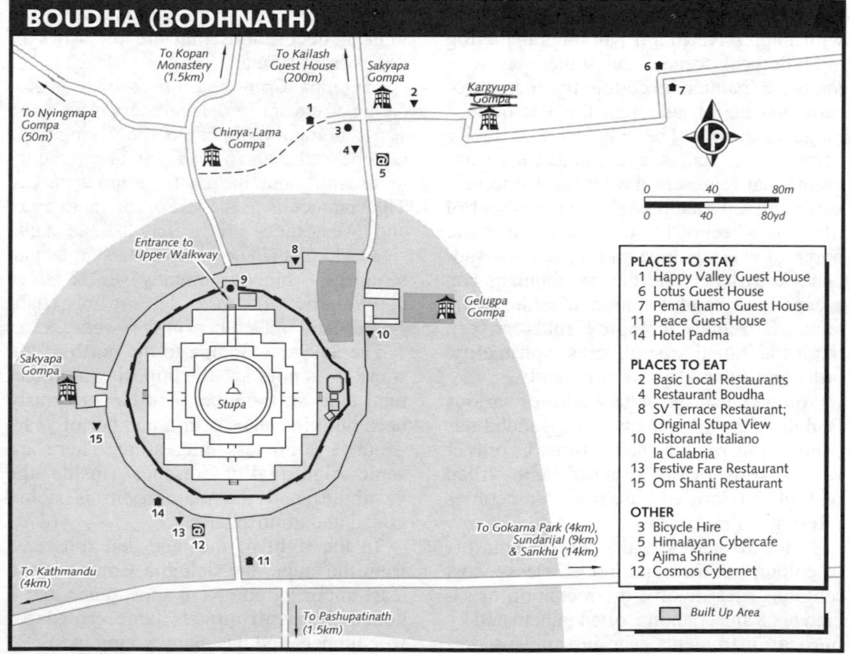

Gompas

Cultural Considerations There are a number of gompas surrounding Boudha that can be visited as long as you are respectful and discreet.

Do not forget to remove your shoes and hat before you enter a gompa. Ask before taking photos and avoid taking photos during a service. Smoking is not permitted anywhere in the main compounds. Do not step over or sit on the monks' cushions, even if no-one is sitting on them. During ceremonies, enter quietly and stand by the wall near the main entrance; do not walk around in front of the altar, or between the monks, or cross the central area of the temple.

It is appropriate to make an offering to the *lama* (Tibetan Bhuddist monk), especially if you do take photographs. A *khata* (white scarf) is traditional, but these days rupees are also appreciated; monasteries depend for their existence on the donations of the faithful.

Decorations All the gompas are decorated with impressive mural paintings depicting mythological scenes, and sometimes with *thangkas* (painted on cotton, framed in brocade and hung), although there is quite a range in quality. The subjects are usually deities, great lamas, ritual *mandalas* (diagrams that represent the forces of the universe and aid meditation) and the wheel of life. The wheel of life is represented in the porch of every gompa and represents Buddha's knowledge and the way humans can escape their conditioning and achieve nirvana. Extremely complex rules govern these traditional arts; all stress spirituality, order and symmetry, not originality.

You will also see huge statues of various Buddhas (the Tibetans believe Buddha has been reincarnated many times), prayer wheels, strategically arranged lamps filled with ghee (clarified butter) and sometimes offerings of rice.

To the Western eye, the gompas are riots of colour, but awesome nonetheless. Most religious rites involve the recitation of sacred texts and chanting, often punctuated by musical instruments. The instruments dramatise and underline particular passages, usually in a quite unmusical way. Drums and cymbals crash, and trumpets and oboes moan repetitively. The result can be both dramatic and moving.

The Gompas The **Sakyapa Gompa** is the only gompa that opens directly onto the stupa (on the western side). There are some fine paintings and a magnificent Tara covered in beautiful embroideries. Don't miss the massive prayer wheel on the left of the entrance.

Named after a lama who had trained in China, **Chinya-Lama Gompa** is on the right of the path that leaves to the north of the stupa.

Nyingmapa Gompa is one of the most recently completed (1984) and impressive gompas. It has a large and thriving community – there are lots of young novices. The gompa is a large, reddish-ochre building (designed after a monastery in Tibet) surrounded by lower, white buildings that form a large courtyard. There are some very fine interior decorations that are the work of artists from Bhutan.

Kargyupa Gompa is also known as Ka-Nying Sheldrup Ling Monastery. This large white gompa is equal to the Nyingmapa Gompa in size and has a richly decorated interior with some fine paintings and thangkas. The entrance is to the left of the main gates and Westerners are welcome; the lama speaks English. The gompa hosts an annual seminar on Vajrayana training (see the boxed text 'Tantric Goddesses' later in this chapter), usually in October for two weeks.

The **Sakyapa Gompa** to the north of the stupa, does not have the imposing architectural unity of the others – it has obviously been built in stages over a number of years – but it is no less interesting. There are some high-quality frescoes (inside the vestibule) and the main room is richly gilded and atmospheric.

To the right of the lane that runs east from the stupa, the **Gelugpa Gompa** is the least imposing gompa in appearance, but it nonetheless still attracts large crowds of worshippers and has many young monks.

Boudha Stupa

There does not seem to be any agreement on how old the site is, but it is likely that the first stupa was built some time after 600 AD, after the Tibetan king, Songtsen Gampo, was converted to Buddhism by his two wives: the Nepali princess Bhrikuti (sometimes regarded as an incarnation of the Green Tara) and Wencheng Konjo from China (the White Tara). The current stupa was probably built after the depredation of the Mughal invaders in the 14th century.

Stupas were originally built to house holy relics, or to commemorate an event or place, with a structure that symbolises Buddhist beliefs. They are never hollow. It is not certain if there is anything interred at Boudha, but some believe that there is a piece of bone that once belonged to Gautama Buddha.

The base of the stupa takes the shape of a *mandala* (symbolising earth); on this four-tiered base sits the dome (symbolising water); then comes the spire (symbolising fire); the umbrella (symbolising air); and the pinnacle (symbolising ether). Buddha's watchful eyes gaze out in four directions from the square base of the spire. There is a third eye between and above the two normal eyes and the 'nose' is not a nose at all but the Nepali number one, signifying the unity of all life. The spire is made up of 13 steps, representing the 13 stages on the journey to nirvana.

Around the base of the stupa's circular mound are 108 small images of the Dhyani Buddha Amitabha. A brick wall around the stupa has 147 niches, each with four or five prayer wheels bearing that immortal mantra *'om mani padme hum'*. On the northern side of the stupa is a small shrine dedicated to Ajima, the goddess of smallpox.

Special Events

The *losar* (Tibetan New Year) in February is celebrated by large crowds of pilgrims, who come to watch the lamas perform their rites. Long copper horns are blown, a portrait of the Dalai Lama is paraded around, and masked dances are performed.

Places to Stay

There are a number of guesthouses in the tangle of lanes north and east of the stupa, but prices are marginally higher than in Kathmandu.

At the bottom of the scale is the ***Peace Guest House***, just inside the main entrance to the stupa compound from the main road. It's about as basic as they come, but you can't beat the price of Rs 80 for a bed in a five-bed room.

A small step up the scale is the ***Kailash Guest House*** *(☎ 480741)*, on the road leading north from the Sakyapa Gompa. It's quite basic, but the management is friendly, and the singles/doubles not bad at Rs 170/220 with shared bathroom, and Rs 250 for a double with bathroom.

The ***Lotus Guest House*** *(☎ 472320)* is a very pleasant option if you want to escape the madness of Kathmandu for peace and quiet and if you want to be close to Boudha. Rooms are spotlessly clean and there is a nice garden. Rooms with shared bathroom cost Rs 250/350, and Rs 290/390 with private bathroom, good value for Boudha.

Right across the lane you'll find the new, multistorey ***Pema Lhamo Guest House*** *(☎ 495662)*, which has good rooms at Rs 350 with shared bathroom, and Rs 550 with private bathroom.

Also good, but way more expensive, and with excellent rooftop views out over the stupa – and the airport – is the ***Happy Valley Guest House*** *(☎ 471241, ⓔ happy@mos.com.np)*, a modern hotel near the northern Sakyapa Gompa. This hotel is a very well-appointed and has friendly management. Rooms cost US$20/35, and there are larger carpeted singles at US$35.

The modern ***Hotel Padma*** *(☎ 479052, ⓔ hotelpadma@wlink.com.np)* is right by the stupa but doesn't take advantage of this excellent position as all rooms are inside with no views. The rooms are large and comfortable, with phone and bathroom. The cost is US$18/25, but a 20% discount seems fairly usual.

Places to Eat

There are a number of restaurants around the stupa itself. Unfortunately, the views are often more inspiring than the food. An exception is the ***Original Stupa View***, which really does have a stupendous view, as well as excellent food. Main meals including an interesting range of vegetarian and Italian dishes are around Rs 180 to Rs 2600. Right next door is the ***SV Terrace Restaurant***, where the food is cheaper but less imaginative.

Also with good rooftop views and worth a try is the ***Ristorante Italiano la Calabria***, on the eastern edge of the enclosure. Despite the name, this place is actually Tibetan. A Sherpa lunch of soup costs Rs 100, and you can get pasta at Rs 120. Farther around the stupa enclosure is the ***Festive Fare Restaurant***, which has a number of tables with good views. The menu is fairly standard tourist fare.

Om Shanti Restaurant, also on the stupa enclosure, has a few tables that overlook the stupa. This place is otherwise pretty ordinary, although it is cheap. Tibetan dishes are Rs 30 to Rs 50, Indian dishes are Rs 40 to Rs 100.

For those on a shoestring budget, there are plenty of small Tibetan eating houses in the streets behind the stupa – any place with a curtain across an open door is probably one. The ***Restaurant Boudha*** is typical of these places.

Getting There & Away

Buses to Boudha run regularly from Kathmandu's City bus station (Rs 5, 1 hour). The tempos that leave from Kantipath in Kathmandu (routes 2 and 28) are slightly quicker and more expensive. Bicycles and taxis are better options. It is an interesting short walk between Boudha and Pashupatinath (see Getting There & Away under Pashupatinath earlier in this section for more information).

Grayline buses go to Boudha; a trip here is usually combined with Pashupatinath, and is also sometimes combined with a trip to Swayambhunath. (See Organised Tours in the Kathmandu chapter for details.)

KOPAN MONASTERY (9KM)

The Kopan Monastery (☎ 481268, fax 481267), a popular centre for courses on Buddhism and other Tibetan-related subjects, stands on a hilltop to the north of Boudha. You can visit Kopan on a walk between Boudha and the Gokarna Mahadev Temple; locals will point the way.

The centre has short courses on Tibetan medicine, thangka painting and other subjects, but the major attraction for Westerners is the 10-day residential course introducing Buddhist psychology and philosophy that is held every November. The cost is about US$300 including accommodation and food, but the participants must observe strict disciplinary rules. See Courses in the Facts for the Visitor chapter for more details.

GOKARNA MAHADEV TEMPLE (10KM)

Only a short distance north-east of Boudha, the Sundarijal road turns off from the Sankhu road and after a couple of kilometres of twists and turns takes you to the old Newari village of Gokarna. The village is surrounded on three sides by the Gokarna Forest Reserve and is notable for its fine riverside Shiva temple.

Narsingha

The image of Vishnu as Narsingha or Narsimha is a common one in the valley. In his man-lion incarnation the god is traditionally seen with a demon stretched across his legs, in the act of killing the creature by disembowelling it. You can find Narsingha at work at Changu Narayan, in front of the palace in Patan, just inside the Hanuman Dhoka entrance in Kathmandu and at the Gokarna Mahadev Temple.

The demon was supposedly undefeatable as it could not be killed by man or beast, by day or night or by any weapon. Vishnu's appearance as Narsingha neatly overcame the first obstacle, for a man-lion is neither a man nor a beast. He then waited until evening to attack the demon, for evening is neither day nor night. And instead of a weapon Narsingha used his own nails to tear the demon apart.

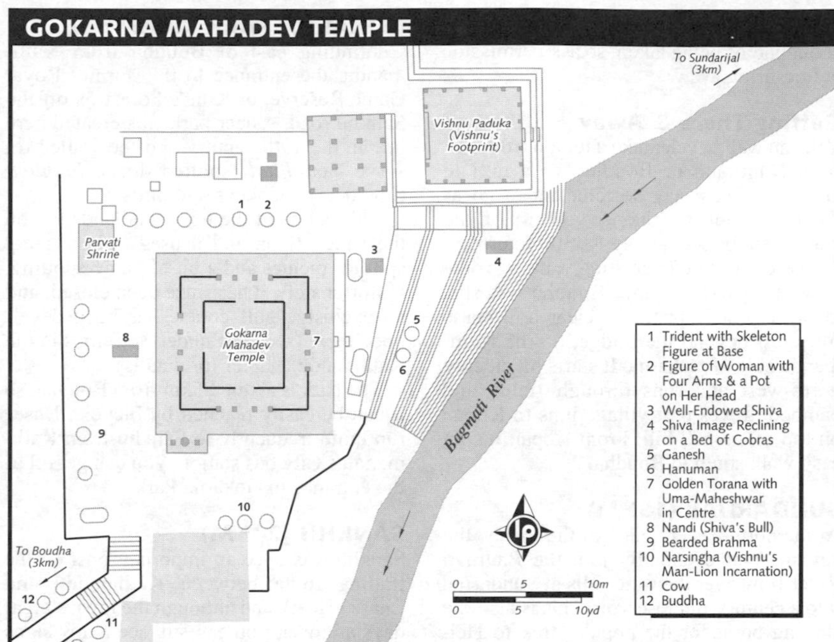

Built in 1582, the triple-roofed Mahadev (Great God) or Gokarneshwar (Lord of Gokarna) Temple stands on the banks of the Bagmati River; its inner sanctum enshrines a particularly revered Shiva lingam. Over the temple entrance is a golden torana, with Shiva and Parvati making an appearance in the centre in the Uma Maheshwar position (where Parvati sits on Shiva's thigh and leans against him) with a figure of the Garuda above them.

The temple's great interest is the surprisingly varied collection of sculptures and reliefs all around the site. They even line the pathway down from the road to the temple courtyard, starting with a Buddha figure at the top, and feature a varied collection of gods and goddesses, some dating back more than a thousand years.

The sculptures include figures from Hindu mythology, including Narad, Aditya (Sun God), Chandra (Moon God) and Kamadeva (God of Love). There's a bearded image of Brahma, Ganesh makes his usual cheerful appearance and Vishnu appears as Narsingha, making a particularly thorough job of disembowelling a nasty demon.

Shiva's bull, Nandi, stands beside the temple, and as well as the inevitable lingams dotted around there's even a nude figure of Shiva, complete with erect lingam. Durga makes three appearances, one of them as Ajima. The finest of the Gokarna statuary is in the small shrine house, which is in the north-western corner of the courtyard. This 8th-century sculpture of the beautiful goddess Parvati shows her at her radiant best; you can see why Shiva fancied her!

To one side of the main temple, just above the river, is the small, open, single-storey **Vishnu Paduka**. This relatively recent addition shelters a metal plate bearing Vishnu's footprint. Outside, set into the steps above the river, is an image of Shiva reclining on a bed of cobras, just like the reclining Vishnu images at Budhanilkantha and Balaju.

The temple guardians here can be touchy about photos being taken, so ask permission before firing away.

Getting There & Away

You can walk, cycle, take a tempo (route 28 from Kantipath or Boudha) or a taxi to Gokarna. Taxis may be reluctant to go as the road is quite rough once you turn off the main road. Expect to pay Rs 500 return.

There's also an interesting walking route between Gokarna and Boudha via the monastery at Kopan. The clear trail starts from just beyond the bridge, on the Kathmandu side of Gokarna. It starts off steeply north-west and runs through fields and bamboo groves past village inns to Kopan on top of a small hill. From Kopan it's an easy walk south to Boudha.

SUNDARIJAL (15KM)

At the north-eastern edge of the valley, the streams that eventually join the Bagmati River flow over the waterfalls at Sundarijal into a century-old reservoir. This is also the starting point for the popular trek to Helambu. The main reservoir that supplies drinking water to the valley is about a two-hour walk uphill from here. A smaller trail forks off before the reservoir to a small rock cave, where a 13th-century image of the Mahadevi (Great Goddess) can be found.

See Treks from Nagarkot in the Nagarkot Route section later in this chapter for details of the long valley-rim walk to Sundarijal from Nagarkot.

Buses leave from Kathmandu's City bus station (Rs 20). Otherwise, it's a pleasant bicycle ride along the quiet roads past Gokarna.

Sankhu & Vajra Jogini Route

The route to Sankhu follows the old Tibetan trade route past Boudha. After Boudha the road to Sundarijal turns off to the north-east and the road to Sankhu continues to the east.

GOKARNA PARK (10KM)

Continuing east of Boudha from Kathmandu, the entrance to this former Royal Game Reserve, or King's Forest, is off the Sankhu road. A deer park was created here late in the 19th century and the walled reserve has *chital* (spotted deer), *laghuna* (hog deer), monkeys and birds.

This is one of the few woodlands left on the valley floor, and it used to be a great spot for picnics and a bit of game-spotting. Unfortunately, it has since been closed, and an exclusive golf course has been developed there (see Golf under Activities in the Kathmandu chapter for details).

The park is about 2.5km from Boudha, so it can be easily reached by bicycle. Buses run quite frequently to Sankhu from Kathmandu's City bus station; you can get off at the entrance to Gokarna Park.

SANKHU (20KM)

Sankhu was once an important post on the trading route between Kathmandu and Lhasa (Tibet), and although the town's great days are over, you can still see many signs of its former prosperity. The town was first settled in the Licchavi era and there are many old homes decorated with woodcarving. Although many traditional aspects of Newari life continue here, the most persuasive reason to visit is the beautiful Vajra Jogini Temple complex, an easy walk or bicycle ride about 2km north-east of town.

Getting There & Away

Buses to Sankhu leave from Kathmandu's City bus station (Rs 25, two hours).

It's easy to reach Sankhu by bicycle. The road is sealed and flat (with a few minor exceptions), and roughly follows the Manohara River. It's an attractive and interesting ride taking about 1½ hours beyond Boudha. Rather than backtrack all the way, in the dry season at least it is possible to cross the Manohara River and climb to the fascinating Changu Narayan Temple (see the following Changu Narayan Route section for details). See Treks from Nagarkot in the Nagarkot Route section for details of the interesting walk down to Sankhu.

MARK KIRBY

Patan's Durbar Square contains the most visually stunning display of Newari architecture in Nepal.

ANDERS BLOMQVIST

Sundari Chowk's superbly crafted royal tank (Tusha Hiti) is a must-see in Patan's Durbar Square.

RICHARD I'ANSON

Nepali-style baroque at Golden Gate, Bhaktapur

ANDERS BLOMQVIST

Drying rice at Dattatraya Temple, Bhaktapur.

MARK KIRBY

Early morning peace shrouds Bhaktapur's Durbar Square.

VAJRA JOGINI (22KM)

Perched high above the valley, in a grove of huge, old trees, this complex of temples is well worth visiting. The main temple was built in 1655 by Pratap Malla of Kathmandu, but it seems likely the site has been used for much longer than that. The origins of the Tantric goddess who is worshipped in this bewitching spot are hard to determine.

The climb up the stone steps to the temples is steep and hot, but there are a number of waterspouts where you can cool off. About halfway up there is a shelter and some carvings of Kali and Ganesh. There is a natural stone, which represents Than Bhairab, sacrifices are made at its foot.

As you enter the main temple compound you will see several bells (the Tantric female equivalent to the vajra or thunderbolt) on your right. There are two temples and the one nearest to the entrance is the Vajra Jogini Temple, a pagoda with a three-tiered roof of sheet copper. There is some beautiful repoussé work on the southern facade. The struts are carved with animals and gods from the Buddhist pantheon. The goddess' image cannot actually be seen through the door.

The two-tiered temple farthest from the entrance enshrines a chaitya and commemorates Ugra Tara, or Blue (Nilo) Tara, a Buddhist goddess. The woodcarving around the doors is very fine. There are various chaityas around the platform and a gilt lion on a pillar. In the north-western corner of the courtyard (the far left when you enter) is the entrance to a cave, which is used for Tantric practices, and a Tibetan inscription. Behind the temples and up some stairs are buildings that were once used as pilgrim resthouses and priests' houses.

Getting There & Away

At Sankhu, turn left at the bus stop and walk north through the village (where there is some beautiful woodcarving). Just after the road turns to the right, take the road on the left which runs out of the village (under an ugly concrete archway). There are some fine stone carvings of Vishnu and Ganesh after the arch. The road then forks: The left fork is the traditional approach for pedestrians and follows the small river; the right fork is drivable (though rough) and is OK for bicycles.

Tantric Goddesses

The name Vajra Jogini suggests a close association with Tantric beliefs. A *vajra* (*dorje* in Tibetan) is the Buddhist thunderbolt symbol that looks a bit like a hollow dumbbell, and Vajrayana is the name for the Tantric form of Buddhism. Tantric beliefs developed as a synthesis of ancient pre-Hindu religions and new ideas that rejected many orthodox Hindu and Buddhist beliefs. Tantric believers hold that endless rebirths on the journey to nirvana can be avoided by incorporating magical rites with all the energies of existence – both good and bad – under the strict tutelage of a lama. Sex as well as sexual imagery play a central role.

Hinduism was initially a patriarchal religion introduced by the Aryan invaders of India, and overriding the existing earth goddesses. The development of shaktis or the female consorts of the new male gods allowed the resurgence of the female forces. These goddesses have enjoyed tremendous popularity in the Kathmandu Valley, sometimes completely overshadowing their male counterparts, especially in Tantric belief. A parallel development in Buddhism produced the female counterparts to the Dhyani Buddhas.

A Jogini is the female counterpart to a Bhairab, one of the wrathful forms of Shiva. In other words, a Jogini is the wrathful form of Shiva's partner Mahadevi (Great Goddess), who is Parvati in a more peaceful manifestation. Among some of Mahadevi's fearsome manifestations are those such as Kali, Durga, Annapurna and Taleju.

So who is Vajra Jogini, you might ask? A Tantric goddess is the simple answer – a unique Nepali goddess possibly combining elements from Hinduism, Buddhism and perhaps even earlier religions.

There's a car park at the foot of the steps to the temple complex. If you get there by bicycle, it will be necessary to pay a few rupees to someone to look after it for you. It's quite a stiff climb to the temples.

Changu Narayan Route

THIMI (10KM)

Thimi is the fourth-largest town in the valley, outranked only by Kathmandu, Patan and Bhaktapur. It's a typical Newari town and its 'capable people' (the name of the town is derived from this Newari expression) operate thriving cottage industries producing pottery and papier-mâché masks. They also grow vegetables for the markets of Kathmandu.

The town's main road runs north-south between the old and new Bhaktapur roads (which form the northern and southern boundaries of the town). In the centre of the southern square stands the 16th-century **Balkumari Temple**. Balkumari was one of Bhairab's shaktis and a much less magnificent Bhairab Temple is found nearby (see the boxed text 'Tantric Goddesses'). Thimi also has a 16th-century **Narayan Temple** and a 15th-century **Mahadev Temple**.

Just to the north of Thimi is **Nade**, from here a stone pathway leads up through an archway to **Ganesh Dyochen**. Nearby is a locally popular triple-roofed **Ganesh Temple**. Farther north is **Bode**, with the interesting 17th-century **Mahalakshmi Temple**.

Special Events

In the Bisket Jatra (Nepali new year's day) ceremony, 32 deities are carried to the Balkumari Temple in palanquins. The arrival of the Ganesh image from Nade is the high point of the colourful festivities (a great deal of bright red powder gets thrown around). A similar but smaller ceremony also takes place at the Mahalakshmi Temple in Bode.

CHANGU NARAYAN TEMPLE (22KM)

The beautiful and historic temple of Changu Narayan stands on a hilltop at the eastern end of the valley, about 4km north of Bhaktapur. Although the temple dates from 1702, when it was rebuilt after a fire, its origins go right back to the 4th century and there are many important stone images as well as sculptures dating from the Licchavi period.

Despite the temple's beauty and interest it attracts relatively few visitors because of its comparative inaccessibility, although these days you can drive or catch a bus right to the temple via Bhaktapur. Alternatively, it makes a pleasant walk from that town or an interesting destination on the walk down from Nagarkot.

The double-roofed temple is dedicated to Vishnu in his incarnation as Narayan and is exceptionally beautiful, with quite amazingly intricate roof struts depicting multi-armed goddesses. It is fronted by a figure of Garuda said to date from the 5th century. The man-bird mount of Vishnu has a snake around his neck and kneels with folded hands facing the temple. Stone lions guard the wonderfully gilded door, which is flanked by equally detailed gilded windows. Two pillars at the front corners carry two traditional symbols of Vishnu, the sankha and the chakra.

Despite the beauty of the temple itself, it is, in Nepali terms, relatively new. The much older images found in the temple courtyard are of equal interest. There are various images of Vishnu carrying the symbols associated with the god in his four hands. In the north-western corner there is an image of Vishnu astride the Garuda, which is illustrated on the Rs 10 banknote. Beside the Garuda figure that faces the front of the temple is one of the oldest Licchavi stone inscriptions in the valley.

Other images include one of Vishnu as Narsingha, his man-lion incarnation, in the act of disembowelling a demon. Another shows him as Vikrantha, the six-armed dwarf who transformed into a giant capable of crossing the universe in three gigantic steps. Behind these two images is a small black slab showing Narayan reclining on the serpent Ananta at the bottom and Vishnu with 10 heads and 10 arms in the centre. This beautifully carved image dates from the 5th or 6th century.

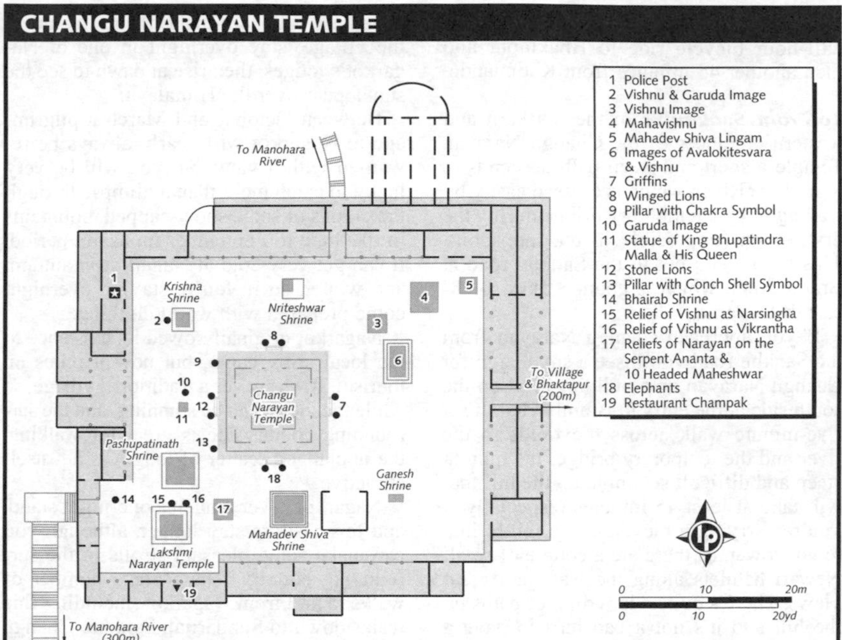

Other points of interest include the statues of King Bhupatindra Malla and his queen, kneeling in a gilded cage in front of the temple. In the centre of the brick paving of the courtyard, triangular bricks are used, while out towards the edge there are older, rounded-corner bricks.

The village of Changu stands below the temple hill and has some Licchavi remains.

Places to Stay & Eat

The small ***Restaurant Champak*** is in the south-western corner of the temple complex. By the car park at the end of the road at the entrance to Changu village, the ***Lovely Coffee House*** has drinks and snacks, and great views out over the valley to Bhaktapur.

Getting There & Away

Bus & Taxi Public buses run regularly between Changu Narayan and Bhaktapur. A taxi from Kathmandu costs around Rs 600 return, and from Bhaktapur around Rs 180.

Walking & Cycling Either of these transport alternatives offers a good way to appreciate the area around Changu Narayan.

To/From Bhaktapur It takes about two hours on foot or about an hour by riding a mountain bike to get to Changu Narayan from Bhaktapur. It's a wonderful downhill run on the way back, but quite a steep climb on the way there. A long spur runs down from the eastern edge of the valley and the temple tops the final bump of this lengthy ridge. There's a sealed road from Bhaktapur right to the village of Changu, which is only a short stroll from the temple, and you can easily get a taxi to Changu Narayan from Bhaktapur. A number of walking trails, inconsistently signposted, lead to Changu Narayan from Bhaktapur and once you get out of the town the hill is clearly visible.

If you're on foot or bicycle, you can continue to Boudha, Sankhu, Gokarna or other attractions in the north-east of the valley.

From Changu Narayan it's an exhilarating half-hour bicycle ride to Bhaktapur and then another 45 minutes from Kathmandu.

To/From Sankhu From the northern and western entrances of the Changu Narayan Temple a short and steep path descends to Manohara River, which is crossed easily by wading or by a temporary bridge during the dry season (impossible in the monsoon). This brings you out to the Sankhu road at Bramhakhel, which is about 3.5km south-east of Gokarna.

If you approach Changu Narayan from the Sankhu road you'll see a small sign for Changu Narayan on a building wall on the south side at the entry to Bramhakhel. It's a five-minute walk across the fields to the river and the temporary bridge. It's quite a steep and difficult scramble up the hill that will take at least 45 minutes (especially if you're carrying a bicycle). You might like to go slower, as there are a couple of small Newari hamlets along the way, and great views. There's quite a labyrinth of paths up the hill and it's not a bad idea to have a guide (and bicycle carrier). You will probably find small boys offering their carrying services – establish a price in advance.

To/From Nagarkot A third way of reaching Changu Narayan is by the pleasant downhill stroll from Nagarkot (see Treks from Nagarkot in the Nagarkot Route section following). Walking down from Nagarkot to Changu Narayan and then on to Bhaktapur is a much more interesting walk than the straightforward walk down to Bhaktapur.

Nagarkot Route

The route to Nagarkot goes by Thimi and Bhaktapur before climbing steeply up to the village on the valley rim.

NAGARKOT (30KM)

There are various places around the edge of the Kathmandu Valley that offer great mountain views, but the resort village of Nagarkot is generally held to be the best. Mountain watchers make their way up to the village, stay overnight in one of Nagarkot's lodges, then rise at dawn to see the sun appear over the Himalaya.

Between October and March a pilgrimage to Nagarkot will nearly always be rewarded with a view, but you will be very lucky to catch more than a glimpse through the clouds of some snow-capped mountains in the June to September monsoon period. It can get very cold at Nagarkot in autumn and winter, so if you're staying overnight come prepared with warm clothing.

Nagarkot originally owed its existence to the local army camp, but now it relies on tourism. It was never a traditional village, so while the views can be stunning, and the surrounding countryside is great for walking, the unplanned scatter of lodges is not itself attractive.

Nagarkot is very much a one-night stand, and few visitors stay longer, although you can make some pleasant strolls in the surrounding country. There are a number of walks to and from Nagarkot, including fine walks down to Sundarijal, Sankhu, Changu Narayan or Bhaktapur in the valley or south to Banepa (beyond the valley).

Orientation

Nagarkot is on a ridge on the eastern rim of the valley and the view extends all the way from Dhaulagiri in the west to past Mt Everest (little more than a dot on the horizon) to Kanchenjunga in the east. An easy hour's walk (4km) south from the village will give an even better 360° view from a lookout tower on a ridge.

The main centre of Nagarkot – in reality a small cluster of guesthouses – is a 10-minute walk north of the main road that runs in a loop through to the army camp. Right in the centre of things is a lookout, between the huge Club Himalaya Resort and the Tea House Restaurant.

Nagarkot accommodation is spread out along the dirt track that heads north from the bus stop at the town's one and only intersection. The winding road takes a sharp turn at the cluster of shops that mark the Nagarkot bus stop. From here a dirt track veers left and after a few hundred metres comes to a hilltop group of hotels, which are the most popular and best situated at Nagarkot. They cluster around the Mahakali shrine, and many have rooms that offer Himalayan views straight from your bed. At the worst you'll just have to take a few steps outside to bring the whole panorama into view.

Accommodation

Accommodation can be in short supply late in the day during high season, in which case you may have to settle for whatever you can get, which will probably mean a room without a view. In low season there are fewer visitors and prices are highly negotiable.

Most places have electricity, but hot water and heating are hard to come by, especially at the budget end of the market. A torch (flashlight) is useful (for an early-morning start to the lookout tower) and warm clothing (even a sleeping bag) can be worthwhile. There's not much to do in the evenings, so bring a book.

Nagarkot has a fair selection of lodges, guesthouses and hotels, most of them far from pretty. They usually offer a range of facilities at a range of prices, and most are expensive for the facilities you get – but what price the view? There's not much choice in the food department. Most people eat at their lodge, and most are unimpressed with the cuisine.

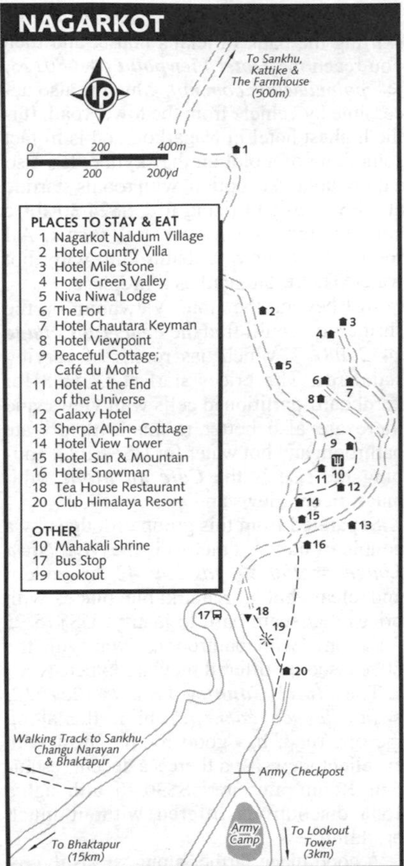

Places to Stay

Heading north from the intersection, the first place you come to is the uninspiring ***Hotel Snowman*** *(☎ 290746)*. Even with discounts of 40% it's overpriced. The full tariff is US$18/25 for plain singles/doubles with private bathroom. Deluxe rooms with views go for US$30/40.

The ***Hotel Sun & Mountain*** *(☎ 290871)*, the next place along, is a modern and unremarkable place with rooms that all face the wrong direction! It's also way overpriced at US$35/40, but discounts are available. The similar ***Hotel View Tower*** is behind it.

Next is a budget hotel, close to the Mahakali shrine. The ***Hotel at the End of the Universe*** *(☎ 610874)* is a good little place. It has some standard rooms from US$4/6, including some pleasant bamboo-walled cottages with private toilet. There are also some modern brick rooms with hot shower at US$15. While none of the rooms has a view, the restaurant does. With a carpeted bench around low tables it's a popular gathering place in the evening.

Just below, the ***Galaxy Hotel*** *(☎ 290797, fax 259142)* has very comfortable rooms with bathroom for US$20/25, although discounts are often available. Most rooms are reasonably pleasant, and have at least partial views, so you may consider the cost worthwhile.

Continue beyond the Mahakali shrine, skirting the bank official's house, and then you reach the ***Hotel Viewpoint*** *(☎ 680123, ⓔ vpoint@wlink.com.np)*, which is also accessible by vehicle from the lower road. It is the highest hotel in Nagarkot, and is in fact something of a blot on the skyline. It's also a more upmarket option, with rooms starting at US$14/20 and rising to US$24/30 for a combination of comfort and views. All rooms have private bathroom with hot water. The restaurant has a fireplace.

Just beyond the Hotel Viewpoint on the shrine side you'll find the ***Peaceful Cottage*** *(☎ 290877)*, which has rooms of varying standards. The prices start at US$6/8 for hardboard-partitioned cells with views, and there are also better rooms with private bathroom and hot water for US$12/22. Topping the rise is the ***Café du Mont***, with magnificent views and average food.

Separated from this group of lodges by a couple of hundred metres is the ***Niva Niwa Lodge*** *(☎ 290797, fax 259142)*, a modern and clean but unremarkable place, with prices that seem hard to justify: US$75/95 for rooms with bathroom. Even with the 20% discount offered they are expensive.

The ***Hotel Country Villa*** *(☎ 221012, ⓔ hcvilla@col.com.np)*, a bit farther along the dirt road, has good rooms, most with excellent views, and there's a decent restaurant. Room rates are US$30/40, although a 15% discount is offered without much prodding.

A good place farther along still is the relaxed ***Nagarkot Naldum Village***, with small bamboo cottages with stunning views – from bed – at US$20 with private toilet (also with views!). This place is a bit of a walk, but if you're after peace and quiet it could be ideal, and the ***Greenpeace Restaurant*** here is not bad.

There's another good place about 1km past Nagarkot Naldum Village on the very rough track to Sankhu. ***The Farmhouse*** *(☎ 228087, ⓔ nfh@mos.com.np)* is in a beautiful, Newari-inspired building with just 12 rooms. It's well away from the sprawl of Nagarkot and is highly recommended. It's run by Kathmandu's Hotel Vajra, and the rates are reasonably high, although meals are included. Rooms with shared bathroom are US$25/40, with private bathroom US$32/50 – all plus 12% tax.

The road that forks off to the right by the Hotel Snowman leads to a few more hotels. First up is the little ***Sherpa Alpine Cottage*** *(☎ 680015)*, which has some very precarious looking timber cottages. These are cosy and at Rs 350 aren't bad value for Nagarkot.

Accessed off a steep side track and just beyond the Hotel Viewpoint, ***The Fort*** *(☎ 680149, ⓔ fort@mos.com.np)* is a large place built in Newari style. The front rooms have excellent views; the whole place is geared towards tour groups. The rooms cost US$57/63, and a 20% discount is offered in the low season.

Farther along is the ***Hotel Chautara Keyman*** *(☎ 419798, ⓔ keyman@wlink.com.np)*, which is rather big and ugly, and is expensive at US$48/60. The individual cottages are much better and these also cost US$48/60. A discount of up to 20% may be available if things are slow.

At the end of the dirt road, perched on the edge of a steep slope, is ***Hotel Green Valley*** *(☎ 290878)*. It's nothing flash, but it has a couple of cheap rooms with shared bathroom and views at Rs 280. Singles/doubles with private bathroom cost Rs 450/650.

The ***Hotel Mile Stone*** *(☎ 290888, fax 260024)* next door to the Hotel Green Valley is a good little place with just four cottages. These are excellent value at Rs 250 with private bathroom, and the cosy restaurant is also good.

South of the bus stop, towards the army camp and perched right on the ridge is ***Club Himalaya Resort*** *(☎ 680080, fax 680068)*, which is run by the Kathmandu Guest House. A large construction like this really does nothing for the rural ambience. Having said that, the building has been well thought out: Each room has a private balcony with view, and there are also views from the atrium-type lobby with its restaurant and indoor swimming pool and Jacuzzi. The rooms are large and well furnished, and cost US$75/90, plus 12% tax.

Places to Eat

Above the main intersection is the modern ***Tea House Restaurant***, with a nice terrace aimed at day-trippers (it's relatively expensive). It is an attractive building, with good views, and it's open from 6 am to 8 pm. Main meals are around Rs 150, and even a Coca-Cola is Rs 30.

A new addition to the scene is the ***Naked Chef*** (which is also known as ***Kilroys at Nagarkot***). It will come as no surprise to find that this place is associated with the restaurant Kilroys of Kathmandu.

There are a couple of basic eating houses at the foot of the viewing tower, so you can at least get a drink or something to eat after making the trip on foot from Nagarkot.

Getting There & Away

There's a road right to Nagarkot from Bhaktapur, so you can take a bus or taxi all the way there. Walking to, or preferably from, Nagarkot is an interesting alternative; there are several possible routes (see Treks from Nagarkot following).

Buses operate to a somewhat unreliable schedule from Bhaktapur, departing every hour or so and costing Rs 14. The bus can be very slow (taking up to two hours) and extremely crowded. The roof is not only less crowded but also offers fine views. A taxi from Bhaktapur costs about Rs 600 one way and Rs 900 return.

Grayline (☎ 413188) has afternoon tours to Nagarkot (from Kathmandu) if there's four or more people, or just take a taxi.

TREKS FROM NAGARKOT

There are a number of trekking routes to and from Nagarkot. If you only want to walk one way it's a good idea to take the bus to Nagarkot and walk back down. The following walks are all written heading downhill from Nagarkot.

To Bhaktapur

Until the road from Nagarkot to Bhaktapur was built, the walking trail was the only way to go. Now with buses running back and forth it's neither necessary nor all that enjoyable. You would be better off taking one of the alternative routes, but if you do want to walk back down it's relatively easy to take the wide, easy trail that runs north of the road and short-cuts across the road turns. The trail eventually joins the road on its final gradual ascent (halfway to Bhaktapur); you can follow this and turn off at the eastern end of Bhaktapur or simply catch a bus, should one come by. It takes about two hours to walk down, and perhaps twice that to walk up.

Going down, you leave the main road to descend through a pine forest, then follow a stream to a cluster of bamboo trees near the city reservoir, where you rejoin the main road. From here you enter the town at the eastern end and continue to Tachupal Tole.

To Changu Narayan Temple

Walking down to Changu Narayan is a much more interesting alternative to the walk down to Bhaktapur. From Nagarkot it is very easy to see the long spur which extends into the Kathmandu Valley. At the very end of the spur the ridge line gives one final hiccup and then drops down to the valley floor. The beautiful temple of Changu Narayan is on the top of this final bump on the ridge line.

The walking trail from Nagarkot follows the road to Bhaktapur along a ridge, branching off at a sharp hairpin bend. It's easier to take the bus from Nagarkot down to this bend rather than walk all the way down to Changu Narayan. The short ride saves you the tedious part of the walk, where the walking trail runs close to the road.

From the bend, the trail climbs uphill through a pine forest for about 20 minutes until it reaches the top of the ridge and then it simply follows the ridge line, undulating gently down to Changu Narayan. The walking trail passes through small Chhetri villages with wonderful views over the valley to the Himalaya beyond. Finally, the shining roof of Changu Narayan appears above the village of Changu itself, from where a stone-paved street leads to the temple. From the hairpin bend (where you leave the Nagarkot to Bhaktapur road) it takes about one to 1½ hours to walk to the temple (see

Changu Narayan Temple in the Changu Narayan Route section previously).

From Changu Narayan you can descend to the Manohara River to the north and take the road back to Boudha and Kathmandu. Alternatively, you can continue south to Bhaktapur, either by the direct trail or by the road running slightly to the east.

To Sankhu

Fewer walkers follow the trail to Sankhu, just north of the Nagarkot to Changu Narayan ridge line in the north-east of the valley. The picturesque Newari town of Sankhu is surrounded by rich agricultural land and is easily visible from Nagarkot and from the trail down to Changu Narayan. The trail follows the same ridge line then drops steeply down the hillside in a north-westerly direction, joining the Boudha to Sankhu road at Bramhakhel.

From Sankhu, buses run to Kathmandu via Boudha every couple of hours.

To Sundarijal

It takes two easy days or one very long one to reach Sundarijal from Nagarkot on a trail which follows the valley rim. From Sundarijal you can take the road to Gokarna, Boudha and Kathmandu or you can continue for another day along the rim to Shivapuri and Budhanilkantha. Some trekking agencies operate treks on this valley-rim walk, but it is also possible to find accommodation in village inns. There are many confusing trail junctions, so ask directions frequently.

The trail starts from the Mahakali shrine in Nagarkot, heading north-east, and passes the village of **Kattike** (about one hour) and then turns more northerly to **Jorsim Pauwa** (about one hour). Walk farther down through **Bagdhara** with its village inns to Chowki Bhanjyang (about one hour). From Chowki Bhanjyang, another hour's walk will take you farther north through **Nagle** to **Bhotichaur**, which makes a good place to stop overnight in a village inn.

The walk continues by returning towards **Chowki Bhanjyang** for a short distance and then taking the fork by a *chautara* (porters' resting place) uphill and then more steeply uphill to cross a ridge line before dropping down on the middle of three trails to **Chule**. The trail contours around the edge of the valley, crossing several ridge lines running down into the valley, before dropping down to **Mulkarkha** and the trail past the reservoir and along the pipeline to Sundarijal. The last part of this trail to Sundarijal is the first part of the popular Helambu Trek (see the Trekking chapter).

To Banepa

The town of Banepa is outside the valley and is the major junction town on the way to Dhulikhel on the Arniko Hwy (the road to the Tibetan border). From Nagarkot, you start this walk near the lookout tower south of town, at the southern part of the ridge and follow a steep descent to the south-east. Following a precise trail is difficult, but that is no problem – all the trails lead to Banepa. A few kilometres north of Banepa the trail passes through the old Newari town of Nala with its interesting temples.

From Banepa, you can take a bus back to Kathmandu or to Dhulikhel. See the following section for more information on Banepa and Nala.

Dhulikhel & Arniko Highway Route

The Arniko Hwy to Dhulikhel passes by Thimi, skirts the southern side of Bhaktapur and then climbs out of the valley before dropping down to Banepa, continuing on to Dhulikhel, the Tibetan border and to Lhasa. See also Touring Routes in the Mountain Biking chapter for this trip.

BANEPA (29KM)

Just outside the valley, the small town of Banepa is a busy crossroads, with a statue of King Tribhuvan marking the centre of town. Dhulikhel is just beyond Banepa; the temple town of Panauti is about 7km south; the interesting village of Nala is to the north-west; and Chandeshwari, with its legendary old temple, is only 1km or so north-east –

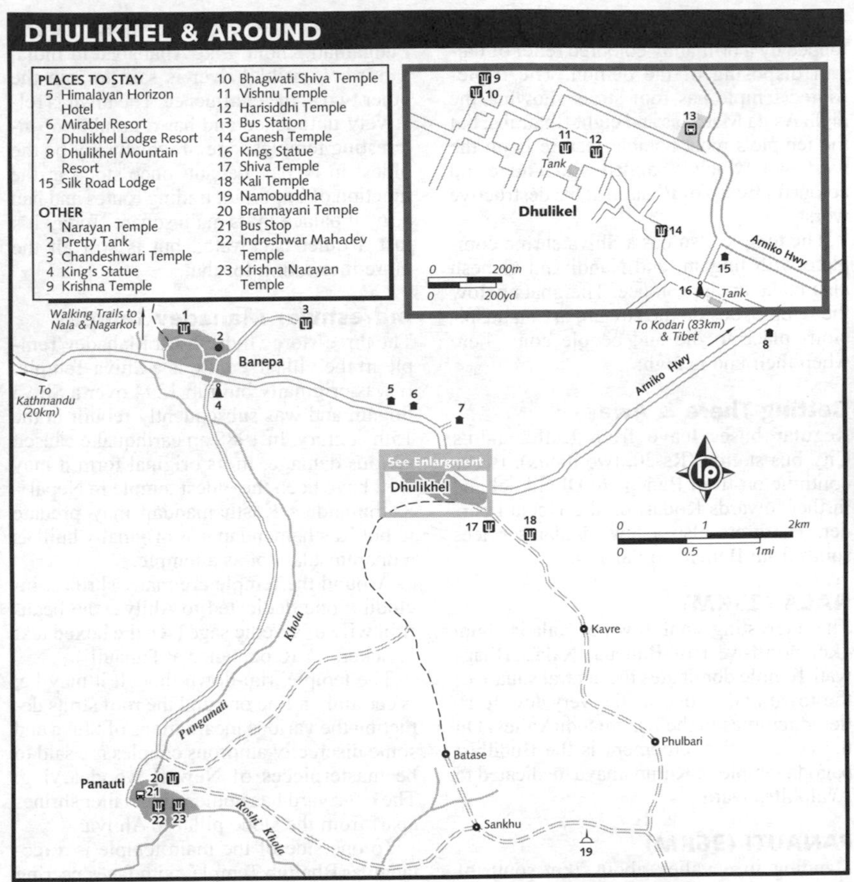

yet Banepa itself is of very limited interest. Indeed, the main road – all that most visitors see – is a dusty, noisy affair and waiting for a change of bus at that busy crossroads is often decidedly unpleasant.

Banepa itself has few buildings of interest, although there are some pleasant squares and quieter laneways in the older part of town to the north-west. The old town square has two Narayan temples with virtually back-to-back worshipful Garuda statues. Right beside the turn-off to Chandeshwari is a pretty tank with bas-reliefs of gods at one end.

Chandeshwari Temple

Only 1km or so north-east of Banepa the temple to the goddess Chandeshwari perches on the very edge of a gorge. The road out of Banepa runs gently uphill, then just as gently downhill through open fields and to a short village street, past an old tank and right to the arched entrance gate to the temple.

Legend has it that the people of this valley were once terrorised by a demon known as Chand, when Parvati, in her demon-slaying mode, got rid of the nuisance she took the name Chandeshwari, 'Slayer of Chand', and this temple was built in her honour.

The temple is entered through a doorway topped by a brilliantly coloured relief of Parvati disposing of the demon. The triple-roofed temple has roof struts showing the eight Ashta Matrikas and eight Bhairabs, but the temple's most notable feature is on the west wall, which is painted with a huge and colourful fresco of Bhairab at his destructive worst.

The temple also has a Shiva shrine complete with lingam, and Nandi and Ganesh also make an appearance. The ghats below the temple, beside the stream, are an auspicious place to die and people come here when their end is nigh.

Getting There & Away

Regular buses leave from Kathmandu's City bus station (Rs 20, two hours). Buses continue on from Banepa to Dhulikhel and farther towards Kodari on the Tibetan border. There are also a few regular services south from Banepa to Panauti.

NALA (33KM)

The interesting small town of Nala is about 4km north-west of Banepa. Nala's Bhagwati Temple dominates the central square of the town and is one of the very few four-tiered temples in the Kathmandu Valley. On the edge of the settlement is the Buddhist pagoda temple of Karunamaya, dedicated to Avalokiteshvara.

PANAUTI (36KM)

Standing in a valley about 7km south of Banepa, the small town of Panauti is at the junction of the rivers Roshi Khola and Pungamati Khola. Like Allahabad in India, a third 'invisible' river is said to join the other two at the confluence. The town is relatively untouched and has a number of interesting temples, one of which may be the oldest in Nepal. Panauti once stood at the junction of important trading routes and had a royal palace in its main square. Today it's just a quiet backwater, but is still all the more interesting for that.

Indreshwar Mahadev Temple

The three-storey Indreshwar Mahadev Temple in the village centre is a Shiva Temple. It was originally built in 1294 over a Shiva lingam and was subsequently rebuilt in the 15th century. In 1988 an earthquake caused serious damage. In its original form it may well have been the oldest temple in Nepal – Kathmandu's Kasthamandap may predate it, but Kasthamandap was originally built as a dharamsala, not as a temple.

Around the temple are many shrines, including one dedicated to Ahilya, the beautiful wife of a Vedic sage (see the boxed text 'Trickery & Repentance at Panauti').

The temple, run-down though it may be, is certainly a fine one and the roof struts depicting the various incarnations of Shiva and some discreetly amorous couples are said to be masterpieces of Newari woodcarving. The courtyard has numerous smaller shrines apart from the stone pillar to Ahilya.

To one side of the main temple is a rectangular Bhairab Temple, with faces peering out of the three upstairs windows, rather like

Trickery & Repentance at Panauti

Legends relate that Ahilya was seduced by the god Indra, who tricked her by assuming the shape of her husband. When the sage returned and discovered what had happened he took a bizarre revenge upon Indra by causing Indra's body to become covered in yonis, female sexual organs! Naturally, Indra was somewhat put out by this and for many years he and his wife Indrayani repented at this auspicious confluence of rivers. Eventually, Parvati, Shiva's consort, took pity upon Indrayani and turned her into the invisible river, which joins the two visible ones in Panauti. More years passed and eventually Shiva decided to release Indra from his strange problem. Shiva appeared in Panauti as a great lingam and when Indra bathed in the river the yonis disappeared. The lingam is the one which stands in the temple.

the Shiva-Parvati Temple in Kathmandu's Durbar Square. A small, double-roofed Shiva Temple stands by the north-western corner, while a Vishnu shrine with a 2m-high image of the god faces the temple from the west. Look for the pots and pans hanging under the roof eaves of the main temple. They're donated to the temple by newlyweds to ensure a happy married life.

Other Temples

Across Pungamati Khola is the 17th-century **Brahmayani Temple**; a suspension bridge crosses the river at this point. Brahmayani is the chief goddess of the village and her image is drawn around the town each year in the chariot festival. This temple was restored with French assistance in 1982–3.

On the town side of the river, actually at the junction where the two rivers meet, is a **Krishna Narayan Temple** with some woodcarvings of similar age and style to the Indreshwar Mahadev Temple. The riverbank stone sculptures are also of interest, but unfortunately the late 1980s were cruel to Panauti: as well as the earthquake there were also severe floods, which swept away the cremation ghats at the river junction.

Special Events

Panauti celebrates a chariot festival at the end of the monsoon each year, when images of the gods from the town's various temples are drawn around the streets in temple carts. The festival starts from the town's old Durbar Square.

There are a number of important religious sites across the subcontinent that play host to huge religious *melas* (religious fairs that attract enormous crowds of pilgrims, worshippers and sadhus). Every 12 years (next in 2010), the Magh Sankranti festival (in mid-January, or the Nepali lunar month of Magh) is celebrated with a great mela in Panauti.

Places to Stay & Eat

There are a few basic hotels around the main intersection by the bridge but the best option is the ***Hotel Panauti*** *(☎ 61055)*, about a five-minute walk away. It has comfortable rooms at Rs 300 with shared bathroom and Rs 500 with private bathroom. There's also a decent rooftop terrace and cafe; this is definitely the best place in town to eat.

Getting There & Away

Buses run regularly from Banepa to Panauti (Rs 8). These leave from the middle of Banepa at the *chowk* (marketplace) with the king's statue in it. See Treks from Dhulikhel later in this section for some information on walking to Panauti.

DHULIKHEL (32KM)

Only 3km south-east of Banepa is the interesting small town of Dhulikhel. It's popular as a Himalayan viewpoint, in part because the road to Dhulikhel is easier than the steep and winding road to Nagarkot, but also because Dhulikhel is a real town, not just a tourist resort. It's also a good centre for short day treks – many visitors come here to stretch their legs before setting off on longer treks.

Dhulikhel is a district headquarters and has a number of government offices, a high school and even a small jail. Its population is Newar, although there are people of many other groups in the surrounding villages. The prime Himalayan viewpoint is the parade ground, on the ridge just south-east of the centre. An even better view can be found from the hill topped by a Kali Temple, about a 30-minute walk along the Namobuddha trail.

A new highway to Sindhuli in the eastern Terai is being constructed with Japanese assistance. The highway starts in Dhulikhel and when finished (some time before 2004, at a guess) will considerably shorten the travelling time between Kathmandu and the towns of the eastern Terai. What the likely huge increase in heavy vehicle traffic will do for the peaceful ambience of Dhulikhel – and the narrow and inadequately engineered Arniko Hwy back to Kathmandu – is not yet clear.

Temples

The old part of the town, west of the bus stop, is an interesting area to wander around, with some fine old Newari buildings and several interesting temples. The town's main square has a tank, the small, triple-roofed **Harisiddhi Temple** and a **Vishnu Temple** fronted by two worshipful Garudas in quite different styles. One is a kneeling stone Garuda topping a low pillar, while the second Garuda is in bright metal, flanked by two kneeling devotees, and is more like the bird-faced Garudas of Indonesia than the conventional Nepali Garudas.

Walking in the other direction you pass the post office and the mountain viewpoint, and after 5km you reach the junction where the road turns west to Namobuddha. Continue straight on from the junction and dip down to a picturesque little **Shiva Temple** at the bottom of a gorge. Water flows through the site, where the main sanctum is a squat, square block decorated with coloured tiles and topped with a metal dome with four *nagas* (snake deities) arching down from the pinnacle. The temple is fronted by figures of Nandi on pillars, and kneeling devotees. To one side is a fine image of Ganesh, while in a second small shrine only the feet remain of three images, the result of the work of art thieves. Below that is a tank, but this is a temple with everything – if you look around you can find images of Hanuman, Saraswati, Shiva and Parvati, lingams, tridents and much more.

Dhulikhel's final temple attraction is the **Kali Temple** high up the hill towards Namobuddha. Climb up here for the excellent view, not for the temple, which is of little interest.

Places to Stay – Budget

The ***Nawa Rangu Guest House*** *(☎ 61226)*, on the way towards the post office and Shiva Temple, is a curious place, with a restaurant hung with interesting naive-style paintings, and basic trekking lodge-style rooms and bathroom facilities. The food is generally good. Basic singles/doubles are Rs 120/180.

On the Arniko Hwy there are a couple of possibilities, neither of them very attractive. The ***Silk Road Lodge*** *(☎ 61269)* has some mountain views, but also gets the traffic noise. Doubles cost Rs 150 with shared bathroom.

About 1km south-east of the main chowk, on the track that leads to Namobuddha, is the ***Snow View Guest House*** *(☎ 61229)*. It's a friendly place set in a pleasant garden with mountain views. Rooms are basic but comfortable, and range from Rs 200 for a double with shared bathroom up to Rs 700 for a carpeted double room with private bathroom.

Places to Stay – Mid-Range & Top End

Just off the main road, near the Dhulikhel bus stop, is the ***Dhulikhel Lodge Resort*** *(☎ 61114, ⓔ dlr@dhuli.mos.com.np)*. This is a large, modern place, with good rooms and superb views. There's also a block of newer rooms, but some don't have the views. It is aimed at groups who want to get out of Kathmandu for a day or so; singles/doubles cost US$70/80, discounts of up to 30% make it good value. The restaurant is popular with day-tripping groups.

A few hundred metres farther on towards Banepa there are a number of other resort-type places, offering varying degrees of luxury. The top-end ***Mirabel Resort*** *(☎ 61972, ⓔ mirabel@ccsl.com.np)* is a rather out-of-place Mediterranean-style resort, but it is very well done and offers the top accommodation in Dhulikhel. There are two restaurants, a bar, and a terrace with excellent views. The rooms have views, a balcony, fridge, TV and phone and cost US$90/100.

Farther again is the ***Himalayan Horizon Hotel*** *(☎ 61296, ⓔ hi.horizon@dhulikhel.wlink.com.np)*. The building is a bit of a monster but it does feature traditional woodcarving and all the rooms face straight out on to the Himalayan peaks. There's a restaurant/terrace area in front of the hotel with equally good views, plus a beautiful garden running down the hill. Rooms in this comfortable hotel are US$51/55, and there are larger deluxe rooms for US$62/66; a substantial discount applies in the low season. The restaurant is relatively expensive, but has excellent food, including a variety of Nepali dishes.

The flash ***Dhulikhel Mountain Resort*** *(☎ 61466, ⓔ dmrktm@wlink.com.np)* is one of a number of upmarket places beyond Dhulikhel downhill towards Tibet. This one is 4km beyond the village and the Himalayan views from here are also superb. Rooms cost US$76/78, although a 20% discount is usually offered. Accommodation is in luxurious, thatched cottages set in a very pleasant garden, and there's heating and solar-heated hot water.

There's a few other 'resorts' in this area, but they have little to recommend them.

Getting There & Away

Regular buses to Dhulikhel leave from Kathmandu's City bus station (Rs 25, two hours). The buses skirt Bhaktapur at the eastern end of the valley and then climb over the Sanga Pass out of the valley, before dropping down to Banepa then climbing again to Dhulikhel, 32km from Kathmandu. The fare is around Rs 7 for the short ride from Banepa to Dhulikhel.

A taxi from Kathmandu costs about Rs 800, and about Rs 550 from Bhaktapur.

The walk to Dhulikhel from Nagarkot is an interesting alternative. After watching the sunrise at Nagarkot you can walk down through Nala to Banepa, from where you can take a bus the last few kilometres to Dhulikhel. See Treks from Nagarkot in the Nagarkot Route section previously for more information.

TREKS FROM DHULIKHEL

To Namobuddha

The trek from Dhulikhel to Namobuddha or Namura is a fine walk in itself and also a good leg-stretcher for longer treks. It takes about three hours each way, so it makes a good day walk. The walk can be made either as a return trip or as a loop to avoid backtracking. If you start early enough you can even continue on from Namobuddha to Panauti and return from there via Banepa by bus.

Namobuddha is a relatively easy trek, which can even be made during the monsoon. From Dhulikhel the trail first climbs up to the Kali Temple lookout then drops down through the village of **Kavre** and past a number of village inns. It then climbs again through pine woods past **Phulbari** and up and down a couple of more hills before reaching the Namobuddha hill. Asking directions is no problem, as any Westerner heading in this direction is assumed to be going to Namobuddha!

Surprisingly, there is very little known about the stupa at Namobuddha as it is an important destination for Buddhist pilgrims.

A legend relates that a Buddha came across a tigress close to death from starvation and unable to feed her cubs. The sorrowful Buddha allowed the hungry tigress to consume him. If you climb to the top of the hill from the stupa, you will reach the site where this event is supposed to have taken place – a stone tablet on the hill here depicts it. An important festival is held at this site in November.

From Namobuddha the circuit walk continues downhill through **Sankhu** and past a couple of water mills, then climbs for about one hour to **Batase**. Next it passes through another pine wood and drops down to cross a stream before climbing up again back to Dhulikhel.

To Panauti

Another interesting walk leads from Dhulikhel to the small village of Panauti. This pleasant two-hour stroll starts off south from Dhulikhel then turns west, crosses rice fields and runs along the course of a small stream. It eventually meets the Banepa to Panauti road a little north of the town. Panauti is a beautiful little town, with numerous temples and magnificent woodcarvings – see Panauti earlier in this section.

From Panauti you can take a bus to Banepa, just 7km north, and from there back to Dhulikhel or to Kathmandu.

ARNIKO HIGHWAY BEYOND DHULIKHEL

While the following eight destinations are well beyond the confines of the Kathmandu Valley, they can be visited as part of an overland vehicle tour from Kathmandu in a relatively short period.

The Arniko Hwy provides Nepal's overland link with Tibet and China. Many people

Slippage

When road workers first tackled the Himalaya, they decided to follow the rivers, which had already done the hard work of cutting through the mountains. They have now realised that the zone just above the rivers is particularly vulnerable to erosion from below and landslides from above – which is why Nepali houses and traditional trails are often built along the top of ridges. As a result, many of the roads that were developed by foreign countries' agencies have turned out to be serious liabilities for the Nepalese government, who must fund their ongoing maintenance.

who make the trek into the Solu Khumbu region and the Everest Base Camp travel out along the highway, taking the turn-off to Jiri, which is the last stop before you have to start walking.

Past Barabise the road is particularly vulnerable to landslides and during the monsoon large sections are swept away; it's very unlikely to be open between May and August. Even when the highway is passable it's of limited use in breaking India's commercial stranglehold on Nepal. (It is an enormous distance from Lhasa to the industrial centres of China, so it is, in most cases, still cheaper to ship Chinese goods via Kolkata – Calcutta – than to truck them over the mountains.)

After Dhulikhel the road descends into the beautiful **Panchkhal Valley**, reaching the town of Panchkhal after about a 20-minute drive. About five minutes' drive beyond Panchkhal a dirt road takes off to the left, giving road access to the Helambu region.

About 8km later you arrive at **Dolalghat**, a thriving town at the confluence of the Indrawati and Sun Kosi Rivers (the departure point for many rafting trips). The turn-off to Jiri is another 14km away, on the right.

Lamosangu (80km)

Lamosangu is a few kilometres after the Jiri turn-off, on the Arniko Hwy, and it is an interesting Sherpa town, which has some decent trade stores (compared with Barabise, Tatopani and Kodari). There are standard dal bhaat shops, but nothing to do. There's basic accommodation if you're stuck.

Next you pass a magnesite mine (one of the few mines in the country), which was only developed because of its placement – beside a sealed road.

Barabise (102km)

Barabise is the next bustling bazaar town, the final stop for buses from Kathmandu, and the largest settlement along the road – it's not a place to linger. Barabise also marks the end of the sealed section of the Arniko Hwy, which continues in the form of an unsurfaced track. In the dry season, passing trucks kick up the top layer of dust, causing choking dust storms. In the wet, the dust transforms into mud. Landslides are more frequent as the side of the gorge steepens, especially during and after heavy rain.

There's nothing to do in Barabise but sit and watch street life go past, or perhaps curse the bus drivers for your lack of sleep!

The ***Himalaya Hotel*** has doubles for around Rs 80 and serves reasonable dal bhaat. ***Barabise Guest House*** has doubles for Rs 100, some of which are at the rear of the building, so take one of these if you want to avoid being woken at the crack of dawn by noisy bus drivers. Both places are in the middle of town on the left-hand side heading towards Tibet.

Borderlands Resort (105km)

Tucked away in a bend of the Bhote Kosi River, ***Borderlands*** *(☎ 01-425836, ⓔ info@borderlands.net)* offers a quiet and isolated retreat. It consists of a central bar and dining area, and a number of thatch-roofed safari tents dotted around a verdant garden. Activities offered include rafting, canyoning and trekking, and there are more sedentary pursuits such as yoga and meditation.

Accommodation costs US$40 per person twin share, which includes meals and transport from Kathmandu. Packages that include activities seem to be better value; drop in to the resort's office in Kathmandu (near the Kathmandu Guest House) for more details.

The Last Resort (109km)

In a beautiful spot on a ridge above the Bhote Kosi River lies the ***Last Resort*** *(☎ 01-439501, ⓔ rivers@ultimate.wlink.com.np)*. Access is by suspension bridge across the river, and it's here that Nepal's only bungy jump is set up. The 'ultimate bungy' is a mighty 160m drop into the gorge of the Bhote Kosi, and is proving immensely popular. The cost of the jump is US$80, which includes lunch and transport to and from Kathmandu. If you want to stay overnight at the resort the cost of the jump is US$105, which includes meals.

The resort also offers canyoning (US$40 per day), as well as rafting on the Bhote Kosi, trekking and rock climbing.

Accommodation at the resort is in comfortable safari tents, with the focus being the soaring stone-and-slate dining hall and Instant Karma bar. Cost of accommodation without activities is US$35, which includes meals and transport to and from Kathmandu.

Like Borderlands, the Last Resort does a range of packages that combine any or all of the above activities, so it's not a bad idea to call into its office in the centre of Thamel for more information.

After the Last Resort the road deteriorates into a dusty (or muddy) track, which for the large part winds across the landslips of the previous monsoon.

Tatopani (118km)

The next point of interest is Tatopani, a small village with a string of small guesthouses, which survive by housing visitors to the hot springs. It is in a more picturesque setting and is much quieter than Barabise.

The thing to do here is go to the hot springs. Five minutes' walk north of the bazaar, look for a sign (with a direction arrow) on a building on the right-hand side. You then descend some steps to the springs, which come out as a set of showers (great after a hard bicycle ride from Dhulikhel). There is also a small gompa above the town, marked by the usual prayer flags, which has a fine view.

Sonam Lodge has doubles for around Rs 80, and dal bhaat is available. The lodge is reasonably clean, and the owner is friendly. ***Sherpa Lodge*** has doubles for around Rs 60, and, once again, dal bhaat is available. Both places are very similar, and both are at the southern end of town.

Kodari (121km)

Kodari is nothing more than a collection of shabby wooden shanties perched perilously on the edge of the gorge on the Nepali side of the **Friendship Bridge**. It is possible to continue past the Nepali checkpoint and across the bridge. Stop in the middle to pose for photos on the red line drawn across the road. You can then continue straight past the Chinese guards and under the barrier into Tibet, which looks just like Nepal. With a bicycle, you can continue for a steep 8km until you reach Chinese customs, on the edge of Khasa (Zhangmu), the first settlement. A visa is needed to progress farther, but some people have managed to leave their bicycles at the barrier and check the town out for a couple of hours. There's not much to see.

Places to Stay & Eat There's one very basic lodge, ***Laxmi Lodge & Bhojanalaya***, which serves dal bhaat and has beds for Rs 50 per person.

Much better is the new ***Kodari Eco-Resort & Roadhouse*** *(☎ 01-249104, ⓔ kodari@mail.com.np)*. It consists of two parts: The ***Roadhouse*** has a restaurant and is on the main road. Comfortable singles/doubles are let on a share basis for US$10 per person including breakfast. The Roadhouse is also the reception for the ***Eco Resort***, which is a 10-minute walk up the hill behind the road. It consists of three comfortable stone cottages (12 rooms in all) built in local style, and with excellent views of Zhangmu and the Friendship Bridge. Rooms cost US$40/50 with private bathroom.

Charikot

If you take the turn-off from the Arniko Hwy to Jiri, the first town you come to is Charikot, a pleasant place on a ridge, with a stunning view. Just before the town sign, ***Sagun Guest House*** has friendly staff and good food. A double room costs Rs 85.

Because of its position on the edge of town, this guesthouse is quiet, but misses the view. The ***Laxmi Lodge & Restaurant*** is in the main square and offers excellent views. It's a charming traditional building, with spiral staircases leading to wooden balconies. Rooms at the front cost around Rs 100 and rooms at the back, with no view, are Rs 60.

Jiri (143km)

Jiri, also quite a pleasant place, has many lodges to choose from. The bus stops at the far end of town so you will need to walk back up to find somewhere to stay. The OK ***Sagarmatha Lodge & Restaurant*** has doubles for Rs 80. On the far side of town – farthest from the bus stop – ***Sherpa Guide Lodge*** has doubles for Rs 80. This is among the cheapest and best places in town.

Buses to Jiri leave from Kathmandu from 6 am onwards (Rs 160, 10 to 12 hours).

Godavari & Pulchowki Route

The road to Godavari is sealed and there's quite a bit of traffic, so this is not one of the best bicycle rides around the valley. There are quite a number of things to see, however.

If you have access to a car it is worth considering a trip to the top of nearby Pulchowki, especially in spring (March, April and May) when the rhododendrons are in bloom.

BISHANKHU NARAYAN (15KM)

If you're looking for an excuse to get off the beaten track, the shrine of Bishankhu Narayan may do nicely. The shrine itself is something of a disappointment, despite the fact that it is one of the most important Vishnu shrines in the Kathmandu Valley. A steep stairway leads to the shrine in a tiny cave – more a fissure in the rock – and there's nothing much to see. On the way, however, you pass through an attractive village, and there are some good views from the shrine itself.

The unsealed road to Bishankhu Narayan takes off to the north from the undistinguished village of Bandegaon then veers to the south-east and crosses a small stream. After 1km you come to a small village. The road forks at the 'village green'; take the left fork and continue for less than 1km to reach the shrine.

GODAVARI (22KM)

Godavari is not really a town, although there are a number of points of interest in the area, such as the Royal Botanic Gardens, St Xavier's College, Godavari Kunda, and Pulchowki Mai, plus a controversial marble quarry. The sealed road from Kathmandu continues to the foot of the hills and to St Xavier's College – the awful scars from the quarry are also clearly visible. Here a partially sealed road continues to the south; the main road veers left (north-east) to the gardens.

Royal Botanic Gardens

The main entrance to the gardens is flanked by white-painted walls. Though this is a quiet and peaceful spot, few of the trees and plants are labelled, so unless you already know what you're looking at you won't end up any the wiser. There really aren't many persuasive reasons for visiting unless you're a keen botanist. The gardens are open from 10 am to 5 pm daily and entry is Rs 2.

Godavari Kunda

A dirt road continues past the entrance to the botanical gardens and after 100m or so you come to the Godavari Kunda – a sacred spring – on your right. It's a curious spot, and although none of the architecture or sculpture is particularly inspiring, it is revered by Hindus. Every 12 years (next in 2003) thousands of pilgrims come here to bathe and gain merit. Clear mountain water collects in a pool in an inner courtyard, then flows through carved stone spouts into a larger pool in the outer courtyard.

Pulchowki Mai

If you return towards the marble quarry and take the partially sealed road to the south,

Pulchowki Mai is a couple of hundred metres past St Xavier's College and virtually opposite the main gates to the quarry. The site is dilapidated and somewhat overshadowed by the quarry. There's a three-tiered pagoda to a Tantric mother goddess flanked by a temple to Ganesh. There are two large pools before the temple compound, fed by nine spouts that represent the nine streams that flow off Pulchowki.

Places to Stay

Signposted off the road a few kilometres before Godavari is the ***Central Godavari Resort*** *(☎ 560675, ⓔ godavari@godavari.wlink.com.np)*. This modern place consists of a number of attractive buildings, which sprawl down a hillside, with idyllic views over rice paddies to the valley and mountains beyond. The 53 rooms are large and well furnished, and have TV, heater, fan and phone. There's also a large restaurant, pool, sauna and Jacuzzi. Singles/doubles cost US$150/165, but a discount of 15% is usually possible.

Getting There & Away

There are local minibuses between Lagankhel in Patan and Godavari (Rs 10, one hour). It would be quite feasible to ride a mountain bike – the road is good – but if you're going to make the effort, there are more interesting rides in the valley.

PULCHOWKI

This 2760m-high mountain is the highest point around the valley and, not surprisingly, there are absolutely magnificent views from the summit. This is also home to one of the last surviving 'cloud forests' in central Nepal. The mountain is also famous for its spring flowers, in particular its magnificent red and white rhododendrons.

Unfortunately, there's a telecommunications tower on the summit and an army camp. The open shrine to Pulchowki Mai may once have been a pretty spot, but it's now covered in rubbish. The views and the superb forest, however, make the journey worthwhile.

The unsealed road is rough in places but quite OK for a normal car if you take it slowly. It takes about 45 minutes from the bottom. You would need to be very keen to undertake the climb on a mountain bike, though it could certainly be done.

Chapagaon & Lele Route

The road to Lele is an ideal mountain-bike trip. It's sealed to Chapagaon and there are great views and some attractive villages along the way. By bicycle it's quite a stiff climb in places – which is all the better for the return trip. Allow the best part of a day, although it is only an hour's bicycle ride from Kathmandu's Ring Rd to Chapagaon.

CHAPAGAON (13KM)

Chapagaon is a prosperous village with a number of shops, temples and shrines strung along the road. Near the entrance to the village is a Ganesh shrine. There are two dilapidated two-tiered temples (one looks as if it has been hit by a truck) dedicated to Narayan and Krishna, and there's also a Bhairab shrine with erotic carvings on its struts.

Vajra Varahi

A small temple complex – an important Tantric site – lies about 500m east of the main road. When you enter Chapagaon take the path on your left after the two-tiered temples. Notice the disused irrigation system, with stone channels and bridges, behind the village. The temple lies in a grove of trees and was built in 1665, but it is now surrounded by less-distinguished shelters and an unfortunate amount of litter. Nonetheless, it's an interesting and atmospheric place that has probably been a centre for worship for millennia. Photography is banned.

Getting There & Away

Local minibuses leave from Lagankhel in Patan to Chapagaon (Rs 12, one to 1½ hours). By mountain bike, Chapagaon is about an hour from Kathmandu's Ring Rd (note the comparison with the bus time!).

About 10 minutes' drive after Chapagaon the road starts to climb into the foothills. The sealed road continues to the Leprosy Mission and Tika Bhairab in the Lele Valley. If you are running out of enthusiasm, an unsealed road takes off to the left – there's a pipal tree and chautara. The road is in poor condition but you are rewarded with fantastic views across the valley to the Ganesh himal. If you keep going you cross a saddle and enter the tranquil Lele Valley.

LELE (19KM)

Lele Valley seems a million miles from the hustle and bustle of Kathmandu, and there are few visitors. It's a peaceful, beautiful valley that in many ways seems untouched by the 20th (or 21st) century.

The Tika Bhairab is a huge, multicoloured painting on a brick wall. The shrine lies at the confluence of two rivers and is marked by a huge sal tree.

The Malla Hotel in Kathmandu operates the very pleasant ***Malla Alpine Resort*** *(☎ 410966, fax 418382)*, signposted at Kalitar, a few kilometres beyond Lele along a rough dirt track. The 18 rooms, set in eight bungalows, offer some great views, and just so you don't have to rough it too much there is also a pool, sauna, bar and restaurant. Singles/doubles cost US$61/72, plus tax.

Bungamati Route

The road to Bungamati, one of the most picturesque small towns in the valley, provides yet another ideal mountain-biking expedition. The road to Bungamati is the continuation of the main road that runs through Jawlakhel (the Tibetan refugee camp on the outskirts of Patan), on the other side of Kathmandu's Ring Rd.

KHOKNA

Khokna is not as appealing as Bungamati, as it was seriously damaged in the 1934 earthquake, but it has retained many traditional aspects of Newari life. It is famous for producing mustard oil. There is no central square, unlike in Bungamati, but there's plenty of action in the main street, including women spinning wool. The main temple is a two-tiered construction dedicated to Shekali Mai, a mother goddess.

From Karya Binayak Temple in Bungamati, Khokna is a 10-minute walk across the paddy fields. Take note of the water tank surrounded by a low brick wall on the outskirts of the village, because if you don't want to retrace your steps to Bungamati, the track that returns to the main road takes off from here.

BUNGAMATI (10KM)

Bungamati is a classic Newari village dating from the 16th century. It is perched on a spur of land overlooking the Bagmati River and is shaded by large trees and stands of bamboo. Fortunately, the village streets are too small and hazardous for cars. Visitors are rare, so tread gently.

Temples

Bungamati is the birthplace of Rato Machhendranath, regarded as the patron of the valley, and the large **Rato Machhendranath** shikhara-style temple in the centre of the village square is his home for six months of the year (he spends the rest of his time in Patan). The process of moving him around Patan and backwards and forwards to Bungamati is central to one of the most important annual festivals in the valley. See Rato Machhendranath in the special section 'Festivals of Nepal' for details.

The chowk around the temple is one of the most beautiful in the valley – here one can see the heart of a functioning Newari town. There are many chortens and a huge prayer wheel, clearly pointing to the capacity of Newari religion to combine elements from different sources.

Between Bungamati and Khokna, the **Karya Binayak Temple** is dedicated to Ganesh. The temple is not particularly interesting and Ganesh is simply represented by a natural stone, but the view is spectacular. From this point, surrounded by trees, you can look over the Bagmati Valley to the foothills, or back to Bungamati, tumbling down the opposite hill.

Getting There & Away

Buses to Bungamati leave from Jawlakhel in Patan (Rs 11, 1½ hours).

By bicycle from Patan, continue over Kathmandu's Ring Rd from the main road through Jawlakhel. After you cross the Nakhu Khola, veer left. The right fork takes you through to the Chobar Gorge, where you can cross the Bagmati River and return to Kathmandu by a different route. It's a pleasant ride along a gradually climbing ridge to get to Bungamati.

Approximately an hour after leaving Kathmandu's Ring Rd by bicycle along the road to Bungamati you'll come out at a viewpoint marked by a single, large tree. It's worth pausing here to take in the lie of the land. To the left lies Bungamati, then swinging to the right comes Karya Binayak; Khokna is about 1km away. Follow the road down to Bungamati and take the right fork, which passes to the left of a large pond. The footpath then veers to the left and climbs up to the distinctive, white shikhara temple and the town square.

To get to Karya Binayak, retrace your steps to the first pond you came to, follow the path around it and take the right fork. It's then a five-minute walk across the rice paddies to the temple.

Kirtipur, Chobar & Dakshinkali Route

KIRTIPUR (5KM)

Strung out along a ridge south-west of Kathmandu, the small town of Kirtipur is a relatively neglected and timeless backwater despite its proximity to the capital. At one time it was associated with Patan and then became a mini kingdom in its own right. During the 1768 conquest of the valley by Prithvi Narayan Shah it was clear that Kirtipur, with its superbly defensible hilltop position, would be the key to defeating the Malla kingdoms, so it was here the Gorkha king struck first and hardest. Kirtipur's resistance was strong, but eventually, after a bitter siege, the town was taken and the inhabitants paid a terrible price for their courageous resistance. The king, incensed by the long struggle his forces had endured, ordered that the nose and lips be cut off every male inhabitant in the town. Fortunately, for a small minority, he was practical as well as cruel, and those who could play wind instruments were spared. It is said that the news of this barbaric act considerably dampened any plans for resistance among the inhabitants of the other valley towns and therefore Patan, Bhaktapur and Kathmandu quickly fell.

At one time there were 12 gates into the city; traces of the old city wall can still be seen. Today the Kirtipur Cottage Industry Centre is a major industry for the town. As you wander through Kirtipur, you can see dyed yarn hanging from upstairs windows and hear the background clatter of the town's hand looms. Many of the town's 9000 inhabitants are weavers or farmers; the lower-caste people generally live outside the old city wall, lower down the hill. Kirtipur's hilltop position offers fine views over Kathmandu, with the Himalaya rising behind.

The campus of Nepal's Tribhuvan University, named after King Tribhuvan, stands below Kirtipur hill and has the best library facilities to be found in Nepal.

Temples

Kirtipur's ridge is actually two hills, with a lower saddle between them. The **Chilanchu Vihara** tops the southern hill and has a central stupa with four smaller stupas, numerous statues and bells and Buddhist monastery buildings around it.

At the bottom of the saddle where the hills meet is the **Bagh Bhairab Temple**, sacred to both Hindus and Buddhists. This famous triple-roofed temple is decorated with swords and shields from the Newari troops defeated by King Prithvi Narayan Shah. They can be seen attached to the walls of the temple, sheltered by the upper roof. The temple's principal image is of Bhairab in his tiger form. Look for the temple's torana to the left of the entrance door with an image of Vishnu astride the Garuda and, below him, Bhairab between Ganesh and Kumar.

Animal sacrifices are made early on Tuesday and Saturday mornings.

From the saddle, a long stone stairway, flanked by stone elephants, leads to the triple-roofed **Uma Maheshwar Temple**, or Hindu Kvat. The elephants wear spiked saddles to keep children from riding them! Curiously, the main image of Shiva and Parvati is a standing one, not in the standard Uma Maheshwar pose. To the left of the central image of the god and his consort is a smaller image in the standard pose. The temple was originally built in 1673 and had four roofs until it was badly damaged by the earthquake of 1934. Following its restoration the temple itself is not of great interest – the stairway and the fine views from the top are better. From this hilltop you can see the nearby villages of Panga and Nagaon.

Getting There & Away

Bus, Minibus & Taxi Numerous buses and minibuses depart from Kathmandu's City bus station (Rs 8, 45 minutes). They terminate at the university, from where you can stroll up the hill to the town itself. Alternatively, and much more comfortably, it's a short trip by taxi (around Rs 230).

Walking & Cycling It takes around 1½ hours to reach Kirtipur by mountain bike, and it's quite a long, steep hill from the Dakshinkali road (first left after Kathmandu's Ring Rd bridge over the Bagmati River). After about 1km from the bridge, turn right at the road flanked by two low, brick gatehouses. Continue up the hill for 1km or so and take the left fork where the minibuses park (take the right fork to the university). You'll notice a modern Thai-designed Buddhist temple to the left of Kirtipur's Naya Bajaar (New Bazaar), which has grown up at the foot of the Kirtipur hill.

Instead of simply returning to Kathmandu the same way, you can continue from Kirtipur to Chobar and the Chobar Gorge then back through Patan, which is mostly rideable, but also an interesting walk. From the Chilanchu Vihara at the south-eastern end of Kirtipur, go down the hill by the mound known as the Mazadega (built with the intention of being the foundations of a stupa). At the base of the hill follow the Pharping Rd around and take the trail leading towards Chobar, just past the Thai temple. You can't go wrong, since Chobar tops the prominent hill to the south-east.

A diversion farther south from the trail described above will take you through the small village of **Panga**, which has a number of temples, none of great age or interest. A path continues from Panga to **Nagaon**, an even smaller village. The trail to Chobar meets Pharping Rd just before the base of the hill, but you can turn off this and follow a narrow footpath straight up the hill until you come into the centre of the interesting small village of Chobar, right on the top of the hill.

After you've visited Chobar's Adinath Lokeshwar Temple (see following) continue down the other side of the hill towards the river. Aim for the large cement works, clearly visible beside the river. The **Chobar Gorge** and the Jal Binayak Temple are immediately to the north of the cement works. See Chobar Gorge later in this section for the walk from there to Patan.

CHOBAR (6KM)

The picturesque little village of Chobar tops a hill overlooking the Bagmati River where it flows through the Chobar Gorge. Although the gorge is a regularly visited attraction, far fewer people come to Chobar itself. Perhaps they're put off by the steep hill.

Adinath Lokeshwar Temple

Chobar's main attraction is the temple of Adinath Lokeshwar. The temple was originally built in the 15th century and reconstructed in 1640. Inside the main sanctuary the face of Rato Machhendranath can be seen peering out. The temple is dedicated to this popular valley deity and is sacred to both Hindus and Buddhists. Six Buddha faces are lined up beneath the temple's golden torana, but the most interesting feature is the many metal pots, pans and water containers, which are fixed to boards hanging all around the temple roofs. These kitchen utensils are donated to the temple by newlyweds in order to ensure a happy married life.

Getting There & Away

Transport to Pharping and Dakshinkali runs by Chobar, but see under Kirtipur and Chobar Gorge in this section for details of walking between Kirtipur and Patan via Chobar and the Chobar Gorge.

CHOBAR GORGE (6KM)

The picturesque Chobar Gorge is south of Patan where the Bagmati River cuts through the edge of the Chobar hill, the highest hill along this side of the valley. The pretty village of Chobar tops the hill and a stone-paved track runs from the river's edge right to the top of the hill, where the Adinath Lokeshwar Temple forms the centre of the settlement. Down by the river, just south of the gorge, is another important temple, the Jal Binayak.

The valley's first cement factory is a more recent and less pleasing addition to the scenery. A high percentage of solid particles in the valley's hazy air can be attributed to this place. A neat little suspension bridge spans the river; it was manufactured in Aberdeen in Scotland in 1903. From the bridge there are fine views of the gorge on one side and the Jal Binayak Temple on the other.

Jal Binayak Temple

Just below the gorge on the riverbank stands one of the valley's most important Ganesh shrines. The triple-roofed temple dates from 1602, although there was probably a temple here even earlier. On the temple's platform there is an aged and worn image of Shiva and Parvati in the Uma Maheshwar pose, which predates the temple by 500 years.

The temple's Ganesh image is simply a huge rock, projecting out the back and bearing very little likeness to an elephant-headed god. The temple's roof struts depict eight Bhairabs and the eight Ashta Matrikas (Mother Goddesses) with whom Ganesh always appears. On the lower roof Ganesh himself appears on some of the struts, with beautiful female figures standing beside him and tiny, brightly painted erotic depictions below. A bronze figure of Ganesh's 'vehicle', in this case a shrew rather than a rat, stands respectfully in the courtyard and faces the shrine.

Getting There & Away

The Chobar Gorge is usually visited en route to Pharping and Dakshinkali by road. A more interesting way to reach Chobar Gorge is to walk there from Kirtipur via the village of Chobar. See Kirtipur earlier in this section for more details.

From the gorge you can cross the bridge and walk up the hill, turning north towards Patan. A road suitable for cars ends at a small village at the top of the hill and you can follow this road, past the Nakhu jail and across the Nakhu Khola, finally crossing Kathmandu's Ring Rd and entering Patan at Jawlakhel.

Legend of the Chobar Gorge

Eons ago the Kathmandu Valley was the Kathmandu Lake. In that long-ago time the hill of Swayambhunath was an island; gradually the lake dried up to leave the valley we see today.

Legends relate that the change from lake to valley was a much more dramatic one, for Manjushri is said to have taken his mighty sword and with one blow cut open the valley edge to release the pent-up waters. The place where his sword struck rock was Chobar on the southern edge of the valley and the result was the Chobar Gorge.

Countless snakes were washed out of the valley with the departing waters, but Kartotak, 'king of the snakes', is said to still live close to the gorge in the Taudaha pond.

Whether or not the great serpent is still there, the pond is certainly a place where ducks like to pause on their long annual migration from Siberia to India. A hill known as Dinacho (which means 'Meditation Point') or Champa Devi rises beyond the pond.

SEKH NARAYAN TEMPLE (18KM)

The Sekh Narayan Temple is the centrepiece of an interesting collection of temples, pools and carvings. The pools – beside the road to Pharping, where it makes a sharp left-hand (south) turn (coming from Kathmandu) – are often used by local women for washing clothes. The main temple is above the pools and is sheltered under a multicoloured, overhanging cliff. This combination of elements forms an interesting juxtaposition between the work of humanity and the gods. In true Nepali style, a Buddhist monastery has been built next door.

The temples and carvings have suitably diverse ages. The Sekh Narayan Temple, one of the most important Vishnu temples in the valley, was built in the 17th century, but it is believed that the cave has been a place of pilgrimage for much longer. Beside the shrine is a bas-relief of Vishnu Vikrantha, also known as the dwarf Vamana. This possibly dates from the Licchavi period, or the 5th or 6th century.

Half-submerged in one of the crystal-clear ponds is a sculpture of Aditya, the sun god, framed by a stone arch and with a lotus flower at each shoulder. This dates from the 12th or 13th century. Finally, the Tibetan gompa is a 20th-century addition. Hindus believe that Gautama Buddha was Vishnu's 10th incarnation, but it's not known if this is the connection.

Sekh Narayan is close to Pharping and is probably best reached by foot from the village if you haven't got your own transport.

PHARPING (19KM)

Pharping is a thriving, traditional Newari town, surprisingly untouched by the swarms of tourists that visit Dakshinkali. The main road skirts the village, so there are few vehicles in the village proper. Before King Prithvi Narayan Shah unified Nepal this was another tiny city-state.

Vajra Jogini Temple

On a hillside overlooking Pharping is the 17th-century Vajra Jogini Temple, dedicated to the same goddess as the Vajra Jogini Temple near Sankhu and built at about the same time. See the boxed text 'Tantric Goddesses' in the Sankhu & Vajra Jogini Route section for a discussion on the goddess' origins. The pagoda-style temple is in a courtyard surrounded by relatively modern two-storey, Newari-style living quarters. Vajra Jogini is featured in the temple's toranas.

The temple is just a short walk behind Pharping on the hill that overlooks the town. The main gompa at Gorakhnath (see following) is only a few hundred metres to the west up a flight of steps. It is also possible to walk an interesting circuit from Dakshinkali to Gorakhnath, Vajra Jogini, Pharping and back to Dakshinkali in less than two hours. See Getting There & Away under Dakshinkali later in this section.

Coming from Kathmandu and after Sekh Narayan, you approach Pharping past a soccer field. The main road swings left around the field, but if you continue straight ahead you will come first to Vajra Jogini (on the side of the hill), then Gorakhnath.

Gorakhnath

Several gompas and temples have sprung up around the Gorakhnath cave, which is behind Pharping. The white Tibetan gompa (which is perched high on the hill like an eagle's nest, at the centre of a web of prayer flags) is particularly interesting.

There are magnificent views overlooking Pharping, the Bagmati River and the valley. You can even see the Himalaya on a clear day. Somewhere in the complex is a cave which the Tibetans associate with Padmasambhava, the Bodhisattva sometimes credited with introducing Buddhism to Tibet.

Gorakhnath is an easy walk from Pharping and Vajra Jogini, and a bit of a scramble from Dakshinkali. It can be combined with an interesting walk that takes in all these places (see Dakshinkali following) or reached by road.

Places to Stay & Eat

Perched on a ridge a few kilometres before Pharping, the ***Hattiban Resort*** *(☎ 371397, ⓔ nepal@intrek.wlink.com.np)* offers some of the best views in the entire valley. The small resort is set in a pine forest, and is reached by a rough, steep and winding 2km track from the main road, although you can leave your vehicle in the (guarded) car park at the bottom and take the resort 4WD up the track. The resort buildings are pleasant, being timber-lined, and the restaurant has an excellent terrace. There are 24 rooms, each with balcony and bathroom. Singles/doubles cost US$66/77; the food is fairly pricey at around US$10 for a main meal.

Right by the main gate to Dakshinkali and also with good views, is the quiet and very modest ***Dakshinkali Village Inn*** *(☎ 290653, fax 330889)*, with decent rooms and a good restaurant. The rooms cost US$15/25, although discounts are usually offered, depending on the time of year. The garden setting is very pleasant.

In Pharping itself there are a couple of small restaurants. The ***Snowland*** is a good little Tibetan restaurant, but all food is made to order and so it doesn't pay to be in a hurry. The *momos* (dumplings) with soup (Rs 20) here are excellent. Close by is the ***Asura Cave*** restaurant.

Getting There & Away

Buses leave throughout the day for Vajra Jogini Temple from Kathmandu's City bus station (Rs 16, two hours).

DAKSHINKALI (20KM)

At the southern edge of the valley, in a dark, somewhat spooky location in the cleft between two hills and at the confluence of two rivers, stands the bloody temple of Dakshinkali. The temple is dedicated to the goddess Kali, Shiva's consort in her most bloodthirsty incarnation, and twice a week faithful Nepalis journey here to satisfy her bloodlust. The six-armed main image of Kali in the temple is of black stone and she tramples upon a male figure.

Sacrifices are always made to goddesses, and the creatures to be sacrificed must be uncastrated male animals. Saturday is the major sacrificial day of the week, when a steady parade of buffaloes, chickens, ducks, goats, sheep and pigs come here to have their throats cut or their heads lopped off. Tuesday is also a sacrificial day, but the blood does not flow quite as freely as on Saturday. During the annual celebrations of Dasain in October the temple is literally awash with blood and the image of Kali is bathed in it. See the boxed text 'A Bad Day for Goats' in the 'Festivals of Nepal' special section in the Facts for the Visitor chapter.

After their rapid dispatch the animals are butchered in the stream beside the temple and their carcasses will later be brought home for a feast; otherwise, a picnic may be held on the hillside. Non-Hindus are not allowed into the compound where Kali's image resides, but it is OK to take photos from outside. The temple itself is not particularly interesting, although there are some fine brass nagas forming a canopy over the compound.

This is one of the most important sites in the valley, so on the sacrificial days it is crowded with Nepali families – and tourists. Most big hotels and the tour companies cart busloads of camera-laden visitors along. Tours to the 'exciting animal sacrifices' are big business for Kathmandu travel agencies. As a result, there are a number of village inns, and a good number of hustlers selling souvenirs and goodness knows what else. Be prepared to pay picturesque sadhus for the privilege of taking their photograph.

Despite the carnival spirit, witnessing the sacrifices is a strange and, for some, confronting experience. The slaughter is surprisingly matter-of-fact, but it creates a powerful atmosphere. Unfortunately, many tourists behave poorly, perching vulture-like from every available vantage point in order to get the most gory possible photos. However extraordinary the sights might seem, this is a religious ceremony, and the participants should be treated with respect, not turned into a sideshow.

For accommodation and food nearby see Pharping previous.

Getting There & Away

Bus & Car Buses only operate on Tuesday and Saturday – the most important days for sacrifice – and though there are plenty of them, they are very crowded. If you have a car, allow 45 minutes for the journey. On other days catch a bus to Pharping and it's an easy 1km downhill walk or ride from there.

Cycling It is an enjoyable, but exhausting two-hour bicycle ride from Kathmandu. The views are exhilarating, but it is basically uphill all the way – so mountain bikes are the way to go. Tuesday is probably the better day to pick as the traffic is not too heavy. Make sure you get an early start, as the shrine is busiest early in the morning. You're advised to pay someone a couple of rupees to mind your bicycle in the car park.

Walking Consider making the interesting two-hour circuit from Dakshinkali to Gorakhnath, Vajra Jogini, Pharping and back to Dakshinkali. Take the path that runs above the left (southern) side of the sacrificial compound, which brings you out into a cleared part of the gorge with several picnic shelters. There's a steep scramble up a goat track that follows a ridge on the right (north-western) side of the gorge. At the top you come out on a plateau – you'll immediately see the white monastery surrounded by prayer flags on a nearby hill. Make your way through the paddy fields, on the narrow paths between the rice. It takes about 40 minutes to get to Gorakhnath. Vajra Jogini is a few hundred metres down some steps to the east of the gompa, and a short walk to Pharping. From Pharping follow the main road about 1km downhill to Dakshinkali.

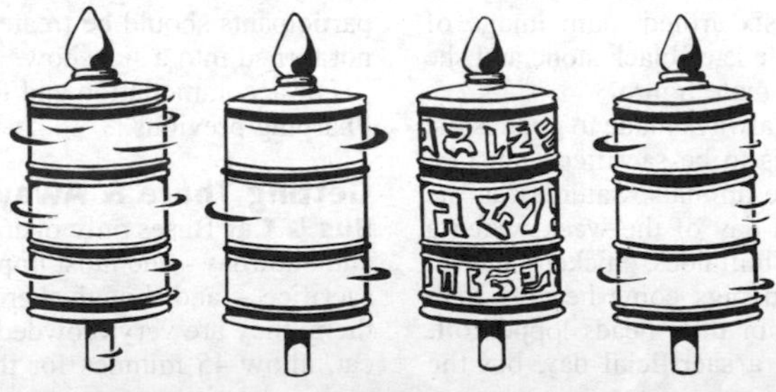

Pokhara

☎ 061

Pokhara is the most popular destination in Nepal after Kathmandu. Its fame rests on the natural beauty of its lakeside location and its proximity to the mountains, not on any great historical or cultural endowment. It's the starting point for some of the most famous treks in Nepal, and there are also plenty of short walks and day trips, suitable for children or weary trekkers, that can be made around the valley.

Pokhara has an enormous number of good-value hotels and restaurants, and although it is undoubtedly a tourist town, it has a relaxed and peaceful atmosphere, completely removed from the hectic bustle of Kathmandu and even further removed from the outright chaos of many Indian cities. It's an oasis where leisurely meals, good books and short walks can easily fill several days – ideal if you are recovering from (or gearing up for) a trek or travel in India. It is the combination of the magnificent location, good-value accommodation and food, and (not least) the proximity of local village life that accounts for much of Pokhara's appeal.

After travelling elsewhere in Nepal or in India, Pokhara has an almost Disneylandish unreality about it. The climate is mild; incredible snow-capped mountains are reflected in a sheltered lake; cool Western music drifts from every restaurant; menus offer everything in the world except *dal bhaat* (rice and lentils; although you can get that too if you want it); hotel rooms are clean, and open onto sunny gardens; there's very little traffic; village life persists, but everyone speaks English; and it's very relaxed.

The first tourists to discover Pokhara were hippies in the early 1970s. In Pokhara many of them discovered the perfect venue for doing the things they were best at: getting stoned, eating, growing their hair, talking, and staring into the middle distance while looking cool. They came for a week and stayed for months. The world has changed since then (and so have the drug laws and visa regulations), but Pokhara retains something of the laid-back, hedonistic style of that time, although rampant Thamel-style development threatens to overwhelm the Lakeside area.

Highlights

- Relaxing in Pokhara's peaceful Lakeside area, and enjoying the backdrop of the snow-capped Himalaya
- Spending a few hours at Gorkha's fort, palace and temple complex; a triumph of Nepali architecture offering superb views of the surrounding valleys and mountains
- Stretching your legs and doing one of the numerous day or longer walks around Pokhara

Viewed from Pokhara, the Himalaya is indeed a mighty mountain range, looming over the horizon much closer than it does in Kathmandu. Only foothills separate the town from the full height of the mountains, while the magnificent 8000m peaks of the Annapurna Range utterly dominate the view to the north (weather permitting, of course). Whereas in the Kathmandu Valley the high temples are all around you, in the Pokhara Valley you are surrounded by mountains.

The valley has three large lakes: Rupa Tal and Begnas Tal, are slightly to the east of town, while the third and largest lake, Phewa Tal, is the focal point for Pokhara's tourist industry.

Pokhara stands at 884m above sea level, about 400m lower than Kathmandu. The autumn and winter temperatures are generally much more comfortable than in often-chilly Kathmandu, but the monsoon rains can be twice as heavy, and the humidity can often be uncomfortably high.

Although the Pokhara Valley is chiefly inhabited by Bahuns and Chhetris, the hills around Pokhara are predominantly inhabited by Gurungs. These people continue to play an important part in the Gurkha regiments in India and overseas, and their earnings have a major impact on the local economy – many of the new hotels around Lakeside are being built with Gurkha money.

Pokhara's development has been relatively recent and rapid. With the eradication of malaria in the 1950s it became safer to live here. The construction of the airstrip in the 1950s and the hydroelectric power dam (with Indian aid) in 1968, plus the building of the roads to Kathmandu and the Indian border in the early 1970s, catapulted Pokhara into the 20th century. As a tourist destination it's now zooming into the 21st with unprecedented – and seemingly uncontrolled – development.

ORIENTATION

Pokhara is a surprisingly sprawling town, stretching in a north–south direction for about 5km. Starting f rom the north, there's the busy bazaar area, which also contains the oldest part of Pokhara – the town as it was before electricity, roads and the construction of the airport totally transformed it. South of the bazaar is the bus station and farther south is the airport.

Most of Pokhara's local shops and the post office are around the Mahendrapul (or Mahendra Pool) Bridge in the bazaar area. The bazaar is a long and strung-out affair. The campus of Privthi Narayan University is also found in that area.

West of the bus station and airport is Phewa Tal, and along its eastern shore is the Lakeside area, which is where Pokhara's great and growing number of tourist hotels and restaurants are predominantly located. It's a long walk from place to place in Pokhara and if you go from south to north it's uphill all the way.

Starting at the south-eastern end of the lake, near the airport, there's a hydroelectric station. This area is often rather confusingly called Damside (although the dam and the lake are continuous) or Pardi. The tourist office is here, and there are several hotels in the Damside area, although Lakeside has more.

Finally there's the Lakeside area itself, also known as Baidam, where the majority of foreign visitors to Pokhara stay. Along the Lakeside road there's a continuous and increasingly tawdry stretch of hotels, restaurants and shops. In this book, Lakeside has rather arbitrarily been divided into three sections: Lakeside East (or Ammat) ending at the Royal Palace; Lakeside West (or Pallo Patan) ending just before the intersection known as Camping Chowk, where the main road returns eastward to town; and Lakeside North (or Khaharey).

INFORMATION

Tourist Offices

At the time of research Pokhara's tourist office (☎ 20028) was set to move to its new location at Damside. In its previous incarnation it offered virtually nothing of use to the public and the staff spoke only limited English; hopefully things have changed.

Visa Extensions

For visa extensions, the immigration office is convenient to the Lakeside and Damside hotels. It's open 10.30 am to 1 pm Sunday to Thursday (10.30 am to noon Friday) for applications and from 3 pm for passport pick-ups. Trekking permits can be extended at this office.

Money

For those staying at Lakeside, the Nepal Grindlays Bank is convenient. Although it is only open standard banking hours, you can make cash and travellers cheque advances against Visa and MasterCard credit cards. There's also a Nepal Grindlays ATM not far away outside the Hotel Snowland at Lakeside. Alternatively, there are plenty of private moneychangers strung out the whole length of Lakeside that are open seven days a week.

Post & Communications

The post office is a long way from the Lakeside and Damside hotels in the bazaar area near Mahendrapul Bridge, but many of the bookshops at Lakeside offer stamps and will post letters and cards for Rs 2 each.

If you want to make either overseas phone calls or calls to Kathmandu, there's a

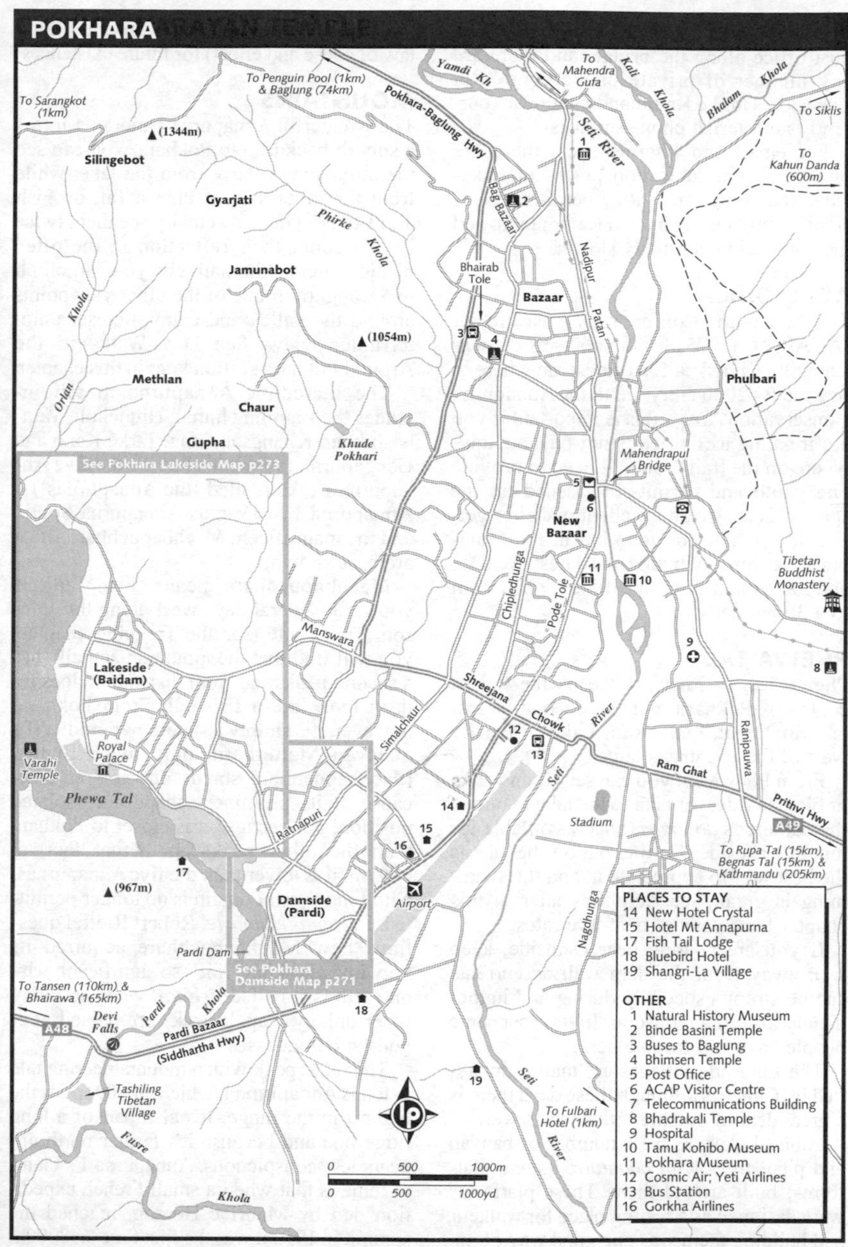
POKHARA
To Sarangkot (1km)
To Penguin Pool (1km) & Baglung (74km)
Pokhara-Baglung Hwy
Yamdi Kh
To Mahendra Gufa
Kali Khola
Bhalam Khola
To Siklis
To Kahun Danda (600m)
Seti River
(1344m)
Silingebot
Gyarjati
Bag Bazaar
Phirke Khola
Nadipur
Bhairab Tole
Jamunabot
Bazaar
Patan
Khola
(1054m)
Methlan
Orlan
Chaur
Phulbari
Gupha
Khude Pokhari
See Pokhara Lakeside Map p273
Mahendrapul Bridge
New Bazaar
Chipledhunga
Pode Tole
Tibetan Buddhist Monastery
Manswara
Lakeside (Baidam)
Shreejana
Chowk
River
Simalchaur
Royal Palace
Varahi Temple
Phewa Tal
Ram Ghat
Seti
Ranipauwa
Prithvi Hwy
Stadium
Ratnapuri
A49
To Rupa Tal (15km), Begnas Tal (15km) & Kathmandu (205km)
(967m)
Damside (Pardi)
Airport
Nagdhunga
Pardi Dam
See Pokhara Damside Map p271
To Tansen (110km) & Bhairawa (165km)
A48
Devi Falls
Pardi Khola
Pardi Bazaar (Siddhartha Hwy)
Tashiling Tibetan Village
Seti River
To Fulbari Hotel (1km)
Fusre Khola
0 500 1000m
0 500 1000yd
PLACES TO STAY
14 New Hotel Crystal
15 Hotel Mt Annapurna
17 Fish Tail Lodge
18 Bluebird Hotel
19 Shangri-La Village
OTHER
1 Natural History Museum
2 Binde Basini Temple
3 Buses to Baglung
4 Bhimsen Temple
5 Post Office
6 ACAP Visitor Centre
7 Telecommunications Building
8 Bhadrakali Temple
9 Hospital
10 Tamu Kohibo Museum
11 Pokhara Museum
12 Cosmic Air; Yeti Airlines
13 Bus Station
16 Gorkha Airlines

telecommunications building east of the post office along the bridge, and there are any number of private phone centres in Lakeside. Unlike Kathmandu, there are currently no Internet phone services.

For email and Internet users there are plenty of communication places in Lakeside. The going rate – Rs 7 per minute – is significantly higher than in Kathmandu, and the connection is usually slower.

ACAP Office

The Annapurna Conservation Area Project (ACAP; ☎ 32275) has a small office near Camping Chowk at Lakeside. Come here to pay the Rs 2000 entry fee to the Annapurna Conservation Area – this is important if you are trekking as the fee is not payable anywhere on the trail. You will need to provide one photo and permits are issued on the spot. This is also an excellent place for getting information on trekking in the Annapurna region, including the latest weather and trail conditions. The office is open 9 am to 4.30 pm daily.

PHEWA TAL

Phewa Tal, or Phewa Lake, is the tourist centre of Pokhara and the second-largest lake in Nepal. Only Rara Lake in the far west of the country is larger.

From Phewa Tal you can set off on walks or bicycle rides, or take to the lake in one of the numerous *doongas* (boats) available for rent at Lakeside. Getting out on the lake is the best way to appreciate it, and the swimming is great. See Activities later in this chapter for details of boat-hire rates.

If you are boating near Damside, keep well away from the dam wall as currents can be strong especially during and immediately after the monsoon. In the past some people have had trouble here.

The Lakeside villages are mainly inhabited by Chhetris although these days there is a great deal of outside influence as well.

Along Lakeside are a number of banyan and pipal trees with *chautaras* (stone platforms) built around them. These platforms were designed as a resting place for walkers, and building them was one good way of improving one's *karma* (Buddhist and Hindu law of cause and effect) for future existences.

MOUNTAINS

The wonderful Annapurna panorama forms a superb backdrop to Pokhara. You can see the mountains clearly from the lake, while from the other side of Phewa Tal, by Fish Tail Lodge, you can actually see them twice if you count their reflection in the often placid waters. Alternatively, you can climb to Sarangkot or one of the other viewpoints around the valley and enjoy a closer uninterrupted view. See Day Walks in the Around Pokhara section later in this chapter.

The incredible **Annapurna massif** includes the Lamjung himal, Hiunchuli, Varahashikhar, Khangsar Kang, Tarke Kang and Gangapurna mountains but it's the five Annapurna peaks (called 'the Annapurnas') – Annapurna I to IV plus Annapurna South, and the magnificent Machhapuchhare – that are best known.

Machhapuchhare means 'Fish Tail'. If you walk several days west along the Jomsom Trek route (see the Trekking chapter) you will find that the mountain actually has a second peak, and from that side it does indeed look like a fish tail. From Pokhara, however, it's simply a superb pyramid: a Himalayan Matterhorn, only much higher. Machhapuchhare stands out not only because of its prominent shape and isolated position, but because it is closer to Pokhara than the other peaks. In actual fact, at 6997m, it is lower than the five Annapurnas. Climbing this mountain is no longer permitted. In *Nepal Namaste*, Robert Rieffel questions how Machhapuchhare acquired its holy image asking 'If it's so significant, why on earth is it called *fish tail* when so many other unholy Nepali peaks are named after gods and goddesses?'.

The other peak with a mountaineering tale to tell is **Annapurna I**, which, at 8091m, is the highest in the range. It's also part of a long ridge line and because it's farther north appears less conspicuous. Annapurna I's claim to fame is that when a small French expedition, led by Maurice Herzog, reached the summit in 1950 it was the first time an 8000m peak had been climbed. Herzog's *Annapurna*, a mountaineering classic, traces the hardships of organising a climb in what was then a remote, inaccessible and little-known area. The harrowing aftermath of the climb, when a severe storm caught the retreating mountaineers, resulted in Herzog losing most of his fingers and toes from frostbite.

To the west of the Annapurnas is the **Dhaulagiri** at 8167m. The Kali Gandaki River, which cuts the deepest gorge in the world, flows between Dhaulagiri and the Annapurnas and actually predates the rise of the Himalaya. For a while, before more precise measuring methods were available, it was thought that Dhaulagiri was the world's highest mountain.

TEMPLES

Pokhara, unlike the towns of the Kathmandu Valley, is not noted for its temples. In fact there are very few of even minor note.

In the lake there's a small island with the double-roofed **Varahi Temple** dedicated to Varahi, who is Vishnu in his boar incarnation.

The streets of the bazaar area become steadily more attractive and traditional as you move north from the newer area around the bus station to what was the centre of the original settlement of Pokhara. In the northern part of the bazaar area, right on the main road in the oldest part of town, is the small, double-roofed **Bhimsen Temple**. Very much in the Newari style of the Kathmandu Valley, it has some small and not very notable erotic carvings on the roof struts.

Slightly farther north, atop a small hill with a park at its base, is Pokhara's best-known temple, the **Binde Basini Temple**. The pleasant and shady setting is actually more impressive than the white shikhara-style temple itself. The temple is dedicated to Durga (Parvati) in her Binde Basini Bhagwati manifestation, and interestingly the image of the goddess is in the shape of a saligram (see the boxed text 'Saligrams' in the Trekking chapter).

MUSEUMS

Pokhara has three museums, all worth a quick look if you're in the area. The **Pokhara Museum** is north of the bus station on the main road and has exhibits on local history. Of greatest interest are the ethnic exhibits. Entry is Rs 5, and it's open daily except Tuesday. The **Tamu Kohibo Museum**, close by but on the opposite side of the Seti River, focuses on Gurung culture.

At the northern end of town, on the Privthi Narayan University campus, is the **Natural History Museum**, also known as the Annapurna Regional Museum. It has some interesting although somewhat dated exhibits on the environmental problems of the area. The natural history section has cement models of Nepali wildlife (you don't have to feed them) and a large butterfly, moth and insect collection. The museum is open 9 am to 1 pm and 2 to 5 pm Sunday to Monday; there is no entry charge, but make a donation.

SETI RIVER

The Seti River flows right through Pokhara but in places it runs completely underground, sometimes dropping to 50m below ground level. *Seti* means 'white' and the water's milky colour comes from limestone in the soil.

There's a good view of this elusive river from the bridge at the northern end of the bazaar (north of Mahendrapul Bridge); an even more dramatic viewpoint can be found just beyond the airport runway. From the far side of the airport, follow the trail to the river where a footbridge crosses the canyon. The bridge is only about 10m wide but the river flows past a good 30m below, although it is difficult to actually see.

Another good view of the river can be found at the rear of the Pokhara Museum or from the Tamu Kohibo Museum.

DEVI FALLS

Also known as Patale Chango, Devin's or David's Falls, this waterfall is about 2km south-west of the airport on the main Siddhartha Hwy and just before the Tashiling Tibetan Village.

The Pardi Khola (Pardi stream) is the outflow from Phewa Tal, and at Devi Falls it suddenly drops down into a hole in the ground and disappears. One of its alternative names comes from a tale about a tourist named David disappeared down the hole, taking his girlfriend with him! There's a Rs 10 charge to visit the falls.

The river emerges from its subterranean hideaway 200m farther on and then joins the Fusre Khola before flowing into the Seti River.

TIBETAN SETTLEMENTS & MONASTERY

There are a number of Tibetan settlements around Pokhara and you see many Tibetans around the lake selling their crafts and artefacts. The **Tashiling Tibetan Village**, where they weave Tibetan carpets, is only 2km south-west of the airport.

There's also a larger settlement known as **Tashipalkhel** at Hyangja, a short drive or an hour or two's walk north-west of Pokhara on the Baglung road. The large monastery here is interesting, although to get to it you have run the gauntlet past a dozen or more handicraft stalls. Also of interest here is the carpet weaving centre, where you can see all stages of the process, and buy the finished article. The ***community guesthouse*** close to the monastery would make a good overnight stop (Rs 150 a double).

The hilltop **Tibetan Buddhist Monastery** is a comparatively recent construction with a large Buddha statue and colourful wall paintings. Cross Mahendrapul Bridge from the bazaar area and follow the road, which is paved at first, to the monastery.

POKHARA

ACTIVITIES

Boating

Boats on Phewa Tal cost Rs 100 to Rs 150 an hour. They are most expensive opposite Varahi Temple, but get cheaper as you head south to Damside. You can simply paddle yourself around lazily or jump overboard for a swim in the pleasant waters. Rowboats are available for Rs 140/300 per hour/half-day, sail boats are Rs 200/600, and pedalos are Rs 350 per hour. If rowing yourself is too strenuous, a boat plus boatman will cost from around Rs 170 per hour. Kayaks are available for roughly Rs 200 per hour. You can also get rides across to the other side of the lake for Rs 250/400 one way/return.

Swimming

Swimming in the lake is pretty good for starters, but it's best to have a boat to fully enjoy the lake.

The swimming pool at Shangri-la Village is open to nonguests on weekends for Rs 550 all day, and this includes an excellent buffet spread. (See Places to Stay – Top End later in this section for details.)

The Penguin Pool, a few kilometres from town along the road to Baglung, is a decent public swimming pool. Entry is Rs 150.

Walking

The Pokhara area offers some fine walking possibilities ranging from day walks, such as the climb up to Sarangkot or the Peace Pagoda, to short three- or four-day treks. See Day Walks in the Around Pokhara section later in this chapter for details.

Meditation & Yoga

A few places in Lakeside offer the more sedentary pursuits of meditation and yoga.

Ganden Yiga Chopen Meditation Centre (☎ 22923) This centre in Lakeside North holds three-day meditation courses.

Nepali Yoga Centre (☎ 28886) On the main road into Pokhara from Lakeside, and near the Himalayan Encounters office, this centre holds daily Hatha yoga classes.

Sadhana Yoga (☎ 26839) North of Yogi's Yogashram, this centre holds 21-day (US$270), six-day (US$86) and one-day courses (US$15).

Yogi's Yogashram This place in Lakeside North offers morning and afternoon Hatha yoga sessions (Rs 300) and weekly introductory and advanced Hatha yoga courses.

Paragliding

If you feel the need to throw yourself off Sarangkot, Sunrise Paragliding offers just the chance, although novices have to do tandem jumps (US$60). It's possible to do a three-day course (US$200), which qualifies you for solo flight. Contact Sunrise Trekking (☎ 21174, ⓔ sunrise@mos.com.np) at the Alka Guest House, Lakeside.

Powered Glider Flights

The Avia Club Nepal (☎ 412830, ⓔ nepal@aviaclub.mos.com.np), which has an office at the airport, offers exciting ultralight flights around the area. Flights range from 15 minutes (US$45) to one hour (US$170).

PLACES TO STAY

There are four accommodation areas in Pokhara: around the bus station and bazaar; by the airport; at Damside (Pardi); and at Lakeside (Baidam).

There's really no reason to stay in the bazaar area – it's crowded, dirty and noisy. Several of Pokhara's larger and more expensive hotels are near the airport, but the advantages of comfortable hotels have to be weighed against the disadvantage of being a long walk from Lakeside.

Damside, at the south-eastern end of the lake, is more popular, and many of the touts who meet the tourist buses from Kathmandu will insist that this is the place to go. They will be at pains to point out that the distinction between Damside and Lakeside is meaningless. In one sense they're right (it is a continuous body of water we're talking about), but in several others they're wrong because Damside has a completely different atmosphere from Lakeside.

Firstly, there is quite a difference between being able to look out across the lake proper, as you can at many places in Lakeside, and looking out on the narrow neck of water by the dam. Damside is a modern, rather desolate area, and there are fewer farmhouses, fields and trees interspersed between the hotels. Many of the buildings are of the bleak concrete five-storey variety and there is a limited range of restaurants – most people eat in their hotels. Finally, you're at least a 15-minute walk from the action at Lakeside.

On the other hand, there are a couple of pleasant mid-range hotels in Damside, and some people prefer to escape the Lakeside scene. They are further rewarded by the best mountain views – the farther south you go, the less the mountains are obscured by the intervening foothills.

The major accommodation site is Lakeside, where you'll find an enormous number of budget to mid-range lodges and guesthouses. If you take any of the roads heading east off the Lakeside road, you quickly escape to land where the buffalo roam. Within two minutes you can be in a cheap and comfortable guesthouse among vegetable gardens and Chhetri farmhouses, although tourist development is rapidly reducing the land available for traditional practices.

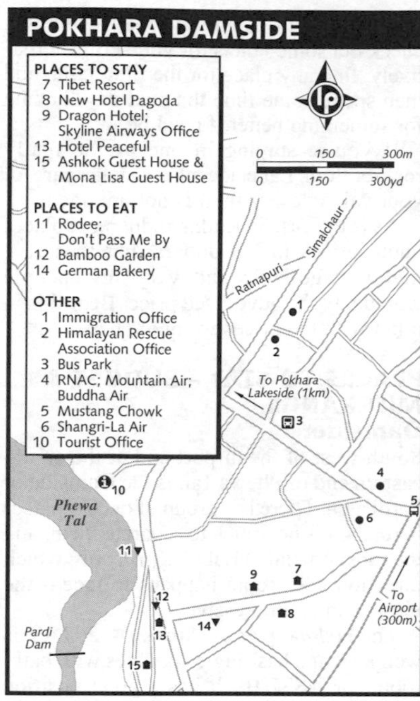

There are so many places to stay, and they change so quickly, that making individual recommendations (especially among budget and mid-range places) is a chancy game. Listen to other travellers' recommendations, and if you arrive by bus avoid the clutches of the touts. There is absolutely no reason to get sucked in by these characters who will, apart from anything else, get a 50% commission from the hotel they take you to. The best thing you can do is grab a taxi to somewhere central in Lakeside, have a drink and a bite to eat at one of the restaurants and then ask to leave your bag somewhere safe (most restaurants will happily do this) while you check out some hotels for yourself. Alternatively, find any place for the first night, and then spend some time the next day looking for something better if need be.

If you're staying in one of the really rock-bottom Lakeside places take care of your valuables, as theft is not unknown.

As is the case in Kathmandu, most places quote prices in US dollars, but these are highly negotiable and very few people would pay the advertised price. Bear this in mind with the prices we quote here.

PLACES TO STAY – BUDGET & MID-RANGE

Damside

South-west of the airport and at the south-eastern end of Phewa Tal, is the Damside or Pardi area. There is a group of decent places here, there's not much to separate them, and the most crucial variable is probably which direction your room happens to face – the views can be impressive.

The ***Ashok Guest House*** *(☎ 20374)* is well kept and has singles/doubles with bathroom for US$7/10. It has a good position right by the lake. The ***Mona Lisa Guest House*** is similar.

The ***Dragon Hotel*** *(☎ 20391, ⓔ dragon@mos.com.np)* is a reasonable mid-range option. Rooms with air-con and bathroom are supposedly US$40/50, plus 12% government tax, but a 50% discount is offered. There's a restaurant, bar and roof garden.

The pleasant and modern ***Tibet Resort*** *(☎ 20853, ⓔ tibetres@cnet.wlink.com.np)* has a big garden. Rooms with bathroom are reasonable value at US$23/34, although expect to pay 30% less. This is one of the best Damside places to stay, even though you can't actually see the lake from here.

The ***New Hotel Pagoda*** *(☎ 21802)*, which has views and very clean rooms, is also good value. Rooms with shared bathroom are US$6/8, or US$10/12 with a private bathroom, but negotiation is also possible.

The ***Hotel Peaceful*** *(☎ 20861)* is also decent. Comfortable rooms are US$5/8 with shared bathroom, US$8/12 with private bathroom.

Lakeside

Although the majority of the Lakeside (Baidam) places are firmly in the budget range, there's also a fair sprinkling aiming for the mid-range with en suite bathrooms, carpets and comfortable beds.

Many of the budget lodges and guesthouses along the lake have similar facilities and prices. Prices tend to vary with demand, rising and falling with the season and the number of travellers passing through. There's usually hot water available in the bathrooms and many places offer very pleasant garden areas, often right in front of your room.

Basic doubles cost around Rs 150 for a room with shared bathroom, or from Rs 250 with private bathroom. Every year sees the opening of a rash of new concrete hotels with totally uninspiring architecture, often built on the spot where a comfortable little single-storey guesthouse has been pulled down. They're relatively expensive with rates starting at about US$10, but there's usually room for bargaining, especially if you plan to stay more than a couple of days.

You can stay close to the centre of things, on or near the main Lakeside road, or opt for a quieter location either back from the main road or way down at the northern end of the lake. The price you'll pay for peace and quiet is a slightly longer walk to get to the restaurants and other activities by the water. The farther north you go (towards the foothills), the more restricted the views of the mountains are.

The following suggestions represent just a handful of standard places, plus some of the pricier alternatives.

Lakeside East The ***New Annapurna Guest House*** *(☎ 25011)* is well back from the road, along a footpath opposite the Fish Tail Lodge access road. It is quiet and well kept, and the coffee bushes in the garden supply the kitchen with fresh beans. Rooms cost from US$4 to US$20, depending on views and facilities.

In the same area, and set back from the road, is the ***Base Camp Resort*** *(☎ 21226, ⓔ basecamp@mos.com.np)*, a good, modern upmarket place. A number of two-storey

GARETH McCORMACK

Sarangkot offers stunning views across Pokhara Valley and Machhapuchhare.

MARK KIRBY

Phewa Tal, Pokhara, the perfect rejoinder to the folly of white-water rafting.

PAUL HARDING

Taking time out in Royal Chitwan NP.

GREG ELMS

Shake, rattle 'n' roll...

HUGH FINLAY

Tiger Tops, Royal Chitwan NP

OLIVIER CIRENDINI

Ten tonne cutie-pie!

PAUL DYMOND

One-horned rhino keeps a (blurry) eye on the two-legged onlookers.

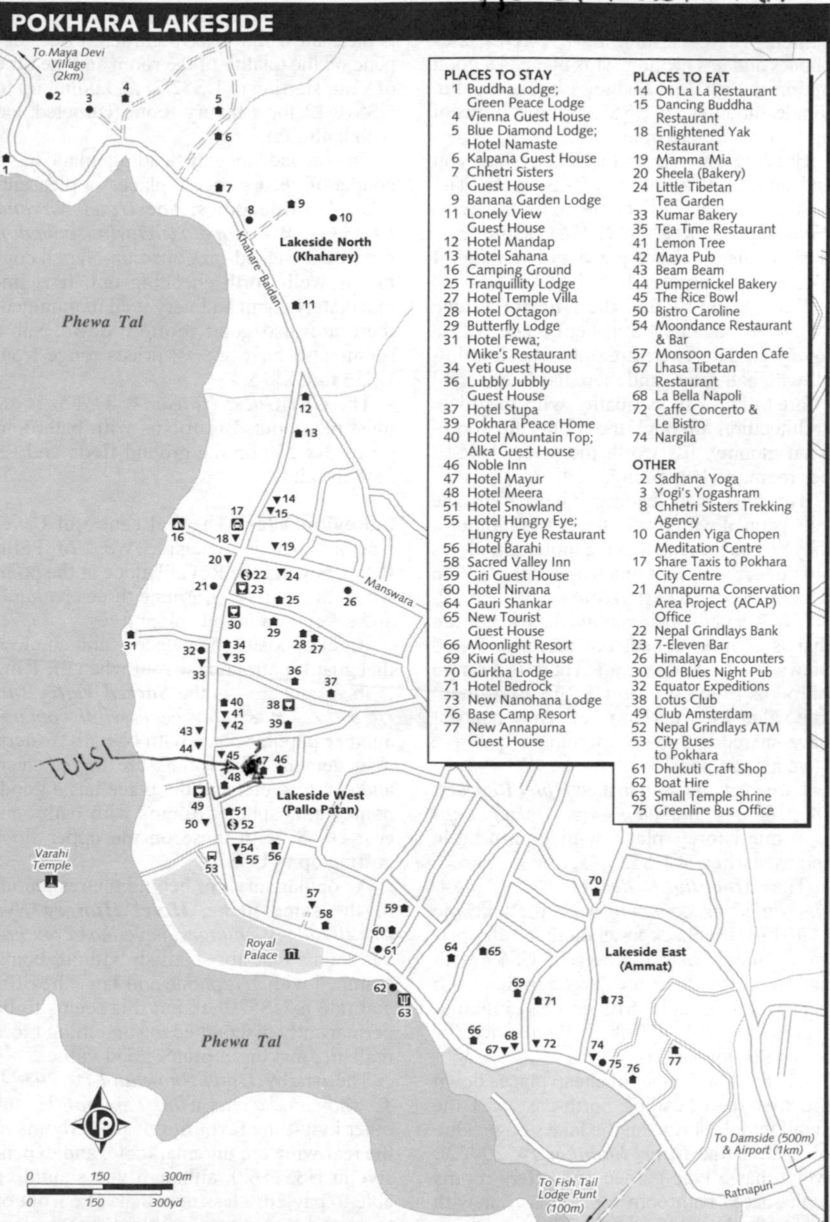
POKHARA LAKESIDE
PLACES TO STAY
1 Buddha Lodge; Green Peace Lodge
4 Vienna Guest House
5 Blue Diamond Lodge; Hotel Namaste
6 Kalpana Guest House
7 Chhetri Sisters Guest House
9 Banana Garden Lodge
11 Lonely View Guest House
12 Hotel Mandap
13 Hotel Sahana
16 Camping Ground
25 Tranquillity Lodge
27 Hotel Temple Villa
28 Hotel Octagon
29 Butterfly Lodge
31 Hotel Fewa; Mike's Restaurant
34 Yeti Guest House
36 Lubbly Jubbly Guest House
37 Hotel Stupa
39 Pokhara Peace Home
40 Hotel Mountain Top; Alka Guest House
46 Noble Inn
47 Hotel Mayur
48 Hotel Meera
51 Hotel Snowland
55 Hotel Hungry Eye; Hungry Eye Restaurant
56 Hotel Barahi
58 Sacred Valley Inn
59 Giri Guest House
60 Hotel Nirvana
64 Gauri Shankar
65 New Tourist Guest House
66 Moonlight Resort
69 Kiwi Guest House
70 Gurkha Lodge
71 Hotel Bedrock
73 New Nanohana Lodge
76 Base Camp Resort
77 New Annapurna Guest House
PLACES TO EAT
14 Oh La La Restaurant
15 Dancing Buddha Restaurant
18 Enlightened Yak Restaurant
19 Mamma Mia
20 Sheela (Bakery)
24 Little Tibetan Tea Garden
33 Kumar Bakery
35 Tea Time Restaurant
41 Lemon Tree
42 Maya Pub
43 Beam Beam
44 Pumpernickel Bakery
45 The Rice Bowl
50 Bistro Caroline
54 Moondance Restaurant & Bar
57 Monsoon Garden Cafe
67 Lhasa Tibetan Restaurant
68 La Bella Napoli
72 Caffe Concerto & Le Bistro
74 Nargila
OTHER
2 Sadhana Yoga
3 Yogi's Yogashram
8 Chhetri Sisters Trekking Agency
10 Ganden Yiga Chopen Meditation Centre
17 Share Taxis to Pokhara City Centre
21 Annapurna Conservation Area Project (ACAP) Office
22 Nepal Grindlays Bank
23 7-Eleven Bar
26 Himalayan Encounters
30 Old Blues Night Pub
32 Equator Expeditions
38 Lotus Club
49 Club Amsterdam
52 Nepal Grindlays ATM
53 City Buses to Pokhara
61 Dhukuti Craft Shop
62 Boat Hire
63 Small Temple Shrine
75 Greenline Bus Office
To Maya Devi Village (2km)
Khahare Baidan
Lakeside North (Khaharey)
Phewa Tal
Manswara
Lakeside West (Pallo Patan)
Varahi Temple
Royal Palace
Lakeside East (Ammat)
Phewa Tal
To Damside (500m) & Airport (1km)
To Fish Tail Lodge Punt (100m)
Ratnapuri
0 150 300m
0 150 300yd

bungalows are grouped around an attractive garden. There is satellite TV, IDD telephones and gas heating. This place is a good option if Fish Tail Lodge is booked solid. Singles/doubles are US$72/75; discounts of up to 35% are possible.

Heading away from the lake's edge you end up in a pleasant village-like area. The first place you will come to is the ***New Nanohana Lodge*** *(☎ 22478)*, a modern, fairly undistinguished place with a range of rooms with bathroom from US$4 to US$10.

Keep going to find the ***Gurkha Lodge*** *(☎ 20798)*, a small, well-kept place with a lovely garden. There are only five doubles, all with bathroom, and there has been a real effort to build in sympathy with the local architecture, although the rooms are somewhat gloomy. It's worth the price: US$12 per room, no bargaining.

The next road leading inland from the lake is lined with places to stay, and though they're convenient, and the mountain views are good, there's not much atmosphere. The decent ***Kiwi Guest House*** *(☎ 22052, ⓔ kiwi@cnet.wlink.com.np)* has a garden that is a bit cramped, but there are good views from the hotel roof. There is a range of rooms from US$7 to US$30, all of them fair value for what you get. The cheapest have shared bathroom, the most expensive have air-con and TV.

POKHARA

Large yet undistinguished ***Hotel Bedrock*** *(☎ 21876, ⓔ hotel@pisang.wlink.com.np)* is a multistorey place with comfortable rooms starting at US$25/45.

The ***Moonlight Resort*** *(☎ 422044, ⓔ mlight@mos.com.np)* is on the lakeside road, but is set back far enough to offer privacy. Good, basic rooms cost US$9 with bathroom, or there are larger rooms with better facilities at US$10, or US$15 including air-con, although the official price for air-con is double this.

There are a number of cheap places down the first road heading north-east past the small temple shrine on the lake's edge. One of these is the ***Gauri Shankar*** *(☎ 20422)*, which has a nice garden and offers rooms with shared bathroom for US$3/4, or with private bathroom for US$6/10.

The ***New Tourist Guest House*** *(☎ 21479)* is pleasant with a decent garden. Prices depend on the quality of the room and the time of year, starting at US$2/3, and going up to US$10/12 for a luxury room (carpeted and with bath tub).

The second laneway heading inland has a couple of cheap, decent places in pleasant, relaxed surroundings. The ***Hotel Nirvana*** *(☎ 23332, ⓔ nirvana@cnet.wlink.com.np)*, run by a switched-on Canadian-Nepali couple, is well worth checking out. It is immaculately clean and very well maintained; there are also good rooftop views. Some rooms also have views; prices range from US$6 to US$15.

The ***Giri Guest House*** *(☎ 24955)* is almost next door. Big rooms with bathroom go for Rs 250 on the ground floor, and Rs 350 upstairs.

Lakeside West The real centre of Lakeside activity is Lakeside West or Pallo Patan, beyond the Royal Palace at the point where the road forks around three chautaras and several enormous pipal trees.

Right opposite the palace – and so close that guards patrol on the roof when the King is in residence – is the ***Sacred Valley Inn*** *(☎ 31792, ⓔ svalley@cnet.wlink.com.np)* another popular place with Nepali-Western management. The rooms are large, clean and comfortable, and the place has a good, homey atmosphere. Rooms with bathroom cost US$8, with those on the upper floor costing up to US$12.

A popular survivor behind the restaurant of the same name, ***Hotel Hungry Eye*** *(☎ 20908, ⓔ hungry@eye.mos.com.np)* has rooms that are smallish without being cramped with TV, phone and fan. The official rate is US$20/30, but this seems to be permanently discounted to something more realistic, making it pretty good value.

The nearby ***Hotel Snowland*** *(☎ 20384, ⓔ snowland@cnet.wlink.com.np)* is another long-time favourite. The old rooms in the rear wing are unremarkable, and expensive at US$15/20, although you should be able to pay 20% less than that. The front of the hotel consists of a block of modern deluxe rooms, all with a view of the lake, and these go for US$35/45, again with a 20% discount.

There's a good upper-mid-range option on the nearby eastbound road. ***Hotel Barahi*** *(☎ 23017, ⓔ barahi@cnet.wlink.com.np)* has a huge garden and a wing of very comfortable deluxe rooms with air-con at US$55/64. There are also some older but still comfortable rooms at US$25/31 with private bathroom.

The road running eastward from the next chautara (beside the incongruous Cape Cod–style Hotel Meera) has a number of options, but the laneway itself is not as pleasant as some. Right at the end is the modern ***Noble Inn*** *(☎ 24926)*, a recent replacement of an old-style place. It is modern, with a pleasant garden and OK rooms for US$5/8 with shared/private bathroom.

The ***Hotel Mayur*** *(☎ 22285, fax 25261)* is in the same lane. The top-floor views are excellent, and the modern rooms are well kept. The cost is Rs 300/350 for rooms on the lower floor, Rs 400/500 for rooms upstairs.

Something of an eyesore, ***Hotel Meera*** *(☎ 21031, ⓔ meera@cnet.wlink.com.np)* is totally inappropriate in this setting. Nevertheless, the rooms are good and the front-room views are excellent. The cost is US$35/45 with TV and air-con. Discounts are offered.

The next eastward lane (just before the next chautara) is very pleasant and retains some of the old Pokhara atmosphere, although it is only just clinging to it as the concrete monsters rise.

Along this lane, ***Pokhara Peace Home*** *(☎ 23205)* is not a bad place. It has a pleasant garden with a village feel, and rooms cost Rs 200 with shared bathroom, Rs 250/350 with private bathroom.

Alka Guest House *(☎ 23357, ⓔ sunrise @mos.com.np)* is in a good position right on the main road. The rooms (doubles only available) are at the back, well away from the road, and are good value at Rs 200 with shared bathroom, and Rs 300 with a private bathroom.

Nearby, the ugly ***Hotel Mountain Top*** *(☎ 20779, ⓔ hmtpkr@mos.com.np)* is an unmissable four-storey monstrosity, not an uncommon sight these days. Admittedly, the comfortable rooms have superb views and they're not bad value. Singles/doubles with shared bathroom are US$15/20, and cost US$25/33 with private bathroom, but low-season discounts can bring this down by 50%.

Up the side road beside Hotel Mountain Top there are a few more guesthouses to choose from, including the ***Lubbly Jubbly Guest House*** *(☎ 22881)*. It's a pleasant little place with a very nice open-air sitting and eating area, although there isn't much garden. Rooms are good value at Rs 150 with shared bathroom, Rs 250 for a larger double with private bathroom.

Another concrete monster, ***Hotel Stupa*** *(☎ 22608, ⓔ hstupa@mos.com.np)* is as good as any if that's the sort of place you want. It's not bad value at US$20/35, but be sure to request a discount as official prices are much higher than this.

The ***Yeti Guest House*** *(☎ 21423)* is set back from the road in a large garden. It's basic, but quite OK at Rs 150 for rooms with shared bathroom, Rs 250 with private bathroom.

One of the few hotels on the western side of the road is the ***Hotel Fewa*** *(☎ 20151, ⓔ mike@fewa.mos.com.np)*, it is superbly situated right on the edge of the lake. It is owned and run by Mike of Mike's Breakfast fame in Kathmandu. The rooms have been recently renovated, and the lakeside location is hard to match. At US$20/25 for rooms with bathroom, the price is not bad – you are definitely paying a premium for the location. There's also six new Nepali-style cottages, which are very tastefully done, and these are good value at US$40/50.

Back on the eastern side of the road, the ***Tranquillity Lodge*** *(☎ 21030)* is a pleasant modern hotel set in a well-tended, shady garden. Rooms are large and comfortable, and moderately priced at US$15/25. There's certainly room for bargaining, especially out of season – expect to pay around Rs 600 for a double.

The nearby ***Butterfly Lodge*** *(☎ 22892, ⓔ butterfly@cnet.wlink.com.np)* is quite popular. There's a decent sized garden and, interestingly, all profits go to charity. Rooms start at Rs 350 for a double.

A little farther along, find ***Hotel Octagon*** *(☎ 26978, ⓔ hoteloctagon@hotmail.com)*. This unusual modern place was built as a house, and the owner lets out the four large rooms on the upper floor. Consequently it has a homely feel, and it's shoes off as in any Nepali house. The two rooms with shared bathroom are US$6, those with private bathroom are US$10.

Next door is the ***Hotel Temple Villa*** *(☎ 21203, ⓔ adv@cnet.wlink.com.np)*, a small and pleasant lodge also in a quiet location. It is clean, and the rooms are large and comfortable. They're reasonable value at US$5 to US$10 for a double with shared bathroom, or US$10 to US$20 with private bathroom.

Lakeside North Things certainly become quieter, cheaper and more basic once you go north of Camping Chowk to Lakeside North (Khaharey). The farther north you go the quieter it gets, and before long you're out in the rice paddies (although every year there are fewer paddies and more concrete). Once you get this far north the lake shore becomes much closer, you are tucked in under the foothills and don't get great views of the mountains, but the compensation is the much better lake views.

For those with tents the best bet is to make a deal with one of the lodges to camp in their garden. Alternatively, there's the ***camping ground*** *(☎ 24052)*, in a great spot by the lake near Camping Chowk. The facilities are very basic and there's not much shade, although it is a nice grassy site and is a good option if you have a large vehicle. It costs Rs 40 to pitch a tent and Rs 60 per vehicle.

The places along the main road into Pokhara aren't very appealing. Not surprisingly, the road lacks the peaceful rural atmosphere of the best parts of Lakeside, and although the traffic isn't particularly heavy, buses, tractors and taxis pass by frequently. Most of the hotels around here are new and are two or three-storey monstrosities with mid-range prices.

Hotel Sahana *(☎ 22614, fax 25050)* is a modern place with rooms set around a garden. It's quite pleasant – not bad value when the 15% discount is taken from the official price of US$15/25 for singles/doubles.

The modern ***Hotel Mandap*** *(☎ 27088)* has lake views from the top floor and is good value. Ground-floor rooms are Rs 300, while those on the top floor are Rs 450.

The ***Lonely View Lodge*** *(☎ 269940)* is a basic and friendly little place with cheap rooms.

The popular ***Banana Garden Lodge*** *(☎ 21880)* is slightly elevated and so has good views. Rooms start at Rs 100.

The new ***Chhetri Sisters Guest House*** *(☎ 24066, ⓔ sister3@cnet.wlink.com.np)* is the newest place in this area. It is owned by three sisters who organise women porters and guides for women trekkers. They have expanded their operations with the opening of this new guesthouse, 100m beyond their trekking office and former guest house (now a private residence, despite the guesthouse sign). The rooms are relatively expensive at US$10/15 with a shared/private bathroom, but there is a Rs 200 dorm option.

Kalpana Guest House is slightly back from the road, and being right among the rice fields, has a very rural ambience. It's clean, well run and good value at Rs 150/200 with shared bathroom.

Hotel Namaste is farther along, and farther back from the road. It is reached by a foot track, and you'd definitely need a flashlight (torch) if venturing out at night. It's a very basic place, but is certainly quiet and private. Right next door is the similar ***Blue Diamond Lodge***. Both have rooms starting at around Rs 150.

Vienna Guest House, above and behind the Hamlet Lodge, has excellent lake views due to its elevated position. The rooms are large and spartan but quite OK, and there's a large verandah for relaxing. It's good value at Rs 200 for a double with bathroom.

Right out on a point, perched on the edge of the road 5m above the lake shore, are a couple of small, cheap lodges, which are very popular, partly because of their superb location. ***Buddha Lodge*** has rooms with shared bathroom from around Rs 150, while the ***Green Peace Lodge*** is slightly fancier. A bicycle would be handy here as they are a good 20-minute walk from the nearest restaurants (although the Green Peace has a restaurant).

If you really want to escape, continue another 2km or so, around the next point, and you come to the very mellow and comfortable ***Maya Devi Village***. It consists of circular, thatched cottages and is surrounded by rice paddies. Rooms start at Rs 350 and you can get meals here.

PLACES TO STAY – TOP END

Lakeside

Pokhara's only top-end Lakeside hotel (so far) is the ***Fish Tail Lodge*** (☎ 22171, ⓔ *fishtail@lodge.mos.com.np*). It's beautifully positioned and isolated from the Lakeside development; guests are shuttled over to the hotel by a rope-drawn pontoon. The hotel takes its name from the English translation of Machhapuchhare. From the hotel there are superb views of the mountains, particularly at dawn when the mountains are reflected in the still waters of the lake. The buildings have been imaginatively designed with references to the local architecture, and they sit in attractive gardens. The rooms have all the usual luxury mod cons and cost US$90/100, plus 12% tax. There's also a newer wing of deluxe rooms, which are more expensive and less attractive, but with limited views; these cost US$105/115. A 25% discount applies to all rooms in the low season. The hotel is extremely popular, so it is worth booking well in advance if you want to stay there. There's a pleasant bar and restaurant and the food is pretty good. Cultural shows are held nightly at 6 pm (Rs 200) and these are also open to nonguests.

The Western Shore

On the other side of the lake, along the Panchase ridge from the Peace Pagoda and with superb mountain views, is ***Raniban Retreat*** *(☎ 31713, ⓔ sales@raniban.com)*. Its stone cottages are well furnished, and the restaurant is also pretty good. Rooms with private bathroom are US$45/50.

Airport Area

Two of Pokhara's large hotels are directly opposite the airport, and three of the best are on the far side of the airport.

The ***Hotel Mt Annapurna*** *(☎ 20037, ⓔ lodrik@mos.com.np)* is Tibetan-owned and decorated in Tibetan style. Unfortunately, the whole place is looking a bit tired these days, and it's not great value, even with discounts. All the rooms have private bathroom and cost US$30/40 for a single/double, plus 12% government tax.

The ***New Hotel Crystal*** *(☎ 20035, fax 20234)* is better but more expensive at US$65/75. All rooms have bathroom and there's a 12% government tax. The facilities are good, but it's a big soulless place that could pretty much be anywhere.

Just south of the airport – and, disconcertingly, right under the approach flight path – is the excellent ***Bluebird Hotel*** *(☎ 228833, ⓔ hotel@bluestar.mos.com.np)*. The whole place has been beautifully done, the rooms are spacious and have air-con and most have excellent mountain views. There's also a swimming pool and a couple of eating options. All this is yours for US$130/150 plus tax.

The nice ***Shangri-la Village*** *(☎ 22122, ⓔ hosangp@village.mos.com.np)*, arguably Pokhara's best hotel, is signposted about 1km past the southern end of the airport. This is a very low-key place, with buildings arranged around a pool and garden, and excellent mountain views. Other facilities include a sauna and health club. The rooms are tastefully decorated, and good use has been made of local furnishings. Singles and doubles are US$150 with air-con, TV and phone. The food here is also good, and the Rs 550 weekend brunch is excellent value, especially for nonguests as, in addition to a full buffet meal, it gives you use of the pool for the day.

Farther south again, but accessed from the Kathmandu road to the east of the airport, is Pokhara's latest hotel folly, ***The Fulbari*** *(☎ 23451, ⓔ resv@fulbari.com.np)*. The location is dramatic, being perched right on the edge of the Seti River gorge, and the mountain views are superb, but one wonders just how they ever hope to fill this 165-room, five-star place. No expense has been spared in its construction; the lobby area makes extensive use of carved wood, the effect is stunning. Rooms come with all the mod cons you'd expect in a place charging US$200/220 plus tax. Facilities include a golf course, pool, health club and tennis courts.

Elsewhere

Also worthy of a mention is the flash award winning ***Tiger Mountain Pokhara Lodge*** *(☎ 01-411225, ⓔ info@tigermountain.com)*. It is set on a ridge about half an hour's drive from Pokhara along the Kathmandu road, and has amazing views over Pokhara and the mountains. Accommodation consists of cottages made from local stone and slate, each with its own balcony and stunning views. The main lodge building has a bar, eating area and library. There's also a dramatically sited swimming pool. The cost is US$100 per person per night, which includes all meals and transfers to and from Pokhara. Discounts apply outside the high season (no discounts from October to November).

PLACES TO EAT

The bazaar area has local restaurants, while other eating possibilities are to be found in the big hotels or among the numerous cheaper hotels, particularly along Lakeside. At most of these travellers restaurants you'll find the standard 'try-anything' menu, which currently means lots of Italian dishes backed up by Indian, Nepali, Mexican, continental and whatever other possibilities present themselves. The range is certainly an improvement over endless dal bhaats or thalis but despite the apparent variety everything very quickly tastes the same! What differs more is the atmosphere and the crowd at any place on any given evening.

Damside

There is not a great range of restaurants in the Damside area, as most people eat at their hotels. ***Don't Pass Me By*** and ***Rodee*** are basic little restaurants right on the edge of the lake, where you can sit outside and enjoy the atmosphere.

There's nothing very German about the ***German Bakery*** but it is a popular breakfast place. The ***Bamboo Garden*** completes the Damside restaurant picture.

Lakeside

Most dining possibilities are along the main road skirting Lakeside.

Starting at Lakeside East, one of the first possibilities is ***Le Bistro***, which has everything from Mexican, Italian, Chinese and Indian to Nepali. And it seems to do a pretty good job of it all. The apple pies are not at all bad either!

Very close by is ***La Bella Napoli***, with decent pizzas and pastas, and other Italian and Western dishes. This place also has decent bakery items.

Also in this area are ***Caffe Concerto***, with good pizzas and Italian ice cream, and the ***Nargila*** for Middle Eastern food.

Lhasa Tibetan Restaurant is a big outdoor place with a standard 'try-anything' menu, in addition to a number of Tibetan specialities. The food is very good and the service is fairly fast. *Sha bhakley*, a Tibetan meat pie, is Rs 100, and *momos* (steamed or fried meat or vegetables wrapped in dough) are Rs 50. Chicken kebabs with *naan* (bread) and salad for Rs 120 are good value, as are the pizzas and cakes.

The ***Monsoon Garden Cafe*** near the Royal Palace is a great little retreat. You can sit under shady trees here and indulge in great home-style cooking; the cakes and desserts are especially good. It is open from breakfast until afternoon tea (fresh scones, jam and cream for Rs 205).

The ***Hungry Eye***, farther along past the Royal Palace near the hotel of the same name, is a long-standing survivor and one of the biggest restaurants in Lakeside. The food is still good (the cakes are excellent), but the service can be chaotic. Pizza ranges from Rs 100 to Rs 200 and a steak is Rs 185.

Next door, ***Moondance Restaurant & Bar*** has average prices and food, but a good atmosphere. There's a fireplace inside. The bar here is popular and there's a pool table, darts and other board games to while away the hours.

Bistro Caroline, run by the same people as Chez Caroline in Kathmandu, is expected to open in 2001. If the food is as good as it is in Kathmandu, this place will be setting the standard here.

The ***Boomerang Restaurant*** is one of a number of outdoor places on the west side of the road. It's also one of a number offering evening cultural shows. There's a nice garden dotted with chairs, tables and thatched shelters – and great views. It's a great place for breakfast (around Rs 80) or lunch, but dinner is less impressive. They have the usual eclectic menu and prices. The ***Fewa Park Restaurant*** next door is fairly similar.

Opposite these places is ***The Rice Bowl***, a fairly standard place with Tibetan and other dishes, and decent views from the top floor.

Beam Beam is also on the west side of the road, and although the garden is much smaller than the Boomerang's, it is still very pleasant – in some ways cosier. Inside, the big TV/video tends to dominate. The service is excellent, and although the menu is pretty standard, the food is good.

The ***Pumpernickel Bakery***, next door, also has a garden. This place has an impressive array of breads and pastries, and is a popular morning spot.

The ***Lemon Tree*** by one of the large trees has a typically broad menu; this place is particularly good for cakes and milkshakes.

The ***Tea Time Restaurant*** on the next corner along is a popular place with a cosy front-verandah eating area in addition to an indoor section.

Mike's Restaurant at the Hotel Fewa offers the best location and arguably the best food in Lakeside. The open-air terrace is right by the lake (the only place with an actual lake frontage), and the food is excellent. The exotic sandwiches with brown bread are well worth the Rs 100 to Rs 140, plus another Rs 40 for soup or salad.

For budget breakfasts try one of the small bakeries, such as ***Sheela*** up near Camping Chowk. This is a very popular little place, with excellent chocolate croissants and buns. The ***Kumar Bakery*** near the Tea Time Restaurant is similar.

The ***Little Tibetan Tea Garden*** is a cosy place on the main road into Pokhara from Camping Chowk. Just so no-one feels left out, they not only do excellent Tibetan food (including that traditional favourite, Tibetan pizza!), but also throw in a few Mexican and Italian dishes.

Also on this stretch of road is ***Mamma Mia***, an excellent mainly Italian place. The pastas here are well worth a try.

Moving north of Camping Chowk, there's the ***Enlightened Yak Restaurant***, upstairs with views of the lake.

Farther along on the opposite side is the ***Dancing Buddha Restaurant***, which has plenty of Osho literature to read, and the ***Oh La La Restaurant*** with its pleasant little bamboo garden.

At the top end of the spectrum, the bar and restaurant at the ***Fish Tail Lodge*** is a fine place for a more expensive night out. The fixed breakfast costs Rs 555, or a buffet lunch or dinner is Rs 750, although these are only laid out when there are sufficient guests. An a la carte dinner for two will probably come to at least Rs 1500. On a clear day it's worth coming over here for a drink in the garden, which has stunning views of Machhapuchhare.

Also popular is the weekend buffet at the ***Shangri-la Village*** (see Places to Stay – Top End earlier in this section).

ENTERTAINMENT

The ***Fish Tail Lodge*** puts on a nightly cultural program featuring Nepali dancing. It runs from 6.30 to 7.30 pm and entry is Rs 200. A number of restaurants in Lakeside do similar shows for free.

There is an increasing number of bars in Pokhara, and the music blares out until 10 or 11 pm each night. There's nothing very bluesy about the ***Old Blues Night Pub***, but the sound system is good (and usually cranked up loud) and the pool tables are quite popular.

Another good bar is the ***Maya Pub***, which has a happy hour in the early evening with two cocktails for the price of one.

Club Amsterdam is a modern bar with a popular outdoor deck.

The ***7-Eleven Bar*** near Camping Chowk is a noisy place with live Indian *ghazal* music (Urdu love songs derived from poetry) in the evenings, although purists of that art form would probably be horrified at the mauling the music receives here.

The ***Lotus Club*** is a disco that gets going around 6 pm and goes until well into the night. Entry is Rs 200.

SHOPPING

Pokhara's large Tibetan population sells many crafts and artefacts. Carpet-weaving is a major local industry for these people.

Saligrams, the fossilised sea creatures found north in the Kali Gandaki Valley, are a popular souvenir, but they are often radically overpriced. You shouldn't pay more than about Rs 100.

GETTING THERE & AWAY

Some travel agencies in Pokhara offer 'through' tickets or package-deal tickets to cities in India. These are dubious value at the best of times and a number of travellers have written to us complaining of various rip-offs perpetrated by unscrupulous Pokhara agents. These range from promises of tourist buses (there are *no* tourist buses running to/from any of the border crossings), to reserved seats that were definitely not reserved, and air-con train sleepers that turned out to be second class.

See India under Land in the Getting There & Away chapter for more information, but if you do decide to buy a package, don't count on everything going smoothly. Make sure you get everything spelt out in a receipt, and hang onto it.

Air

There are many daily services between Kathmandu and Pokhara. As the route is something of a cash cow, all the private companies have jumped on the bandwagon; their offices are opposite the airport near Mustang Chowk and close to Damside. The Skyline Airways office is in the Dragon Hotel in Damside. The flight to Kathmandu takes from 20 minutes to an hour, depending on the aircraft, and costs US$71 ($US61 with RNAC). It's probably easiest to get one of the many agents in Lakeside to do the running around for the ticket.

There are great Himalayan views if you sit on the right-hand side of the plane from Kathmandu to Pokhara, and vice versa.

Bus

The main Pokhara bus station (also known as the bus park) is a dusty (or during the monsoon, muddy) expanse of chaos, with seemingly little organisation. The booking office is at the top of the steps that lead into the bus station on its western edge.

To/From Kathmandu The bus trip between Kathmandu and Pokhara takes six to eight hours and most departures are early in the morning. The road is in a pretty good condition the whole way.

Greenline (☎ 27271), with an office in Lakeside, offers a daily air-con service to Kathmandu, which is a steep Rs 600 but includes breakfast at Kurintar about halfway.

Public buses (from the bus station) cost Rs 125; tickets for the large tourist buses start from Rs 150 and the tourist minibuses cost Rs 200. It's dubious whether the extra expense of tourist buses is worthwhile. The minibuses are quicker (often considerably scarier as a result), but the full-sized tourist buses aren't significantly different to public express buses in terms of time and comfort.

The tourist buses are, however, more convenient when you consider where they pick you up and drop you off. In Kathmandu they pick up and drop off at the Thamel end of Kantipath. In Pokhara, the tourist buses pick up Kathmandu-bound passengers outside their hotels, although all tourist buses coming from Kathmandu terminate at a makeshift terminus at Mustang Chowk, between Damside and the airport. Taxis await all tourist bus arrivals, and everything is pretty orderly, although there are still plenty of touts.

To/From Royal Chitwan National Park Public buses between Pokhara and Tadi Bazaar in the eastern Terai cost Rs 90, or there are minibuses for Rs 150. Greenline also offers air-con buses on this route for Rs 480, including breakfast. See the Royal Chitwan National Park section in the Terai chapter for more details.

To/From the Indian Border Day/night buses to Sunauli and Bhairawa near the Indian border depart from the main Pokhara bus station (Rs 180/220, 9 hours), or there are day minibuses (Rs 250). Buses depart for Birganj (Rs 150/175, 10 hours) and Nepalganj via Mugling (Rs 280/350, 15 hours).

Pokhara agents may try to tempt you with the offer of tourist buses to the border. Be warned there are no tourist buses; so while you do get picked up outside your hotel, you go from there to the bus station where everyone else gets on!

The road to India is called the Siddhartha Hwy because it ends close to Lumbini where the Buddha, Siddhartha Gautama, was born. See the Getting There & Away chapter for more details on transport to India.

To/From Trekking Routes Pokhara is the base for popular treks such as the Annapurna Sanctuary Trek, Jomsom Trek and the Annapurna Circuit, plus a number of other lesser known alternatives. See the Trekking chapter for details.

For the start of the Jomson Trek, the Pokhara-Baglung Hwy goes all the way to Beni, so most trekkers take the bus as far as Nayapul (just before Baglung), from where it's just a 20-minute walk to Birethanti. Buses for Baglung and Beni leave the local bus station roughly every half-hour from early morning until mid-afternoon, the trip to Nayapul costs Rs 45 and takes about two hours.

To Besisahar, for the start of the Annapurna Sanctuary Trek, there is one bus daily at around 7 am from the main Pokhara bus station (five hours).

GETTING AROUND

Motorcycle

Renting a motorcycle costs around Rs 400 per day. However, Pokhara and the surrounding roads will not be improved by the growing number of motorcycles.

Taxi

It's a long way between the bazaar and Lakeside; a taxi costs around Rs 100. It's a bit of a battle to extract fair prices when catching a taxi from Lakeside to the airport or bus station. Expect to pay as much as Rs 100. Buses shuttle between the lake, airport and bazaar with fares costing around Rs 5 per person.

Share taxis run from Camping Chowk in the northern part of Lakeside into Pokhara's city centre.

Bicycle

There are lots of bicycle rental places along the lake, by the dam or by the airport. Ordinary bicycles cost around Rs 50 per day, mountain bikes around Rs 100. You can also rent children's bicycles. Pokhara looks deceptively flat but actually slopes steadily uphill as you move north. If you ride a bicycle from the lake to the Binde Basini Temple at the northern end of the bazaar area, you'll find it's a wonderfully long freewheel on the way back.

Around Pokhara

For those with limited time, less enthusiasm for walking or with small children, the area around Pokhara also has some fine short treks ranging from half-day and day walks to longer treks lasting from two or three days to a week.

There are plenty of rental shops in Pokhara, and prices are similar to those in Kathmandu. The range of equipment is probably not quite as large however, so if you want anything out of the ordinary you are best off bringing it from home or Kathmandu.

DAY WALKS

Sarangkot

This very pleasant walk up to Sarangkot, at an elevation of 1592m, is probably the most popular short excursion from Pokhara. It can be a good, early morning stroll to admire the mountain views, a leg stretcher before you start out on a longer trek or a place you pass through on the first or last hours of one of the longer treks from Pokhara.

Sarangkot has a number of accommodation and eating options – such as the ***New Horizon Lodge*** (☎ *29363*), ***View Top Restaurant & Lodge***, ***Lake View Lodge*** and ***Hotel Mountain Prince***. None of these actually has mountain views, but it's only a short walk to the viewpoint, so you can climb up to Sarangkot in the evening, stay overnight and catch the view at dawn, or simply walk up for breakfast.

Sarangkot once had a *kot* or fort, the remains of which can be seen on the very top of the ridge just a few minutes walk above Sarangkot. At the viewpoint itself you pay a donation to enter the old fort, where there's a platform equipped with powerful binoculars for viewing the mountains and Pokhara (tokens are available from the attendant).

Getting There & Away There are a number of routes to Sarangkot, but the easiest way is to walk up from the Binde Basini Temple in the bazaar area of Pokhara and on the return leg head straight down from the top to Phewa Tal.

From the temple head west and follow the bitumen road that runs about halfway up before it turns to dirt. You can short-cut many

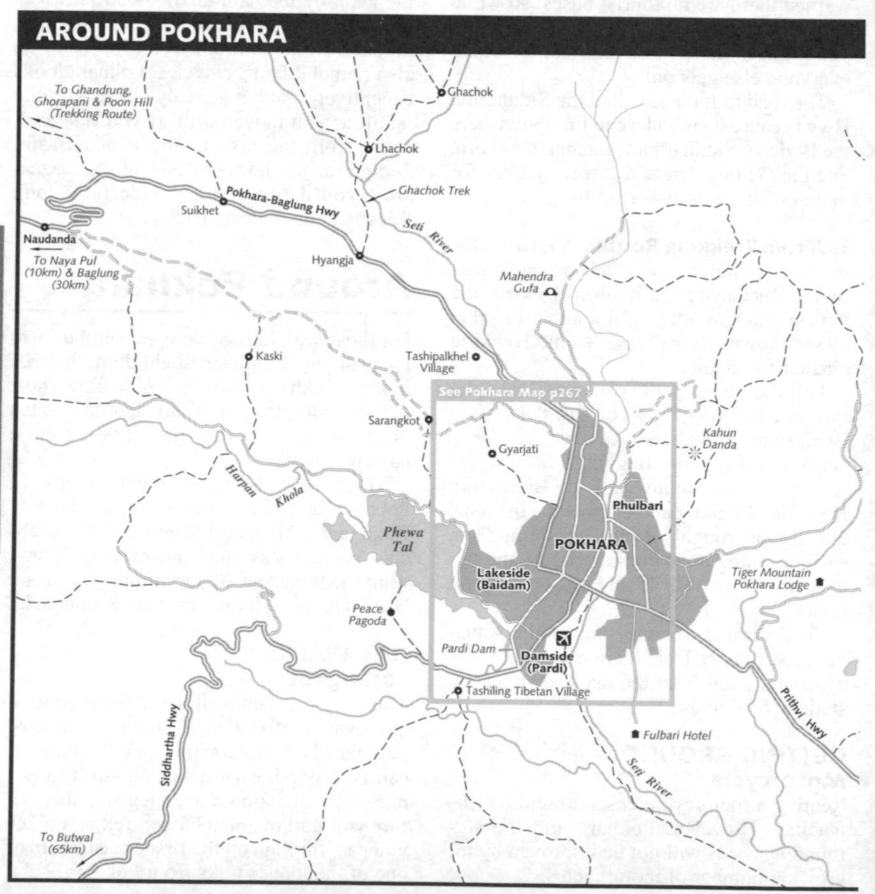

of the sharp corners. On the way up you pass several places where women work at handlooms. It takes about two hours to walk to Sarangkot from Binde Basini Temple, versus three or four hours from the Lakeside area *if* you don't get seriously lost!

By motorcycle or mountain bike, just follow the road all the way. It actually passes below Sarangkot and continues just below the ridge line, before a track branches off to the right leading back the 1km or so to Sarangkot.

The view back down over Phewa Tal is equally fine and from the top of Sarangkot it takes about two hours to walk down to the lake. It's easy to get lost on the way up from the lake but coming down from Sarangkot is straightforward: You make a very steep descent down stone stairs all the way down the hillside and through the forest. If you're exhausted when you reach the lake, there are often boatmen waiting to paddle you back to the Lakeside area.

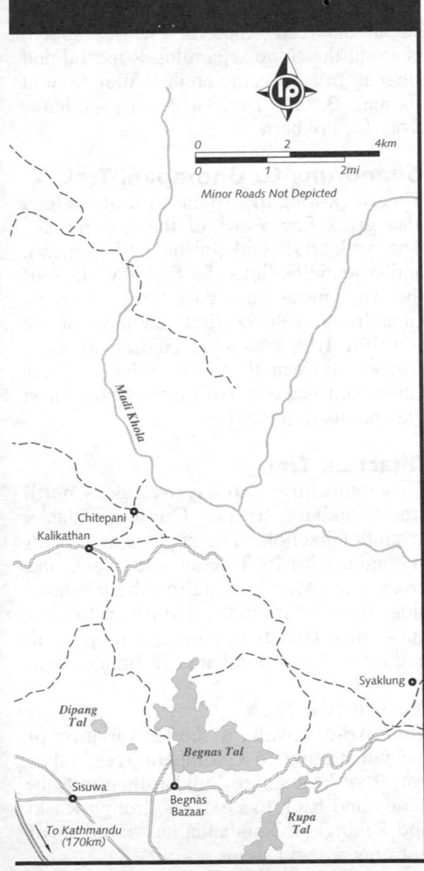

An alternative to the routes via the Binde Basini Temple or the Phewa Tal is the walk from Bhairab Tole in the northern part of Pokhara's bazaar via the village of Gyarjati. Another hour beyond Sarangkot will take you to Kaski or Kaskikot at 1788m. The hill is topped by a **Bhagwati temple**.

Kahun Danda

To the north-east of the bazaar area of Pokhara is Kahun Danda (*danda* means hill). It takes about three hours to walk to this popular viewpoint at 1560m and there's a lookout tower on top of the ridge. The walk starts from the Mahendrapul Bridge and continues through Phulbari and up the gradual slope to the top. The remains of the 18th-century **Kanhu Kot** stand on the hilltop.

Mahendra Gufa & Bat Cave

The limestone cave of Mahendra Gufa has some very limited stalactites as well as stalagmites, and is hardly worth the effort. The cave is lit by electric light, so you don't need a guide, although they are available at the gate for Rs 30.

More interesting is the so-called Bat Cave, about a 10-minute walk from Mahendra Gufa. We're not talking caped crusaders here, but real bats, thousands of them, which hang from the ceiling of this cave. Unlike Mahendra Gufa, the Bat Cave is unlit and so you will need a good flashlight (torch) or you could hire one of the would-be guides (no fixed rate) who hang around the entrance.

Both caves are open from 7 am to 6 pm daily and there's a Rs 10 entry charge to each. You could walk to the caves from Pokhara, although the route is basically through a residential area of Pokhara and so is not particularly interesting. Getting there by bicycle or taxi is a better bet.

Rupa Tal & Begnas Tal

These two lakes are the second- and third-largest in the valley, but few travellers visit them even though they're only 15km east of Pokhara.

Buses run regularly from Pokhara to Begnas Bazaar, the small market centre at the very end of the ridge that divides the two lakes. From there it's a pleasant stroll along the ridge to the other end of either lake. This is actually the final part of the Annapurna Skyline Trek.

Places to Stay & Eat As this is part of a major trekking route there are a number of basic trekking lodges in the area – just wander along the ridge until you find something.

One of the nicest is the ***Rupa View Point***, well signposted off the main trail and with views over Rupa Tal. It's a traditional family home with a couple of extra rooms that were built for trekkers, and the welcome is warm. Doubles cost Rs 150.

At the top of the scale is the beautiful ***Begnas Lake Resort*** *(☎ 061-60030, ⓔ villas@begnas.mos.com.np)*, nestled right on the shore of Begnas Tal, near the saddle with Rupa Tal. It consists of very tasteful stone bungalows with wooden floors made of local material, and it's set in a garden of fruit trees, which supply the resort with much of its needs. The views of the lake and mountains are excellent, and there's a small swimming pool, which is filled with fresh lake water. Singles/doubles cost US$100/110. The resort is accessible by boat (ring ahead to the hotel) or by road (local buses and 4WD) from Begnas Bazaar.

POKHARA

SHORT TREKS

See also the boxed text 'Trekking Around Pokhara' in the Trekking chapter.

Annapurna Skyline Trek

The three- or four-day Annapurna Skyline Trek has also been dubbed the 'Royal Trek', as Britain's Prince Charles walked it some years ago. It's a fine trek to do with children as it doesn't reach any great altitude, it doesn't entail any particularly long walking days and there's always plenty to see. It's not a heavily trekked area, however, so there is no village inn accommodation en route, except around the Begnas Tal end.

There are several possible variations on the route but basically the walk starts from the Kathmandu-Pokhara (Prithvi) Hwy, a few kilometres east of Pokhara, climbs up to a ridge and then for most of the walk follows ridges with fine views of the Annapurnas before leading back down into the Pokhara Valley.

The walk passes through some small villages such as Kalikathan, Shaklung and Chisopani before it drops down to the stream that feeds Rupa Tal. The final stretch is along the ridge separating Rupa Tal and Begnas Tal, emerging on the valley floor at Begnas Bazaar from where buses leave from for Pokhara.

Ghandrung to Ghorapani Trek

This week-long trek to the west of Pokhara also gives fine views of the Annapurnas. The walk starts and finishes at Birethanti, and essentially links the first few days of the Annapurna Sanctuary Trek as far as Ghandrung with the first few days of the Jomsom Trek as far as Ghorapani, then crosses between those two villages. Near Ghorapani is Poon Hill, one of the finest viewpoints in the region.

Ghachok Trek

This interesting two-day trek goes north from Pokhara to the Gurung villages around Ghachok. The walk starts from Hyangja, with its Tibetan settlement, and crosses the Mardi Khola (on the left-hand side after the fork in the Seti River) to Lhachok, then Ghachok, before turning south and returning to Pokhara via Batulechaur.

Naudanda Trek

This two-day walk, a shorter variation of the Ghandrung to Ghorapani Trek, takes you from Hyangja to Suikhet then to Naudanda and back to Pokhara through Kaski and Sarangkot. Naudanda has a variety of guesthouses and shops.

Kathmandu to Pokhara

For many people, the 206km-long highway between Kathmandu and Pokhara, the Prithvi Hwy, will be their first taste of Nepal's Middle Hills, and although for most of the way the road follows rivers at the bottom of deep valleys there are still some magical views – rock gorges and river rapids, precipitous hills, tiered rice terraces and glimpses of the Himalaya.

Migrants from around Nepal (especially the Kathmandu Valley) have been attracted by the economic opportunities, albeit minimal, offered in the roadside towns that have sprung up along the route. Most of these towns contain the usual unattractive collection of shanties and two-storey concrete boxes. There are, however, some interesting places (west of Mugling and off the main road) that are worth visiting, including Gorkha, which was the original capital for the Shah dynasty, and Bandipur, which is an old Newari trading settlement.

The countryside is inhabited by Bahun, Chhetri, Magar and Gurung peoples. The large multistoreyed houses, especially east of Mugling, are most likely owned by Bahuns and Chhetris, but around Mugling the region is dominated by Magars, and to a lesser extent, Gurungs. Historically, the Magars had their own independent kingdoms in western Nepal. Both Magars and Gurungs played a major role in Prithvi Narayan Shah's armies (which unified Nepal), and have since been recruited in large numbers by both the British and Indian armies to serve in the so-called Gurkha regiments.

Partly thanks to the money that these Gurkhas earn, much of the region seems relatively prosperous, although some Magar families are desperately poor. Land holdings are small, but the region seems to have avoided major problems such as overpopulation, deforestation and land degradation. The intensive, traditional forms of agriculture – based on rice cultivation and a small number of domestic animals – seem to be quite sophisticated and sustainable.

KATHMANDU TO NAUBISE

The road leaves from the western end of Tripureshwar Marg and runs through straggling roadside bazaars. About 10km from town, all heavy traffic stops at a police checkpoint to pay a toll at Thankot, and 4km later the road crosses the rim of the valley. In clear weather there are views (from east to west) of the Ganesh himal, himal Chuli, and the twin peaks of Manaslu himal. You also look down over incredible terracing rising from the Trisuli River and Mahesh Khola.

The road from the rim of the valley to Naubise is in generally good condition, with the occasional bad spot. It snakes dramatically down the steep hillside in a series of switchbacks. This is a notoriously dangerous and congested section of road, and is further enlivened by the antics of the drivers (mainly trucks and buses) as they jockey for position. Everyone tries to overtake everyone else, seemingly unhindered by minor impediments such as blind corners or oncoming vehicles, and vehicles topple over the edge with alarming regularity. A tunnel from Thankot to Naubise has been mooted as a way of bypassing this section, but it exists only on paper for the foreseeable future.

At Naubise, the Tribhuvan Hwy joins the road after its spectacular journey from Hetauda (see the boxed text 'Travelling Along the Mahendra Highway – Eastern Terai' in the Terai chapter for details of that route).

NAUBISE TO MUGLING

From Naubise, the road follows the small Mahesh Khola to the point where it joins the Trisuli River just past Baireni (52km from Kathmandu). It then continues along the Trisuli Valley through the small town of Gajuritar.

Around **Malekhu** the gorge is still attractively forested. Just before Malekhu, a bridge over the river leads to Trisuli Bazaar, superseding the old, winding, single-lane road that leaves the valley at Kakani.

Just after Malekhu there are a number of small restaurants, which are good places to break the journey. The ***Hill Top Restaurant***

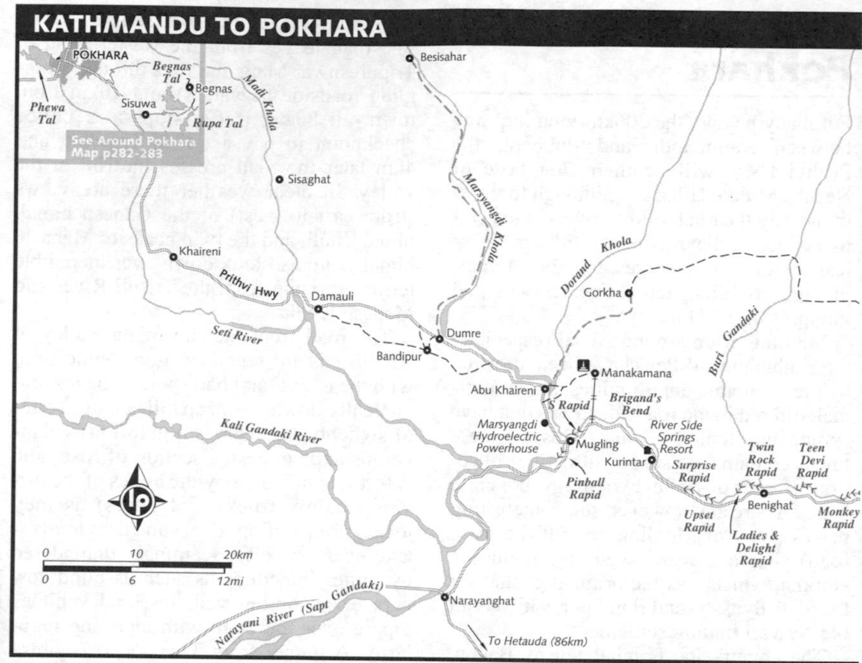

has a great view over the river where many rafting trips start, and has good food that is also reasonably priced. The ***Blue Heaven Restaurant***, which is about 75km from Kathmandu and 4km before Benighat, is virtually on the beach.

At **Benighat**, the large Buri River flows into the Trisuli from the north, giving rafters the volume of water required for plenty of excitement. The road continues to follow the westward-flowing Trisuli to Mugling, where it meets the equally large Marsyangdi Khola, which flows south-east.

About 8km before Mugling is **Kurintar**, and here you will find the surprisingly sophisticated ***River Side Springs Resort*** *(☎ 056-29429, ⓔ nangint@ccsl.com.np)*. It consists of a number of comfortable cabins and an airy central lodge building; it has a swimming pool just a stone's throw from the river. It's a popular weekend getaway for Kathmandu expats. The cost for cabins is US$50/60, which have fan and bathroom and a small verandah. A 50% discount is available to residents of Nepal.

Also in Kurintar is ***Manakamana Village Resort*** *(☎ 01-252560, ⓔ om@hons.com.np)* with rooms at US$15/20, or US$20/25 with air-con.

MUGLING

Mugling is at the junction between the most important road from the plains (from Narayanghat) and the Kathmandu-Pokhara (Prithvi) Hwy, so it is a popular stop for buses and trucks. It's 110km from Kathmandu and 96km from Pokhara, and it lies at an elevation of just 208m, making it the lowest town between Kathmandu and Pokhara.

The town is also at the junction of the westward-flowing Trisuli and the eastward-flowing Marsyangdi Rivers, which together form the Narayani, a major tributary of the Ganges. This is the finishing point for most of the serious white-water rafting

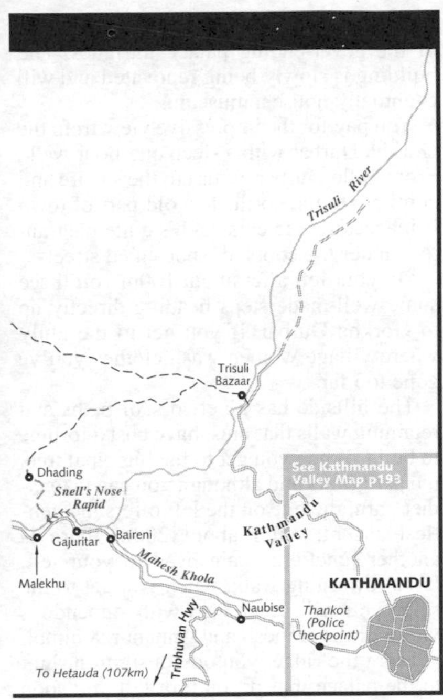

trips on the Trisuli, and the launching place for the more sedate trips down the Narayani to Narayanghat and the Royal Chitwan National Park.

Most buses travelling between Kathmandu and Pokhara stop here for a meal break, so there are plenty of hawkers and hangers-on milling around. Keep an eye on your gear, and don't leave valuables on the bus.

Places to Stay & Eat

There are literally dozens of restaurants that serve good dal bhaat for around Rs 50. Most are owned by Thakalis, and there is little to distinguish one restaurant from another.

Mugling would not be a pleasant place to spend a night. There are plenty of hotels, but few are interested in having a Westerner stay, since their main business is prostitution. One that does accommodate the occasional stranded backpacker is the ***Hotel Machhapuchare***, towards the western end of town, near the toll barrier. Avoid the noisy front rooms, and instead take one at the rear, which go for Rs 220 with private bathroom. The restaurant downstairs is popular with some of the tourist minibuses that do the Kathmandu to Pokhara run.

For those who are able to afford it, there is a slightly incongruous motel on the Pokhara side of town just over the bridge. The ***Motel du Mugling*** (*☎ 056-29434*) is attractively sited by the confluence of the two rivers. It is very comfortable and has a pleasant terrace with views. The restaurant here does decent food. The singles/doubles are well fitted out, and not bad value at US$15/20.

MUGLING TO ABU KHAIRENI

Leaving Mugling, a suspension bridge crosses the Narayani River just below the junction of the Trisuli and Marsyangdi Rivers. About 3km farther on you reach the **Marsyangdi Hydroelectric Powerhouse**. Water is diverted to the building you see beside the road from a dam 12km away. The road from here to Abu Khaireni winds through a narrow gorge of the Marsyangdi, and it's probably the most scenic part of the whole trip.

Next you reach Abu Khaireni, 8km from Mugling, another roadside bazaar town. It is at the intersection of the road to Gorkha, and is the starting point for the climb to the **Manakamana Temple**. To get to the temple, turn right off the highway on the road to Gorkha; continue for 1km until you see the Manakamana Hotel on the right; turn right and cross the suspension bridge over the river, and then keep climbing for three or four hours!

The soft alternative is the new Austrian-built **cable car**, which terminates right by the highway near Mugling (see the boxed text 'Manakamana Cable Car').

GORKHA

☎ 064

Gorkha, 24km north of the Kathmandu-Pokhara (Prithvi) Hwy, is accessible by a good sealed road that intersects with the highway at Abu Khaireni, 8km west of Mugling. The countryside is spectacular and Gorkha itself is well worth visiting.

Manakamana Cable Car

A few kilometres from Mugling is the Manakamana cable car, which whisks pilgrims up to the Manakamana Temple (one of the most popular temples in Nepal) on the top of the ridge across the Trisuli River. The cable car was built by an Austrian company and is very popular, especially on Saturdays when you may have to wait for an hour or more to get on.

In addition to regular passenger cars there are three freight cages, which transport sacrificial animals up to meet their maker (no charge!).

Trivia buffs might like to know the following: the trip time is eight minutes and 40 seconds, it's 2.8km in length and the vertical rise is 1034m.

Nepalis pay Rs 200/250 one way/return; for foreigners it's US$8/10 plus 12% tax. The lift operates from 9 am (8 am Saturday) to 5 pm daily but stops in the middle of the day from noon to 1.30 pm.

Hardy souls who want to climb up to the temple from the road should see under Mugling to Abu Khaireni for details.

Gorkha Durbar

Gorkha Durbar, a fort, palace and temple complex, is the centrepoint and highlight of Gorkha. Some of the building is believed to date from the reign of King Ram Shah (1606–36), but later generations have made alterations, often utilising Newari artisans.

The complex is a triumph of Nepali architecture – perched like an eagle's nest high above the town in a perfect defensive position – with superb views of plunging valleys and the soaring Himalaya. It is very easy to imagine an ambitious prince looking out over this dramatic landscape and dreaming of ruling all he could see – and more.

To get to Gorkha Durbar, walk north from the bus station until you come to several small temples (Vishnu, Krishna and Ganesh) surrounding a tank. Head to your right until you come to a square, to the right of which is **Tallo Durbar**, a large, square Newari-style building that was built in 1835 and housed a Rana who had been banished from Kathmandu for playing a role in one of the never-ending palace intrigues. The building is slowly being renovated and will eventually house a museum.

You pay for the impressive view from the Gorkha Durbar with a steep one-hour walk. From Tallo Durbar, return to the square and continue to the north. The old part of town is inaccessible to cars, so it's quite pleasant to wander the cobbled, shop-lined streets.

On your left after about 100m you'll see some well-made steps heading directly up to Gorkha Durbar. If you get to the gully where village women wash clothes you've gone too far.

The hillside has a network of paths and retaining walls that must have cost a fortune to build. When you get to the big pipal tree, the path forks and although you can take either path, the one on the left offers the gentlest ascent. After about 200m there is another junction; again head to your left. It's a rewarding walk; when you get to the ridge you will be greeted with stupendous views of the Ganesh and Annapurna himal.

From the ridge, you obviously turn right to the palace, but if you turn left you soon come to **Tallokot**, a small, old fort now used as a sacrificial site.

Photography is not permitted once you are inside the Gorkha Durbar complex, and this rule is strictly enforced by soldiers, so you may want to try to capture something on film from here. Officially you are not allowed to wear leather inside the complex, so wear sandshoes or a thick old pair of socks if you are going to do some serious exploration, though this rule is not strictly enforced.

If you enter from the west, the first building on your left is the **Kalika Temple** (note the 'Star of David' window), which has some superb woodcarving. Only a special caste of Brahmin priests and the king can enter, but sacrifices are made outside.

The main palace, called the **Dhuni Pati**, has latticed windows all around the top floor but unfortunately you're not allowed to enter, so you can only imagine the breezy rooms that lie behind. This was Prithvi Narayan's birthplace and an 'eternal' flame has been burning inside ever since his rule.

Next, walk up a few steps. You'll see a **priests' house** on the left and two bells on the right. Between the latter are stairs descending to a cave where a reclusive saint named Gorkhanath once lived.

Beyond the priests' house is a four-faced **Shiva lingam**. You can descend to servants' quarters and a temple on the next level, then down again to a crude but dramatic repainted carving of Hanuman, the monkey god, and six carved stelae.

From here it's another half-hour walk east to **Upkallot**, the highest point on the ridge, with the ruins of a fort, and a telecommunications tower. The views over the palace and across to the Himalaya are stupendous.

Places to Stay

There are some cheap, basic accommodation options near the Gorkha bus station. The small ***New Amrit Lodge*** is very basic, but it's a friendly place and some rooms have sensational views. Doubles/triples with shared bathroom cost Rs 120/180.

The ***Hotel Gorkha Prince*** (☎ *20131*) is just across the road from the Amrit and is much bigger with a variety of rooms. The inner ones can be gloomy, so ask to see more than one. Singles/doubles with shared bathroom cost Rs 120/180, slightly more with private bathroom.

The ***Gurkha Inn*** (☎ *20206*), close by, has a very pleasant garden setting, and the views from the terrace are excellent. The building itself is Nepali mock-Tudor in style, but it is also very pleasant and airy. The rooms are comfortably furnished and cost US$21/31, although heavy discounts are available, depending on demand.

The ***Hotel Gorkha Bisauni*** (☎ *20107*) is a couple of hundred metres farther down the hill. The rooms, with phone and TV, are quite comfortable, and are good value at US$10/12 with a shared bathroom and US$17/22 with private bathroom. Discounts are available.

The ***Gorkha Hill Resort*** (☎ *20325*) has a superb site 4km before town (800m down a dirt road to the east of the main road at Laxmi Bazaar). The ageing but well-kept resort has a very pleasant garden setting,

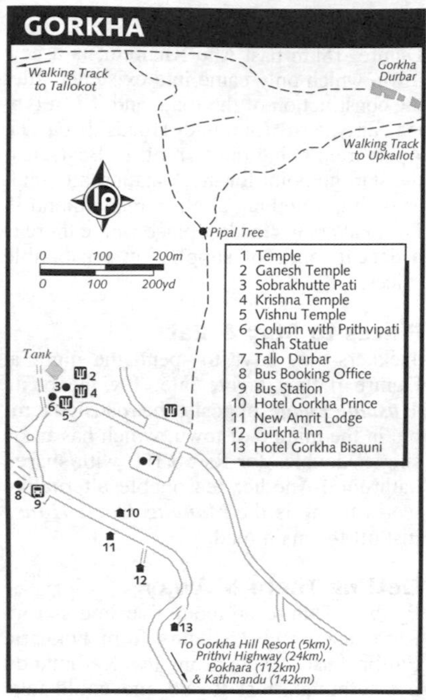

and there are great views across to Gorkha. Though not cheap, the resort is worth the US$34/44 charge.

Getting There & Away

The bus station is in the square in the centre of town, and the booking office for night buses is in the group of shops on the west side of the square. There are two buses a day to and from Pokhara (Rs 75, 4½ hours), and at least seven day buses to and from Kathmandu (Rs 92, five hours). Buses from Gorkha all leave early in the morning. There are also direct buses from Gorkha to Birganj (Rs 140, six hours, four daily), Sunauli (Rs 160, six hours, one daily) and Narayanghat (Rs 65, two hours, many daily).

If you are dropped off at Abu Khaireni, 8km from Mugling on the Kathmandu-Pokhara (Prithvi) Hwy, there are local minibuses to Gorkha (Rs 15). It's an enjoyable drive on a good road, but there's a steep climb for cyclists.

POKHARA

DUMRE

Dumre, 18km past Abu Khaireni, is a new town, which only came into existence after the construction of the road, and it is a typical, dirty, dusty (or muddy) roadside bazaar. Apart from being the turn-off to Besisahar, the starting point for the Annapurna Circuit Trek, it has nothing at all to recommend it. For trekkers it's the last place where there is a decent range of supplies at reasonable prices.

Places to Stay & Eat

Trekkers may have to spend the night at Dumre if they arrive late. Try the basic ***Mustang Lodge***, opposite the roadside temple in the middle of town, which has basic singles/doubles for Rs 50/100 with shared bathroom. Another reasonable alternative worth trying is the ***Manang Guest House*** just off the main road.

Getting There & Away

By bus, Dumre is about five hours from Kathmandu and 2½ hours from Pokhara. Public buses leave from the Kathmandu bus terminal, cost Rs 90 and could take longer that five hours; the fare from Pokhara is Rs 60. The tourist buses that travel between Pokhara and Kathmandu cost around Rs 150.

Many people start their trek by catching shared 4WDs or trucks to Besisahar. Expect to pay around Rs 500, although porters and local people pay less. The road is very rough and the journey can take up to five hours, though three hours is more common.

BANDIPUR

☎ 065

Straddling a dramatic ridge overlooking Dumre and with excellent views of the Marsyangdi Valley, and a broad sweep of the Himalaya from Dhaulagiri to Langtang, Bandipur is a beautiful Newari hilltop village just south of the Kathmandu-Pokhara (Prithvi) Hwy. It was once a major Newari trading centre on the route between Tibet and India, and its bazaar still hints at those days. Narrow stone-paved roads pass between temples and multistoreyed houses. With the construction of the main highway, and eradication of malaria in the Terai, Bandipur has been bypassed by the last 40 years. The result is that the town today is a perfect place to get a feel for Newari village life before the advent of concrete and consumerism. This is virtually virgin tourism territory – kids here still greet visitors with a 'namaste' without asking for a pen, sweets or one rupee – so visitors need to tread carefully.

Things to See

There are no real sights as such. The **Khagda Devi Temple** is just off the northern end of the bazaar, while the **Mahalaxmi Temple** is a short way to the east. More impressive, for the views if nothing else, is the **Thani Mai Temple**, which is perched at the top of the **Gurungche Hill**, about a 30-minute walk south-west of the bazaar. For easier views without much effort, head for the **Tundikhel**, the only area of flat land in town.

There is a **silk farm** an easy 30-minute walk south of the village, just off the trail which eventually leads to the Seti River. The staff don't speak much English but they'll happily show you around. Due to the risk of infection, you have to remove your shoes and step through an insecticide-powder dip to go into the rooms where the worms do their business.

If Bandipur has a 'must see' it is **Siddha Gufa**, supposedly the largest cave in Nepal. It lies below the town, about a 1½-hour walk, and is in fact much closer to the highway than Bandipur. The cave is probably best visited when leaving Bandipur, as you can continue down to the highway at Bimalnagar, and then grab a passing bus to Dumre, 1km to the west. The lower part of the path from the cave down to Bimalnagar is somewhat overgrown and can be a bit of a scramble. The cave itself is large and long (at least 200m) and you will need a guide with a decent flashlight or lantern to fully appreciate it. The limestone formations within the cave are impressive and undamaged. Guest houses in Bandipur should be able to arrange a guide – count on spending around Rs 300.

Places to Stay & Eat

There are a number of very basic lodges in the bazaar, although many are actually hostels for the Notre Dame School, an English-medium boarding school in Bandipur, which attracts pupils from all over the country. Don't expect any luxuries such as running water, but the reception is welcoming.

Pick of the bunch is probably the ***Bandipur Guest House*** *(☎ 20103)*, in a funky old building at the south end of the bazaar. Rooms cost Rs 150, and the meals are good.

Other than that, try the ***Raksha Hotel***, midway along the bazaar.

At the opposite end of the scale, and somewhat incongruous in old-time Bandipur, is the ***Bandipur Mountain Resort*** *(☎ 20125)* at the western end of Tundikhel. This place has a block of 10 very comfortable rooms at US$50 per person full board, or there are 10 double tents at US$35 per person.

For food it's dal bhaat tarakari all the way, twice a day. Eating at your guesthouse is probably your best bet.

Getting There & Away

The traditional way of getting to Bandipur was the old trade route, which heads off the highway about 500m west of Dumre. This is a three-hour walk up through some very pretty countryside; you may prefer to do this on the way down – or not at all.

The 7km link road up to Bandipur heads off the main highway about 3km west of Dumre. It is surfaced for about 1km, but then is as rough as guts for the rest of the way, although blacktop is coming (or that's the local rumour, anyway).

There is a daily bus to Narayanghat (at 9 am), and one or two daily buses to Pokhara (at 11 am, sometimes 2 pm). Failing that, there is an irregular trickle of tractors with large trailers bringing supplies up from Dumre and you can get a ride on the load – far from comfortable, but you will get there.

DUMRE TO POKHARA

From Dumre it is just 16km to the district headquarters of **Damauli**. This place has a bustling bazaar.

Soon after Damauli the road crosses a large bridge over the Madi Khola, and follows the Seti River for the remaining 54km to Pokhara. The next town is **Khaireni**, where a German-assisted agricultural project is based.

After Khaireni, the road passes the turn-off to Rupa Tal and Begnas Tal, which are the second- and third-largest lakes of the Pokhara Valley. **Sisuwa** is the last place en route to Pokhara, 12km away.

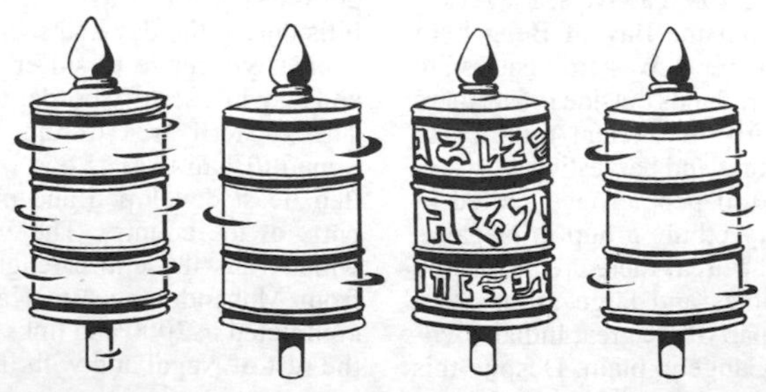

The Terai

When people think of Nepal, they tend to think of soaring snow-clad mountains rather than hot subtropical plains. Despite this, nearly half the country's population lives on a narrow strip of flat and fertile land that lies wedged between the Indian border and the mountains. This is known as the Terai (sometimes spelt Tarai).

With the Kathmandu Valley as well as the world's highest mountains a few hours away by bus, it is not surprising that the Terai is often just a transit zone for those travelling overland to and from India. While there is nothing here quite as startling as 8000m-high mountains, the region does have a beauty of its own, and some fascinating possibilities for travellers. The most well-known spots are the magnificent Royal Chitwan National Park, famous for its elephant safaris and wildlife; Lumbini, the birthplace of Buddha; and Janakpur, the birthplace of Sita (Rama's wife, from the *Ramayana*).

A dawn ride on an elephant through forests where you may come across tigers, rhinos, crocodiles and peacocks is unforgettable. Nor could anyone forget the neat mud-walled huts and brilliant saris amid the vivid green rice paddies that stretch the length of the Terai, or the strange waterlogged world of the Sapt Kosi's flood plain, with its birds, thatched villages, hyacinths and lilies.

Large sections of the Terai are still forested; the land is cut by numerous rivers, often grey and turbulent with melted snow and silt. These rivers burst from the hills onto the plains, a mere 100m above sea level yet over 1000km from the Bay of Bengal. In most parts of the Terai, Western visitors are rare and in the farmlands outside towns there is little to disturb the ancient routines of ploughing, planting and harvesting.

While many hill people have settled in the region (every ethnic group in Nepal is represented in the area) there are also some indigenous peoples and large groups that are culturally a part of the great Indian civilisations of the Gangetic plain. Despite this extraordinary diversity, the people of the Terai remain distinctively Nepali: unhurried, good humoured and friendly.

Highlights

- Going on an elephant safari at the beautiful national parks of Royal Chitwan and Royal Bardia, and spotting the royal Bengal tiger and the Indian one-horned rhinoceros
- Visiting peaceful Lumbini, the birthplace of Siddhartha Gautama, known as Buddha, the founder of Buddhism
- Soaking up the beauty of the Sapt Kosi flood plain, best seen from the Koshi Tappu Wildlife Reserve
- Joining pilgrims at Janakpur, one of the best places to absorb the atmosphere of a Hindu pilgrimage centre, with its temple to Sita and the festival of Sita Bibaha Panchami in November/December

Unfortunately, most of the border towns are new and unattractive, with Dickensian-looking industries on their outskirts, streets choked with buses and trucks, and little in the way of history or culture. The exception to this are the pilgrim centres of ancient Janakpur, with its sadhus and temples, and Lumbini, which remains more significant for what it was rather than what it is.

Chitwan should not be missed, and in the cool season (November to February) it is definitely worth travelling there from the hills during the day and seeing the country, even if you have to suffer a crowded bus and stay in a scruffy border town overnight. The western area of the Terai (west of Sunauli/Bhairawa) is one of the least visited, least developed and most interesting parts of the country. The Mahendra Hwy, which runs the entire length of the Terai from Mahendranagar to Kakarbhitta, was completed in 2000 and links the region with the rest of Nepal and with India.

HISTORY

Over the centuries, parts of the Terai have been under the sway of both the Nepali and Indian empires. Some regions were inhabited by sophisticated agricultural and urban communities as early as 800 BC, but the empires have come and gone, and at times the countryside has been completely reclaimed by forest. The stories of the area's decline are largely unknown, but disease and war certainly played a role – some parts were most recently depopulated as a result of the Muslim invasions of the 14th century. Malaria was a major problem here until the 1960s.

Without doubt the Terai's most famous son is Siddhartha Gautama – Buddha – who was born in 563 BC at Lumbini. Siddhartha was the son of Suddhodana who ruled a small state from Kapilavastu. The ruins near Taulihawa, west of Lumbini, are believed to be his capital. Archaeologists have identified many successive levels of human habitation at the site (see the Taulihawa & Tilaurakot section later in this chapter for more details).

The Terai's most famous daughter is Sita, who is believed to have been born where present-day Janakpur stands. The daughter of Janak, the king of Mithila (also known as Videha), Sita is famous for her faithful marriage to Rama, the hero of the Hindu epic the *Ramayana*, written in the 1st or 2nd century BC. The kingdom of Mithila lives on in the rich culture and language of Nepal's eastern Terai and India's northern Bihar region.

By 321 BC the Mauryan empire based at Patna in India was on the rise, swallowing the small principalities around it. Under the emepror Ashoka, the empire controlled more of the subcontinent than under any subsequent ruler until the British. Ashoka was one of Buddhism's greatest followers and missionaries, so it was perhaps inevitable that Ashoka would visit nearby Lumbini, then a thriving religious centre. In 245 BC he erected a stone pillar at Lumbini that can still be seen today. Some believe he travelled as far as Kathmandu.

The next great empire to rise in the region was the Gupta empire, again originally based in Patna, which flourished between AD 300 and 600, and extended its influence to Kathmandu and beyond. In the early 13th century, invading Mughals occupied large parts of northern India, driving many Hindu refugees towards Nepal and the Kathmandu Valley. It is believed that one of these groups founded the Malla dynasty which, under King Yaksha Malla, had extended its power from Kathmandu south to the Ganges River by the 15th century.

The next (and current) Kathmandu-based dynasty, the Shah, won control in 1768 and continued to expand Nepali borders until the kingdom was twice the size it is now, extending south into the Gangetic plain and east and west along the Himalaya. Eventually the Shahs and their famous Gurkha soldiers ran up against the British East India Company. In 1816, after two years of inconclusive war, the Nepalis were forced to sign a treaty that greatly reduced their territory. Land (including the city of Nepalganj) was returned to Nepal as a reward for its support for the British during the 1857 Indian Uprising (or War of Independence as it is known in India today).

Most of the Terai was heavily forested until the 1960s, although limited areas were settled, and indigenous Tharu groups were widely dispersed through the region. However, the drainage and spraying programs begun in 1954 markedly reduced the incidence of malaria, which allowed mass migration both south from the hills and north from India. Fertile soils and easy accessibility led to rapid development. The Terai is now the most important and the fastest-growing region for agricultural and industrial production in Nepal.

GEOGRAPHY

The Nepali Terai lies at the northern rim of the great Gangetic plain, which ranges from 60m to 300m above sea level and never exceeds more than 40km in width. The Gangetic plain runs table-flat from deep in India to the foothills of the Himalaya – the Chure hills (known as the Siwalik hills in India), which abruptly jump 1000m.

Several flat, wide 'valleys' known as the Inner Terai lie behind the first range of hills. These include the valley along the Narayani

River (including part of Royal Chitwan National Park) and the Rapti River (east of Nepalganj).

The border with India, being a political creation, does not conform to any particular geographic barrier. To further blur the demarcation, the inhabitants on both sides come and go as they please.

The Terai accounts for 17% of Nepal's total area, but it is, in effect, the country's granary. In general, the soils are highly fertile and this, in addition to abundant water resources, permits the intensive cultivation of a wide variety of crops.

Unfortunately, outside the national parks the native forests are rapidly disappearing and suitable land is heavily exploited. Crop yields are already declining in some areas. The consequences of rapid population increase, deforestation and overworking the land are likely to be disastrous.

During the monsoon, parts of the Terai are subject to serious flooding. The relationship between deforestation in the hills and increased siltation and flooding on the plains is controversial, but there is no doubt that population growth in the hills and industrial development in the Kathmandu Valley are having a serious impact on downstream water quality. This is most critical in the dry season when many streams become mere trickles or dry up completely, and water flows are much reduced in even the major rivers.

CLIMATE

The Terai has a humid, subtropical climate with well over 1500mm of rainfall in most places. The most pleasant time to visit is November to February when you can expect daytime temperatures to average in the mid- to high 20°Cs, with cool nights. From April to September temperatures above 40°C are common and are combined with the additional discomfort of the monsoon from June to September.

FLORA

The Terai is subtropical, and the flora reflects this. Rapid development has led to large-scale deforestation, but fortunately a surprising amount of forest remains.

Substantial areas are still cloaked in sal *(Shorea robusta)* forests. These forests characteristically grow on well-drained soils and form relatively homogeneous communities. Sal is a magnificent, highly

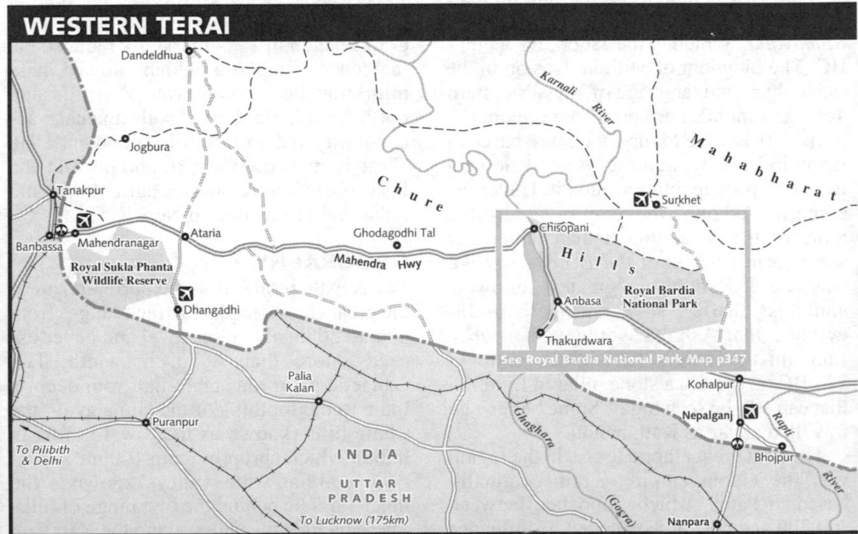

valued hardwood. It grows straight and true (averaging 30m when mature), and has long been used by builders and woodcarvers. The longevity of the buildings and the carvings in the Kathmandu Valley is due to the strength and durability of this wood.

On swampier ground there are scrubby forests of khair *(Acacia catechu)* and shisham *(Dalbergia sissoo)*. Simal trees *(Bombax ceiba)* stand out above the others. Simal trees are notable for their spring display of large red flowers and when they are old they develop huge buttresses at their base.

There are also grasslands that form a diverse and complex community of over 50 species. Elephant grasses (the *Saccharum* family) can grow up to 8m high, but there are also shorter species such as khar that are vital for thatching.

FAUNA

The fauna of the Terai is striking although, as always, shy. From the road, the most obvious species are the handsome black-faced, grey *bandar* (langur monkeys) and the common, brown-red rhesus monkeys. You may also catch a glimpse of some of the many species of deer – including the *chital* (spotted), *mirga* (barking), *jarayo* (sambar), *laghuna* (hog), and swamp deer. The *nilgai* (blue cow), Asia's largest antelope, is also quite common, but you won't see it unless you make an effort.

The largest mammal is the *hathi* (Asian elephant), although it seems that there are now only a few individuals surviving in the wild at Royal Bardia National Park and Royal Sukla Phanta Wildlife Reserve. Not far behind in scale and impressiveness is the great *gaida* (Indian one-horned rhinoceros), which can be seen in the national parks and reserves at Chitwan, Bardia and Sukla Phanta.

There are a number of carnivores in the area, the most magnificent being the *bagh* (royal Bengal tiger) that, with thanks to the Terai's national parks, seems to have escaped extinction. There are also *chituwa* (leopards), wild dogs, jackals, civets, a few species of mongoose and cats.

You may also find *bhalu* (sloth bears), wild boars, porcupines, hares, bats, squirrels and *sarpa* (snakes) – some of which are poisonous (the cobra, krait and viper).

The rivers and lakes are home to mugger and gharial crocodiles and the extraordinary rare Gangetic dolphin.

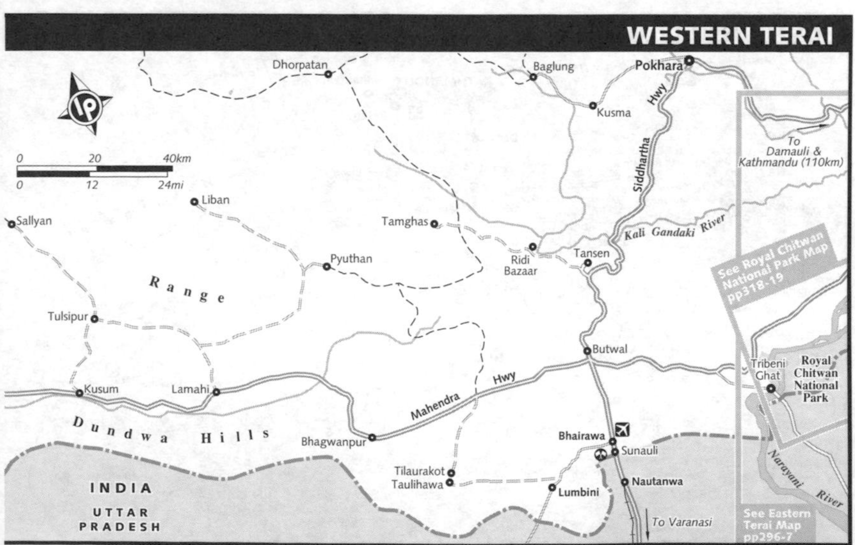

The Terai is a birder's delight, with more than 450 migrant and local species including cormorants, herons, egrets, storks, cranes, ibis, ducks, kites, goshawks, hawks, eagles, osprey, falcons, kestrels, quail curlews, sandpipers, snipes, gulls, terns, pigeons, parakeets, cuckoos, owls, kingfishers, woodpeckers, swallows, orioles, drongos, babblers, flycatchers, warblers...

The invertebrates range from butterflies to mosquitoes.

ECONOMY

Agriculture, as elsewhere in Nepal, is the major contributor to the economy, although the Terai is also home to most of the country's manufacturing industries (with the exception of the carpet industry). More than half the gross domestic product is produced in the Terai.

Many of the Terai's advantages stem from a single fact: it's flat! Development has been assisted by the relative ease with which roads and services can be established. Roads are crucial for industry, but they also enable health and education services, as well as fertilisers and improved seeds, to be delivered more efficiently.

Cash crops such as sugar cane, jute, tobacco and tea are grown alongside staples such as rice, wheat and maize. Land-holdings are much larger than in the hills, but the average size is still under two hectares – hardly a Texan cattle ranch – and they are getting smaller as the population grows. Surplus food is sold to markets in the Kathmandu Valley, although a considerable amount is also given directly to less-fortunate relatives in the hills.

Mechanised transport, proximity to Indian raw materials and the Indian market, and the availability of hydroelectric power has allowed the development of some industry. This is largely concentrated between Birganj and Hetauda, and around Biratnagar. Jute mills, tanneries and leather factories, biscuit and cigarette factories, drug manufacturers as well as a sugar refinary are in this area.

POPULATION & PEOPLE

The population has increased rapidly since the 1950s. In 1991 (the most recent census), 46.6% of the population of Nepal – or over 8.6 million people – lived in the Terai. Current estimates put the population of the Terai at around 11 million. As a result of migration from the mountains and hills, as well as a

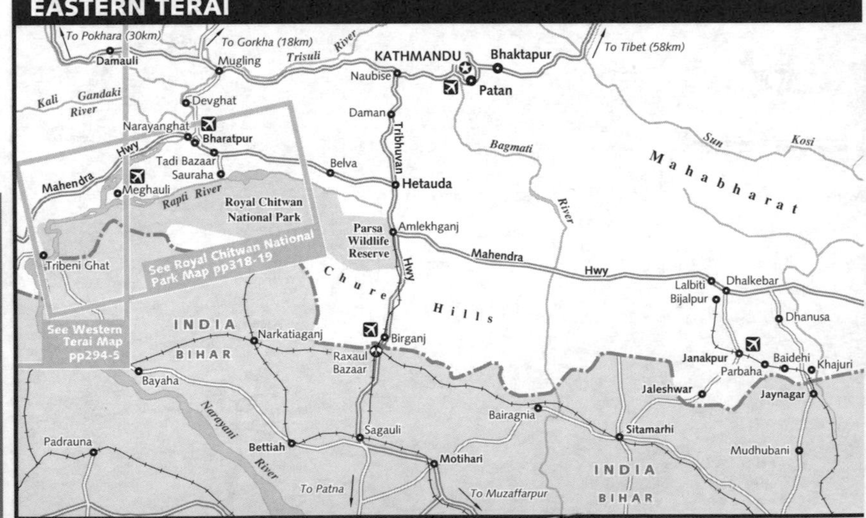

high birth rate, the population is increasing rapidly and will probably overtake that of the hills. Unfortunately, it is now clear that the Terai will not be able to absorb excess population from the hills indefinitely, and yet the hill population has continued to grow. Population pressures are rapidly mounting.

Internal migration has meant that the indigenous people of the Terai have been joined by people from every ethnic group in the country. Not surprisingly, many people are closely related to Indian groups in Bihar and Uttar Pradesh; Indo-Aryan subsistence farmers with dark skin, and who hold Hindu beliefs that are sometimes combined with forms of animism.

The largest ethnic group on the Terai is the Tharu (see People in the Facts about Nepal chapter for details). There are quite a number of smaller ethnic groups, none exceeding 40,000 people. They include the Danuwar, Darai, Djanghar, Koche, Majhi, Rajbansi, Satar and Tajpuri.

LANGUAGE

Apart from Nepali, the most widely spoken language of the Terai is Maithili, a language and culture shared with people on the Bihar side of the border. It is spoken by around two million Nepalis, especially around Janakpur and Biratnagar. The next most common language, Bhojpuri, is also used on both sides of the border and is spoken by around 1.5 million people in Nepal, especially around Birganj – this language mingles with Maithili. Abadhi is another Indian-based language, spoken by around 250,000 Nepalis in around Bhairawa and Nepalganj.

INFORMATION

There are tourist information centres near the borders at Kakarbhitta (☎ 023-20208), Birganj (☎ 051-22083), and at Bhairawa (☎ 071-20304) as well as Janakpur (☎ 041-20755), but they are of little practical help.

Most services, including post, telephone and electricity, are more widely and efficiently available in the Terai than in the rest of the country outside the major cities.

Remember not to drink water or use ice in the Terai unless you know it has been boiled or properly treated. Skip the dairy products (with the exception of curd) and salads, and peel the fruit. Wash your hands before eating. (See the Health section in the Facts for the Visitor chapter for more details.)

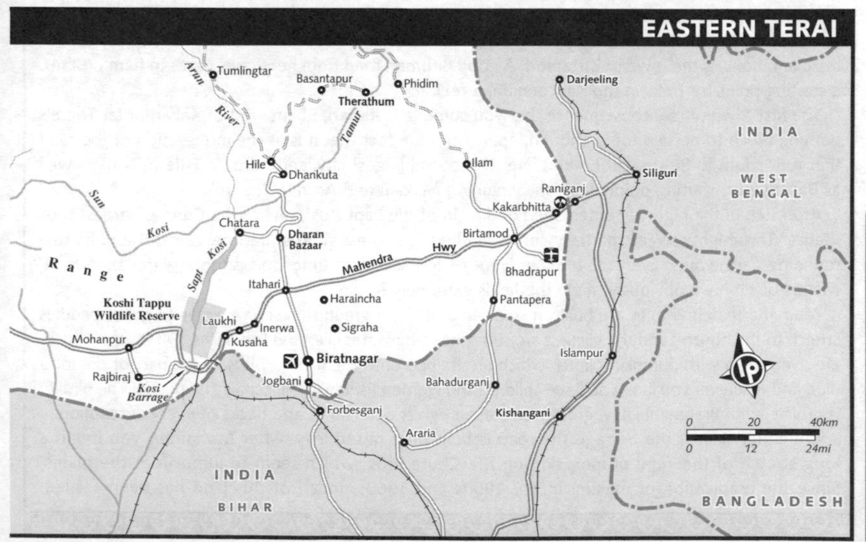

GETTING THERE & AWAY

The Terai is easily accessible from West Bengal, Bihar and Uttar Pradesh in India and from Kathmandu and Pokhara in Nepal. Bus and plane services are frequent and relatively cheap. The long-distance express buses are even reasonably comfortable, if not entirely safe. The Indian railway system runs close to the border at several points, but most people use the buses – they are much quicker.

Air

Royal Nepal Airlines (RNAC), Buddha Air, Mountain Air, Skyline Air, Necon Air, Yeti Air, Cosmic Air, Gorkha Airlines and Shangri-La Air all fly to a number of towns in the Terai from Kathmandu. For more details see the Nepal Air Fares chart in the Getting Around chapter, and the relevant Getting There & Away sections for each town.

Land

Roads enter the Terai at numerous border crossings in the south. Most travellers going to or from Nepal cross at Nautanwa (India) to Sunauli/Bhairawa (Nepal), but the other crossings open for foreigners to use are Raxaul Bazaar (India) to Birganj (Nepal), Jamunaha (India) to Nepalganj (Nepal), Banbassa (India) to Mahendranagar (Nepal) in the far west, and in the extreme east of the country from Siliguri (India, near Darjeeling) to Kakarbhitta (Nepal). See the Getting There & Away chapter for details.

GETTING AROUND

Bus

Although airlines service all the major centres, most normal mortals travel by bus. This can be a serious penance, for although the price is not high in rupees, it can be in terms of comfort and sanity! The express buses (often running at night only) are usually OK, although wherever possible you should check with a local as to which are the best companies.

Unfortunately, most day buses are of the stopping-all-stations variety and they can be horrifically crowded. Bodies occupy or cling to every possible centimetre. Under

Travelling Along the Mahendra Highway – Eastern Terai

Kakarbhitta to Narayanghat

The start of the Mahendra Hwy in the east is **Kakarbhitta**. About 17km farther west, past several tea plantations, is the town of **Birtamod**. A good bitumen road from here goes north to **Ilam** (78km), a starting point for treks in the Kanchenjunga region.

The first town of real consequence that you come to is **Itahari**, 90km west of Kakarbhitta. There's nothing much to be said for it, though, apart from the fact that it is at the intersection of the road that runs south to **Biratnagar** (24km), Nepal's second largest city, and north to **Hile** (93km) as well as **Basantapur**, starting points for Kanchenjunga, Makalu and Arun Valley treks.

After Itahari the highway enters the flood plain of the **Sapt Kosi**, one of the Ganges' largest tributaries. This mighty river is partially controlled by the impressive **Kosi Barrage** (a dam) and its surrounding earthworks. Even so, the low-lying region seems at times to be more water than land. Metres of silt have obviously made the fields extremely fertile.

Mud and thatch villages are built on small areas of high ground. In spring, emerald green paddies stretch to the horizon and the villages are surrounded by water lilies and hyacinths. Often, the houses are overgrown with pumpkin plants, which are trained onto the roofs. Fish is a vital part of the local diet, and wherever you look you'll see children and women fishing in the canals and ponds. The birdlife is prolific, with Brahmani kites, greater and lesser egrets and cranes and ducks of every description.

On either side of the barrage the road is built on a raised levy. After **Mohanpur** you begin a long stretch of the Terai proper, skirting the **Chure hills**, which seem to jump from the plains. Since the eradication of malaria in the 1950s and 1960s, much of this land has been settled.

these circumstances, the most comfortable place to be is the roof, although you will need to protect yourself from the elements. The problem is that if you travel by night you miss the views, and yet if you travel by day, you run the risk of missing the views anyway because you are jammed inside a bus and suffering extreme discomfort.

Whether you travel by day or night, you will get plenty of excitement. Combine high speeds with poorly maintained vehicles, suicidal overtaking manoeuvres, animals, trucks, children, rickshaws, unmarked roadworks, invincible pedestrians and the potential outcome is obvious, and also usually graphically illustrated by wrecked trucks and buses alongside the road. Though buses can't plummet over cliffs on the plains of the Terai, they can wind up to some pretty scary and impressive speeds.

See the Getting Around chapter for more details on bus travel.

Car

If you are travelling in a group, or if you have the necessary funds, it is worth considering hiring a car and driver (or motorcycle) in Kathmandu to explore the Terai. When shared among a group, this is reasonably priced at around US$35 per day, plus petrol, for a small car that seats three passengers, and has obvious advantages.

Bicycle

Another alternative is to ride a bicycle, preferably a mountain bike that is sufficiently sturdy to deal with rough roads. Cycling conditions are ideal: Motorised traffic is relatively sparse on the Mahendra Hwy, there are villages at regular intervals, the climate during winter is mild and dry, and the countryside is beautiful and mostly flat.

Getting to the Terai from Kathmandu you either have to tackle the daunting Tribhuvan Hwy via Daman (at an altitude of 2322m!), or the section of the Kathmandu-Pokhara (Prithvi) Hwy that is between Kathmandu and Mugling, which is very busy and dangerous. Consider catching buses over these scary sections.

See the Mountain Biking chapter for more details.

Travelling Along the Mahendra Highway – Eastern Terai

Many of the settlers have come from the hills, but have swiftly adapted to their new environment and have prospered. Frequently, houses have been built on stilts to cope with the annual floods.

Nearly 110km past the Kosi Barrage you reach Dalkebar; the turn-off to **Janakpur** (24km south of the highway), one of the Terai's most interesting cities. The countryside is intensively cultivated and densely populated. As you travel farther west, however, there are fewer people, fewer bright Indian saris and more trees. Between Dalkebar and **Amlekhganj** there is an almost unbroken stretch of magnificent sal forest.

At Amlekhganj, the Mahendra Hwy briefly joins the Tribhuvan Hwy for the 26km run north to **Hetauda**. From Hetauda, the road runs west along the edge of the Mahabharat Range and the north bank of the Rapti River. There are some rich, cultivated fields, but a great deal of forest remains. On the other side of the Rapti lies the **Royal Chitwan National Park**, famous for its tigers and rhinos.

After Belva, the valley begins to broaden and this area, called the Inner Terai for obvious reasons, is flat, fertile and heavily populated. The villages along here are Tharu and Gurung, among other hill peoples. About 55km west of Hetauda, you come to the small roadside town of **Tadi Bazaar**, the departure point for Royal Chitwan National Park.

The road from Tadi to **Narayanghat** (15km) is not particularly interesting; there's a lot of development, and Narayanghat and Bharatpur run together and sprawl a long way. All buses heading for Kathmandu travel west to Narayanghat and then turn north, following the Narayani River through the hills to Mugling (36km) on the Kathmandu-Pokhara (Prithvi) Hwy.

Eastern Terai

There are a number of different routes that travellers can chose from when travelling through Nepal. Information in the Eastern Terai is ordered from east to west; from Kakarbhitta to Narayanghat.

The main east-west link across the entire Terai is the Mahendra Hwy, which is generally in excellent condition. A number of attractive hill towns are accessible from the highway, including Ilam (which is accessible from Birtamod); Hile, Dharan Bazaar and Dhankuta (accessible from Itahari); and Daman, which is between Hetauda and Naubise. A description of the journey along the eastern portion of the Mahendra is provided in the boxed text 'Travelling Along the Mahendra Highway – Eastern Terai' earlier in this chapter.

KAKARBHITTA

☎ 023

The sole reason for the existence of Kakarbhitta is its proximity to India. This is the border post for road traffic going to or from Siliguri and Darjeeling. In fact, it's not much more than a glorified bus stop, and it's difficult to imagine that anyone would want to stay longer than the time it takes to make a bus connection.

The surrounding countryside is attractive, however, and you can tell you're not far from Darjeeling when you see the tea plantations on the outskirts of town.

Orientation & Information

There is a tourist office (☎ 20208) just inside Nepal, past customs on the northern side of the road (on the right if you're coming into Nepal from India).

The border is open to tourists from 7 am to 7 pm. As you move away from the border the main bus parking area is a dusty (or muddy) quadrangle on your right, followed by the bazaar and village.

The Nepal Rastra Bank isn't signposted, but it's the unmistakable pink monstrosity on the south side of the road. There are two banks on the Nepali side, but only the Nepal Rastra Bank changes money; it's open from 7 am to 7 pm daily. There is one moneychanger in the far corner of the bus park, though this place only accepts cash.

Places to Stay & Eat

There are plenty of places to stay around the bazaar, but the quality of these is pretty variable. If you want to get a decent night's sleep, steer clear of the places that front onto the bus park.

The ***Kanchan Hotel*** *(☎ 70015)* is not a bad choice. The rooms are clean, and the restaurant serves decent food. The cost is Rs 180 for a double with shared bathroom or Rs 280 with bathroom. Bigger rooms with TV and phone cost Rs 500.

The ***Hotel Deurali*** close by is typical of the bazaar cheapies, and has double rooms with shared bathroom at Rs 150.

The ***Hotel Rajat*** *(☎ 70033)*, one block behind the rear of the bus park, is the best hotel on offer. There's a few doubles with shared bathroom at US$4, large rooms with TV and phone at US$13 and deluxe rooms at US$20. However, these prices are highly negotiable. The hotel also has a bright and airy restaurant on the ground floor.

Getting There & Away

Air The nearest airport is at Bhadrapur, 10km south of Birtamod, which is 13km west of Kakarbhitta. Daily flights go to Kathmandu (US$99) with Buddha Air, Cosmic Air, Gorkha Airlines (☎ 023-20549), Mountain Air and Necon Air.

To/From India There are plenty of land connections to destinations both in Nepal and India. Many people buy through tickets between Kathmandu and Darjeeling, but this is relatively expensive and is unnecessary. With a through ticket you travel the Kakarbhitta to Kathmandu section at night and miss the sights. Also many travellers are ripped off buying through tickets between India and Nepal – bookings fail to materialise or are for lower quality services than those paid for. Admittedly, these problems are not nearly as common on this route as they are on some others. See the Getting There & Away chapter for more details.

It's a 10-minute walk from Kakarbhitta to the Indian border post of Raniganj; rickshaws cost about Rs 10 (INRs 6). From Raniganj there are direct share taxis to Darjeeling (INRs 100, four hours), Kalimpong (INRs 70, three hours) and Siliguri (INRs 70, one hour).

To/From Other Parts of Nepal There is plenty of competition for your business if you plan to buy a bus ticket, so it's worth shopping around. The prices won't vary, but the departure times and the quality of the buses can. Night buses can be booked at the office in the front of the bus park.

Night buses for Kathmandu and Pokhara leave between 3 and 5 pm (Rs 408, 13 hours). Not only would this be an epic and unpleasant journey, but you would miss the views. If time and weather allow, consider catching a day bus to Janakpur and stopping there; buses leave between 6.30 and 9 am (Rs 185, five hours). The road is quite interesting between Itahari and Janakpur; it runs across the flood plain of the massive Sapt Kosi. See the boxed text 'Travelling on the Mahendra Highway – Eastern Terai' in this chapter for more details.

There is one night bus for Birganj (Rs 256, eight hours) and there are day buses to Biratnagar (Rs 77, 3½ hours).

The overnight buses from Kathmandu all arrive in Kakarbhitta before 10 am; they leave Kakarbhitta for Kathmandu between 3 and 5 pm. Night buses to Kakarbhitta leave from the Kathmandu Bus Terminal at 4 and 5 pm. Book a day in advance.

ILAM

☎ 027

Ilam is an attractive small town at the centre of Nepal's tea industry; the climate of the surrounding hills is similar to Darjeeling's. Few Westerners visit, but there is some reasonable accommodation available, some tea plantations to see and there are good walks in the area.

Places to Stay & Eat

The cheapest places are around the bus park at the bottom end of the town. These can be noisy however, as buses start around 4 am. Of these places, the ***Maivalley Guest House*** is among the better ones. The ***Deurali Lodge*** *(☎ 20228)* is another bus-park cheapie; both places cost less than Rs 200 for a double.

The ***Tamu Guest House*** is a bit farther away and so escapes the noise. The rooms are OK and cost Rs 180 for a double.

Danfe Guest House is set in among the tea plantations, and offers real peace and quiet. Rooms are basic but clean, and good value at Rs 130/250 for a single/double. The guesthouse is a few minutes' walk from the bus park; take the stairs up at the rear corner of the bus park, turn right onto the track, then left at the T-junction.

The ***Green View Guest House*** *(☎ 21030)* is the best on offer. The rooms are large, clean and modern; most do indeed have a green view – tea plantations. Large doubles are Rs 280 with shared bathroom and Rs 380 with bathroom.

There's not much in the restaurant stakes. There are a few basic Nepali ***eateries*** along the road between the bus park and the main *chowk* (intersection).

Getting There & Away

The road from the Terai is in good condition and is sealed all the way; it's also very steep and the views are spectacular. Buses leave from Birtamod on the Mahendra Hwy 13km west of Kakarbhitta. They depart from 7 am to 1 pm (Rs 102, five hours).

The road is being pushed farther into the hills beyond Ilam, and currently the road goes beyond Taplejung. Buses run regularly between Birtamod and Taplejung.

BIRATNAGAR

☎ 021

The fact that Biratnagar is the second-largest city in Nepal, and an industrial centre, actually makes it sound worse than it is. It's an energetic, bustling place with the crowds and shops you would expect of a city with several hundred thousand inhabitants. However, there's just nothing much to attract the visitor unless you are particularly interested in Nepal's somewhat shaky industrial development, or the strongest, most-politicised

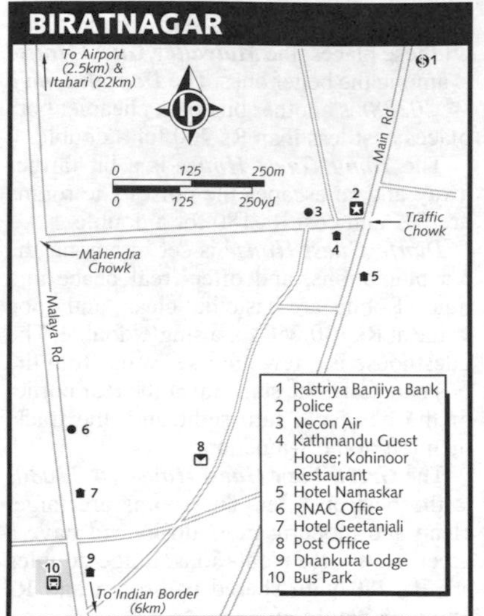

unions in the country. The border crossing to the south is not open to tourists.

The countryside and surrounding villages are interesting, but difficult to explore without private transport. One possibility is to continue north along Main Rd (where you'll find the Hotel Namaskar and Rastriya Banjiya Bank) – this veers left when you leave town. Continue westwards until you reach a T-junction, then turn right (north) along a dirt road that parallels the sealed road and continue through Sigraha and Haraincha until you reach the Mahendra Hwy to the west of Itahari.

Jute used to be grown in large quantities, and can still be seen, but the industry has been in decline for years. There are numerous ethnic groups in the region, but the most distinctive are the Tharus and Danuwars. The Danuwars are very similar in culture and appearance to the Tharu, but the women wear a distinctive embroidered sari.

Places to Stay & Eat

There's quite a range of places at varying prices. Bear in mind, however, that anywhere on Main Rd or near the bus park will be pretty noisy.

The ***Dhankuta Lodge***, which is opposite the bus park, is clean and reasonable offering singles/doubles at Rs 130/150 or Rs 180/250 with bathroom. Avoid the front rooms, which cop the bus park noise.

The ***Hotel Geetanjali*** *(☎ 27335)* is also close to the bus park on Malaya Rd. Set in a pleasant garden, the hotel charges Rs 230 for doubles without bathroom and Rs 280 with bathroom. There's no restaurant, but decent Indian food is available.

The ***Kathmandu Guest House*** near Traffic Chowk has quiet if gloomy rooms at Rs 140/200 with bathroom. It's good value. The ***Kohinoor Restaurant*** in the same building is worth a try.

Up the scale somewhat is the nice ***Hotel Namaskar*** *(☎ 21199, fax 25988)* on Main Rd near Traffic Chowk, a 15-minute walk from the bus park. The hotel has a range of rooms from Rs 380 to 1000. At the top price you get air-con and a private sitting room, but the cheaper rooms are clean and quite adequate, and all rooms have bathroom. There is also a good, reasonably priced restaurant here.

Getting There & Away

Biratnagar is serviced from Kathmandu at least once daily by RNAC (☎ 25576), US$77. Necon Air (☎ 25987), Buddha Air (☎ 24693) and Mountain Air also fly this route and charge US$87.

There are plenty of buses to Kathmandu, Kakarbhitta and Janakpur. Night buses to Kathmandu leave at 4.30 pm (Rs 374, 12 hours). There are day buses to Kakarbhitta (Rs 77, 3½ hours), Janakpur (Rs 137), Birganj (Rs 214, eight hours), Dhankuta (Rs 89) and Dharan Bazaar (Rs 27).

ITAHARI

Itahari is an undistinguished town at the intersection of the Mahendra Hwy and the Biratnagar to Dhankuta road. There is an interesting market held along the dusty lanes south-east of the main intersection.

The hotel pickings are extremely slim. Best of a bad lot is ***Jaya Nepal Hotel*** near the traffic roundabout. Doubles with shared bathroom go for Rs 160, singles/doubles with bathroom are Rs 280/380. The restaurant is OK and serves passable food.

Getting There & Away

All the long-distance, east–west buses stop in Itahari. There are also plenty of local buses that go to Biratnagar (Rs 15, one hour) and Dharan Bazaar (Rs 10, 30 minutes). One bus a day leaves for Dhankuta (Rs 53, five hours).

DHARAN BAZAAR

☎ 021

Dharan Bazaar lies right at the foot of the Chure hills, but the transformation from the Terai is dramatic. It's a bustling bazaar town catering to the hill people of eastern Nepal. It has grown rapidly despite suffering a major earthquake in 1988.

There are no sights of note, but if you're heading into the mountains this will be your best chance for final purchases. A small number of trekkers bound for Hile and Basantapur come through town, and **Chatara**, the finishing point for raft trips on the Sun Kosi, is only about 15km to the west. Baraha Chhetra, 5km north of Chatara, is the site for an annual religious festival in late October or early November.

Places to Stay & Eat

There are a few possibilities for places to stay and eat, but none of them are really all that flash.

The ***Hotel Family Inn*** *(☎ 20848)*, close to busy Bhanu Chowk in the centre of town (where the buses stop). Reasonable doubles with shared bathroom cost Rs 230 or so-called deluxe rooms are Rs 380 with bathroom. Avoid the ***Hotel Navayug*** next door.

The ***Hotel Aangan***, about 300m west from Bhanu Chowk, is a clean and decent hotel; double rooms with bathroom cost Rs 380. There are also more expensive air-con rooms.

Getting There & Away

Dharan Bazaar is 50km from the attractive hill town of Dhankuta. Hile, the starting point for a number of treks in eastern Nepal, is 12km past Dhankuta. The spectacular road is sealed as far as Hile, but does continue on to Therathum and is being pushed even farther. Buses to Dhankuta cost Rs 53 and take three hours, buses to Basantapur and Therathum (via Hile) cost Rs 110 and take five hours.

There's also one direct nightly bus in each direction to/from Kathmandu. The trip takes 14 hours and costs Rs 369.

DHANKUTA

☎ 026

Although Dhankuta is only 50km by excellent road from the Terai, it seems more like a million miles. The largest, flattest spot in the nearby vicinity is the bus station – it soon becomes quite hard to remember that expanses of waterlogged plains exist.

The town is strung along a ridge that basically runs north–south; the bus station is below the ridge. The sad remnants of the forest that once covered the hill are at the northern end of town. There is a collection of small, but decent, lodges that cater to a largely Nepali clientele, but there's no real reason to stay here, unless you want to catch the colourful *haat bajar* (weekly bazaar) on Thursday. Hile is more interesting and has better walking possibilities.

As you walk downhill (south) along the main street the road forks; the right fork goes down to the bus station, follow the left fork to a spur to see fine views of the Himalaya. The latter involves a pleasant 45-minute walk. After about 15 minutes the main track veers to the left and there is a stile over a barbed-wire fence. Climb the stile and follow the ridge line up to the left. Eventually you'll come to a small shrine. There are plenty of flowers and birds along the way and, of course, good views.

Places to Stay & Eat

There are some small, clean, basic lodges on the main street.

The ***Shaha Lodge*** *(☎ 20281)* and ***Naulo Lodge*** *(☎ 20481)* are both very basic; both cost less than Rs 200 a double.

A good option is the ***Hotel Parchaya*** *(☎ 20425)*, which would be a pleasant place to stay while you explored the surrounding hills. It's clean and bright and there are superb views. To find it, walk north up the ridge until you get to a large pipal tree, which is in the middle of an intersection. The hotel is on the right; two-bed rooms are Rs 80, four-bed rooms cost Rs 150, all with shared bathroom.

The ***Hotel Suravi*** *(☎ 20204)* is about as flash as it gets around here. Singles/doubles with shared bathroom cost Rs 80/160, or rooms with bathroom cost Rs 180/350. The restaurant here is quite decent.

The ***Puchhae Café*** next door to the Hotel Parchaya is a good little place with decent music and a relaxing atmosphere.

Getting There & Away

Plenty of buses travel the spectacular road from Dhankuta to Dharan Bazaar (Rs 53, three hours). From Dhankuta the sealed road continues to Hile, then continues on unsealed to Therathum. Buses for Basantapur cost Rs 70 and take three hours; to Hile it is Rs 15. The road is being pushed farther and farther into the hills, but there are no buses beyond Therathum.

HILE

☎ 026

Hile, a scruffy, bustling, one-street bazaar town strung out along a ridge, is the starting point for Arun Valley treks (possible for individuals) and for treks to Makalu (groups only). Kanchenjunga trekkers (also groups only) usually start at Basantapur. Hile is a good base for day walks in the region.

Nepal's ethnic map is always complicated, but at Hile it is about as complicated as it gets, with Tibetans, Bahuns, Chhetris, and Magars, Tamangs, Rais, Limbus and Indians.

There are some fantastic views of the Himalaya, especially of the Makalu massif, from the ridge above the town. Walk along the Basantapur road past the army base and a few hundred metres past the army checkpoint (there's a boom across the road) you can cut up to the left onto a grassy ridge.

Places to Stay & Eat

There are several decent but basic lodges, with not much to separate them.

The ***Doma Lodge*** *(☎ 20574)* is as basic as they come, but it's clean and friendly. Dorm beds cost Rs 25, doubles are Rs 80 with bathroom.

The ***Hotel Himali*** *(☎ 20340)* is similar, dorm beds cost Rs 30 and singles/doubles with shared bathroom cost Rs 80/120.

The ***Hotel Hillstone*** near the bus stand is Hile's Hilton. Don't expect too much, but it's clean and the rooms are a decent size. Rooms cost Rs 280 for a double with bathroom.

Getting There & Away

Buses to Basantapur and Therathum (about 20km beyond Basantapur and the current roadhead), depart every 45 minutes or so, cost Rs 46 and take around two hours.

There's one daily bus to Kathmandu. It costs Rs 420 and takes about 14 hours.

KOSHI TAPPU WILDLIFE RESERVE

The Koshi Tappu Wildlife Reserve protects a section of the Sapt Kosi's flood plain that lies behind the Kosi Barrage. The Sapt Kosi is one of the Ganges' largest tributaries, and the Kosi Barrage is designed to minimise destructive annual floods. Most of the reserve is surrounded by high embankments that control the spread of the river and funnel it towards the barrage.

The main highway skirts the reserve and crosses the river at the barrage. It's a beautiful, fascinating water world. Small thatched villages perch on what little high ground there is, and wherever you look there are water birds and ponds full of flowering plants, all overwhelmed by fields of rice stretching to the horizon.

Behind the embankments the river continuously changes course, and regularly floods during the monsoon, although only to shallow depths. The vegetation is mainly *phanta* (tall grass) with some scrub and riverine forest. Local villagers are allowed to collect grass for thatching every January, which also clears the way for easier wildlife viewing.

The reserve is home to the last surviving population of wild *arna* (water buffalo), various deer, blue cow antelope, gharial crocodiles and Gangetic dolphins. It is also home to more than 400 species of water birds (migratory and otherwise). These include 20 species of ducks, ibises, storks, egrets, cranes and herons. The migratory species, including the sarus crane from Siberia and the ruddy shelduck from Tibet, take up residence from November to February.

The reserve occasionally hosts bird-watchers between November and February, but very few people visit and the arrival of a tourist out of the blue gives everyone quite a shock. There's one deluxe safari camp, but there's no other formal accommodation, although there is an area where you could camp, and the helpful staff are happy to give visitors the use of a kitchen. The reserve has five elephants, which can be ridden for Rs 1000 for one hour. Canoes can also be arranged.

Orientation & Information

The reserve headquarters at Kusaha is where all visitors must pay an extortionate Rs 3600 entry fee. It's a 3km walk from the highway, outside the eastern embankment, on the eastern side of the barrage.

If you do plan a visit, and especially if you want to stay, ring ahead to get the latest information on access and the availability of facilities. Contact the park headquarters on ☎ 025-21488.

The turn-off to the reserve (signposted) is about 11km north–east of the Kosi Barrage, about 2km before the village of Laukhi. Coming from Itahari, it's about 46km to Laukhi and a farther 2km to the turn-off.

Places to Stay

The only formal accommodation is the ***Koshi Tappu Wildlife Camp***, which is just outside the north-eastern corner of the reserve, 24km north of the barrage near the tiny village of Prakashpur (accessible from Inerwa on the Mahendra Hwy). The camp is located on a small waterway with excellent bird-watching possibilities from the bar! Because so few visitors come to this part of the world, it is an excellent place to escape the crowds for a few days.

The camp is very well set-up, and is in a pleasant established garden. Accommodation is in very comfortable tented rooms, and there's shared bathroom facilities, a separate dining area serving excellent meals, and a bar. There is no electricity, and therefore the evenings are illuminated by atmospheric kerosene lamps.

Accommodation costs US$225/300 for a single/double per night, which includes guided bird walks and an idyllic half-day rafting glide down the wide and slow-moving river. Most guests come on a package from Kathmandu, which involves flying to Biratnagar and transfers to the camp. Bookings can be made through Explore Nepal (☎ 01-226130, ⓔ explore@mos.com.np), PO Box 536, Kamaladi, Kathmandu.

For those who don't mind roughing it a bit, it might be possible to stay in the ***homes*** of a few of the families who live at the park headquarters. This is village accommodation at its most basic. Don't expect any frills and be sensitive to the fact that this is not tourist accommodation and people may be unfamiliar with what tourists usually expect in the way of food and facilities.

There is also basic ***lodge*** accommodation at Bhantabarl, the small village, which is on the eastern side of the barrage.

Getting There & Away

Any buses travelling on the Mahendra Hwy can drop you at the park turn-off, from where it is a further 3km walk to the park headquarters.

For the wildlife camp, if you don't have your own 4WD, take a local bus to Inerwa on the Mahendra Hwy, and from there local buses go regularly to Prakashpur. The wildlife camp is a farther 1km, which you'll have to cover on foot; ask for directions.

JANAKPUR

☎ 041

If you do have the time and the inclination to experience something of the Terai, Janakpur should be at the top of your list. Janakpur is a scruffy, dusty (or muddy) yet interesting town with temples, pools, sadhus, rickshaws and rainbow-coloured saris. It is a tourist town, but the tourists are all devout Indian pilgrims, rather than Western backpackers.

Janakpur's religious significance is due to its role in the famous Hindu epic, the *Ramayana*. It is the legendary birthplace of Sita, an incarnation of Lakshmi, and the place of her marriage to Rama, who is one of Vishnu's most popular incarnations. At times, especially during festivals when strangely resonant vignettes from the *Ramayana* are played out in the streets, it can feel as if the ancient myth has come to life.

Janakpur is situated in what was once the kingdom of Mithila, a region now divided between Nepal and India. The Maithili language, which also has its own unique script, is spoken by approximately two million Nepalis – only Nepali is spoken by a greater number of people.

Janakpur is at least the third city to be built on this site, and most buildings are less than a century old. The city that was mythologised in the *Ramayana* existed around 700 BC, but it apparently sank back into the forest, the population perhaps wiped out by disease. Simaraungarh grew up in its place, but was destroyed by Muslims in the 14th century, and once again the region was reforested. Theologically, Janakpur is paired with Ayodhya, which is near Faizabad in

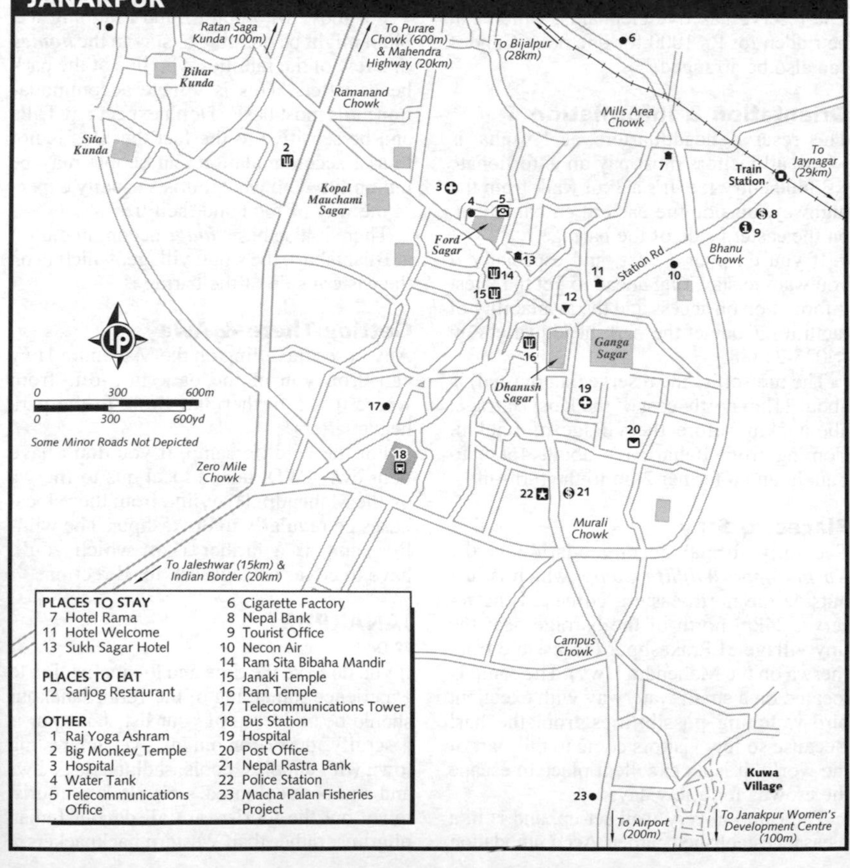

Uttar Pradesh, where Rama is believed to have been born.

Modern Janakpur is a typical Terai town, although Janakpur is perhaps cleaner and less crowded than some others. Narrow lanes are interspersed with temples, *kutis* (pilgrim hostels) and both *sagar* and *kunda* (large and small sacred ponds). Legend says the ponds were created by King Janak for the use of the gods who came to the wedding of Rama and Sita. They take the place of a river for ritual bathing and are also used by the local dhobi caste, who are clothes washers. Thanks to a successful development project, many ponds are also stocked with the fish that provide an important supplement to the local diet.

The town authorities have managed to keep most traffic out of the centre of town, which makes it pleasant to wander around.

It's possible to visit on the way to/from Kakarbhitta. Although the only railway in Nepal connects Janakpur to the Indian town of Jaynagar, tourists are not allowed to cross the border (see the Around Janakpur section later in this chapter).

Orientation & Information

Janakpur is a hopeless tangle of narrow streets, so the best way to get your bearings is from the telecommunications tower to the south-west of the centre and the large, elevated concrete water tank. The town itself lies to the east of the main road that runs through to Jaleshwar at the border.

The Janaki Temple (Janaki Mandir) is just to the south of the water tank, and the bus station is to the south-east of the temple near the telecommunications tower. The train station is about a 20-minute walk to the north-east of the large water tank.

There is a tourist office (☎ 20755) at Bhanu Chowk, not far from the train station. Consider ringing to check the dates for major festivals, although fluency in Nepali is usually necessary. The office is open from 10 am to 5 pm Monday to Friday, but closes an hour earlier from November to January.

Janaki Temple

The *mandir* (temple) to Sita (who is also known as Janaki) is believed to be built over the spot where her father, King Janak, found her lying in the furrow of a ploughed field. It's impressively large yet, surprisingly, you come across it from the winding Janakpur streets almost without warning.

Although it has no great architectural or historical merit – it was built in 1912 and might be described as baroque Mughal – it is nonetheless a fascinating place. There are instances of fine work, especially in some of the carved stone screens, and in the beautiful silver doors to the inner sanctum.

The inner sanctum is opened from 5 to 7 am and 6 to 8 pm to reveal a flower bedecked statue of Sita that was apparently miraculously found in the Saryu River near Ayodhya. She is accompanied by Rama and his three half-brothers, Lakshmana, Bharat and Satrughna.

During the day, there are few people in the temple – some priests, sadhus and, if you're lucky, perhaps some musicians playing in the cloisters – but it comes alive in the evenings when Sita is displayed.

Ram Sita Bibaha Temple

Virtually next door to the Janaki Temple, but built with the traditional Nepali pagoda roof, this rather bizarre temple is built on the spot where Rama and Sita were married. Entry is Rs 1; leave cameras at the gate. The temple itself has glass walls so you can peer in at the kitsch life-sized models of Sita and Rama, his half-brothers and sisters-in-law.

Ram Temple & Danush Sagar

Located in the city's oldest quarter, to the south-east of the Janaki Temple, the Ram is another Nepali-style temple that is the centrepoint for the Rama Navami celebrations. Immediately to its east is the Danush Sagar, which is considered to be one of the holiest ponds and is a popular pilgrimage site.

Other Temples & Ponds

There are numerous temples and ponds scattered around the outskirts of town. It is worth hiring a cycle-rickshaw to see them, although you could track them down on foot if you are feeling energetic. They're reached by brick-paved roads that meander into the paddy fields. If you hire a rickshaw, allow a couple of hours and expect to pay around Rs 100.

Start at the temple that is widely known as the **Big Monkey Temple**. This place is easy to miss as it looks like an ordinary house. It is about 100m south of Ramanand Chowk. Hanuman, the monkey god, is worshipped here in the form of a rhesus monkey, kept in a depressing cage. Despite this, it could well be monkey heaven given that the attendants and pilgrims press food on their mascot. The constant supply of delicacies no longer arouses much interest or excitement, but temptation (or boredom) triumphs and the monkey keeps munching on. The previous monkey grew to 60kg before finally succumbing in 1998 to the affects of gross overfeeding and underexercising; its replacement is well on the way to following it.

Two of the most interesting and attractive ponds can be reached by following the brick-paved roads to the west. They are **Bihar Kunda** and **Ratan Saga Kunda**. The

The Romance of Rama

The *Ramayana*, or romance of Rama, is among the best-loved and most influential stories in Hindu literature. Handsome Rama embodies chivalry and virtue, and his wife, the beautiful Sita, exemplifies devotion and chastity. Together with Rama's ally, the faithful monkey god, Hanuman, they are heroes and exemplars of immense popularity. Like all great mythical archetypes, they have somehow found an enduring place in the human psyche.

It's likely the legend has at least a basis in fact, and was first retold around village hearths. The *Ramayana* was first permanently recorded in Sanskrit, possibly as long as 2400 years ago by a sage and poet, Valmiki. Since then it has become a part of people's lives and imaginations throughout the subcontinent and, in various forms, as far as Bali, where to this day it features in puppetry and dance.

Rama was a reincarnation of Vishnu, born at the request of the gods to do battle with the ghastly demon-king Ravana, the king of Lanka (possibly Sri Lanka). He was reincarnated at Ayodhya (350km west of Janakpur) as the eldest son of a wealthy king. Handsome, virtuous and strong, he grew up as the idol of the people and especially of one of his half-brothers, Lakshmana.

In the kingdom of Mithila, good King Janak discovered baby Sita, the reincarnation of Lakshmi, lying in a furrow of a ploughed field. She too grew up to be wise and beautiful. So many men wanted to marry her that Janak set a test – a successful suitor had to bend the divine bow of Shiva. Rama, of course, drew the bow and he and Sita looked into each other's eyes and knew divine love.

Rama and his three half-brothers were married in a single ceremony – the brothers to neighbouring princesses – and there was much feasting, flowers falling from heaven, gorgeous processions across the plains and so on. But this is where things took a turn for the worse.

After returning to Ayodhya, Rama and Sita were forced to leave the palace because of the intrigues of the detestable hunchback Manthara. While they wandered in exile, Rama and Lakshmana were distracted by a golden deer, and Sita was kidnapped and carried off to Lanka by the demon king. Imprisoned, Sita was forced to defend herself from the disgusting advances of Ravana.

Meanwhile, Rama and Lakshmana formed an alliance with a monkey kingdom. In particular they were served by the indomitable monkey god Hanuman. With Hanuman's loyal assistance, Sita was finally rescued and the demon king, Ravana, was destroyed.

Unfortunately, life didn't improve much for Sita who was forced to undergo an ordeal by fire to prove her chastity. Although Rama, now king of Ayodhya, believed her innocence, his people did not and Sita was forced into exile again. Sita gave birth to Rama's twin sons and the family was later reunited, but Sita decided she had had enough of this mortal coil and was swallowed up by the earth.

There are many versions of the story recorded in many art forms and many different languages, including English. Trying to imagine the power and subtlety of the complete story by reading this condensation is a bit like trying to imagine a tree by looking at a match.

countryside is lush and tropical with coconut palms and huge trees framing the temples and ponds that are scattered across the fertile plains.

Janakpur Women's Art Project

In the Janakpur Women's Development Centre, this women's art project (☎ 21080) promotes traditional Mithila painting skills and seeks to empower local women – who live in a highly restrictive patriarchal society (see the boxed text 'Mithila Painting' later in this chapter).

The centre is on the southern outskirts of Janakpur and incorporates aspects of traditional architecture. The beautiful site is on the edge of an interesting village, a short rickshaw ride and walk from the centre of town. It is possible for visitors to see the women working at ceramics, painting, tapestry, silk-screen printing and sewing, and to purchase some of their striking creations at extremely reasonable prices.

The project includes women of diverse castes and backgrounds and the art that is created reflects this variety; wedding paintings, pregnant elephants, gods, and abstract tattoo designs are just some of the subjects portrayed. Increasingly the paintings are changing to also include scenes from the women's lives, including scenes of childbirth and marriage. In addition to paintings (acrylic on daphne paper) the women are also producing ceramics (plates and figures), papier-mâché, patchwork tapestry, silk-screen prints and woven wall hangings.

In Kathmandu, the project's goods are sold at Sana Hastakala, Mahaguthi, and a number of other reputable craft shops. See the Shopping section in the Kathmandu chapter for more information.

A visit is a must. The centre is open from 10 am to 5 pm daily except Saturday.

To get there, take a rickshaw from town to Macha Palan, a large fisheries project with a red and white sign in Nepali. The rickshaw should cost around Rs 20. Coming from town, a brick road on the left forms a T-junction just before the project. Follow it east to Kuwa village. Turn right at Kuwa village and continue until you reach a large but unprepossessing temple. Turn left immediately before the temple and then right immediately after it. Continue to the south; the road bends to the left, past a tank on the right. The centre is the only building in this vicinity, and it is enclosed behind a high, red-brick wall. While the route sounds complicated, you can ask directions if in doubt and you shouldn't have a problem. It is about a 10-minute walk from Macha Palan to the centre.

Special Events

On the fifth day of the waxing moon in late November/early December, thousands of pilgrims arrive to celebrate Sita Bibaha Panchami; the re-enactment of Sita's marriage to Rama (Vivaha Panchami). This is also the occasion for an important fair and market that lasts a week. Rama's birthday (Rama Navami) in late March/early April is also accompanied by a huge procession.

Most Hindu festivals are major events in Janakpur. Tihar (Deepawali) is an interesting time to be in town, when the Mithila women repaint the murals on their houses. On the day before Holi, Parikrama involves a ritual walk around the town's ring road. Holi itself can get very boisterous and wild; women should take care.

Places to Stay & Eat

Janakpur is desperately in need of a couple of decent hotels.

Despite the fact it is somewhat run-down, the ***Hotel Welcome*** *(☎ 20646, fax 20922)* on Station Rd is not a bad option. The rooms are tolerably grubby. On the plus side, the staff are friendly and helpful and the restaurant is good. Singles/doubles with bathroom are Rs 250/300, for a more comfortable room (although this is relative) with air-con, it's Rs 700/1200. Checkout is 24 hours after check-in.

The ***Sukh Sagar Hotel*** *(☎ 20488)*, very close to the Janaki Temple, has large rooms that are passably clean and reasonable value at Rs 180 with shared bathroom and Rs 140/250 with bathroom. On the ground floor there's a decent local restaurant, which does a passable *dal bhaat* (lentils and rice).

The best on offer is the pleasant ***Hotel Rama*** *(☎ 20059)*, in the northern part of town by Mills Area Chowk. The rooms are a good size, and range in price from Rs 170 (very basic and gloomy) with shared bathroom, Rs 380 for big, airy doubles with fan, bathroom and hot water to Rs 500 with air-cooler and Rs 900 with air-con. There's a reasonable although very dark restaurant here.

The ***Sanjog Restaurant***, down a side alley opposite the Danush Sagar, is basic, but for Janakpur it's about as good as it gets. The menu is very ambitious, although most dishes seem to be unavailable.

Getting There & Away

Necon Air (☎ 20688) has flights four times weekly to Kathmandu (US$65).

Private buses to Kathmandu leave from the chaotic main bus station between 5 and 7 pm. There are half a dozen express night buses to/from Kathmandu that cost Rs 260 and take about nine hours. Night buses to Pokhara also cost Rs 260. There are day buses to Birganj (Rs 116), Biratnagar (Rs 137) and Kakarbhitta (Rs 185).

The train is only useful for sightseeing in the area (see Around Janakpur following for more details).

AROUND JANAKPUR

The fields and villages around Janakpur form a lush and magical mosaic. It's worth exploring them on foot, bicycle, rickshaw or train. Unfortunately, there are no formal bicycle-hire places, but if you ask around something may turn up. Western visitors are rare, so tread gently, and always ask before taking photos.

It doesn't really matter in which direction you choose to go. **Jaleshwar** to the south-west on the Nepali side of the border is a completely uninspiring town, but there are some interesting villages on the way there. Other possibilities include the road that runs south to the airport, which turns to dirt and continues through a number of attractive villages; the road that runs north of the cigarette factory; and also the road that runs west of Purare Chowk. **Dhanusa**, 15km to the north-east, marks the spot where Rama allegedly drew Shiva's magic bow.

Mithila Painting

Mithila culture is essentially a culture of the Gangetic plain, and the Hindu caste structure is strictly upheld. Most people are subsistence farmers, but land-holdings are usually very small and many families live on the edge of starvation. Many are in the grip of moneylenders or *zamindars* (landlords).

Zamindars, usually from the Brahmin (priest) or Kshatriya (warrior) castes, occupy an almost feudal role as major landowners and in their traditional role as moneylenders. Their tenant farmers and debtors are effectively serfs trapped in a system of bonded labour.

Most Mithila people live in small villages, usually with no more than around a hundred households. House walls are made from bamboo or thatch plastered with a mixture of cow dung and mud. The roofs are thatched, sometimes tiled. Most houses have a fenced courtyard, which is also sealed with mud and cow dung.

Mithila women are raised with the expectation that they will be workers in their husband's home, and are frequently married as children. After puberty they are veiled so that their faces cannot be seen by males outside their family.

As a part of their cultural and religious tradition, the women paint striking murals on the external walls of their homes. Inside, pottery storage containers and internal pillars also carry designs. Different castes and different regions have developed distinctive styles and symbols, which are passed down from mother to daughter. Traditionally, painting and decoration is not undertaken purely to create an aesthetic result, nor is it purely cathartic or expressive. Painting largely springs from cultural and religious motives. The act of painting, as a part of a ritual, can be more important than the finished result itself, and completed paintings can act as charms, prayers and meditation aids.

Janakpur is the terminus for two train lines, one of which runs east to **Jaynagar** over the Indian border, and the other which runs north-west to Bijalpur. However, only the first route to Jaynagar carries passengers. They're narrow-gauge trains and are very slow, so they offer an interesting if somewhat crowded method of seeing the countryside.

If you want to travel to or from Jaynagar there are three daily services in each direction, so it is easy to put together a day trip. Trains leave both Janakpur and Jaynagar at 6 and 11 am and 3 pm. Tickets cost Rs 39/15 in 1st/2nd class. It's about 29km (four hours!) to Jaynagar, but tourists are not allowed to cross the border into India, so you will need to get off in one of the villages along the way.

The first stop after Janakpur is **Parbaha** (Rs 12/5 in 1st/2nd class, 8km), and there are interesting villages on either side of the tracks – you could walk back to town. Another interesting stop is **Baidehi**, about an hour (Rs 16/6, 12km) from Janakpur, where you could alight and catch the Janakpur-bound train that comes through an hour later. Alternatively, you could continue as far as you are allowed to go to **Khajuri** (Rs 27/10, 21km), about 8km from Jaynagar on the Nepali side of the border, and catch the afternoon Janakpur train.

BIRGANJ

☎ 051

Birganj is one of the main border crossings between Nepal and India, and is also one of Nepal's most important industrial cities. This is an unfortunate combination. It has been one of the most unattractive places on the planet for some time. For much of the year the climate is oppressively hot, and during the monsoon the heat combines with the humidity to make the place almost unbearable.

There are immigrants from around Nepal and many from India; bear in mind that the only reason these people come to Birganj is that the alternative of remaining in their place of birth is worse. The local language is Bhojpuri, which is spoken on both sides of the border.

Mithila Painting

Paintings often derive from Hindu mythology and can use complex symbols (sometimes with a distinct mandala-like quality), simple apparently abstract figures (including hand stencils, peacocks, pregnant elephants and fish), or can take on a narrative quality (representing religious stories). High castes, including the Kshatriya, have developed extremely elaborate, abstract forms. Lower-caste paintings are often simpler and more realistic, but they have an energetic expressionistic style, and retain a strong sense of formal design.

Mithila paintings from Madubani in Bihar, India, have been discovered by the international art world. The most well known are the elaborate Kshatriya wedding paintings that are presented to the groom as part of the build-up to an arranged marriage.

Until fairly recently, little interest was taken in the art produced on Nepal's side of the border. This changed with the foundation of the Janakpur Women's Art Project in 1989, which had the dual aim of promoting traditional Mithila painting skills and empowering the women painters. The project is housed in the Janakpur Women's Development Centre and it's possible to visit the centre to see the women working and to buy what they produce (see Janakpur Women's art Project earlier for more details.)

SIMON BORG

THE TERAI

Birganj is probably the most important entry point for Indian imports, but most travellers (especially those coming from Varanasi) enter through Sunauli to the west. Birganj remains the most convenient entry point, however, for those coming from Patna or Kolkata (Calcutta).

Fortunately, there are plenty of day and night buses to and from Kathmandu and Pokhara and points south (in India) so there should be no necessity to stay more than a night in Birganj – hopefully not even that.

Orientation & Information

Birganj and Raxaul Bazaar (on the Indian side of the border) virtually run together, though it is a 60-minute rickshaw ride to get between the two bus stations.

The Birganj bus station (in the best or worse part of town, depending on whether you are going or coming) is on the ring road at Bhanu Chowk, about 500m east of the clocktower.

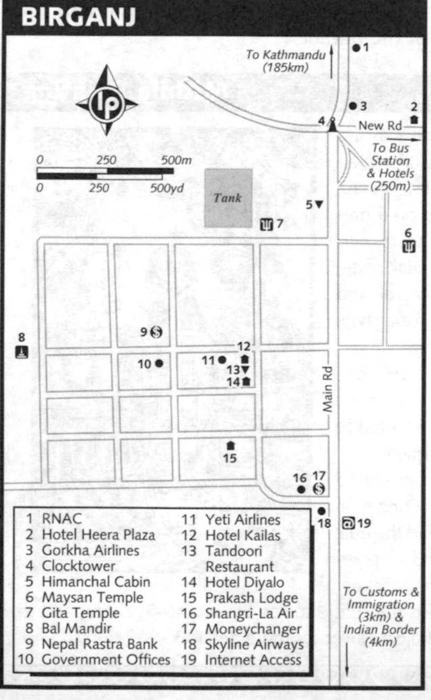

The various official offices on either side of the border are all open between 7 am and 7 pm, as is the bank on the Nepali side.

There's an official moneychanger on Main Rd, and it accepts major currencies (cash and travellers cheques). Indian rupees are interchangeable with Nepalese rupees in Birganj, but get rid of any excess here.

Internet access is available (Rs 2 per minute) from a small place on Main Rd, though there are bound to be others by now.

Things to See

If you do find yourself with a couple of hours to kill in Birganj you could hire a rickshaw for an hour or two (around Rs 40 an hour) and have a bit of a look around. The town has a certain gruesome fascination and there are a couple of modern temples and muddy ponds. The most interesting is the **Bal Temple**, which is a modern Buddhist temple about 1km west from the main road.

Places to Stay & Eat

There are a number of cheap places in the bus station area a few hundred metres east of the clocktower, but it's a noisy area and there's a good chance you won't get any sleep. Most places charge around Rs 200 for a double. Places in this area include the ***Park Hotel, Hotel Welcome Nepal*** *(☎ 24057)* and the ***Buddha Guest House***.

There's another hotel area in the centre of town, clustered around what was the old bus station. The really cheap places are a pretty dismal lot. The ***Prakash Lodge*** is as good (or as bad) as any.

The ***Hotel Kailas*** *(☎ 23084, fax 22410)* has a range of decent rooms and a good, air-con (mercifully) tandoori restaurant. A few smallish singles with shared bathroom start at Rs 100, otherwise singles/doubles with TV, fan and bathroom start at Rs 200/430, rising to Rs 990 with air-con, plus 12% tax.

Almost next door, ***Hotel Diyalo*** *(☎ 22370, e adarsh@atcnet.com.np)* is a well-run hotel with immaculate, reasonably priced rooms (for what you get). There is also a good restaurant. Rooms with bathroom are from Rs 600/700 to Rs 800/900 with air-cooler to Rs 1600/1800 with air-con.

For something better try ***Hotel Heera Plaza*** *(☎ 23988, e giris@atcnet.com.np)*, on New Rd midway between the clock-tower and the bus station. Smallish rooms with TV, carpet and bathroom are on offer for Rs 650/750, rising to Rs 1350/1550 with air-con.

A decent, cheap ***tandoori restaurant*** is between the Kailas and Diyalo hotels.

The ***Himanchal Cabin*** restaurant on Main Rd does South Indian food such as *dosas* (lentil and rice flour pancakes).

Getting There & Away

To/From India It's a 30-minute, rickshaw trip (Rs 20) between the Birganj bus station and the border, and another 30 minutes (and INRs 25) between the border and the Raxaul Bazaar bus station. Expect to pay INRs 90 for the five-hour bus journey to Patna from Raxaul Bazaar.

To/From Other Parts of Nepal There are daily flights between Simara, the airport for Birganj and Kathmandu with RNAC (US$44) and at least six private airlines (US$54).

There are plenty of day and night buses to and from Kathmandu. Night buses leave Birganj between 7 and 9 pm daily, arriving in Kathmandu around 5 am (Rs 207). Day buses leave between 6 and 10 am and cost Rs 190. Tickets can (and should) be booked in advance.

There are also buses leaving for Pokhara (Rs 150/175 in the day/night, 10 hours), Janakpur (Rs 116, day) as well as Tadi Bazaar (for Chitwan; Rs 82).

Despite the fact that the Tribhuvan Hwy from Hetauda to Naubise looks like the best route to Kathmandu, virtually all the buses travel west to Narayanghat before they climb into the hills. There are a couple of buses to Kathmandu via this route, but be warned that while it is very scenic, it is also very slow.

Getting Around

Rickshaws cost around Rs 40 per hour, which is the charge if you get one to take you all the way through to Raxaul Bazaar (this is recommended).

HETAUDA

☎ 057

Hetauda is the starting point for a cableway that carries cement from the Terai to Kathmandu. It's quite an amazing construction, similar in concept to a ski lift. The current cableway dates from 1958 and can carry 25 tonnes per hour; it takes 15 hours for goods to travel the distance.

The town itself is of little interest, so unless you want to catch a bus over the superb Tribhuvan Hwy, there's no need to stop here. If taking the highway, there are spectacular views and this route is well worth considering. You begin to climb into the **Mahabharat Range** the moment you leave Hetauda. The road is in good condition, but it's very narrow, so it's a case of drivers leaning almost constantly on their horns and hoping they won't meet an out-of-control Tata truck around the next blind corner.

The change from the Terai is remarkably sudden; you're soon among forested hills and it is almost impossible to believe the plains are so close. As you gain altitude, you enter magnificent rhododendron forests. The highest point on the road is 2400m, just before you reach Daman. However, most buses heading for Kathmandu and Pokhara turn west to Narayanghat.

Places to Stay & Eat

There's a handful of cheap places around the bus station, but avoid these if you plan on getting any sleep.

The ***Neelam Lodge*** *(☎ 20900)* is on the Daman road north of Mahendra Chowk in the centre of town and is the pick of the cheapies. Beside two big pipal trees, it has clean singles/doubles for Rs 150/200 with bathroom (cold water) – good value. It's about 500m from the main bus station.

The ***Hotel Seema*** *(☎ 20191, e dhiraj@mos.com.np)*, about 200m south of the chowk, is a modern place with decent rooms at Rs 150/300 with shared bathroom, Rs 350/550 with bathroom and Rs 1500/2000 for a deluxe air-con room.

Motel Avocado *(☎ 20429, e avocado@wlink.com.np)*, on the way out of town along the Tribhuvan Hwy towards Daman, has some accommodation in a quiet, pleasant garden (with avocado trees). Rooms in an old Nissen hut are spacious, comfortable and rather idiosyncratic. They come with fans and bathroom, and cost Rs 350/500 (negotiable). There's also a three-storey wing of modern deluxe rooms with air-con for Rs 1500/2000. The restaurant here is quite good, and the motel also has interesting travellers' notebooks on cycling and motorcycling.

Getting There & Away

A Sajha Yatayat bus (Rs 72, eight hours) as well as private buses run the magnificent Tribhuvan Hwy via Daman. The main bus station in Hetauda is to the south-west of the main intersection (known as Mahendra Chowk). Private buses to Daman (more frequent and expensive) leave from the roadside, at a place called Bim Phedi bus stand, about 100m north of Motel Avocado.

A number of private buses go to Kathmandu (Rs 130) and Pokhara (Rs 120) via Narayanghat and Tadi Bazaar. Buses to Tadi Bazaar take around three hours and cost Rs 40. There are numerous buses to Birganj for Rs 30.

DAMAN

Daman is 2322m above sea level, midway between Kathmandu and Hetauda. Its claim to fame is that it has, arguably, *the* most spectacular outlook on the Himalaya – there are unimpeded views of the entire range from Dhaulagiri to Mt Everest. If you have the opportunity to get to Daman, it should not be missed.

There is a viewing tower with a telescope (small entry fee), a couple of basic lodges (no views) and one upmarket lodge.

On the Hetauda side of Daman is a magnificent rhododendron forest (which would be particularly worth seeing in spring) then great views over the Terai to India. Heading north from Daman you travel through the intensely cultivated **Palung Valley**. From here to Kathmandu, every possible inch of the hills is farmed. There are more good views of the Himalaya to enjoy before you reach Naubise on the Kathmandu-Pokhara (Prithvi) Hwy.

Places to Stay & Eat

Daman has a couple of *very* basic lodges (with rooms for less than Rs 100, you get what you pay for).

The only other option is the ***Everest Panorama Resort*** *(☎ 40380, fax 40382)*, a couple of kilometres on the Hetauda side of Daman, and a good bit higher. The spacious rooms all have views (although some are obscured by the large restaurant building), as well as TV and private bathroom. They are somewhat musty, however, and for all of US$70/80 plus 12% tax are somewhat overpriced. On the plus side, there are mountain bikes for hire, and pony rides and fishing expeditions on offer.

Getting There & Away

Daman is about three hours by car from Kathmandu and four hours from Hetauda. Unless you're on your way to/from Birganj, hiring a car and making a day trip from Kathmandu is probably the ideal way to get to Daman, but it won't be cheap (around US$80). If you have a group and it's clear weather, it would be worth it. Alternatively, this is one of the most spectacular (and most gruelling) mountain-bike routes in Nepal (see Rajpath from Kathmandu under Touring Routes in the Mountain Biking chapter for details).

From Daman there is a limited number of buses that pass through en route between Kathmandu and Hetauda. The bus takes about four hours from Kathmandu.

TADI BAZAAR

In the Chitwan Valley between Hetauda and Narayanghat, the small town of Tadi Bazaar (sometimes spelt Tandi Bazaar) is nothing more than a junction town for Sauraha, the budget accommodation centre for the Royal Chitwan National Park. For more details see Royal Chitwan National Park later in this chapter.

Getting There & Away

See the Getting There & Away entry in the Royal Chitwan National Park section for details on transport to/from Tadi Bazaar and the nearby village of Sauraha.

NARAYANGHAT & BHARATPUR

☎ 056

Narayanghat is a fast-growing town on the banks of the large Narayani River, just downstream from the junction of the Kali Gandaki and Trisuli Rivers. It has developed mainly because it lies at the intersection (Pul Chowk) of the Mahendra Hwy, which runs the length of the Terai, and the main road into the hills to Kathmandu and Pokhara. It is also the administrative and trading centre for the whole district. Bharatpur is contiguous with Narayanghat, and has an airport.

Although on the map the most direct route from eastern Nepal to Kathmandu is the road from Hetauda to Naubise, most traffic takes the road from Narayanghat to Mugling. The Tribhuvan Hwy (or Rajpath) from Hetauda to Naubise is a great drive, but its endless narrow corners mean it's not appropriate for trucks and buses.

Narayanghat will, for most people, simply be a *chia* (milk tea) stop en route to Kathmandu, Chitwan or India. Apart from the river there's not much of interest in the town; it's not a bad spot to stop if you are exploring the Terai, and there's an interesting excursion to Devghat, a holy site northwest of town at the confluence of the Kali Gandaki and Trisuli Rivers (see Around Narayanghat later in this chapter).

Places to Stay & Eat

If, due to bad luck or bad management, you are forced to stay the night, there are a few choices. Right by the main intersection, very handy for buses, is the ***Regal Rest House*** *(☎ 20755)*. Doubles with shared bathroom are Rs 200, while singles/doubles with private bathroom and hot water cost Rs 250/350. Don't stay here unless you can get a room at the back, as the road is very busy with buses coming and going at all hours of the day and night. There's also a decent restaurant here.

A much more pleasant option, but also somewhat inconvenient, is ***Gainda Cottages*** *(☎ 20590)* which is on the northern bank of the Narayani (across the bridge and first right). It is not exactly luxurious, and taking mosquito repellent is a good idea, but the welcome is warm, the rooms are clean and there's a courtyard garden area. Rooms are reasonable value at Rs 180/300 with shared bathroom. Simple food is available.

There are some cheaper places around the northern bus station. The ***Hotel River View*** *(☎ 21151)* is a quiet, basic place which does indeed have a river view, although only from the upper floors. The rooms are a bit on the small side, but are good value at Rs 200 for a double with bathroom and mosquito nets.

Other than these places there are a couple of upmarket choices in Bharatpur, and these are handy for the airport, although if you're going to pay this sort of money you'd be better off in Chitwan itself. ***Hotel Narayani Safari*** *(☎ 20130, e nsafari@mos.com.np)* is primarily used as a base for trips to Chitwan. It is well run and has air-con, a swimming pool, tennis court and an excellent restaurant. Rooms officially cost US$50/65, but discounts are offered.

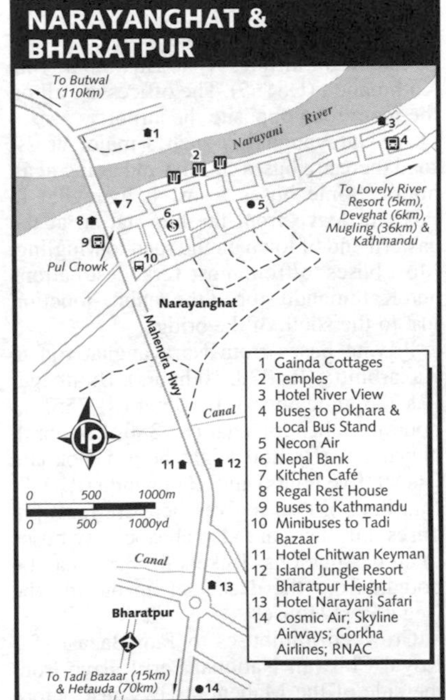

The modern ***Hotel Chitwan Keyman*** *(☎ 20200, fax 22264)* has a quiet rear garden and very comfortable rooms with air-con and TV for US$36/42. A 30% discount is offered, and they throw in breakfast too.

Opposite the Keyman is the comfortable ***Island Jungle Resort Bharatpur Height*** *(☎ 20730, ⓔ island@mos.com.np)*, not surprisingly owned by the Island Jungle Resort in Chitwan. The comfortable rooms, which are set around a garden with a swimming pool, cost Rs 1500 plus 12% tax.

A few kilometres out of town on the Kathmandu road is the ***Lovely River Resort*** *(☎ 01-425042)*, signposted 2km off the road along a dirt track. It's a very pleasant set up on the banks of the Trisuli River. Accommodation is in stone cottages and costs Rs 1200, which includes three meals.

The ***Kitchen Café***, tucked away at the southern edge of the bridge, makes a very pleasant escape from the mayhem out on the main road. There are tables outside in the garden, or you can eat inside.

Getting There & Away

A number of airlines fly to Bharatpur from Kathmandu (US$65). The offices are all on the main road opposite the airport.

As Narayanghat is such a major crossroad there are buses coming and going at all hours. Some buses from Narayanghat to Pokhara leave from the bus station at the eastern end of town on the road to Mugling. Most buses to/from most Terai destinations and Kathmandu stop at the main T-junction just to the south of the bridge.

Private buses from Narayanghat run to Kakarbhitta (Rs 330, 10 hours), Biratnagar (Rs 275, nine hours), Janakpur (Rs 255, six hours), Mahendranagar (Rs 380, 12 hours), Nepalganj (Rs 260, eight hours), Pokhara (Rs 80, five hours) and Kathmandu (Rs 117, four hours). Prices given here are for night buses, but there are also cheaper day buses to all destinations. Tickets for buses can be bought from the desks set up outside the Regal Rest House.

Crowded minibuses to Tadi Bazaar (for Royal Chitwan National Park) leave from the side of the Mahendra Hwy just before the second intersection south of the main T-junction; they cost Rs 12 and take 30 minutes. Taxis to Chitrasali (for Chitwan) cost about Rs 300.

AROUND NARAYANGHAT

Devghat

Also known as Deoghat and Harihara Chhetra, Devghat is an ancient holy site that was first mentioned in the *Skanda Purana* (Skanda was the son of Shiva; this Purana expounds the doctrines and worship of Siva). It's a suitably beautiful spot, with forest-clad hills, a large sandy beach, and a number of shady shrines and temples overlooking the swirling waters where the Kali Gandaki and Trisuli Rivers meet. The confluence of rivers, particularly when they are major tributaries of the Ganges, is always regarded as religiously significant by Hindus, as it is believed a third spiritual river also joins the rivers here.

Many elderly high-caste Hindus come here to quietly live out their days, and finally to be cremated on the river banks, thus gaining religious merit and hopefully avoiding a stay in hell while they await reincarnation. In fact, all sorts of religious rites, including marriages, are performed at Devghat and they often involve large family groups. The atmosphere is peaceful and tranquil, not at all gloomy.

Devghat is one of the main sites for the festival of Magh Sankranti, and pilgrims come from around Nepal and India to immerse themselves in the river (see the Ridi Bazaar section under Around Tansen later in this chapter). This festival takes place on the first day of the Nepali month of Magh, in mid-January, and celebrates the gradually lengthening days and the onset of warmer weather.

Western visitors are rare, and should bear in mind that caste-related ideas of ritual pollution may mean that some of the orthodox pilgrims and inhabitants could be offended by any contact with Westerners. Do not enter homes or temples without invitation and do not touch anything that could be holy (which means almost everything!). There is nowhere to stay, and not even a chia stall, so bring drinks and food.

THE TERAI

Getting There & Away Frequent minibuses run to Narayanghat from the northern bus stop. By road, head north from town on the Mugling road for 3km, turn left on a signposted dirt road just before a police checkpoint and continue for 2km, then take the right fork and continue for another 3km. It's possible to walk along the south-eastern bank of the river, but the track is a bit overgrown and it's easiest to pick up and follow it from the Devghat end.

Royal Chitwan National Park

☎ 056

From the 19th century, the Chitwan Valley was a centre for the hunting trips that British and Nepali aristocrats seemed to find so entertaining. King George V and his son, the Prince of Wales, later Edward VIII, never made it to Kathmandu, but they did find time to slaughter wildlife in the Chitwan forests. In 11 fun-packed days during one safari in 1911, they killed 39 tigers and 18 rhinos.

Nevertheless, the occasional hunting foray into the park did not seriously jeopardise the Terai's wildlife. In fact, the region's status as a hunting reserve probably helped protect it.

Until the late 1950s, the only settlements in the Chitwan Valley were scattered Tharu villages inhabited by people whose apparent immunity to malaria was rumoured to be the result of their heavy drinking! After malaria was largely controlled by liberal applications of DDT from 1954, land-hungry people from the hills were quick to see the potential wealth of the region and much of the the jungle was then rapidly transformed into farmland.

As their habitat disappeared, so did the tigers and rhinos. By 1973 the rhino population of Chitwan was estimated to have fallen to only 100 and there were just 20 tigers left. (Compare those numbers with the British royals' epic hunting trip 60 years earlier.) Fortunately, this disastrous slide was halted when a sanctuary was established in 1964, although this was at the expense of 22,000 people, who were forcibly removed from within its boundaries. The national park was proclaimed in 1973 and since that time the animal population has rebounded. A census conducted in 2000 found that Chitwan contains 544 rhinos and an estimated 80 tigers, quite apart from 50 other species of mammals and over 450 different types of bird.

Today the park offers one of the finest wildlife experiences in Asia, although it cannot be compared to the great wildlife reserves of Africa. The wildlife is not as varied or as great in number, and the high grass and often dense forest mean the animals are much more difficult to find and observe than wildlife in Africa. You have to be extremely lucky to see one of the park's elusive tigers or leopards. However, an elephant safari is an unforgettable experience, and you are almost certain to see rhinos, various species of deer, monkeys and numerous species of birds.

As with many other national parks throughout the world, the park authorities have to tread a careful line between keeping the local people content and protecting the animals of the park. An often heavy-handed army presence, which involves over one thousand soldiers, has kept poaching and woodcutting to a minimum. This no doubt contributes to local resentment, and the two most significant problems are that the park ties up potential farming land and timber resources, and that surrounding crops are often damaged by the park's animals.

The animals do not respect the park's boundaries. Rhinos wander out in November to wreak havoc on rice crops, and then again in February and March when they attack mustard, lentils and wheat. Deer, monkeys and wild pigs also cause a great deal of damage. The little *machans* (lookout towers) you see in many fields outside the park are used by watchers, who spend their nights in the fields waiting to scare off encroaching animals. Fortunately, tiger and crocodile attacks are rare, but there have been fatalities.

On the positive side, in mid-January and February each year neighbouring villagers are allowed into the park to harvest a number of grass species. Grass has numerous traditional uses, including roof thatching, and provides a valuable cash crop. Working for the park lodges also provides local employment. Also, in contrast to the expensive lodges inside the park, where much of the money goes to owners in Kathmandu or overseas, many of the budget Sauraha lodges funnel money straight into the pockets of local families (although canny Kathmandu entrepreneurs are also heavily present in these as well).

There is something for every budget; at one extreme you can spend US$300 a night to stay at the famous Tiger Tops Lodge, while at the other extreme a simple double room in one of the many small lodges in Sauraha, right on the edge of the park in a prime wildlife-viewing area, costs less than US$2 a night.

Numerous travel agents in Western countries, as well as in Pokhara and Kathmandu, offer package tours to the park. This is the best approach if you plan to stay at one of the expensive lodges inside the park as you can book directly at the lodges' Kathmandu

ROYAL CHITWAN NATIONAL PARK

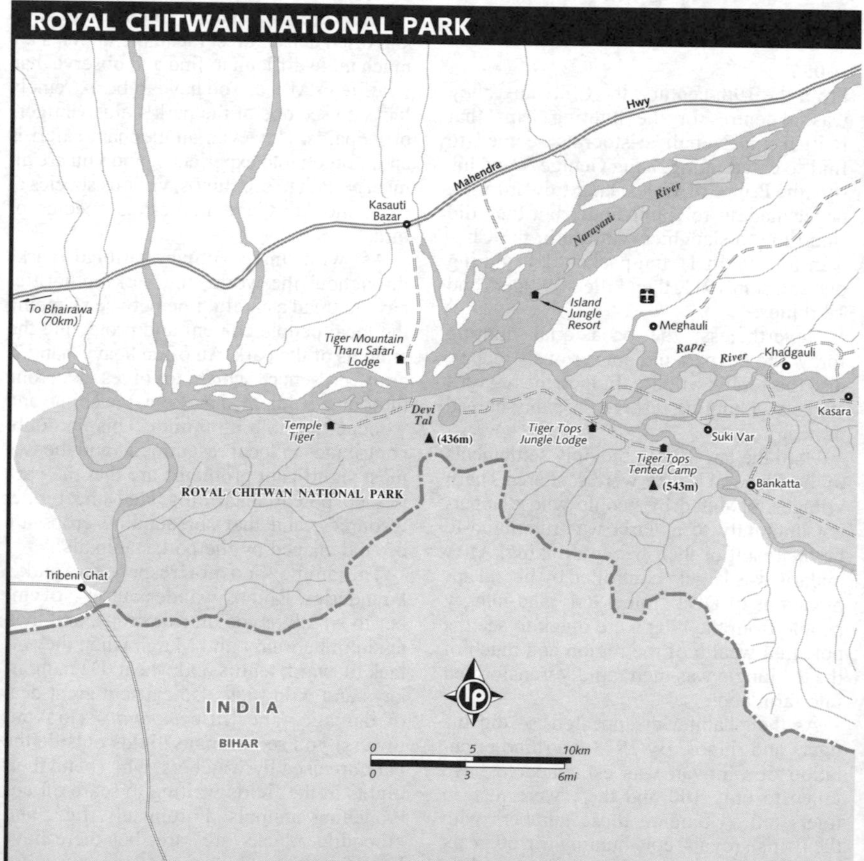

head offices – the package deals usually work out to be better value than the nightly 'walk-in' rate.

However, packages are both unnecessary and relatively expensive if you plan to stay in the budget lodges at Sauraha. The booking agent obviously has to make money on the deal (which adds to the cost), and although you save a little effort, you pay for this by committing yourself to a particular lodge (which you may or may not like) and to a limited time frame.

Many people find the two-night, three-day packages too short, because after you subtract the travelling time (between six and seven hours by bus from Kathmandu or Pokhara) you only have one full day to explore. For most, a visit of two full days is sufficient, although the peaceful atmosphere, good-value accommodation in Sauraha and the range of available activities can easily tempt you into staying longer.

The park is easily accessible from Kathmandu or Pokhara and is actually en route for those heading to/from the Indian border at Birganj as well as points east. It is only a short detour if coming to/from western Nepal or the border at Sunauli.

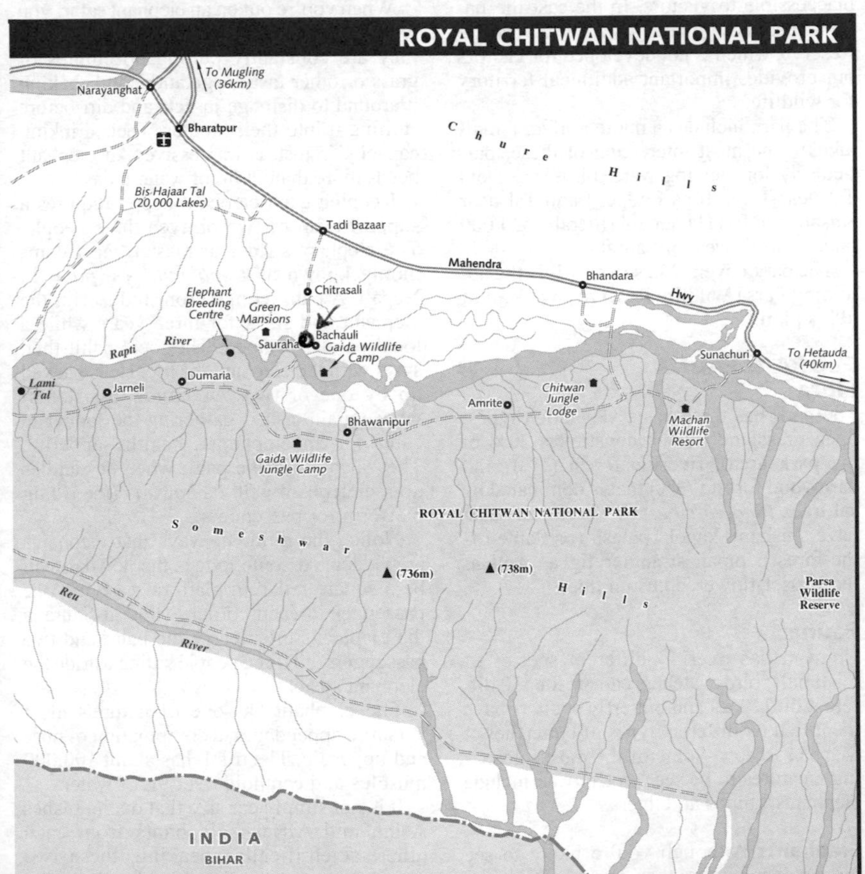

GEOGRAPHY

Along most of the Terai the Gangetic plain runs to the foot of the Chure hills (which then merge with the higher Mahabharat Range), but here the Someshwar hills form the Chitwan Valley, also described as the inner Terai, which lies between the two.

To the north the park comprises a narrow strip of floodplain along the Narayani and Rapti Rivers, a part of the Chitwan Valley and the most visited section of the park. South of this the bulk of the park encompasses the Someshwar hills, which reach a maximum height of 738m, and are largely inaccessible to visitors. In the east the national park is adjoined by the Parsa Wildlife Reserve, which is not developed for visitors but provides important additional territory for wildlife.

The park includes a number of *tal* (small lakes). The most interesting of these, particularly for viewing water birds, are Devi Tal near Tiger Tops Lodge, Lami Tal near Kasara and Bis Hajaar Tal (literally '20,000 lakes') north-west of Sauraha.

The park covers 932 sq km, while the adjoining Parsa Wildlife Reserve covers all of 499 sq km.

FLORA & FAUNA

Flora

The park has three basic vegetation types: open grassland (which constitutes 20% of the park area); riverine forest (7%); and hardwood forest (73%) that is dominated by sal trees *(Shorea ribusta)*. The forests also have shisham, kapok, palash (or flame-of-the-forest), pipal, strangler fig as well as the scarlet-flowered kusum trees.

Fauna

Chitwan has over 43 different species of mammals; bird-watchers can try for 450 different bird types and butterfly spotters have identified 67 different types of butterflies at Machan Resort. Some of the most interesting creatures to be seen in Chitwan include elephants, rhinos and tigers.

Elephants Although you're likely to see more elephants here than any other Chitwan animal, there are no wild elephants in the park. Chitwan's elephants are all trained Asian elephants (also known as Indian).

Training an elephant takes about two years and the Chitwan elephants are usually acquired when they're eight to 20 years old, and can be expected to work until they are 40 or 50. Even elephants born in Nepal (not that there are many) have to go to India to be trained. A trained elephant is not cheap to purchase or to maintain. They typically cost at least US$3000 to buy and then need to be provided with 270kg to 300kg of food a day.

When you're out on an elephant safari you will see how even that isn't enough food; they are constantly pulling up clumps of grass or other tasty vegetation, and shaking it around to dislodge insects and dirt before stuffing it into their mouths. Their drinking capacity is just as impressive: An elephant needs more than 200L of water a day.

Keeping each elephant happy requires a support team of two or even three people. The elephant's rider or master, most commonly known as a *mahout*, is a *pahit* in Nepali. A pahit comes from India with the elephant and stays for three years while a local pahit is trained. The local pahit then stays with the elephant for life. He is backed up by one or two *patchouas* (assistants) whose main task is gathering the fodder to cater for an elephant's healthy appetite. They also assist the pahit when he saddles up the elephant with its *howdah* (the riding platform for passengers).

Notice the different ways that elephants are ridden. At some lodges the howdah will be a square railed-in platform carrying one passenger in each corner, while at Sauraha the elephants often carry the pahit and two passengers, all three people sitting astride the elephant's back.

The elephant has one of nature's most versatile appendages, a combination of nose and upper lip. The trunk has about 100,000 muscles and can hold over 9L of water.

It is not simply ear size that distinguishes Asian and African elephants from each other; scientifically speaking, these two species are not as closely related as you might think. The Asian elephant is noticeably smaller (males reach an average height of 2.75m and females grow to 2.45m), has smaller ears, a bulbous head and a convex back. Only the males, but not all of them, have tusks. The African elephant has enormous ears, a sloping head and a concave back; both the male and female have tusks. The Asian elephant has four nails on each hind foot where the African has only three.

Another major difference, as far as humans are concerned, is the domestication of these huge creatures. Asian elephants are easily trained, while African elephants are not – though some people say that any elephant can be trained, and it is simply that in Africa training elephants has not been widely attempted.

feature	Asian elephant	African elephant
toes	five front four rear	four front three rear
ears	fold forward & India shaped	fold back
tail		bristly
trunk	one 'lip'	two 'lips'
trunk	white patches	white stripes

Elephants have a gestation period of 22 months and the mother is always assisted by another female in looking after the young calf. The calf is fed by its mother for three years and there is usually about seven years between pregnancies, although the elephants are in *musth* (state of sexual excitement) once a year. In the wild, the elephants live in a basically matriarchal society; the bulls do not travel with the herd. Elephants have four teeth and grow six sets during their life. Once the sixth set is worn out, the elephant dies of starvation.

The numerous rivers in the parks have some fine swimming holes and if you're staying at one of the park lodges you'll kick yourself if you pass up the opportunity to lend a hand at elephant bath time. On a hot day in the Terai, there's no better way of cooling off than sitting on an elephant's back in a river and shouting *chhop!* If your accent is right you'll be rewarded with a refreshing cool shower!

Elephant Commands

If you have aspirations of becoming a *pahit* (elephant trainer) you'll first have to learn some elephant commands, although each pahit will have his own particular words and ways of saying them:

sit	*baith*
lie down	*sut*
stand up	*maile*
hold your trunk out for me to climb up	*utha*
stop	*rhaa*
go	*agat*
shower me	*chhop*

Rhinoceroses While elephants are the creatures you see most often in Chitwan, it's the *gaida* (rhinoceros) you spend most time looking for, and with most hope of success. There are two types of rhino in Africa and three in Asia. The great Indian one-horned rhino, found in Chitwan, is larger than the African black rhino, although is smaller than the African white rhino. A fully grown Indian rhino can reach 1.8m at the shoulder and weigh more than two tonnes.

Rhinos are generally solitary creatures although several may occupy the same area. Their diet is chiefly grass and they have very poor eyesight, although their senses of smell and hearing are good. It's their poor sight which leads to the rhino's reputation for having a bad temper. As they cannot see very well, rhinoceroses are prone to assume almost any shape might be dangerous, so they often charge it just in case.

Fortunately for the Indian rhino, its horn is not as large as the African variety and is therefore not so valuable to poachers. Nevertheless, there are many superstitions about rhinos and almost every part of the creature is of value: The urine is considered a charm against both disease and ghosts, a rhino-skin bracelet wards off evil spirits, rhino blood cures menstrual problems and the horn is used for medicinal purposes and is famed as an aphrodisiac. Its value for Arab dagger handles has led to the disastrous decline in rhino numbers in Africa and Asia. Along the riverbanks in Chitwan a rhino marks its territory by dropping excreta in mounds. Since it walks backwards to approach these mounds a waiting poacher used to have easy prey.

More than 600 rhinos currently live in the park and many experts consider the park to be now too small to sustain such a large number. Increasingly, rhinos are wandering outside the park and destroying local crops, and locals aren't shy about killing them if they do. In recent years a number of rhinos have been relocated to other Terai parks, notably Royal Bardia and Sukla Phanta in western Nepal.

Tigers Chitwan's royal Bengal tigers are probably the most elusive of the park's wildlife. Without artificial assistance, such as staking a young buffalo calf out as live bait, you would be very lucky to see a *bagh* (tiger) in Chitwan. Though their numbers have increased considerably since the park was opened, tigers are solitary creatures and they mainly hunt by night.

Tigers require an enormous amount of territory. A male commands an area of about 60 sq km, and a female about 16 or 17 sq km. Both sexes occupy an exclusive territory, although a male's territory may overlap with that of several females. Chitwan is simply not big enough to support the 50 breeding adults that is felt to be the minimum number to prevent interbreeding. This is part of the reason the adjoining Parsa Wildlife Reserve was proclaimed.

Other Mammals Chitwan is also known for more than 50 other mammals. *Chituwa* (leopards) are as elusive as tigers and the night prowling *bhalu* (sloth bears) are also rarely seen.

Chitwan has four types of deer and you will often catch a fleeting glimpse of them as they dash through the undergrowth. There's the tiny *muntjac* (barking deer), the attractive *chital* (spotted deer), the *laghuna* (hog deer) and the big *jarayo* (sambar deer). *Gaur*, the world's largest wild cattle, are also found in the park.

Bandar (langur monkeys) are a common sight, chattering noisily in the tree tops or scattering vegetation down below. The spotted deer often follow the langurs around, taking advantage of their profligate feeding habits. The smaller macaque monkeys are the monkeys commonly found at temples in Nepal and all over the subcontinent. Freshwater or Gangetic dolphins are found in some river stretches in the park, but they are rarely seen.

Reptiles Chitwan has *sarpa* (snakes) of course, including some impressive pythons, as well as turtles and two types of crocodiles. The marsh mugger crocodile is found in marshes, lakes and occasionally in rivers, while the rarer gharial crocodile is exclusively found in rivers. The gharial, which grows to 7m in length and is a harmless fish eater, was in danger of extinction and is still very rare. The gharial breeding centre near Kasara, the park headquarters, has had considerable success, hatching eggs and raising the youngsters to a reasonable size before releasing them into Terai rivers.

WHEN TO GO

Many of the park lodges are closed during the May to August monsoon months when visibility is very poor, the ground is muddy and the flooding rivers make large parts of the park inaccessible. In September the lodges begin to reopen, although at first the rivers are still too high for 4WDs and transfers to the lodges can only be made by elephant.

The best time to visit Chitwan is from October to February when the average daily temperature is about 25°C. There are still cold, misty mornings, however, so a warm jacket is recommended. The Terai can also be extremely hot and sticky, and even in October the humidity leaves everything feeling permanently damp.

After local villagers are allowed into the park to cut the grass, the grasslands are then burnt. While the villagers are crashing about, wildlife is understandably scarce, but February to May is a prime time for wildlife viewing, thanks to the very fact that the grass cover has been removed. Sporadic thunderstorms begin in April and the weather becomes unpleasantly hot.

WHAT TO BRING

Park visitors should come prepared for every eventuality. At times the Terai region can be stiflingly hot, so cool clothes are essential. However, the sun can be fierce and there's not much shade when sitting on an elephant's back, so long sleeves, a shady hat and a good sunscreen are necessary. At the other extreme, the winter months can be surprisingly chilly, particularly if you're out on foot or on elephant back at dawn. So, from November to February you should come prepared for the cold with sweaters and a jacket. Good walking shoes (that you don't mind getting wet) are essential at any time of year and you'll want a swimsuit for the rivers.

Neutral colours are best to ensure you blend into the background and are less likely to alert the wildlife. Reds, yellows and whites are particularly conspicuous.

Insect repellent is another Terai necessity. There is a small risk of malaria – there are plenty of mosquitoes and a wide variety of other voracious insects. Even people who are normally immune to insect attack may discover later that while they were propping up against the bar in the evening, a full-scale attack was being mounted on their ankles.

In addition to camera gear – preferably with a telephoto lens – binoculars are also invaluable to have.

INFORMATION

The park entry fee is Rs 500 per day. If you're staying at a lodge in the park this will usually be included in your overall charge, but if you stay outside the park in Sauraha you have to pay the fee yourself. This can be arranged by most Sauraha guesthouses, or you can easily do it yourself at the ranger's office next to the park visitor centre in Sauraha, where you also book rides on government-owned elephants.

The ticket office and visitor centre are open from 6 am to 5 pm daily. The visitor centre has an interesting, small museum with exhibits about the park, its creation, the problems it faces and its wildlife. The park headquarters are farther west, inside the park at Kasara where there is a small museum of elephant skulls and a gharial crocodile breeding project.

There's no bank in Sauraha, but there are a couple of private moneychangers that accept major currencies (in the form of cash and travellers cheques).

See the Books section in the Facts for the Visitor chapter for books on wildlife and Royal Chitwan National Park.

There's a number of STD/ISD phone services in the village and a couple of these also offer Internet services, although the connection is very slow. Internet connection costs Rs 7 per minute.

Dangers & Annoyances

Come prepared for Nepal's famous *jukha* (leeches). These operate in force during the monsoon and will still be waiting for unwary jungle walkers during the first month or two of the dry season. See the Health section in the Facts for the Visitor chapter for tips on how to deal with these pests.

There is also a small risk of contracting typhus fever from a tick bite. Check with your guide whether they are a problem, and inspect exposed skin after walking.

SAURAHA

Sauraha is just outside the park on the northern bank of the Rapti River, which largely forms the park's boundary. It lies 6km south of Tadi Bazaar (on the Mahendra Hwy).

Sauraha is a simple little village, accessible (for now) only by foot, 4WD or bicycle. It's the sort of place nobody usually visits so it provides a good opportunity to observe Terai rural life. There are verdant rice fields, neat mud-walled houses, barns and a village well in the 'centre' of town. Ox carts rumble by and there's a constant background scene of ducks, chickens and children.

Progress is, however, making its inexorable mark and although it is still a very pleasant place to spend a few days, it is showing signs that it could degenerate into a Terai Thamel. Unfortunately, as elsewhere, there appears to be a complete absence of planning and little or no control over new developments. A new bridge that gives vehicle access from Tadi Bazaar is now finished, and it seems likely that buses will drop you in Sauraha itself; the intrusion of buses and cars into the village certainly won't help the character of the village.

Be wary of being offered a free or cheap 4WD ride to a lodge in Sauraha by a tout. In theory this places you under no obligation, but in practice it's not easy to avoid staying at that particular place. If not taking the bus, you are much better off paying the standard 4WD fare (Rs 30) – hardly a king's ransom – and make it absolutely clear that you intend to check a few different places before you commit yourself. For accommodation in Sauraha see this heading under Places to Stay later.

THINGS TO SEE & DO

Elephant Rides

The greatest thrill at Chitwan is the traditional elephant safari in search of wildlife; seeing a rhino from atop an elephant is an experience not to be missed. You won't want to spend your entire visit aboard an elephant, however. It is not a comfortable mode of travel and your first ride is likely to leave you with aches in muscles you did not know you had, not to mention a new and very interesting selection of bruises!

Government-Owned Elephants Seven government-owned elephants are available at Sauraha for one- to 1½-hour excursions into the park, costing Rs 1000 per person. Howdahs are not used – two or three passengers sit astride the elephant's back. At peak times the number of visitors exceeds the supply of elephants, so it's wise to turn up at the ranger's office near the visitor centre at 6 am, or get your lodge staff to get there even earlier; pre-booking is not possible. Elephant safaris start at 7.30 am and 4 pm, prime wildlife-viewing times.

Privately Owned Elephants The lodges inside the park have their own elephants and elephant safaris are a standard activity; two, three or sometimes four passengers ride on a wooden-railed howdah.

Outside the park it's possible to take rides onboard private elephants, either arranged through your lodge or one of the two private operations, Unique and United, both of which have offices in Sauraha. The going rate for a two-hour safari is Rs 550, but they are restricted to the Kumroj Community Forest, a buffer zone located a 30-minute drive east of Sauraha. Transfers by 4WD are included. Wildlife sightings are usually good here, with rhinos being common, but tiger sightings are very uncommon, not surprising given the proximity of villages and the presence of so many people. If you only have time and money for one ride, you are much better off going into the park proper.

When booking a package tour in Kathmandu, or an elephant ride through a lodge, make sure you check whether your ride will take you inside or outside the park.

Jungle Walks

Visitors are allowed to enter the park on foot, but in order to get the most out of the experience, and for reasons of safety, it is mandatory that you go with a guide. Most lodges (including some in Sauraha) have their own naturalists, but there are also a number of independent guides. These young locals may not have much formal training, but they're often very knowledgeable about the park's wildlife and where to find it.

Walking is the ideal way to see the park's prolific butterflies and birds, and to also see the flora close up. Walks, which are often

WARNING

Tourists and guides have been killed by rhinos. Tigers and sloth bears can also be dangerous. Guides should brief you on safety procedures at the beginning of the walk. Many locals regard these walks as dangerous, but offer themselves as guides to remain employed – if they refuse to take tourists on guided walks they risk losing their jobs. It's a potentially risky activity (for both guides and tourists) that, upon weighing up these risks, is perhaps best avoided.

nothing more than a pleasant stroll through the jungle, can be exhilarating, but they are potentially dangerous if you meet a rhino.

Jungle walks from Sauraha usually cost around Rs 60 per person for two hours, Rs 250 for half a day, and Rs 400 for a full day. Short walks will generally cover grassland and riverine forest; you need a day to get into the jungle. Walks can also be combined with canoe trips.

Canoeing

A canoe trip along the Rapti or Narayani Rivers is the most restful way of seeing the wildlife, particularly water birds, and with a bit of luck you may also see mugger and gharial crocodiles. With a great deal of luck you might catch a glimpse of a freshwater Gangetic dolphin, although they are as rare a sight as tigers.

Canoe trips from Sauraha cost Rs 230 per person, but trips can also be combined with a walk. The standard program is a one-hour float downriver, followed by a three-hour guided walk back to the village (costing around Rs 500 in total). National park fees must also be paid.

4WD Safaris

Animals are surprisingly unconcerned by vehicles, so a 4WD safari can be more exciting than you may expect. It also gives you a chance to get beyond the immediate Sauraha area. Most 4WD rides take three or four hours and include a visit to the park headquarters at Kasara, about 20km west of Sauraha, and the nearby gharial crocodile breeding centre. The cost is around Rs 650 per person. Bear in mind that 4WDs may not be able to get across the river into the park until the water levels drop sufficiently (maybe from around January to April).

Terai Culture

Staying in Sauraha gives you an excellent opportunity to explore the surrounding countryside, either on foot or bicycle. Originally, the area was dominated by Tharu, but over the last decade increasing numbers of hill people have bought up the land. Many villages are now a multicultural mixture. They're full of life (and hordes of children) and give a vivid insight into the rigours and pleasures of subsistence farming. The nearest Tharu village is **Bachauli**, east of Sauraha towards the Gaida Wildlife Camp.

Some lodges arrange visits to nearby villages and a number organise displays of traditional Tharu dances. The stick dance, with a great circle of men whacking their sticks together, is quite a sight. In Sauraha are two 'cultural centres', Tharu Culture Program and Chautari Culture House, where dances are performed each evening at 8 pm during the season. It's very much a tourist experience, but fun all the same. The cost is around Rs 350. Some of the more expensive lodges put on free performances for guests.

Wildlife Breeding Projects

There are two important breeding projects associated with the national park worth visiting: the elephant breeding camp 3km west of Sauraha and the gharial crocodile breeding centre near Kasara. Access to the breeding centre is from outside the park, so you need to take a canoe across the river at the elephant breeding centre, having already paid the national park entry fee.

Cycling

Bicycles are not allowed into the park proper – because apparently nothing infuriates a rhino more than a bicycle – but the surrounding countryside is ideal for touring. You can hire standard Indian-made single-speed bicycles from various shops around the chowk in Sauraha for around Rs 120 per day; these are adequate for negotiating the dusty tracks as long as you are not too ambitious about the distance you want to cover.

Just wandering along the tracks east and west of Sauraha is good fun, but if you like to have a specific destination, consider a trip to Bis Hajaar Tal, about 1½ hours north-west of Sauraha. The lakes are famous for their prolific birdlife. To get there, ride to Tadi, turn left (west) onto the Mahendra Hwy and continue for about 3km until you reach a signposted bridge over the Khageri Khola. Cross the bridge and take the dirt road on the left (south). After another small bridge the road forks; take the right fork and continue for about 5km. You'll see the lakes on the right.

PLACES TO STAY

Basically you can stay either inside the park, or at Sauraha. The places inside the park are all expensive, but at Sauraha there is a range of accommodation costing from US$2 to US$50. When it comes to seeing the wildlife there's little difference between the two options. You've got just as much chance of seeing a rhino whether your room costs US$2 or US$200 a night.

For those who can afford it, the lodges inside the park offer considerable luxury, wildlife-watching activities that are well organised, as well as an all-encompassing safari atmosphere.

Although they can be pretty basic, the Sauraha budget lodges often have an interesting clientele, are scattered around an attractive, partly traditional village, and the full range of wildlife-watching activities can also be easily organised.

Inside the Park

Most visitors to the park lodges arrive on package tours from Kathmandu, often as part of a larger tour of Nepal or the region. Transfers to your accomodation are usually arranged through the lodges (see Getting There & Away in this section for more details). It is necessary to book in advance. Most of the lodges have attractive individual cottages dotted around a central dining room and bar area. Some have 'tented camps' with luxurious, semipermanent tents – usually you won't have a private bathroom, but you certainly won't be uncomfortable.

The lodges generally quote a daily charge that is based on twin-share accommodation. It covers activities (including rides on their privately owned elephants) and all meals, but not park entry or the park's camping fee if you stay in a tented camp. Most also have all-inclusive packages for two or three days that include transport from Kathmandu. The only additional expenses will be for drinks and tips, and a (hefty) surcharge if you want single accommodation.

The ***Tiger Tops*** (*☎ 01-411225, fax 414075, e info@tigermountain.com, postal address: PO Box 242, Durbar Marg, Kathmandu*). which runs three different operations in the park, is the best known and is easily the most expensive of the lodges. The Pioneer Jungle Lodge in Chitwan is operated under the umbrella of Tiger Mountain, a very professional organisation, and enjoys a deservedly high reputation, particularly for its excellent guides as well as its environmentally conscious approach. Whether you think it is worth the amount of money charged probably depends on how much money you have. Although the accommodation is comfortable and the food is good, those expecting to be pandered to with extravagant five-star luxury could be disappointed. Tiger Tops has chosen to not expand or compromise the safari experience with unnecessary technological and consumerist trappings. Children under 12 stay for 50% of the adult rate, and there are big discounts in the low season.

The well-known ***Jungle Lodge***, which charges US$300 per person a night plus tax in the peak season, is the original tree-top hotel. The buildings are on stilts and are constructed from local materials. The recently refurbished rooms are comfortable, with solar-powered lights and fans and solar-heated water. Closed early June to early September.

The ***Tented Camp*** is 3km east of the jungle lodge in the beautiful Surung Valley. It's US$150 per person a night – there are 12 safari tents with twin beds and modern toilet and shower amenities. Closed early May to early September.

Tiger Mountain Tharu Safari Lodge, the newest addition, is open all year round. Built in traditional Tharu style, the long houses are made from timber, grass reeds and mud, and are decorated with wall paintings. The rooms are attractive and comfortable; each has a single and queen-sized bed, and a bathroom for US$100 per person a night. There's also a swimming pool here. The village is actually just outside the park on the northern bank of the Narayani River.

One of the other operators in the park, at the western end, close to Tiger Mountain

Tharu Safari Lodge is ***Temple Tiger*** *(☎ 01-263480, ⓔ temtigrs@mos.com.np, postal address: PO Box 3968, Kamaladi, Kathmandu)*. Accommodation consists of comfortable elevated individual cabins built largely from local materials, and each with a private viewing area over the grasslands. Minimal forest clearance has taken place here, so the atmosphere is really one of a jungle camp. The daily rate is steep at US$250 per person, plus the park entry fee. Children aged three to 12 are charged 50% (children under three stay for free).

Island Jungle Resort *(☎ 01-220162, ⓔ island@mos.com.np, postal address: PO Box 2154, Durbar Marg, Kathmandu)* is also at the western end of the park on a large island in the middle of the Narayani River. The site is superb, one of the best in the park. Accommodation consists of cottages which, although comfortable, are not particularly attractive. The cost is US$110 per person per night, although packages can be considerably cheaper and very good value. There's also tented camp accommodation, which costs US$100 per person. Children aged three to 10 are charged 50%.

Gaida Wildlife Camp *(☎ 01-220940, ⓔ gaida@mos.com.np, postal address: PO Box 2056, Durbar Marg, Kathmandu)* is farther east, not far from Sauraha in the only section of park north of the Rapti River.

The ***Gaida Wildlife Jungle Camp*** is an 8km trip south at the base of the Someshwar hills. The main camp has comfortable thatched huts for US$110 per person, and the jungle camp has safari tents for US$80 per person. The wildlife is not particularly prolific immediately around the main camp, but is very good around the jungle camp, which is open from October to May.

At the eastern end of the park is the rustic place ***Chitwan Jungle Lodge*** *(☎ 01-228458, ⓔ e@chitwanjunglelodge.com, postal address: PO Box 1281, Durbar Marg, Kathmandu)*. Rooms are constructed in traditional Tharu style with mud walls and thatched roofs. There's no electricity but otherwise the lodge has all the mod cons including a restaurant, private bathrooms and a very pleasant open-air bar. The forest is relatively undisturbed in this part of the park and a river with a terrific swimming (and elephant-bathing) hole runs very close by. The rate is US$100 per person, but a package is US$270 for a stay of two nights including land transport from Kathmandu. You can get there by raft for an extra US$50 per person.

Machan Wildlife Resort *(☎ 01-225001, fax 240681, postal address: PO Box 3140, Kathmandu, ⓔ wildlife@machan.mos.com.np)* is a particularly attractive resort at the far eastern end of the park, close to the boundary of the adjoining Parsa Wildlife Reserve. It offers excellent facilities including an attractive natural swimming pool and a video library of wildlife films. The accommodation is in well-designed, timber-frame bungalows with bathrooms, and is decorated with superb Mithila murals. The cost is US$125 per person for the first night, with additional nights costing US$100. Return transfers from Kathmandu cost US$122 by air and US$60 by car.

Sauraha

There are so many lodges, and competition is so intense, that prices in Sauraha are ridiculously low. Many lodges have thus come to depend on 'invisible' add-on charges (commissions or service charges for organising bus tickets and wildlife-watching activities) to make a profit. While there is actually nothing wrong with a charge for services rendered, they can get completely out of hand in Sauraha. Prices are sometimes inflated by ridiculous amounts, particularly since in almost all cases it's easy and straightforward to organise tickets and activities yourself.

With literally dozens of places to chose from, it is impossible to mention them all here. There's a certain lack of originality when it comes to naming these places; it seems they almost all have a three-word name taken from a list of about half a dozen words – jungle, safari, Chitwan, tiger, camp, wildlife and river all feature prominently.

The most important variable is the quality of the staff and your fellow travellers, both of which change, so ask other travellers for recommendations and check places for yourself. The main north–south road is busier and more developed than the east–west roads.

Budget The budget lodges at Sauraha are all very much out of the same mould; clean and simple mud-and-thatch cottages that sleep two and cost around Rs 100 for doubles. Most have a small veranda, and those with a nice garden can really be very pleasant places to stay. The mud-wall architecture keeps things surprisingly cool, and the rooms have insect screens on the windows and/or mosquito nets on the beds. Toilets and bathrooms are shared; hot water is unlikely, but this is not a major problem given the climate.

***Chitwan Safari Camp** (☎ 80024)* has a pleasant garden and a quiet, but good central position. It's old fashioned and simple, and although it is a fraction more expensive than some of the other budget places (Rs 100 to Rs 300 for doubles) you really can't quibble at the price.

The ***Annapurna View Lodge** (☎ 80072)* is another decent budget place with a nice atmosphere. Cottages with two beds cost Rs 100 or Rs 150/300 for a single/double room with bathroom.

Next door, the ***Crocodile Safari Camp*** is busy and friendly with standard rooms for Rs 100 and doubles with bathroom for Rs 300. The restaurant is good, but the garden is fairly ordinary.

Also in this area is the ***Skyline Jungle Camp** (☎ 80024)*, a modern place with standard brick cottages costing Rs 100 or doubles with bathroom for Rs 300. The rooms have a shady, verdant veranda.

The ***Nature Safari Camp** (☎ 80019)*, farther along the same track, is a modern concrete construction, but the rooms as well as bathroom facilities are good. Standard rooms are good value at Rs 100 with shared bathroom, and there are also a few with agreeable outlooks and private bathroom for the nice bargain rate of Rs 250.

The ***Rainforest Guest House** (☎ 80007)*, at the northern end of town, is a quiet and shady budget place with mud and thatch

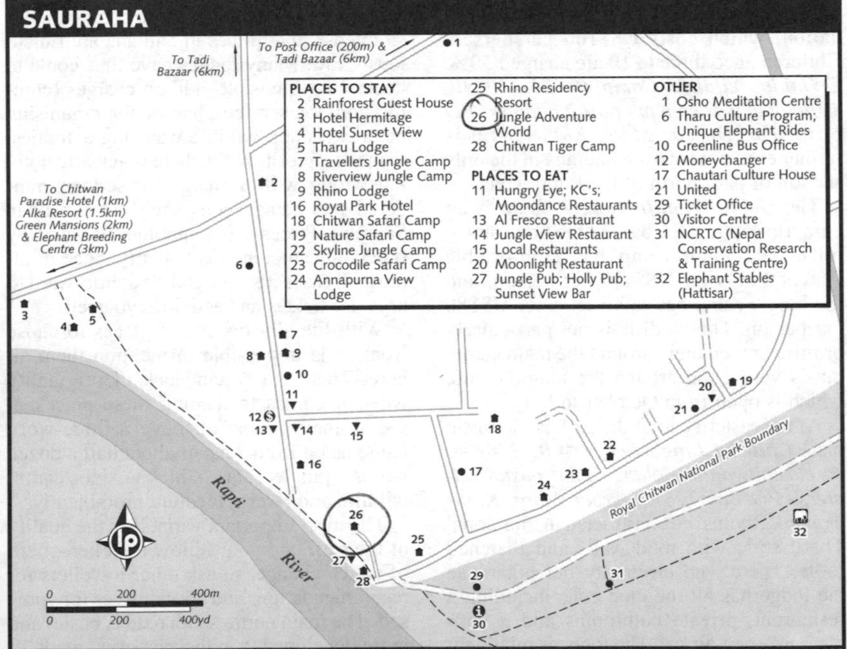

cottages for Rs 100/150, or brick cottages at Rs 300 with bathroom. This place has a large garden but little shade.

Travellers' Jungle Camp (*☎ 80014)* is a friendly place with mud-and-thatch cottages at Rs 100 or brick cottages with bathroom at Rs 300 and Rs 400. This is a good family-run place with helpful owners.

The ***Tharu Lodge*** (*☎ 80055)* is a mellow little place close to the river with a nice garden and river views. It's just off the track leading to the elephant breeding centre. Standard mud-and-thatch cottages cost Rs 100 and brick cottages with bathroom cost Rs 350.

Right next door is the ***Hotel Sunset View***, which is similar, although it's a pity the river views have been blocked by rooms.

Mid-Range An increasing number of lodges are moving upmarket, so if you absolutely can't live without air-con and TV, the following may be for you. Most mid-range places are dependent on the package trade, but they are happy to take on individuals if there are vacancies. Some are pretty good value with slightly more comfortable rooms with bathroom from around US$10/15.

The standard package offered is three days and two nights, including transport, food, accommodation, entry fees, jungle walks, a canoe trip, an elephant ride, a performance of Tharu folk dancing and a tour of a Tharu village. Typically, the packages cost from US$100 if you travel to the park by bus, considerably more if you travel by air or private car – it is possible to spend considerably less if you travel independently and pay as you go. There are also combined rafting/Chitwan trips.

Rhino Lodge (*☎ 80065, e terai@ccsl.com.np)*, a reputable mid-range package-oriented place, has a range of doubles from Rs 600 with bathroom up to Rs 900 on the 2nd floor with views. The big plus about this place is that its bar and restaurant nicely overlook the river.

The ***Riverview Jungle Camp*** (*☎ 80022)* is a decent place, and although central, is not in any way spoilt. It's worth a look, with much larger than usual double cottages for Rs 300 or more substantial brick cottages at Rs 650 with bathroom.

With a river frontage ***Hotel Hermitage*** (*☎ 80090, e hermitage@mail.com.np)* has standard brick cottages at Rs 700 with bathroom. There's also two new two-storey blocks of air-con rooms with TV.

The ***Chitwan Paradise Hotel*** (*☎ 80048, e paradise@mos.com.np)*, farther along the road to the elephant breeding centre, is nicely secluded and has cottages with bathroom at US$15. Interestingly, 40% of the profits go to NIDS, a nongovernmental organisation that supports rural communities. A bicycle would be very handy if you're staying here.

With an excellent position overlooking the river ***Chitwan Tiger Camp*** (*☎ 80060, e tigercmp@col.com.np)* offers bamboo machan rooms on stilts with the best views in Sauraha. Machan rooms are US$10/15 with shared bathroom, standard cottage rooms are US$15/25 with bathroom, and luxury rooms with coolers cost US$25/40. Discounts are possible.

The ***Royal Park Hotel*** (*☎ 80061)* has an excellent location set in a large garden close to the river. The substantial, spacious cottages all have bathroom, fan and hot water, and beautiful slate floors. They also have wheelchair access. The cost is US$20 or US$25 including breakfast. There's also an area set aside for campers, which costs US$2 per person. The bar here is in a great spot with limited river views.

Jungle Adventure World (*☎ 80064, e jaw_resort@hotmail.com)* also has a very pleasant garden setting with excellent river views. The cottages are comfortably furnished and are good value at US$15.

The newest mid-range place, known as ***Rhino Residency Resort*** (*☎ 01-220697, e rhino@residency.wlink.com.np)* is near the national park gate. Air-con rooms are in a manicured garden, and there's a swimming pool and restaurant, all surrounded by a high wall for privacy – it's about as far from a village experience as you can get in Sauraha. Rooms cost US$40/55.

Green Mansions (*☎ 01-221854)*, signposted about 3km west of Sauraha near the elephant breeding centre, is a comfortable, low-key place. Rooms have some nice local touches, such as brass-bowl handbasins and shower bases. It's actually very nicely done, but without your own transport it's a bit far from everything. Doubles cost US$30.

Also west of Sauraha near the Baghmara Community Forest ***Alka Resort*** (☎ *80049,* ⓔ *info@alkaresort.com.np)* is a well-run place with a pleasant jungle-type garden. Rooms are US$25 per person with dinner and breakfast.

PLACES TO EAT

Most places to stay also prepare food, most people seem to eat breakfast at their lodge, preferring to venture out only at lunch time and in the evening.

In Sauraha, eating is centred around the main chowk. There's a handful of small, 1st-floor terrace restaurants above the shops, with limited views over the river. The food is generally standard travellers' fare, and the quality is average. Restaurants here include the ***Jungle View***, ***KC's***, ***Moondance*** and ***Hungry Eye***. Near the park boundary, the ***Moonlight*** is similar.

Al Fresco Restaurant, a flash two-storey place, is a sign of Kathmandu money moving in. The views from the 1st-floor balcony are great. At the time of writing, it was closed and its future was uncertain, but with this location it is bound to reopen.

There are also a few places actually on the flood plain of the river, and they look pretty vulnerable to a severe flood. They are all low-key – a bamboo hut with tables and umbrellas by the river, and are popular places at sunset. These include the ***Jungle Pub***, the ***Sunset View Bar*** and the ***Holly Pub***.

GETTING THERE & AWAY

Air

Yeti Airlines has daily flights from Kathmandu to Meghauli, near the Tiger Tops, Temple Tiger and Island Jungle Resort lodges, for US$82 each way. There are also daily flights with most of the private airlines to Bharatpur (Narayanghat) for US$65 each way. The flights take around 30 minutes.

Bus

Tourist buses that go between Kathmandu or Pokhara and Chitwan cost from Rs 150, the trip typically takes six or seven hours. Any travel agent in Kathmandu or Pokhara can make a booking. Tourist buses (used by the majority of visitors) actually go to Chitrasali, the footbridge over the river midway between Tadi Bazaar and Sauraha. In Sauraha, lodges will book tickets (but beware of inflated prices) or you can book in Tadi at booking stalls near the main intersection.

Greenline (☎ 60126) has a daily air-con service in each direction for Rs 480 including breakfast, leaving Kathmandu, Pokhara and Sauraha (Chitrasali) at 8 am – you can change at Kurintar for Pokhara.

To Sunauli on the Indian border (from Tadi), buses cost Rs 140 and take about five hours and to Birganj buses cost Rs 85 and take about three hours.

Ordinary buses drop you in Tadi Bazaar on the Mahendra Hwy, about 15km east of Narayanghat. Minibuses then run from Tadi Bazaar to Narayanghat, cost Rs 10 and take 30 minutes. From Tadi Bazaar it's 6km to Sauraha (Rs 30 by 4WD).

Car

Visitors to the lodges inside the park usually get to the lodges by car from Kathmandu or Pokhara and this is usually arranged by the lodge operators. Cars typically cost around US$60, and the 160km to 180km trip (depending on where you're going) takes four to five hours.

If you are coming or going from Kathmandu, you should try to convince your driver to take you one way via the Tribhuvan Hwy passing through Daman and Hetauda. However, this route will cost extra as the narrow, winding road will add at least an hour to your travel time. See the Daman and Hetauda sections in this chapter for details of this spectacular route.

The cars usually drop you at the turn-offs from the main road, from where your lodge vehicle will pick you up for the final trip into the park and across the river. This short trip is usually made by 4WD, although in the first month or two after the monsoon ends

(September and October) the river may still be too high for vehicles and the transfer may be made by elephant. It's quite a surprise to arrive at the turn-off and find an elephant waiting for the final amble to the lodge!

Raft

Numerous Kathmandu rafting operators offer trips down the Trisuli River to Chitwan. Most park lodges will organise a rafting trip in conjunction with your stay in the park.

Rafting trips start from Mugling, where the road to Narayanghat and Chitwan turns off from the Kathmandu-Pokhara (Prithvi) Hwy, or from farther up the Trisuli. It takes two or three days to raft down to Chitwan. Don't expect white-water thrills; this section of the river is really more of a gentle drift, although there are some fine views and the sandy beaches along the riverside offer great camping spots.

Prices will range from around US$30 to US$75 per day for rafting only, and rafting and Chitwan trips (four nights, five days) can be as cheap as US$150. Shop around and establish details before you hand over your money; check where the rafting trip begins, what size the groups are, what activities are included at Chitwan and what transport there is from the river to your accommodation at Chitwan. See the Rafting & Kayaking chapter for more information.

Western Terai

This section covers the western portion of the Mahendra Hwy from Narayanghat to Mahendranagar, which is in excellent condition. Tansen (Palpa) is also included in this section, which is between Bhairawa and Pokhara. For a summary of the trip along this portion of the highway, see the boxed text 'Travelling Along the Mahendra Highway – Western Terai' following.

BUTWAL

☎ 071

Lying at the very foot of the Chure hills, Butwal is at first appearances an unattractive, dirty town. The approach in from Tansen, to the north, is dramatic; one moment you're in a narrow mountain gorge, the next you are surrounded by people, dust, rickshaws and Hindi film posters.

If you find yourself stranded for a night, or have a couple of hours to kill waiting for a bus, it's well worth a wander through the old part of town on the west bank of the Tinau River. Historically, Butwal once lay at the start of a trade route to Tibet and so has a good deal more history than most Terai towns. While there are no significant old buildings, the narrow, traffic-free streets of the old part of town are a million miles from new Butwal – kids play cricket in the street, women sit chatting in doorways and there is a general unhurried air. Walk across the main vehicle bridge, then head north through the old streets towards the hills, then cut back across the river on one of the two suspension foot and bicycle bridges.

You can check email at a small place in the Royal Hotel, which is 50m south of Traffic Chowk.

Places to Stay & Eat

There are plenty of cheap hotels at Traffic Chowk on the main road in the centre of town, and this is also where long-distance buses stop. Pick of the cheapies is the ***Hotel New Gandaki*** *(☎ 40928)*, which has scruffy rooms at Rs 150 for a double with shared bathroom and Rs 250 with bathroom.

A quantum leap up the scale, and well worth the price difference, is the modern ***Hotel Kandara*** *(☎ 40380)*. This place is friendly with a nice small garden with car parking at the rear. Clean rooms with bathroom are Rs 280/440 for singles/doubles, Rs 450/800 with carpet and hot water or Rs 1300 for air-con doubles. Avoid the front rooms as they cop the street noise.

Next door is the ***Hotel Siddhartha*** *(☎ 40380)*, a clean and comfortable hotel with rooms at Rs 380/480 with bathroom. The attached ***Nest Restaurant*** is a cheap and reasonable place to eat.

The ***Hotel Sindoor*** *(☎ 40381)* is an upmarket and expensive hotel catering to visiting bigwigs. Though overpriced and a bit gloomy, it's clean, quiet and unquestionably the best place in town. Rooms here are US$25/35; but it wouldn't hurt to ask them for a discount.

Getting There & Away

All the long-distance buses leave from the Traffic Chowk on the main drag.

Buses for Pokhara, Tansen and west Terai are booked at the small shop with the red sign in Nepali at the Hotel Kandara 50m north of Traffic Chowk. The booking office for buses to Kathmandu and places east is about 100m south of Traffic Chowk, outside the small, modern, yellow temple; look for the red sign in Nepali and the scrum of eager people.

There are departures for Kathmandu (Rs 167), Tansen (Rs 38), Pokhara via Mugling (Rs 165, eight hours) and via Tansen (Rs 128, nine hours!). Buses also depart for Nepalganj (Rs 187), Narayanghat (Rs 70) and Mahendranagar (Rs 327).

There are also regular departures for Sunauli/Bhairawa (22km).

SUNAULI & BHAIRAWA

☎ 071

Sunauli (pronounced 'so-**nor**-li') is a small, squalid, grubby collection of offices and hotels right on the Indian border – not a good introduction if you've just entered Nepal, but cheer up, things improve rapidly from here. Bhairawa is a somewhat more substantial, dusty, bustling town nearly 4km inside Nepal; officially Bhairawa's name is Siddharthanagar, but this name is rarely ever used.

There are three points in favour of visiting this part of the world. Firstly, Sunauli is by far the most popular and convenient border crossing between Nepal and northern and western India (including Varanasi, Agra and Delhi). Secondly, Bhairawa is the closest town to Lumbini, the birthplace of Buddha. And thirdly, although Sunauli and Bhairawa are hot and featureless, they are still relaxed and pleasant in comparison to Birganj, the next major crossing point to the east.

Travelling Along the Mahendra Highway – Western Terai

Mahendranagar to Narayanghat

The far west is the least developed and most traditional part of the Terai. It's inhabited by Tharus, Bajis (Abadhi speakers from India), Muslims and more recently, migrants from the hills.

The highway was only sealed and all the bridges were completed in 2000, so the far west of the country has only recently been well connected with the rest. It is around 45km from the border town of **Mahendranagar** to **Ataria**, a scruffy town at a major intersection; roads head south to the district headquarters of **Dhangadhi** (14km) and north way up into the hills to **Dipayal** (155km) and **Baitali** (168km). Between Ataria and Chisopani (80km) there are a number of nondescript Tharu towns. The most interesting spot is **Ghodagodhi Tal** (50km from Ataria), a small lake and bird sanctuary right by the roadside.

The **Karnali River** is one of the largest in Nepal, draining the western third of the country. Thanks to the World Bank, an enormous single-span suspension bridge has been built at **Chisopani**, at the point where the river flows through its last gorge and spills out onto the plains.

After the Karnali River the road runs through the sal forest of the **Royal Bardia National Park**; there are three army checkpoints along this section, and if you are travelling by car you must arrive at the second and third checkpoints a prescribed number of minutes after leaving the previous checkpoint. The army guys are real sticklers for this – if you get there too quickly you've obviously been speeding (speed limit in the park is 40 km/h), too slowly and you've obviously stopped along the way somewhere (also not allowed). You must also pull up right on the white line about 25m before the checkpoint! While travelling through here keep your eyes peeled for monkeys, deer and peacocks.

The collection of wooden shacks known as **Anbasa** is the turn-off for **Thakurdwara**, the main accommodation centre for Bardia. It is 500m east of the Amreni checkpoint (the second checkpoint).

There is some small-scale industry, a couple of banks and government offices and plenty of shops. Most prearranged bookings to or from India involve a night's stopover in Sunauli.

If you are heading straight for other parts of Nepal, it makes sense to grit your teeth and stay in Sunauli (all buses depart from here). If you plan to spend a few days exploring this part of the country (well worth it, especially in the cooler months), then tear yourself away from Sunauli's many and varied delights and head for Bhairawa, which offers some better accommodation and some civility.

Orientation & Information

Both the Nepali and Indian customs and immigration offices are open 24 hours, but between the hours of about 7 pm and 5 am you will have to wake officials up, something they are quite accustomed to. You are free to walk across the border between the Indian and Nepali sides without going through any formalities, although if you try to attempt this with a backpack on you would be asking for trouble.

There is a tourist office (☎ 20304) at the border, but don't expect much. There's also a bank and numerous official moneychangers. Indian rupees (INRs) are accepted in Bhairawa and Sunauli (at the pegged exchange rate of Indian Rs 1 = Nepal Rs 1.60), but offload any excess before leaving here as Indian rupees get harder to get rid of the farther you move from the border.

Bhairawa is a 20-minute rickshaw ride to the north. Most shops and businesses in Bhairawa are strung along Narayan Path or Bank Rd. The Siddhartha Hwy runs along the eastern edge of town to the border.

Places to Stay & Eat

Sunauli There are about a dozen options here, none of them much chop and all expensive for what you get. (Note that there is no point staying on the Indian side as the choice will be limited to only one very tired government tourist bungalow.)

Travelling Along the Mahendra Highway – Western Terai

After leaving the national park you enter an agricultural zone inhabited by Tharus and a growing number of migrants from the hills. As you approach **Kohalpur**, 71km from Chisopani and the turn-off for Nepalganj, there are an increasing numbers of Muslims – the white spires of mosques can be seen in the villages.

Nepalganj is 16km south of Kohalpur, and lies on the flat, hot Gangetic plain at the western end of the Rapti Valley. The Rapti Valley, like the Chitwan Valley, is described as the Inner Terai, and lies along the Rapti River between the Duduwa hills to the south and the Chure hills and Mahabharat Range to the north. The valley is attractive and intensively cultivated – it seems to become more fertile the farther east you travel. There are endless fields of mustard, interspersed with small Tharu settlements and the much grander Newari-style houses of their *zamindars* (landlords). There are a number of grubby and depressing roadside villages with the usual chia shops – the largest being **Kusum** (71km from Nepalganj) and **Lamahi** (52km from Kusum).

About 25km from Lamahi, the road crosses the Rapti River and climbs over the foothills before dropping down into the Terai proper. **Butwal**, where buses turn north to Pokhara along the Siddhartha Hwy, is the next major town, which is 97km from the bridge over the Rapti and 245km from Kohalpur.

The road from Butwal to **Narayanghat** (114km) is not particularly interesting. There are a couple of places where there are quite steep climbs over ridges of the Chure hills, but most of the countryside is flat and monotonous sal forest. The soil is too sandy to be farmed. There are some unattractive strips of roadside development, inhabited mainly by relatively recent migrants from the hills. From Narayanghat there is a road link to Mugling on the Kathmandu-Pokhara (Prithvi) Hwy (see the Kathmandu to Pokhara section in the Pokhara chapter for details).

The *Nepal Guest House* has a reasonable restaurant, is reasonably priced and is passably clean. The place is something of a labyrinth and the rooms vary – ask to see several before you settle in. There are four-bed dorms with beds for Rs 40, singles for Rs 100 with shared bathroom and doubles with fan and bathroom for Rs 170.

The hopefully named *Hotel Paradise* (☎ *22777*) is OK and is right next to the bus park, but make sure you get a room on the side away from the bus park as buses start leaving here at around 4 am. Rooms are Rs 280/400 with bathroom.

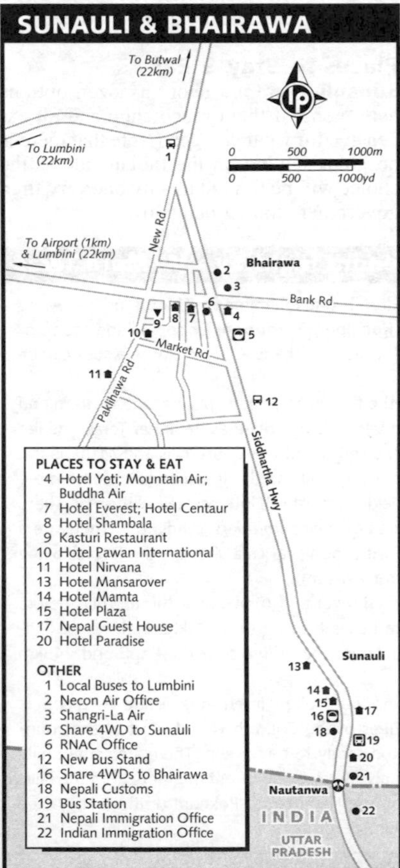

The *Hotel Plaza* is probably one of the better places and has yet to slide into the shabby state that seems to befall most hotels in this part of the world. It's good value at Rs 250/350.

The *Hotel Mamta* (☎ *20312*), about 300m from the border post, does not look very inspiring, but the rooms are reasonably clean. A single bed in a six-bed dorm costs Rs 50 and a room with shared bathroom is Rs 100/180, and with bathroom is Rs 150/250.

Aiming at something approaching luxury, but failing fairly dismally, is the *Hotel Mansarover* (☎ *23686*). Double rooms are Rs 640 with bathroom or and the luxury of air-con and TV is yours for Rs 1600.

Apart from the restaurants attached to hotels, there are a few small restaurants.

Bhairawa The *Hotel Shambala* (☎ *20167*) on Bank Rd is not too bad, and charges Rs 250 for a small double with shared bathroom, Rs 350/450 for rooms with bathroom, and Rs 1000/1200 with air-con, although prices are open to negotiation somewhat. There's also a restaurant here.

Another budget option on Bank Rd is the *Hotel Centaur*, not far from the Hotel Everest (see below). It is a typical no frills place, with rooms for Rs 150, or with bathroom at Rs 200/250.

The *Hotel Everest* (☎ *20317*) on the same road is a modern place with clean and comfortable rooms. The charge is perhaps a bit high at Rs 500/700 with bathroom, but some bargaining may be possible.

The tour groups that occasionally pass through usually stay at *Hotel Yeti* (☎ *20551*, e *htl-yeti@btw.wlink.com.np*) on the corner of Bank Rd and Siddhartha Hwy. It's clean, there's a decent restaurant and, for what it delivers, the prices are reasonable – US$30/35 or US$35/45 with air-con; discounts are offered. The only problem is the hotel overlooks a main intersection (where the buses stop), so it can be a bit noisy.

Hotel Pawan International (☎ *23680*, e *pawanhl@mos.com.np*) on Paklihawa Rd is new and glossy, and seems to be catering to well-to-do Indians passing through. It is good value at US$55/65 for air-con rooms.

The 5-star ***Hotel Nirvana*** *(☎ 20837, e nirva@ccsl.com.np)* on Paklihawa Rd seems very misplaced in scruffy Bhairawa. It's modern, clean, has air-con and is well worth the money if you desire this level of comfort. The restaurant here serves OK meals, and there's a bar. Room rates are US$95/105, but ask for a discount, which may lower this considerably.

The ***Kasturi Restaurant***, near the corner of Bank Rd and Paklihawa Rd, is a pleasant place with high ceilings and excellent vegetarian Indian food, but no alcohol. Dishes such as pulau and korma cost around Rs 50.

Getting There & Away

Air The Bhairawa airport is about 1km west of town.

At least five airlines fly the route between Bhairawa and Kathmandu daily for US$82. Their booking offices are all close to the Hotel Yeti. Skyline Airways has daily flights to Pokhara.

Bus There are plenty of bus connections to destinations in both Nepal and India. Whether you have booked a 'through' ticket or not, be wary as everyone changes buses at the border. There are no 'tourist' buses.

To/From India You catch buses to Indian cities from the Indian side of the border. There are direct buses to Varanasi for INRs 100 to INRs 150, depending on the degree of luxury, and the journey there takes about nine hours.

There are also buses to Gorakhpur where you can connect with the Indian broad-gauge railway (INRs 40, three hours). Coming from Gorakhpur, buses leave every half hour from 5 am to 7 pm; you'll need to catch a bus from Gorakhpur by 3 pm if you want to be sure of catching a night bus to Kathmandu the same day. See the Getting There & Away chapter for more information.

To/From Other Parts of Nepal Travelling north, most buses leave from Sunauli, stopping in Bhairawa, but buses can be booked and boarded at either place. In Sunauli there's a bus booking office at the bus stand; buses can only be booked on the day of departure. This office opens at 3 am. In Bhairawa the bus companies' offices are around the intersection of Bank Rd and the Siddhartha Hwy, although a new bus stand is currently under construction about 500m south of here, and this may be in use by now.

There are day and night buses for both Pokhara (Rs 180/220 day/night, nine hours) and Kathmandu (Rs 189/230), all travelling via Narayanghat. To Narayanghat, where you can change for Chitwan, the trip costs Rs 100.

There are also a number of night buses to Janakpur (Rs 257), Biratnagar (Rs 371) and to Kakarbhitta (Rs 420).

There are plenty of local buses to Butwal for Rs 17. For transport details to Lumbini see Getting There & Away under Lumbini later in this section.

Getting Around

The only time you'll need transport will be to go between Sunauli and Bhairawa – four, hot, flat kilometres. A rickshaw costs around Rs 50 and takes 20 minutes, a share 4WD costs Rs 5.

LUMBINI

Lumbini is believed to be the birthplace of Siddhartha Gautama – the founder of Buddhism, known as Buddha or the enlightened one (see the boxed text 'Siddhartha Gautama' in this section). This is confirmed by the existence of an inscribed pillar erected 318 years after the event by the great Buddhist emperor Ashoka, and the presence of a number of ancient ruins.

Fittingly, Lumbini is an example of the ephemerality of human effort. There is not much to see and it requires a serious effort of the imagination to conjure up the ghosts of the past. Lumbini is not a Bethlehem or Mecca: There is no city, no impressive architecture, no pilgrim-jammed car park, no heavily armed soldiers, no hustlers, and not even a postcard stand.

In the end, it is the absence of all these things and the peacefulness of Lumbini that make a visit worthwhile. In some ways, Tilaurakot to the west (see the Taulihawa & Tilaurakot section later in this chapter), the site of Kapilavastu, the fortress-palace where Buddha was raised as a prince of the royal family, is more evocative.

It's curious that Buddha should have been born and raised on a fertile tropical plain, a place of such contrast to the deserts of the Middle East where so many religions originated; strange that he should have been born a wealthy prince; and almost bizarre that this privileged life and rich countryside should have inspired a belief that suffering is synonymous with existence.

Allow yourself an hour or two to wander around and soak in the atmosphere. The important sights don't take long to cover – the Maya Devi Temple, the Ashokan Pillar, the Sacred Pond and the Tibetan and Theravada *viharas* (monasteries). Due to the enervating heat that afflicts this area for about nine months of the year, the site is probably best appreciated in the early morning or late afternoon, and so it's worth considering an overnight stay.

There are grandiose plans for the development of Lumbini, with the aim of creating a place of pilgrimage, and a tourist attraction. It will be interesting to see whether this can be achieved by government decree. A plan by Japanese architect Kenzo Tange was adopted in 1978, involving canals, gardens, a library and museum, monastic zones, a pilgrim lodge and a hotel. There has been some slow progress.

History

The great Indian emperor Ashoka visited Lumbini in 245 BC, and left a number of his famous inscribed pillars in the region. In AD 403 the region was visited by Fa Hsien, a Chinese pilgrim who described a ruined Kapilavastu and a deserted countryside.

In 636 Hsuan Tang, another pilgrim, described 1000 derelict monasteries and Ashoka's pillar at Lumbini, shattered by lightning and lying on the ground. Derelict it may have been, but the site was still

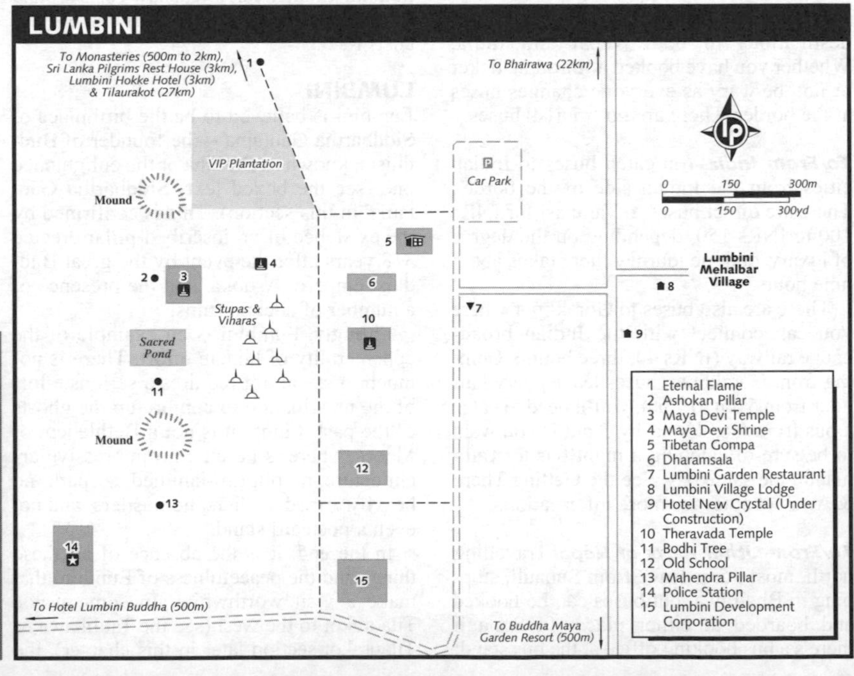

known in 1312 when Ripu Malla visited, possibly leaving the nativity statue that is still worshipped in the Maya Devi Temple.

Mughal invaders arrived in the region at the end of the 15th century, and in common with their zealous actions elsewhere on the subcontinent, it is likely that the remaining 'pagan' monuments at both Kapilavastu and Lumbini were destroyed. The whole region then returned to wilderness and the sites were eventually lost to the jungle, until the governor of Palpa, Khadga Shumsher Rana, who had a keen interest in archaeology, began the excavation of a pillar (which turned out to be Ashoka's Lumbini pillar) in late 1896.

Today, no trace of the Lumbini forest remains, but the pond where Maya Devi, the mother of Buddha, is believed to have bathed can still be seen, although in a much restored form. The brick foundations of stupas and viharas dating from the 2nd century BC can be seen around the pond. The Maya Devi Temple is built on ancient foundations, and these foundations are now the site of an archaeological dig.

After the discovery of Lumbini, the ruins near Tilaurakot were subsequently identified as Kapilavastu. There has been some archaeological work, which has revealed the remains of moated city walls, as well as impressive gates and the foundations for a palace complex.

Most of the surrounding countryside is dominated by extremely poor Muslim peasant farmers nowadays. There are no resident Buddhists in Lumbini.

Ashokan Pillar

Emperor Ashoka is one of the greatest figures in Indian history. Throughout his massive empire he left pillars and rock-carved edicts, which to this day delineate the extent of his power. These structures can be seen in Delhi, Gujarat, Orissa, Uttar Pradesh, Madhya Pradesh – and in Nepal.

The pillar at Lumbini commemorates Ashoka's pilgrimage to the birthplace of Buddha. It is 6m high, although half of it is underground, and it is inscribed with the following words:

> King Ashoka, the beloved of Gods, in the 20th year of the coronation, made a royal visit. A stone railing and a stone pillar were erected in honour of Buddha who was born here. Because Buddha was born here the village of Lumbini was freed from paying tax.

Maya Devi Temple

Until recently the Maya Devi Temple, parts of which were believed to be over 2000 years old, stood on the spot where Buddha is thought to have been born. A huge pipal tree, which was gradually tearing the temple apart, was believed by some to have been the tree that Maya Devi held while giving birth to Siddhartha.

In 1993 the tree was ripped out and the temple demolished to make archaeological excavations possible. At the time of writing, this was still going on and the site has been sheltered by an ugly tin roof. In 1995 archaeologists claim to have found a commemorative stone atop a platform of seven layers of bricks 5m below the old temple floor and dating from the era of Ashoka. Buddhist literature says Ashoka placed a stone on top of bricks at the birthplace of Prince Siddhartha, who was later called Lord Buddha. Ancient writings say Buddha was born when Maya Devi went into labour after bathing in a sacred pond (see the boxed text 'Siddhartha Gautama' following). The recently discovered stone is said to be the correct distance from the nearby pool.

When the temple was demolished the revered centrepiece of the temple, a stone carving showing the birth of Buddha, was moved to an ugly brick structure close by that looks like a public toilet block (4 Maya Devi shrine). Possibly dating from the Malla dynasty (about 14th century AD), the sculpture was the centre of a fertility rite, and it has almost been reduced to formlessness by the wear of constant puja. One can still make out Maya Devi, with her right hand raised to hold the pipal tree branch, as she gives birth. There is also a modern marble interpretation, along with a number of small sculptures left by devotees.

A major Hindu festival is held on the full moon of the Nepali month of Baisakh

Siddhartha Gautama

The region at the foot of the Himalaya was broken up 2500 years ago into a number of small republics and principalities that were vassal states to larger empires based on the Gangetic plain). Siddhartha Gautama was the son of Suddhodana (of the Sakya clan) who ruled the republic of Kapilavastu and Maya Devi (of the Koliya clan), the daughter of the ruler of the neighbouring state of Dewadaha.

It is believed that Maya Devi was 10 months pregnant when she decided to visit her parents' house in Dewadaha. On the way from Kapilavastu, her entourage had to pass through the grove of Lumbini, which was a famous beauty spot with a pond surrounded by sal trees. On the day she reached Lumbini, in May 563 BC, the sal trees were in full bloom, so Maya Devi stopped to enjoy the scene and bathe in the pond. Leaving the water, she suddenly felt labour pains. She walked 25 paces, raised her right hand and caught hold of the drooping branch of a pipal tree, and the baby was born.

Maya Devi returned to Kapilavastu where her son Siddhartha was given a sheltered, privileged upbringing. At the age of 29, while wandering in the town outside the palace walls, he came across an old man, a sick man, a corpse and a hermit. This confrontation with suffering and death impelled Siddhartha to renounce his luxurious life and to leave Kapilavastu.

(April–May), when thousands of local Hindus come to worship Maya Devi as Rupa Devi, the mother goddess of Lumbini, and to celebrate Buddha as the ninth incarnation of Vishnu. The Buddhist celebration of Buddha's birthday, Buddha Jayanti, is celebrated around the same time, but is more low-key. During winter, when it's not too hot, Buddhist pilgrims from the Kathmandu Valley often come to worship on Purnima (the night of the full moon) and Astemi (the eighth night after the full moon).

Other Attractions

The square pool beside the temple is believed to be the spot where Maya Devi bathed before giving birth to Buddha; needless to say, it has been heavily restored. The foundations for a number of stupas and viharas dating from the 2nd century BC to the 9th century AD lie in the vicinity.

There are also two modern temples although, unfortunately, neither are particularly interesting or well maintained – both are slated for demolition under the Lumbini Development Plan. One temple was built by the Nepali government in 1956 and the other was built in traditional Tibetan style in 1968.

The two large mounds on either side of the site are not impressive stupas, as you might suspect, but simply the spoils from modern archaeological digs.

A number of monasteries to the north of the site are complete and are worth visiting. The site is *very* spread out, so without your own transport you'll need to take one of the cycle-rickshaws by the main gate. The roads are bumpy as hell so it's not exactly leisurely. The **Chinese Monastery** is most impressive, and is something straight out of the Forbidden City; even the roof tiles were imported. Also open and worth a look is the **Burmese Monastery** and the recently completed monastery of the Indian **Mahabodhi Society**. Monasteries of Thailand, Vietnam and Korea are also under construction.

There's a small museum at the Lumbini Research Institute. It is open from 10 am to 5 pm Sunday to Thursday and 10 am to 3 pm Friday. Again, you'll need transport to get to it.

Places to Stay & Eat

Most people simply make a day trip from Bhairawa, but there are a couple of places to stay and eat in Lumbini.

Lumbini Village Lodge is in Lumbini Mehalbar, the small market town right by the main entrance to the site. (The village is an undistinguished little place, with a lively

Siddhartha Gautama

He spent the next five years seeking to understand the nature of existence. Mostly he wandered as an itinerant ascetic – no doubt much like the Hindu sadhus of today – but he found that extreme self-denial did not provide him with any answers. Finally, after 49 days meditating under a bodhi tree at Bodhgaya in India he attained enlightenment. From Bodhgaya he travelled to Sarnath, near Varanasi, where he preached his first sermon.

Buddha spent the next 46 years teaching his 'middle way'. Suffering, he taught, is a natural part of life, but suffering is caused by attachment, desire and delusion, and if these negative forces are controlled (by following the noble 'eightfold path'), it is possible to reach nirvana.

Although some people believe Buddha visited the Kathmandu Valley, there is no firm evidence for this. Most of his preaching was undertaken in northern India and across the Gangetic plain. He died at the age of 80 at Kushinagar, near Gorakhpur, about 100km south-east of Lumbini.

Despite his disavowal of divinity, the main sites associated with Buddha's life (Lumbini, Kapilavastu, Bodhgaya, Sarnath and Kushinagar) soon became centres for pilgrimage, and monasteries and temples sprang up. There are, however, only sparse records of Lumbini's and Kapilavastu's histories.

The ruins of Kapilavastu lie at Tilaurakot, 27km west of Lumbini, but Dewadaha has not been conclusively identified.

market on Monday. The rest of the time it's a peaceful corner of the Terai.) For what you get the prices are a bit steep; gloomy cell-like rooms are Rs 150/250 for a single/double. There is reasonable food at around Rs 50 for dal bhaat.

A better bet is the ***Sri Lanka Pilgrims Rest House***, way out about 3km north of the site, beyond the sacred flame and just off the dirt road to Tilaurakot. This clean and modern brick place has spacious dorms on offer with beds at US$5, and you can often have a room to yourself. It would be handy to have a bicycle if you want to travel back and forth to the site.

***Hotel Lumbini Buddha** (☎ 071-80114)* is about 500m south-west of the main site. It's a decent mid-range hotel with rooms from around US$10.

A similar distance south-east of the site is the new ***Buddha Maya Garden Resort*** *(☎ 80220, fax 80219)*, owned and run by the famed Kathmandu Guest House. It consists of a number of dorm rooms for US$12 per bed and comfortable rooms at US$50/70; there's a decent restaurant here. This represents the best value in the area if the price fits your budget.

At the top of the scale is the ***Lumbini Hokke Hotel*** *(☎ /fax 80236)*, close to Sri Lanka Pilgrims Rest House. Built with Japanese pilgrims in mind, most of the rooms have been furnished in traditional Japanese style with tatami floors, paper partitions and Japanese furniture. There are also a number of European-style rooms. All rooms have air-con and bathroom. Considering the luxury, prices are reasonable, with rooms at US$90/120 in autumn and winter (September to March), and US$68/90 at other times. Meals (Japanese only) are US$7 for lunch or dinner.

Just by the main car park is the ***Lumbini Garden Restaurant***, which, judging by its appearance, is not part of the Lumbini Development Plan – it's a modern red-brick eyesore sporting numerous large Coca-Cola ads. The prices are relatively high, but it's the only decent place to eat and the food is OK, though service can be extremely slow. There are a couple of very basic eating places between the two temples.

Getting There & Away

There are regular minibuses that make the 22km journey from Bhairawa to Lumbini for Rs 18, but they are agonisingly slow (1½ hours). The roof is the place to be. The last bus back passes by the main entrance at about 5 pm (but check this time). They leave Bhairawa from the signposted intersection with roundabout, about 500m north of the Hotel Yeti.

If you are in a group, or have the funds, it would be immensely preferable to hire a taxi-4WD (from Rs 300 to Rs 500). These prices include two hours waiting time at the site, which should be sufficient for most people.

The best method of transport for budget travellers is be bicycle, although attempting this – or anything much – in high summer may be a bit ambitious. There are no formal rental places in Bhairawa, but if you ask around (start at your hotel, then try bicycle repair shops) something might turn up.

TAULIHAWA & TILAURAKOT

Tilaurakot is nothing more than a tiny hamlet 3km north of Taulihawa, a bustling Terai centre. Tilaurakot was once, however, capital of the republic of Kapilavastu, where Buddha spent the first 29 years of his life.

Taulihawa is a vibrant town with the usual multicultural mix of peoples found in Terai cities. There is a temple complex known as **Tauleshwar**, now used by Shaivites, in the centre of town.

Although even less visited than Lumbini, Tilaurakot is in many ways actually the more atmospheric of the two spots. There is a small group of farming households outside the ruins of the city walls, which, along with their moat, can be clearly discerned. The whole complex is shaded by large trees and has the peaceful atmosphere of a park.

The scattered foundations that can be seen within the walls give only the most minimal indication that there was once a palace here, but archaeologists have found 13 successive layers of human habitation, dating back to the 8th century BC. Today the only sign of life is a small run-down shrine to a Hindu goddess, Somaya Mai.

The scene outside the walls could be unchanged from what Siddhartha might have seen. Timeless patterns of subsistence farming unfold along the banks of the Banganga River, and on the north side of the river there is an expanse of untouched sal forest. It is not hard to imagine Siddhartha walking out through the imposing gateway of the palace and as he wandered, seeing an old man, a sick man, a corpse and a hermit.

About 400m from the ruins, a small museum displays some of the artefacts that were found at the site – including coins and pottery (closed on Tuesday and Saturday).

Places to Stay & Eat

There are plenty of ***food stalls*** in Taulihawa. The ***Lumbini Hotel***, on the road to Tilaurakot, is very basic but acceptably clean, and singles/doubles cost Rs 80/100. There are no facilities at Tilaurakot.

Getting There & Away

A road links Taulihawa with Lumbini, 27km to the east. The road passes the Lumbini Hokke Hotel (see Places to Stay & Eat in the Lumbini section), and a number of Muslim villages. Slow and crowded local buses link Taulihawa with Bhairawa, but once again a bicycle is the best method of transport.

Tilaurakot is 3km north of Taulihawa. At the end of the bitumen the museum is on the left and the ruins are 400m away down a dirt track on the right. In winter you can cross a ford over Banganga River and continue 14km due north along a dirt road through Sagar Forest, finally joining the Mahendra Hwy 35km west of Butwal and 80km east of Lamahi (also spelt Lumihi).

TANSEN (PALPA)

☎ 075

Tansen is just off the Siddhartha Hwy, between Pokhara and Sunauli/Bhairawa. Historically, it has enjoyed a strategic position on the trade and pilgrim route between the hills and the plains.

Prior to the unification of Nepal under the Shahs, Tansen was the capital of the Palpa kingdom, which was ruled by the Sen dynasty. Prithvi Narayan Shah, the Gorkha king who founded modern Nepal, was the product of an arranged marriage between the Shah and Sen families.

For many years Palpa fought in alliance with Gorkha; together the two states defeated the independent kingdoms of western Nepal. Finally in 1806, the last king of Palpa, known as Prithivipal Sen, was lured

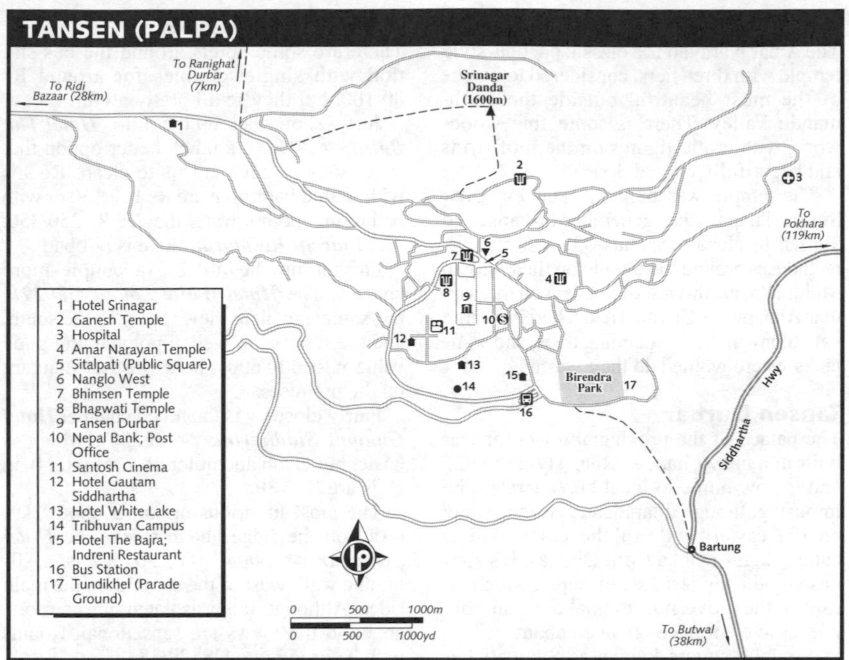

to Kathmandu and beheaded. Palpa was annexed, but Tansen remained the administrative centre for the region. A number of its subsequent governors were high-ranking members of the ruling Shah and, later, Rana families who were exiled from Kathmandu for plotting against the king of the day.

Tansen is still the administrative centre for a large region, but it sees few visitors, and as it is increasingly sidelined by the development on the Terai and at Pokhara, it is gently falling apart.

The town sprawls over a steep ridge, and quite a few of the main streets are too steep for cars, which helps to keep some of the less-pleasant aspects of the 20th century at bay. In the older sections of the town, attractive Newari buildings line cobbled streets that are reminiscent of parts of Kathmandu.

Most of the surrounding countryside is dominated by Magars, but there are also Bahuns and Chhetris. Newars form the majority in Tansen itself. They migrated from the Kathmandu Valley to take advantage of the new opportunities for trade between the hills and India that opened up in the 19th century – traditional crafts and agricultural surpluses were traded for the products of the British industrial revolution (especially cotton fabrics) that were flooding into India from Britain. Tansen is still famous for metalware and dhaka, the woven material that is made into *topis* (Nepali hats).

There are great views over the bowl-shaped **Madi Valley** from the town itself, and a spectacular view of the Himalaya from the nearby hill, Srinagar Danda. There are some interesting walks in the surrounding countryside, including a day trek to the banks of the Kali Gandaki River and the vast, deserted Ranighat Durbar (Ranighat Palace). Tansen is a pleasant place to break the rough journey from Pokhara (110km, six hours!) to Bhairawa (38km, two hours).

Pooja Communication near the bank has email facilities.

Amar Narayan Temple

The Amar Narayan is a classic pagoda-style temple with three tiers, considered to be one of the most beautiful outside the Kathmandu Valley. There is some fine woodwork, with erotic figures on the roof struts and beautifully carved doors.

The temple was built in 1806 by Amar Singh Thapa (the general who annexed Tansen to Nepal). Sadhus often stay in the resthouses around the temple on their way to Muktinath, north-west of Pokhara on the popular Annapurna Circuit Trek. There's a large bat colony in the surrounding trees, and some tanks where women do their washing.

Tansen Durbar

The palace of the provincial governor was built in a heavy-handed Rana style in 1927 and is now home to local bureaucrats. The imposing, though dilapidated, entrance gate on the eastern side of the compound is called Baggi Dhoka (Mul Dhoka). It's supposedly the biggest gate in Nepal, which allowed the governor to make a suitably impressive entrance on an elephant.

A public square known as Sitalpati lies just outside the gate; it is named after the building in the centre, which was, before its renovation, an unusual octagonal shape.

Bhagwati Temple

The Bhagwati Temple, near the durbar, is a rather garish construction that was unsympathetically renovated after an earthquake in 1935, and again in 1974. It was built originally in 1815 to commemorate the Nepali victory over the British at Butwal.

There are some smaller temples in the vicinity, these are dedicated to Shiva, Ganesh and Saraswati.

Srinagar Danda

Srinagar Danda is a 1600m-high hill directly north of town and is a steep half-hour walk from Sitalpati. From the pine-forested top there's a spectacular view over the gorge of the Kali Gandaki River to the Himalaya – the panorama stretches from Kanjiroba in the west, all the way to Dhaulagiri, the Annapurnas, and Langtang in the east.

Places to Stay & Eat

There are some hotels around the bus station with singles/doubles for around Rs 80/100, but they're all pretty awful.

Just a short walk up the hill is ***Hotel The Bajra*** *(☎ 20443)*, a much better option that is reasonably new and quite clean. Rooms with shared bathroom are Rs 100/150 or with bathroom and hot water they're Rs 250/350. The ***Indreni Restaurant*** here is not bad.

Farther up the hill are a couple more choices. The ***Hotel White Lake*** *(☎ 20291)* has some excellent views away to the south, and the rooms are well appointed and good value at Rs 400/600. There's also a restaurant on the premises.

Fairly close by is the much cheaper ***Hotel Gautam Siddhartha*** (☎ 20280), which is basic, but clean and quiet. Rooms with twin beds are Rs 180.

The most luxurious option is about 2km away on the ridge above town. The ***Hotel Srinagar*** *(☎ 20045, fax 20467)* is a 20-minute walk west of the summit on the main ridge. Although rather isolated, it's comfortable and the views are sensational. Rooms with bathroom are US$29/38.

A welcome addition to the eating scene is the new ***Nanglo West*** at Sitalpati. With a very pleasant courtyard, the meals (Indian and continental) are reasonably priced. It's open from 10.30 am to 8.30 pm daily.

Other than that, almost all of the lodges around the bus stand are good for a dal bhaat.

Getting There & Away

There are daily buses to Pokhara (Rs 108) and Butwal (Rs 38).

The scenery along the north–south highway is magnificent, so if you can, find a place on the roof to appreciate the views. If you're inside and coming from Pokhara try to get a seat on the right side of the bus. The road to Butwal is subject to landslides during the monsoon, and traffic is also often disrupted during this time.

AROUND TANSEN

Ridi Bazaar

Ridi is a holy town, mainly populated by Newars, at the confluence of the Kali

Gandaki and Ridi Rivers. The confluence of tributaries to the Ganges is always regarded as holy, and Ridi has been further sanctified by the presence of *saligrams*, black ammonite fossils that have a spiral shape and are regarded as emblems of Vishnu. Saligrams are found in a number of places along the Kali Gandaki, most notably north of Jomsom around Muktinath.See the boxed text 'Saligrams' in the Trekking chapter.

Although Ridi's religious popularity has declined, cremations are still relatively frequent, and pilgrims come for ritual bathing, marriage ceremonies and other rites and rituals. Pilgrims believe that if they fast and worship for three days, and then take a ritual bath in the Kali Gandaki, all their sins will be forgiven.

The most important festival is Magh Sankranti, when many pilgrims come to immerse themselves in the river (see Devghat in the Around Narayanghat section earlier in this chapter). This festival takes place on the first day of the Nepali month of Magh (mid-January) and celebrates the gradually lengthening days and the onset of warmer weather. Worshippers also gather every Ekadashi (the 11th day after the full moon). The festival of Ridi is held in November.

The commercial end of town is across the Ridi River; the Rishikesh Temple is near the bus station. It is believed the temple was founded by Mukund Sen in the early 16th century, but the current temple dates from the 19th century. It is also believed that the statue of Rishikesh (a manifestation of Vishnu) was discovered in the river, and that the figure of the god has gradually aged from boyhood to adulthood.

It is a 13km trek from Tansen to Ridi. You can leave the road just to the west of the Hotel Srinagar, and pick it up again about 7km from Ridi. Alternatively, it is 28km by road. Buses leave Tansen in the morning, cost Rs 55 and take around two hours.

Ranighat Durbar

Sometimes fancifully referred to as Nepal's Taj Mahal, Ranighat Durbar was built by Khadga Shamsher Rana in 1896. Khadga was exiled to Tansen and made governor for plotting to become prime minister. While he was in exile, he consoled himself by building a spectacular palace, supposedly in memory of his wife, Tej Kumari.

The palace is a huge, white baroque building, dramatically perched on a rocky crag above the Kali Gandaki River. It was used for 25 years as a luxurious *dharamsala* (pilgram guesthouse) by aristocrats who ostensibly came to bathe in Kali Gandaki, and no doubt to party and plot with Khadga. Khadga was an ambitious man, and in 1921 he made another abortive attempt to seize power only to be exiled farther away – this time in India. On his departure the building was stripped of its valuable furnishings, and was allowed to fall into ruin. Fortunately, it is now looking much less forlorn than it has for years as it has been largely restored.

The trail to Ranighat begins a short distance to the east of the Hotel Srinagar, at the edge of the pine forest. It's an attractive 7km hike down to the river and takes at least four hours each way – it's a long day trip.

NEPALGANJ

☎ 081

The most important town in western Nepal, Nepalganj at times feels more Indian than Nepali. It's a border town that owes as much to trade (read smuggling) as it does to its position as a major administrative centre. It has more of an air of permanence than some other border towns, and planners have had the good sense to run the highway to the west of the main town. Despite this, it's a distinctly unattractive place with few redeeming features.

Nepalganj is a densely crowded city, and every possible ethnic group in Nepal is represented here. There is an unusually large Muslim community, many of whom settled here to escape the violence of the 1857 Indian Uprising. The Muslim men are distinctive, with their long beards and skull caps, as are the women, some of whom dress in black and are completely veiled. The colourful throngs in the streets, however, include Shaivite sadhus, Tharu women (with tight bodices, bare midriffs and bright skirts), turbanned Sikhs, Bajis (Abadhi speakers from India), Bahuns, Chhetris, Newars, Magars,

Gurungs, Thakuris and even Tibetans (who look a bit hot in their traditional gear).

An increasing trickle of travellers come through Nepalganj on their way to or from western Nepal and Royal Bardia National Park (see later in this chapter), or to Jumla in north-western Nepal. It can also be a useful back-door entry into Nepal from central Uttar Pradesh in India; Lucknow is about four hours away.

Orientation & Information

The airport is 6km north of Birendra Chowk (with the statue) to the east of Surkhet Rd (main north–south road). The long-distance bus station is about 1km north of Birendra Chowk around a T-junction.

The town is about 6km north of the border. The old, vaguely interesting part of town lies to the east of the main road around Tribhuvan Chowk, although virtually all the hotels are on the highway.

The various customs and immigration offices at the border all have different closing hours, but they are all open at least from 8 to 11 am and 1 to 5 pm. There is a moneychanger at the Mankamana Guest House and at least two banks in town.

A couple of places south of Birendra Chowk on Surkhet Rd offer Internet access (with slow connections).

Things to See & Do

The old part of town has the **Bageshwari Mandir**, the garish temple honouring Kali. There's also a vibrant **bazaar** selling everything except kitchen sinks (although one of the metalworkers could probably knock one up if you needed it). It is well worth wandering around the centre of town. The crush of people, the smells, the food, the shops, the film posters and the rickshaws give a vivid taste of the subcontinent.

Places to Stay & Eat

The cheapies are centred around Birendra Chowk, the main intersection with the all to inevitable statue.

The ***New Hotel Punjabi*** *(☎ 20818)* is one of the better choices with large, comfortable, and acceptably clean rooms. Singles/doubles

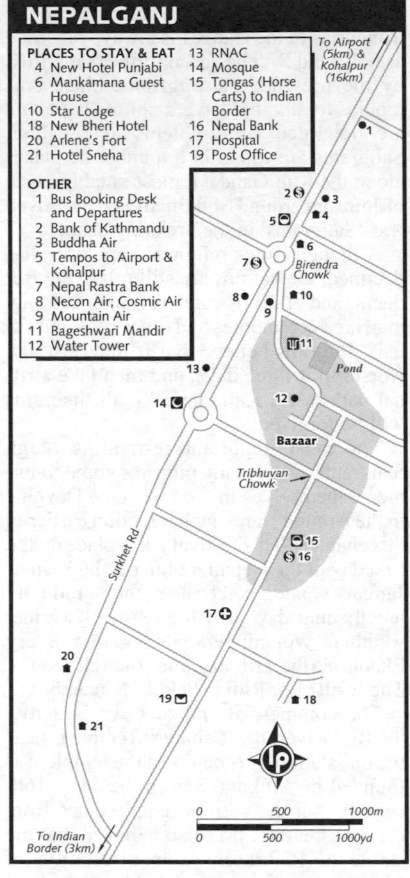

with bathroom cost Rs 250/350; with shared bathroom they are Rs 100/150. The Indian dishes from the restaurant are quite passable.

The nearby ***Mankamana Guest House*** is also acceptable; doubles with bathroom (cold water) cost Rs 150.

The hotels on Garwhari Tole, which connect Birendra Chowk with the old part of town, are somewhat quieter. The ***Star Lodge*** *(☎ 22257)* has rooms at Rs 100/150 with shared bathroom, and Rs 150/200 with private bathroom.

Moving up the scale a bit is the ***New Bheri Hotel*** *(☎ 20213)*, which offers the best value in town. The hotel is near the hospital in a quiet part of town, and has a pleasant garden. Rooms are US$8/10 with bathroom and US$16/20 with air-con, but with discounts you may have to pay only half that. It's a good place.

There are two reasonable upper-end hotels, both south of town on the highway towards the Indian border. There's many more trees around here and the hotels are set back from the road, so there's no problem with noise and parking.

The ***Hotel Sneha*** *(☎ 20119, ⓔ hotel@sneha.wlink.com.np)* has a range of large, clean rooms, and helpful staff. Standard rooms are US$18/24, deluxe rooms with air-con are US$30/36 plus 12% tax. Discounts of 15% are possible. There's a restaurant here and the food is quite passable.

Close by is ***Arlene's Fort*** *(☎ 20704, ⓔ atulgurung@hotmail.com)*, which has a pleasant garden complete with water feature. The rooms are spacious and all have air-con, bathroom and TV. The cost is Rs 1000/1200, good value for a place with air-con in Nepalganj. There's also a restaurant in the garden.

Getting There & Away

Air The distinctly grubby Nepalganj airport is 6km north of town. This is RNAC's western headquarters and so there are a number of flights into the interior. RNAC flys from Nepalganj to Surkhet (US$33, weekly), Simikot (US$88, four times weekly), Kathmandu (US$99, daily), Mahendranagar (US$60, twice weekly) and Jumla (US$57).

Most private airlines have at least one daily flight each between Nepalganj and Kathmandu (US$109). Their offices are all on Surkhet Rd, close to Birendra Chowk.

Bus There's a booking window for bus tickets just a couple of shops south of the intersection where the buses congregate.

There are private buses to Pokhara (Rs 280/350 day/night via Mugling, 12 hours) and Kathmandu (Rs 421, 12 hours). Buses for Mahendranagar leave hourly between 5 and 11 am (Rs 270, six hours). It's advisable to book at least one day in advance.

Local buses for Thakurdwara (for Royal Bardia National Park) leave at noon and 2 pm, and take an interminable five hours to cover less than 100km.

Once across the Indian border, 6km to the south, there are direct buses to Lucknow (seven hours) and share taxis (INRs 150, four hours). The nearest point on the Indian rail network is Nanpara, 17km from the border.

Getting Around

There are shared tempos from Birendra Chowk to the airport for Rs 7, or you can take a 'reserve' for Rs 50. A cycle-rickshaw costs around Rs 50 but takes up to half an hour. To get to the Indian border onboard a cycle-rickshaw costs around Rs 30.

ROYAL BARDIA NATIONAL PARK

☎ 084

The Royal Bardia National Park is the largest untouched wilderness area in the Terai. It's bordered to the north by the crest of the Chure hills and to the west by the large Geruwa River, a branch of the mighty Karnali, one of the major tributaries of the also mighty Ganges.

You stand a better chance of seeing a tiger here than anywhere else in Nepal (including Chitwan). It's a stunning place that seems a very long way from the 21st century – watching the sun rise over the forest from the back of an elephant is like having a box seat at the dawn of time.

About 70% of the 968-sq-km park is covered with open sal forest, with the balance a mixture of grassland, savanna and riverine forest. The grassed areas (phanta) are excellent for viewing wildlife. Most people will visit in the hope of seeing a royal Bengal tiger, but there are also leopards, jungle cats, mongooses, sloth bears, blue cow antelopes, langur and rhesus monkeys and barking, spotted hog and sambar deer. The Indian one-horned rhinoceros was reintroduced from Chitwan in 1986, and though breeding successfully the numbers are still small – 67 according to a 2000 census. There are at least two wild male elephants, and one is thought to be the largest in Asia.

The Geruwa River rushes through a gap in the hills at Chisopani, grey with silt and snow-melt. It's home to the famous mahseer game fish, gharial and mugger crocodiles and the strange and also very rare Gangetic dolphin.

More than 30 different mammals and 250 species of birds have been recorded in the park. Birds include numerous species of herons, storks, geese, ducks and parakeets, as well as peacocks and endangered birds such as the Bengal florican and sarus crane.

In some ways Bardia is like Chitwan; the major difference is the degree of isolation and the limited number of visitors – recent statistics show that of all visitors to national parks and reserves in the Terai, only 5% visit Bardia (92% visit Chitwan!).

The park is most easily visited en route to or from Delhi and western Nepal; with the completion of the Mahendra Hwy it means that, in travelling time, Bardia is now more easily accessible from Delhi than Kathmandu. From Bardia it's a day's travelling to Kathmandu or Pokhara, with direct buses to each. This means you need a minimum of four days: day one to get from Kathmandu or Pokhara to Bardia; days two and three to explore the park, the river and the surrounding villages; and day four to return from Bardia to Pokhara, Kathmandu or western Nepal.

SIMON BORG

Peacocks provide much inspiration for Nepali folklore and imagery.

Orientation & Information

The park headquarters are at Thakurdwara, about 20km south-west along a bumpy dirt road from Anbassa on the Mahendra Hwy. Anbassa is nothing more than a road intersection and a motley collection of temporary wooden shacks on the highway. It is about 500m south of the Amreni checkpoint, where the highway actually enters the park, and this in turn is 8km from Chisopani. Virtually all tourist activity is centred around the western spur of the park that takes in the forest and grasslands around the Geruwa River; the large eastern portion of the park is untouched.

The park office (☎ 297129) is open from 8 to 10 am and 2 to 5 pm daily; the park itself is open from 6.30 am to 5.30 pm (7 pm in summer). Entry is Rs 500 a day, and you can get a fishing permit for Rs 300 per rod. The national park also offers elephant rides at Rs 1000 per person from the park headquarters at Thakurdwara. The only trouble here is that you need at least 30 minutes by elephant to reach the 'core' area of the park for the best wildlife viewing. It's also possible to enter the park on foot, although you need to take an experienced guide, something your lodge can arrange. Keep in mind that walking in the park is a potentially dangerous activity, and should only be undertaken if you are accompanied by an experienced guide.

Also at the park headquarters is a small holding area for marsh mugger and gharial crocodiles that have been bred in captivity and are due to be released into the river. There's also a small museum.

Places to Stay & Eat

Development at Bardia is still very low-key, with just a handful of basic Chitwan-style 'jungle cottages' and a few more upmarket options. There is no electricity, and levels of

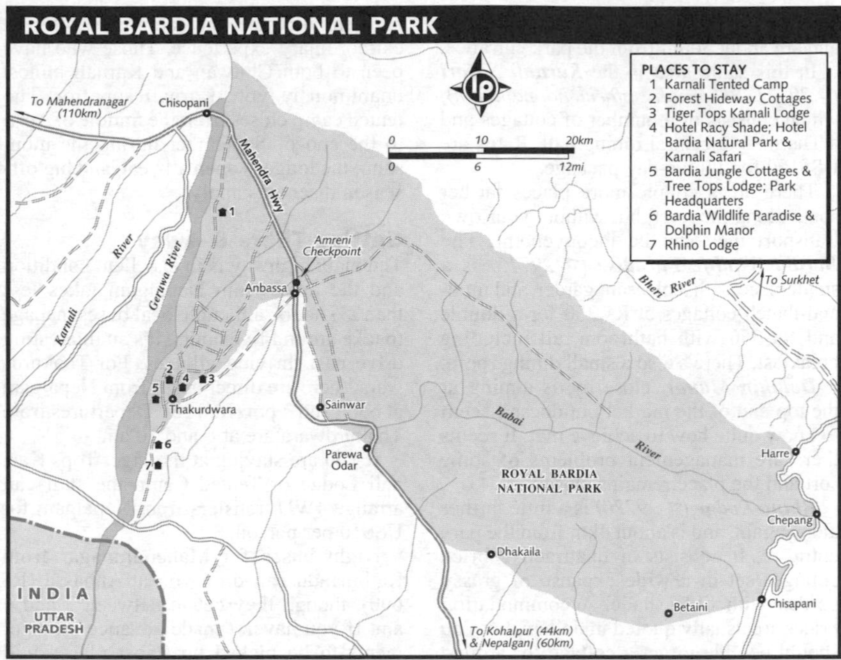

accommodation can be very basic but this is a perfect spot to hole up for a few days and allow yourself to be lulled by the relaxing pace and atmosphere of Terai village life.

One of the best places is the solar powered ***Forest Hideaway Cottages*** *(☎ 29716, ⓔ hideway@forest.wlink.com.np)*, about 500m along the northern park boundary from the park headquarters and run by a helpful Scottish-Nepali couple. This place is also a licensed moneychanger (cash and travellers cheques, no cards), and you can also make international and local phone calls. It's a comfortable little place set in a shady garden. There's a variety of mud-and-thatch cottages – basic cottages with two beds, mosquito nets and shared bathroom are Rs 350 for a double with breakfast, larger cottages are Rs 500, also with breakfast and shared bathroom. Large cottages with a bathroom shared between two rooms are Rs 600 with breakfast. You can also camp here for Rs 150 for a double with breakfast, or Rs 75 in your own tent (no breakfast). Basic but perfectly adequate meals are available, and there's a bar. Safaris by 4WD can be arranged for Rs 1500 per person for four hours, and rafting day trips cost Rs 2000 per person. Bicycles, useful for exploring the surrounding villages, can be hired for Rs 150 per day.

Bardia Jungle Cottages *(☎ 29714)* is also very good; it's right opposite the park entrance. It has a large, shady garden and good facilities, including an enclosed restaurant. Comfortable cottages go for Rs 250 with shared bathroom, Rs 400 with bathroom. Meals are also available here.

Tree Tops Lodge nearby is a very new place and so doesn't yet have a garden or shade, but this will come with time. Large cottages with shared bathroom are Rs 250, with bathroom Rs 300.

There are a couple of more basic places, including the ***Hotel Racy Shade*** and the adjacent ***Hotel Bardia Natural Park***. Both have just a few mud-and-thatch cottages, and are about 500m from the park entrance.

In this same area is the ***Karnali Safari*** *(☎ 29721, ⓔ karnali_safari@hotmail.com)*, which consists of a number of cottages and a Tharu-style central dining hall. Rates are US$150 for a three-day package.

There are a couple more places farther south along the river, but without your own transport they can be inconvenient. The ***Bardia Wildlife Paradise*** *(☎ 29715)* is a small place with a pleasant garden and mud-and-thatch cottages at Rs 250 for a double and Rs 350 with bathroom, all including breakfast. There's also a small dining room.

Dolphin Manor, close by, is aiming at the top end of the market but doesn't seem to know quite how to achieve that. It seems there are management problems of some sort and the place remains closed.

Rhino Lodge *(☎ 29720)* is a little farther along again, and is about 4km from the park entrance. It consists of unattractive brick cottages set in a wide expanse of grassy garden with little shade. Accommodation prices are usually quoted in dollars, but you should be able to get a cottage for around Rs 400 with bathroom.

At the top of the range is the ***Tiger Tops Karnali Lodge***, run by Tiger Mountain *(☎ 01-411225, ⓔ info@tigermountain.com, postal address: PO Box 242, Durbar Marg, Kathmandu)*, the same company that runs the Tiger Tops Lodge in Chitwan. The lodge is right on the park boundary and is built out of local materials in Tharu-village style – simply outstanding. The staff are knowledgeable and helpful, without being intrusive.

The lodge also has the only accommodation inside the park – the ***Karnali Tented Camp***, which has a superb location overlooking the Geruwa River, in the north-west corner of the park not far from Chisopani. A camp it may be, rough it is not. The beds are comfortable, the food is good and the water is hot. Again activities revolve around elephants, but another highlight is a float down the river – a bird-watcher's delight.

Although it isn't cheap at US$150 a night per person including all meals and activities (elephant rides, guided walks) not including park entrance fee, the camp does offer an extraordinary experience. Those who have been to both Chitwan and Karnali almost unanimously vote Karnali superior. The tented camp closes from the middle of April to the end of September during the monsoon; the lodge is open all year, and big off-season discounts apply.

Getting There & Away

The main highway is in excellent condition and the drive from Nepalganj takes less than 2½ hours, although local buses manage to take around five hours. It's an interesting drive past thriving villages. For Thakurdwara, there are direct buses from Nepalganj at noon and 2 pm (Rs 120). Departures from Thakurdwara are at 8 and 10 am.

If you are staying at the Tiger Tops Karnali Lodge or Tented Camp the staff can arrange 4WD transfers from Nepalganj for US$10 per person.

Night buses for Mahendranagar from Kathmandu can drop you at Anbassa (Rs 600), though they get in between 3 and 6 am. If you haven't made advance arrangements to be picked up (most places will send a 4WD for you), there's little option but to sit out the rest of the night and wait for transport. There's no electricity or telephones in Anbassa. Day buses to/from Mahendranagar are Rs 200 and take four hours.

For Kathmandu, there are numerous night buses coming from western Nepal, although it is only possible to get a reserved seat on the one from Chisopani, and your lodge will have to arrange this. It comes through Anbassa around 2 pm. There are also direct night buses to Pokhara (Rs 600) and Birganj.

AROUND ROYAL BARDIA NATIONAL PARK

Chisopani

At the north-western end of Bardia, the Karnali River bursts out of the hills and enters the plains. Here a massive modern bridge spans the river, connecting the far western parts of the country. The single-span bridge, built by the Japanese and funded by the World Bank, is something of an engineering marvel and looks somewhat incongruous here. You may also wonder at the cost of a construction like this and whether better use could not have been made of the available funds. Still, it looks nice.

The town such as it is consists of a collection of timber shacks and shelters on the western bank of the river. There's a few basic ***eating houses***, and you could probably find somewhere to sleep if stuck. Surprisingly there's a daily direct bus to Kathmandu that leaves at 1.30 pm.

ROYAL SUKLA PHANTA WILDLIFE RESERVE

Sukla Phanta is smaller and more isolated than Bardia, yet is similar in some respects. In the extreme south-west of the country, it covers 305 sq km of riverine flood plain, which includes *phanta* (open grass plains), forest (primarily sal), a lake as well as the Bahini River.

The reserve is home to tigers (35 at the last estimate), leopards, rhinos (a few relocated here from Chitwan in late 2000), various species of deer (including an important colony of swamp deer, thought to number about 2000), gharial and mugger crocodiles, otters and wide range of birdlife.

The large swamp deer are found in large herds and it's not unusual to see three or more herds on even a short wildlife drive in the southern part of the park in the *sukla phanta* (literally white grass plains) found in this area. Although the deer are found in large numbers, Indian poachers are a real problem. Army guards are stationed in this part of the park, however they have to patrol by bicycle, which limits their efficacy.

This is probably one of the least-visited reserves in Nepal, but if you are travelling between Nepal and India it is not too difficult to make a diversion, especially if you can afford to stay at the tented camp.

Information

The ranger's office (☎ 099-21309) is 3km past the airport (accessible by rickshaw from Mahendranagar). Entry is Rs 500 a day, plus Rs 2000 for a vehicle. It is possible to organise elephant rides for Rs 1000, but it's best to book in advance.

The main vehicle track within the park is closed from mid-June to mid-September.

Places to Stay

Silent Safari *(☎ 099-21230, fax 22220, postal address: PO Box 1, Mahendranagar)* is the only company operating in the park. It is run by an ex-army colonel, the very personable Hikmat Bisht, a keen naturalist who has spent many years in and around the park and now divides his time between the camp (even when there are no guests) and his house in Mahendranagar. Visitors who come here are generally keen bird-watchers who don't mind roughing it a bit. Accommodation is in comfortable safari tents, and the price (US$175 per person) includes meals, wildlife drives and walks. Visits to local Tharu villages can also be arranged. The camp is open from October to June, and advance bookings are essential.

Getting There & Away

Silent Safari will pick up guests from the airport at Mahendranagar (US$10).

If you don't have a vehicle, it's possible to rent one in Mahendranagar for around Rs 4000 for a day.

MAHENDRANAGAR

☎ 099

Mahendranagar is an uninspiring, shabby village that owes its existence to the nearby border crossing. There's absolutely nothing to see here, and the locals are quite unused to dealing with tourists, so a few words of Nepali will be very useful. The surrounding countryside is inhabited by traditional Tharu communities, although here, as elsewhere, there is an increasing number of hill people.

With the finishing off the Mahendra Hwy in 2000 it seems likely that increasing numbers of visitors will enter Nepal here from Delhi rather than making the alternative trek to Gorakhpur and entering via Sunauli.

Orientation & Information

The town is laid out to the south of the main highway with the bus station actually on the highway, about a 10-minute walk from the centre of the village. The main landmark is the King Mahendra Square with streets one to five leading off from one side.

Mahendranagar is about 5km from Mahakali River, which forms the Nepal-India border. The border is open 24 hours a day for pedestrians, but the barrage on the Indian side for vehicles is only open from 7 to 8 am, noon to 2 pm and 4 to 6 pm. It's a little-used border and the crossing is straightforward and quite fast.

Places to Stay & Eat

There are a few cheap hotels on the main street. The ***Hotel New Anand*** *(☎ 22393)* is the best of them; it's friendly and has double rooms for Rs 300 with bathroom, and hot water by the bucket. Food is also available.

Across the road from the New Anand is the cheaper ***Shiv Shankar Guest House*** *(☎ 21447)*. Rooms here are a bit rough, but would do at a pinch, and cost Rs 150 for a double with bathroom.

Mahendranagar's Hilton is ***Hotel Sweet Dream*** *(☎ 22313)*, on the highway about a five-minute walk east of the bus station. The rooms in this recently built hotel are large and have carpets. The cost is Rs 300 for a double with bathroom, or Rs 500 with air-cooler, which is pretty good value. There's also a restaurant here.

Getting There & Away

Air RNAC flys to Nepalganj (US$60) and Kathmandu (US$149) twice a week.

Bus The last of the 22 bridges between Mahendranagar and Chisopani was finished in 2000, finally putting this part of the country within easy striking range.

There are daily direct buses from Kathmandu to Mahendranagar, which depart at 12.30 pm. From Mahendranagar departures are around 2 pm. The trip costs Rs 695 and takes 15 hours. There are also buses from Mahendranagar to Nepalganj (Rs 270, four to five hours).

To/From India Buses leave Mahendranagar roughly every half hour for the border to the west. It's a 1km walk (or rickshaw ride) between the Nepali and Indian posts, and then a farther few kilometres to the Indian town of Banbassa.

Banbassa is on the Indian metre-gauge rail system, and the onward connections are poor. It is much better served by buses with direct connections to Delhi (nine hours), Bareilly (the nearest broad-gauge station, three hours), Nainital (seven hours), Almora (eight hours), Dharamsala (15 hours) and Agra (10 hours).

Trekking

For the people in the hills of Nepal, walking has always been the main method of getting from A to B. There were no roads venturing into the hill country from the Terai and India until the Tribhuvan Hwy to Kathmandu was constructed in the 1950s. Pokhara was not connected to the outside world by road until the 1970s. Even today the vast majority of villages can only be reached on foot, although every year the roads penetrate farther into Nepal's endless ranges of hills.

The Nepali people, making their way from village to village on the well-worn trails, were only joined by Western visitors when Himalayan mountaineering came into vogue. It was the accounts of those pioneering mountaineers, who had to make their way to the base of the great peaks on foot, that inspired the first trekkers. The word 'trekking' was first applied to Nepali hiking trips in the 1960s and the enormous popularity of trekking today has developed since that time.

Trekking in Nepal means a walking trip following trails, many of which have been used for communication and trade for centuries. Trekking is not mountaineering, although some of the popular trekking trails are used by mountaineering expeditions on their approach marches. A trekking trip can be any length you choose – there are popular treks around the Kathmandu and Pokhara valleys that only take a day to complete, there are also treks of two or three days, or there are longer treks lasting from a week to a month. You could even string a series of popular treks together and walk for months on end.

The two major attractions that account for the enormous popularity of trekking are the scenery and the people. The flora and fauna found along the way are other attractions.

There is no question that Nepal offers some of the most spectacular and beautiful scenery in the world. Of course it's the mountains that are best known, and the exploits of mountain photographers have made Everest, Machhapuchhare, Ama Dablam, and other mountains instantly recognisable to keen trekkers all over the world. Nepal has a near monopoly on the world's highest peaks – eight of the 10 highest are found in Nepal and a number of the popular trekking routes offer you wonderful views or even visits to the base camps used by mountaineering expeditions. Mountain flights may give you superb views, but there is absolutely nothing like waking up on a crystal-clear Himalayan day and seeing an 8000m peak towering over you, seemingly just an arm's length away.

The mountains may be the most obvious scenic attraction, but trekkers soon find there are plenty of other treats for the eye. The hill country is often breathtakingly beautiful with pretty villages, attractive houses, neat fields and interesting temples. As you climb higher the subtropical lowlands give way to meadows, stretches of forest, swift-flowing rivers and deep canyons before you reach the cold and often barren regions at the foot of the great peaks. The views change with the seasons, whether it is the cycle of planting and harvesting or the brilliant displays of wildflowers in spring and autumn.

Highlights

- Making it as close to the top of Everest as possible without actually being a mountaineer, and waking to see the famous peak towering over you
- Staying in the mountain villages and meeting people from Nepal's diversity of ethnic groups
- Stopping off on the Jomsom Trek at Muktinath, a pilgrimage centre high in the mountains visited by both Buddhists and Hindus
- Trekking through some of the most spectacular scenery in the world

Trekking in Nepal is not like hiking through the often uninhabited countryside of a North American, Australian or European national park. Local people are constantly passing by on the trails, and along many routes there are regularly spaced villages to pause in. In the villages you can meet people from a diversity of ethnic groups. The outgoing nature, general friendliness and good humour of Nepalis is often noted by trekkers. Colourful festivals can make trekking at certain times of year even more enjoyable.

Of course, your trekking companions can be another important part of the trekking experience. A long trek can be a great opportunity to enjoy yourself with good friends. Despite stories you may have heard about the Himalaya being overrun with hordes of trekkers the reality is generally very different. Certainly there may be many trekkers during the peak seasons on the most popular routes, particularly the Jomsom Trek, but compared to the crowds visiting national parks in the west the numbers are often minuscule.

Preparations

PLANNING

Although Nepal offers plenty of opportunity for short treks lasting a day or less, most treks last considerably longer. From Pokhara or around the Kathmandu Valley you can do a variety of two-, three- or four-day walks, but Nepal's most popular treks take at least a week. For the very popular Everest Base Camp and Annapurna Circuit Treks you have to allow three weeks. Don't take on one of these classic long treks too lightly; the end of the first week is not the time to discover that you're not keen on walking.

When to Go

Put simply, the best time to trek is October to May (dry season); the worst time is June to September (monsoon). This generalisation does not allow for the peculiarities of individual treks. Some people even claim that the undeniable difficulties of trekking during the monsoon are outweighed by the virtual absence of Western trekkers.

The first two months of the dry season, October and November, are probably the ideal period for trekking. The air, freshly washed by the monsoon rains, is crystal clear, the mountain scenery is superb and the weather is still comfortably warm. At low altitudes in October it can actually be quite balmy, and trekkers may find they complete a whole trek in only T-shirts.

December, January and February are still good months for trekking, but the cold can be bitter at high altitudes. Getting up to the Everest Base Camp can be a real endurance test and Thorung La pass on the Annapurna Circuit is usually blocked by snow.

March and April offer better weather than winter but at the price of hazy visibility on long-distance views. By this time of year the weather has been dry for a long time and dust is starting to hang in the air. The poorer quality of the Himalayan views is compensated for by the superb wildflowers such as Nepal's wonderful rhododendrons.

By May it starts to get very hot, dusty and humid, and the monsoon is definitely just around the corner. From June to September the trails can be dangerously slippery due to the monsoon rains, and raging rivers often wash away bridges and stretches of trail. Nepal's famous *jukha* (leeches) are an unpleasant feature of the wet season, but with care, trekking can still be possible and there are certainly fewer trekkers on the trail.

Independent Trekking

At one extreme, independent trekking can mean simply trekking from lodge to lodge along the main trekking trails with one or more friends. The popular trekking trails all have accommodation along their entire length. People have even walked the complete Annapurna Circuit without a sleeping bag, although this is asking for trouble and is definitely not recommended.

For most moderately fit people, guides and porters are not necessary on the Annapurna or the Mt Everest treks. A good guide/porter will enhance your experience, but a bad one will just make life more

CHRIS KLEP

A warm welcome awaits trekkers in Pangka, Sherpa country in the Solu Khumbu region.

STAN ARMINGTON

Good balance is the key!

JOHN BORTHWICK

Sure-footed Sherpas can carry enormous loads.

RICHARD I'ANSON

Trekking along the lush Tamur Kosi Valley in the remote eastern Terai is not only for the hardy.

GARETH McCORMACK

Buddhist prayer flags without the wind in their sails, Kyanjin Gompa, Langtang Valley

BRETT SHEARER

Sending prayers off to the heavens.

GARETH McCORMACK

Watch for the signs.

ANDREW PEACOCK

Pack-yaks ease the burden of trekking in the Everest region.

Independent Trekking with Children

A few years ago we decided to have a family holiday in Nepal. We had both travelled and trekked extensively in Nepal – without kids – and thought it would be a good place to return to with our two children – Ella aged six and Vera 2½. It turned out to be an excellent choice, although there were moments when we doubted our sanity in carting two kids halfway across the world, exposing them to all manner of bugs, not to mention the pollution of Kathmandu, just so we could see some mountains with snow on them.

One of the main goals of our trip was to do a week-long trek in the mountains. Many people we spoke to thought it was perhaps a bit of an ambitious thing to undertake with two small children, but this just made us more determined to give it a go – we could always turn back if it didn't work out. Our base point was to be Pokhara, seven bumpy and dusty but cheap hours by bus, or one easy, spectacular and not-too-expensive hour by plane (we opted for the latter) from Kathmandu.

As we were travelling on a fairly tight budget, we didn't think we could afford an organised trek where everything is taken care of for you. Instead we organised it all ourselves. We approached many of the trekking agencies in Pokhara, and finally settled on one that we felt had its act together sufficiently to arrange for porters and transport to the trail head. Our plan was that we would have three porters – two to carry rucksacks, and a third to carry Vera most of the time, and Ella when she got tired of walking. As it turned out, Ella walked virtually the whole way, which was a great effort, and Vera was carried in a *doko* (a large, conical, cane basket) on a porter's back. She felt safe being up off the ground, and was emboldened enough to pull faces at trekkers and locals we passed along the trail. Her mode of travel certainly made her a curiosity to locals and foreigners alike. To wedge her in safely we sat her first in her child-pack, placed this in the basket, and then filled the gaps with sleeping bags and items of warm clothing we shed as the day wore on.

The porters were great with the kids, and although we felt a bit like a travelling show at times, it was worth hiring enough porters to free us of any major load. At around US$5 per porter per day, it was money well spent.

Overall the trek went very well, but we realised early on that we had overestimated how far we would be able to walk in one day. Once we slowed down and basically let Ella set the pace, things were fine. The walking itself was not too strenuous, largely because of our slow pace, but we did get up to 3500m, and even at this altitude the children's breathing was being affected. In six days we were able to comfortably walk from Birethanti to Ghorapani/Deorali on the Jomsom Trek, cut across to Ghandruk on the Annapurna Circuit and return to Birethanti.

Staying in the teahouses along the way was a highlight for the kids. On arrival they would disappear into the candle-lit, smoky interiors of the kitchen, and usually emerge beaming some time later, brandishing a boiled potato or some other morsel kindly given by the hard-working women of the house.

The major problem we faced on the trek was a bout of giardia that Vera contracted, and this led to our second-biggest problem; what to do with all the soiled disposable nappies. They're a major nuisance to get rid of at the best of times; in small villages in the mountains they are a disaster. The only really sound solution is to use cloth nappies. On a practical level this is very difficult (although not impossible), so with the disposables you need to roll the used ones up very tightly, store them in a strong plastic bag and carry them out to a place where you can dispose of them properly. This is not as offensive as it sounds!

Empty, plastic mineral water bottles are another problem in the mountains, and it's recommended that you buy iodine tablets to purify your water. Some powdered flavouring helps to disguise the awful taste, but our two children steadfastly refused anything other than plain bottled water.

Hugh Finlay

complicated (see Guides & Porters later this section).

There are many factors that influence how much you spend on an independent trek. In most places, dorm accommodation costs around Rs 20 to Rs 50, a simple meal of rice and dal around Rs 30 to Rs 50 – note that as you get farther from the road on the Annapurna Circuit and in the Everest region, prices can be more than twice as high. After a long day hiking, however, most people will weaken when confronted by a cold beer, an apple pie or a hot shower and these will dramatically add to your costs. Around US$3 to US$10 per day in the Annapurnas and Everest region is about right, including the occasional luxuries you might treat yourself to.

According to some studies, competition on the Annapurna Circuit is so intense, and the need for money so desperate, that lodges have been known to provide food and accommodation at below cost. In almost all lodges prices are fixed and are more than reasonable. Remember this – and the real value of the rupee – if you start to get carried away with bargaining.

Organised Trekking

Organised treks can also vary greatly in standards and costs. Treks arranged with international travel companies tend to be more expensive than trips arranged within Nepal.

International Trekking Agencies At one extreme there are big international adventure travel companies that market trips in the West. You book your trek through them and everything is organised before you leave home. The cost will probably include flights to and from Nepal, accommodation in Kathmandu before and after the trek, tours and other activities as well as the trek itself. A fully organised trek provides virtually everything: tents, sleeping bags, food, porters and an experienced English-speaking *sirdar* (trail boss), sherpa guides and usually a Western trek leader. All you need to worry about is a day-pack and camera.

Companies organising trekking trips in Nepal include some well-known names such as Mountain Travel, Wilderness Travel or Above the Clouds in the USA, World Expeditions or Peregrine Adventures in Australia,

Organised Trekking with Children

Taking children trekking in Nepal can be surprisingly enjoyable. Both of our children's treks were of the organised variety. Tackling a long, high-altitude trek like the Annapurna Circuit with small children might be asking too much. With our children we planned on shorter treks (we didn't want them getting fed up) which avoided very high altitudes. We also opted for organised treks to make it easier for both sides so we didn't have to worry about finding food and shelter and the kids were likely to eat better.

Our first trek with children was the short Annapurna Skyline Trek (see the Pokhara chapter for details) when our daughter Tashi was eight and our son Kieran was six. Back home, like most kids, they seemed to think getting from the car to the video recorder a long walk, but in fact they walked the whole way and still had energy for frantic games with the porters and local village kids after we set up camp each night.

Our enthusiasm must have been catching because three years later we found ourselves back in Nepal, this time with seven friends and neighbours and six children (two aged six, two aged eight, one 10-year-old and one 11-year-old). This time we opted for the Helambu Trek as it is reasonably short, does not go too high and is not too heavily trekked. Malla Treks in Kathmandu, who organised the trek for us, made it even more interesting by sending along a bunch of Nepali children, who also happened to be on school vacation. Our resulting 'international trek' was a great learning experience, and once again our kids turned out to be hardier than we'd expected. On one day only, when a misunderstanding with the porters resulted in us having to climb a 3500m pass late in the day, did the two six-year-olds need a little carrying. Apart from that, the whole noisy mob walked the entire eight days.

Tony Wheeler

and Explore Worldwide in the UK. Although the trek leaders may be experienced Western walkers from the international company the actual organisation in Nepal will probably be by a locally based trekking company.

Local Trekking Agencies It's quite possible to arrange a fully organised trip when you get to Nepal (and save a lot of money), but if you have a large group it's best to make the arrangements well in advance. Many trekking companies in Nepal can put together a fully equipped trek if you give them a few days notice. With the best of these companies a trek may cost upwards of US$60 or US$70 a day and you'll trek in real comfort with tables, chairs, and dining tents, toilet tents and other luxuries.

There are more than 300 trekking agencies in Nepal, ranging from those tied up with international travel companies, down to small agencies that specialise in handling independent trekkers. These small agencies will often be able to fix you up with individual porters or guides. A group trek organised through one of these smaller trekking agencies might cost US$30 to US$50 a day. Group treks staying at village inns along the route can be cheaper still (around US$25 a day including a guide and food).

Some trekking agencies that have been recommended include:

Adventure Nepal Trekking (☎ 01-412508, fax 222026) Tridevi Marg, Thamel, PO Box 915, Kathmandu
Ama Dablam Trekking (☎ 01-415372/3, fax 416029) Lazimpat, PO Box 3035, Kathmandu
Annapurna Mountaineering & Trekking (☎ 01-222999, fax 226153) Durbar Marg, PO Box 795, Kathmandu
Asian Trekking (☎ 01-415506, ⓔ asiant@asian-trekking.com) Keser Mahal, Thamel, PO Box 3022, Kathmandu
Bhrikuti Himalayan Treks (☎ 01-417459, fax 413612) Nag Pokhari, PO Box 2267, Kathmandu
Chhetri Sisters (☎ 061-24066, ⓔ sisters3@cnet.wlink.com.np), Lakeside North, Pokhara
Crystal Mountain Treks (☎ 01-412656, fax 412647) Naxal, Nag Pokhari, PO Box 5437, Kathmandu
Himalayan Hill Treks & River Tours (☎ 01-520609, ⓔ brian@hilltrek.mos.com.np) Patan, PO Box 1066, Kathmandu
International Trekkers (☎ 01-371397, fax 371561) Chabahil, PO Box 1273, Kathmandu
Journeys Mountaineering & Trekking (☎ 01-225969, fax 229262) Kantipath, PO Box 2034, Kathmandu
Lama Excursions (☎ 01-425812, fax 425813) Chanddol, Maharajganj, PO Box 2485, Kathmandu
Malla Treks (☎ 01-410089, ⓔ trekinfo@mallatrk.mos.com.np) Lekhnath Marg, PO Box 5227, Kathmandu
Mountain Travel Nepal (☎ 01-411225, ⓔ info@tigermountain.com) PO Box 170, Kathmandu
Nepal Himal Treks (☎ 01-413305) Baluwatar, PO Box 4528, Kathmandu
Sherpa Co-operative Trekking (☎ 01-224068, fax 227983) Durbar Marg, PO Box 1338, Kathmandu
Sherpa Society (☎ 01-484218, ⓔ passang@mos.com.np) Chabahil, Chuchepati, PO Box 1566, Kathmandu
Sherpa Trekking Service (☎ 01-220423, fax 227243) Kamaladi, PO Box 500, Kathmandu
Sisne Rover Trekking (☎ 061-20893, ⓔ sisne@mos.com.np) PO Box 257, Lakeside, Pokhara
Thamserku Trekking (☎ 01-354491, fax 354323) Basundhara, Ring Rd, PO Box 3124, Kathmandu
Treks & Expedition Services (☎ 01-418347, fax 410488) Kamal Pokhari, PO Box 3057, Kathmandu
Venture Treks & Expeditions (☎ 01-221585, fax 220178) Kantipath, PO Box 3968, Kathmandu
Yeti Mountaineering & Trekking (☎ 01-410899) Ramshah Path, PO Box 1034, Kathmandu

Books & Maps

Books and maps are readily available in Kathmandu and Pokhara bookshops.

See Lonely Planet's *Trekking in the Nepal Himalaya* by Stan Armington for the complete story on trekking here. It has comprehensive advice on equipment selection, an excellent medical section oriented towards trekking and the mountains, and comprehensive route descriptions not only of the popular treks covered more briefly in this book, but also of a number of interesting but less heavily used routes.

The best series of maps of Nepal is the 1:50,000 series produced by Erwin Schneider for Research Scheme Nepal Himalaya and originally printed in Vienna. Most sheets are now published by Nelles Verlag in Munich, Germany. They cover the Kathmandu

Valley and the Everest region from Jiri to the Hongu valley and have a contour interval of 40m. The 1:100,000 Schneider maps of Annapurna and Langtang have a contour interval of 100m. They're available from many map shops overseas and at many bookshops in Kathmandu.

The Finnish government has assisted the survey department with the production of an outstanding series of 1:50,000 and 1:25,000 maps covering a large portion of eastern and central Nepal. They are available in some bookshops and from the Survey Department in Balawatar, Kathmandu, on the road towards the airport.

All of these maps are available at bookshops in Kathmandu and some speciality map shops overseas stock a selection. Most are available online from Omni Resources at www.omnimap.com.

What to Bring

Equipment It's always best to have your own equipment since you will be familiar with it and know for certain that it works. If there is some equipment that you do not have, however, you can always buy or rent it from one of Nepal's many trekking shops. Much of the equipment available is of excellent quality (but check items carefully) and the rental charges are generally not excessive, but large deposits are often required (usually equal to a generous valuation of the equipment itself). Never leave your passport as a deposit.

Rental rates vary depending on quality, but per day prices are roughly as follows:

item	rate (Rs)
mattress	10–20
sleeping bag	30–50
down jacket	25–50
pack	30–50
tent	100–200

Kathmandu is still the centre for trekking equipment and there are many outlets around Thamel. Pokhara and Namche Bazaar also have trekking equipment places. The equipment available in Nepal used to be mainly expedition leftovers, but now there is also a great deal of new equipment. Some trekking gear, including sleeping bags, down jackets, duffel bags, rucksacks, camera cases, ponchos and wind jackets are manufactured in Kathmandu and sold in Thamel trekking shops at very reasonable prices. Much of this locally produced gear is decorated with well-known brand names such as North Face, Karimor, Lowe Pro and Gore-Tex, but don't be deceived into thinking you're getting top-quality merchandise at a bargain price. Even so, most items are well made and will stand up to the rigours of at least one major trek.

Approximate retail prices for new Nepali-made gear complete with fake brand names are as follows:

item	cost (Rs)
sleeping bag	5500
down jacket	5000
rain/wind jacket	1300
pile jacket	1200–1500
day pack	1000–2500
expedition pack	3500
duffel bag	350–450

Clothing The clothing you require depends on where and when you trek. If you're going to the Everest Base Camp in the middle of winter you must be prepared for very cold weather and take down gear, mittens and the like. But if you're doing a short, low-altitude trek early or late in the season the weather is often likely to be fine for T-shirts and perhaps a sweater, or better yet a pile jacket, to pull on in the evenings. If you don't have your own sleeping bag or down jacket, these can be rented in Kathmandu; these may not be particularly clean.

Apart from ensuring you have adequate clothing to keep warm, it's important that your feet are comfortable and will stay dry if it rains or snows. Uncomfortable shoes or blistered feet are the worst possible trekking discomfort. Make sure your shoes fit well and are comfortable for long periods. Running shoes are adequate for low-altitude (below 3000m), warm-weather treks where you won't encounter snow, though they lack ankle support. Otherwise the minimum standard of footwear is lightweight trekking boots; these can be bought new (imported) in Kathmandu at Rs 2000 to Rs 3000.

Other Gear In winter or at high altitudes a high-quality sleeping bag will be necessary. However, if you are going on an organised trek check exactly what equipment is supplied; it's a waste of time bringing your own sleeping bag if the company supplies one. If you need to hire one, it could be grubby; check for fleas or worse.

Rain is rare during most of the trekking season, though weather patterns in the Bay of Bengal can cause massive rainstorms during the autumn, and there are sure to be a few rainy days in spring. You should be prepared for it by carrying waterproof gear, or at least an umbrella. The rainy season just before and after the monsoon also brings leeches and it's nice to have some salt or matches to deal with them.

Take a torch (flashlight) for those inevitable calls of nature on moonless nights.

Cigarettes and matches are popular small gifts to have with you on treks if you are travelling with porters, but beware of encouraging children begging for 'one rupee' or a 'school pen'.

Money Except in Solu Khumbu and on the Annapurna treks, changing foreign money is likely to be very difficult if not impossible. Bring enough money for the whole trek and don't count on being able to change Rs 1000 notes easily.

Guides & Porters

If you can't (or don't want to) carry a decent-sized pack, if you have children or elderly people in your party, or if you plan to walk in regions where you have to carry in food and tents, help should be considered.

If you make arrangements with one of the small trekking agencies in Kathmandu expect to pay Rs 150 to Rs 200 per day for a guide, Rs 300 to Rs 750 per day for a porter.

Finding Guides & Porters Many people hire a porter for independent trekking, and there is no doubt this has many advantages.

Porters can ease the load!

To hire a guide, look on bulletin boards, hire someone through a guesthouse or agency, visit a trekking company or check with the office of the Kathmandu Environmental Education Project (KEEP). Chhetri Sisters Guesthouse (☎ 061-24066, ⓔ sister3@cnet.wlink.com.np) at Lakeside North, Pokhara, organises women porters and guides for women trekkers.

It's fairly easy to find guides and porters, but it is hard to be certain of their honesty and ability. Unless you have first-hand recommendations, you're best to hire someone through a guesthouse or agency. A porter or guide found at a street corner can easily disappear along the trail with all your gear even if they are carrying a slew of letters from past clients certifying to their honesty.

Arranging expeditions where guides, porters, tents and food are required can be very time-consuming and can quickly become extremely complicated. In such cases you're definitely best off putting this in the hands of a professional.

There is a distinct difference between a guide and a porter. A guide should speak English, know the terrain and the trails, and supervise porters, but will probably not be interested in carrying a load or doing menial tasks such as cooking or putting up tents. Porters are generally only hired for load-carrying, although an increasing number speak some English and know the trails well enough to act as guides.

If halfway through a trek you decide you do need some help (illness, problems with high altitude or ordinary old blisters might contribute) it will generally be possible to find someone. Most lodges can arrange a porter, particularly in large villages or near a hill-country airstrip where there are often porters who have just been paid off from a trekking party and are looking for another load to carry. Large organised trekking parties carry most of their own food and as the food is used up, fewer porters are needed and the extra porters are paid off along the route – so you can find experienced porters in the most unlikely places.

Obligations to Guides & Porters An important consideration when you decide to trek with a guide or porters is that you place yourself in the role of an employer. This means that you may have to deal with personnel problems, including medical care, insurance, strikes, requests for time off, salary increases and all the other aspects of being a boss. Be as thorough as you can when hiring people and make it clear from the beginning what the requirements and limitations are. After that, prepare yourself for some haggling – it's almost impossible to protect against it.

When hiring a porter you are responsible (morally if not legally) for the welfare of those you employ. Many porters die or are injured each year (see the boxed text 'Porters, Exploitation & IPPG') and it's important that you don't contribute to the problem.

The main points to bear in mind when hiring a porter are:

- Ensure that adequate clothing is provided for any staff hired by you. This needs to be adequate for the altitudes you intend to trek to, and to protect against bad weather. Equipment should include adequate footwear, headwear, gloves, windproof jacket and trousers, sunglasses, and blanket, sleeping mat and tent at altitude.
- Ensure that whatever provisions you have made for yourself for emergency medical treatment is available to porters working for you.
- Ensure that porters who fall ill are not simply paid out and left to fend for themselves (it happens!).
- Ensure that porters who do fall ill and are taken down and out in order to access medical treatment are accompanied by someone who speaks the porter's language and also understands the medical problem.

Whether you're making the arrangements yourself or dealing with an agency, make sure you clearly establish where you will go, how long you will take, how much you are going to pay and what you will supply along the way. Traditionally you pay for a guide's food and accommodation, porters pay for their own food. With a guide, agree on a daily rate for food rather than pay as you go. Arrangements where you pay for the guide or porter's accommodation and food can end up being surprisingly expensive. The amount of food a hungry Nepali porter can go through, when you're footing the bill, can be simply stunning. You need to increase the allowance at higher elevations where food is more expensive.

You may also be responsible for outfitting guides and porters to cope with cold and snow. If you are going above the snow line you must make absolutely certain that porters have goggles, shoes, shelter and appropriate clothing. There are still regular horror stories about ill-equipped porters tackling the Thorung La (the pass between Manang and Muktinath on the Annapurna Circuit). Frostbite, snow blindness and death have resulted.

When you do provide equipment for porters, be sure to make it clear whether it is a loan or a gift. In reality it will be very hard to get back equipment that you have loaned unless you are very determined and thick-skinned. The porters and sherpas have special techniques to make you feel guilty and petty when you ask for the return of equipment. If you're hiring your own porters, contact KEEP for information about the porter clothing bank, a scheme that allows you to rent protective gear for your porter.

DOCUMENTS & FEES

Trekking Permits

Permits are not required for trekking in the Everest, Annapurna and Langtang regions.

Porters, Exploitation & IPPG

Porters are the backbone of the trekking industry in Nepal, and yet every year there are incidents (all preventable) involving porters suffering from acute mountain sickness (AMS), snow blindness, frostbite and even dying. It seems they are well down the pecking order with some trekking companies who simply don't look after the porters hired by them. This certainly does not apply to all companies, but there are plenty, especially at the budget end of the scale, who are more worried about their own profit than the welfare of those they rely on to generate that profit.

Porters often come from the lowland valleys, are poor and poorly educated and are often ignorant of the potential dangers of the areas they are being employed to work in. Stories abound of porters being left to fend for themselves, wearing thin cotton clothes and thongs when traversing high mountain passes in blizzard conditions. At the end of each winter a number of porters' bodies are discovered in the snow melt – they become tired, ill or affected by altitude, and simply sit down in the snow, get hypothermia and die. If you are hiring a porter independently, you have certain obligations to meet. If you are trekking with an organised group using porters, be sure to ask the company how they ensure the well-being of porters hired by them.

In order to prevent the abuse of porters, the International Porter Protection Group (IPPG) was established in 1997. Its aim is to improve health and safety for porters at work, to reduce the incidence of avoidable illness, injury and death, and to educate trekkers and trekking/travel companies about porter welfare. IPPG operates a clothing bank for porters, with branches in Lukla and in the office of the Himalaya Explorers Club (next to KEEP) in Thamel. Visit the IPPG Web site at www.ippg.net.

These three regions cover the vast majority of trekking routes taken by visitors to Nepal.

Treks in more remote areas (see table following) do require a permit. If you are trekking with an organised group this will be arranged for you. If you're doing it independently it is possible to obtain the permit the same day, although you must make your application as early as possible in the morning. Be prepared for a distinctly tiring battle with bureaucracy.

Trekking permits are issued in Kathmandu and Pokhara, and can only be extended in those cities. Permits can be obtained from Kathmandu's immigration office, open 10 am to 1 pm Sunday to Thursday and 10 am to noon Friday for applications. You have to go back later to retrieve your passport.

Trekking permits and application forms are colour coded depending on the region in which you plan to trek; be sure to get the right form when you start the process. Two passport photos are required with each of the applications; fees, though quoted in US dollars, are payable only in rupees.

If you plan to trek in two different remote areas, two trekking permits are needed.

area	fee
Everest, Annapurna & Langtang	No permit required
Jumla (& others)	US$5 per week for first four weeks, US$10 per week after that
Kanchenjunga* & Lower Dolpo*	US$10 per week for first four weeks, US$20 per week after that
Upper Mustang* † & Upper Dolpo* †	US$700 for up to 10 days, groups only
Manaslu* †	US$75 per week low season, US$90 high season
Humla*	US$90 for seven days, then US$15 per day

* Treks to these regions must be fully equipped treks arranged by a trekking agency.

† A government liaison officer must accompany treks to this region.

National Park & Conservation Fees

If you trek in the Annapurna, Manaslu, Kanchenjunga or Makalu regions, you will enter a conservation area and must pay a conservation fee, and if your trek enters a national park, you must pay a national park fee.

You can buy an entrance ticket for all national parks and conservation areas in advance at the Annapurna Conservation Area Project (ACAP; ☎ 225393, ext 363) office in the basement of the Sanchaya Kosh shopping centre on Tridevi Marg at the entrance to Thamel in Kathmandu. The office is open from 9 am to 5 pm daily. You can also pay the national park fee when you arrive at the park entrance station, but *you must pay the conservation fee in advance*. Currently, the (once-only) fee is Rs 1000 (US$15) for national parks; Rs 2000 (US$30) for Annapurna; and Rs 1000 for Makalu-Barun and Kanchenjunga conservation areas.

Conservation fees for the Annapurna area are also payable in Pokhara at the ACAP office (☎ 061-32275), opposite Nepal Grindlays Bank at Lakeside. Bring Rs 1000 and one photograph. Fortunately the permit is issued on the spot and you should accomplish the task quickly unless there is a long queue.

RESPONSIBLE TOURISM

Trekking, Firewood & Forest Depletion

The depletion of forest is a severe problem throughout the Himalaya, and is a particular problem in Nepal. In this regard, trekkers can definitely do their part to aid Himalayan conservation. Minimise the use of firewood by staying in lodges that use kerosene or fuel-efficient wood stoves and solar-heated hot water. Avoid using large open fires for warmth – wear additional clothing instead. Keep showers to a minimum, and spurn showers altogether if wood is burnt to produce the hot water.

Consolidate cooking time (and wood consumption) by ordering the same items at the same time as other trekkers. *Dal bhat* (rice and lentils) is usually readily available for large numbers of people, does not require special lengthy cooking time and is nutritious and inexpensive. Remember that local meals are usually prepared between 10 and 11 am, so eating then will usually not require lighting an additional fire. Treat your drinking water with iodine, rather than boiling it.

Those travelling with organised groups should ensure kerosene is used for cooking.

Garbage & Waste

While trekkers certainly contribute to the problems of firewood use and the appearance of rubbish along the trails, they are not the only culprits. As modern nonbiodegradable packaging becomes increasingly common in Nepal, garbage is starting to appear even along the village trails that are untravelled by Western trekkers.

You can do several things that will reduce the amount of rubbish and pollution in the hills. One important contribution you can make is to reduce the volume of waste plastic in village rubbish heaps by not drinking bottled mineral water; instead carry a water bottle and treat the water with iodine. ACAP is developing a number of drinking water depots along the Annapurna Circuit in order to help alleviate the problem created by discarded plastic bottles.

Independent trekkers should always carry their garbage out or dispose of it properly. You can burn it, but you should remember that the fireplace in a Nepali home is a sacred institution and throwing rubbish into it would be a great insult.

Toilet paper is a particularly unpleasant sight along trails; if you must use it, carry it in a plastic bag until you can burn it. Better yet, carry a small plastic trowel to bury your faeces (well away from any streams) and a small plastic water container so that, like the vast majority of people in the world, you can clean yourself with water instead.

Those travelling with organised groups should ensure that toilet tents are properly organised and that rubbish is carried out. Check on the company's policies before you sign up.

USEFUL ORGANISATIONS

Several organisations are attempting to deal with the environmental problems created by trekking, including the Annapurna Conservation Area Project, which has done a great deal to encourage sustainable development in the Annapurna region. ACAP has its offices in Thamel, Patan and Pokhara.

Two other organisations in Thamel in Kathmandu offer free, up-to-date information on trekking conditions, health risks and minimising your environmental impact.

KEEP has a library, an excellent notice board and sells iodine bottles, biodegradable soap and other such environmentally friendly equipment.

The Himalayan Rescue Association (HRA) Trekkers' Information Centre has information about AMS and useful notebooks with up-to-date information from other trekkers. Both KEEP and the HRA offices are excellent places to visit and advertise for trekking companions.

See under Information in the Kathmandu chapter for contact details for all of these useful organisations.

Another good source of impartial information in Kathmandu for independent trekking, are the slide shows held in the Kathmandu Guest House by Chris Beall, a British freelance photographer, writer, and trek leader. The shows cost Rs 300 (including tea/coffee and biscuits), and if they are on you'll see posters up at the Kathmandu Guest House.

Most Thamel bookshops stock *Trekking Gently in the Himalaya* by Wendy Brewer Lama (Rs 30), which is a small booklet with essential tips for trekkers.

HEALTH

See under Health in the Facts for the Visitor chapter for more detailed information on staying healthy while trekking. Acute mountain sickness (AMS) or altitude sickness is the major concern on high-altitude treks, but for the majority of trekkers health problems are likely to be minor, such as stomach upsets and blisters. While paranoia is not at all required, common-sense precautions are.

Basic rules for healthy trekking include taking care that water is always safe to drink. The best method is to treat water with iodine, as this is safe (although not exactly delicious!) and does not require the use of firewood or kerosene to boil water. Diarrhoea is one of the comparatively minor problems that can ruin a trek so watch what you eat and ensure your medical kit has a medication such as Lomotil or Imodium (for emergencies only) and an antibiotic like Norfloxacin. The food on an organised trek is unlikely to cause any problems, but village-inn trekkers are at risk.

At high altitudes the burning power of the sun is strong, so make sure you have a pair of good sunglasses, and a maximum protection sunscreen. If there is any likelihood that you'll be walking over snow, sunglasses are insufficient; you need mountaineering glasses with side pieces, or at the very least, rig up pieces of cardboard on the frames of your glasses to reduce glare. Ensure that your porters also have adequate eye-wear.

Blisters can take the fun out of trekking so make sure your shoes and socks are comfortable and come prepared with Band-Aids just in case they aren't. Many people suffer from knee and ankle strains, particularly if they are carrying their own pack. If you have a predisposition for these injuries, carry elastic supports or bandages.

Make sure you are in good health before departing as there is very little medical attention along the trails and rescue helicopters are not only very expensive but *must* be cleared for payment in advance! Your embassy can do this if you have registered with them. See under Everest Base Camp Trek for more information on possible medical assistance along the way. In general, Himalayan hospitals can offer only very limited facilities and expertise.

Be ever-alert for the symptoms of AMS. The Himalayan Rescue Association (HRA) in Thamel, Kathmandu can offer valuable advice on trekking issues and has an excellent pamphlet on AMS.

TREKKING SAFELY

In the mid-1970s it was possible to claim that Nepal was totally immune from theft, assaults and other assorted vices of Western 'civilisation'. Unfortunately that claim can no longer be made.

[Continued on page 369]

MOUNTAINEERING IN THE HIMALAYA

The word 'Himalaya' is Sanskrit for 'Abode of Snows', and Nepal's stretch of the Himalaya has eight peaks over 8000m, including the highest of them all, mighty Mt Everest (8848m). Known to the Tibetans as Qomolangma and to the Nepalis as Sagarmatha, the world's highest place was the overpowering attraction for Nepal's first modern tourists – the mountaineers.

Most of the important Nepali peaks were conquered during the 1950s and 1960s, so although it's no longer possible to be the first to set foot on top, this has certainly not diminished the attraction of Himalayan mountaineering. Climbing these giants today is an adventurous sporting activity, whereas 40 years ago it required huge sponsored expeditions.

There are 14 peaks over 8000m in the world, and of the 10 highest no fewer than eight are in Nepal, although some of these straddle the national border – Everest straddles the border between Nepal and China (Tibet) and Kanchenjunga (8598m) straddles that of Nepal and India.

Nepal's magnificent mountains can be enjoyed in three distinctly different fashions. The easiest way is to simply look at them: This can be done by air – on regular flights or on the daily tourist-season mountain flights – or you can admire them from the various popular mountain viewpoints such as Nagarkot or Dhulikhel near Kathmandu or Sarangkot above Pokhara. Getting to these viewpoints is covered in the appropriate chapters.

HIGHEST PEAKS AROUND THE WORLD

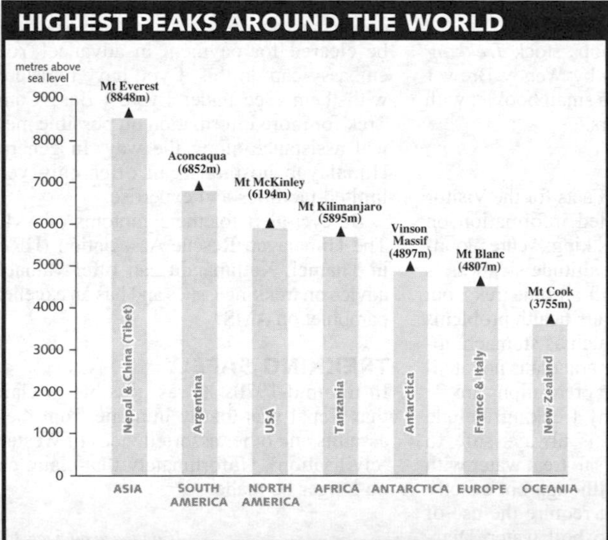

Inset: A mountaineer climbing high on the south ridge of Mt Pumori (7161m), Khumbu himal. (Photo: Grant Dixon)

Mountain Flights

Every morning during the clear dry-season months, all the major airlines offer mountain flights, with panoramic dawn views of the Himalaya. Each passenger on the modern aircraft operated by the private airlines is guaranteed a window seat. The hour-long flight from Kathmandu costs US$99 with Royal Nepal Airlines (RNAC) and US$109 with the private airlines. If the weather is clear, the views are stunning.

If simply looking at the mountains isn't enough you can get right in among them by trekking. Trekking is not mountain climbing: Apart from high passes on certain treks and the approach to the Everest Base Camp, you are unlikely to go above 3500m. Trekking along some routes, however, does provide breathtaking views. More information is given in the Trekking chapter.

Finally, there is mountain climbing, and while getting to the top of an 8000m peak is strictly for the professionals, there are plenty of 'trekking peaks' that small-scale amateur expeditions can readily attempt. This is not to say that mountaineering in Nepal is easy – climbing mountains this high always involves an element of risk – but getting to the top of a Himalayan peak does not always necessarily require millionaire status or big commercial backers.

History

Mountaineering became a fashionable pursuit in Europe during the second half of the 19th century. Having knocked off the great Alpine peaks, Europeans found the much greater heights of the Himalaya an obvious new challenge. An Englishman named WW Graham made a mountaineering visit to Nepal in 1883 and reached the top of a 6000m peak. He was followed by another Englishman, Tom Longstaff, who climbed Trisuli (7215m) in 1907. For the next 20 years this remained the highest summit reached in the world. An Italian attempt on K2, in Pakistan, two years later became the first of the huge Himalayan expeditions involving hundreds of porters.

First Attempts on Everest During the 1920s and 1930s, reaching the top of Mt Everest came to be seen as the major goal of mountaineers. Apart from the difficulties inherent in reaching such heights there were also political constraints. Nepal continued to be totally isolated, and all attempts on Everest were made from the Tibetan side.

British assaults were made in 1921, 1922 and 1924. The 1922 expedition used oxygen to reach 8326m, while the 1924 expedition fell just 300m short of the top, reaching 8572m without the use of oxygen. Apart from numerous climbers and support staff, the 1924 expedition utilised at least 350 porters. Such massive numbers of porters and support staff set a pattern that was to continue until recent years.

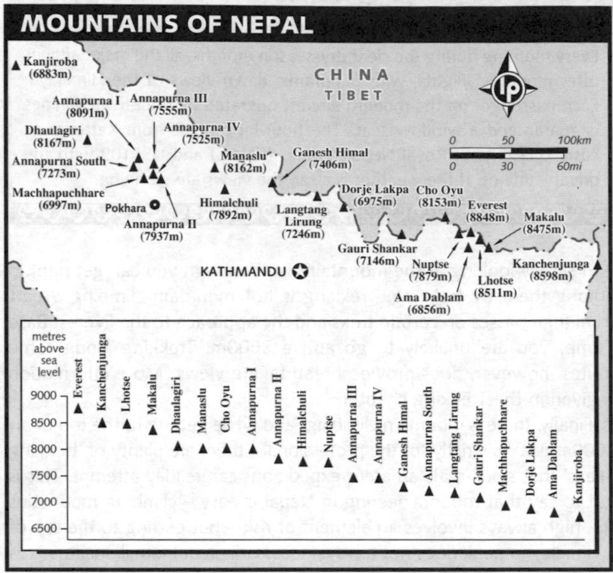

The discovery in 1999 of the body of British climber George Mallory frozen near the summit is a new chapter in one of the enduring mysteries of mountaineering history. In 1924, Mallory and his climbing partner, Andrew Irvine, disappeared within sight of the top. Did they reach the summit? No-one can be sure. However, Mallory did leave behind his famous explanation of mountaineering – he said he was climbing Everest 'because it's there'. Further expeditions followed through the 1920s and 1930s but no real progress was made, although the 8000m level was achieved a number of times. Maurice Wilson added his name to the Everest legend, and to the Everest death roll, when he died during a bizarre solo attempt on the mountain in 1934.

Post WWII Attempts The West's new-found affluence after its recovery from WWII, together with more modern equipment, vastly improved oxygen apparatus, new mountaineering skills and the reopening of Nepal, led to a golden age of Himalayan mountaineering.

There hadn't been any Himalayan mountaineering in the 1940s, and through the 1930s only two significant summits had been reached – Kamet (7761m) in 1931 and Nanda Devi (7822m) in 1936. The Kamet summit group included HW Tilman, and the Nanda Devi group included Eric Shipton, whose descriptions of their trekking and mountaineering experiences helped to spark the current interest in trekking. Shipton was said to have planned his lightweight expeditions on the back of an envelope.

The prewar failures were abruptly reversed in the 1950s, beginning with Maurice Herzog's valiant French expedition on Annapurna in

1950. His team's horrific storm-plagued struggle turned an already extremely difficult climb into an epic of human endurance – but for the first time mountaineers reached the top of an 8000m peak. After descending the mountain they had a month-long struggle through the monsoon with the expedition doctor having to perform amputations of frostbitten fingers and toes as they went.

Herzog's book *Annapurna* (1952) remains a classic of mountaineering literature. It's indicative of how things have changed in Nepal that Herzog had trouble even finding his way to the mountain! Today thousands of trekkers pass by the Annapurnas every year, and where Herzog once had to search desperately for supplies for his hungry climbers, there are now comfortable lodges offering bed and breakfast to trekking parties.

Conquest of Everest Mount Everest was also getting its share of attention, and in 1951 a climber who would soon become very famous took part in an exploratory expedition to the mountain – he was New Zealander Edmund Hillary. Another name, soon to be equally famous, appeared on the list of climbers on the Swiss Everest expedition of 1952 when Sherpa climber Norgay Tenzing reached 7500m. The conquest of Everest finally took place in 1953 when the British team led by John Hunt put those two climbers, Tenzing and Hillary, atop the world's highest peak.

Repeat performances came much easier than the first time, and the second success came in 1956 when a Swiss party reached the summit. In 1960 it was the People's Republic of China that managed the feat, this time from the Tibetan side. A huge US expedition with the climbers backed up by nearly 1000 porters got to the top in 1963, and in 1965 it was the turn of an Indian expedition. Another huge party, this time from Japan, was on top of Everest in 1970 and one utterly fearless climber ensured his place in the Everest history books by making an extremely rapid descent on skis! Further attempts included the massive Italian expedition that reached the summit in 1973, and the victorious Japanese party of women who celebrated International Women's Year by putting a female climber on top in 1975.

The success of the 1953 British expedition to Everest began a trend towards larger and larger expeditions. Proponents of this form of 'siege' mountaineering believed that this was the only way to conquer the great Himalayan peaks. A series of camps would be established higher and higher up the mountain with constant 'carries' of supplies eventually resulting in climbers reaching the top. This theory of Himalayan climbing reached its ultimate expression with the 1973 Italian Everest expedition when 64 climbers were backed up by 100 sherpas and nearly 2000 porters. Helicopters ferried supplies and, hardly surprisingly, this massive effort put nine people on the summit in two parties.

The few climbers who did reach the summit from these expeditions required a huge pyramid of supporters below them. The effect on the country could be devastating as forests fell to provide firewood for the expeditions and vast amounts of mountaineering equipment and garbage were left behind. The Everest Base Camp has been aptly titled the 'world's highest garbage dump'. Lightweight expeditions had been successful, but Helmut Bhul's solo climb to the summit of Nanga Parbat in Pakistan and his lightweight expedition to the top of Broad Peak were looked upon as aberrations requiring superhuman effort rather than as pointers towards a different way of doing things.

New-Style Mountaineering Inevitably, a reaction set in, and while the checklist of important summits was methodically knocked over by huge and expensive expeditions, young climbers were perfecting a wholly different style of climbing on the peaks of Europe and North America. Getting to the top was no longer the sole aim: You had to reach the top with style.

The 'easy' ridge routes to the top were ignored while climbers scaled the most difficult faces, combining athletic skills and high-tech equipment. British mountaineer Chris Bonington was the chief protagonist of this style of climbing and his brilliant conquest of the southern face of Annapurna in 1970, followed by an expertly organised race up the hitherto unthinkable south-western face of Everest in 1975, was a supreme example of this trend.

Lightweight Expeditions Attempting the difficult faces and routes was one trend, but lightweight expeditions were another. In 1978, the Austrian expedition to Everest put Reinhold Messner and Peter Habler on top without the use of oxygen. Once this 'impossible' feat had been achieved other climbers found they could do the same. Freed from the necessity of carting heavy oxygen cylinders up the mountains, much smaller parties could now attempt the big mountains.

Only two years later Reinhold Messner made a solo ascent of Everest, climbing the north face on the Tibetan side in the fastest ascent ever made.

In early 1990, Tim McCartney-Snape, an Australian, went several steps further. He walked and climbed from sea level, at the Bay of Bengal, to the top of Mt Everest, alone and without oxygen.

Mountaineering Today

Himalayan mountaineering today not only provides a great deal of free publicity for Nepal's tourism industry, it's also a very useful source of income for the government. If you want to attempt a Himalayan peak there's a fee to be paid to the government even before you get your climbing permit, and the higher and more famous the mountain the higher the fee. Everest is currently US$50,000 for an expedition of seven climbers (plus an additional US$20,000 if the ascent is via the most commonly used route, the south-east ridge) and is usually 'booked out' for years ahead. Every year, 600 to 900 climbers come to Nepal to try their luck, but there are still many sizeable peaks that have not been successfully climbed, and some that haven't even been attempted.

Today, mountaineering is a sport pure and simple – there's no noise made about its scientific value. In fact, the successes and failures of the

How High is Mt Everest?

Using triangulation from the plains of India, the Survey of India established the elevation of the top of Everest at 29,002 feet (8839m). In 1954 the Survey of India revised the height to 29,028ft (8848m) using the unweighted mean of altitudes determined from 12 different survey stations around the mountain.

On 5 May 1999, scientists supported by the National Geographic Society and Boston's Museum of Science recorded GPS data on the top of Mount Everest for 50 minutes. Their measurements produced a revised elevation of 29,035 feet (8850m). Bradford Washburn, renowned mountain photographer/explorer and honorary director of Boston's Museum of Science, said the latest data had been received 'with enthusiastic approval' by the US National Imagery and Mapping Agency and China's National Bureau of Surveying and Mapping. Nepal, however, continues to favour the 8848m elevation.

As part of the same survey, GPS readings from the South Col indicated that the horizontal position of Everest is moving steadily and slightly north-eastward at about 6cm a year.

various expeditions are regularly reported on the sports pages of *The Kathmandu Post*. Of course it's also a decidedly dangerous sport: Over 400 climbers have reached the top of Everest, but about 100 climbers have died in the attempt. Some other mountains in Nepal have an even worse record: Almost as many climbers have lost their lives climbing Annapurna as have managed to reach the top.

Fees These vary with the altitude of the peak. Currently, the fee for an expedition of seven climbers is US$1500 for peaks lower than 6501m, and rises by US$1000 for every 500m increase in height. Peaks between 7501m and 8000m attract a fee of US$4000, and for peaks over 8000m (apart from Everest) the fee is US$10,000. Fees must be paid two months in advance of any climb. A different scale of fees applies to trekking peaks (see Trekking Peaks later in this section).

Permits To climb any of the 133 mountain peaks that are open to expeditions, a mountaineering team should obtain permission from the Ministry of Tourism's Mountaineering Section (☎ 256231, ⓔ tourisminb@mos.com.np), Bhrikuti Mandap, Kathmandu. Every one of these teams must be represented by a licensed trekking agency in Nepal.

Trekking Peaks

There are many smaller mountains in Nepal called 'trekking peaks' (5587m to 6654m) that keen and experienced trekkers can climb. Most Everest Base Camp trekkers make the ascent of Kala Pattar for the view of Everest and at 5545m this would be a substantial peak anywhere else in the world. In his book *Many People Come, Looking, Looking* (1980), Galen Rowell tells of a little jaunt up a 6500m peak as a prelunch side trip while crossing the Thorung La on the Annapurna Circuit Trek.

Climbing gear can be bought or rented in Kathmandu. Tents, stoves, sleeping bags and down gear should pose no problems, but socks, shoes, clothing and freeze-dried food are likely to be harder to find.

Bill O'Connor's book *The Trekking Peaks of Nepal* gives a detailed description of the climb to each of the peaks plus the trek to the mountain. Equipment, applications, procedures, weather, health and other matters are also comprehensively covered.

Nepali Trekking Peaks

peak	height	region
Chulu East	6584m	Manang
Chulu West	6419m	Manang
Ganja La Chuli (NayaKanga)	5844m	Langtang
Hiunchuli	6441m	Annapurna
Imja Tse (Island Peak)	6183m	Solu Khumbu
Khongma Tse (Mehra Peak)	5849m	Solu Khumbu
Kusum Kanguru	6367m	Solu Khumbu
Kwangde	6011m	Solu Khumbu
Lobuje	6119m	Solu Khumbu
Mardi himal	5587m	Annapurna
Mera Peak	6654m	Solu Khumbu
Paldor	5896m	Langtang
Parchamo	6187m	Rolwaling
Pisang	6091m	Manang
Pokhalde	5806m	Solu Khumbu
Ramdung	5925m	Rolwaling
Singu Chuli (Fluted Peak)	6501m	Annapurna
Tharpu Chuli (Tent Peak)	5663m	Annapurna

By Himalayan standards these are only minor peaks, but some of them provide challenging snow- and ice-climbing.

Fees The fee scale for climbing trekking peaks depends on the group size. For one to four people it's US$350. For five to eight people there's a flat fee of US$350 for the group plus US$40 per person. For nine to 12 people (the maximum group size) it's US$510 plus US$25 per person.

Permits To climb trekking peaks, a permit is required from the Nepal Mountaineering Association (NMA; ☎ 01-434525, ⓔ peaks@nma.wlink.com.np), PO Box 1435, Nagopokhari, Kathmandu. The office is opposite the Biman Bangladesh Airlines office, east of the top end of Durbar Marg; the Web site is at www.nma.com.np. Permits must be applied for in advance and are only valid for one month, although weekly extensions are available for 25% of the total fee. All people ascending trekking peaks must be accompanied by a *sirdar* (leader) who is registered with the NMA.

RICHARD I'ANSON

SCOTT DARSNEY

SCOTT DARSNEY

The experience of hard-core mountaineering in the Himalaya is truly awesome. The less intrepid among us can still take on the trek to Everest Base Camp and enjoy the Himalayan beauty.

CHRIS KLEP

ANDREW PEACOCK

ANDERS BLOMQVIST

ANDERS BLOMQVIST

Looking for a natural high? Nepal is the thrill-seeker's nirvana.

[Continued from page 361]

Usually, the farther you get from population centres the fewer problems there will be, although assaults in remote places are not unheard of. Several basic rules should be followed: Don't trek alone, don't make ostentatious displays of valuable possessions and don't leave lodge doors unlocked or valuables unattended.

See also Dangers & Annoyances in the Facts for the Visitor chapter.

Choosing Companions

You should not trek alone. It's useful to have someone to watch your pack – when you have to run off the trail into the bushes, or even when you are in a lodge and go out to the toilet. It's also good to have someone around in case you injure yourself or fall sick while walking. Almost all deaths, disappearances and incidents of violent crime have involved trekkers travelling alone. A companion could help convince a would-be thief to direct his attention elsewhere and can send for help if you fall or are injured. Women should choose all trekking companions carefully and treat with caution any offer of a massage in a remote hotel.

If you do not already have a travelling companion, then you should find either a guide or another trekker in Kathmandu or Pokhara to trek with. If you're looking for a Western companion, check hotel bulletin boards or just chat with someone who sits next to you in a restaurant and perhaps your schedules and ambitions will coincide. Unless you have a friend to trek with, or are prepared to take a chance on finding a companion in Nepal, booking a group trek may be a good option.

Trail Conditions

Walking at high altitudes on rough trails can be dangerous. Watch your footing on slippery trails, and never underestimate the capacity of the weather to change extremely rapidly for the worse – at any time of the year. If you are crossing high passes where snow is a possibility, never walk with less than three people, and carry a supply of emergency rations, have a map and compass (and know how to use them), and have sufficient clothing and equipment to deal with cold, wet, blizzard conditions.

Register with Your Embassy

All embassies and consulates strongly recommend that their citizens register with them before they head off into the wilderness. They have standard forms that record your name, rough itinerary, insurance details and next of kin, and can obviously speed up a search or a medical evacuation. These are usually kept at the embassies' reception desks and take two minutes to complete. You can avoid a trip to the embassy by filling in a registration form at either the KEEP or the HRA Trekkers' Information Centre in Kathmandu. These organisations regularly forward the forms to the appropriate embassies.

Altitude

Walking the trails of Nepal often entails a great deal of altitude gain and loss, and it is as well to remember that even the base of the great mountains of the Himalaya can be very high. Most treks that go through populated areas stick to between 1000m and 3000m, although the Everest Base Camp Trek and the Annapurna Circuit Trek both reach over 5000m. On high treks like these it is wise to ensure adequate acclimatisation, and the old maxim of 'walking high, sleeping low' is good advice; your night halt should be at a lower level than the highest point reached in the day.

Treks

ROUTINES & CONDITIONS

Most trekkers want to get away from roads as quickly as possible, and although roads reach farther into the hill country every year, it is in fact still possible to leave them quickly behind. Nepali trails are often steep and taxing. The old adage that 'the shortest path between two points is a straight line' appears to have been firmly drummed into Nepalis, irrespective of any mountains that may get in the way! In compensation, the trails are often very well maintained. Busy trails up steep slopes are often flagged with stones every step of the way.

A typical day's walk lasts from five to seven hours and involves a number of ascents and descents. It's rare to spend much time at the same level. On an organised camping trek the day is run to a remarkably tight schedule. A typical pattern would be: up at 6 am, start walking at 7 am, stop for lunch at 10 am, start after lunch at noon, stop walking at 3 pm. Nepalis rise early, eat very little for breakfast, eat a large lunch in the late morning and a second meal before dark, then retire early – you will be best off following a similar schedule.

Although a little rudimentary knowledge of the Nepali language will help to make your trek easier and more interesting, finding your way is rarely difficult on the major trekking routes and English is fairly widely spoken. See the Language chapter for some useful Nepali words and phrases.

Accommodation

Organised treks camp each night and all you have to do is eat and crawl into your tent. Even erecting the tent is handled by the trekking crew who put it up for you at the site selected by your sirdar or group leader.

Independent trekkers usually stay in the small lodges, guesthouses or village inns that have appeared along almost all the main trails. At first this sort of accommodation was simply a matter of local inns letting you unroll your sleeping bag on the floor. Today along some of the most popular trails the lodges are quite luxurious and offer private rooms, extensive menus and even showers. It's possible to make quite long treks relying entirely on local food and accommodation. Nevertheless, it's still a good idea to carry a sleeping bag as lodges sometimes run out of bedding at peak season, and their bedding can contain unwanted sleeping companions.

Food

On a typical organised trek your only concern with food is sitting down to eat it. The porters carry all the food along with them, and there will be a cook with well-drilled assistants who can turn out meals of stunning complexity. Baking a cake on a kerosene stove is just one of the tricks trekking party cooks often perform to display their virtuosity.

Independent trekkers will find numerous places to eat along the most popular trails, although it's often wise to carry some emergency food supplies such as cheese, dried fruit or chocolate bars. Food may vary from dal bhaat at simple village inns to surprisingly good meals on the more popular trails. KEEP and other environmentally concerned organisations point out that dal bhaat is nutritious, easily prepared, available everywhere, and requires a minimum of fuel for preparation. In most places you will be offered a second helping of dal bhaat for free. You lessen your impact on the environment and usually eat better if you try to adapt to the local diet. On the Everest and Annapurna treks it's unlikely that you will walk more than an hour or two without coming across some sort of establishment that can offer tea, soft drinks, beer, and often a full meal.

The standard of cuisine on the Jomsom Trek is so Westernised that it has been dubbed 'the apple pie trail' because that dish features on so many village-inn menus. It's surprising how many places even have cold beer available as well; before you complain about the price contemplate the fact that somebody had to carry that bottle of beer all the way there and will probably have to carry the empty bottle back again!

If you're going right off the beaten track and exploring remote areas like Makalu and Kanchenjunga in the east or Jumla and Dolpo in the west, you must be very self-sufficient. In these relatively untouched areas there is probably very little surplus food for sale and the practice of catering to Western trekkers has not yet developed. Village inns are rare and when they occur are very rudimentary and sanitation conditions leave a lot to be desired.

CHOOSING A TREK

There are countless long treks in Nepal, many of which still see only a handful of Western walkers each year. Many of the previously off-limits areas have been opened up for trekkers in organised groups including upper Mustang, upper Dolpo, Manaslu, Humla and the Kanchenjunga Base Camp in the north-east of the country.

The six very popular longer treks described in this chapter are: the Everest Base Camp, Helambu, Langtang, Jomsom, Annapurna Circuit and Annapurna Sanctuary Treks.

Everest Base Camp Trek This trek takes about three weeks and reaches a maximum height of 5545m at Kala Pattar, a small peak offering fine views of Mt Everest. Although the final part of the trek is through essentially uninhabited areas, small lodges operate during the trekking season so it's quite suitable for independent trekkers. The flights in or out of Lukla at the start and/or finish of the trek can be a real problem.

Helambu Trek A one-week trek that can start from and finish in the Kathmandu Valley, which does not offer superb mountain scenery but is culturally interesting. The maximum height reached is 3490m and there is plenty of accommodation along the route, although it's still a good idea to carry a sleeping bag.

Langtang Trek This can last up to 10 to 12 days if you walk in and out, but it can be varied by crossing a high pass down to the Helambu region. There are fine views, interesting villages, and although there are some relatively uninhabited stretches, accommodation is available. The maximum height reached is 4300m.

Jomsom Trek This trek from Pokhara up the Kali Gandaki valley is among the most popular in Nepal with superb scenery, interesting people and the best trailside accommodation in the country. It takes a week to reach Muktinath, the end point of the trek. Walking back takes another week or you can fly from Jomsom. Muktinath, the high point of the trek, is at 3800m.

Annapurna Circuit It takes nearly three weeks to walk the entire Annapurna Circuit; for scenery and cultural diversity this is the best trek in Nepal. It crosses to the north of the main Himalayan Range, on to the Tibetan plateau, and crosses a 5416m pass. The last week of the trek is the Jomsom Trek in reverse.

Annapurna Sanctuary Trek This trek, which goes into the centre of the Annapurna Range, also starts from Pokhara, and offers unparalleled mountain scenery. The trek takes 10 to 14 days and reaches a maximum height of 4095m at the Annapurna Base Camp. Accommodation along the way is not a problem.

EVEREST BASE CAMP TREK

Everybody knows of Mt Everest and that's the simple reason why the Everest Base Camp Trek is so popular. The trek has a number of stunning attractions, but it also has some distinct drawbacks that might well deter potential trekkers were it not for the undeniable plus point of being able to say you've been to the base of the highest mountain in the world.

The attractions include spectacular scenery and the outgoing Sherpa people of the Solu Khumbu, the region where Mt Everest and its attendant lesser peaks are located. The drawbacks include the long, hard slog to get there as well as the acclimatisation problems that are caused by the region's considerable altitude.

It's not until you get right into the Solu Khumbu region that the Everest trek really gets interesting. The first part of the trek is not only a hard slog, but is also pretty sparse in the breathtaking views department. The hard slog comes about because the trek doesn't follow valleys – like the Annapurna treks – instead the Everest trek cuts across the valleys. So for day after day it's a tiring process of dropping down one side of a steep valley and climbing up again on the other. By the time you reach the base camp your ascents will total almost 9000m, the full height of Everest from sea level!

The Everest trek starts in Nepali-speaking Hindu lowlands and ends in the Tibetan-Buddhist highlands where the Sherpas are renowned for their enterprise, hard work, civic responsibility and devotion to the practice of Buddhism. In their often inhospitable land, the potato, a relatively recent introduction, is the main crop, but these days trekking and mountaineering is the backbone of the Sherpa economy. More than half the population in the region is now involved with tourism and Namche Bazaar looks more like an alpine resort than a Sherpa village.

The Everest trek may not be quite as good as the Pokhara area for village-inn treks, but plenty of accommodation is available during the trekking season even in the normally uninhabited areas, which are around the high peaks.

Flights In & Out

Most Everest trekkers opt to fly one way to avoid having to repeat all those ups and downs. This introduces its own problems as flights to Lukla are notorious for cancellations, waiting lists and short-tempered trekkers. If you have the time, walk in from Jiri and fly out from Lukla. If you want to make a shorter trip you can fly in to Lukla, trek to Everest and then fly out, taking around 15 days to trek to Kala Pattar or you can just visit Thami, Namche Bazaar and Tengboche in a week or so.

Emergency Facilities

There are small hospitals in Jiri, Phaplu and Khunde (just north of Namche Bazaar); while the HRA has a medical facility in Pheriche.

Access: Kathmandu to Jiri (via Lamosangu)

The Everest trek has been getting steadily shorter over the years. The members of the 1953 British expedition that put Hillary and Tenzing on the top started their walk to Everest at Bhaktapur in the Kathmandu Valley. Today you can take the Kodari road to Lamosangu, 78km from Kathmandu, and turn off there to Jiri, a farther 110km. Buses to Jiri leave from the Kathmandu City bus station in the mornings (Rs 200, around 10 to 12 hours). Keep a close eye on your luggage.

Jiri at 1860m is a relatively new town that has expanded since the road was completed. It has a weekly market on Saturday and there are many hotels in the town centre near the bus stop and also on the ridge near the market site. The bus stops at the far end of town so you need to walk back to find somewhere to stay. The ***Sherpa Guide Lodge***, ***Jiri View***, older ***Cherdung Lodge*** and ***Jirel Gabila*** are clustered together in the centre of the village. Room prices are in the Rs 100 to 200 range except for the ***Gauri Himal*** (☎ 049-29158), which has rooms from Rs 350 to 800.

Day 1: Jiri to Shivalaya

The walk starts with a climb to the ridge top at 2370m then drops down to Shivalaya at 1750m. Before the Jiri road was opened the trek used to go through Those (pronounced 'toe-say'), which at that time was the busiest market town between Lamosangu and Namche Bazaar. It is still possible to walk from Jiri to Those and Shivalaya.

Day 2: Shivalaya to Bhandar

From Shivalaya you climb again to Sangbadanda at 2150m, Kosaribas at 2500m, then to Deorali, a pass at 2705m. There are hotels here, or you can descend again to Bhandar at 2150m. This Sherpa settlement has a *gompa* (Tibetan Buddhist monastery) and a number of hotels. It's possible to take a short detour between Sangbadanda and Bhandar to visit Thodung at 3090m where there's a cheese factory, established with Swiss aid in the 1950s.

Day 3: Bhandar to Sete

The trail drops down to the Likhu Khola, crosses the river at 1490m, and tracks along it to Kenja at 1570m. The trail now starts the long climb to Lamjura Bhanjyang. The first part of the climb is quite steep, then it traverses to Sete, an abandoned gompa at 2575m. From here on the villages are almost all inhabited by Sherpas and have both Nepali and Sherpa names (the Sherpa village names are given in brackets).

Day 4: Sete to Junbesi

It's a long but gradual climb to the Lamjura Bhanjyang at 3530m. You're rewarded with frost and often snow along the trail in winter or with lovely flowering rhododendrons in the spring. Goyom at 3300m on your way to the pass is a good lunch stop. The pass is the highest point between Jiri and Namche Bazaar and from the top you descend to Tragdobuk at 2860m, then to the pretty Sherpa village of Junbesi (Jun) at 2675m. Junbesi has a monastery, some good hotels and is a good place for a rest day with some interesting walks in the vicinity.

Day 5: Junbesi to Nuntala

The trail climbs to a ridge at 2980m where for the first time you can see Everest, then on to Salung at 2980m. A lower trail from

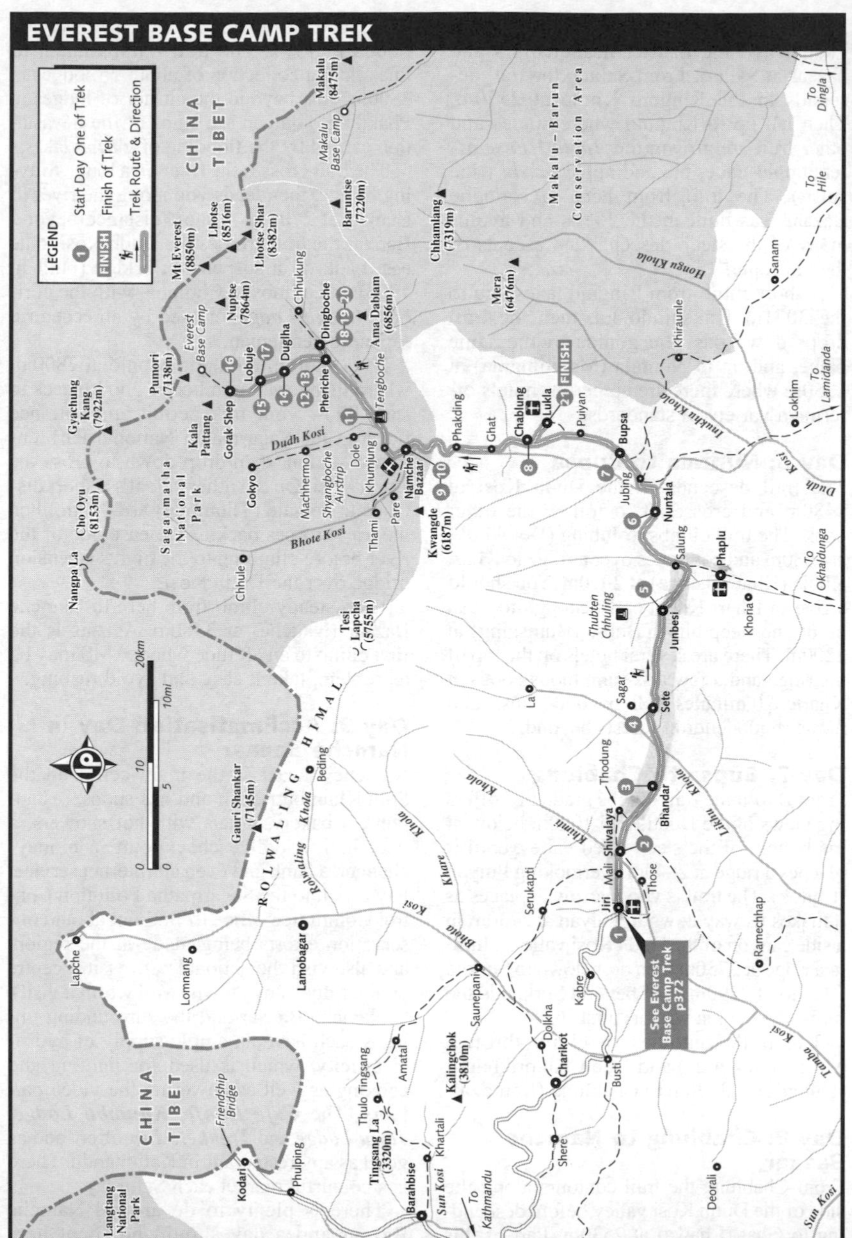
EVEREST BASE CAMP TREK
LEGEND
Start Day One of Trek
FINISH
Finish of Trek
Trek Route & Direction
CHINA
TIBET
Makalu (8475m)
Makalu Base Camp
Mt Everest (8850m)
Lhotse (8516m)
Lhotse Shar (8382m)
Baruntse (7220m)
Chamlang (7319m)
Makalu – Barun Conservation Area
To Dingla
To Hile
Pumori (7138m)
Everest Base Camp
Nuptse (7864m)
Chhukung
Ama Dablam (6856m)
Dingboche
Gyachung Kang (7922m)
Kala Pattang
Gorak Shep
Lobuje
Dugla
Pheriche
Tengboche
Mera (6476m)
Hongu Khola
Sanam
Cho Oyu (8153m)
Sagarmatha National Park
Gokyo
Machhermo
Dudh Kosi
Dole
Khumjung
Namche Bazaar
Shyangboche Airstrip
Phakding
Ghat
Chablung
Lukla
Puiyan
Khiraunle
Inukhu Khola
To Lamidanda
Lokhim
Dudh Kosi
Nangpa La
Chhule
Bhote Kosi
Thami
Pare
Kwangde (6187m)
Bupsa
Jubing
Nuntala
Salung
Phaplu
To Okhaldunga
Khoria
Tesi Lapcha (5755m)
ROLWALING HIMAL
Thubten Chhuling
Junbesi
La
Sagar
Sete
Thodung
Likhu Khola
Khimti Khola
Bhandar
Shivalaya
Mali
Jiri
Those
Serukapti
Ramechhap
Gauri Shankar (7145m)
Beding
Rolwaling Khola
Khare Khola
Bhota Kosi
Lapche
Lomnang
Lamobagar
Saunepani
Kabre
Dolkha
Charikot
See Everest Base Camp Trek p372
Tamba Kosi
Busti
Kalingchok (3810m)
Amatal
Thulo Tingsang
Tingsang La (3320m)
Khartali
Shere
Deorali
Sun Kosi
Friendship Bridge
Kodari
Phulping
Barahbise
To Kathmandu
Langtang National Park
0 10 20km
0 5 10mi

Junbesi leads to the hospital and airstrip at Phaplu and the district headquarters and bazaar at Salleri. From Salung the trail descends to the Ringmo Khola at 2570m. Then it's up to Ringmo where apples and other fruit are grown; the ***Apple House*** offers apple juice, pie and apple *rakshi* (rice spirit). The trail from here to Namche Bazaar was built in the 1980s and avoids many of the steep descents and ascents of the old route.

A short climb from Ringmo takes you to the 3071m Trakshindo La, then the trail drops down past the gompa of the same name, and on to Nuntala (Manidingma) at 2250m where there are numerous hotels offering a variety of standards.

Day 6: Nuntala to Bupsa

The trail descends to the Dudh Kosi at 1480m and crosses it to follow the other bank. The trail climbs to Jubing (Dorakbuk) at 1680m and continues over a ridge to Khari Khola (Khati Thenga) at 2070m. You should arrive in Khari Khola early enough to push on up the steep hill to Bupsa (Bumshing) at 2300m. There are several hotels on the top of the ridge and a few less sumptuous hotels at Kharte, 20 minutes walk beyond Bupsa, and in the rhododendron forests beyond.

Day 7: Bupsa to Chablung

From Bupsa the trail climbs gradually, offering views of the Dudh Kosi 1000m below at the bottom of the steep-sided valley, until it reaches a ridge at 2840m overlooking Puiyan (Chitok). The trail is very narrow in places as it makes its way down to Puiyan at 2730m in a side canyon of the Dudh Kosi valley. Climb to a ridge at 2750m then drop down to Surkhe (Buwa) at 2290m. Just beyond Surkhe is the turn-off to Lukla with its airstrip.

The trail continues to climb through Mushe (Nangbug) and then Chaunrikharka (Dungde) at 2630m to Chablung (Lomdza).

Day 8: Chablung to Namche Bazaar

From Chablung the trail contours along the side of the Dudh Kosi valley before descending to Ghat (Lhawa) at 2530m. Part of this village and the old trail were washed away by floods in 1997. The trail climbs again to Phakding, a collection of about 25 lodges at 2800m. Just beyond the cluster of lodges at Phakding, you can see signs of the devastation caused by the flooding of glacial lakes.

The trail crosses the river on a long, swaying bridge, then leads you along the river to Benkar at 2700m. A short distance beyond Benkar the trail crosses the Dudh Kosi to its east bank on a suspension bridge (built in 1996) and climbs to Chomoa, with the curious ***Hatago Lodge***, created by an eccentric Japanese gentleman.

It's a short climb up to Monjo at 2800m, where there are a number of good places to stay. Show your trek permit and entrance ticket at the Sagarmatha National Park entrance station, then drop down to cross the Dudh Kosi. On the other side it's a short distance to Jorsale (Thumbug) at 2810m, then the trail crosses back to the east side of the river before climbing to the high suspension bridge over the Dudh Kosi.

It's a steady climb from here to Namche Bazaar (Nauche) at 3480m. As this is the first climb to an altitude where AMS may be a problem, take it easy and avoid rushing.

Day 9: Acclimatisation Day in Namche Bazaar

Namche Bazaar is the main centre in the Solu Khumbu region and has shops, restaurants, a bakery, hotels with hot showers, a pool hall, a police checkpoint, a moneychanger, a bank and even an Internet service. Pay a visit to the Sagarmatha Pollution Control Committee office to find out about conservation efforts being made in the region, and also visit the national park visitor centre on the ridge above town (well worth a visit).

Namche Bazaar and the surrounding villages each have an ample supply of hydroelectricity, which is used for lighting and cooking as well as powering the video parlours. The ***Cafe Danfe***, ***Khumbu Lodge***, ***Tawa Lodge*** and ***Trekkers Inn*** offer food as good as any restaurant in Kathmandu. There is a colourful market each Saturday.

There is plenty to do around Namche Bazaar and a day should be spent here

The Yeti

Like Big Foot in North America, the Loch Ness monster in Scotland or even the elusive bunyip in Australia, the yeti or abominable snowman is much hunted but little seen. The yeti is a shy humanoid creature that lives high in the most remote regions of the Himalaya. There are countless yeti legends told by the Sherpas and other hill peoples. They tell of its legendary strength, its ability to carry off yaks and even abduct people.

Nobody has ever managed to get a clear photograph of the yeti; footprints in the snow are generally the only indication that a yeti has been by, although hastily gnawed yak bones also add to the yeti legend.

Of course, there are plenty of scientific explanations for yetis. The footprints may have been a human print or some other natural footprint that has appeared to grow larger as the snow melts. Rigorous studies have been made of the yeti scalps found in various monasteries, in particular the one at the Khumjung Monastery, and they have all turned out to be fakes. Keep your camera loaded though, a good photo of a yeti (even a small yeti) will probably be worth a fortune.

There are regular 'sightings' reported in the press every year and various incidents that have no obvious answer are sometimes attributed to the yeti, such as the one in 1998 where a local woman was murdered between Mong La and Dole on the Gokyo Trek. After much intensive investigation the official police explanation was a yeti attack, and was reported on regional radio as such!

Beware the yeti!

acclimatising. Remember that the victims of AMS are often the fittest and healthiest people who foolishly overextend themselves. It's important to do a strenuous day walk to a higher altitude as part of your acclimatisation, coming back down to Namche to sleep. For this purpose the day walk to Thami (to the west) is worthwhile.

Day 10: Namche Bazaar to Tengboche

The slightly longer route from Namche Bazaar to Tengboche via Khumjung and Khunde is more interesting than the direct one. The route starts by climbing up to the Shyangboche airstrip. Above the airstrip is the ***Everest View Hotel***, a Japanese scheme to build a deluxe hotel with great views of the highest mountains on earth. The hotel has had a chequered history, but is once again open, with rooms at US$135, plus an extra charge for oxygen if needed!

From the hotel or the airstrip you continue to Khumjung at 3790m and then rejoin the direct trail to Tengboche. The trail descends to the Dudh Kosi at 3250m where there are three small lodges and a series of picturesque water-driven prayer wheels. A steep ascent brings you to Tengboche at 3870m. The famous gompa, a photographer's favourite with its background of Ama Dablam, Everest and other peaks, was burnt down in 1989. It has been rebuilt as a large, impressive structure. There's a camping area, a number of places to stay, and during the November–December full moon the colourful Mani Rimdu festival is held here with much singing and dancing.

Day 11: Tengboche to Pheriche

Beyond Tengboche the altitude really starts to tell. The trail drops down to Devuche, crosses the Imja Khola and climbs past superb *mani* stones (carved with the Tibetan Buddhist chant *om mani padme hum*) to Pangboche at 3860m. The gompa here is worth visiting and the village is a good place for a lunch stop.

The trail then climbs to Pheriche at 4240m where there is an HRA trekkers' aid post and possible medical assistance. Pheriche has a number of hotels and restaurants that may feature exotic dishes left over from international mountaineering expeditions.

Day 12: Acclimatisation Day in Pheriche

Another acclimatisation day should be spent at Pheriche. As at Namche, a solid day walk to a higher altitude is better than just resting; Dingboche and Chhukung at 4730m are possible destinations. You could also make a day trip to Nangkartshang Gompa or up past Dingboche. Either walk offers good views.

Day 13: Pheriche to Duglha

The trail climbs to Phalang Karpo at 4340m then Duglha at 4620m. It's possible to continue on to Lobuje, and many people do so. The HRA doctors at Pheriche urge everyone to stay a night at Duglha to aid acclimatisation.

Day 14: Duglha to Lobuje

From Duglha the trail goes directly up the terminal moraine (debris) of the Khumbu Glacier for about one hour then left into a memorial area known as Chukpilhara, before reaching the summer village of Lobuje at 4930m. The altitude, the cold and the crowding combine to ensure less than restful nights.

Day 15: Lobuje to Gorak Shep

The trail continues to climb to Gorak Shep at 5160m. The return trip from Lobuje to Gorak Shep takes a couple of hours, enough time to continue to Kala Pattar (Black Rock) – or you can overnight in Gorak Shep and reach Kala Pattar the next morning. At 5545m this small peak offers the best view you'll get of Everest without climbing it.

Although there is usually accommodation at Gorak Shep it's nothing to write home about, so it's a better plan to return to Lobuje for the night. The altitude hits nearly everybody; getting back down to Lobuje or even better, to Pheriche, makes a real difference.

Day 16: Gorak Shep to Lobuje

If you want to actually get to the base camp then it's about six hours round trip from Gorak Shep, and there's no view, so if you only have the energy for one side trip, then make it Kala Pattar.

The descent to Lobuje is easy, but it seems endless because of the many uphill climbs from Gorak Shep. The night, however, will be much more comfortable than the previous one.

Day 17: Lobuje to Dingboche

Staying the night at Dingboche instead of at Pheriche makes an interesting accommodation alternative. It's a 'summer village' at 4410m with numerous large lodges.

Days 18 to 20: Dingboche to Lukla

The next three days retrace your steps down to Lukla via Tengboche and Namche Bazaar. There is extreme pressure for a seat on flights out of Lukla, so be sure to have an advance booking, and be there the evening before your flight to reconfirm (the airline offices are generally open from 5 to 6 pm, but sometimes it's 6 to 7 pm). Then be prepared for a torrid time at the airstrip as frustrated trekkers vie for the limited seats. This is especially so when flights have been cancelled for a few consecutive days due to poor visibility, and there is a huge backlog of passengers all wanting to get back to Kathmandu. Lukla has a number of places to stay including the relatively expensive ***La Villa Sherpani*** and the ***Sagarmatha Resort***. Life at Lukla seems to revolve around watching flights come and go.

Day 21: Back to Kathmandu

If the gods are with you, your flight comes in and your reservation hasn't been cancelled. Then, after it took you so many days to get here by road and foot, your aircraft only takes 35 minutes to fly you back.

Alternative Routes & Side Trips

See the Other Treks section later in this chapter for information on the long trek south from the Solu Khumbu region to Hile, an interesting alternative to going straight back to Kathmandu. Alternatives to hanging around in Lukla waiting for flights or walking all the way back to Jiri are also possible but not very satisfactory. Going down to Phaplu, two or three days south of Lukla, is unlikely to get you out any faster. It's a four- or five-day walk down to Lamidanda from where there are several flights a week to Biratnagar and Kathmandu.

Experienced trekkers can consider taking the little-frequented Barabise to Mali route in, avoiding the Jiri road completely.

Another interesting side trip is the nine-day round trip from Namche Bazaar to Gokyo and back. This trek ends at another Kala Pattar with fine, but different, views of Everest. You can even combine both Kala Pattars by crossing the 5420m Cho La, but you had better bring your ice axe and your crampons and know how to use them.

A shorter side trip from Namche Bazaar is to Thami, the gateway to Tesi Lapcha and the Rolwaling himal. You can do a round trip to Thami in one very long day, although it's better to stay overnight in order to catch the morning views.

HELAMBU TREK

See the Helambu & Langtang Treks map later in this section for this trek. Although not as well known and popular as the Everest Base Camp Trek or the Annapurna Circuit, this trek offers a number of distinct advantages. The trek is north of the Kathmandu Valley, so is easily accessible from Kathmandu. Indeed you could leave your hotel in Kathmandu and set foot on the Helambu trail within an hour. The Helambu Trek only takes a week so it is ideal for people who do not have the time for one of the longer treks. And since it stays at relatively low altitudes it also does not require fancy cold-weather equipment and clothing.

The Helambu Trek starts from Sundarijal at the eastern end of the Kathmandu Valley and doesn't climb above 3500m. The trek makes a loop through the Sherpa-populated Helambu region to the north-east of Kathmandu and only the first day's walk is repeated on the return trip. The trek's main drawback is that it doesn't offer fine Himalayan views like other treks, but it can be trekked on a village-inn basis as there are guesthouses and lodges in many of the villages along the trail. The Sherpa people of the Helambu region are friendly and hospitable, just like their better-known kinfolk of the Solu Khumbu region.

As in Solu Khumbu, the potato is a vitally important crop and not only forms a large part of the local diet but is also exported to the Nepali lowland in exchange for rice and other produce.

Wherever you trek in the region, you will enter the Langtang National Park. The army is particularly conscientious about collecting the Rs 1000 park entrance fee. On this trek there are park checkposts at Magen Goth, Khutumsang and Sermathang that won't let without you pass without a park permit (see Documents & Fees earlier in this chapter).

Emergency Facilities

There is a national park radio at Magen Goth. Telephones are available at Tarke Gyang.

Access: Kathmandu to Sundarijal

There's no direct bus to Sundarijal, 15km from Kathmandu, but you can get to the start of the trail by taxi, or get a bus to Jorpati, just beyond Boudha (Bodhnath), and catch a Sundarijal bus at the road junction. At Sundarijal you enter the Shivapuri Watershed & Wildlife Reserve (Rs 300 entry).

Day 1: Sundarijal to Chisopani

From Sundarijal the trail starts off up concrete steps beside the pipeline that brings drinking water down to the valley. Eventually the trail leaves the pipeline from near the dam and reaches Mulkharka, sprawling up the ridge around 1895m, 600m above Sundarijal. There are superb views back over the valley and some convenient tea shops for rest and refreshment.

The trail continues to climb, but less steeply, through Chisopani at 2300m then the trail drops down to Pati Bhanjyang at 1770m. Chisopani is rather like a grubby little truck stop without the trucks but the mountain views in the morning can be very fine. Take care of your possessions here, it's still rather close to the Kathmandu Valley.

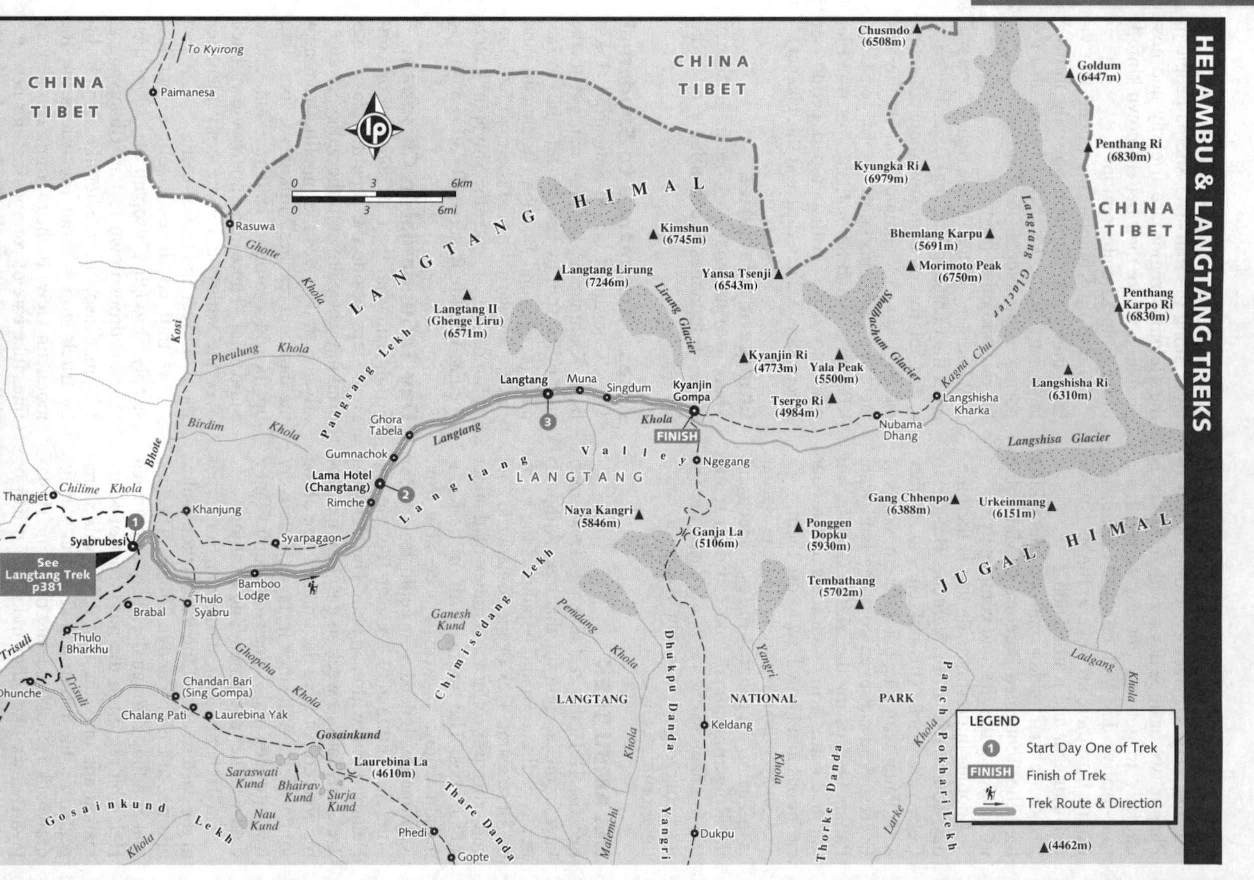
HELAMBU & LANGTANG TREKS
LEGEND
Start Day One of Trek
FINISH Finish of Trek
Trek Route & Direction
CHINA
TIBET
To Kyirong
Paimanesa
0 3 6km
0 3 6mi
LANGTANG HIMAL
JUGAL HIMAL
LANGTANG NATIONAL PARK
Langtang Valley
LANGTANG
Chusmdo (6508m)
Goldum (6447m)
Penthang Ri (6830m)
Penthang Karpo Ri (6830m)
Kyungka Ri (6979m)
Bhemlang Karpu (5691m)
Morimoto Peak (6750m)
Langtang Glacier
Kimshun (6745m)
Langtang Lirung (7246m)
Yansa Tsenji (6543m)
Lirung Glacier
Shalbachum Glacier
Langtang II (Ghenge Liru) (6571m)
Kyanjin Ri (4773m)
Yala Peak (5500m)
Tsergo Ri (4984m)
Langshisha Ri (6310m)
Kagna Chu
Langshisha Kharka
Nubama Dhang
Langshisa Glacier
Rasuwa
Ghotte Khola
Kosi
Bhote
Pheulung Khola
Pangsang Lekh
Birdim Khola
Langtang
Muna
Singdum
Kyanjin Gompa
Khola
FINISH
Ghora Tabela
Langtang
Gumnachok
Lama Hotel (Changtang)
Rimche
Ngegang
Langtang Lekh
Naya Kangri (5846m)
Gang Chhenpo (6388m)
Urkeinmang (6151m)
Ponggen Dopku (5930m)
Ganja La (5106m)
Thangjet
Chilime Khola
Khanjung
Syabrubesi
See Langtang Trek p381
Syarpagaon
Bamboo Lodge
Thulo Syabru
Brabal
Thulo Bharkhu
Trisuli
Dhunche
Tembathang (5702m)
Ganesh Kund
Chimisedang Lekh
Pemdang Khola
Dhukpu Danda
Yangri
Ladgang Khola
Ghopcha Khola
Chandan Bari (Sing Gompa)
Chalang Pati
Laurebina Yak
Gosainkund
Laurebina La (4610m)
Saraswati Kund
Bhairav Kund
Surja Kund
Nau Kund
Gosainkund Lekh
Khola
Phedi
Gopte
Thare Danda
Keldang
Malemchi Khola
Dukpu
Yangri Khola
Thorke Danda
Larke Khola
Panch Pokhari Lekh
(4462m)

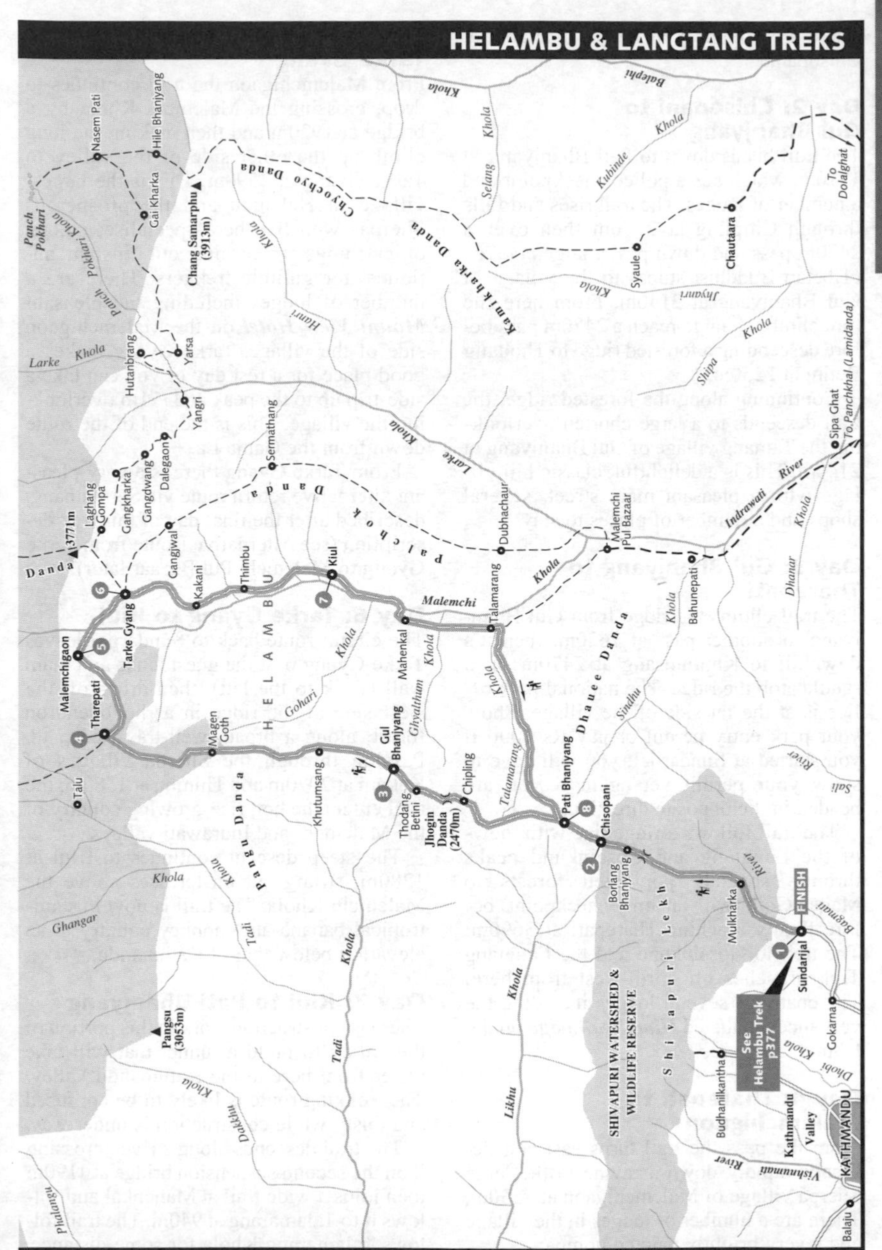
HELAMBU & LANGTANG TREKS
Nasem Pati
Hile Bhanjyang
Gai Kharka
Chang Samarphu (3913m)
Panch Pokhari
Panch Pokhari Khola
Chyochyo Danda
Kamikharka Danda
Balephi
Kubinde Khola
Selang Khola
Jhyanri Khola
Syaule
Chautaara
To Dolalghat
Hutanbrang
Yarsa
Yangri
Larke Khola
Hanri Khola
Shipa Khola
Sipa Ghat
To Panchkhal (Lamidanda)
Indrawati River
Dhanar Khola
Laghang Gompa
Gangkharka
Gangdwang
Dalegaon
Semathang
Palchok Danda
Gangwal
Dubhachaur
Malemchi Pul Bazaar
Bahunepati
Danda
3771m
Tarke Gyang
Thimbu
Kakani
Kiul
HELAMBU
Malemchi Khola
Talamarang
Mahenkal
Malemchigaon
Tharepati
Dhauee Danda
Talamarang Khola
Sindhu
Gohari Khola
Ghyalthum Khola
Magen Goth
Gul Bhanjyang
Pati Bhanjyang
Chisopani
Thodang Betini
Chipling
Jhogin Danda (2470m)
Khutumsang
Talu
Pangu Danda
Borlang Bhanjyang
Mulkharka
FINISH
Sundarijal
Bagmati River
Sali River
Ghangar Khola
Tadi Khola
Shivapuri Lekh
SHIVAPURI WATERSHED & WILDLIFE RESERVE
See Helambu Trek p377
Gokarna
Pangsu (3053m)
Likhu Khola
Budhanilkantha
Dhobi Khola
Kathmandu Valley
KATHMANDU
Vishnumati River
Dakkhu Khola
Phalangu
Balaju

There are a number of lodges available at Chisopani.

Day 2: Chisopani to Gul Bhanjyang

The trail heads down to Pati Bhanjyang at 1770m, which has a police checkpoint and a number of lodges. The trail rises and falls through Chipling at 2170m then over a 2470m pass and down past a large *chorten* (Tibetan Buddhist stupa) to the village of Gul Bhanjyang at 2140m. From here the trail climbs again to reach a 2470m pass before descending a forested ridge to Thodang Betini at 2250m.

Continuing along the forested ridge, the trail descends to a large chorten overlooking the Tamang village of Gul Bhanjyang at 2140m. This is a delightful, classic hill village with a pleasant main street, several shops and a number of places to stay.

Day 3: Gul Bhanjyang to Tharepati

The trail climbs the ridge from Gul Bhanjyang to another pass at 2620m, then it's downhill to Khutumsang at 2470m, in a saddle atop the ridge. The national park office is at the far side of the village. Show your park entry permit or pay Rs 1000 if you started at Sundarijal; you will have to show your permit yet again if you are headed in the opposite direction.

The trail follows a ridge line with views of the Langtang and Gosainkund peaks through sparsely populated forests to Magen Goth (with an army checkpoint) before finally reaching Tharepati at 3690m. The trail to Gosainkund and the Langtang Trek branches off north-west from here. Tharepati has several lodges including the very nicely situated ***Himaliya Lodge*** on the Khutumsang side.

Day 4: Tharepati to Malemchigaon

From the pass the trail turns east and descends rapidly down a ravine to the large Sherpa village of Malemchigaon at 2530m. There are a number of lodges in the village and a very brightly painted gompa.

Day 5: Malemchigaon to Tarke Gyang

From Malemchigaon the trail continues to drop, crossing the Malemchi Khola by a bridge at 1920m and then making the long climb up the other side of the valley to Tarke Gyang at 2590m. This is the largest village in Helambu and the prosperous Sherpas who live here specialise, among other things, in turning out 'instant antiques' for gullible trekkers. There are a number of lodges including the pleasant ***Mount View Hotel*** on the Malemchigaon side of the village. Tarke Gyang makes a good place for a rest day or you can take a side-trip up to the peak at 3771m overlooking the village. This is the end of the route down from the Ganja La.

From Tarke Gyang there is a very pleasant alternative return route via Sermathang, described after the final day of this trek description (see Alternative Route from Tarke Gyang to Malemchi Pul Bazaar later).

Day 6: Tarke Gyang to Kiul

The circuit route back to Sundarijal leaves Tarke Gyang past the guesthouse and mani wall (walk to the left), then drops off the west side of the ridge in a rhododendron forest, along a broad, well-travelled path. Passing through the Sherpa villages of Kakani at 2070m and Thimbu at 1580m, the trail enters the hot, rice-growing country of the Malemchi and Indrawati valleys.

The steep descent continues to Kiul at 1280m, strung out on terraces above the Malemchi Khola. The trail is now in semi-tropical banana-and-monkey country at an elevation below that of Kathmandu.

Day 7: Kiul to Pati Bhanjyang

There is construction work in this portion of the valley to build a tunnel that will take water from here to the Kathmandu Valley. The trekking route is likely to be confused and dusty while construction is under way.

The trail descends along a river, crossing it on the second suspension bridge at 1190m then joins a wide trail at Mahenkal and follows it to Talamarang at 940m. The trail follows Talamarang Khola for some distance, then (it's hard to find at times) climbs steeply to Batache and then Thakani, on the ridge top, at 1890m. From here the trail follows the ridge to Pati Bhanjyang at 1770m where the Helambu circuit is completed.

Day 8: Back to Sundarijal

The final day largely retraces the route of the first day's walk.

Alternative Route from Tarke Gyang to Malemchi Pul Bazaar

An alternative route can be followed from Tarke Gyang through Sermathang and then along a long ridge through Dubhachaur to join the road at Malemchi Pul Bazaar, south of Talamarang. This route is very pleasant as far as Malemchi and attracts relatively few trekkers. There are numerous lodges at Sermathang and Malemchi but the choice is limited elsewhere.

From Malemchi the final stretch is along a dusty roadway that brings you out on the Kathmandu to Kodari road at Panchkhal, from where you will have to take a bus 55km back to Kathmandu via Dhulikhel. You can usually get a ride on a bus or truck down the road from Malemchi and this route does avoid having to duplicate the final stretch from Pati Bhanjyang through Sundarijal. The route begins at Tarke Gyang (see Day 6 of the Helambu Trek).

(Another Helambu alternative is to start and finish from Malemchi Pul Bazaar, via Panchkhal on the main road, completing the shorter loop, which goes through Malemchi, Talamarang, Kiul, Tarke Gyang as well as Sermathang and Malemchi.)

Day 1: Tarke Gyang to Sermathang The easy trail descends gently through a beautiful forest to Sermathang at 2620m, the centre of an important apple-growing area. Sermathang is more spread out than the closely spaced houses of Tarke Gyang; there are fine views of the valley of the Malemchi Khola to the south. If you do the trek in the reverse direction this is where you must pay the Rs 1000 entry fee to the Langtang National Park. There are lodges at Sermathang.

Day 2: Sermathang to Malemchi Pul Bazaar From Sermathang the trail continues to descend to Dubhachaur at 1610m then steeply down to Malemchi at 880m where it meets the road. The village has a collection of lodges and village inns. Buses run frequently along the road (known as the Helambu Highway) from Malemchi via Bahunepati and Sipa Ghat to Banepa where you change to a bus or taxi to Kathmandu.

LANGTANG TREK

The Langtang Trek, while offering many of the benefits of the Helambu Trek, also gives you the opportunity to get right in among the Himalayan peaks and to walk through remote and relatively unpopulated areas. If you want real adventure then the Langtang and Helambu Treks can be linked by high-altitude passes, either via the Gosainkund lakes or across the Ganjā La at 5106m (see Langtang Trek to Helambu Trek Crossings later in this section).

Langtang Lirung at 7246m is visible to the north of Kathmandu on clear days. The Langtang Trek can take up to two weeks (although a three-day approach to the heart of the Langtang Valley is suggested here) and lead to the foot of glaciers high in the Langtang Valley. The trail passes through Tibetan and Tamang villages and offers fine views of the Ganesh himal across to the north-west. Although the trek passes through comparatively lightly populated and undeveloped areas, it is still possible to stay at village inns at various points along the route. Ascending from just 541m at Trisuli Bazaar to 3800m at Kyanjin Gompa the trail passes through an ever-changing climate and offers trekkers an exceptional diversity of scenery and culture.

Wherever you trek, you will enter the Langtang National Park and the army will collect a Rs 1000 park entrance fee. Checkposts are at Dhunche and at Ghora Tabela.

Emergency Facilities

There are national park radios at Ghora Tabela and Langtang, and there are telephones at Dhunche and Thulo Syabru. The Yeti Guest House in Kyanjin Gompa has a satellite phone that can be used to summon a helicopter in an emergency.

Access: Kathmandu to Syabrubesi

It's 72km from Kathmandu to Trisuli Bazaar, which takes about four hours by car or six by bus. The road is paved but very winding with fine mountain views. Ranipauwa is the only large village along the route. From Trisuli, the 50km road leading to Dhunche is steep, winding and rather hairy, passing through Betrawati and Thare. There are two buses per day from Kathmandu to Dhunche (Rs 64, nine hours). Dhunche is a pretty village at 1950m and here you must pay the entrance fee to Langtang National Park, though it's better to buy the permit in Kathmandu before starting your trek.

There is a direct bus from Kathmandu to Syabrubesi, about 15 km (a one-hour drive) past Dhunche. The road descends from Dhunche, gently at first, then in a series of steep loops to a bridge across the Bhote Kosi. Syabrubesi is a string of shops and lodges along the road just past the bridge. A bus departs Syabrubesi for Kathmandu at 7 am. You can book a seat in advance at a roadside ticket office.

Day 1: Syabrubesi to Lama Hotel

Start the trek from the camping area below Syabrubesi (New Syabrubesi) and trek northward past some abandoned government buildings to a suspension bridge over the Bhote Kosi, just north of the junction with Trisuli Khola. Turn right at the eastern end of the bridge and walk into the small settlement of Old Syabru.

The trek becomes a pleasant walk through trees where langur monkeys frolic, passing a side stream and small waterfall before reaching three *bhattis* (village inns) beside a stream at Doman, 1680m. The trail then makes a steep climb over a rocky ridge to Landslide Lodge at 1810m, where the route from Thulo Syabru joins from above. Over the rest of the day's walk and the following morning, you will pass few settlements, but the forest abounds with birds.

It's then a long climb in forests to another trail junction with a sign pointing to Syabru (Thulo Syabru). This is a new national park trail that local people rarely use. Beyond the trail junction the trail climbs gently to Bamboo Lodge, a cluster of three hotels (none made of bamboo) at 1960m. Beyond Bamboo Lodge the trail crosses the Dangdung Khola, then climbs to a steel suspension bridge over the Langtang Khola at 2000m.

On the north bank of the Langtang Khola the route climbs alongside a series of waterfalls formed by a jumble of house-sized boulders. Climb steeply to a landslide and the ***Langtang View & Lodge*** at Rimche, 2400m, and then ascend farther to Changtang, popularly known as Lama Hotel, at 2470m.

Day 2: Lama Hotel to Langtang

The trail continues to follow the Langtang Khola, climbing steeply, at times very steeply, to Ghora Tabela at 2970m, where there are fine views of Langtang Lirung. Although there is no permanent settlement here, there is the good ***Lovely Lodge***; your national park entry permit will be checked again here.

From Ghora Tabela the trail climbs more gradually to Langtang at 3450m. The national park headquarters is here and Langtang and the villages around are in Tibetan style with stone walls around the fields and herds of yaks. The best lodge here is the ***Village View Lodge***.

Day 3: Langtang to Kyanjin Gompa

It only takes the morning (passing through small villages) to climb to Kyanjin Gompa at 3800m where there is a monastery, lodges (best is the ***Hotel Yala Peak***) and a cheese factory. There are a number of interesting walks from the gompa and if you are intending to continue over the Ganja La to Helambu you should spend some time here acclimatising. From the gompa you can climb to 4300m on the glacial moraine to the north for superb views of Langtang Lirung. Day walks can also be made to Yala or farther up the valley for more spectacular views.

LANGTANG TREK TO HELAMBU TREK CROSSINGS

There are a number of alternative routes back to Kathmandu from Kyanjin Gompa on the Langtang Trek. There are occasional helicopter flights from the nearby STOL (short take off and landing) airstrip but these are usually chartered sightseeing trips and it's unlikely that you could get a seat on one. You can simply retrace your route back down the valley or, if the season and weather permits, attempt the high route via the Gosainkund Lakes to join the Helambu Trek. If you are a very experienced trekker, with a tent, stove and food, you could tackle the Ganja La.

WARNING

The Ganja La is one of the more difficult passes in Nepal and should not be attempted without a knowledgeable guide, adequate acclimatisation, good equipment and some mountaineering experience.

Across the Ganja La

Walking from the Kyanjin Gompa at the end of the Langtang route south to Tarke Gyang in Helambu involves crossing the 5106m Ganja La. The pass is usually blocked by snow from December to March and at any time a bad weather change can make crossing the pass decidedly dangerous. The walk takes five days; between Kyanjin and Tarke Gyang there is no permanent settlement. The final climb to the pass on both sides is steep and exposed. During most of the year there is no water for two days south of the pass, so you must be prepared for all these complications.

Via Gosainkund

The trek via Gosainkund is another way of crossing between the Langtang and the Helambu Treks. Again, adequate preparation is necessary, but there are village inns along the route, so finding food and accommodation is not a problem in the trekking season. There is often snow on the Gosainkund trail, so this route does become impassable during much of the winter.

It takes four days to walk from Dhunche, near the start of the Langtang Trek (and an alternative starting point to the one we give), to Tharepati in the Helambu region. The trek can also be made from Helambu or it can be done by turning off of the Langtang Trek from Thulo Syabru, and it is an excellent choice as a return route from the Langtang Trek.

Gosainkund is the site for a great pilgrimage in August each year – this is the height of the monsoon, not a pleasant time for trekking. The large rock in the centre of the lake is said to be the remains of a Shiva shrine and it is also claimed that a channel carries water from the lake directly to the tank at the Kumbeshwar Temple in Patan, 60km to the south.

Day 1: Dhunche to Chandan Bari The first day takes you from Dhunche at 1950m to Chandan Bari (Sing Gompa) at 3330m. The route from Thulo Syabru to the gompa can be confusing.

Day 2: Chandan Bari to Laurebina Yak The walk climbs steeply with fine mountain views then heads for Laurebina Yak, which has lodges.

Day 3: Laurebina Yak to Gosainkund Lakes The trail drops down to Saraswati Kund at 4100m, the first of the Gosainkund lakes. The second lake is Bhairav Kund and the third is Gosainkund itself at an altitude of 4380m. There are several lodges, a shrine and numerous *paths* (small stone shelters for pilgrims) on the north-western side of the lake.

Day 4: Gosainkund Lakes to Gopte The trail climbs from the Gosainkund lakes still higher to the four lakes near the Laurebina La at 4610m, then it drops down again to Gopte at 3440m where there are seasonal village inns.

It was in the Gopte area that an Australian trekker got lost in 1991 and was not found for 43 days. Nearby is the place where a Thai International Airbus became lost in 1992 and crashed into a mountain.

Day 5: Gopte to Tharepati The final day's walk descends to a stream and then climbs to Tharepati at 3690m, where this trail meets up with the Helambu Trek.

Back to Kathmandu From Tharepati you're on the Helambu Trek and can either take the direct route south to Pati Bhanjyang and Kathmandu or east to Tarke Gyang and then complete the circuit back to Kathmandu.

JOMSOM TREK

See the Annapurna Treks map later in this section for this trek. The Jomsom Trek is essentially the final third of the Annapurna Circuit. It follows the Kali Gandaki valley between the soaring peaks of Annapurna and Dhaulagiri and then emerges north of the main Himalayan range, on the dry, desert-like Tibetan plateau. The final destination is the holy temple of Muktinath, a further day's walk past Jomsom. Return to Pokhara either by retracing your steps down the Kali Gandaki valley or by flying from Jomsom to Pokhara.

Access: Pokhara to Naya Pul

Like many other treks in Nepal this one is getting shorter as roads gradually extend farther into the mountains. Eventually it will probably be possible to drive all the way to Jomsom. A road has been pushed through the hills from Pokhara to Baglung to the west. Buses leave for Baglung from the bus stop in Bag Bazaar at the northern end of Pokhara. Take the bus up the ridge to Naudanda and then down into the Modi Khola valley and get off at Naya Pul (New Bridge); the fare is Rs 60, or Rs 750 for a taxi.

Alternative Access Points It's still possible to walk all the way from Pokhara to

Trekking Around Pokhara

Pokhara is the starting or finishing point for some of the best trekking in Nepal; the long Annapurna Circuit trek is the most popular trek in the country.

The reasons for the area's popularity are numerous but topping the list is convenience. You can start your trek from Pokhara – there's no long, uncomfortable bus rides or problematic flights to the starting point. Also, because the Annapurna Range is so close to Pokhara you are in the mountains almost immediately.

The treks in this part of the country offer a great deal of cultural and geographic diversity; indeed the Jomsom and Annapurna Circuit treks both go to the north of the Himalayan watershed, into the dry desert area that is properly part of the Tibetan plateau. Finally, these treks are the best in Nepal for independent trekkers and a network of lodges and guesthouses can be found all along the main trails. The entire region is administered by the Annapurna Conservation Area Project (ACAP), which is working to conserve the natural and cultural resources of the area.

The Pokhara area also offers a number of one-day treks or short three- or four-day treks. These are covered in the Around Pokhara section of the Pokhara chapter. There are three popular longer treks, all of which follow the same route at some point.

The **Annapurna Sanctuary Trek** takes you right in among the mountains of the Annapurna Range to the Annapurna Base camp. This trek takes about 10 days. The **Jomsom Trek** takes about seven days in each direction, but it is possible to fly back to Pokhara from Jomsom. Most trekkers continue a day farther to the holy temple of Muktinath. Finally, the **Annapurna Circuit Trek** takes a full three weeks and completely encircles the Annapurna Range. The last seven days of the circuit walk from Muktinath to Pokhara are the same as the Jomsom trek, but in reverse.

The Annapurna Range is the centre for all of these Pokhara treks. For most of Nepal's length, the Himalaya form the border between Nepal and China. However, the Annapurnas are different: The border is well to the north so the Jomsom and Annapurna Circuit Treks both go north of the Himalayan watershed, into the high-altitude desert, which is characteristic of the Tibetan plateau.

Birethanti of course. You can reach Naudanda by walking through Sarangkot (see the Pokhara chapter for details) and along the ridge to Kaski, which has the ruins of a small palace, and on to Naudanda. There are fine views of the whole Annapurna Range and back over Pokhara and Phewa Tal from this large village. Naudanda has a choice of hotels. From Naudanda, follow the road for a bit, then turn off past Khare to Chandrakot and drop to Birethanti.

You can also avoid the long climb over the Ghorapani hill by taking the bus on to Baglung. From here it's a two-day walk up the Kali Gandaki valley to Tatopani. You can also continue on a rough, unpaved road by bus or taxi to Beni and save another half day of walking.

Day 1: Naya Pul to Tikedungha

From Naya Pul it's a short walk up Modi Khola to the large village of Birethanti at 1000m, where you can really see how civilised this trek is. Birethanti has a bakery, bank and even sidewalk cafes! A trail east to Ghandruk turns off here. Birethanti has excellent hotels but you may want to continue farther to shorten the next day's long climb. Sticking to the northern side of the Bhurungdi Khola, the trail climbs to Hille and nearby Tikedungha at 1525m. Both Tikedungha and Hille have places to stay.

Day 2: Tikedungha to Ghorapani

From Tikedungha the trail drops down and crosses the Bhurungdi Khola, then climbs very steeply up a stone staircase to Ulleri, a large Magar village at 1960m. It continues to ascend, but more gently, through fine forests of oak and rhododendron to Banthanti at 2250m and then Nangathanti at 2460m. Another hour's walk brings you to Ghorapani at 2750m.

Only a short walk beyond Ghorapani is the Deorali pass and village (*deorali* also means 'pass') with spectacular views, and this is where most people stay. An hour's climb from here will take you to Poon (or Pun) Hill at 3210m, one of the best Himalayan viewpoints in Nepal. There are hotels at Ghorapani and at Deorali. *Ghora* means 'horse' and *pani* means 'water' and indeed, long caravans of pack horses are regularly seen all along the Jomsom Trek.

A trail also runs from Ghorapani/Deorali to Ghandruk. This part of the trek is plagued by leeches during the monsoon and there may be snow on the trail in the winter.

Saligrams

The black fossils of marine animals known as saligrams are found at several points along the Kali Gandaki, most notably in the area north of Jomsom around Muktinath, but also at Ridi Bazaar and Devghat. These ammonite fossils date back to the Jurassic period over 100 million years ago and provide dramatic evidence that the mighty Himalaya was indeed once under water.

Saligrams are considered holy emblems. They are sometimes believed to represent Vishnu, and are often held during worship and when making a vow. In Pokhara, the image of the goddess Durga (Parvati) in her Binde Basini Bhagwati form is a saligram.

You will see many saligrams on sale in Pokhara or along the Jomsom trail. Think twice before buying them; firstly, it is actually illegal to collect them, because the government is concerned about potential damage to Nepal's fossil record; secondly, they're overpriced; and thirdly, adding rocks to your backpack is never a good idea!

Day 3: Ghorapani to Tatopani

The trail descends steeply to Chitre at 2420m where there are more lodges. From here the hills are extensively terraced as the trail drops down through Sikha, a large village with shops and hotels at 1980m, and then descends gently to Ghara at 1780m. A farther steep descent of 380m takes you to Ghar Khola village where the trail crosses the river on a suspension bridge and then climbs up above the Kali Gandaki before crossing that too. There's also an ACAP checkpost here.

Turning north the trail soon reaches Tatopani at 1190m. It's a busy population centre, although a monsoon flood in the late

1980s washed away a number of lodges and bathing pools, and the remainder of the village sits precariously on a shelf above the river. Tatopani offers some of the best food along the whole trail, and you can even get a cold beer to go with it. *Tato* means 'hot' and *pani* is 'water', a name earned courtesy of the hot springs by the river. Tatopani is a popular destination for a shorter trek out of Pokhara. At the south end of the village is the trail to the hot springs and a police checkpost where you must register.

Day 4: Tatopani to Ghasa

The trail follows the Kali Gandaki valley all the rest of the way to Jomsom.

From Tatopani the route climbs across several recent landslides and ascends gradually to Dana at 1400m. This is where the difficult track branches off to Maurice Herzog's base camp, used for his historic ascent of Annapurna in 1950.

The trail continues to climb to Rupse Chhahara at 1560m and at one stage takes a precarious route through a steep, narrow section of the gorge. A new suspension bridge crosses the river at 1620m and then the trail crosses back again at 1880m, then through Ghasa at 2120m, the first Thakali village.

Day 5: Ghasa to Larjung

A steep climb through forest takes you to the Lete Khola, then to the village of Lete at 2430m, with a superb view of the eastern flank of Dhaulagiri, and finally to Kalopani at 2530m. Kalopani has great mountain views and some comfortable lodges to view them from.

From Kalopani the trail crosses to the east side of the Kali Gandaki, before crossing back again at Larjung. This village at 2570m has interesting alleyways and tunnels between the houses, an attempt to avoid the fierce winds that often whistle down the Kali Gandaki valley.

Kali Gandaki

A river cuts a channel between the peaks of Annapurna I and Dhaulagiri, thus qualifying the Kali Gandaki valley for the title of the world's deepest gorge. The two 8000m-plus mountaintops are only 38km apart and the river flows between them at a height of less than 2200m.

The Kali Gandaki valley is also the home for the Thakalis, an ethnic group noted for their trading and business expertise, particularly in the running hotels and lodges not only here in their homeland but also in Pokhara and elsewhere in Nepal.

Day 6: Larjung to Marpha

Khobang at 2580m is a village with a gompa above it, and the mountain views on this stretch are the best to be seen.

Tukuche at 2590m is one of the most important Thakali villages, once a meeting place for traders from Tibet. Despite the growth of tourism in this area Tukuche is still a quieter, smaller place than it was during the era of trade with Tibet.

From here the landscape changes as you enter the drier and more desert-like country north of the Himalayan watershed. It also gets windier; gentle breezes from the north in the early morning shift to a gale from the south as the morning wears on. Marpha, at 2680m, virtually huddles behind a ridge to keep out of the wind! The village also has some of the most luxurious accommodation to be found along the trail and is thus a good alternative to staying in Jomsom. A government-established project between Tukuche and Marpha is able to grow fruit and vegetables for the whole region.

Day 7: Marpha to Kagbeni

The trail continues along the valley side, rising gradually before crossing over a low ridge to Jomsom. At 2713m, Jomsom is the major centre in the region and it has a hospital, an ACAP visitor centre and a police checkpost (where you must register and get your ACAP permit stamped). This is the last of the Thakali villages; those farther north are inhabited by people of Tibetan descent.

Jomsom has regular flights to Pokhara for US$50.

If you have time left in the day, it's worth following the trail along the river all the way to the medieval-looking village of Kagbeni at 2810m. This obviously Tibetan-influenced settlement has a number of good lodges, and is as close as you can get to Lo Monthang, the capital of the legendary kingdom of Mustang farther to the north, without paying a US$700 permit fee.

In 1999 a new bridge and trail was constructed up the west bank of the Kali Gandaki. This trail provides an alternative to the original trail up the east bank.

Day 8: Kagbeni to Muktinath

From Kagbeni the trail climbs steeply to rejoin the direct trail before Khingar is reached at 3200m. The trail climbs through a desert landscape then past meadows and streams to the interesting village of Jharkot at 3500m. A farther climb brings you to Ranipauwa, which is the accommodation area of Muktinath, at 3710m.

Muktinath is a pilgrimage centre for Buddhists and Hindus. You'll see Tibetan traders as well as *sadhus* (holy men) from the far south of India. The shrines, in a grove of trees, include a Buddhist gompa and the Vishnu temple of Jiwala Mayi. An old temple nearby shelters a spring and natural gas jets that provide Muktinath's famous eternal flame. It's the earth-water-fire combination that accounts for Muktinath's great religious significance.

Back to Pokhara or Jomsom

From Muktinath you can retrace your steps to Pokhara, or simply trek back to Jomsom and hope to catch a flight from there. It is possible to continue beyond Muktinath and cross the Thorung La to walk the rest of the Annapurna Circuit but this long walk is better made in the opposite direction – it's a long, hard climb of 1600m from Muktinath to the pass.

ANNAPURNA CIRCUIT TREK

Since it opened to foreign trekkers in 1977, the three-week trek around Annapurna has become the most popular trek in Nepal. It passes through country inhabited by a wide diversity of peoples, it offers spectacular mountain scenery and it goes to the north of the main Himalayan range on to the high and dry Tibetan plateau. To many independent trekkers it also offers the considerable advantage of having accommodation available each night. The only drawback perhaps are the tedious checkpoints on this trek – between ACAP and the police there is a checkpoint to pass almost every day!

The circuit is usually walked in a counterclockwise direction because of the steepness of the track to the Thorung La when going in a clockwise direction. For many people, this is too much to manage in one day. The Thorung La at 5416m is often closed by snow from mid-December to mid-March and bad weather can move in at any time. Trekkers should be prepared to turn back due to the weather or if they suffer from AMS. If you take porters over this pass you must make sure they are adequately equipped for severe cold and snow.

After you cross the Thorung La from Manang to Muktinath the final seven days of the circuit trek are the same as the Jomsom Trek from Pokhara, but in reverse. Completing the Annapurna Circuit in 16 days allows for only one rest and acclimatisation day at Manang. It's very easy to slot a few additional days into the schedule.

Access: Kathmandu to Besi Sahar

It's a long and somewhat tedious drive from Kathmandu to the turn-off at Dumre. Starting from Pokhara is much easier since Dumre is 137km from Kathmandu but only 70km from Pokhara. From Dumre, at 440m, buses and 4WDs run regularly to Besi Sahar at 820m.

Day 1: Besi Sahar to Bahundanda

The trail drops, then climbs to Khudi at 830m. This is the first Gurung village you reach (many of Nepal's Gurkha soldiers are Gurungs). The Khudi trail offers fine views of Himalchuli (to the north-east) and Ngadi Chuli (aka Manaslu II, and before that, Peak 29) as it climbs to Bhulbhule at 840m. You enter the Annapurna Conservation Area here and must register at the ACAP checkpoint.

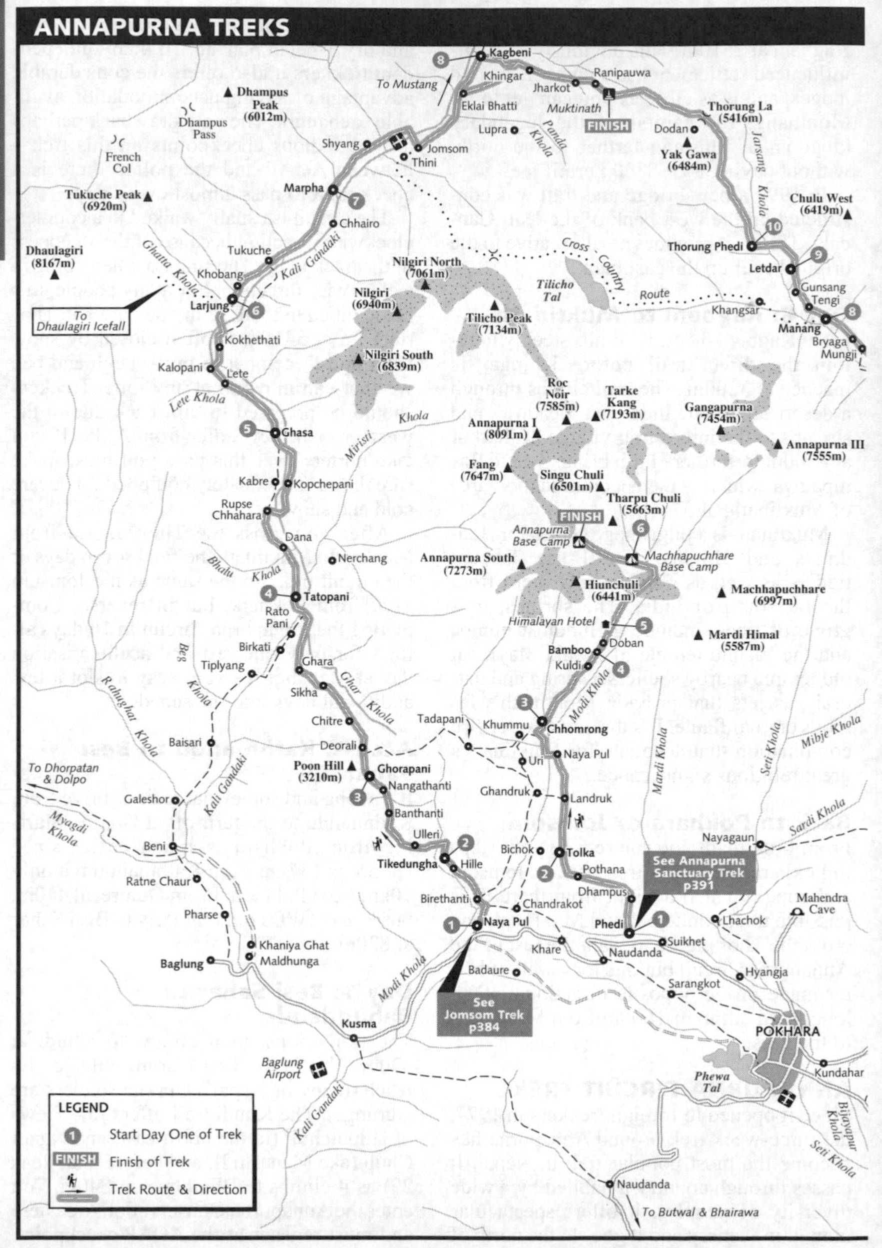

ANNAPURNA TREKS
Kagbeni
Khingar
To Mustang
Eklai Bhatti
Jharkot
Ranipauwa
Muktinath
FINISH
Thorung La
(5416m)
Dodan
Yak Gawa
(6484m)
Jarsang Khola
Panda Khola
Lupra
Dhampus Peak
(6012m)
Dhampus Pass
French Col
Shyang
Jomsom
Thini
Marpha
Chhairo
Tukuche Peak
(6920m)
Tukuche
Kali Gandaki
Khobang
Dhaulagiri
(8167m)
Ghatta Khola
To Dhaulagiri Icefall
Larjung
Chulu West
(6419m)
Thorung Phedi
Letdar
Gunsang
Tengi
Manang
Bryaga
Mungji
Khangsar
Cross Country Route
Tilicho Tal
Nilgiri North
(7061m)
Nilgiri
(6940m)
Tilicho Peak
(7134m)
Nilgiri South
(6839m)
Kokhethati
Kalopani
Lete
Lete Khola
Ghasa
Miristi Khola
Roc Noir
(7585m)
Tarke Kang
(7193m)
Gangapurna
(7454m)
Annapurna I
(8091m)
Annapurna III
(7555m)
Fang
(7647m)
Singu Chuli
(6501m)
Tharpu Chuli
(5663m)
Kabre
Kopchepani
Rupse Chhahara
Dana
Nerchang
Annapurna Base Camp
Machhapuchhare Base Camp
Annapurna South
(7273m)
Hiunchuli
(6441m)
Machhapuchhare
(6997m)
Bhalu Khola
Tatopani
Rato Pani
Birkati
Tiplyang
Beg Khola
Rahughat Khola
Ghara
Sikha
Ghar Khola
Himalayan Hotel
Doban
Bamboo
Kuldi
Mardi Himal
(5587m)
Modi Khola
Chitre
Deorali
Poon Hill
(3210m)
Ghorapani
Nangathanti
Tadapani
Khummu
Chhomrong
Uri
Naya Pul
Mibje Khola
Seti Khola
Mardi Khola
Baisari
To Dhorpatan & Dolpo
Galeshor
Kali Gandaki
Myagdi Khola
Banthanti
Ulleri
Ghandruk
Landruk
Beni
Tikedungha
Hille
Bichok
Tolka
Pothana
Sardi Khola
Nayagaun
See Annapurna Sanctuary Trek p391
Ratne Chaur
Birethanti
Chandrakot
Dhampus
Mahendra Cave
Pharse
Naya Pul
Phedi
Lhachok
Suikhet
Khaniya Ghat
Maldhunga
Baglung
Khare
Naudanda
Badaure
Hyangja
Modi Khola
Sarangkot
See Jomsom Trek p384
Kusma
POKHARA
Baglung Airport
Phewa Tal
Kundahar
Kali Gandaki
Bijayapur Khola
Seti Khola
Naudanda
To Butwal & Bhairawa
LEGEND
Start Day One of Trek
FINISH
Finish of Trek
Trek Route & Direction

ANNAPURNA TREKS

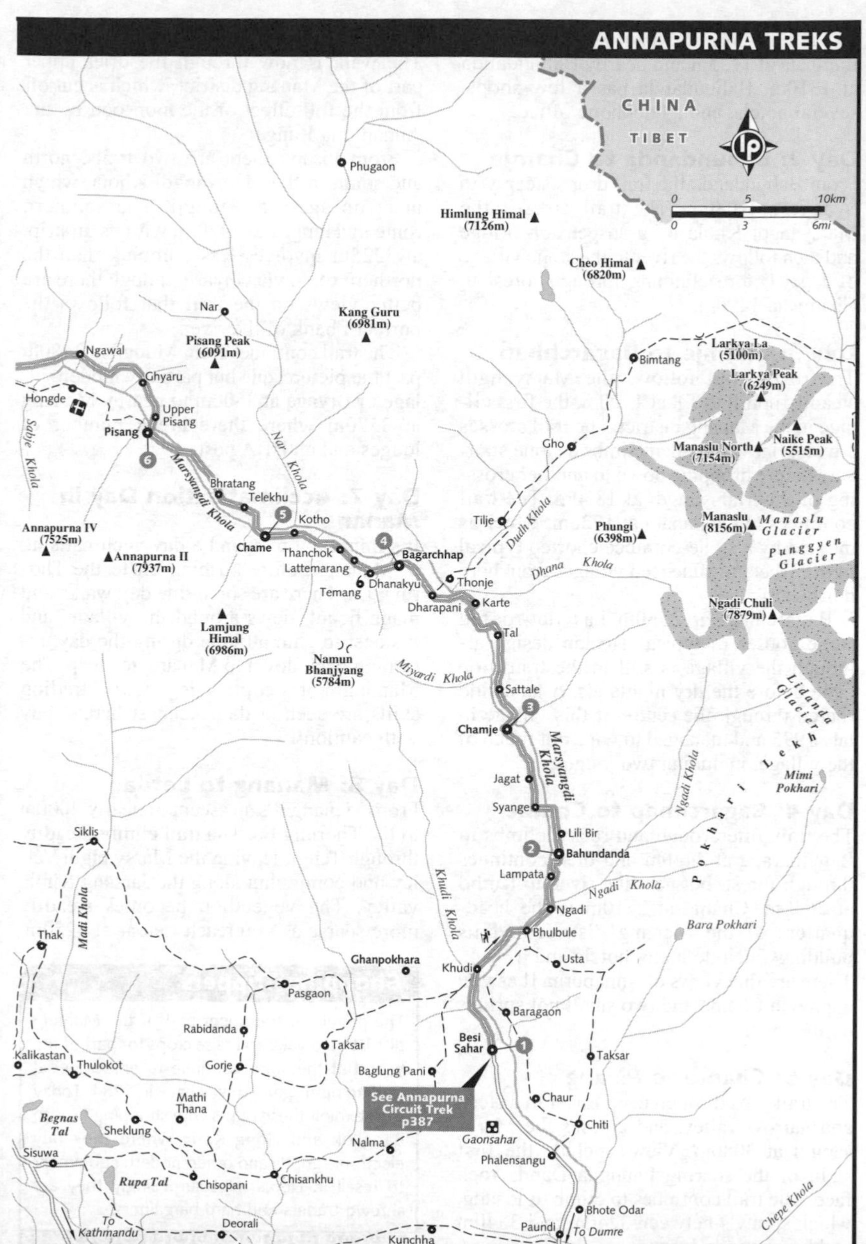

The trail goes to Ngadi before reaching Lampata at 1135m and nearby Bahundanda at 1310m. Bahundanda has a few shops, several hotels, and a telephone office.

Day 2: Bahundanda to Chamje

From Bahundanda the trail drops steeply to Syange at 1080m. The trail crosses the Marsyangdi Khola on a suspension bridge and then follows the river to the stone village of Jagat before climbing through forest to Chamje at 1400m.

Day 3: Chamje to Bagarchhap

The rocky trail follows the Marsyangdi steadily uphill to Tal at 1700m, the first village in the Manang district. The trail crosses a wide, flat valley then climbs a stone stairway before dropping down to another crossing of the Marsyangdi at 1850m. The trail continues to Dharapani at 1920m, which is marked by a stone-entrance chorten typical of the Tibetan-influenced villages from here northwards.

Bagarchhap at 2160m has flat-roofed stone houses of typical Tibetan design although the village is still in the transition zone before the dry highlands. A landslide roared through the centre of this village in late 1995 and managed to wipe out much of the village, including two lodges.

Day 4: Bagarchhap to Chame

The trail, often rough and rocky, climbs to Lattemarang at 2440m and then continues through forest, but near the river, to Kotho at 2640m. Chame at 2710m is the headquarters of the Manang district and its buildings include many hotels and a bank. There are fine views of Annapurna II as you approach Chame and two small hot springs by the town.

Day 5: Chame to Pisang

The trail runs through deep forest in a steep and narrow valley, and crosses the Marysangdi at 3080m. Views include the first sight of the soaring Paungda Danda rock face. The trail continues to climb to Pisang, which sprawls between 3240m and 3340m and has many lodges.

Day 6: Pisang to Manang

The walk is now through the drier upper part of the Manang district, which is cut off from the full effect of the monsoon by the Annapurna Range.

From Pisang there are two trails, north and south of the Marsyangdi Khola, which meet up again at Mungji. The southern route by Hongde at 3420m, with its airstrip, at 3325m involves less climbing than the northern route via Ghyaru, though there are better views on the trail that follows the northern bank of the river.

The trail continues from Mungji at 3480m past the picturesque but partially hidden village of Bryaga at 3500m to nearby Manang at 3570m where there are a number of lodges and an HRA post.

Day 7: Acclimatisation Day in Manang

It's important to spend a day acclimatising in Manang before pushing on to the Thorung La. There are some fine day walks and magnificent views around the village, and it's best to gain altitude during the day, returning back down to Manang to sleep. The Manangbhot people's legendary trading skills are seen at their keenest here – buy with caution!

Day 8: Manang to Letdar

From Manang it's an ascent of nearly 2000m to the Thorung La. The trail climbs steadily through Tengi, leaving the Marsyangdi Valley and continuing along the Jarsang Khola valley. The vegetation becomes steadily more sparse as you reach Letdar at 4250m.

Shopping Trippers

The people of the upper part of the Manang district herd yaks and raise crops for part of the year, but they also continue to enjoy special trading rights gained way back in 1784. Today they exploit these rights with shopping trips to Bangkok and Hong Kong where they buy electronic goods and other modern equipment to resell in Nepal. Not surprisingly they are shrewd traders and hard bargainers.

Day 9: Letdar to Thorung Phedi

Cross the river at 4310m and then climb up to Thorung Phedi at 4420m. There are two hotels here – at the height of the season as many as 200 trekkers a day may cross over the Thorung La and beds can be in short supply. Some trekkers find themselves suffering from AMS symptoms at Phedi. If you find yourself in a similar condition you must retreat downhill; even the descent to Letdar can make a difference. Be sure to boil or treat water here; the sanitation in Letdar and Thorung Phedi is poor, and giardiasis is rampant. There is a satellite phone here that you can use for US$5 per minute in an emergency.

Day 10: Thorung Phedi to Muktinath

Phedi means 'foot of the hill' and that's where it is, at the foot of the 5416m Thorung La. The trail climbs steeply but is regularly used and easy to follow. The altitude and snow can be problems; when the pass is snow-covered it is often impossible to cross. It takes about four to six hours to climb up to the pass, marked by chortens and prayer flags. The effort is worthwhile as the view from the top is magnificent. From the pass you have a tough 1600m descent to Muktinath at 3800m.

Many start out for the pass far too early at 3 am. This is not necessary and is potentially dangerous due to the risk of frostbite if you are hanging around waiting in the cold snow for too long. A better starting time is around 5 to 6 am.

Back to Pokhara

The remaining seven days of the trek simply follow the Jomsom Trek route but in the opposite direction.

ANNAPURNA SANCTUARY TREK

See the Annapurna Treks map earlier in this section for this trek. The walk up to the Annapurna Base Camp is a classic walk right into the heart of the mountains. The walk ends at a point where you are virtually surrounded by soaring Himalayan peaks. At one time this trek was a real expedition into a wilderness area, but now there is a string of lodges that operate during the trekking season. The return trip can take as little as 10 or 11 days but it's best appreciated with a full 14 days, and the walk to the base camp can be tacked on as a side-trip from the Jomsom or Annapurna Circuit Treks.

There are several possible routes to the sanctuary, all meeting at Chhomrong. The diversion from the Jomsom and Annapurna Circuit Treks is made from near Ghorapani to Ghandruk.

The route to the Annapurna Sanctuary is occasionally blocked by avalanches. Check with the ACAP office in Chhomrong for a report on current trail conditions, and do not proceed into the sanctuary if there is heavy rain or snow.

Warning – Theft

There is a theft racket throughout the Annapurna region, particularly in Dhampus and Tikedunga, but it can happen anywhere. Thieves often cut the tents of trekkers and remove valuable items during the night. Thus trekking groups have taken to pitching their tents in a circle like an old-time wagon train and posting a guard with a lighted lantern throughout the night. If you stay in a hotel, be sure that you know who is sharing the room with you, and lock the door whenever you go out – even for a moment (and that includes going to the toilet). The thieves watch everyone in order to decide who has something worth taking or is likely to be careless. If necessary they will wait patiently all night to make their move.

Access: Pokhara to Phedi

The walk from Pokhara leaves the route to the Jomsom trek at Phedi – you can take a bus or taxi.

Day 1: Phedi to Tolka

From Phedi the trail climbs to Dhampus at 1750m, which stretches for several kilometres from 1580m to 1700m and has a number of widely spaced hotels. Theft is a real problem in Dhampus, so take care.

The trail climbs to Pothana at 1990m and descends steeply through a forest towards

Bichok. It finally emerges in the Modi Khola valley and continues to drop to Tolka at 1810m.

Day 2: Tolka to Chhomrong

From Tolka the trail descends a long stone staircase, and then climbs a ridge to the Gurung village of Landruk at 1620m. The trail descends again for about 10 minutes, and then splits – north takes you to Chhomrong and the sanctuary, or you can head downhill to Ghandruk.

The sanctuary trail turns up the Modi Khola valley. Ask someone in Landruk about the bridge at Naya Pul. It was washed away during the 2000 monsoon and it still may be necessary to take an alternate route to reach Chhomrong. If the bridge is still out, descend to the Modi Khola, climb a bit and follow a trail north along the west bank to join the normal route near Naya Pul at 1340m. The trail continues from Naya Pul up to Jhinu Danda at 1750m and up again to Taglung at 2190m, where it joins the Ghandruk to Chhomrong trail.

Chhomrong at 2210m, is the last permanent settlement in the valley; it has a choice of hotels, and an ACAP office.

Day 3: Chhomrong to Bamboo

The trail drops down to the Chhomrong Khola, then climbs to Kuldi at 2470m where there is an abandoned ACAP checkpoint and information centre. The trek now enters the upper Modi Khola valley, where ACAP controls the location and number of lodges and also limits their size. If the lodges are full up, you may have to sleep in the dining room, or perhaps the lodge owner can erect a tent for you. In winter, it is common to find snow anywhere from this point on. Continue on to Bamboo at 2310m, which is a collection of three hotels. This stretch of trail has many leeches early and late in the trekking season.

Day 4: Bamboo to Himalayan Hotel

The trail climbs through Bamboo, then rhododendron forests to Doban at 2540m and on to ***Himalayan Hotel*** at 2840m.

Day 5: Himalayan Hotel to Machhapuchhare Base Camp

From Himalayan Hotel it's on to Hinko at 3100m. There is accommodation in Deorali at 3170m, on the ridge above Hinko. This is the stretch of trail that seems to be most subject to avalanches.

At Machhapuchhare Base Camp (which isn't really a base camp since climbing the mountain is not permitted) at 3700m there is seasonal accommodation. These hotels may or may not be open, depending on whether the innkeeper (and the supplies) have been able to reach the hotel through the avalanche area.

Day 6: Machhapuchhare Base Camp to Annapurna Base Camp

The climb to the Annapurna Base Camp at 4130m takes about two hours, and is best done early in the day before clouds roll in and make visibility a problem. There are four lodges here, which get ridiculously crowded at the height of the season.

Back to Pokhara

On the return trip you can retrace your steps, or divert from Chhomrong to Ghandruk and on to Ghorapani to visit Poon Hill and follow the Annapurna Circuit or the Jomsom trek route back to Pokhara.

The Ghorapani to Ghandruk walk is a popular way of linking the Annapurna Sanctuary Trek with treks up the Kali Gandaki valley. It's also used for shorter loop walks out of Pokhara (see the Around Pokhara section of the Pokhara chapter for more information).

OTHER TREKS

The treks described earlier in this chapter are used by the vast majority of trekkers. Yet other alternatives will take you to areas still relatively unvisited. These are described briefly below. (For more treks still see Lonely Planet's *Trekking in the Nepal Himalaya.*)

Kanchenjunga Base Camps

The trekking route up to the Kanchenjunga North and South Base Camps in the extreme north-eastern corner of the country is open to trekkers, but you have to go with a recognised agency. The starting point can be Basantapur or Taplejung by road, or Tumlingtar or Taplejung by air.

Makulu Base Camp

It's a long but fine trek from Hile or Tumlingtar up the Arun River to the Makalu Base Camp in eastern Nepal. The area is protected by the Makalu-Barun National Park and its conservation area.

Solu Khumbu to Hile

As an alternative to flying back to Kathmandu from Lukla, or walking back to Jiri, the Everest Base Camp Trek can be extended by walking for 11 days east and then south to Hile. From Hile you can then travel by road through Dhankuta and Dharan to Biratnagar from where there are buses and flights to Kathmandu.

Mustang

Mustang has lured trekkers for many years, and has only recently been opened. It was closed, both because of guerrilla war along the border with Tibet, and because of the ecological sensitivity of the region. The area is part of the Tibetan plateau, and is high, dry and beautiful. It lies to the north-west of the Kali Gandaki, beyond Kagbeni, which is the farthest point north on the Jomsom Trek. It is only possible to enter with an organised group, and permits are a steep US$700 for 10 days, with extra days at US$70.

Dolpo

Trekking to the Dolpo region has only been permitted since mid-1989. The region lies west of the Kali Gandaki valley. A special permit is needed, and you must be well equipped and self sufficient. From Baglung near Pokhara it's a tough 14-day trek to Phoksundo Lake, and beyond it is 'inner Dolpo' the site of Shey Gompa. A special permit (US$700) is required to trek into this area.

Rara Lake

The eight-day round-trip trek from Jumla north to the Rara Lake and back still gets very few trekkers, largely because trekking here requires real planning: flights are difficult to get on, porters are hard to find and little food is available.

Mountain Biking

This chapter was originally written by John Prosser. It has been updated for the last two editions by Peter Stewart, a keen mountain biker and adventurer, who has explored many of Nepal's biking routes and ridden through many parts of wider Asia. Peter Stewart owns Himalayan Mountain Bikes, and organises cycling tours and events such as the annual Himalayan Mountain Bike Championship Series in Kathmandu.

Highlights

- Biking to heights that initially seem unachievable, with the world's greatest 8000m peaks looming in the distance
- Winding your way through and around the cities and towns of the Kathmandu Valley, which seem to have almost been designed with the mountain bike in mind
- Covering in a day what takes days on foot, at a pace that allows intimacy with your surroundings, the people and their culture
- Exploring mountain villages reached via thrilling mountain trails

Ah, mountain biking! Strong wheels, knobbly tyres, a wide selection of gears and overall strength – the mountain bike is an ideal, go anywhere, versatile machine for exploring Nepal. These attributes make it possible to escape paved roads, and to ride tracks and ancient walking trails to remote, rarely visited areas of the country. Importantly, they allow independent travel – you can stop whenever you like – and they liberate you from crowded buses and claustrophobic taxis.

Nepal's tremendously diverse terrain and its many tracks and trails are ideal for mountain biking. It's only in recent years that Nepal has gained recognition for the biking adventures it offers – from easy village trails in the Kathmandu Valley to challenging mountain roads that climb thousands of metres to reach spectacular viewpoints, followed by unforgettable, exhilarating descents. The Terai has flat, smooth roads, and mountain biking is an excellent way of getting to the Royal Chitwan National Park. For the adventurous there are large areas of the country still to be explored by mountain bike.

The Kathmandu Valley still offers the best and most consistent biking in Nepal, with its vast network of tracks, trails and back roads. Mountain biking offers the perfect way to visit the people of the Kathmandu Valley and their wealth of temples, stupas and medieval towns. A mountain bike really comes into its own when you get off the beaten track and discover idyllic Newari villages that have preserved their traditional and rural lifestyle. Even today, it's possible to cycle into villages in the Kathmandu Valley that have rarely seen a visitor on a foreign bicycle. Each year more roads are developing, opening new trails to destinations and villages that were previously accessible only on foot.

Many trails are narrow, century-old walkways that are not shown on maps, so you need a good sense of direction when venturing out without a guide. To go unguided entails some risks, and you should learn a few important words of Nepali to assist in seeking directions. It's also important to know the name of the next village you wish to reach. However, it's no simple task to gain the right directions, and any mispronunciations can result in misdirections. The most detailed Kathmandu Valley map is commonly referred to as the 'German map' (also Schneider and Nelles Verlag), and is widely available in Kathmandu. The maps by Karto Atelier are also excellent.

TRANSPORTING YOUR BICYCLE

If you plan to do more than use roads it may be a good idea to bring your own bicycle. Your bicycle can be carried as part of your baggage allowance on international flights. You are required to deflate the tyres, turn the handlebars parallel with the frame and remove the pedals. Passage through Nepali customs is quite simple once you reassure airport officers that it is 'your' bicycle and it will also be returning with you, though this requirement is never enforced.

On most domestic flights, if you pack your bicycle correctly, removing wheels and pedals, it is possible to load it in the cargo hold. Check with the airline first.

Local buses are useful if you wish to avoid some of the routes that carry heavy traffic. You can place your bicycle on the roof for an additional charge (Rs 50 to Rs 100 depending on the length of the journey and the bus company). If you're lucky, rope may be available and the luggage boy will assist you. Make sure the bicycle is held securely to cope with the rough roads and that it's lying as flat as possible to prevent it catching low wires or tree branches. Unless you travel with foam padding it is hard to avoid the scratches to the frame but a day pack may come in handy. Supervise its loading and protect the rear derailleur from being damaged. Keep in mind that more baggage is likely to be loaded on top once you're inside. A lock and chain may also be a wise investment.

EQUIPMENT

Most of the bicycles you can hire in Nepal are low-quality Indian so-called mountain bikes, not suitable for the rigours of trail riding. Quality, imported bicycles are slowly becoming available for rent through tour operators. Some of the better rental shops can supply helmets, pannier bags and luggage racks. See Getting Around in the Kathmandu and Pokhara chapters for more information on bicycle hire.

If you bring your own bicycle it is essential to bring tools and spare parts, as these are largely unavailable in Nepal. Unfortunately, carrying a complete bicycle tool kit and spares for every situation may be impractical. An established mountain bicycle tour operator (such as Himalayan Mountain Bikes in Kathmandu), which has mechanics, workshop and a full range of bicycle tools can help. Fortunately, what the standard local bicycle repair shops lack in spare parts and knowledge of the latest faddish equipment they make up for in their ability to improvise. For basic adjustments their standard of skill is usually high, but you still need to maintain a watchful eye on your equipment during repairs. On the trails you're on your own, so plan for all situations and be ready to improvise.

Sleeping bags, mats and tents can be hired in Kathmandu cheaply. More thin layers of clothes offer better protection and convenience than thick, bulky items. These days a greater number of mountain bike clothing items are being manufactured locally and are of good quality. They are a good buy and may save you luggage space on the way.

Although this is not a complete list, a few items that may be worth considering bringing with you include:

- basic range of bicycle tools
- bicycle bell
- cycling gloves, tops and shorts
- energy bars and electrolyte water additives
- fleecy top for evenings
- helmet
- lightweight clothing (eg, Coolmax and Gortex)
- medium-sized money bag for valuables
- minipump
- spare parts (including inner tubes)
- stiff-soled shoes that suit riding and walking
- sun protection
- sunglasses
- torch (flashlight)
- warm hat and gloves
- water bottles or hydration system (eg, Camelbak)
- windbreaker

ROAD CONDITIONS

Traffic generally travels on the left-hand side, even though it's not uncommon to find a vehicle approaching you head-on, and smaller vehicles giving way to larger ones. Bicycles are at the bottom of the hierarchy, and will definitely come off second best if they mess with Tata trucks! Nepali roads carry a vast array of vehicles: autorickshaws, tempos (three-wheeled vehicles), buses, motorcycles, cars, trucks, tractors... Once you've thrown in a few holy cows, wheelbarrows, dogs, wandering children, chickens and rickshaws all moving at different speeds and in different directions you have a typical Nepali street scene. In the past few years the introduction of newer and faster vehicles has added a new element of risk – speed.

The centre of Kathmandu, unfortunately, is becoming a very unpleasant place to ride because of pollution, heavy traffic and the increasingly reckless behaviour of young motorcyclists. If you are sensitive to traffic fumes, consider bringing some sort of mask.

Extreme care should be taken near villages as young children play on the trails and roads. Local pedestrians seem to have a philosophy of 'others can watch out for me', thus they (and drivers) rarely look and appear to have little awareness of surrounding traffic. The onus seems to fall on the approaching vehicle to avoid an incident. On the trails, animals should be approached with caution. Don't even try to predict what a buffalo, dog or chicken will do. A good bicycle helmet is a sensible accessory, and you should ride with your fingers poised on the rear brake lever.

A few intrepid mountain bikers have taken bicycles into trekking areas hoping to find great riding. What they have discovered is that these areas are generally not suitable for mountain biking and they carry their bicycles for at least 80% of the time. Trails are unreliable, and are subject to avalanche and frequent obstacles. In addition, there are always trekkers, porters and local people clogging up the trails. Bicyclists just add one more problem to these heavy-traffic areas in peak season. To say 'I did it' may be enough, but there are other equally great locations that can be ridden. Courtesy and care on the trails should be a high priority when biking.

Riders who have taken bicycles to such places as the Everest Base Camp or around the Annapurna Circuit will know of the long carries. If you decide to indulge in such a bicycle trek, have a good shoulder pad and be thoughtful of others sharing the trail so that opportunities for future bicyclists are preserved. While mountain bikes are being banned from many trails around the world, Nepal remains mainly unrestricted, and this is a great attraction of biking here. Some regions are under review, however. The issue is whether trekkers are being hindered by mountain bikers.

TRAIL ETIQUETTE

Arriving in a new country for a short time where social and cultural values are vastly different from those of your home country does not allow much time to gain an appreciation of these matters. So consider a few pointers to help you develop respect and understanding. For more information, see Dos & Don'ts under Society & Conduct in the Facts about Nepal chapter.

Clothing

Tight-fitting Lycra bicycle clothing, although functional, is a shock to locals, who maintain a very modest approach to dressing. Such clothing is embarrassing and also offensive to Nepalis.

A simple way to overcome this is by wearing a pair of comfortable shorts and a T-shirt over your bicycle gear. This is especially applicable to female bicyclists, as women in Nepal generally dress conservatively.

Safety

Trails are often filled with locals going about their daily work of farming, carting food, portering, playing, passing the time of day and shepherding their stock. A small bell attached to your handlebars and used as a warning of your approach, reducing your speed, and a friendly call or two of *'cycle ioh!'* ('cycle coming!') goes a long way in keeping everyone on the trails happy and safe. Children love the novelty of the bicycles, the fancy helmets, the colours and the strange clothing, and will come running from all directions to greet you. They also love to grab hold of the back of your bicycle and run with you. You need to maintain a watchful eye so no-one gets hurt.

Conservation

When it comes to caring for the environment, the guidelines that apply to trekkers also apply to mountain bikers. For more detailed information, see the Trekking chapter; see also Conservation in the Facts about Nepal chapter.

ORGANISED TOURS

A small number of companies offer guided trips on mountain bikes. They provide high-quality bicycles, local and Western guides, pannier bags, helmets and all the necessary equipment. There is usually a minimum of four bicyclists per trip, although for shorter tours two is often sufficient. For the shorter tours (two to three days) vehicle support is not required, while for longer tours vehicles are provided at an extra cost.

The following companies are the only outfits with good-quality imported mountain bikes that can also be hired independently of a tour. Any others fall a long way back in standards and safety.

Dawn Till Dusk
(☎ 01-418286, ⓔ dtd@wlink.com.np) In the Kathmandu Guest House compound, Dawn Till Dusk runs tours at prices similar to HMB's.

Himalayan Mountain Bikes (HMB)
Kathmandu: (☎ 01-437437, ⓔ bike@hmb.wlink.com.np) The Thamel office is at the entrance to Northfield Cafe and is known as Adventure Centre Nepal.
Pokhara: (☎ 061-23240) This company pioneered mountain biking in Nepal, and has operated since 1998. HMB offers a full range of tours ranging in length from one day (around US$30) to three or four days ($US45 to US$50 per day), up to 21-day fully catered trips (around US$80 per day). It also offers customised group tours.

TOURING ROUTES

The Scar Road from Kathmandu

The Scar Road can be considered one of the Kathmandu Valley's classic mountain bike adventures. It's got the lot and offers a challenging ride for all levels of experience. It's a 70km round trip which for the average bicyclist will take around six hours.

Leaving Kathmandu, head towards Balaju, on the Ring Rd only 2km north of Thamel, and onto the Trisuli Bazaar road. At this point you start to climb out of the valley on a sealed road towards Kakani, 23km away at an altitude of 2073m. The road twists and turns at an even gradient past the Nagarjun Forest Reserve, which provides the road with a leaf canopy. Once you're through the initial pass and out of the valley, the road continues north-west and offers a view of endless terraced fields to your left. On reaching the summit of the ridge, take a turn right (at a clearly marked T-junction), instead of continuing down to Trisuli Bazaar. (If you go too far you reach a checkpoint just 100m beyond.) At this point magnificent views of the Ganesh *himal* (range with permanent snow) provide the inspiration required to complete the remaining 4km of steep and deteriorating blacktop to the crown of the hill just past the Tara Gaon Kakani Hotel in Kakani, for a well deserved rest.

It is possible to spend the night at this hotel, or at one of the basic village inns, so as to take advantage of sunrise and sunset from this great spot. (See Kakani in the Around the Kathmandu Valley chapter for details.)

After admiring the view from the hotel's garden terrace or a road-side tea shop, descend for just 30m beyond the gate and take the first left on to a 4WD track. This track will take you through the popular picnic grounds frequented on Saturday by Kathmandu locals. Continue through in an easterly direction towards Shivapuri. The track narrows after a few kilometres near a metal gate on your left. Through the gate, you are faced with some rough stone steps and then a 10-minute push/carry up and over the hilltop to an army checkpoint. Here it's necessary for foreigners to pay a reserve entry fee of Rs 300. Exit the army camp, turning right where the Scar Road is clearly visible in front of you. You are now positioned at the day's highest point – approximately 2200m.

Taking the right-hand track you start to descend dramatically along an extremely steep, rutted single trail with several water crossings. The trail is literally cut into the side of the hill, with sharp drops on the right that challenge a rider's skill and nerve. As you hurtle along, take time to admire the view of the sprawling Kathmandu Valley below – it's one of the best. Maybe stop to look!

The trail widens, after one long gnarly climb before the saddle, then it's relatively flat through the protected Shivapuri watershed area. This beautiful mountain biking section lasts for nearly 25km before the trail descends into the valley down a 7km spiral on a gravel road. This joins a paved road, to the relief of jarred wrists, at Budhanilkantha, where you can buy refreshments. Take a moment to see the Sleeping Vishnu just up on your left at the main intersection. From here it's back to civilisation as the sealed road descends gently for the remaining 15km back into the bustle of Kathmandu via Lazimpat.

Kathmandu to Dhulikhel

This two- or three-day circular tour takes you through a classic selection of valley sights. The first day from Kathmandu to Dhulikhel, an interesting hilltop town at 1500m, is 32km; the second day is 58km.

From Thamel, head out of town in the direction of Pashupatinath and once on the Ring Rd proceed towards Tribhuvan Airport.

Proceed along the northern fringe of the Pashupatinath complex, and look for the trail running to the northern end of the airport runway. From the north-east corner of the runway, ask for directions to the 'Pepsi' and from there head almost due east into the town of Bhaktapur.

If you stay on the Ring Rd instead, follow the western boundary of the airport past the very end of the airport runway to the south. Here the road descends just after branching left followed by a straight run through to the edge of Bhaktapur and the beginning of the Arniko Hwy. A basic map of the area will assist you here.

The Arniko Hwy was built by the Chinese and carries an enormous amount of traffic, including the dilapidated Chinese-donated electric trolleybuses. The minor roadway running parallel to the highway to the north, and into Bhaktapur, will be a much nicer route. The nicer ride along the old road takes you via the village of Sano Thimi (Small Thimi), which is famous for its pottery and handicrafts. To find the old road, take the first left off the main highway onto a narrower sealed road that heads back towards the airport on its east side. At the next main intersection (1.8km on), turn right before continuing on to complete the 16km to the medieval town of Bhaktapur.

Mountain bikes are a great way to explore Bhaktapur's narrow streets. After time in this magical past kingdom, continue east. Facing Bhaktapur's 30m-high Nyatapola Temple, in Taumadhi Tole, take the exit from the square on your right-hand side. This narrow street twists and turns on its way out of the city. After leaving the brick-paved streets, join a tarmac road and then continue straight on, bearing south-east.

The tarmac ends and the road continues in the form of a compacted track towards the rural village of Nala. This route is an excellent alternative to the Arniko Hwy and takes you through a beautiful corner of the valley. The track climbs gradually, and becomes progressively steeper near the top. A gentle 3km downhill gradient brings you to rural Nala with its pretty temples.

From Nala head right, via the Bhagvati Temple, and continue for a couple of kilometres to Banepa. Turn left and continue along the paved main road for a further 5km to Dhulikhel, which is visible on your right-hand side as you approach, after passing through a truck and bus checkpoint. This completes the first day.

For more information on Dhulikhel, see the Around the Kathmandu Valley chapter.

Dhulikhel to Namobuddha & Kathmandu Namobuddha is a popular destination from Dhulikhel, and offers superb trail riding with spectacular views of the Himalaya. To start your ride from Dhulikhel's main square, which has a small tank, head south-east along a paved road in the direction of the Kali Temple set on a hillside above the town. The paved road ends and starts to climb the hill in the form of a rough 4WD track. The track twists its way up a testing 3km to reach the temple, which is a spectacular viewpoint. From the temple you can see the track snake its way across the terraced landscape.

Continue along the track, which provides fun downhill runs before it starts a 5km climb towards Namobuddha. After completing the climb, descend for a short while until you reach a T-junction at Kavre village. Turn right and Namobuddha will appear shortly after on the left, so completing a 12km journey from Dhulikhel. Refreshments are available in the small shops near the stupa, which provides an interesting place to rest before continuing to Panauti. It's worth doing the 15-minute walk to the monastery above the stupa. The stupa is frequented by many Buddhists and Hindus alike as a major pilgrimage point of the Kathmandu Valley.

Leaving Namobuddha you continue down the track, which takes you through a series of turns – a great mountain bike descent. The track finally drops to the bottom of the valley and undulates for 14km from the village of Shanku to the historic town of Panauti. This ancient Newari town has some of the oldest temples in Nepal – cross the footbridge if you want to explore further. (See the Around the Kathmandu Valley chapter for information about Panauti.)

Leaving Panauti you join a paved road that's a flat run along the valley to the main road at Banepa. From this point you can return to Kathmandu, 26km via the Arniko Hwy, or ride the 3.5km back to Dhulikhel and then continue to Kathmandu, thus you will have completed a 58km circuit.

Dhulikhel to Kodari

From Dhulikhel, it is possible to continue 82km along the Arniko Hwy to the Friendship Bridge that marks the Tibetan border at Kodari (1500m). This is a three- or (more likely) four-day return trip from Dhulikhel.

Dhulikhel to Lamosangu From Dhulikhel you immediately begin an adrenaline-filled descent (almost 900m) into the Panchkhal Valley, on a slick sealed road, with majestic views of the Himalaya adding to a thrilling ride. A couple of short climbs interrupt the descent as you cycle to Dolalghat, a popular starting point for Sun Kosi rafting trips. On the downhill watch for overtaking buses on the blind corners.

From Dolalghat (60km from Kathmandu) there is a short 2km climb, and after 20km you cross the bridge over the Indrawati River and climb out of the Panchkhal Valley to join the Bhote Kosi, on your left, which you follow for the rest of the journey. Owing to landslide damage there is a mixture of surfaced and unsurfaced roads. Traffic can be quite heavy along this section. This is a delightful on-road trip with interesting sights, and is also the road to Jiri, a popular starting point for the Everest Base Camp trek. The road climbs at a gentle gradient as it follows the river.

A couple of kilometres past the turn-off to Jiri is Lamosangu, 27km from Dolalghat. Lamosangu provides a far more pleasant place to spend the night than Barabise due to the fact that fewer buses stop here. About here you have several options in choosing your next overnight stop. Your choice will depend largely on your progress on the bicycle. Lamosangu is 87km from Kathmandu while Barabise is 90km. A much more upmarket destination is ***Borderlands resort***, a farther 13km from Barabise, on a dirt road. Many find the riverside safari camp a high point of this ride. A few kilometres farther is the ***Last Resort***, another good spot to stay. See the Arniko Highway Beyond Dhulikhel section in the Around the Kathmandu Valley chapter for more on this whole area.

Lamosangu to Kodari & Tatopani The next day's ride continues past Barabise where the road changes into a compacted dirt track with a top layer of dust. Recent roadwork along here has improved things, but still the dust cover is transformed into choking clouds when buses pass; in wet weather it all turns to mud. Care should be taken during heavy rains as this section of the road is particularly susceptible to landslides. The valley's sides begin to steepen and it gradually changes into a beautiful gorge with spectacular waterfalls.

The track climbs practically the entire 27km to Tatopani and a farther 5km to Kodari at the edge of the Friendship Bridge and the border with Tibet . As it climbs from Tatopani to the Friendship Bridge, this section of the ride is probably the most beautiful. It is possible (but dependent on border guards) to cycle beyond the bridge and climb a rough and steep track to the Chinese customs checkpoint (8km), just outside of Khasa, which is visible from the bridge. It should be possible to return as far as Borderlands or Lamosangu the same day, taking advantage of a mainly downhill ride. Otherwise, you can stay in Tatopani and visit the hot springs there. Again, see the Around the Kathmandu Valley chapter for information on accommodation.

Tatopani to Dhulikhel The ride back to Dhulikhel is 43km and includes the long climb out of Dolalghat, for which you should allow plenty of time. An option here is to jump on a local bus with your bicycle. Depending on how you feel after the climb, you can stay in Dhulikhel or complete the trip by returning the 32km to Kathmandu.

The Rajpath from Kathmandu

The Tribhuvan Hwy (or Rajpath as it is popularly known) was the first highway to connect Kathmandu with the rest of the world. The road switchbacks 150 spectacular kilometres from Kathmandu to Hetauda. Most traffic from the Terai and India uses the highway that runs between Narayanghat and Mugling which, although longer, is actually quicker. The Rajpath has a great mixture of light traffic and magnificent scenery, culminating at Daman with an incomparable Himalayan view. It is a classic ride over a 2488m pass on a rough sealed road.

The ride begins on the Kathmandu-Pokhara (Prithvi) Hwy, which gives the only access to the valley. After leaving the valley, the highway descends to Naubise, at the bottom of the Mahesh Khola valley, 27km from Kathmandu, where the Rajpath intersects with the Kathmandu-Pokhara (Prithvi) Hwy. Take the Rajpath, which forks to the left and is well signposted for Hetauda. Start a 35km climb to Tistung at a height of 2030m. You climb through terraced fields, carved into steep hillsides. On reaching the pass at Tistung you descend for 7km into the beautiful Palung Valley before the final steep 9km climb to Daman, at a height of 2322m.

This day's ride (almost all climbing) takes between six and nine hours in the saddle. Thus, with an early start it is possible to stay in Daman, which will give you the thrill of waking up to the broadest Himalayan panorama Nepal has to offer. On a clear morning you can see from Dhaulagiri to Everest, a view worth the pedal. The following day the road climbs a farther 3km to the top of the pass, at 2488m. At this point, you could savour the very real prospect of an exhilarating 2300m descent in 60km!

As you descend towards the Indian plains, laid out before you to the south, notice the contrast with the side you climbed, as the south side is lush and semitropical. With innumerable switchbacks and a bit of speed you should watch out for the occasional bus and truck looming around a blind corner. The road eventually flattens out after the right turn to cross a newly constructed bridge and the first main river crossing. The rest of the journey is a gently undulating route alongside a river; a farther 10km brings you to Hetauda. (See Hetauda in the Terai chapter for details on accommodation.) After a night's rest can continue along the Rajpath towards India or turn right at the statue of the king in the centre of town and head towards Royal Chitwan National Park.

Hetauda to Narayanghat & Mugling

Hetauda is just to the east of Royal Chitwan National Park, which has a wide selection of accommodation, both in the park and in the town of Sauraha, as well as a great range of activities. See Royal Chitwan National Park in The Terai chapter for more details. You are prohibited from riding inside the park, but are allowed to ride directly to your resort.

This is vastly different riding from that of Kathmandu, or the other rides described in this chapter, and in the summer months (say May to September) it can be a very hot ride. From Hetauda, as you cycle along the flat, smooth road towards Narayanghat enjoying the lush subtropical scenery, watch for resort signposts on your left. Machan Wildlife Resort's turn-off is 40km from Hetauda, and the resort is reached after a farther 4km of beautiful trail riding with three river crossings. Alternatively, a farther 23km from the Machan turn-off brings you to the Chitwan Jungle Lodge turn-off. A farther 14km brings you to Tadi Bazaar and the turn-off for Sauraha, reached by an interesting 6km 4WD track.

Narayanghat, 20km from Sauraha on the banks of the Narayani River, gives a choice of further routes. From here you can return to Kathmandu or Pokhara via Mugling. Although some may say this section from Narayanghat to Mugling is best avoided on a bicycle because of heavy bus and truck traffic, it is nonetheless a very beautiful section of road to ride, and traffic during many times of the day can be light. The alternative is to catch a bus. If you're heading to Pokhara (96km) it may be a good idea to miss the busy highway between Mugling and Pokhara by catching a bus in Mugling. Here, the road is much improved and vehicles travel a lot faster in what are still quite dusty conditions.

Kathmandu to Pokhara via the Mahendra Highway

A surprisingly large number of bicyclists show an interest in this ride. No doubt the scenery of great Himalayan vistas, the Trisuli River, quaint townships, numerous bridge and river crossings and changing landscapes add to its attraction. That fact that you can escape a bus ride and arrive in Pokhara safely on your own two wheels is a big plus. The downside is that you are almost guaranteed to see the remains of a truck or bus crash any time you travel this road. The message is pretty obvious: Take care on this notorious stretch of road.

The bike ride begins on the Kathmandu-Pokhara (Prithvi) Hwy, which gives the only access to the valley. After leaving the valley at Thankot, the highway descends to Naubise, at the bottom of the Mahesh Khola Valley, 27km from Kathmandu.

Following the thrilling if not hair-raising descent (watching for oil slicks after on-the-spot truck repairs), you are on your way for either one long day or two comfortable days of biking to Pokhara. Mugling is about the halfway mark at 120km. It's is a largely downhill run from Kathmandu and so you can reach here comfortably within four to five hours. At Mugling you'll find all the food and supplies you need plus accommodation for an overnight stay. There are also lots of small food stops along the way at some very scenic spots.

To make Pokhara in a day takes around 12 to 14 hours of steady biking so an early start is needed if you decide to go for it. It's a good idea to calculate the daylight hours available during the season you make this trip. Approaching and entering Pokhara after dark is not advised.

From Mugling you keep to the right as you exit the town and within 300m you will cross the Trisuli River bridge. The second half of your journey to Pokhara is mostly uphill but still offers some excellent downhills. From Mugling you have an overall altitude gain of about 550m over 96km. Again there are numerous roadside cafes and food stops to keep the carbohydrates supplied. The final approach to Pokhara, with the Annapurna Ranges as a backdrop, certainly adds some inspiration after a long day of biking.

Around Pokhara

Pokhara is famous for its beauty, relaxed atmosphere, spectacular views of the Annapurnas and Manaslu himal, as well as the splendour of the unclimbed Machhapuchhare. The surrounding area provides excellent opportunities for trail riding around lakes and rivers and towards the mountains. The riding, however, is less consistent or contiguous than that around Kathmandu, and this means shorter trips. The area is also less populated than the Kathmandu Valley, so although there are fewer trails, villages and temples to explore, the rides are more tranquil and the traffic is hardly noticeable.

Pokhara to Sarangkot & Naudanda

The ride to Sarangkot, visible directly north from Pokhara Lakeside, provides an excellent, challenging day trip. This is in fact the bicycle leg of the Annapurna Triathlon.

Leave early and ride along Lakeside (towards the mountains) to the last main intersection and sealed road. Turn right; this is the road that returns to central Pokhara. After 2km you turn left and continue straight on (north). This intersection is the Zero Km road marker. After a farther 2km there is a smaller sealed road to the left, signposted as the road to Sarangkot. This winds its way along a ridge into Sarangkot, providing outstanding views of the Himalaya, which seems close enough to reach out and touch. After 6km a few tea shops mark a welcome refreshment stop just where the stone steps mark the walking trail to the summit. From here it's a 4WD track that closely hugs the edge of the mountain overlooking Phewa Tal. Continue until you join a Y-intersection which doubles back sharply to the right and makes the final climb to Sarangkot Point.

From this point you could also continue straight ahead, riding the narrower motorcycle trails leading to Kaski and Naudanda. After the Sarangkot turn-off the trail soon begins to climb to Kaski, towards the hill immediately in front of you. The section to Kaski takes around 30 to 60 minutes, and you may need to push your bicycle on the steeper section near the crown of the hill. Over the top you follow the trail through to Naudanda. You are now at around 1590m, having gained around 840m altitude from Pokhara. The trail is rocky in parts and will test your equipment to the extreme, so don't consider riding this trail on a cheap hire bicycle.

The view from the ridge at Naudanda is spectacularly beautiful. Dhaulagiri, Manaslu, the Annapurnas and Machhapuchhare create a classic Himalayan panorama, especially on a cool, clear morning. To the south you can look down over Pokhara and Phewa Tal.

Naudanda to Beni & Pokhara Having reached Naudanda from Sarangkot Point you have the choice of continuing west or east. Heading west, the sealed Pokhara-Baglung Hwy continues along the spine of the ridge and connects Pokhara with Lumle (a popular starting point for trekking in the Annapurnas). If you choose to head towards Lumle and on to Beni you have a mostly downhill run on sealed roads except for the last 10km into Beni. Riding on to Birethanti may be a good option if Beni is too far. This is an initial 5km up followed by a 20km switchback downhill. There are nice lodges in Birethanti (walk in from Birat) for an overnight stop before you return to Pokhara.

From Naudanda it is 32km to Pokhara. You can either return via the Sarangkot trail (described earlier in this chapter) or follow the highway back. The latter starts with a twisting 6km descent into the Madi Khola Valley. The highway has an excellent asphalt surface and descends gently as it follows the river, allowing an enjoyable coast almost all the way back to Pokhara.

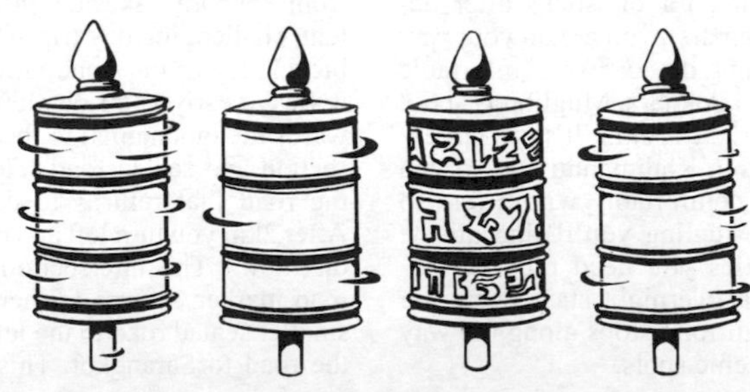

Rafting & Kayaking

The bulk of this chapter was researched and written by David Allardice, the owner and operator of Ultimate Descents International, a company that organises rafting and kayaking journeys in Nepal. Some of the information under Planning was written by Ravi Fry; it was updated by David Allardice.

Nepal has earned the reputation of being one of the best places in the world for rafting and kayaking. Its mountain scenery has drawn trekkers as well as climbers for many years; these same mountains shape an incredible variety of white-water challenges for paddlers.

A series of the world's most outstanding river journeys are found here, ranging from steep, adrenaline-charged mountain streams to classic big-volume wilderness expeditions. The combination of spectacular rivers, mountain scenery and a rich cultural heritage makes Nepal an obvious river-runner's destination.

No other country has such a choice of trips on wild rivers with warm water, a subtropical climate (with no bugs!) and huge beaches with white sand that are ideal for camping.

There has been a continuous increase in the number of kayakers coming to Nepal and it is justifiably recognised as a mecca for boating. Some companies offer trips that cater specifically to kayakers, where you get to explore the river with rafts carrying all your gear and food, and often camp near choice play spots.

The opportunities for kayak expeditions are exceptional. Apart from the rivers discussed later in this chapter, of note and at the right flows are the Modhi Kola, Madhi Khola, Tamba Kosi, Karnali headwaters, Thuli Bheri, Balephi Khola and tributaries of the Tamur.

PLANNING

Anyone who is seriously interested in rafting and kayaking, and especially anyone contemplating a private expedition, should get hold of *White Water Nepal*, an excellent guidebook by Peter Knowles, with David Allardice as the consultant on rafting. It should be possible to get copies of the book in Kathmandu. It has very detailed information on river trips, with 60 maps, river profiles and hydrographs, plus advice on equipment and health, in short it has all the information a prospective river-runner could want.

Anyone who plans to raft or kayak independently should contact local rafting companies to get some up-to-date information. Himalayan rivers are dynamic, and rivers and their rapids change every monsoon.

Highlights

- Winding along the Sun Kosi through the beautiful Mahabharat Range in eastern Nepal
- Journeying down the Karnali, the longest and largest river in Nepal, with awesome challenging rapids and plenty of wildlife
- Having a full-on adrenaline rush rafting the Bhote Kosi, the steepest river rafted in Nepal
- Sharing a peaceful moonrise over a picturesque river with your friendly fellow river-runners

When to Go

The best times for rafting are September to early December, and March to early June. From early September to early October, and May to June, the rivers can be extremely high with monsoon run-off. Any expeditions attempted at this time require a very experienced rafting company with an intimate knowledge of the river and strong teams, as times of high flows are potentially the most dangerous times to be on a river.

From mid-October onwards the weather is settled, and this is one of the most popular times to raft. In December many of the rivers become too cold to enjoy unless you have a wetsuit, and the days are short with the start of winter – the time to consider shorter trips. The summer season from

March to early June has long hot days and lower water flows to begin with, which generally means the rapids aren't as powerful. The rivers rise again in May with the pre-monsoon storms and some snow-melt, then it's high-water time again.

From June to August the monsoon rains arrive. The rivers carry 10 times their low-water flows, and can flood with 60 to 80 times as much water. High flows obviously make rivers much more difficult. Few rivers should be attempted at flood levels.There is a definite relationship between volume, gradient and difficulty. River levels can fluctuate dramatically at any time, although as a general rule weather patterns in Nepal are quite stable.

Learning to Raft

For many people a rafting trip in Nepal will be their first white-water experience. There are many different kinds of rafting trips, and it is important to select a river that suits your interests and ability. The style of trip, the difficulty of the river and the length of time you have are all factors to consider.

Any raft can be paddled, or rigged with an oar frame and rowed. With an oar frame the guide normally sits in the middle and rows, while the other passengers enjoy the scenery – and hold on through the rapids. With a paddle raft the guide normally sits at the back calling instructions and steering, while the crew provides the power. Most active people prefer the teamwork and group participation of paddle rafting. With a strong team a paddle raft can probably run harder rapids than an oar raft, and the sense of achievement cannot be compared.

Learning to Kayak

Nepal is an ideal place to learn to kayak and there are quite a few learner kayak clinics on offer with different companies. Teaching yourself to kayak is fraught with problems. At the very best you'll learn horrendous techniques that will yield little satisfaction and will probably have to be relearned later. At the very worst you'll hurt yourself. A qualified instructor is highly recommended.

In terms of learning possibilities and the communication required in teaching, the best instruction clinics tend to be staffed with both Western and Nepalese instructors. Kayak clinics normally take about four days, which gives you time to get a good grounding in the basics of kayaking, safety and river dynamics.

Permits

Rafters and kayakers are not required to have rafting permits for certain rivers. There's a list of rivers where rafting is permitted (including all the rivers in the following section), but this is constantly being expanded, so it's best to check the situation when you arrive.

Equipment

If you go on an organised rafting trip everything should be arranged for you. Normally, all specialised equipment is supplied. Quality equipment is important, for both safety and comfort. Modern self-bailing rafts are essential. Good life jackets and helmets are mandatory on any white-water trip. Modern plastic and alloy paddles are preferable to locally made wooden ones. The roll-top dry bags will keep your gear dry even if the raft flips, and waterproof camera containers will allow you to take photos all the way down the river. The company should also supply tents. Ask how old the equipment is.

Usually you will only need light clothing, with a slightly warmer change for nights. A swimsuit, a sunhat, sunscreen, and light tennis shoes or sandals that will stay on your feet are all necessary, but can be bought in Kathmandu. For overnight trips a sleeping bag is necessary, but these can easily be hired. Temperatures on some rivers vary, so check with the company you are booking with – they will recommend what to bring. In winter you will definitely need thermal clothing for running rivers.

Most airlines will carry short kayaks on the same basis as surfboards or bicycles; there's no excess baggage charge, so long as you are within the weight limits. If you are a group, negotiate a deal at the time of booking. If there are only one or two of you, just turn up, put all your bulky light gear in the kayak, with heavy items in your carry-on luggage, and smile sweetly! If you phone the airline in advance they have to quote the rule book and start talking air cargo, which is expensive.

SAFETY

Safety is the most important part of any river trip. Safety is a marriage of the right technical skills, teamwork, planning and local knowledge. Unfortunately, there are no minimum safety conditions enforced by any official body in Nepal. This makes it very important to choose a professional rafting and kayaking company. It seems that not all rafting companies are created equal.

If you choose an organised trip, ask what first-aid gear, supplies, spare parts and repair equipment are carried. On a river it's important that the guides are capable of dealing with any situation that occurs, more so if it is a long wilderness expedition. Many a trip has gone astray because of lack of preparation, not having the right equipment, or insufficient training to deal with the variety of situations that can arise.

This section outlines some of the factors you should consider in ensuring a safe trip, and is based on the experience of many international guides. For more information on choosing a safe company, see Organised Tours later in this chapter.

River Grading System

Rivers are graded for difficulty on an international scale from class 1 to 6, with class 1 defined as easy-moving water with few obstacles, and class 6 as nearly impossible to negotiate and a hazard to life. Anyone who is in reasonable physical shape and isn't afraid of water can safely go on rivers graded class 1 to 3. For more difficult and exciting class 4 rivers, you should be active, confident in water, and have rafting experience. Class 5 is a very large step up from class 4; expect long continuous sections of powerful white water, strenuous paddling, steep constricted channels, powerful waves and the possibility of overturning a raft. Swimming in a class 5 rapid poses a significant risk.

Nepal has a reputation for extremely difficult white water, which is well justified at times of high water flow (during the monsoon), but at most flows there are many class 3 and 4 rivers. There are also many easier class 1 and 2 rivers where you can float along admiring the scenery and running a few small rapids.

Raft Numbers

There should be a minimum of two rafts per trip. If anyone falls out of a raft the second raft can help with the rescue (the victim is known as a 'swimmer'). In higher water, three rafts are safer than two. Many experts also agree that one or two safety kayakers can replace the second raft, though the kayakers need to be white-water professionals with the training, skill and experience not only to run the most difficult rapids on the river, but also to be able to perform rescues in these rapids. Kayakers may also teach you to kayak on the easier sections of some rivers. Among safety kayakers, there is no substitute for skill; having more kayakers along does not necessarily mean a safer trip if these people are not capable and experienced. Good safety kayakers are invaluable on steeper rivers where they can often get to a swimmer in places no other craft could manage a rescue.

Check how many people have booked and paid for a trip, as well as the maximum number that will be taken.

Raft Guides

The most important aspects of rafting safety are both the skills and judgement of the raft guides and the teamwork of the group on the trip. The person leading the trip must be a qualified guide with a minimum of 50 days of rafting experience. This person should also have done at least five previous trips on the river on which they are guiding. All raft guides should have done the river before.

If possible, speak with the guide who will lead the trip to get an impression of the people you will be spending time with and the type of trip they run. Ask them about their previous experience. Overseas experience or training allows the guides to keep up with the latest advances and safety training. Kayaking experience adds additional depth to a guide's skills. All guides should have a current first aid certificate and be trained in cardiopulmonary resuscitation.

Many Western river guides have worked in Nepal, shared ideas, strengthened local skills and improved the standard of trips. They pioneered many of the runs that have now become classics. There is rightly a strong sense of pride among Nepalese companies and guides. Local Nepalese companies now run trips with only Nepalese guides. Employment of local guides should be encouraged, but international safety standards should not be compromised. Himalayan rivers are some of the most powerful rivers run commercially in the world, and expedition guides need to be of the highest standards. The standard of the best Nepalese guides is world class, but among the worst guides it is not what it should be. Many guides do not have river-rescue or first-aid qualifications yet they are leading multiday wilderness trips in Nepal.

There are some international companies running trips in Nepal that supply their own experienced Western leaders who run trips in association with local guides.

On the River

Your guide should give you a comprehensive safety talk and paddle training before you launch off downstream. If you don't get this it is probably cause for concern.

- Listen to what your guide is telling you. Always wear your life jacket in rapids. Wear your helmet whenever your guide tells you, and make sure that both the helmet and jacket are properly adjusted and fitted.
- Keep your feet and arms inside the raft. If the raft hits a rock or wall and you are in the way, the best you'll escape with is a laceration.
- If you do swim in a rapid, get into the 'white-water swimming position'. You should be on your back, with your feet downstream and up where you can see them. Hold on to your paddle as this will make you more visible. Relax and breathe when you aren't going through waves. Then turn over and swim at the end of the rapid when the water becomes calmer. Self rescue is the best rescue.

ORGANISED TOURS

There are about 100 companies in Kathmandu claiming to be rafting and kayaking operators. A few are well-established companies with good reputations, and the rest are newer companies, often formed by guides breaking away and starting their own operations, and sometimes people with very little experience of rivers. Although these new companies can be enthusiastic and good, they can also be shoestring operations that may not have adequate equipment and staff. Most of the small travel agencies simply sell trips on commission; often they have no real idea about the details of what they are selling and are only interested in getting bums on seats. To further confuse the situation, there are also sometimes complicated subcontracting arrangements between companies. It is immensely preferable to deal with the rafting company directly.

If a group has recently returned from a trip, speak to its members. This will give you reliable information about the quality of equipment, the guides, the food and the transportation. Question the company about things such as how groups get to and from the river, the number of hours spent paddling or rowing, where the camps are set up (near villages?), food provided (rafting promotes a very healthy appetite), who does the cooking and work around the camp, the cooking fuel used (wood?), what happens to rubbish, hygiene precautions, and night-time activities. Many companies have a photo file or video in their office which can give you an impression of the equipment, safety and how trips are operated. Ask a lot of questions.

If your time is limited you may choose to book a trip before you leave home. However, all the operators accept bookings in Kathmandu. Booking in Kathmandu gives you the opportunity to meet your fellow rafters and guides before you make a commitment. Trips depart on a regular basis (there's at least one long trip a week during the season), and the best companies will refer you to a friendly competitor if they don't have any suitable dates.

Rafting trips vary from quite luxurious trips where you are rowed down the river and staff do everything for you (pitch camp, cook and so on), to trips where you participate in the running of the expedition including pitching tents, loading the rafts and helping with the cooking. The quality of the rafting equipment is another variable, and can make a huge difference to the comfort and safety of participants.

Trips range in price from US$15 to US$60 a day, and generally you get what you pay for. At US$15 you don't get much at all. It is better to pay a bit more and have a good, safe trip than to save US$100 and have a lousy, dangerous trip. Bear in mind that trips in Nepal are generally less than half the cost of similar trips in the USA, so in relative terms all the prices are extremely reasonable. If you plan to do a more difficult trip it's particularly important to choose a company that has the experience, skills and equipment to run a safe and exciting expedition.

With the constant change in rafting companies it's difficult to make individual recommendations; the fact that a company is not recommended here does not necessarily mean it will not deliver an excellent trip. Nonetheless, the following companies have been recommended for their professionalism.

Prices for rafting tours range from US$30 to US$60 a day.

Equator Expeditions (☎ 01-354169, ⓔ equator@mos.com.np) Thamel, Kathmandu; also in Pokhara. Specialises in long participatory rafting and kayaking trips as well as kayak instruction.

Himalayan Encounters (☎ 01-417426, ⓔ rafting&trekking@himenco.wlink.com.np) Kathmandu Guest House compound, Thamel, Kathmandu; also in Pokhara. This company is associated with Encounter Overland, and has earned a solid reputation through many Trisuli and Sun Kosi trips.

Himalayan Wonders (☎ 01-426720, ⓔ himalayan@wonders.wlink.com.np) Namche Bazaar Bldg, Thamel, Kathmandu. This reliable company is at the budget end of rafting.

Raging River Runner (☎ 01-430257, ⓔ ragriver@ccsl.com.np) Jyatha, greater Thamel. A recommended budget company.

Ultimate Descents International (☎ 01-439525, ⓔ ultimate_descents@xtra.co.nz) Contact The Last Resort office, Thamel. David Allardice's Ultimate Descents International specialises in rafting and kayaking trips and kayak instruction with a combination of Western leaders and Nepalese guides. Check out its Web site: www.ultimatedescents.com

Ultimate Descents Nepal (☎ 01-419295, ⓔ info@udnepal.com) Adventure Centre Nepal, Thamel. Specialises in long participatory rafting trips as well as kayak instruction.

Ultimate Rivers (☎/fax 01-439526, ⓔ rivers@ultimate.wlink.com.np) Next to the Kathmandu Guest House. Ultimate Rivers specialises in participatory rafting and kayak instruction.

There has been some confusion over the name Ultimate Descents. The name Ultimate Descents and the company's logo are registered and protected worldwide by Ultimate Descents International. Ultimate Descents Nepal is a local Nepali company. Both companies have solid reputations, but these two companies should not be confused.

CHOOSING A RIVER

Before you decide what river you'll do, you need to decide what it is you want out of your river trip. There are trips available from two to 12 days on different rivers, all offering dramatically different experiences.

The Future of River-Running in Nepal

In the past 15 years a number of rivers have stopped flowing freely because of construction of hydroelectric projects. Nepal sees hydro development as a means of stimulating growth and the economy. If this is done responsibly, with consensus among the river-running community and other concerned parties, then there will still be many world-class river runs. But under the present government this may not be the case. A new river project on the Marsyangdi will take water out at Philesangu and drop it back in at Bhote Odar, which will make the Marsyangdi a series of shorter sections. There are projects planned for the Karnali, Arun and Bhote Kosi Rivers. If there is no cohesive action soon to preserve some of Nepal's rivers for future generations, the future of rafting and kayaking here does not look bright.

First off, don't believe that just because it's a river it's going to be wet'n'wild. Some rivers, such as the Sun Kosi, which is an incredible full-on white-water trip in September and October, are basically flat and uneventful in the low water of early spring. On the flip side, early spring can be a superb time to raft rivers such as the Marsyangdi or Bhote Kosi, which would be suicidal during high flows. The Karnali is probably the only river that offers continually challenging white water at all flows, though in the high-water months of September and May, it's significantly more challenging than in the low-water months.

There is much more to rivers than just white water, but the climate in Nepal being what it is, many companies will promote whichever river they're running at the time as the pinnacle of white-water excitement. Not all companies run all rivers, especially the more technical and demanding ones, and some companies shouldn't be running any rivers at all, but such is life. Buyer beware.

Longer trips such as the Sun Kosi (in the autumn), the Karnali and the Tamur offer some real heart-thumping white water with the incredible journeying aspect of a long river trip. With more time on the river, things are more relaxed, relationships progress at a more natural pace, and memories become entrenched for a lifetime. Long after the white water has blurred into one white-knuckled thrill ride, the memories of a moonrise over the river and the friends you inevitably make will remain. River trips are much more than gravity powered roller-coaster rides; they're journeys traversed on very special highways. For many people they become a way of life.

If a long trip is simply impossible because of financial or time constraints, don't undervalue the shorter ones. Anyone who has ever taken a paddle-raft or kayak down the Bhote Kosi (at any flow) would be hard pressed to find anything better to do with two days in Nepal. There are also medium-length options which are perfect for people who want to experience river journeying but have limited time.

This section describes the main commercially rafted rivers in Nepal. It is by no means a complete list, and private boaters who have the experience, equipment and desire to run their own expeditions are best advised to consult the aforementioned guidebook, *White Water Nepal*.

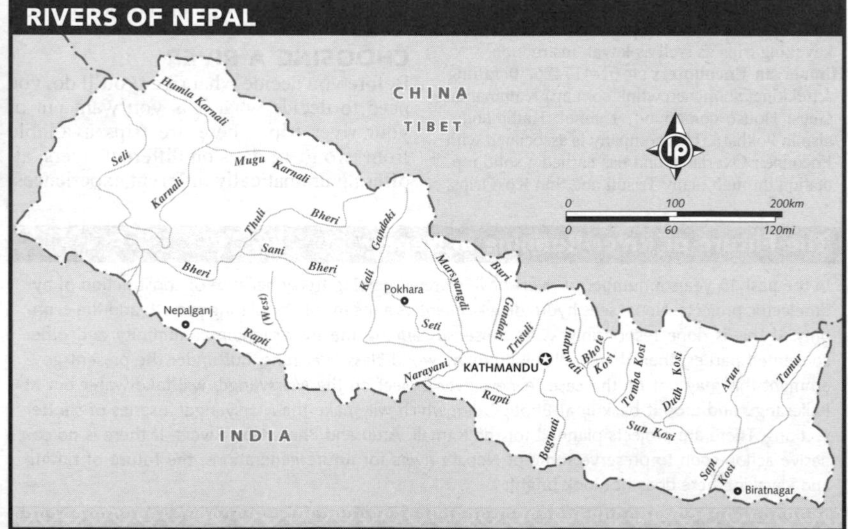

Karnali

The Karnali is a gem, combining a short trek with some of the prettiest canyons and jungle scenery in Nepal. Most experienced river people who have boated the Karnali find it one of the best all-round river trips they've ever done. In high water, the Karnali is a serious commitment, combining *huge*, though fairly straightforward, rapids with a seriously remote location. At low water the Karnali is still a fantastic trip. The rapids become smaller, but the steeper gradient and constricted channel keep it interesting.

Being the longest and largest river in all of Nepal, the Karnali drains a huge and well-developed catchment. Spring snow-melts can drive the river up dramatically in a matter of hours – as the river rises the difficulty increases exponentially. The river flows through some steep and constricted canyons where the rapids are close together, giving little opportunity to correct for potential mistakes. Pick your company carefully.

The trip starts with a long but interesting bus ride to the remote far west of Nepal. If you're allergic to bus rides, it's possible to fly to Nepalganj and cut the bus transport down to about four hours on the way over, and two hours on the way back. From the hill town of Surkhet a lovely two-day trek brings you to Sauli, from where it is a two-hour trek to the Karnali River. Once you start on the Karnali it's 180km to the next road access at Chisopani, on the northern border of the Royal Bardia National Park.

The river section takes about seven days, giving plenty of time to explore some of the side canyons and waterfalls which come into the river valley. Better-run trips also include a layover day, where the expedition stays at the same camp site for two nights. The combination of long bus rides and trekking puts some people off, but anyone who has ever done the trip raves about it. Finish with a visit to the Royal Bardia National Park at the end for what is an unbeatable combination.

Sun Kosi

This is the longest river trip offered in Nepal, traversing 270km through the beautiful Mahabharat Range on its meandering way from the put-in at Dolalghat to the take-out at Chatara, which is far down on the Gangetic plain. It's quite an experience to begin a river trip just three hours out of Kathmandu, barely 60km from the Tibetan border, and end the trip looking down the hot, dusty gun barrel of the north Indian plain just nine or 10 days later. Because it's one of the easiest trips logistically, it's also one of the least expensive for the days you spend on a river.

The Sun Kosi starts off fairly relaxed, with only class 2 and small class 3 rapids to warm up on during the first couple of days. Savvy guides will take this opportunity to get teams working together with precision, as on the third day the rapids become more powerful and frequent, and those on high-water trips find themselves astonished at just how big a wave in a river can get.

While the lower sections of large-volume rivers are usually rather flat, the Sun Kosi reserves some of its biggest and best rapids for the last days. At the right flow it's an incredible combination of white water, scenery, villages, and quiet and introspective evenings along what many people consider to be one of the world's great 10 classic river journeys.

Upper Sun Kosi

Not to be confused with the Bhote Kosi, which finishes at Lamosangu, the upper Sun Kosi is a fun 20km stretch of easy class 2 water and beautiful scenery. From Khadichour to Dolalghat the river is crystal blue, with brilliant beaches on which to picnic. It's a great place for a short family trip or learner kayak clinics.

Trisuli

With easy access just out of Kathmandu, the Trisuli is where many commercial trips operate. This is the cheapest trip available in Nepal – if you sign on to a US$15-a-day raft trip, this is where you'll end up.

What makes the Trisuli so cheap is also what makes it one of the least desirable rafting trips in the country. The easy access is provided by the Prithvi Hwy, which is the only highway connecting Kathmandu and India, and it runs right alongside the river.

During most flows the rapids are straightforward and spread well apart. The large number of companies operating on the river drives the prices down, but it also detracts considerably from the experience of the trip. Beaches are often heavily used and abused, with garbage, toilet paper and fire pits well assimilated into the sand. This, combined with the noise and pollution of the highway, makes the Trisuli a less than ideal rafting experience.

It's not all bad news though. During the monsoon months the Trisuli changes character completely as huge run-offs make the river swell and shear like an immense ribbon of churning ocean. There are fewer companies running at this time of the year, and the garbage and excrement of the past season should by now be well on its way to Bangladesh as topsoil.

The best white water is found on the section between Baireni and Mugling, and trips on the Trisuli can be combined with trips to Pokhara or Chitwan.

Kali Gandaki

The Kali Gandaki is an excellent alternative to the Trisuli, as there is no road alongside, and the scenery, villages, and temples all combine to make it a great trip.

The rapids on the Kali Gandaki are much more technical and continual than on the Trisuli (at class 3 to 4 depending on the flows), and in high water it's no place to be unless you are an accomplished kayaker experienced in avoiding big holes. At medium and lower flows, it's a fun and challenging river with rapids that will keep you busy for three days.

This is one of the holiest rivers in Nepal, and every river junction on the Kali Gandaki is dotted with cremation sites and aboveground burial mounds. If you've been wondering what's under that pile of rocks, we recommend against exploring. Because of the recent construction of a dam at the confluence with the Andhi Khola, what was once a four- to five-day trip has now become a three-day trip, starting at Baglung and taking out at the dam site. At very high flows it will probably be possible to run the full five-day trip to Ramdhighat by just portaging the dam site. This option would add some great white water and you could visit the wonderful derelict palace at Ranighat, which is slowly being restored. It is a fantastic place to stop and also have a look around.

If you are able to raft to Ramdhighat on the Siddhartha Hwy between Pokhara and Sunauli, you could continue on to the confluence with the Trisuli at Devghat. This adds another 130km and three or four more days. The lower section below Ramdhighat doesn't have much white water, but it is seldom rafted and offers a very isolated area with lots of wildlife.

Seti

The Seti is an excellent two-day trip in an isolated area, with beautiful jungle and plenty of easy rapids. Beware of companies who market this as a hot white-water trip. While it's a beautiful river valley well worth rafting, it's not a white-water bonanza.

The logical starting point is Damauli on the Kathmandu-Pokhara (Prithvi) Hwy between Mugling and Pokhara. This would give you 32km of rafting to the confluence with the Trisuli River. This is an excellent trip for learner or intermediate kayakers.

It is possible to raft a higher section, starting at Dule Gouda, which would add another 30km, but considering the quality of the rapids it probably isn't worth it. Beware if you decide to try the upper section of the river, as it disappears underground above Dule Gouda! Perhaps this is what they refer to as class 6.

Bhote Kosi

Just three hours from Kathmandu, the Bhote Kosi is one of the best short raft trips to be found anywhere in the world.

The Bhote Kosi is the steepest river rafted in Nepal – technical and totally committing. With a gradient of 80 feet per mile (24m per 1.6km), it's a full eight times as steep as the Sun Kosi, which it feeds farther downstream. The rapids are steep and continual class 4, with a lot of continual class 3 in between.

The normal run is from around 95km north-east of Kathmandu (north of Barabise) to the dam at Lamosangu. The river has been kayaked above this point, but a raft trip here would not be recreational. At high flows several of the rapids become solid class 5, and consequences of any mistakes become serious.

This river is one of the most fun things you can do right out of Kathmandu and a great way to get an adrenaline fix during the low water months, but it should only be attempted with a company that has a lot of experience on the Bhote Kosi, and is running the absolute best guides, safety equipment and safety kayakers. Most trips are two days, but usually the whole river is rafted on the second day, so if you are already up there then it can be done as a day trip.

Camping on the Bhote Kosi is limited, with few good beaches, so some companies have created unique river camps and resorts between Barabise and Tatopani (see the Around the Kathmandu Valley chapter for details). Rafting the Bhote Kosi out of one of these camps makes a lot of sense as you get a bit more river time and can relax at the end of a day's rafting or kayaking in pristine surroundings and comfort. The environmental impact of trips is limited by staying at fixed camps, and the camps create local employment and business. These camps and resorts also offer other activities so you can mix and match what you do.

Marsyangdi

The Marsyangdi is one of the best whitewater runs in the world. The trip starts with a stunning bus ride from Dumre to Besisahar. From here it is a beautiful trek up to the village of Ngadi, with great views of the Manaslu and the Annapurnas ahead of you the whole time. The scenery is fantastic.

From Ngadi downstream to the end of the trip at Bimalnagar, it's pretty much solid white water. Rapids are steep, technical and consecutive, making the Marsyangdi a serious undertaking. Successful navigation of the Marsyangdi requires companies to have previous experience on the river and to use the best guides and equipment. Rafts must be self bailing, and should be running with a minimum of weight and gear on board. Professional safety kayakers should be considered a standard safety measure on this river.

If you're looking for a four- to five-day trip with lots of demanding white water and great mountain scenery, the Marsyangdi is hard to beat.

Tamur

Newly opened and seldom run, this river combines one of the best short treks in Nepal with some really challenging whitewater action. The logistics of this trip make it a real expedition, and while it is a little more complicated to run than many rivers in Nepal, the rewards are worth the effort.

Most expeditions begin with a stunning four-day trek from Basantapur up over the Milke Danda Range to Dobhan. At Dobhan three tributaries of the Tamur join forces, combining the waters of the mountains to the north. The first 16km of rapids is intense, with one rapid feeding into the next, and the white water just keeps coming after that. The best time to raft the Tamur is probably when flows are at medium, which is between mid-October and mid-November.

Other Rivers

The **Bheri**, which is in the west, is a great float trip with incredible jungle scenery and lots of wildlife. This is one of the best fishing rivers and can be combined with a visit to the Royal Bardia National Park.

The **Arun** from Tumlingtar makes an excellent three-day wilderness trip, although the logistics of getting to the starting point are pretty complicated.The **Upper Seti** just outside Pokhara makes an excellent day trip when it is at high flows.

There is a plethora of rivers in Nepal that could be rafted and kayaked, but getting government permission is another matter. Things change quickly and capriciously in this part of the world, and the best advice is to check local information sources (several of them) to see what's running.

Language

It's quite easy to get by with English in Nepal; most of the people the average visitor will have to deal with in the Kathmandu Valley and in Pokhara will speak some English. Along the main trekking trails, particularly the Annapurna Circuit, English is widely understood.

However, it's interesting to learn at least a little Nepali and it's quite an easy language to pick up. Nepali is closely related to Hindi and, like Hindi, is a member of the Indo-European group of languages. If you want to know a bit more Nepali than the phrases and vocabulary included in this chapter, the Lonely Planet *Nepali phrasebook* is a handy introduction to the language.

Although Nepali is the national language of Nepal and is the linking language between all the country's ethnic groups, there are many other languages spoken. The Newars of the Kathmandu Valley, for example, speak Newari; other languages are spoken by the Tamangs, Sherpas, Rais, Limbus, Magars, Gurungs and other groups. In the Terai, bordering India, Hindi and Maithili, another Indian language of this region, are often spoken (see the table on this page for a breakdown of the languages spoken by Nepalis as their first language).

Even if you learn no other Nepali, there is one word every visitor soon picks up – *namaste* (pronounced 'na-ma-stay'). Strictly translated it means 'I salute the god in you', but it's used as an everyday greeting encompassing everything from 'Hello' to 'How are you?' and even 'See you again soon'. Properly used, it should be accompanied with the hands held in a prayer-like position, the Nepali gesture which is the equivalent of Westerners shaking hands.

Studying Nepali

Nepali pronunciation is relatively straightforward. Peace Corps and other aid workers pick up a working knowledge of the language very quickly and there are language courses available which will enable you to get by with just four to eight weeks of intensive study. See the Courses section in the Facts for the Visitor chapter for details.

Languages of Nepal

Language	% of Total Population
Nepali	50.3
Maithili	11.9
Bhojpuri	7.5
Tharu	5.4
Tamang	4.9
Newari	3.4
Rai	2.4
Magar	2.3
Abadhi	2.0
Limbu	1.4
Gurung	1.2
Sherpa	0.7
Other	8.6

Pronunciation

Vowels

a	as the 'u' in 'hut'
ā	as the 'ar' in 'garden', with no 'r' sound
e	as the 'e' in 'best' but longer
i	as the 'i' in 'sister' but longer
o	as the 'o' in 'sold'
u	as the 'u' in 'put'
ai	as the 'i' in 'mine'
au	as the 'ow' in 'cow'

Consonants

Most Nepali consonants are quite similar to their English counterparts. The exceptions are the so-called retroflex consonants and the aspirated consonants. Retroflex sounds are made by curling the tongue back to touch the roof of the mouth with the tip as you make the sound; they are indicated in this guide by an underdot, eg, **ṭ**, *Kaṭhmanḍu.*

Aspirated consonants are sounded more forcefully than they would be in English and are made with a short puff of air; they are indicated in this guide by an 'h' after the consonant, eg, **kh**, *khānuhos* (please).

Both retroflex and aspirated consonants are best learned by having a Nepali demonstrate them for you. You could start with the word *kaṭhmanḍu*, which contains both retroflex and aspirated consonants.

Greetings & Civilities

Hello/Goodbye.	*namaste*
How are you?	*tapāilai kasto chha?*
Excuse me.	*hajur*
Please (give me).	*dinuhos*
Please (you have).	*khānuhos*
Thank you.	*dhanyabad*

Unlike in the West, verbal expressions of thanks are not the cultural norm in Nepal. Although neglecting to say 'Thank you' may make you feel a little uncomfortable, it is rarely necessary in a simple commercial transaction; foreigners going round saying *dhanyabad* all the time sounds distinctly odd to Nepalis.

Basics

I	*ma*
Yes. (I have)	*chā*
No. (I don't have)	*chhaina*
OK.	*theekcha*
Where?	*kahā?*
here	*yahā*
there	*tyahā*
good/pretty	*ramro*
Do you speak English?	*tapāi angreji bolna saknu hunchha?*
I only speak a little Nepali.	*ma ali nepāli bolchhu*
I understand.	*ma bujhchu*
I don't understand.	*maile bujhina*
Please say it again.	*pheri bhanuhos*
Please speak more slowly.	*tapāi bistārai bolnuhos*
I don't need it.	*malai chahiṇa*
I don't have it.	*ma sanga chhaina*
Wait a minute.	*ek chhin parkhanos*

Getting Around

bus	*bus*
taxi	*taxi*
boat	*nāu*
ticket	*tikaṭ*
How can I get to ...?	*... kolāgi kati paisā lāgchha?*
Is it far from here?	*yahābata ke tādhā chha?*
Can I walk there?	*hiḍera jāna sakinchhu?*
I want to go to ...	*ma ... jānchhu*
Where does this bus go?	*yo bus kahā jānchha?*
How much is it to go to ...?	*... jāna kati parchha?*
I want a one-way/return ticket.	*jāne/jāne-āune tikaṭ dinuhos.*
Does your taxi have a meter?	*tapāi ko taxi mā meter chha?*

Accommodation

Where is a ...?	*... kahā chha?*
guesthouse	*pāhuna ghar*
hotel	*hoṭel*
camp site	*shivir*
lodge	*laj*
What is the address?	*thegānā ke ho?*
Please write down the address.	*thegānā lekhunuhos*
Can I get a place to stay here?	*yahā bās paunchha?*
May I look at the room?	*kothā herna sakchhu?*
How much is it per night?	*ek rātko, kati paisā ho?*
Does it include breakfast?	*bihānako khāna samet ho?*
room	*kothā*
clean	*safā*
dirty	*mailo*
fan	*pankhā*
hot water	*tāto pāni*

Around Town

bank	*baink*
... embassy	*... rājdutāvas*
museum	*samgrāhālaya*
police	*prahari*
post office	*post afis*
stamp	*tikaṭ*
envelope	*kham*
tourist office	*turist afis*

What time does it open/close?	*kati baje kholchha/ banda garchha?*
I want to change some money.	*paisā sātnu manlāgchha*

Trekking

Which way is ...?	*... jāne bato kata parchha?*
Is there a village nearby?	*najikai gaun parchha?*
How many hours/ days to ...?	*... kati ghanṭā/din?*
Where is the porter?	*bhariya kata gayo?*
I want to sleep.	*malai sutna man lagyo*
I'm cold.	*malai jado lagyo*
Please give me (water).	*malai (pani) dinuhos*

way/trail	*sāno bāṭo*
bridge	*pul*
downhill	*orālo*
uphill	*ukālo*
left	*bāyā*
right	*dāyā*
cold	*jāḍo*
teahouse	*bhatti*

Food & Drink

I'm a vegetarian.	*ma sākāhari hun*
What is this/that?	*yo/tyo ke ho?*

food/meal	*khāna*
bread (loaf)	*(pau) roṭi*
rice/cooked rice	*chāmal/bhāt*
meat	*māsu*
green, leafy vegetable	*sāg*
vegetable (cooked)	*tarakāri*
lentils	*dāl*
egg	*phul/anḍā*
fruit	*phala*
sugar	*chini*
salt	*nun*
pepper	*marich*
curd	*dhai*
milk	*dudh*
tea	*chia*
drinking water	*khāna pāni*

Emergencies

Help!	*guhār!*
It's an emergency!	*āpaṭ paryo!*
There's been an accident!	*durghaṭanā bhayo!*
Please call a doctor.	*dākṭarlai bolāunuhos*
Where is the (public) toilet?	*shauchālaya kahā chha?*
I'm lost.	*ma harāye*

Shopping

Where is the market?	*bazār kata parchha?*
What is it made of?	*kele baneko?*
How much?	*kati?*
That's enough.	*pugyo*
I like this.	*malai yo ramro lagyo*
I don't like this.	*malai yo ramro lagena*

money	*paisa*
cheap	*sasto*
expensive	*mahango*
less	*kam*
more	*badhi*
little bit	*alikati*

Health

Where can I find a good doctor?	*rāmro dākṭar kaha pāincha?*
Where is the nearest hospital?	*yahā aspatāl kahā chha?*
I don't feel well.	*malāi sancho chhaina*
I have diarrhoea.	*dishā lāgyo*
I have altitude sickness.	*lekh lāgyo*
I have a fever.	*joro āyo*
I'm having trouble breathing.	*sās pherna sakdina*

medicine	*ausadhi*
pharmacy	*ausadhi pasal*

I have ...	*malāi ... lāgyo*
asthma	*damko byathā*
diabetes	*madhu meha*
epilepsy	*chāre rog*

Times & Dates

What time is it?	*kati bajyo?*
It's one o'clock.	*ek bajyo*
minute	*minet*
hour	*ghantā*
day	*din*
today	*āja*
yesterday	*hijo*
tomorrow	*bholi*
now	*ahile*
week	*haptā*
month	*mahinā*
What day is it today?	*āja ke bār?*
Today is ...	*āja ... ho*
Monday	*som bār*
Tuesday	*mangal bār*
Wednesday	*budh bār*
Thursday	*bihi bār*
Friday	*sukra bār*
Saturday	*sani bār*
Sunday	*āita bār*

Numbers

1	*ek*
2	*dui*
3	*teen*
4	*chār*
5	*panch*
6	*chha*
7	*sāt*
8	*āṭh*
9	*nau*
10	*das*
20	*bees*
30	*tees*
40	*chālis*
50	*pachās*
60	*sāṭṭhi*
70	*saṭari*
80	*assi*
90	*nabbe*
100	*saya*
200	*dui saya*
500	*panch saya*
1000	*hazār*
100,000	*lākh*
one million	*das lākh*
ten million	*crore*

Glossary

Beware of the different methods of transliterating Nepali and the other languages spoken in Nepal. There are many and varied ways of spelling Nepali words. In particular the letters 'b' and 'v' are often interchanged.

General

ACAP – Annapurna Conservation Area Project
Adi Buddha – the original self-generated Buddha of Tantric Buddhism who created the Dhyani Buddhas
Aditya – ancient Vedic sun god, also known as Surya
Agni – ancient Vedic god of the hearth and fire
Agnipura – Buddhist symbol for fire
AMS – acute mountain sickness, also known as altitude sickness
Ananda – Buddha's chief disciple
Annapurna – the goddess of abundance and an incarnation of *Mahadevi*
Ashoka – Indian Buddhist emperor who spread the religion throughout the subcontinent
Ashta Matrikas – the eight mother goddesses
aunsi – new moon
Avalokiteshvara – as Gautama Buddha is the Buddha of our era, so Avalokiteshvara is the *Bodhisattva* of our era
avatar – incarnation of a deity living on Earth

bagh chal – traditional Nepali game
bahal – Buddhist monastery, usually two-storeys high and built around a courtyard; many are now used as schools
bahil – simpler version of a *bahal*
bajra – see *vajra*
bakba – Tibetan clay mask
bandh – the severest form of strike where all shops, schools and offices are closed and vehicles don't use the roads; see also *julus* and *chakka jam*
bazaar – market area; a market town is also called a bazaar
betel – mildly intoxicating concoction of areca nut and lime, which is wrapped in betel leaf and chewed
Bhadrakali – Tantric goddess who is also a consort of *Bhairab*
Bhagavad Gita – Krishna's lessons to Arjuna, part of the *Mahabharata*
Bhairab – the 'terrific' or fearsome Tantric form of Shiva with 64 manifestations
bhatti – teahouse or village inn
Bhot – Nepali for Tibet
Bhote – high-altitude desert valleys north of the Himalaya bordering Tibet; Nepali term for a Tibetan
bodhi tree – a pipal tree under which Buddha was sitting when he attained enlightenment, also known as 'bo tree'
Bodhisattva – one near-Buddha who renounces the opportunity to attain *nirvana* in order to aid humankind
Bön – the animist religion of Tibet prior to Buddhism
Brahmin – the highest Hindu caste, said to originate from Brahma's head
bright fortnight – two weeks of the waxing moon, as it grows to become the full moon; see also *dark fortnight*

chaitya – small *stupa*, which usually contains a *mantra* rather than a Buddhist relic
chakka jam – literally 'jam the wheels', in which all vehicles stay off the street during a strike; see also *bandh* and *julus*
chakra – *Vishnu*'s disc-like weapon, one of the four symbols he holds
chautara – stone platforms around trees, which serve as shady places for porters to rest
Chhetri – the second caste of Nepali Hindus, said to originate from Brahma's arms
chirag – ceremonial oil lamp
chorten – Tibetan Buddhist stupa
chowk – (pronounced choke) historically a courtyard or marketplace; these days used more to refer to an intersection or crossroads
chuba – long woollen Sherpa coat

Dalai Lama – incarnation of a *Bodhisattva* and the spiritual leader of Tibetan Buddhists
danda – hill
dark fortnight – two weeks of the waning moon, as the full moon shrinks to become the new moon; see also *bright fortnight*
Dattatraya – deity who is thought of as an incarnation of *Vishnu*, *Shiva*'s teacher, or the Buddha's cousin
deval – temple
Devanagari – Sanskrit Nepali script
Devi – the short form of *Mahadevi*, the *shakti* to *Shiva*
dhaki – hand-woven cotton cloth
dhami – priest claiming occult powers; a sorcerer
dharamsala – resthouse for pilgrims
dharma – Buddhist teachings
dhoka – door or gate
dhyana – meditation
Dhyani Buddha – the original Adi Buddha created five Dhyani Buddhas, who in turn create the universe of each human era
doko – basket carried by porters
doonga – boat
dorje – see *vajra*
durbar – palace
Durga – fearsome manifestation of *Parvati*, *Shiva*'s consort
Dwarapala – door guardian figure
dyochen – a form of temple enshrining Tantric deities
dzopkyo – male cross between a *yak* and a cow; also zopkiok
dzum – female offspring of a *yak* and a cow; also zhum
dzu-tch – large *yeti* that eats cattle

ek – Nepali number one; a symbol of the unity of all life

freaks – 1960s' term from the overland era for the young Western travellers who could be found congregating in Bali, Kabul, Goa and Kathmandu

gaine – a beggar musician
ganas – *Shiva*'s companions
Ganesh – son of *Shiva* and *Parvati*, instantly recognisable by his elephant head
Ganga – goddess of the Ganges
ganja – hashish
Garuda – the man-bird vehicle of *Vishnu*
Gautama Buddha – Buddha of our era
Gelugpa – one of the four major schools of Tibetan Buddhism; its adherents are sometimes referred to as the *Yellow Hats*
ghanta – Tantric bell; the female equivalent of the *vajra*
ghat – steps beside a river; a 'burning ghat' is used for cremations
gompa – Tibetan Buddhist monastery
gopi – cowherd girl (Krishna had a lot of fun with his gopis)
gufa – cave
guhya – vagina
Gurkha – Nepali soldiers who have long formed a part of the British army; the name comes from the region of Gorkha
Gurkhali – British army name for the Nepali language
Gurung – western hill people from around Gorkha and Pokhara

Hanuman – monkey god
Harisiddhi – fearsome Tantric goddess
harmika – square base on top of a *stupa*'s dome upon which the eyes of Buddha are painted; the eyes face the four cardinal directions
hathi – elephant
himal – range or massif with permanent snow
hiti – water conduit or tank with water-spouts
hookah – water pipe for smoking

incarnation – a particular life form; the form mortals assume is determined by *karma*
Indra – king of the Vedic gods; god of rain

Jagannath – *Krishna* as Lord of the Universe
Jambhala – god of wealth; look for his money bag and his attendant mongoose
janai – sacred thread, which high-caste Hindu men wear looped over their left shoulder and which they replace each year
jatra – festival
jayanti – birthday
jhankri – faith healers who perform in a trance while beating drums

Jogini – mystical goddesses, counterparts to the 64 manifestations of *Bhairab*
jukha – leech
julus – a procession or demonstration; see also *bandh* and *chakka jam*

Kali – the most terrifying manifestation of *Parvati*
Kalki – *Vishnu*'s 10th and as yet unseen incarnation during which he will come riding a white horse and wielding a sword to destroy the world
Kalpa – day in the age of Brahma
Kam Dev – Shiva's companion
Kamasutra – ancient Hindu text on erotic pleasures
Karkotak – chief *naga* of the Kathmandu Valley
karma – Buddhist and Hindu law of cause and effect, which continues from one life to another
Kartikkaya – god of war and son of *Shiva*, his vehicle is the cock or peacock; also known as Kumar or Skanda
kata – Tibetan prayer shawl, often presented to an important Buddhist when introduced
Kaukala – a form of Shiva in his fearsome aspect; he carries a trident with the skeleton of *Vishnu*'s gatekeeper impaled upon it; this act was the result of banning *Shiva* from *Vishnu*'s palace!
KEEP – Kathmandu Environmental Education Project
Khas – Hindu hill people
khat – see *palanquin*
khola – stream or tributary
khukuri – traditional curved knife of the *Gurkhas*
kinkinimali – temple wind bells
kosi – river
kot – fort
Krishna – fun-loving eighth incarnation of *Vishnu*
Kumari – living goddess, a peaceful incarnation of *Kali*
kunda – water tank fed by springs
kundalini – female energy principle

la – mountain pass
laliguras – Nepali word for rhododendron, the national flower
lama – Tibetan Buddhist monk or priest
lathi – bamboo staves used by police during a protest
lingam – phallic symbol that represents *Shiva*'s creative powers

machan – a lookout tower used to view wildlife
Machhendranath – patron god of the Kathmandu Valley and an incarnation of *Avalokiteshvara*
Mahabharata – one of the major Hindu epics
Mahadeva – another name for *Shiva*; literally 'Great God'
Mahadevi – literally 'Great Goddess', sometimes known as Devi; the *shakti* to *Shiva*
maharishi – great teacher
Mahayana – literally 'Greater Vehicle'; form of Buddhism prevalent through East Asia, Tibet and Nepal
mahseer – game fish of the Terai rivers
Malla – royal dynasty of the Kathmandu Valley responsible for most of the important temples and palaces of the valley towns
mandala – geometrical and astrological representation of the world
mandir – temple
mani – stone carved with the Tibetan Buddhist chant *om mani padme hum*
Manjushri – the god who cut open the Chobar Gorge so that the Kathmandu Lake could become the Kathmandu Valley
mantra – prayer formula or chant
Mara – Buddhist god of death; has three eyes and holds the *wheel of life*
math – Hindu priest's house
mela – a country fair
mithuna – Sanskrit term usually referring to a depiction of gods engaged in intercourse in erotic art; *yab-yum* in Tibetan

naga – serpent deity; the nine nagas have control over water, and are often seen over house entrances to keep evil spirits away
nagini – female *naga*
Nagpura – Buddhist symbol for water
nak – female *yak*
namaste – traditional Hindu greeting (hello or goodbye), often accompanied by a

small bow with the hands brought together at chest or head level, as a sign of respect
Nandi – *Shiva*'s vehicle, the bull
Narayan – *Vishnu* as the sleeping figure on the cosmic ocean; from his navel Brahma appeared and went on to create the universe
Narsingha – man-lion incarnation of *Vishnu*
Newari – people of the Kathmandu Valley
nirvana – final escape from the cycles of existence

om mani padme hum – sacred Buddhist *mantra*, which means 'hail to the jewel in the lotus'

padma – lotus flower
Padmapani – literally 'Lotus in Hand'; a manifestation of *Avalokiteshvara* as he appears in many Nepali religious buildings, holding a tall lotus stalk
pagoda – multistoreyed Nepali temple, which was exported to China and Japan
palanquin – portable covered bed usually shouldered by four men
Parvati – *Shiva*'s consort
pashmina – goat wool blanket or shawl
Pashupati – *Shiva* as Lord of the Animals
path – small raised platform to shelter pilgrims
pipal tree – see *bodhi tree*
pith – open shrine for a Tantric goddess
pokhari – large water tank
prajna – female counterparts of male Buddhist deities
prasad – food offering
prayer flag – each carries a sacred *mantra* that is 'said' when the flag flutters
prayer wheel – cylindrical wheel inscribed with a Buddhist prayer or *mantra* that is 'said' when the wheel spins
Prithvi – Vedic earth goddess
puja – religious offering or prayer
Puranas – Hindu holy books of around 400 BC
puri – town
purnima – full moon

Qomolangma – Tibetan name for Mt Everest; literally 'Mother Goddess of the World' (also spelt Chomolongma)

rajpath – road or highway, literally 'king's road'
raksha bandhan – yellow thread worn on the wrist that is said to bring good fortune
Ramayana – Hindu epic
Rana – of the hereditary prime ministers who ruled Nepal from 1841 to 1951
rath – temple chariot in which the idol is conveyed in processions
Red Hats – name given collectively to adherents of the Nyingmapa, Kargyupa and Sakyapa schools of Tibetan Buddhism
rikhi doro – golden thread worn around the waist by *Shiva* devotees

sadhu – wandering Hindu holy man; generally a Shaivite who has given up everything to follow the trail to religious salvation
Sagarmatha – Nepali name for Mt Everest
sal – tree of the lower Himalayan foothills
saligrams – black ammonite fossils of Jurassic-period sea creatures
sanyasin – religious ascetic who has cut all ties with regular society
Saraswati – goddess of learning and creative arts, and consort of Brahma, who is often identified by her lute-like instrument
satal – pilgrim's house
seto – white
Shaivite – follower of *Shiva* whose face is covered in ashes with three horizontal lines painted on the forehead, and who carries a begging bowl and *Shiva*'s symbolic trident
shakti – dynamic female element in male-female relationships; also a goddess
Sherpa – of the Buddhist hill people famed for stalwart work with mountaineering expeditions; literally 'People from the East'; with a small 's' sherpa means trek leader
Sherpani – female *Sherpa*
shikhara – Indian-style temple with tall corncob-like spire
Shitala Mai – ogress who became a protector of children
Shiva – the most powerful Hindu god, the creator and destroyer
sindur – red dust and mustard oil mixture used for offerings
sirdar – leader/organiser of a trekking party
STOL – short take off and landing aircraft used on mountain airstrips

stupa – hemispherical Buddhist religious structure
Sudra – the lowest Nepali caste, said to originate from Brahma's feet
sundhara – fountain with golden spout

tabla – hand drum
tahr – wild mountain goat
tal – lake
Taleju Bhawani – Nepali goddess, an aspect of *Mahadevi* and the family deity of the *Malla* kings of the Kathmandu Valley
Tantric Buddhism – form of Buddhism that evolved in Tibet during the 10th to 15th centuries
Tara – White Tara is the consort of the Dhyani Buddha Vairocana; Green Tara is associated with Amoghasiddhi
teahouse trek – independent trekking between village inns
tempo – small, three-wheeled, automated minivan commonly used in Nepal
Thakali – people of the Kali Gandaki Valley who specialise in running hotels
thangka – Tibetan religious painting on cotton
third eye – symbolic eye on Buddha figures, used to indicate the Buddha's clairvoyant powers
tika – red sandalwood-paste spot marked on the forehead, particularly for religious occasions
tole – street or quarter of a town, sometimes used to refer to a square
topi – traditional Nepali cap
torana – pediment above temple doors, which can indicate the god to whom the temple is dedicated
Tribhuvan – the king who in 1951 ended the *Rana* period and Nepal's long seclusion
trisul – trident weapon symbol of *Shiva*
tumpline – leather or cloth strip worn across the forehead or chest of a porter to support a load carried on the back
tunal – carved temple strut
tundikhel – parade ground

Uma Maheshwar – *Shiva* and *Parvati* in a pose where *Shiva* sits cross-legged and *Parvati* sits on his thigh and leans against him
Upanishads – ancient Vedic scripts, the last part of the *Vedas*
urna – the bump on the forehead of a Buddha or *Bodhisattva*

vahana – a god's animal mount or vehicle
Vaishnavite – follower of *Vishnu*
Vaisya – caste of merchants and farmers, said to originate from Brahma's thighs
vajra – the 'thunderbolt' symbol of Buddhist power in Nepal; *dorje* in Tibetan
Vajra Jogini – a Tantric goddess, *shakti* to a *Bhairab*
Vasudhara – the wife of Jambhala the god of wealth; she rides a chariot drawn by a pig
Vedas – ancient orthodox Hindu scriptures
Vedic god – ancient Hindu god described in the *Vedas*
vehicle – the animal with which a Hindu god is associated; *Shiva*'s vehicle is a bull, *Ganesh*'s is a mouse, and *Vishnu*'s is the man-bird *Garuda*
vihara – Buddhist religious buildings and pilgrim accommodation
Vishnu – the preserver, one of the three main Hindu gods

wheel of life – this is held by *Mara*, the god of death; the wheel's concentric circles represents Buddha's knowledge and the way humans can escape their conditioning and achieve *nirvana*

yab-yum – Tibetan term for Tantric erotica
yak – main beast of burden and form of cattle found above 3000m
yaket – Tibetan wool jacket
yaksha – attendant deity or nymph
Yama – Vedic god of death; his messenger is the crow
Yellow Hats – name sometimes given to adherents of the *Gelugpa* school of Tibetan Buddhism
yeti – abominable snowman
yogi – yoga master
yoni – female sexual symbol, equivalent of a *lingam*

zamindar – absentee landlord and/or moneylender

Food & Drink

See also Food in the Facts for the Visitor chapter.

arak – fermented drink made from potatoes or grain

buff – water buffalo, popularly known as buff, is the usual substitute for beef given that cows are sacred and (officially at least) can't be eaten

chang – home brew of the Himalaya, a mildly alcoholic concoction made from barley, millet or rice and what may be untreated water (proceed with caution); also known by its Tibetan name, *thon*
chapati – unleavened Indian bread
chatamari – (Newari) rice-flour pancake topped with meat and/or egg
chia – milk tea
choyla – (Newari) roasted, diced *buff* meat, usually heavily spiced and eaten with *chura*
chura – (Newari) beaten rice (think of flat Rice Bubbles!), served in place of rice
curd – yogurt is known throughout the subcontinent as curd; the buffalo milk curd of Nepal can be very good

dal – lentil soup; the main source of protein in the Nepali diet
dal bhaat tarakari – staple meal of Hindu Nepalis, consisting of lentil soup, rice and curried vegetables

ghee – clarified butter
gundruk – traditional Nepali soup with dried vegetables
gurr – made from raw potatoes ground and mixed with spices and then grilled like a large pancake and eaten with cheese

kachila – (Newari) raw buff mince mixed with oil, ginger and spices

kwati – (Newari) soup made from sprouted beans and eaten during festivals

lassi – refreshing drink of curd mixed with sugar and what may be untreated water (proceed with caution)

makhan – butter
momo – typical Tibetan dish made by steaming or frying meat or vegetables wrapped in dough; similar to Chinese dim sum or Italian ravioli; also known as *kothe*
momoch – (Newari) another version of *momo*

rakshi – (Newari) distilled rice wine, made from traditional recipes and extremely variable in quality: it can be anything from smooth firewater to paint stripper!

samay baji – (Newari) ritual feast of *chura*, *choyla*, boiled egg, black soybeans, diced ginger and *wo*
sekuwa – (Newari) barbecued meat: *buff*, pork, fish or chicken
sha bhakley – Tibetan meat pie
sikarni – sweet curd dessert that may include nuts and dried fruit
sukuti – (Newari) spicy nibble of dried roasted meat

tama – traditional Nepali soup made from dried bamboo shoots
tawkhaa – (Newari) a jelly of curried meat that is served cold
thon – see *chang*
thugpa – traditional thick Tibetan meat soup
tsampa – ground grain, usually barley, mixed with tea, water or milk and eaten dry – either instead of rice or mixed with it; the staple dish in the hill country

wo – (Newari) lentil-flour pancake

Thanks

Many thanks to the travellers who used the last edition and wrote to us with helpful hints, useful advice and interesting anecdotes.

A Michael & L Abraham, Russell Adams, Prof Dan Adler, Simon Aggus, Lars Agren, N Ahleuins, Petra Ahrens, Jim Aitken, Chris Albert, Jon Aldridge, April Alexander, Alexej Alvariza, Karim Ammeraal, Gillian Anderson, Ola Andersson, Nuno Andre Gomes, Davide Andrea, Steve Anyon-Smith, M & R Apers, Julia Archer, Rafa Artavia, Barry Arthur, Tim Ashbaugh, Martin Ashley, Ken Ashley Johnson, Jorg Ausfelt, Laura Ayala, T Baars, Claude Bachmann, Charles Back, Bobbie Bailey, G Bailey, Sue Bailey, Stacey Bainbridge, Sarah Baines, Graham Baker, Mark Baker, Egbert Bakker, Rashed Bakri, Les Ballard, Eve Ballenegger, Steve Ballinger, Uldis Balodis, John Bament, Helen Banks, Kedar Bantawa, Dom Barry, Jean Barthes, Andy Baschong, David Basham, Kevin Bateman, Jo Batterham, C Beallor, Rob Becker, Simon Q Beckmann, Tamara Bekef, Andrew Bell, Doody Bell, Jeff Bell, Nicole Bellefleur, V O Bellers, Silke Belzer, Mara Benedict, Bernarda Benka Pulka, Alan Bennett, Sharon & Jonnie Benzimra, Jonas Berg, Jonas Bergenholtz, Ami Berger, Marten Berglund, WH Bergner, Isabelle Bermyn, Jeremy Bernstein, Uday Bhattarai, John Bielinski, Vicki Bielski, Stuart Biggs, Carol Bishop, Jeppe Blak-Nielsen, Gary Blanchard, Lawrence Blieberg, Karin Blokziel, Mirjam Blom, Kurt Bockhorst, Pamela Bode, Jackie Borges, R Borras, Robert Bough, Marielle Bourgeois, Nick Bourne, Antoinette Bouwens, John Bower, Angelique Braat, Audrey & Roy Bradford, Christine & Gabrielle Bradley, Kylie Brehany, Sarah & Ian Brenchley, Robert Brenner, Karel Brevet, Mark Briffa, Karen Briggs, Belinda Brown, Rhona Brown, Tim Brown, Rob Buchanan, Gerlinde Buder, Christine Bull, Cath Bulling, Christopher Bullock, Mat Burbury, Marie-Claire Bureau, Andrew Burke, Jane Burren, Fiona Burton, LE Butler, Sheridan Butler, Julian & Jane Cabrera, Francesca Camisoli, Mariano Cano, Lyn Caron, Kathleen Carothers, Elaine Andrews-Carra, Giovanna Caruso, Joanna Cary, George Casley, Andrew Caulkett, Dan Cavanagh, T Chalhoub, Jack Chang, A Chapman, Ruben Chaston, Ushman Chauhan-Jacobsen, Anita Chauvin, Darryl Cherney, Cynthia Chow, Pierre Christen, Sharee & Brett Christie, Monika Christofori, Lenka Chromcova, Pia Cipikoff, Alex Clark, Dean Clark, Fintan Clarke, Christina Cleaver, Dudu Cohen, Laurie Cohn, Ailsa Colston, Natalie Cook, Stuart Cooke, Phillipe Cornelis, Alexandra Correia, J Correiro, Kevin Cosgriff, Jane Costello, Juan I Costero, R Coulter, Christiano Covelli, Anne Cox, Fraser Crayford, Michael Cridland, Norma Crooks, Sean Cross, Onn Crouvi, Ian Cruickshank, Cristobal Cubedo, Wendy Custance, Curt Custard, Verle Cuudde, Sophie Dackanbe, Ake Dahloff, Michel J van Dam, Adam Danek, Jim Daniels, Christopher & Victoria Darue, John Darwin, Laura Davidson, Tania Davis, Will Davis, Harry Dawson, Lyn Day, Wim De Becker, Armando De Beradinis, Kerin Deeley, Dale & Heather Deller, Laurens den Dulk, Dorine Derks, Alex Derom, Dan Diaz, Geneveve Diver, Rachel Dodds, Anthony Doerga, Maya Doe-Simkins, N Dolkar, R Domrow, Simon Donald, Eshed Doni, Elizabeth Donnelly, Neelke Doorn, Jeremy Dore, Damien Dougherty, David Duchovney, Diana Duckworth, Dr James MacGregor Duff, Stephan Dufresne, Shiva Dulal, Laurent-jan Dullaart, Emma Duncombe, James Dunn, Tim Dunn, Judy Dunne, Silvia Durrsperger, Jack Dyson, Michael Eckert, Dawn Edmonds, Janet Edwards, Mrs Nimrod & Mr Eitan, Tamsin Emmens, Isabelle & Dirk Engels, Naomi Engleman, Achara & Don Entz, Daniel Ericson, XCI Escarra, Susan Esmonde, Brooks Evans, K Evans, Ruth Evans, Ruth & Neil Evans, Sue Evans, Melissa Faircloth, Cox Family, Barbara Fannen, Kian Feng, Anthony Fewenstein, Pam & Alan Fey, Jan Fietzke, The Finlays, Shawna Fisher, Mary Fletcher, Carl Flint, Andre Foerste, Adam Ford, Michael Foskett, Flamers Fothersby, Rechelle Fowler, Cathrine Fragell Darre, Mike Frame, Brooke Francis, Grant Fraser, Camilla Fredberg, Eva Fredriksen, A Freeman, Bernd Friese, Ingrid Fruh, Sabra Frye, Dave Fuller, Peter Gaeng, Kendra Galiano, Ken Gallant, Ian Gardner, Jason Garman, Gary Garthwait, J Gays, Pauli Gerritsen, Alan Gibson, Darren Gidding, Kristina Gidlof, Tori & Glen Gilbert, Paul Gill, Amanda Gilliam, Robert Gillman, Paul Glendenning, Anna Goarst, Sunita Godbole, P Godfrey, Bea Goemans, William Goldberg, Sharon Gorman, Sabijin Gorter-Wijnheijmer,

Katherine Gouga, Joanna Grabiak, Sascha Grabow, Jenni Gray, Jurek Grebosz, David Green, Anna Greenhous, Jolanda Griens, A Grimholm, Jennifer & Kerry Grimson, Helen Grinstead, Nienke Groen, Gill Grolimund, Kim Gronemeier, G Groothengel-de Wolff, Hans Guggenheim, John & Isabel Guise, Alexandra Gulemeester, Deah Gulley, Prema Gurung, Laurent Guyonvarch, J Van Haard, Luke Haas, Thorsten Hackl, Christian Hadorn, Mari Hagberg, A Halferty, Keri Hallam, W Hamer, Raphael Hamers, Paul Hamilton, Stuart Hamilton, Deborah Hammond, Sheila Hannon, Zwen Harbers-Thijssen, Judith Harmke, Joop Harms, C Harper, D Harrison, Stacie Hartung, Patrick Harvey, Ben Harwood, James Hatcher, Steven Hatcher, Ayana Haviv, Vincent Hayes, Ken Healy, Kevin & Trea Heapes, Joyce Hee, Bernie Hejilek, Pete Helfrich, Victoria Henkin, Victory Henkin, Eleanor Henly, Jeff Hennier, Marion Hercock, Itai Hermelin, Olegario Hernbndez, Sandra Hesse, Marco Heusdens, Anna Hicks, Matthew Hildebrand, Kaye Hill, R Hill, Ignace Hindrick, Laura Hinton, Paula Hirschoff, Kathy Hirsh, Caroline Holden, Jacquelyn Holker, Zoe Holloway, Catherine Holman, R Holtes, Jayne, Simon & Sally Holtham, Birgitta Holzel, Andrew Hopewell, Martin Hopper, Hotel Horizon Kathmandu, Hobbe Horse, Mark Horsley, Bela Horvath, Jayne Hoskins, Marcelo Houacio Pozzo, Jocelyn Houghton, Rod How, M Howard, Adrian Howe, Peter Hruska, Raimo Hubner, Mike & Nadine Hudson, Harriet Hughes, Bram Hulzebos, Sally Humphrey, Kelly Hunt, Mark Hunter, Christopher Hurren, Haya Husseini, Amy Huxtable, Stewart Huxtable, Dirk Huyge, Kathy Illsley, Barbara Int-Hout, Julja Istanbul, Valentina Ivancich, Angela Jackson, Aurianne Jacobs, Paul Jacobs, Robert H Jacoby, Jean Jacques, Rutger Jagersma, Trond Jakobsen, Julia Jakubovics, Amanda James, Bob James, Keith James, Eric James Rayner, Marjon Janmaat, Isle Janneman, Johnny Johansen, Dave John, Matthew John Nash, Brent Johnson, Fred Johnson, Patricia Johnson, Hayley Johnston, Brett Jones, June Jones, Rachael Jones, Sture Jonsson, Richard Juterbock, Ulrich Kaden, Denise Kahan, Dan Kalafatas, Juray Kaman, Gerhard Kanne, Sue Kapiak, Steven Karp, Renko Karruppannan, Gideon Katz, S Kaur, Ray Kearns, Guy Kedar, David Keitz, Jitso Keizer, Kahe Kell, Greg Kennedy, Daniel Kern, George Kerr, Vaugan Killin, Cathy Kim, Rebecca King, Ruth King, Tara King, Linda Kirk, Per Kjaer Johansen, P Klekatka, Neil Klemp, Tania Knight, V J Knowles, Patricia Knox, Vivian Ko, Alan & Andrea Koeninger, Hans Kolb, Ivan Kolker, Errol Korn, Christopher Kowollik, Marcia J Kramer, Tom Krienheder, Birgitt Krohn, Albert Kromkamp, Jakob Kroon, Mike Krosin, Mike Kryne, Werner Kulp, Rajendra Kumar Chitrakar, Vicky Kuperman, Igal Kutin, Roger La Haye, Beryl Laatunen, Paul Lachapelle, Robby Lacuzzi, Brian Lacy, Raymond Lae, Olivier & Catherine Lair, Astrid Langhorne, Tim Langmaid, Jan Lann, Pete Larrett, J K Larsson, Baron Sergio de Lasseter, Anne Laudisoit, Kevin Law-Smith, Jeffrey Lee, Hanan Leib, Ruth Leimeister, Jenni Leitch, DA Lentz, Bennett Lerner, Hagar Leschner, Lauren Lesko, Michael Leventhal, Jennifer Lewis, Marita Liabo, Dana Lieberman, Micah Lieberman, Samuel Lievens, D Linington, Mike Linnett, U W Lippelt, D Litchfield, Brian Locker, Claudia Loetscher, Elspeth Logan, Manoeal Lopez, Marjolein B Loppies, Claudia Lotscher, Kate Lovatt, Debbie Lovell, C Lovelock, Jonni Lu Pool, Jennifer Lund, Alison Lynas, Laura Lyne McMurchie, Rachel MacHenry, Selvaggia Macioti, Ruth Mackay-Shea, Joan Mackie, Kathy Madson, Jennifer Magarity, Stefano Maggini, Julia Mair, Jan Malik, Delian Manchev, Joshua Mandell, Chris Manley, Doreen Manning, Jane Mara, Steve Marcus, Roland J Marsden, Francine Marshall, Anadi Martel, Paloma Marugan, Kate Mason, Manfred Mauler, Brian Maxwell, Myles & Cathy Mayne, Trevor Mazzucchelli, Jim & Lorraine McAndrew, Jill McCallum, Eoin McCarney, Rachel mcEleney, Hamish McKee, Laura Mclean, Liz McMillan, Heather McNeice, Ian McRae, Michael Meadows, Colin Megson, Sander Meijsen, Kirsten Mellor, Karin Mendoza, Stacy Mercier, Dean van der Merwe, Peter Meyer, Marcel Michiels, Alan Middlebrook, David Migdal, Ramsey & Jane Mikhail, Karsten Mikkelsen, Teri Millane, David Millent, Rosemarie Milsom, Toby Milwright, Lucy Minato, Ardalan Mirahmadi, Naomi Mitchell, Kerstin Mockrish, Christine Moffett, Dennis Mogerman, Marjorie Mogg, Vicki Moncrief, Anita Moore, Charlie Moore, Craig Moore, SP Moore, Vincenzo Morelli, Giles Morrison, Dave Mountain, Cindy Moyer, Dallas MsMillan, Claudia Mueller, Andrea Munch, Joe Murphy, Patrick Murphy, Geraldine Murray, Kate Murray, Thara Nagarajan, Terry Nakazono, Timothy Nalden, Sue Napier, J Nathan, Doris Neilson, Dieter Neujahr, Lily Neve, Jon Nevill, Chris Nevmever, Bonnie Ng, Serene Ng, Martin Nicholson, Maureen Nienabar, Uri & Nomi Nir, Yoav Noam, V Noonan,

Don NovoGradac, Richard Nutter, Jon O'Donnell, Yasu Ohyagi, Paul O'Kelly, Conny Olde Olthof, Helle Olesed, Jolanda Onderwater, Grace Onions, Stefan Orani, Reg Ormond, W Osada, Joe Osentoski, Raymond Ostelo, Mark Outerbridge, Lori Panther, Harling Park, Israr & Richard Parker, James Parkinson, Nancy Parshall, Sarah Pasela, Dipak Patel, Sangita Patel, G Paul, Emma Pavey, Sharon Peake, Sarah Pearce, Steve Pearcy, Denni & Michael Pearson, Josh Pedersen, Claire Pellit, Julian Peltenburg, Michael Perring, Oskar Persson, D Pessers-Boeve, Jon Petrie, Andreas Pfletschinger, Barbara Pfyffer, Bernard Phelps, Jan Piebe Tjepkema, Fabrizio & Alessia Piemontese, Liezel Pilling, David Pindar, John Piper, Luis Pitta, Lidy van der Ploeg, Lorraine Plunkett, Mandy Pocock, John Polush, Bas Pos, Joel et Maria Teresa Prades, Juergen Preimesberger, Nicholas Prescotte, Susan Preston-Martin, Michael Price, Duncan Priestley, Emma Pritchett, Martin Pronk, Judy Prudy, Carter Quinby, Montse Quintana, Kelly Rae, Kirat Rai Yayokkha, Helen Ranger, Debra Rappaport, Jaliya Rasaputra, K M Rebeiro, Matt Redman, Simon Reed, Jose Remmers, Michelle Renbaum, Jan Rensen, Assaf Reznik, Elizabeth Rhoades, Bob Rickard, Sue Ridley, Evan Rieder, Joe Rizzo, Ben Roberts, Steve Roberts, Natasha Robinson, Pinhas Rodan, Ellie Roelofs, Thomas Rohland, Herwig Rombauts, Rick Ronald, Leif Ronby Pedersen, Heikki Ronka, EL Roobottom, Michael Rose, Etta Rosen, Howard Rosenthal, Mark Ross, Keith Rossborough, Ruth Rosselson, Adriano Rossi, Stephen Rowland-Jones, Michael Rubio, Jay Ruchamkin, Meriel Rule, Gabriela Rutz, Dominique Ryan, Alex Sacker, Eyal Sadeh, CMR Sally, Nicole Salzer, Mimi Samuel, Claire Sansom, Menno Sasker, Wiebke Sautter, Elizabeth Savir, John Saynor, Karl Schabert, Joseph Schaller, Karl Scharbert, Michael Schell, Martin Schichtel, Silvia Schikhof, Steve Schlick, Valentin Schmitt, Duncan Schofield, Milo Schram, Raph Schramm, Peter Schroeder, Thorsten Schuller, Penny Schwartz, Carole Scriha, Bill Searl, Laura Seidman, Frank Selbmann, Eugene Semb, K Shah, Grishma Shah-Elzinga, Surendra Shahi, Jean Shannon, Peter & Florence Shaw, Dave Sheaffer, Noa Shefet, Mark Shepherdson, PT Sherpa, Dana Shields, P Shimazaki, Sainath G Shinde, Dan Shingleton, Valerie Shipps, Chris Shorten, Ailsa Siemens, Diana Silbergeld, Barbara Siliquini, Hugues Simard, Dave Simms, Mrs F & Mr Sims, Renu Singh, Randheer Singh Geera, Serge Sintzoff, Laura Skilton, Mrs AR & Mr Skipper, Nathalie van der Slikke, Chris Slocombe, Ageeth Smid, Daphne Smith, Eleanor Smith, L Smith, Lorraine Smith, Sandy Smith, Sue Smith, Vanessa Smith Holburn, Christopher Snyder, Yael Soffer, Nils Sondermann, Lee Soo May, Mary & John Spesia, Ben Spiegelberg, Lisa Spratling, Tom Stace, Marc Stafford, Tracy Starr, Martin Stebbing, Davi Stein, Vlrik & Lorina Stenwall, Matthew Stephens, Robert Stewart, Ben Stewart-Koster, Leonie Stockwell, Beneticte Stokkeby, Kasper Stokman, AJ Street, Chris Strom, Jan Strubbe, Koen Stynen, C Suan, Jon Sumby, Martin Suttcliffe, Ron Szili, Susan C Tabler, Wainer Tabone, Ramon Tak, Fredrik Tamsen, Georgina Tan, Lisa Tapert, Marie Tarrant, Alice Teasdale, Edward Telford, Barbara Temsamani, Ulrike Teutriene, Anurag Thapa, Hari Thapaliya, Elke Thape, Jenny Thatcher-Eldredge, Belinda Thomas, Fern Thomas, Karyn Thomas, Martine Thompson, Neil Thompson, Louise Thornley, AR Thorp, Pat Tillman, Hari Timilsina, Zoltan Tompa, Tonny Tornblom, Jennifer Tradewell, Sarah Treaddell, Bo Trkulja, Carol Tsang, Monica Tse, Tatyana Tsinberg, Fredrik Tukk, Ian Tupper, Mark Turin, Michael Tyrrell, Boaz Ur & Lachover, John Urquhart, Frans van Assendelft, Kees Van Boven, Hennie van der Male, Maarten van Egmond, Ingrid van Klingeren, Henk van Lambalgen, Harrie van Lammeren, Karen Van Riemsdyk, Harold van Voorveld, Michel van Woudenberg, Mark J Vanderstelt, Renuka Vasudevan, Phil Vaughan, Richard Vaughan, Mostafa Vaziri, Bep vd Meyden, Jerry van Veenendaal, Mike Venables, Gert Venghaus, Aron Wahl, David Wajand, Ali Wale, Alex Walker, Colin A Walker, Leith Wallace, Melanie Walsh, Birgit Walter, Sue Wang, Adam Ward, Mike Watson, John Wealend, Paul Weaver, Susan Werner, Frank Werning, Peter Westgate, Brad Wetmore, John Whelpton, Alvin & Gregg White, Tony White, Karen Whitlow, RD Wicks, C Widness, Ellen Wild, Lowell Wiley, Andrew Wilkins, Madeline F Wilks, Mark Williams, Thomas Willim, Jon Willis, Katherine Willis, Janet Willoughby, Anne Wilshin, A P Wilson, Kay Wilson, Rosalind W Wilson, Alison Wolsey, Orange Wong, Stella Wood, Julian Woodridge, Joyce Wu, Cindy Yeo, Karl Yeomans, Jennifer Yoder, Chan Yu Ying, Michelle Yuen, Sandy Yujuico, Kim Zumwall

Index

Abbreviations

CA = Conservation Area NP = National Park WR = Wildlife Reserve

Text

Bold indicates maps.

Bold indicates maps.

Boxed Text

MAP LEGEND

CITY ROUTES

Freeway .... Freeway
Highway .... Primary Road
Road .... Secondary Road
Street .... Street
Lane .... Lane
.... On/Off Ramp
.... Unsealed Road
.... One-Way Street
.... Pedestrian Street
.... Stepped Street
.... Tunnel
.... Footbridge

REGIONAL ROUTES

.... Tollway, Freeway
.... Primary Road
.... Secondary Road
.... Minor Road

BOUNDARIES

.... International
.... State
.... Disputed
.... Fortified Wall

HYDROGRAPHY

.... River, Creek
.... Canal
.... Lake
.... Dry Lake, Salt Lake
.... Spring; Rapids
.... Waterfalls

TRANSPORT ROUTES & STATIONS

.... Train
.... Underground Train
.... Metro
.... Tramway
.... Bus Route
.... Cable Car, Chairlift
.... Walking Trail
.... Walking Tour
.... Path
.... Pier or Jetty

AREA FEATURES

.... Building
.... Park, Garden
.... Market
.... Sports Ground
.... National Park
.... Cemetery
.... Campus
.... Plaza

POPULATION SYMBOLS

CAPITAL .... National Capital
CAPITAL .... State Capital
CITY .... City
Town .... Town
Village .... Village
.... Urban Area

MAP SYMBOLS

.... Place to Stay
.... Place to Eat
.... Point of Interest
.... Airfield
.... Airport
.... Bank
.... Border Crossing
.... Buddhist Temple
.... Bus Terminal, Stop
.... Camping Ground
.... Cave
.... Embassy, Consulate
.... Gompa
.... Hindu Temple
.... Hospital
.... Internet Cafe
.... Lookout
.... Monastery
.... Monument
.... Mountain
.... Museum
.... Pass
.... Petrol/Gas Station
.... Police Station
.... Post Office
.... Pub, Bar
.... Shopping Centre
.... Stately Home
.... Stupa
.... Swimming Pool
.... Taxi
.... Telephone
.... Temple
.... Tourist Information
.... Trail Head
.... Transport (General)

Note: not all symbols displayed above appear in this book

LONELY PLANET OFFICES

Australia
Locked Bag 1, Footscray, Victoria 3011
☎ 03 8379 8000 fax 03 8379 8111
email: talk2us@lonelyplanet.com.au

USA
150 Linden St, Oakland, CA 94607
☎ 510 893 8555 TOLL FREE: 800 275 8555
fax 510 893 8572
email: info@lonelyplanet.com

UK
10a Spring Place, London NW5 3BH
☎ 020 7428 4800 fax 020 7428 4828
email: go@lonelyplanet.co.uk

France
1 rue du Dahomey, 75011 Paris
☎ 01 55 25 33 00 fax 01 55 25 33 01
email: bip@lonelyplanet.fr
www.lonelyplanet.fr

World Wide Web: www.lonelyplanet.com *or* AOL keyword: lp
Lonely Planet Images: lpi@lonelyplanet.com.au